Lecture Notes in Computer Science 2185

Edited by G. Goos, J. Hartmanis and J. van Leeuwen

Springer
Berlin
Heidelberg
New York
Barcelona
Hong Kong
London
Milan
Paris
Tokyo

Martin Gogolla   Cris Kobryn (Ed.)

«UML» 2001 –
The Unified
Modeling Language

Modeling Languages, Concepts, and Tools

4th International Conference
Toronto, Canada, October 1-5, 2001
Proceedings

 Springer

Series Editors

Gerhard Goos, Karlsruhe University, Germany
Juris Hartmanis, Cornell University, NY, USA
Jan van Leeuwen, Utrecht University, The Netherlands

Volume Editors

Martin Gogolla
University of Bremen, Department of Mathematics and Computer Science
Database Systems Group
P.O. Box 33 04 40, 28334 Bremen, Germany
E-mail: gogolla@informatik.uni-bremen.de

Cris Kobryn
Telelogic Technologies
P.O. Box 23 20, Fallbrook, CA 92088, USA
E-mail: cris.kobryn@telelogic.com

Cataloging-in-Publication Data applied for

Die Deutsche Bibliothek - CIP-Einheitsaufnahme

The unified modeling language : modeling languages, concepts, and tools ;
4th international conference ; proceedings / "UML" 2001, Toronto, Canada,
October 1- 5, 2001. Martin Gogolla ; Cris Kobryn (ed.). - Berlin ;
Heidelberg ; New York ; Barcelona ; Hong Kong ; London ; Milan ; Paris ;
Tokyo : Springer, 2001
 (Lecture notes in computer science ; Vol. 2185)
 ISBN 3-540-42667-1

CR Subject Classification (1998): D.2, D.3, K.6

ISSN 0302-9743
ISBN 3-540-42667-1 Springer-Verlag Berlin Heidelberg New York

Springer-Verlag Berlin Heidelberg New York
a member of BertelsmannSpringer Science+Business Media GmbH

http://www.springer.de

© Springer-Verlag Berlin Heidelberg 2001
Printed in Germany

Typesetting: Camera-ready by author, data conversion by PTP- Berlin, Stefan Sossna
Printed on acid-free paper   SPIN 10840541   06/3142   5 4 3 2 1 0

Preface

In the four years since the Object Management Group adopted the Unified Modeling Language (UML) in 1997, it has become widely accepted throughout the software industry and successfully applied to diverse domains. During this time it has become the de facto standard for specifying software blueprints, which continue to increase in value as we evolve from analysis and design models to multi-view architectures. Indeed, it is becoming difficult to find a software project with more than ten developers who don't use UML in some way to specify part of their architecture.

Despite its rapid and widespread acceptance, however, the UML 1.x series of revisions has not been without its problems. Some of the major issues commonly cited include: excessive size, gratuitous complexity, limited customizability, nonstandard implementations, and lack of support for diagram interchange. Such substantive problems can only be addressed by major revisions to UML. Fortunately, the Object Management Group realizes this and has issued four Requests for Proposals for UML 2.0.

UML 2.0 represents both a wonderful opportunity and a serious responsibility for the UML community. It is an opportunity to resolve the serious shortcomings listed above; it is also a responsibility to ensure that the second version of the language does not suffer from "second system syndrome." This conference, whose objective is to bring together researchers and practitioners to share their visions for the future of UML, is an ideal place to explore how we can exploit the opportunity and share the responsibility for UML 2.0. Now in its fourth year, the ≪UML≫ conference series remains the premier forum for presenting and discussing innovative ideas that will make UML easier to learn, apply, and implement.

In total 122 abstracts and 102 papers were submitted to this year's conference, of which 32 were selected by the program committee for presentation. As in 2000, this year's conference included a two-day tutorial and workshop session, in which nine tutorials and five workshops were scheduled. The primary purpose of these sessions was to provide a more informal forum for discussing state-of-the-art research in UML. Topics included: Agile modeling, teaching UML, concurrency, rigorous development methods, OCL, software architecture, concurrent, distributed, and real-time applications, tools, requirements, time-critical systems, meta-modeling, quality assurance, effective diagrammatic languages and executable UML. A short description of the workshops and tutorials can be found in these proceedings and details at the conference web site: http://www.cs.toronto.edu/uml2001/.

We would like to express our deepest appreciation to the authors of submitted papers, tutorials, workshops, and panels, and the program committee members and the additional referees. Jaelson Castro together with Manuel Kolp did an excellent job of managing all matters of the conference organization. Heinrich Hußmann chaired the workshop and tutorial submissions. We would also like to thank Werner Damm, John Mylopoulos and James Rumbaugh for agreeing to present invited talks at the conference. Mark Richters and Oliver Radfelder at the University of Bremen are thanked for their contribution to setting up the conference web site and in organizing and handling the electronic submission process. The ConfMan program (`http://confman.unik.no/~confman/ConfMan/`) was used to gather and organize submitted papers and reviews, and Mark Richters extended it to deal with an online preference selection process for the PC members. Ralf Kollmann at the University of Bremen organized the preparation of the final version of the conference proceedings. We would also like to thank the ≪UML≫ steering committee for their advice, Jean-Michel Bruel and Robert France for maintaining the mailing list, and last year's program chair, Andy Evans, for lots of helpful emails and hints.

July 2001   Martin Gogolla
                                                              Cris Kobryn

Organization

Executive Committee

General Chair:	Cris Kobryn (Telelogic Technologies, USA)
Conference Chair:	Jaelson Castro (Universidade Federal de Pernambuco, Brazil)
Program Chair:	Martin Gogolla (Universität Bremen, Germany)
Tutorial/Workshop Chair:	Heinrich Hußmann (Technische Universität Dresden, Germany)

Organizing Team

Publicity Chair (Europe):	Jean-Michel Bruel (University of Pau, France)
Publicity Chair (Americas):	Robert France (Colorado State University, USA)
Program Organization:	Ralf Kollmann (Universität Bremen, Germany)
	Oliver Radfelder (Universität Bremen, Germany)
	Mark Richters (Universität Bremen, Germany)
Local Organization:	Manuel Kolp (University of Toronto, Canada)

Program Committee

Colin Atkinson (DE)
Jean Bezivin (FR)
Marco Boger (DE)
Grady Booch (US)
Jean-Michel Bruel (FR)
David Bustard (UK)
Betty Cheng (US)
Derek Coleman (US)
Steve Cook (UK)
Desmond D'Souza (US)
John Daniels (UK)
Bruce Douglas (US)
Gregor Engels (DE)
Andy Evans (UK)
Robert France (US)
Brian Henderson-Sellers (AU)
Pavel Hruby (DK)
Peter Hruschka (DE)

Heinrich Hußmann (DE)
Jean-Marc Jezequel (FR)
Stuart Kent (UK)
Haim Kilov (US)
Steve Mellor (US)
Richard Mitchell (UK)
Ana Maria Dinis Moreira (PT)
Pierre-Alain Muller (FR)
Gunnar Övergaard (SE)
James Rumbaugh (US)
Bernhard Rumpe (DE)
Andy Schürr (DE)
Bran Selic (CA)
Keng Siau (US)
Perdita Stevens (UK)
Alfred Strohmeier (CH)
Jos Warmer (NL)
Alan Wills (UK)

Additional Referees

João Araújo
Toby Baier
Julian Bradfield
Benoit Baudry
Didier Buchs
Olivier Burgard
Benoit Caillaud
R. G. Clark
Birgit Demuth
Massimo Felici
Frederic Fondement
Falk Fünfstück
Sudipto Ghosh
Nabil Hameurlain
J.H. Hausmann
Reiko Heckel
Annig Lacayrelle
Katharina Mehner
Manfred Muench
Thierry Nodenot

Francois Pennaneach
Noël Plouzeau
Mohamed Kandé
Anneke Kleppe
Thomas Kühne
Jochen Küster
Juliana Kuester-Filipe
Frank-Ulrich Kumichel
Stefan Sauer
Ansgar Schleicher
Lothar Schmitz
João Costa Seco
Shane Sendall
Zixing Shen
Gerson Sunyè
Anne Thomas
Yuhong Tian
Yves Le Traon
Guido Wimmel

Sponsors

 IEEE Computer Society
http://www.computer.org

 IEEE-CS Technical Committee
on Complexity in Computing (TCCX)
http://www.elet.polimi.it/tccx/

Corporate Donors

 Telelogic Technologies
http://www.telelogic.com

Rational Software Corporation
http://www.rational.com

Academic Supporters

 Universidade Federal Pernambuco
http://www.ufpe.br

 Universität Bremen
http://www.uni-bremen.de

 University of Toronto
http://www.toronto.edu

 Technische Universität Dresden
http://www.uni-dresden.de

Table of Contents

Architecture and Patterns

Analysis and Testing

Performance and Databases

Invited Talk

Graph Transformations

Real-Time and Embedded Systems

Associations and Ontology

Statecharts

Invited Talk

Components

Use Cases

Workshops and Tutorials

The Preacher at Arrakeen

Jim Rumbaugh

Rational Software Corporation

Abstract. In the Dune novels, Paul Atreides fights a battle for survival against nefarious forces and succeeds in uniting the Universe under his control. Eventually, however, a bureaucratic and militaristic religion grows up around his legend. Disillusioned by the atrocities committed in his name, Paul abandons his throne and returns in disguise as the mysterious Preacher at Arrakeen to denounce the bureaucracy, fanaticism, and tyranny of his out-of-control followers. Sometimes that's how I feel about UML. This talk (sermon?) will denounce the excesses of the UML cult and see if it can be saved from its friends.

M. Gogolla and C. Kobryn (Eds.): UML 2001, LNCS 2185, p. 1, 2001.

An Action Semantics for MML

José M. Álvarez[1], Tony Clark[2], Andy Evans[3], and Paul Sammut[3]

[1] Dpto. de Lenguajes y Ciencias de la Computación.
University of Málaga, Málaga, 29071, Spain
alvarezp@lcc.uma.es
[2] Dpt. of Computer Science, King's College,
Strand, London, WC2R 2LS, United Kingdom
anclark@dcs.kcl.ac.uk
[3] Dpt. of Computer Science, University of York,
Heslington, York, YO1 5DD, United Kingdom
andye@cs.york.ac.uk, pauls@cs.york.ac.uk

Abstract. This paper describes an action semantics for UML based on
the Meta-Modelling Language (MML) - a precise meta-modelling language designed for developing families of UML languages. Actions are
defined as computational procedures with side-effects. The action semantics are described in the MML style, with model, instance and semantic
packages. Different actions are described as specializations of the basic
action in their own package. The aim is to show that by using a Catalysis like package extension mechanism, with precise mappings to a simple
semantic domain, a well-structured and extensible model for an action
language can be obtained.

1 Introduction

The UML actions semantics has been submitted by the action semantics consortium to "extend the UML with a compatible mechanism for specifying action
semantics in a software-independent manner" [1]. The submission defines an
extension to the UML 1.4 meta-model which includes an abstract syntax and
semantic domain for an action language. This language provides a collection
of simple action constructs, for example write actions, conditional actions and
composite actions, which can be used to describe computational behaviours in
a UML model. A key part of the proposal is a description of the semantics of
object behaviour, based on a history model of object executions.

Unfortunately, the action semantics proposal suffers from a problem commonly met when developing large meta-models in UML - how to structure the
model so as to clearly separate its different components. Failure to achieve this
results in a meta-model that is difficult to understand and to modify, particularly, to specialize and extend. In addition, meta-models based on the current
UML semantics suffer from a lack of a precisely defined semantic core upon
which to construct the meta-model. This means that it is often hard to ascer-
tain the correctness of the model, and to overcome this, significant work must

M. Gogolla and C. Kobryn (Eds.): UML 2001, LNCS 2185, pp. 2–18, 2001.

be invested in clarifying the semantics before any progress can be made. On the positive side, the basic semantic model used in the action semantics, with its notion of snapshots and history and changes seems quite appropriate to define the different changing values of a system. In addition, the actions defined in the submission thoroughly cover the wide range of actions necessary for a useful action language. Thus, if a way can be found to better restructure what is a significant piece of work, then clearly there will benefits to all users and implementors of the language.

The purpose of this paper is to show how the definition of a precise semantic core and the use of a Catalysis [2] like package extension mechanism can result in a better structured and adaptable definition of the action semantics. The work is based on an extension of the Meta-modelling Language (MML) [6], a precise meta-modelling language developed to enable UML to be re-architected as a family of modelling languages. However, it must be clear that this is not an intent to solve the general problem of model executability, but only a proposal to describe executability features in a MML context.

1.1   The Basics of the MML Model

MML is a metamodeling language intended to rearchitect the core of UML so it can be defined in a much simpler way and it can be easily extended and specialised for different types of systems. Among other basic concepts, MML establishes two orthogonal distinctions, the first one being a mapping between model concepts (abstract syntax) and instances (semantic domain). The second is the distinction between model concepts and concrete syntax and applies both to models and instances. The syntax is the way concepts are rendered. Models and instances are related by a semantic package that establishes the satisfaction relationship between instances and models. A similar relationship is defined between between model concepts and concrete syntax.

These distinction are described in terms of a language definition pattern, see Figure 1. Each component in the pattern is defined as a package. As in UML, a package is a container of classes and/or other packages. In addition, packages in MML can be specialised. This is the key mechanism by which modular, extensible definitions of languages are defined in terms of fundamental patterns, and is similar to the package extension mechanism defined in [2]. Here, specialization of packages is shown by placing a UML specialization arrow between the packages. The child package specializes all (and therefore contains all) of the contents of the parent package.

Another important component of the MML is its core package, which defines the based modelling concepts used in UML: packages, classes and attributes. Currently, the MML model concepts package does not provide a dynamic model of behaviour. Thus, in order to define a semantic model for the action semantics in the MML, an extension must be made to the core MML package. This is described in the following sections.

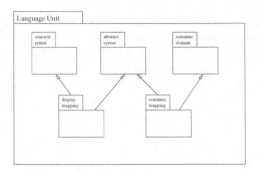

Fig. 1. The MMF Method

2   Principles of the New Action Semantics

Two basic goals have led to the redefinition of the action semantics. The first one is to include the action semantics as the dynamic core of MML, and possibly substitute the static core. This implies the definition of model and instances views and separation between concepts and syntax. The second goal is to have this action semantics as simple as possible and as easy to extend and specialize as possible. For the goal of simplicity, it is necessary to define as few new concepts as possible. One of the ways to do this is to reuse whenever possible the concepts already defined in the other packages of MML. It is also important to abstract out the fundamental concepts common to all actions and to be as removed as possible from the implementational aspects of actions. MML is designed to be easily extensible, as will the action semantics if we include it as another part of MML. As the actions semantics will be another package in MML, it has to follow the structure of the rest of packages, that is, the package should be composed of model, instance and semantics packages, with the model and instance packages further divided in packages for concepts, syntax and the mapping between concepts and syntax.

2.1   New Basic Concepts

The dynamic core tries to model the evolution of the values of the objects in the system with time. This is in contrast with the view of the static model that considers instances to be attached to a single value. The approach taken to define the dynamic model considers a history as a sequence of values, often called snapshots, being the execution of the actions responsible for the progression from one value to the next. A snapshot can be related to the whole system, as it is in the first approach to actions in the MMF document, or to a single object as it is in this approach. Only those acts causing the change of a value will be considered to be actions. For example, to write a new value in an instance slot will be an action as the value of the instance slot is different before and after the execution of the action. However, the reading of the value of a variable will not be considered as an action as no element in the system changes its value. These kind of acts will be considered to be expressions. In the current definition of MML, expressions are defined to model the OCL. There is also a subclass of expression called method, which is used to model the static methods of classes. Thus, the basic notion of an action is of a model element that relates a series of values with a series of elements. These input values will be used in the action execution to update some of the values of the elements associated with the action. The specific semantics of every action will be described in every subclass action in terms of its class diagram and well-formedness rules. Unlike in the previous proposal for action semantics, there is no concept of action execution history with a step for every state in the execution. In this model, the action execution is simply the occurrence of the action. If it is a compound action, it can be decomposed into simpler actions.

2.2   Time

Time was introduced in the previous action semantics definition to define a timing order in the dynamic model. In our point of view, time is not a concept general to every type of systems, so will not be used in the basic dynamic model. However, particular systems as real-time systems can easily extend this model to cope with the notion of time as best fitted to its purposes.

3   Actions

An Action represents a computational procedure that changes the state of an element in the system. In order to execute, an action requires some input values that will be used to compute the new values for other elements in the system.

Methods in MML are also used to define computational procedures. Methods are side-effect free - they simply evaluate a set of parameters against an OCL expression to obtain a result. Any method can be defined just by changing the body expression.

Actions are not side-effect free since they change the value of an element. Actions will not have a body expression that specifies what the action does. However, new action classes that specialize the basic Action class will be defined. Their particular behaviour will be described by means of well-formedness rules.

With this approach, a new action cannot be defined by just changing the expression that defines it, but there is a set of standard basic actions on top of which new actions are constructed.

The actions package specializes the staticCore package.

3.1   Concepts

The abstract class Action specializes Classifier. Every action has a set of input parameters and can produce output values. As the order of the parameters and results is significant, these associations are ordered. An action will be executed

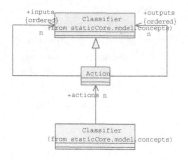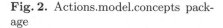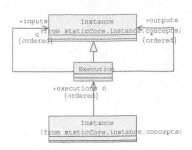

Fig. 2. Actions.model.concepts package

Fig. 3. Actions.instances.concepts package

on the behalf on an object. Therefore there is another association between Action and Classifier, describing the Class that the host object belongs to.

Methods

[1] The method allActions() returns the set of all actions of Class, including those of its parents.

```
uml.staticCore.model.concepts.Class
allActions() : Set(Action)

    parents->iterate(p s = actions | s -> union(p.allActions()->
    reject(c | actions->exists(c' | c'.name = c.name)))
```

[2] This method returns the set of immediate subactions of this action. The actual set returned is defined in concrete descendants of Action.

```
context uml.actions.model.concepts.action
subactions() : Set(Action)
```

[3] This method returns all subactions of an action, nested to any depth.

```
context uml.actions.model.concepts.action
allSubactions() : Set(Action)

    self.subactions()->
    union(self.subactions().allSubactions()->asSet)
```

[4] This method returns true if the action is a subaction, at any depth, of another given action.

```
context uml.actions.model.concepts.action
isSubactionOf(otherAction: Action):Boolean

    otherAction.allSubactions()->includes(self)
```

3.2 Instances

The Execution class is defined in the Instances package. An Execution instance represents the actual execution of an action. The execution is associated with the actual inputs values used to execute the action and the actual output results.

Though there is no notion of time, and consequently, time ordering in the dynamic model, there is a causal relationship between the execution of the action and the values used in it. As the action cannot execute until all the input values are calculated, the values after the action execution cannot be accessed for the calculation of the input parameter values.

An Execution also has an association with the object on whose behalf it is executed.

Well-formedness Rules

[1] A calculation used to generate a parameter value for an execution cannot access an instance that is the output of that execution or follows that output in the element history.

```
context uml.actions.instance.concepts.Execution inv:
```

> *To be formalized.*

4 Primitive Actions

A primitive action is an action that cannot be decomposed into simpler actions. There are several subclasses of primitive action, each tailored to the kind of elements they act upon: null action, variable actions, object actions and slot actions.

These actions specializes the Action class. Their different behaviour will be determined by means of well-formedness rules.

Well-formedness rules

[1] A primitive action has no subactions.

```
context uml.primitiveActions.model.concepts.PrimitiveAction
subactions(): Sequence(Action)

    Set{}
```

4.1 Null Action

The null action, as its name states, makes no change to the system. It is included because the compound actions have to have at least one subaction.

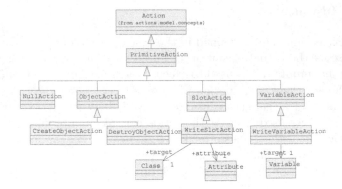

Fig. 4. Primitiveactions.model.concepts package

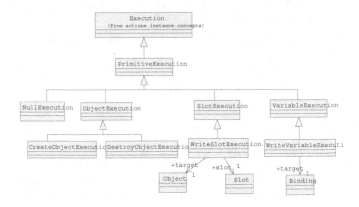

Fig. 5. Primitiveactions.instances.concepts package

Well-formedness rules

[1] A NullAction has no input nor output elements.

```
context uml.primitiveActions.model.concepts.NullAction inv:

    self.inputs->size = 0 and
    self.outputs->size = 0
```

[2] A NullExecution has no input parameters nor output values.

```
context uml.primitiveActions.model.concepts.NullExecution inv:

    self.inputs->size = 0 and
    self.outputs->size = 0
```

4.2   Variable Actions

The only possible action on variables is to write a new value to that variable. A variable must be accessible from the action so that it can be used. Accessibility will be discussed in the group actions section.

The variable whose value is updated is the target of the action. The only input parameter to the action is the value to be assigned to the variable.

The input value for the execution of a *WriteVariableAction* will be the same as the value of the variable after the execution of the action.

Well-formedness rules

[1] A WriteVariableAction has a single input parameter.

```
context uml.primitiveActions.model.concepts.WriteVariableAction inv:

  self.inputs->size = 1
```

[2] The type of the updated variable must be the same as the type of the input value.

```
context uml.primitiveActions.model.concepts.WriteVariableAction inv:

  self.inputs->at(1).oclIsKindOf(self.target)
```

[3] The variable must be accessible by the action.

```
context uml.primitiveActions.model.concepts.WriteVariableAction inv:

  self.target.isAccesibleBy(self)
```

[4] A WriteVariableExecution has a single input parameter.

```
context uml.primitiveActions.instance.concepts.WriteVariableExecution
inv:

  self.inputs->size = 1
```

[5] The value of the updated variable after a WriteVariableExecution is the input value.

```
context primitiveActions.intance.concepts.WriteVariableExecution inv:

  self.inputs->at(1) = self.outputs->at(1)
```

[6] The output value of the execution belongs to the history of the variable.

```
context primitiveActions.intance.concepts.WriteVariableExecution inv:

  self.target.history->includes self.outputs->at(1)
```

Methods

[1] This method checks whether the given action is within the scope of this variable.

```
context uml.constraints.model.concepts.Variable
isAccesibleBy(a : Action) : Boolean

  self.scope.subactions()->include(self)
```

4.3   Object Actions

An object cannot change its value, but it can be dynamically created and destroyed. There are two actions for Objects, one to create a new object of a given class and another one to destroy an object. Some languages include dynamic object typing, allowing the Class of an object to be changed in execution time. If the reclassify action is to be included in the action semantics, then when an object is reclassified as belonging to another class, the element in the system whose value changes must be known. The reclassify action is not considered further here.

Both the create and destroy object actions have a single input parameter, which is the class the object belongs to. Neither of them have output values.

The execution of a create object action has a result, the created object. This action does not execute any further job, that is it does not execute any initialization on the slots of the new object. The execution of a destroy object action has no output values. An element value cannot be accessed by any other action execution or expression calculation after it has been destroyed.

Well-formedness rules

[1] The element created by a CreateObjectAction must be an object.

```
context uml.primitiveActions.model.concepts.CreateObjectAction inv:

  self.outputs->size = 1 and
  self.target.oclIsKindOf(Class)
```

[2] A CreateObjectAction has a single input.

```
context uml.primitiveActions.model.concepts.CreateObjectAction inv:

  self.outputs->size = 1
```

[3] The input of a CreateObjectAction is the class of the created object.

```
context uml.primitiveActions.model.concepts.CreateObjectAction inv:

  self.inputs.olcIsKindOf(Class)
```

[4] The element destroyed by a DestroyObjectAction must be a object.

```
context uml.primitiveActions.model.concepts.DestroyObjectAction inv:

  self.outputs->size = 1 and
  self.outputs.oclIsKindOf(Class)
```

[5] A DestroyObjectAction has a single input.

```
context uml.primitiveActions.model.concepts.DestroyObjectAction inv:

  self.inputs->size = 1
```

[6] A CreateObjectExecution has no prevalues and one postvalue.

```
context uml.primitiveActions.instance.concepts.CreateObjectExecution
inv:

  self.inputs->size = 0 and
  self.outputs->size = 1
```

[7] A CreateObjectExecution has a single input parameter.

```
context uml.primitiveActions.instance.concepts.CreateObjectExecution
inv:

  self.parameter->size = 1
```

[8] The output of a CreateObjectExecution is a new object of the specified class.

```
context uml.primitiveActions.instance.concepts.CreateObjectExecution
inv:

  self.outputs->at(1).isTypeOf(self.value)
```

[9] A DestroyObjectExecution has one input value and no output values.

```
context uml.primitiveActions.instance.concepts.DestroyObjectExecution
inv:

  self.inputs->size = 1 and
  self.outputs->size = 0
```

[10] A DestroyObjectExecution has a single input parameter.

```
context uml.primitiveActions.instance.concepts.DestroyObjectAction
inv:

  self.inputs->size = 1
```

[11] The input value of a DestroyObjectExecution is an object.

context Class uml.primitiveActions.instance.concepts.DestroyObjectExecution inv:

    self.inputs->at(1).isTypeOf(Object)

[12] An object cannot be accessed by any other action execution or expression calculation after it has been destroyed.

context uml.primitiveActions.instance.concepts.DestroyObjectAction inv:

    To be formalized

4.4   Slot Actions

As for variables, the only available action on slots is to write a new value on them. In MML, an attribute can be of any type including Classifiers. Therefore, the allowable actions on slots should be the same as those on instances of the classifier to which the attribute belongs.

Well-formedness rules

[1] A WriteSlotAction has a single input parameter.

context uml.primitiveActions.model.concepts.WriteSlotAction inv:

    self.inputs->size = 1

[2] The attribute must be a valid attribute for the class.

context uml.primitiveActions.model.concepts.WriteSlotAction inv:

    self.target->attributes->include(self.attribute)

[3] The type of the updated slot must be the same than the type of the input value.

context uml.primitiveActions.model.concepts.WriteSlotAction inv:

    self.inputs->at(1).oclIsKindOf(self.slot)

[4] A WriteSlotExecution has a single input parameter.

context uml.primitiveActions.instance.concepts.WriteSlotExecution inv:

    self.inputs->size = 1

[5] The slot must be a valid slot for the object.

context uml.primitiveActions.model.concepts.WriteSlotExecution inv:

    self.target->slots->include(self.slot)

[6] The value of the updated variable after a WriteSlotExecution is the input value.

```
context primitiveActions.intance.concepts.WriteSlotExecution inv:

  self.inputs->at(1) = self.outputs->at(1)
```

[7] The output value of the execution belongs to the history of the variable.

```
context primitiveActions.intance.concepts.WriteSlotAction inv:

  self.target.history->includes self.output->at(1)
```

5   Compound Actions

In contrast to the primitive actions, other actions are complex and they can be divided into subactions. There are three types of compound actions, group actions, conditional actions and loop actions, each of them defining one of the basic language constructors.

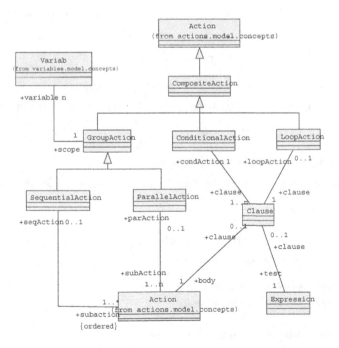

Fig. 6. Compositeactions.model.concepts package

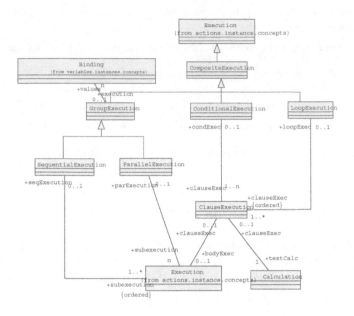

Fig. 7. Compositeactions.instances.concepts package

Well-formedness rules

[1] A composite action does not update any value.

```
context uml.compositeActions.model.concepts.compositeAction inv:

    self.target->size = 0
```

[2] A composite action has no input parameters.

```
context uml.compositeActions.model.concepts.compositeAction inv:

    self.parameter->size = 0
```

[3] A composite execution has neither a prevalue nor a postvalue.

```
context uml.compositeActions.model.concepts.compositeAction inv:

    self.preValue->size = 0 and
    self.postValue->size = 0
```

[4] A composite execution has no input parameters.

```
context uml.compositeActions.instance.concepts.compositeExecution
inv:

    self.parameter->size = 0
```

5.1   Group Actions

A group action is simply intended to give a scope to a number of subactions. The scope includes the variables the actions have access to and the kind of ordering in the action execution. A group action is associated with a number of variables. These variables are accessible to all the subactions in the group action and not accessible by any action outside of it.

There are two types of group action: sequential actions and parallel actions. The subexecutions in a sequential execution have to execute in the order that they are included in the corresponding sequence. This implies that an execution, or a value calculation for that execution cannot access a value modified by a previous execution.

In a parallel execution all the subexecutions can happen concurrently and the same value can be accessed to calculate values for different execution, but the value can only be modified by a single execution.

Well-formedness rules

[1] Subactions executions in a group execution happen sequentially.

    context uml.compositeActions.instance.concepts.sequentialAction inv:

>   To be formalized.

Methods

[1] The subactions of a parallel action are its subactions.

    context uml.compositeActions.model.concepts.parallelAction
    subactions(): Set(Action)

>   self.subAction

[2] The subactions of a sequential action are its subactions.

    context uml.compositeActions.model.concepts.sequentialAction
    subactions(): Sequence(Action)

>   self.subaction

5.2   Clauses

A clause comprises a test and an body. The test is an expression that returns a boolean value and the body is an action.

When a clause executes, the test is always calculated, but the action may not execute, depending on the context of the clause and the value yielded by the test.

5.3   Conditional Actions

A conditional action is composed of a set of clauses. In the execution of a conditional action, all the clause tests are calculated concurrently. As they are side effect free, the order is not relevant to the final calculations. Only one of the clauses whose test has yielded true in its calculation is chosen to execute its action.

Well-formedness rules

[1] The subactions of a conditional action are its body subactions.

```
context uml.compositeActions.model.concepts.conditionalAction
subactions(): Set(Action)

    self.clause.body
```

[2] A conditional execution has as many test calculations as its corresponding action has text expressions.

```
context uml.compositeActions.instance.concepts.conditionalExecution
inv:

    self.clauseExec->forAll(c | c.testCalc->size = 1)
```

[3] A conditional execution only executes one of its clause's bodies, and the test for that clause must yield true.

```
context uml.compositeActions.instance.concepts.conditionalExecution
inv:

    self.clauseExec->collect(c | c.bodyExec->size = 1)->size = 1 and
    self.clauseExec->forAll(c | c.bodyExec->size = 1 implies
    c.testCalc = true)
```

5.4   Loop Actions

A loop action has a single clause with its test expression and body action. The loop execution consists of successive clause calculations. For a clause calculation, the test is evaluated and if it yields true, the action is executed. After the execution of action, there is another clause calculation. When the test yields false in a clause calculation, the action is not executed and the loop execution is terminated.

Well-formedness rules

[1] The only subaction of a loop action is its body action.

```
uml.compositeActions.model.concepts.loopAction subactions():
Set(Action)

    self.body
```

[2] A loop execution has one test calculation more than body executions.

```
context uml.compositeActions.instance.concepts.loopExecution inv:

    self.testCalc->size = self.bodyExecution->size + 1
```

[3] The test only yields false on the last iteration of a loop execution.

```
context uml.compositeActions.instance.concepts.loopExecution inv:

    self.clauseExec->subSequence(1, self.clauseExec->size - 1)
    ->forAll(c | c.testCalc = true) and
    self.clauseExec->at(self.clauseExec->size).testCalc = false
```

6   Changes in Current MML

Some changes to the current definition of MML have to be done to include the dynamic model.

In first place, an instance is no longer related to a single value, but to a number of values, each of them denoting the new value after the execution of an action on the instance. To include this new point of view, in the instance package of the staticCore, the association between Instance and Value is replaced by a one to one association between Instance and a new class, History. The History is in turn associated with a number of values that reflect the successive changes on the instance.

The current concept of Expression only covers those used for OCL. It has to be extended to include subclasses that calculate non- boolean values or return the value of elements in the system that actions need to execute. The reading of the value of a variable is an example of these new classes.

7   Conclusions and Future Work

In this paper we have proposed a restructured meta-model architecture for the action semantics, based on the meta-modelling language (MML). The focus of the work has been to develop a consistent approach to constructing the meta-model, in which abstract syntax and semantics are clearly delineated. The result is a definition that supports a simple methodological approach to extension. Whenever a new action is added to the abstract syntax of the language, a structure preserving addition is made to the semantic domain. This *pattern* of construction is a vital weapon in the meta-modellers armory, and is essential if large meta-models of language are to be constructed successfully.

With respect to other work that has been done in this area, Kleppe and Warmer [4] have concurrently a similar approach to refactoring the action semantics, based on the MML. Our work differs from theirs in that we have attempted to define a more generic model of behaviour, which makes no assumptions about the ordering of actions. Thus, our model is more adaptable, and could form the foundation of a number of different languages with alternative semantic models. This ability is essential in order to support families of related UML action languages.

Clearly, there are a number of future directions of work possible. In particular, the development of additional meta-modelling patterns is currently impacting on the MML. These patterns provide a number of fundamental structures that are commonly repeated across language definitions. For example the container/contained pattern is commonly found in many language models, as are patterns which describe properties of generalisable modelling elements and instansiable elements. It is expected that a refactoring of the meta-model using these patterns would further improve its structure and clarity.

References

1. Action Semantics Consortium: Response to OMG RFP ad/98-11-01. Action Semantics for the UML. Revised September 5, 2000 (2000) www.umlactionsemantics.org
2. D'Souza D., Wills A. C.: Object Components and Frameworks with UML – The Catalysis Approach. (1998) Addison-Wesley.
3. Clark T., Evans A., Kent S., Brodsky S., Cook S.: A Feasibility Study in Rearchitecting UML as a Family of Languages using a Precise OO Meta-Modeling Approach. (2000) www.puml.org
4. Kleppe A., Warmer J.: Integration of static and dynamic core for UML: A study in dynamic aspects of the pUML Object-Oriented meta modelling approach to the rearchitecting of UML, (2001) TOOLS Europe 2001
5. Brodsky S., Clark A., Cook S., Evans A., Kent S. (2000) A feasibility Study in Rearchitecting UML as a Family of Languages Using a Precise OO Meta-Modeling Approach. Available at http://www.puml.org/mmt.zip.
6. Clark A., Evans A., Kent S. (2000) Engineering Modelling Languages: A Precise OO Meta-Modeling Approach. Available at http://www.puml.org/mml

The Essence of Multilevel Metamodeling

Colin Atkinson and Thomas Kühne

AG Component Engineering
University of Kaiserslautern
D-67653 Kaiserslautern, Germany
{atkinson,kuehne}@informatik.uni-kl.de

Abstract. As the UML attempts to make the transition from a single, albeit extensible, language to a framework for a family of languages, the nature and form of the underlying meta-modeling architecture will assume growing importance. It is generally recognized that without a simple, clean and intuitive theory of how metamodel levels are created and related to one another, the UML 2.0 vision of a coherent family of languages with a common core set of concepts will remain elusive. However, no entirely satisfactory metamodeling approach has yet been found. Current (meta-)modeling theories used or proposed for the UML all have at least one fundamental problem that makes them unsuitable in their present form. In this paper we bring these problems into focus, and present some fundamental principles for overcoming them. We believe that these principles need to be embodied within the metamodeling framework ultimately adopted for the UML 2.0 standard.

1 Introduction

The UML is an object-oriented language for describing artifacts in some domain of interest to the user. Like all languages, it needs to define the meaning of its descriptive concepts, the rules for putting them together, and the syntax to be used to represent them. In this respect, defining a graphical language to be used for modeling is conceptually no different to defining a textual language to be used for programming. Concepts like concrete syntax, abstract syntax and semantics are therefore also applicable for the definition of the UML.

For pragmatic reasons, early versions of the UML relied on natural language as the primary vehicle for describing the notation. However, in view of the well known limitations of natural language for this purpose, more recent versions of the UML have attempted to improve on this by using an abstract syntax accompanied by formal constraints. However, designing the abstract syntax for the UML has proven to be problematic in several ways [1].

Since the UML is a general purpose modeling language it is in principle suitable for describing its own properties. The motivation for using the UML to help describe its own semantics is the same as for any application of the UML—to provide a compact, easy to understand, and mostly graphical description of a domain or system of interest. However, a simple but significant problem stands

M. Gogolla and C. Kobryn (Eds.): UML 2001, LNCS 2185, pp. 19–33, 2001.

in the way of this goal—the UML's instantiation model does not scale-up cleanly to multiple modeling levels. As long as there are only two levels—one with classes (M_1) instantiating another level with objects (M_0), the UML instantiation mechanism works well. However, when the UML concepts are employed to describe the level from which the class level is instantiated, i.e., the UML metamodel level (M_2), they do not support a natural modeling approach. In particular, they fail to adequately describe an M_1-level model element that represents a class (for further instantiation) as well as just an object.

Unfortunately, the metamodeling approaches currently used or proposed for the UML are based on an instantiation mechanism which treats an instance of a model element as just an object. Although an instance can also represent a class[1], the properties that it receives by virtue of the instantiation mechanism are only those of an object. Thus, for instance, when an M_1-level element is instantiated from an M_2-level element all of the attributes and associations defined for the M_2-level element becomes slots and links of the M_1-level element, and thus are not available for further instantiation. If an M_1-level element wishes to have attributes and/or associations, these must either be defined explicitly or must be inherited. The inability of the instantiation mechanism to carry information concerning attributes and associations across more than one level of instantiation is the source of pernicious problems in the currently proposed UML metamodeling frameworks.

In this paper we examine the nature of the most serious of these problems, which we refer to as the "ambiguous classification" and the "replication of concepts" problems, and discuss some of the attempts to compensate for them in existing metamodeling approaches. We then introduce a fundamentally different approach to metamodeling which rectifies these problems and provides a sound basis for a multi-level modeling architecture. This approach is based on the premise that the definition of modeling elements should inherently recognize the possibility of instantiation sequences that span more than two modeling levels, and should allow attributes and associations to be obtained purely through instantiation. Finally we describe the key concepts upon which such a mechanism is based and explain how it overcomes the identified problems.

2   Symptoms of Shallow Instantiation

The current UML instantiation model, which for the purposes of this paper we call "shallow instantiation", is based on the premise that a class can only define the semantics of its direct instances, and can have no effect on entities created by further instantiation steps. This view of instantiation, which of course makes sense in traditional two-level environments, leads to two fundamental problems when scaled up to multiple metalevels.

---

[1] In the UML instances of a metaclass that specializes Classifier are viewed as elements which can themselves be instantiated.

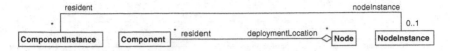

Fig. 1. Defining components and nodes

2.1 Ambiguous Classification

Traditionally, object-oriented modeling has only been concerned with two levels, the object (M_0) level and the class (M_1) level, where every element at the M_0-level is an instance-of[2] exactly one M_1 element. When a metamodeling level (M_2) is introduced, the situation is less clear-cut.

As an illustration of the problems that arise when this model of instantiation is scaled up to multiple levels, consider Fig. 1, which shows a simplified extract of the current UML metamodel related to the definition of nodes and components. These classes are regarded as residing at the M_2-level in the typical multi-level modeling architecture. In the UML, a component is an executable code module that can be deployed independently on physical computational resources known as nodes. A node is a run-time physical object that generally has at least a memory, and also often processing capability, upon which components may be deployed. The UML metamodel contains information about the nodes and component concepts in two places: The core package contains the M_2-level classes Node and Component and an association between them with role name resident for Component. The common behavior package of the metamodel, on the other hand, contains the M_2-level classes ComponentInstance and NodeInstance, and an association between them with a role name resident for ComponentInstance. This association enables component and node instances to be linked with each other. Note, however, that an additional constraint in the metamodel specifies that only component and node instances whose classifiers are linked with an resident/deploymentLocation relationship may be linked with each other. Figure 1 therefore illustrates how the UML metamodel captures the notions of nodes and components.

The problems of shallow instantiation reveal themselves when lower level classes are instantiated from the metamodel. Figure 2 shows a typical scenario containing M_1-level classes C and N, and M_0-level objects CI and NI. Class N is an instance-of the M_2-level element Node and since Node inherits from Classifier, class N can be used to instantiate an actual node instance NI. Similarly, class C is an instance-of the M_2-element Component and since Component inherits from Classifier, class C can be used to instantiate an actual node instance CI. One of the fundamental properties of component instances and node instances is that the former reside on the latter in a running version of the system. Therefore, one would like to define at the metamodel (M_2) level the fact that component instances, i.e., instances of ComponentInstance (at the M_0-level) have links to the

---

[2] As in the UML, specification, we use "instance-of" to refer to direct instantiation only, and "indirect instance-of" to refer to the relationship between an instance and one of the superclasses of its class.

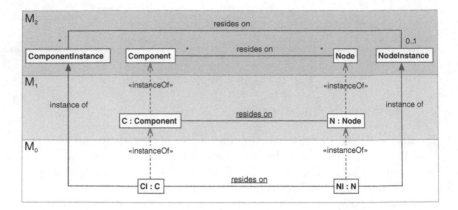

Fig. 2. Using the metamodel to define component and node instances

nodes instances (at the M_0-level) that they reside on. Not making such a statement at M_2 puts the responsibility on the modeler who creates a component type at M_1 to establish an association to a corresponding node type. Simply defining an association between Component and Node at the M_2-level, called, e.g., resides on, however, will not work because of the limitations of shallow instantiation. The problem is that when an instance of Node is created such as N, the association resides on becomes a link to an instance of Component such as C. This is highlighted in Fig. 2 by underlining its name and is actually desired since it specifies which component type may reside on a particular node type. Because this is a link, however, it can have no effect on actual node instances and component instances instantiated from N and C.

The only way in which the actual M_0-level component instances and node instances are able to obtain a link to capture which component instance resides on which node instance is by instantiating an association. This is why NodeInstance and ComponentInstance—as M_2-level representatives for "typical" component and node instances—feature the resides on association, supporting resides on links between node and component instances at the M_0-level.

This strategy of introducing representative types at the M_2-level is the adopted practice not only in the current version of the UML, but also in more recent proposals for the UML metamodel [2]. However, this approach clearly raises a dilemma—are objects at the M_0-level (e.g., NI) instances of their M_1-level classifiers (e.g., N), or instances of the representative instance at the M_2-level (e.g., NodeInstance), or both? From a modeling perspective a node instance is created by a class of type Node, as opposed to a (meta-)class called NodeInstance. In terms of the example used in the MML approach [3], the same dilemma occurs with regard to whether the object fido is an instance-of class Dog or of (meta-)class Object. In this example, one faces the need to express that fido is classified by Dog but also should be recognized as an Object (see the lower part of Fig. 3). In [3], this "ambiguous classification" problem is labeled the "multiple of" problem, because there are potentially two valid classifiers for one instance at the M_0-level.

In effect one of the instance-of relationships is serving as the *logical* instantiation link, while the other is serving as the *physical* instantiation link. Interestingly, for NI the relationship which is naturally viewed as the primary one from the perspective of the modeler (the logical one to N) is not the same as the relationship which is naturally viewed as the primary one from the perspective of a CASE tool (the physical one to NodeInstance).

In essence, the multiple classification problem arises because one wants to make statements at the M_2-level about how node and component instances (at the M_0-level) are shaped and how they may be connected with each other. Yet, one is prohibited from doing so in a natural way by the semantics of shallow instantiation.

2.2   Replication of Concepts

The ambiguous classification problem arises because the traditional semantics of instantiation prohibits a model element from influencing anything other than its immediate instances. Had we been able to specify an association resides on between Component and Node at level M_2 with the ability to create an effect on M_0 elements, there would have been no need for the ComponentInstance and NodeInstance elements.

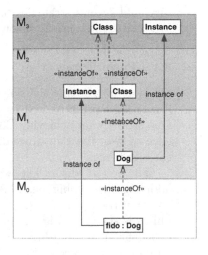

Because shallow instantiation fails to carry information across more than one instantiation link it is often necessary to duplicate information at multiple levels. This is known as the "replication of concepts" problem. As an illustration of this problem, consider how the "fido the dog" problem mentioned in the pre-

Fig. 3. Replication of concepts

vious subsection would appear when all metamodeling levels are considered. Fig. 3 shows the typical scenario in which fido is an instance-of Dog , Dog is an instance-of Class and Class (at the M_2-level) is an instance-of Class (at the M_3-level).

For the reasons explained in the previous subsection, with shallow instantiation model elements usually have more than one instance-of relationship in order to obtain additional "auxiliary" properties. In the case of the UML, all model elements instantiated from a class are also viewed as being instances of the metaclass Instance, or one of its subclasses. This is illustrated in Fig. 3. Identifying fido to be an Instance as well as a Dog can also be interpreted as defining the semantics of instantiation. This is the approach to the definition of semantics adopted in the MML work [3].

The same pattern is repeated again at the level above to define the properties exhibited by the model element Dog. The relationship between Dog and its classifier Class now represents a logical instance-of, and its real physical classifier is now considered to be Instance (this time at the M_3-level). In effect, the semantics of instantiation have to be redefined at each level (other than the lowest level).

The replication of model elements and concepts at multiple levels causes two main problems, First, it means that the size of the models are increased, making them more complex and difficult to understand. This phenomenon can be seen in the MOF and the UML, where a large proportion of the model elements and concepts are the same. Second, when fundamental concepts such the instance-of relationship are redefined and recreated for every level, inconsistencies can easily arise, leading to subtle differences in instantiation semantics at different levels.

3   Compensating for Shallow Instantiation

The problems described above have not gone unnoticed by the research community, and several strategies have been developed to try to cure the symptoms. We review these briefly below.

3.1   PowerTypes

One way of relieving the symptoms of shallow instantiation is to use the inheritance mechanism as well as instantiation to capture instance-of relationships. One strategy for achieving this is the powertype concept [4]. It avoids the presence of two direct instance-of relationships for one element by making one of them indirect.

The way in which the powertype approach addresses the ambiguous classification problem (illustrated in Fig. 2) by use of polymorphism is shown in Fig. 4. As can be seen, NI is a defined to be a direct instance-of N and an indirect instance-of NodeInstance

Object NI obtains its features from NodeInstance not by being a *direct* instance-of it (see Fig. 2) but by being an *indirect* instance-of it. As N receives all features from NodeInstance by inheritance, it can shape NI as necessary. In this case an association resides on from NodeInstance would enable NI to be linked to component instances.

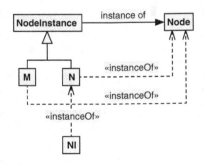

Fig. 4. Node as a powertype of NodeInstance

In general, a powertype is defined to be a type (e.g., Node) whose instances (e.g., N and M) are subtypes of another type[3] (e.g., NodeInstance). In this example, therefore, the powertype of NodeInstance is Node. Note that also associations involving Node, such as resides on), can have an effect on N because Node is viewed as its classifier.

The important contribution of the powertype approach is to exploit the fact that NI does not need to be a direct instance-of NodeInstance but that it suffices

---

[3] Type, here, can be taken to be synonymous with classifier.

to model it as an indirect instance. More generally, the powertype concept recognizes that one sometimes needs to characterize a concept as being an instance-of a special type *and* to be subtype of another special type, as opposed to an "either/or" choice.

However, the powertype concept, as is, does not fit within the strict four layer modeling architecture of the UML. Although Node is assumed to be the classifier of N it resides at the same level. In other words, Node would have to be moved to level M_2 in order to exploit the powertype concept within the UML. This is, in effect, done by the approach described in the following section.

3.2 Prototyipcal Concept Pattern

Like the powertype approach, the Prototypical Concept Pattern [5] solves the ambiguous classification problem by combining the inheritance and instantiation mechanisms, but does so in a way that is compatible with ordinary shallow instantiation semantics. Instead of requiring a new relationship type to express that Node is the powertype of NodeInstance, Node is modeled as the classifier of NodeInstance. Figure 5 shows how to apply the Prototypical Concept Pattern to classify NI as both being an instance-of N and an indirect instance-of NodeInstance.

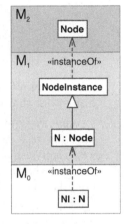

Fig. 5. The Prototypical Concept approach

The instance NI is, of course, an instance-of its class N (see Fig. 5). It is, however, also an indirect instance of NodeInstance because N inherits from NodeInstance. An association to ComponentInstance defined for NodeInstance, therefore, would create a link in NI to a component instance e.g., CI.

Figure 6 shows the complete scenario for the component/node model. Note how N receives the required resides on link (with the is allowed to reside on interpretation) by virtue of being an instance-of Node. The idea of a prototypical concept, which conveys certain properties upon all its subtypes has a long tradition in programming languages. The root class Object is used in the libraries of such languages as SMALLTALK, EIFFEL, and JAVA.

The potential problem with this approach is that the inheritance link between a new class (e.g., N) and its prototypical concept (e.g., NodeInstance) relies on a convention. There is no means available within the UML metamodel to enforce its presence. Moreover, this approach does not solve the replication of concepts problem.

3.3 Nested Metalevels with Context Sensitive Queries

The two previous approaches tackle the problem of ambiguous classification by using specialization to handle one of the classification dimensions. They also as-

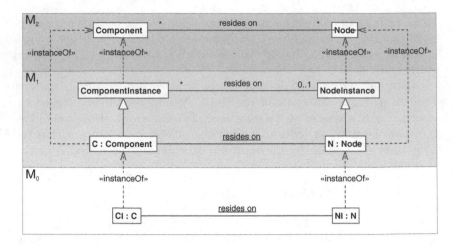

Fig. 6. Applying the Prototypical Concept Pattern

sume either a flat modeling framework (powertypes) or the linear metamodeling framework that currently underpins the UML (prototypical concept pattern).

One way of tackling the symptoms of shallow metamodeling in a way which does not rely on specialization is to organize the level in a more sophisticated way than just a linear hierarchy. In the nested metalevels approach of [3] one assumes that a level M_x which is meta to both M_{x-1} and M_{x-2} sees no level boundary between M_{x-1} and M_{x-2}.

This is depicted by Fig. 7. From the perspective of level M_2, N is an instance-of Node and NI is an instance-of NodeInstance. The level boundary between M_1 and M_0 is non-existent for level M_2. This view is justified by the fact that not all instance-of relationships are of the same kind [6]. The ambiguous classification problem is resolved by giving the physical instance-of relationships between Node and N, and NodeInstance and NI first class status, while the "instance of" relationship between N and NI are viewed as only being links be-

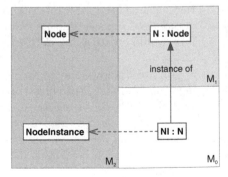

Fig. 7. Nested metalevels

tween instances. Although the instance-of relationship between NI and NodeInstance would be non-strict [7] under normal circumstances, it is not here because levels M_0 and M_1 are assumed to be a single level from the perspective of level M_2.

The drawback of this approach, however, is that the instance-of relationship between NI and N has second-class status. In the "fido the dog" example fido would be an instance-of Object and not of Dog. This is not only counterintuitive for someone focusing on the levels M_1 and M_0, but also implies that this second-class instance-of relationship has to be manually created between NI and N by some M_2-level mechanism.

Since a user not concerned with metamodeling would prefer to view NI as an instance-of N (or fido as an instance-of Dog) Álvarez et al. propose to make queries concerning classifiers context dependent [3]. Asking NI for its class would therefore yield N at the modeling level and NodeInstance at the metamodeling level. To achieve an adequate representation of the model for both kinds of users, Álvarez et al. propose a mapping G, which maps models between meta-levels and transforms them accordingly.

While this approach sidesteps the multiple classification problem and is probably faithful to how model representations of current case-tool vendors are designed, it still clings to the instantiation semantics of the traditional two level (M_1 and M_0) modeling approaches. As a consequence, the class features of a model element still have to be defined manually at each level. For instance, there is no way for the class Node to automatically influence the model element NI. Thus, the representative instance (introducing NodeInstance) approach is still required. Moreover, the nested metalevels approach does not provide an answer to the "replication of concepts" problem.

4   Deep Instantiation

Although they go someway to alleviating the symptoms of shallow instantiation semantics, none of the approaches described in the previous section satisfactorily solve both the "multiple classification" and "replication of concepts" problems. Moreover, they all involve uncomfortable levels of complexity. We believe that these approaches only partially relieve the symptoms, without curing the underlying problem. As mentioned previously, the underlying cause of the symptoms is the reliance on the old "two-levels only" modeling philosophy, i.e., the shallow instantiation assumption. For this reason we believe the solution lies in a more fundamental enhancement of existing modeling frameworks.

It is well known that model elements in a multiple level framework can represent both objects and types. This is in fact the basis of the very concept of metamodeling. Odell [4] captures this property by stating that objects are also types, while Atkinson uses the term "clabject" [7] to refer to a modeling element with both class and object facets. The capability of instances to be types is also inherent in the definition of the MOF [8].

Although the dual object/class properties of many modeling elements is widely acknowledged, it is not adequately supported by the traditional shallow instantiation model. On the contrary, the traditional instantiation model is "shallow" precisely because the class facet of a model element always has to be explicitly documented for each model element that represents a type. In other words, a class can never receive attributes and associations from its classifier, only slots and links.

We believe the solution to the problems outlined in the previous sections is to define an instantiation mechanism that recognizes and fully supports the class/object duality of instantiatable modeling elements within a multi-level modeling framework. In other words, an instantiation mechanism is needed in which a modeling element's class features can be acquired automatically by the instantiation step rather than always having to be defined explicitly. We refer to such an instantiation mechanism as deep instantiation. Only with a deep instantiation approach will it be possible to coherently define the instance and class facets of elements once and only once.

4.1 Potency

The key to achieving deep instantiation is to add the concept of "potency" to every model element at every level in a modeling framework. The potency of a model element is an integer that defines the depth to which a model element can be instantiated. Thus a model element of potency 0 corresponds to an object, a slot, a link, or any concept that is not intended for further instantiation (e.g., an interface or an abstract class). On the other hand, an element of potency 1 corresponds to a class, an attribute or an association that is intended to be instantiated only once. By extension, an element of potency 2 can support instantiation twice. In other words, it gives rise to instances with a potency of 1. The act of instantiating a modeling element obviously reduces its potency by one. This approach therefore unifies the concepts of class and object into a single concept "modeling element", distinguishing types (classes) and instances (objects) by their respective potency.

Another important property possessed by every model element is its level. As its name implies, the level of a model element is an integer representing the model level in which the element resides. Thus, an M_0 element has level value 0, and an M_1 element has value 1, etc.

Together, the level and potency properties of model elements allow many of the properties of the desired instantiation mechanism to be expressed in a very concise and concrete way. Instantiation, within a strict multi-level modeling framework, takes a model element with level l $(l > 0)$ and potency p $(p > 0)$ and yields an element with level $l - 1$ and potency $p - 1$. Since instantiation reduces both values by 1, it can only be applied to model elements whose potency and level are greater than 0. More formally,

$$\forall m \in ModelingElement : m.l > 0 \wedge m.p > 0 \Rightarrow$$
$$n.l = m.l - 1 \wedge n.p = m.p - 1, \text{where } n = @^4 m.$$

Elements whose potency is 0 cannot be instantiated, regardless of their level number. The potency property of a model element, hence, subsumes the isAbstract attribute (defined for GeneralizableElement in the UML) which designates a model element as being uninstantiatable. A model element which has an isAbstract slot containing the value *true* has a potency of 0. Another good example of a model element with potency 0 is the inheritance relationship between two elements, as it can not be further instantiated.

---

[4] Using an instantiation notation adopted in MML.

Many characteristics of the meta-modeling architectures in use today, such as the OMG's MOF and UML architectures can be concisely captured in terms of constraints on, and relationships between, the level and potency values. The fact that M_0 is assumed to be the bottom level for all elements, is captured by the rule that potency of a model element cannot be greater that its level, i.e,

$$\forall m \in ModelingElement : m.p \leq m.l$$

The fact that a modeling architecture only recognizes a certain number of levels is captured by a simple bound on the value of level, i.e.,

$$\forall m \in ModelingElement : 0 \leq m.l < 4$$

Finally, the semantics of shallow instantiation could be captured by the constraint that the potency of elements cannot be greater than one.

4.2   Single and Dual Fields

The semantics of instantiation is intimately related to the properties of attributes and slots[5]. When an element x is instantiated to create an element y (i.e., $y = @x$), the semantics of instantiation dictates that every attribute of x becomes a slot of y, with the same name and a value of the appropriate type. However, any *slots* in x have no effect on y, which we previously identified as the source of numerous problems.

Together, the potency and level values of a model element allow numerous simplifications of multi-level modeling. One of the most significant is the unification of the attribute and slot concepts. A slot is just an attribute that happens to have potency 0. In order to provide a convenient way of talking about attributes and slots in a general (unified) sense, and to avoid confusion arising from the semantic baggage associated with the existing terms, we introduce the concept of a field. A field with potency 0 represents a slot, and therefore must have a value. However, a field of higher potency may or may not have a value, depending on whether it is a simple field or a dual field.

A simple field is a field which does not have a value unless it has potency 0 (and thus corresponds to a traditional slot). Thus when an element x is instantiated to create an element y, any simple fields (of potency 2 or above) become an identical simple field of y, but with a potency decremented by one. On the other hand, a field of x with potency 1 becomes a field of y with potency 0 and a value.

A dual field is a field which has a value even for potencies greater than zero. When an element x is instantiated to create an element y, any dual fields of x become identical dual fields of y, but with a potency decremented by one and with a possibly new value. A dual field therefore has no counterpart in traditional

---

[5] Methods types and their instances, of course, are also affected by the semantics of instantiation, but since they are basically the same as for attributes and slots they are not discussed further here.

modeling approaches. The semantics of a dual field can best be thought of in terms of a set of simple fields. Basically, a dual field of potency n corresponds to a set of n simple fields, all identical except that they all have different potencies $(n, n - 1, \ldots, 0)$, and the field of potency 0 has a value. The instantiation of an element with such a set of simple fields will yield a model element with $n - 1$ similar fields. This is because the field with potency 0 cannot by definition be instantiated and thus disappears when the element it belongs to is instantiated.

Because they are model elements in their own right, fields also have their own level and potency values. Obviously the level of a field must match that of the model element to which it belongs, but the potency does not have to match. Clearly it makes sense to permit a model element to have fields with a lower potency, since these will simply disappear after the appropriate number of instantiation steps. However, perhaps surprisingly, it also makes sense for a model element with potency n to have fields with a potency higher than n. For instance, a regular abstract class corresponds to a model element of potency 0 with fields of potency 1. These fields cannot be instantiated, however, until a model element with a potency greater than zero inherits the fields.

Clearly, providing a clean and consistent notation for these concepts is essential for its ultimate acceptance. At present the notation is at an early stage of evolution, but for the purposes of this paper we adopt the convention illustrated below. The potency of a model element is represented as a superscript and the level as a subscript. In addition, fields of potency 0 (which have a value) are distinguished by being underlined. We are aware of the fact that underlining is currently being used to denote static attributes but argue strongly for correcting this decision. Our potency 0 fields *exactly* correspond to instantiated attributes, whereas the correspondence between static attributes and instantiated attributes is only partial. Thus simple fields are underlined if their potency is 0, whereas dual fields are always underlined. The visualization of the level subscripts is optional, if clear from the context. Also, with one exception, it is only mandatory to explicitly indicate potency values greater than one. The exception are dual fields of potency 1 where the potency value has to be shown in order to distinguish the field from an ordinary field of potency 0.

Element^2_2
$\underline{\text{DualField}^1_2}$
SimpleField^2_2

Fig. 8. Elements with potencies and levels

4.3   Modeling with Deep Instantiation

In this section we demonstrate how the few simple concepts introduced in the previous section have the power to radically change the way in which metamodeling is performed, and how they provide a much simpler and conceptually coherent solution to the modeling scenarios introduced in the previous sections.

Fig. 9 shows a new version of the component/node scenario modeled using deep instantiation semantics rather than shallow instantiation. In order to illustrate how the concepts introduced in the previous subsection help simplify the presentation of components, nodes and their properties we have added a few additional concepts not present in the UML metamodel. However, the intention of these should be clear.

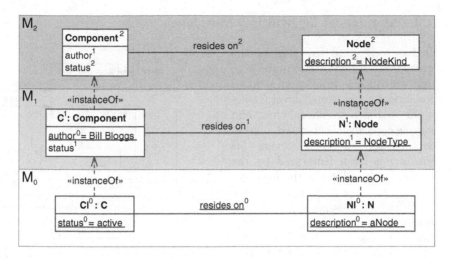

Fig. 9. Components and nodes with deep instantiation

Field author is a potency 1 field of Component which becomes a potency 0 field in C and obtains a value. This, therefore, represents the normal attribute/slot semantics familiar in regular two-level modeling. Status, however, is a potency 2 simple field of Component. When C is instantiated from Component it becomes a potency 1 field (i.e. a regular attribute). Thus, when CI is instantiated from C, status becomes a potency 0 field (i.e. a regular slot) and assumes a value.

The description field of Node is a dual field rather than a simple field. This means that even though it has potency 2 in Node it also has a value. When N is instantiated from Node, the potency of description is reduced by one, but since it is a dual field it still has a value. Finally, when NI is instantiated from N, description becomes a potency 0 field with a value. There is consequently no difference between dual fields of potency 0 and simple fields of potency 0.

The problem of the proliferation of elements, associations, and links is also neatly solved by potencies. In Fig. 9 the resides on relationship between Component and Node has potency 2 rather than the traditional potency 1. This means that when C and N are instantiated from Component and Node, resides on becomes a relationship of potency 1. As a consequence it is available for further instantiation, and thus can give rise to potency 0 relationships (i.e. links) between instances of C and N. The need to introduce artificial metaclasses such as Component Instance and Node Instance, is therefore avoided. Note that the M_1-level resides on association precisely specifies which component types may reside on a particular node type. There is no need to allow links between component and node instances in general, which have to be restricted by an additional rule to achieve the effect that deep instantiation naturally provides. Also, in contrast with the prototypical concept approach, all properties associated with component instances and node instances can be defined simply and directly at the M_2-level in a way that is enforceable and controllable by tool vendors.

4.4   Metamodel for Multiple Metalevels

It has long been the goal of the graphical modeling community to capture all the fundamental ideas for modeling in a multilevel framework within a small, coherent and simple core, usually termed a meta-metamodel. So far, however, this vision has been frustrated by the problems described in the first section of this paper. For instance, the MOF, which is supposed to be the meta-metamodel for the UML, duplicates many of the same modeling concepts as the UML (because of the replication of concepts problem) and equivocates on the proper positioning of modeling elements [8].

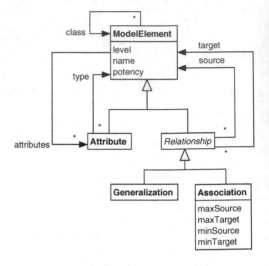

Fig. 10. The MoMM

We believe the concepts described above provide the ingredients for this vision to finally be fulfilled, and for a truly concise meta-metamodel of strict multi-level modeling to be defined. A preliminary version of the MoMM (**M**etamodel for **M**ultiple **M**etalevels) is illustrated in Fig. 10.

The key point to note about this meta-metamodel is that since every model element, anywhere in the metamodeling architecture, is intended to have level and potency values, these have to represented as dual fields of the basic model element. They must be dual fields because all elements in an instantiation chain, up to a maximum of three, need a level and potency value.

5   Conclusion

Given the OMG's goal to make the next version (2.0) of the UML supportive of a family of languages, the nature of the metamodeling framework will be critical in its future success. As a consequence, there has been a significant increase in the level of research into the optimal modeling architecture. However, all existing approaches proposed to date suffer from the limitations imposed by the model of shallow instantiation inherited from the traditional two-level roots of object technology. As a consequence they all suffer from a number of fundamental problems that seriously undermine the semantics of the metamodeling architecture.

The basic problem is that the traditional two-level semantics of instantiation does not scale up for metamodeling hierarchies with more than two levels. The original UML modeling concepts are sufficient to allow modeling at the M_1-level, but fail to address the needs at level M_2. This problem causes a number of symptoms in existing multi-level modeling architectures, such as the UML, including the "ambiguous classification" problem (or multiple-of problem as it is known in the MML work), and the "replication of concepts" problem.

Although various strategies have been developed for softening the impact of these problem, none is entirely successful in removing all of the symptoms. In this paper we have therefore put forward a number of principles that we believe offer a fundamental solution to these problems, and thus offer the way for a clean, simple and coherent semantics for metamodeling. We have demonstrated how these ideas can simplify the descriptions of real modeling scenarios currently found in the UML. Furthermore, the principles lead to a simple, linear hierarchy in which every modeling element can be assigned its proper location, i.e., the doctrine of strict metamodeling is supported.

This work is at a preliminary stage, and is currently ongoing at the Component Engineering group (AGCE) at the University of Kaiserslautern. However, we hope the ideas might be helpful in the search for the optimal UML 2.0 modeling framework.

References

1. Brian Henderson-Sellers. Some problems with the UML V1.3 metamodel. In *Proceedings of the 34th Annual Hawaii International Conference on System Sciences*. Institute of Electrical and Electronics Engineers, 2001.
2. Tony Clark, Andy Evans, Stuart Kent, Steve Brodsky, and Steve Cook. A feasibility study in rearchitecting UML as a family of languages using a precise OO meta-modeling approach. http://www.cs.york.ac.uk/puml/mml/mmf.pdf, September 2000.
3. José Álvarez, Andy Evans, and Paul Sammut. MML and the metamodel architecture. Workshop on Transformations in UML (WTUML'01), associated with the fourth European Joint Conference on Theory and Practice of Software (ETAPS'01), Genova, Italy, January 2001.
4. Jim Odell. Power types. *Journal of Object-Oriented Programming*, May 1994.
5. Colin Atkinson and Thomas Kühne. Processes and products in a multi-level metamodeling architecture. *submitted for publication*, 2001.
6. Jean Bézivin and Richard Lemesle. Ontology-based layered semantics for precise OA&D modeling. In Haim Kilov and Bernhard Rumpe, editors, *Proceedings of the ECOOP'97 Workshop on Precise Semantics for Object-Oriented Modeling Techniques*, pages 31–37. Technische Universität München, TUM-I9725, 1997.
7. Colin Atkinson. Meta-modeling for distributed object environments. In *Enterprise Distributed Object Computing*, pages 90–101. IEEE Computer Society, October 1997.
8. OMG. Meta object facility (MOF) specification. OMG document formal/00-04-03, Version 1.3, March 2000.

Mapping between Levels in the Metamodel Architecture

José M. Álvarez[1], Andy Evans[2], and Paul Sammut[2]

[1] Dpto. de Lenguajes y Ciencias de la Computación, University of Málaga,
Málaga, 29071, Spain
alvarezp@lcc.uma.es
[2] Dept. of Computer Science, University of York,
Heslington, York, YO10 5DD, United Kingdom
andye@cs.york.ac.uk, pauls@cs.york.ac.uk

Abstract. The Meta-Modeling Language is a static object-oriented modeling language whose focus is the declarative definition of languages. It aims to enable the UML metamodel to be precisely defined, and to enable UML to evolve into a family of languages. This paper argues that although MML takes a metamodeling approach to language definition, it cannot be described as strict metamodeling. This has significant implications for the nature of the metamodel architecture it supports, yet without contravening the OMG's requirements for the UML 2.0 infrastructure. In particular it supports a rich generic nested architecture as opposed to the linear architecture that strict metamodeling imposes. In this nested architecture, the transformation of any model between its representations at two adjacent metalevels can be described by an information preserving one-to-one mapping. This mapping, which can itself be defined in UML, provides the basis for a powerful area of functionality that any potential metamodeling tool should seek to exploit.

1. Introduction

The Unified Modeling Language (UML) has been rapidly accepted as a standard notation for modeling object-oriented software systems. However, the speed at which UML has developed has led to some issues, particularly regarding its customisability and the precision of its semantics [1]. UML is therefore evolving, with an impending revision (UML 2.0 [2]) seeking to resolve these and other issues.

The customisability issue has arisen in part because UML has proven so popular. UML was originally designed as a general-purpose language that was not intended for use in specific domains [3]. However as UML has become more widespread, there has been considerable demand for it to be applicable in specialised areas. As it currently stands, UML is a monolithic language with little provision for customisability. Any new features would need to be added to the single body of language, leading to an increasingly unwieldy language definition. There is also potential for conflicts between the requirements of different domains, which may not be resolvable within a monolithic language definition [Cook, 4]. An alternative approach (which the OMG has set as a mandatory requirement for UML 2.0 [5])

M. Gogolla and C. Kobryn (Eds.): UML 2001, LNCS 2185, pp. 34–46, 2001.

allows the language to naturally evolve into a family of distinct dialects called 'profiles' that build upon a core kernel language. Each profile would have its own semantics (compatible with the kernel language) specific to the requirements of its domain.

The semantics issue concerns the fact that the current specification for UML (version 1.3) [6] uses natural language to define its semantics. Thus there is no formal definition against which tools can be checked for conformance. This has resulted in a situation where few tools from different vendors are compatible [Warmer, 4]. A formal precise semantics is essential for compliance checking and interoperability of tools.

Another key requirement for UML 2.0 is that it should be rigorously aligned with the OMG four-layer metamodel architecture [5]. In this architecture, a model at one layer is used to specify models in the layer below. In turn a model at one layer can be viewed as an 'instance' of some model in the layer above. The four layers are the meta-metamodel layer (M3), the metamodel layer (M2), the user model layer (M1) and the user object layer (M0). The UML metamodel (the definition of UML) sits at the M2 layer, and as such it should be able to be described as an instance of some language meta-metamodel at the M3 level. Although the relationship between UML and MOF (the OMG's standard M3 language for metamodeling) loosely approximates this [6], the lack of a precise formal UML metamodel severely limits the potential value of such a relationship.

In line with these key requirements for UML 2.0, the Precise UML group [7] have proposed 'rearchitecting UML as a family of languages using a precise object-oriented metamodeling approach' [8]. The foundation of their proposal is the Meta-Modeling Facility, which comprises the Meta-Modeling Language (MML), an alternative M3 layer language for describing modeling languages such as UML, and a tool (MMT) that implements it.

Whilst MML takes a metamodeling approach, it cannot be described as 'strict' metamodeling, and this has profound implications for the metamodel architecture. This paper (an expanded version of an earlier paper [9]) attempts to provide clarification of the exact nature of this architecture, in particular demonstrating that the linear hierarchical model is inappropriate; instead an alternative model for this architecture is offered. It also argues that when viewed in this modified architecture, any model can be represented at a number of different metalevels, and that a precise definition can be given to the transformation of a model between those metalevels. This transformational mapping should be a key feature of any metamodeling tool.

The paper is structured as follows: Section 2 gives an overview of MML; Section 3 describes the 'nested' metamodel architecture supported by MML; Section 4 defines the mapping that describes the transformation between metalevels in this architecture; Section 5 demonstrates the application of this mapping with a simple example; and Section 6 outlines conclusions and further work.

2. The Meta-modeling Language

MML is a 'static OO modeling language that aims to be small, meta-circular and as consistent as possible with UML 1.3' [10]. The MML metamodel partitions the fundamental components of language definition into separate packages. It makes two key orthogonal distinctions [8]: between 'model' and 'instance', and between 'syntax' and 'concepts'. Models describe valid expressions of a language (such as a UML 'class'), whereas instances represent situations that models denote (such as a UML 'object'). Concepts are the logical elements of a language (such as a class or object), and (concrete) syntax refers to the representation of those concepts often in a textual or graphical form (for example the elements of a class diagram or XML code). MML also defines appropriate mappings between these various language components, in particular a semantic mapping between the model and instance concepts, and mappings between the syntax and concepts of both the model and instance components.

The MML metamodel defines the minimum number of concepts needed to define itself, and wherever possible uses the existing syntax and concepts of UML 1.3. This meta-circularity eliminates the need for another language to describe MML, thus closing the language definition loop. The clean separation of language components and the mappings between them is fundamental to the coherence and readability of the MML metamodel.

The key extensibility mechanism in MML that provides the means of realising UML as a family of languages is the notion of package specialisation based on that of Catalysis [11]. In the Catalysis approach, packages may be specialised in the same way as classes; all the contents of the parent package are inherited by the child package, where they can themselves be specialised. This allows the definition of language components to be developed incrementally over a number of packages [10].

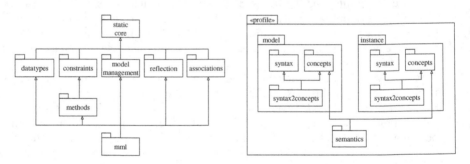

1a. Profile Packages   **1b.** Profile Framework

Fig. 1. The MML Architecture

The architecture of the MML metamodel is founded on the separation of language components and the notion of package specialisation described above. The metamodel is split into a number of key profile packages, each of which describe a fundamental aspect of modeling languages, and which are combined through an inheritance hierarchy to give the complete MML definition (Fig. 1a adapted from [8]). In turn, each of the profile packages shares the same framework of sub-packages as depicted in Fig. 1b (adapted from [8]).

These sub-packages represent the basic language components and the appropriate mappings between them, and contain modeling constructs such as classes and associations. A simplified form of the *static core* profile is depicted in Fig. 2, by way of illustration. The *model.concepts* packages describe constructs that denote valid language metamodels (such as the UML metamodel), and the *instance.concepts* packages describe constructs that denote valid instances of those metamodels (such as UML models). Constraints are applied to the constructs where appropriate through the use of OCL (the Object Constraint Language).

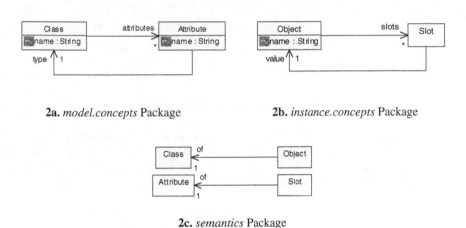

2a. *model.concepts* Package   2b. *instance.concepts* Package

2c. *semantics* Package

Fig. 2. Simplified 'Static Core' Profile

A key idea to grasp for the discussion that follows is that MML serves two distinct functions: it is both a metamodeling language (such that the UML metamodel instantiates the MML metamodel) and a kernel language (it defines a subset of elements needed in the UML metamodel). Ultimately then, the aim is for the UML 2.0 metamodel to be both a specialisation and instance of the MML metamodel.

3. Strict Metamodeling and the Four-Layer Architecture

This section argues that MML does not in fact fit into a *strict* metamodeling architecture, and that instead of being a problem, this actually makes MML more powerful. It also argues that this deviation from strict metamodeling does not contravene the mandatory requirements for UML 2.0 [5].

In a strict metamodeling architecture, every element of a model must be an instance of *exactly one* element of a model in the *immediate* next metalevel up [12]. As MML stands, it satisfies the 'exactly one' criterion, but every element does not instantiate an element from the immediate next metalevel up.

This is illustrated in Fig. 3 below. The concepts in the *model.concepts* packages (*e.g.* Class) and the concepts in the *instance.concepts* packages (*e.g.* Object) are all in the same metalevel (M3) since they are all part of MML. In line with the strict metamodeling mandate, instantiations of elements from the *model.concepts* packages belong to the metalevel below (M2) – these will be the elements that form the UML metamodel. However, instantiations of elements from the *instance.concepts* packages belong to the metalevel below that (M1), since these will form models that must satisfy the languages defined at the M2 level.

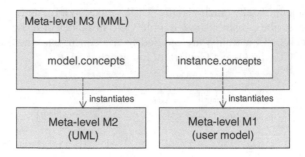

Fig. 3. Instantiation of the MML Metamodel

In fact, since UML extends MML (through specialisation), this pattern is repeated for the relationship between M2, M1 and M0. So the Four-Layer Metamodel Architecture does not in fact resemble the linear hierarchy shown in Fig. 4a but the nested structure shown in Fig. 4b. If Fig. 4a was the true representation, any metalevel could only describe elements from the metalevel immediately below it; for example MML (level M3) could describe elements from the UML metamodel (M2) but not elements from user models (M1). In the nested architecture however, a model can describe elements from *every* metalevel below it. This is a very powerful feature since it means that if a tool implements the MML metamodel, then it can not only be used to define languages such as UML, but user models and objects as well. How this is achieved is the subject of subsequent sections.

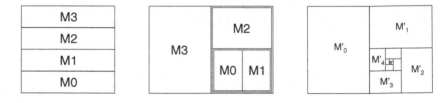

4a. Linear Four-layer   **4b.** Nested Four-layer   **4c.** Nested Generic

Fig. 4. Metamodel Architectures

Theoretically, the nested structure of the metamodel architecture (according to MML) is not confined to four levels; it could be applied at any number of levels, as depicted in Fig. 4c. In effect, the four-level metamodel architecture is a specialisation of this generic nested architecture.

In fact, the fundamental metalevel of this architecture is not the bottom level as suggested by the OMG metalevel 'M0', but the top level, since only the top level is represented by classifiers (*e.g.* classes and packages) – all other metalevels are represented by instances. An alternative notation for the levels of the metamodel architecture (M'_1 *etc.*) is introduced in Fig. 4c to emphasise this, and also to distinguish these levels from the four OMG metalevels.

This nested metamodel architecture might be seen as being at odds with the requirements set out by the OMG for the UML 2.0. However, the UML 2.0 Infrastructure RFP [5] states:

> Proposals shall specify the UML metamodel in a manner that is strictly aligned with the MOF meta-metamodel by conformance to a 4-layer metamodel architecture pattern. Stated otherwise every UML metamodel element must be an instance of exactly one MOF meta-metamodel element.

It should be noted that this does not specify a *strict* metamodel architecture, and every UML metamodel element is intended to be an instance of exactly one MML meta-metamodel element (where an MML meta-metamodel element is equivalent to a MOF meta-metamodel element). This paper therefore argues that the nested metamodel architecture outlined in this section fulfils the infrastructure requirements.

4. Mapping between Metalevels

As described in Section 2, MML makes a fundamental distinction between *model* concepts and *instance* concepts. However, any model element can in fact be thought of as an instance element (for example, a class can always be thought of as an instance of the metaclass *Class*). These two representations of the same entity are related by a one-to-one information preserving mapping, arbitrarily referred to as '*G*' (Fig. 5a). In effect the *G* mapping represents the crucial notion of *meta*-instantiation. In fact an entire model can be represented by another model at a metalevel below it through the application of this same *G* mapping (Fig. 5b).

5a. Mapping between Model Elements   **5b.** Mapping between Models

Fig. 5. Mapping between Metalevels

Thus for a model X:

$$X(M'_n).G = X(M'_{n+1}) ; \qquad (1)$$

the mapping between a model and its representation two metalevels below is given as:

$$X(M'_n).G.G = X(M'_{n+2}) ; \qquad (2)$$

and in order to translate to a metalevel up:

$$X(M'_n).G^{-1} = X(M'_{n-1}) . \qquad (3)$$

It can be seen that model information does not have two representations, but an infinite hierarchy of representations, corresponding to the nested generic metamodel architecture of Fig. 4c. It will be shown that the further down a model is in the metalevel hierarchy, the larger and more complex it is. However, as with the metamodel architecture, only the first few metalevel representations hold any real practical value.

How might this mapping be modeled?   One approach would be to include a method in every model element that would create the appropriate element to represent it at the next metalevel below;   for example *Class* would have a method $G()$ that would create an instance of *Object* with a slot '*of* = *Class*'. This is an intuitive way of viewing the transformation, but would result in a single confusing model that contained both representations simultaneously.   Instead what we need is a way of separating these two representations.   This can be achieved by modeling the *G* mapping as a package that specialises both the metamodel for elements that can appear in a model at M'_n and the metamodel for elements of its equivalent model at M'_{n-1} (Fig. 6).   This mapping package has visibility (through specialisation) of both metamodels, so it can define how one model is a valid *G* transformation of another model by means of appropriate associations between elements of the metamodels, and constraints on those associations.   This model of mapping, which is also used in the *semantics* packages of the MML metamodel [8] and will provide the basis of the OMG's Model Driven Architecture [13], is based on the Catalysis [11] model of refinement.

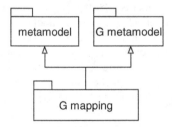

Fig. 6. The *G* Mapping Package

The two metamodels in Fig. 6 are in fact identical (one is a copy of the other), but they must be shown as separate packages as the mapping needs to refer to elements from two metamodels.   For illustrative purposes, this paper assumes the metamodel (*i.e.* the M'_0 layer in the metamodel architecture) to be that of Fig. 2.   Thus the only valid elements are classes, attributes, objects and slots.   There are obviously severe limitations to the expressibility of this metamodel, but fewer concepts aid clarity.   The following points must be considered regarding this metamodel:

- the name attribute on an Object instance is optional, so unnamed objects are valid;
- datatypes (such as String) are not modeled explicitly for the sake of simplicity, but do feature in the associated models;
- slots do not have a name; instead they are simply 'of' a named attribute.   Thus in Fig. 5a, the syntax '*name* = Dog' actually represents an unnamed slot 'of' the attribute *name*, whose value is 'Dog'.   This relationship between slots and attributes is introduced as it is closer to the relationship between objects and classes, and thus provides consistency between different elements as the *G* mapping is applied.

The associations of the *G* mapping are defined in Fig. 7;   in this class diagram, the *Object* metaclass in *G metamodel* has been renamed as *GObject* to distinguish it from

Object in *metamodel*. Note how every element in *metamodel* maps to *Object* in *G metamodel*. Translating to natural language, the *G* mapping maps classes, attributes, objects and slots to instances of *Class, Attribute, Object* and *Slot*.

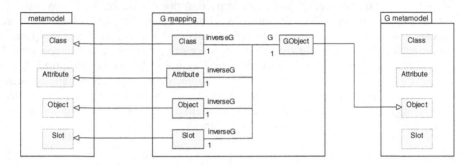

Fig. 7. The *G* Mapping Class Diagram

The OCL constraints on each of the metaclasses are given in Table 1. There is considerable commonality in these constraints and these could potentially abstracted into a generic pattern. It should be noted that these constraints only cover one direction of the *G* mapping transformation (*i.e.* what models are valid *G* transformations of other models), but constraints could be added to cover the reverse direction (*i.e.* what models are valid inverse *G* transformations of other models). One limitation that arises through the use of constraints (or methods) is that constraints only talk about *instances* of their associated model element, not model elements themselves. Because of this, there is no way of translating down from or up to level M'_0 (the true model level) – thus Equations 1 to 3 above only hold for $n>0$.

Table 1. The *G* Mapping Constraints


```
context Class inv:
   G.of.name = "Class"
   G.slots -> exists (s |
      s.of.name = "name" and
      s.value = self.name)
   self.attributes -> forAll(a |
   G.slots -> exists (s |
      s.of.name = "attributes" and
      s.value = a.G
```

```
context Attribute inv:
   G.of.name = "Attribute"
   G.slots -> exists (s |
      s.of.name = "name" and
      s.value = self.name)
   G.slots -> exists (s |
      s.of.name = "type" and
      s.value = self.type.G
```

```
context Object inv:
   G.of.name = "Object"
   G.slots -> exists (s |
      s.of.name = "of" and
      s.value = self.of.G
   G.slots -> exists (s |
      s.of.name = "name" and
      s.value = self.name)
   self.slots -> forAll(s |
   G.slots -> exists (s1 |
      s1.of.name = "slots" and
      s1.value = s.G
```

```
context Slot inv:
   G.of.name = "Slot"
   G.slots -> exists (s |
      s.of.name = "of" and
      s.value = self.of.G
   G.slots -> exists (s |
      s.of.name = "value" and
      s.value = self.value.G
```

5. Application of the *G* Mapping

The application of the *G* mapping can be demonstrated by introducing a simple example. First however, a subtle but important point must be made. When a class such as *Dog* in Fig. 8 is drawn in a class diagram, it must conform to some metamodel. It is the metamodel therefore that resides at the top level (M'_0), so only the metamodel can contain true classes – every other level must be represented by instances. Therefore the class box for *Dog* does not in fact represent a true class, but an instance of the metaclass *Class*. It is no coincidence that this difference between the apparent representation of an element and its 'true' representation is modeled by the *G* mapping. It is important therefore to realise that every class diagram and object diagram has the *G* mapping implicit in its syntax.

Fig. 8. User Model and User Objects

To illustrate this, in Fig. 8 we have a class *Dog*, and two instantiations of *Dog*. However, as described above, if the metamodel of Fig. 2 resides at the M'_0 level, then the true representation of the *Dog* model and instance is that of Fig. 9a. It is helpful to see how the elements in this view of the model fit in the metamodel architecture; this is shown in Fig. 9b. This is the view of a system that a modeling tool takes – it implements the metamodel, and translates user models and objects down to the M'_1 and M'_2 level respectively.

A metamodeling tool might view a system quite differently however. It would implement a meta-metamodel (such as the MOF or MML metamodel), and take a metamodel (such as the UML metamodel) as an instance at the M'_1 level. User models and user objects can still be included in the system, but they must be translated a further metalevel down. If the basic Fig. 2 metamodel is assumed to be both the meta-metamodel and the metamodel, then it too must be translated a metalevel down (Fig. 10), so that it can be represented at the M'_1 level.

The corresponding view of the user model and user objects is now two metalevels removed from that of Fig. 8. The complete model is too large to include here, so only a small segment (representing the *Dog* class only) is shown in Fig. 11a; the position of the various elements of the system is again shown in Fig. 11b. It can thus be seen how the complexity and size of a model increases rapidly the lower it is represented in the metalevel hierarchy. However, the gain is the potential for a metamodeling tool where the metamodel can be changed as required, so long as it conforms to the meta-metamodel (the only fixed model in the system), which can also be used for user modeling. A user would never have to understand a model such as that of Fig. 11a; their model would be translated on-the-fly to the representation appropriate for them (Fig. 8).

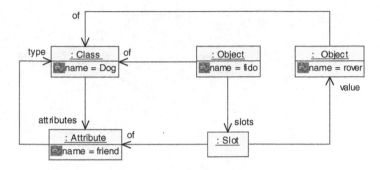

9a. Model

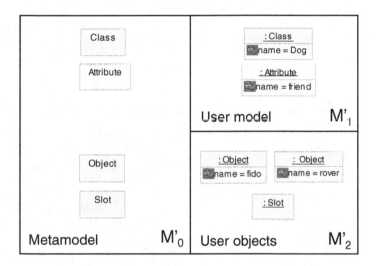

9b. Position in the Metamodel Architecture

Fig. 9. User Model and User Objects at Metalevels M´₁ and M´₂

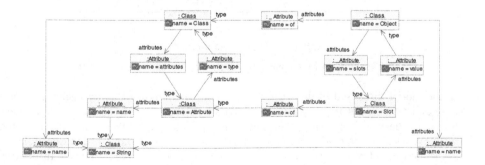

Fig. 10. Metamodel at Metalevel M´₁

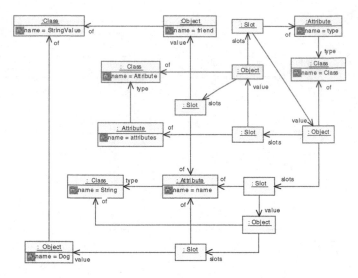

11a. Model

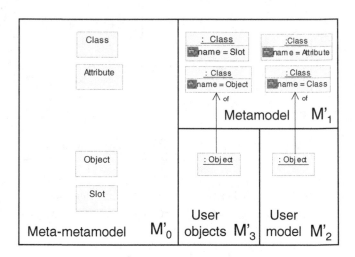

11b. Position in the Metamodel Architecture

Fig. 11. User Model and User Objects at Metalevels M'_2 and M'_3

In the model discussed in this section, *fido* can be thought of as an instance of both *Dog* and *Object*, but if (as MML suggests) an object can only be 'of' a single class, how can these two notions of instantiation be modeled? The crucial idea is that whenever a query is made on a model (such as 'what is *fido*.of?'), that query has an associated metalevel as well as the model elements themselves. This is in contrast with current thinking that queries can only be made about a model from the top metalevel (M'_0). In the Fig. 11 view of the system, if the '*fido*.of' query is applied at the M'_0 level, the answer is returned as *Object*. However, the '*fido*.of = *Dog*' relationship is also modeled, but at the M'_1 level. Thus if the mapping *G* is applied to the query '*fido*.of' itself, the result would be the *Dog* object. The *G* mapping can similarly be applied to any operation, whether side effect free or not.

6. Conclusion

The Meta-Modeling Language (MML) is a static object-oriented modeling language whose focus is the declarative definition of other languages such as UML. MML takes a metamodeling approach to defining languages, in line with the OMG's requirement that UML 2.0 must be aligned with their Four-Layer metamodel architecture. However, the architecture supported by MML cannot be described as a *strict* metamodel architecture, since not all elements instantiate elements from the *immediate* metalevel up. Instead, MML supports a powerful nested metamodel architecture, which this paper argues does not contravene the mandatory requirements for UML 2.0.

A key aspect of this architecture is that a model can be represented at any metalevel. The transformation between the representation of any model at one metalevel and its representation at the metalevel below it can be described by an information preserving one-to-one mapping (*G*). This mapping would have the following potential uses in a metamodelling tool:

- to enable metamodeling tools to be used as modeling tools;
- to translate representations of models 'on the fly' to a metalevel most appropriate for visualising them (*e.g.* a *Class* object is visualised as a class);
- to translate queries and manipulations on models to any metalevel;

This mapping is so fundamental that it should be brought out explicitly. It should not be part of MML, rather it should be a separate part of the Meta-Modeling Facility, something that defines some core functionality for any tool that is MML compliant. It is planned to continue this work by implementing a simple metamodeling tool that is able to translate models using the *G* mapping.

References

1. Kobryn C.: UML 2001 : A Standardization Odyssey. Communications of the ACM, 1999 [42, 10]
2. UML 2.0 Working Group web site:
    http://www.celigent.com/omg/adptf/wgs/uml2wg.htm
3. Rumbaugh J., Jacobson I., Booch G.: The Unified Modeling Language Reference Manual. Addison-Wesley, 1999
4. Cook S., Mellor S., Warmer J., Wills A., Evans A. (moderator): Advanced Methods and Tools for a Precise UML. Available at [7]
5. Request for Proposal: UML 2.0 Infrastructure RFP. Available at [2], 2000
6. OMG Unified Modeling Language Specification. Available at [15], 1999
7. Precise UML group web site: http://www.puml.org/

8.   Brodsky S., Clark A., Cook S., Evans A., Kent S.: A Feasibility Study in Rearchitecting UML as a Family of Languages using a Precise OO Meta-Modeling Approach. Available at [7], 2000
9.   Alvarez J., Evans A., Sammut P.: MML and the Metamodel Architecture. Available at [7], 2001
10. Clark T., Evans A., Kent S., Sammut P.: The MMF Approach to Engineering Object-Oriented Design Languages. Available at [7]
11. D'Souza D., Wills A.: Objects, Components and Frameworks with UML: The Catalysis Approach. Addison-Wesley, 1998
12. Atkinson C., Kuhne T.: Strict Profiles: Why and How. In [14], 2000
13. Soley R. & OMG: Model Driven Architecture White Paper. Available at [15], 2001
14. Evans A., Kent S., Selic B.: Proceedings of <<UML>> 2000 – The Unified Modeling Language, Advancing the Standard: 3rd International Conference (LNCS 1939). Springer-Verlag, 2000
15. OMG web site: http://www.omg.org/

An Execution Algorithm for UML Activity Graphs

Rik Eshuis* and Roel Wieringa

University of Twente, Department of Computer Science
P.O. Box 217, 7500 AE Enschede, The Netherlands
{eshuis,roelw}@cs.utwente.nl

Abstract. We present a real-time execution semantics for UML activity graphs that is intended for workflow modelling. The semantics is defined in terms of execution algorithms that define how components of a workflow system execute an activity graph. The semantics stays close to the semantics of UML state machines, but differs from it in some minor points. Our semantics deals with real time. The semantics provides a basis for verification of UML activity graphs, for example using model checking, and also for executing UML activity graphs using simulation tools. We illustrate an execution by means of a small example.

1 Introduction

A workflow model specifies an ordering on activities performed in an organisation. Typical ordering constructs are sequence, choice and parallelism. A useful notation for specifying this ordering is provided by UML activity graphs [14]. Figure 1 shows an example activity graph. Ovals represent activity states and rounded rectangles represent wait states. In an activity state, some activity is busy executing whereas in a wait state, an external event is waited for, e.g. a deadline must occur, or some third party must send some information. An activity state is called an action state in UML [14]. The workflow starts in the black dot (the initial state) and ends at the bull's eye (the end state). A bar represents a fork (more than one outgoing edge) or a join (more than one entering edge). A diamond represents a choice (more than one outgoing edge) or a merging of different choices (more than one entering edge).

The semantics in the current version 1.3 of UML is not yet entirably suitable for workflow modelling because in the UML 1.3 version, the semantics is specified in terms of state machines. (In UML 2.0, the semantics will be defined independently from state machines.) For example, in UML 1.3 an activity is defined as an entry action of a state. An entry action is executed to completion when its state is entered [14, p.2-144]. But in Fig. 1 this means that the two activities *Register* and *Evaluate* are executed simultaneously in the same run-to-completion step! This is not what we would like the activity graph of Fig. 1

---

* Supported by NWO/SION, grant nr. 612-62-02 (DAEMON).

M. Gogolla and C. Kobryn (Eds.): UML 2001, LNCS 2185, pp. 47–61, 2001.

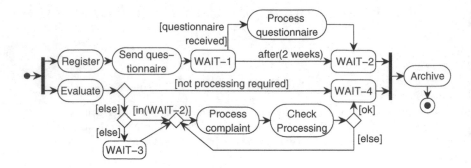

Fig. 1. Processing Complaints (adapted from Van der Aalst [1])

to say. What we would like to express by Fig. 1 is that *Register* and *Evaluate* start simultaneously, not that they should stop at the same time.

The underlying problem is that in UML 1.3, an activity graph is viewed as model of a software system that executes the activities. We want to use activity graphs for workflow modelling and therefore see an activity graph as a model of a workflow system (WFS). In workflow modelling, the activities are performed by actors (people or applications) external to the WFS, not by the WFS itself. It is the task of the WFS to monitor these activities, to manage the flow of data between them, and to route work items through a collection of actors, but it is not the task of the WFS to *execute* the activities. So in Fig. 1 the WFS executes the state transitions, i.e. the arrows in the diagram. The activities (nodes in the diagram) are executed by actors external to the WFS.

In this paper we present a formal execution semantics of UML activity graphs intended for workflow modelling that incorporates the above ideas. To show that our semantics is executable, we give our semantics in terms of an execution algorithm. Constraints are written in OCL and simple set theory.

The remainder of the paper is structured as follows. In Section 2 we explain in more detail how a WFS works. In Section 3 we define the syntax of activity graphs we use in this paper. In Section 4 we present our semantics in terms of execution algorithms for the components of the WFS that we identified in Section 2 and give a small example. In Section 5 we discuss related work. We end with conclusions and future work.

2   Workflow Systems

Purpose. A workflow system manages the flow of a case through an organisation. A case is the handling of a specific customer request to provide a certain service, e.g. the handling of an insurance claim in order to accept and pay the claim or to decline the claim. In a *case*, a certain set of activities is done in a certain sequence. An *activity* is an amount of work that is uninterruptible and that is performed in a non-zero span of time by an actor. An actor is either a user or an application. In an activity, the actor updates *case attributes*, which are stored in a database. The sequence of the activities of a certain class of cases is specified in a *workflow model*. The WFS uses the sequencing information in the workflow model to route the case after an activity has terminated or event has occurred.

Events can be generated by the user of the WFS, the application used by this user, or by the database. The WFS reacts to the events by routing the case. We distinguish four kinds of events.

- A typical kind of event in a workflow is a *termination event*, which denotes that a certain activity has terminated (it is not important who the actor was) and that therefore the next activity can be started. What this next activity is, is determined by the WFS based on the WFS model. The WFS then routes the case to the next activity. Termination events are not defined in UML 1.3.
- In a slightly confusing terminology, a *completion event* is defined in the UML as the event when a wait state is entered[1] [14, p.2-147].
- An *external event* is a discrete change of some condition in the environment. This change can be referred to by giving a name to the change itself or to the condition that changes:
  - A *named external event* is an event that is given an unique name [14, p.2-131].
  - A *value change event* is an event that represents that a boolean condition has become true [14, p.2-131]. For example, in Fig. 1 the condition [questionnaire received] denotes a value change event.
- A *temporal event* is a moment in time to which the system is expected to respond, i.e. some deadline [14, p.2-131]. For example, in Fig. 1 the label after(2 weeks) denotes a deadline, after which the WFS is supposed to react by skipping the Process questionnaire activity. Temporal events are generated by the WFS itself. We assume that the WFS has an internal clock that measures the time.

In general, the state of a case is distributed over several actors. Each distributed part has a local state. Multiple instances of the same local state can be active at the same time. The (global) state of a case is therefore a bag, rather than a set, of local states.

Architecture. Our semantics is motivated by the following architecture of workflow systems (Fig. 2) [8,11,15]. It also resembles the architecture of UML state machines [14, p.2-149]. A WFS consists of two components, an event manager and a router, that act in parallel. These two components communicate with each other by means of a queue. The event manager receives events and puts them in the queue. The event manager is also responsible for generating temporal events.

---

[1] In UML 1.3 a completion event occurs when all entry actions and do-activities in the current state have completed. In this paper, however, wait states have no entry actions. Do-activities in UML 1.3 are activities performed by the software system. However, the activity states in our activity graph represent activities done by actors, not by the WFS. So we do not use do-activities.

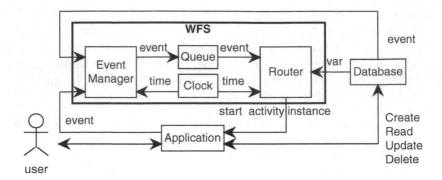

Fig. 2. Abstract execution architecture of a workflow system.

The router takes an event from the queue and routes the case. During routing typically new activities are started and new events are generated. It takes time for the router to process an event. Hence, when a new input event arrives, the router may be busy processing another input event. One of the outcomes of the routing may be that some new activities need to be started. This message is sent to the relevant actors. The assignment of activities to actors (resource management) falls outside the scope of this paper. The database typically generates change events. The user and/or the application typically generates termination and named external events. Only the router generates completion events.

3   Syntax

A UML activity graph consists of nodes and edges. Some of the nodes are only used to connect simple edges into more complex edges. Such nodes are called pseudo nodes and the complex edges they construct are called compound transitions in the UML [14, p.2-147]. The semantics is defined in terms of compound transitions. First we discuss the syntax of UML activity graphs. Next we discuss activity hypergraphs. An activity hypergraph is derived from a UML activity graph by replacing the pseudo state nodes by compound transitions.

UML activity graphs. In Section 1 we already explained the most important state nodes. In addition, a subactivity state node can be used to specify a compound activity. Each subactivity state node must have a corresponding activity graph that specifies the behaviour of the compound activity. In this paper we assume all subactivity state nodes have been eliminated from the activity graph by substituting for each subactivity state node its corresponding activity graph. The transitive closure of the hierarchy relation between activity graphs must therefore be acyclic.

Combining fork and merge, we can specify workflow models and patterns in which multiple instances of the same state node are active at the same time [2]. Figure 3 shows two example activity graphs in which a state node can have

multiple active instances. In the upper activity graph,
B can be instantiated more than once whereas in the
lower activity graph, C can be active twice at the same
time if both A and B have terminated. State nodes
(including pseudo state nodes) are linked by directed,
labelled edges, expressing sequence. Each label has the
form $e[g]/a$ where e is an event expression, g a guard
expression and a an action expression. All three components are optional. An edge leaving an action state
node cannot have an event label [14, p.2-164], since

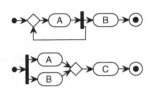

Fig. 3. Example activity
graphs that can have mul-
tiple state instances

that would mean the atomic activity can be interrupted. The only action expression we allow is the sending of external events (broadcast). (Other action
expressions would change the case attributes, which we do not want, since we
want case attributes to be changed by actors, not by the WFS.) Special event
labels when($time = texp$) and after($texp$) denote an absolute and a relative temporal event, respectively, where $texp$ is a natural number denoting time units.

We do not treat object flow states since their semantics will be revised probably. Instead, we have local variables in our model that are stored in the database.
We also have left out dynamic concurrency in our present definition, but it can
be dealt with as indicated in our full report [6]. And we have left out swimlanes
since these do not seem to impact the execution semantics.

Activity hypergraphs. To define a semantics for activity graphs, we must first
flatten the activity graph into an activity hypergraph. Figure 4 shows the result
of flattening Fig. 1 into an activity hypergraph. Figure 5 shows a meta model of
activity hypergraphs. An activity hypergraph is a rooted directed hypergraph,
consisting of nodes and hyperedges. A hyperedge is an edge that can have more
than one source and more than one target.

A node is either an action state node, a wait state node, an initial state
node, or a final state node. Every action state node has an associated activity.
We use the convention that in the activity graph, an action state node is labelled
with the name of its activity. If we use this name to indicate the node, we write

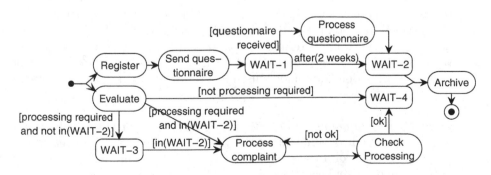

Fig. 4. Activity Hypergraph of Fig. 1

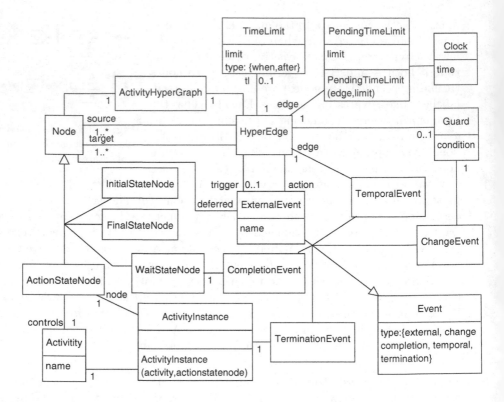

Fig. 5. Metamodel of activity hypergraphs

it in sans serif and if we use it to indicate the activity, we write it in *italic*. Different action state nodes may bear the same label, since they may have the same associated activity.

A hyperedge can have a trigger event, a guard and send actions. The trigger event must be a named external event. The only variables the guard can refer to are the case attributes of the workflow. A temporal event for a hyperedge is specified by declaring a time limit (class TimeLimit). At runtime a specification of a temporal event is translated into a deadline (class PendingTimeLimit) on the global clock (object Clock). If a hyperedge has a temporal event it must have no trigger event. Finally, termination events are implicitly specified by the fact that one of the source state nodes of an hyperedge is an action state node. In that case the action state node must have terminated before the hyperedge can be taken.

Mapping activity graphs to activity hypergraphs. An activity graph is mapped into a hypergraph by eliminating the pseudo state nodes of the activity graph using the concept of a compound transition [9,14]. Figure 6 shows some of the most common mappings. Roughly speaking, for every xor-node every pair of entering and exiting edges maps into one compound transition. In Fig. 4 for ex-

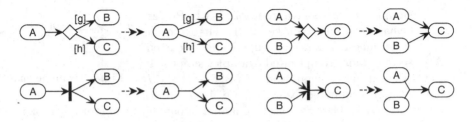

Fig. 6. Example eliminations of pseudo state nodes

ample, the decision node after Check processing has been replaced by two edges, one entering WAIT-4, the other one entering Process complaints. And for every and-node, all its entering and exiting edges map into the same compound transition. For example, in Fig. 4 the fork between the initial state node and Register and Evaluate has been replaced by one compound transition (or hyperedge), that has as source the initial state node, and as targets both Register and Evaluate. If xor-nodes are connected to and-nodes the mapping becomes slightly more complicated. The full report [6] gives all details.

4   Semantics

An execution of an activity hypergraph consists of a series of global states connected by transitions. A global state (or *configuration*) is a bag of currently active nodes. Remember that we need a bag of nodes rather than a set to allow multiple instances of a node to be active.

To define a transition we need the concept of relevance. A hyperedge is *relevant* in a configuration iff all its source state nodes are currently active, i.e. in the configuration, and all source action state nodes have terminated. For example, in Fig. 4 the hyperedge leaving Register is relevant iff the *Register* activity has terminated. Note that a wait state node does not have to be completed to make its leaving hyperedges relevant [14]. We call a node *finished* if it is either terminated (action state node) or completed (wait state node). The rules for taking a hyperedge are as follows.

– A hyperedge with either a trigger event or a temporal event, is taken when its trigger or temporal event occurs, it is relevant, and its guard is true.

For example, the hyperedge from WAIT-1 to WAIT-2 can only be taken if the temporal event after(2 weeks) has occurred.

– A hyperedge that has no trigger event but whose guard refers to some case attributes, is taken when
   • there occurs a change event that makes the guard true, and the hyperedge is relevant, or,
   • the last of the sources of the hyperedge have finished, it is relevant, and its guard is true by definition.

For example, the hyperedge from WAIT-1 to Process questionnaire can only be taken if the change event that makes [questionnaire received] true has occurred. As a second, more complicated example, suppose in Fig. 7 the current configuration is [A,B] and A and B have not yet terminated. Now suppose A terminates

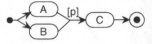

Fig. 7. Example enabling

but B does not. Then the bag of enabled hyperedges will still be empty, so the termination event of A will not trigger the hyperedge leaving $\{A,B\}$. Suppose next B terminates. Then the bag of enabled hyperedges will contain the hyperedge leaving $\{A,B\}$ and entering C. But this hyperedge will only be taken if the guard p is true. If p is not true, the hyperedge can only be taken when next a change event occurs that makes p true.

- A hyperedge that has no trigger event and no guard, is taken when the last of its sources has finished and it is relevant.

If a hyperedge is taken, its source state nodes become inactive and its target state nodes become active.

We now give the details of our execution semantics for activity hypergraphs in terms of the abstract execution architecture depicted in Fig. 2. We present execution algorithms for both the event manager and the router. The components share the following variables:

- variable I represents the current bag of input events for the event manager,
- variable Q represents the event queue for the router,
- variable C represents the current configuration, which is a bag of state nodes,
- variable TL represents the set of temporal events that are scheduled to occur (pending time limits).

Event Manager. The event manager (Fig. 8) polls the current bag of input events in an infinite loop. If there are input events, these are put in the queue (operation + denotes bag union). Besides, the event manager generates time outs (lines 3-8) if the global clock has reached a certain value and adds these to the queue. Note that we do not use timers to generate time outs, since we

```
proc EventManager()  ≡
1.   while true do
2.      if I ≠ bag {} then Q:=Q+I; fi;
3.      foreach tl ∈ TL do
4.         if Clock.GetTime() ≥ tl  then
5.            var te:=new TemporalEvent(tl.edge);
6.            Q:=Q + bag { te } ;
7.         fi
8.      od
9.   od
```

Fig. 8. Procedure EventManager

```
while true do
1   Pick a non-deferred event from the queue
2   If it is a termination or completion event update F
3   Compute a step
4   Take a step:
    4.1  Update Q with the generated events
    4.2  Update TL by removing irrelevant scheduled time-outs and
         adding scheduled time-outs that have become relevant
    4.3  Create new activities
    4.4  Generate completion events
    4.5  Generate change events for the in predicate
    4.6  Update F and C
od
```

Fig. 9. Global structure of router

regard these to be implementation level constructs. Timers should not be used to specify temporal events but merely to help implementing them. It is possible that the event manager is slow and that a temporal event occurrence is added to Q after the global clock has reached its limit.

Router. In the router, we introduce an extra local variable F to store the bag of finished state nodes from C. Bag F is used to remember which state nodes from C have terminated or completed but could not yet been left (e.g. because some guard was false, or another source state node has not yet completed or terminated). For example in Fig. 7, when A terminates we add A to F. Note that keeping the termination event in the queue would mean the system gets stuck, since two termination events are needed before the hyperedge leaving {A,B} can be taken, and yet the router can handle only one (termination) event at a time. The global structure of the router is shown in Fig. 9. We next present each piece of the code, followed by an explanation of its meaning.

1   Pick a non-deferred event from the queue:
    proc Router() ≡
    1.   **var** F: bag Node;// the finished state nodes: $C.includes(F)$
    2.   F:=bag {};
    3.   **while** true **do**
    4.   **if** ($Q\neq$ bag {}) **then** // there is an event to route
    5.   **var** event : Event;
    6.   event:=choose(highest(Q));// pick an event with the highest priority
    7.   **if** ($!C \rightarrow$ exists(n:Node|$n.deferred \rightarrow$ includes(event))) **then**
                                        // event is not deferred
    8.   **var** enabled,step : bag HyperEdge; // the bag of hyperedges that are
                                                enabled and taken respectively
    9.   **var** newC : bag Node;// the new configuration
    10.   **var** newF : bag Node;// the new bag of finished state nodes

The router polls the queue in an infinite loop (lines 3-4). If the queue is not empty, the router picks the event with the highest priority (6). If there is more than one event that has highest priority, a nondeterministic choice between the candidate events is made. Note that usually some kind of fairness constraint must be imposed upon the queue to ensure that every event in the queue will eventually be processed. Here we have omitted such a constraint, since it is not present in UML 1.3. We assume operations *highest* and *choose* on finite bags. Operation *highest* returns the elements with the highest priority in the bag and operation *choose* returns nondeterministically an arbitrary element from a given finite bag. If the picked event is not deferred in the current configuration (7), it is processed (8-61). We use help variables $newC$ and $newF$ since below we refer to both the old and the new values of C and F.

2 If it is a termination or completion event update F:

11.	$newF := F$;
12.	**if** (*event.type=termination*) **then**
13.	$newF := newF$ + bag {*event.activityinstance.node*}
14.	**elsif** (*event.type=completion*) **then**
15.	$newF := newF$ + bag {*event.waitstatenode*}
16.	**fi**;

Bag $newF$ is initialised with F. If the event is a termination or completion event, $newF$ is updated with the corresponding node.

3 Compute a step:

17.	$enab := ComputeEnabled(C, event, newF)$;
18.	$step :=$ a maximal, consistent subbag of $enab$;

The next step *step* is a maximal, consistent subbag of the bag *enab* of enabled hyperedges. We use procedure ComputeEnabled that we explain below in Fig. 10 to fill *enab*. Both the consistency and the maximality constraint are taken from the UML definition [14, p.2-151].

Roughly speaking, a bag of enabled hyperedges is inconsistent, given a configuration C if not all of them can be taken together, since the union of their sources is not contained in C. For example, in Fig. 1 if the current configuration contains Evaluate and the current event denotes termination of activity *Evaluate* then either the hyperedge to WAIT-4, or to Process Complaint or to WAIT-3 is taken, but none of these three hyperedges can be taken simultaneously, since then three instances of Evaluate would need to be active (and terminated!). So these three hyperedges are inconsistent.

Given a bag *enab* of enabled hyperedges, a consistent step *step* is maximal if there is no hyperedge $h \in enab$ but $h \notin step$ such that $step + bag\{h\}$ is consistent. So as many hyperedges as possible should be taken. In particular, if at least one hyperedge is enabled, the step cannot be empty. If more than one step exists, a random choice is made.

4.1 Update Q with the generated events:

19.	**var** *generated*: set *Event*;// events generated when the step is taken
20.	*generated* := bag {};
21.	**foreach** $e \in step$ **do** $generated := generated$ + $e.action$ **od**;
22.	$Q := Q$ - bag {*event* } + *generated*;

Queue Q is updated with the bag of generated events. We use a help variable *generated* because Q is a shared variable that is also updated by the event manager. We assume that the assignment is atomic.

Next, we compute the value of help variables *newF* and *newC*.

```
23.          newF:=newF - exited(C,step);
24.          newC:=nextconfig(C,step);
```

The new bag *newF* of finished state nodes and the next configuration *newC* are computed. Given a configuration C and a step S, $exited(C, S)$ denotes the bag of states that are exited when S is taken. Similarly, $entered(C, S)$ denotes the bag of states which are entered when S is taken. The next configuration when S is taken in configuration C will be $nextconfig(C, S) = C - exited(C, S) + entered(C, S)$.

4.2 Update *TL* by removing irrelevant scheduled time-outs and adding scheduled time-outs that have become relevant:

The code for this part is split in three.

```
25.          var OffTL: set PendingTimeLimit; // irrelevant timeouts
26.          var OldRelevant : bag HyperEdge;
27.          OldRelevant:=rel(C,F) - rel(newC,newF);
28.          foreach tl ∈ TL do
29.             if (tl.edge ∈ OldRelevant) then // tl has become irrelevant
30.                OffTL:=OffTL + bag { tl };
31.                OldRelevant:=OldRelevant - bag { tl.edge };
32.             fi
33.          od
```

First the set of irrelevant time outs is computed. A scheduled time out becomes irrelevant, if the hyperedge that the scheduled time out corresponds to is no longer relevant in the new configuration, i.e. the source of the hyperedge is no longer contained in the new relevant configuration. Consider for example the activity graph in Fig. 1. If the old configuration C contains WAIT-1 and the change event [questionnaire received] occurs, then the next configuration C' will contain Process questionnaire instead of WAIT-1. Hence, hyperedges leaving WAIT-1 are no longer relevant, and the scheduled time out after(2 weeks) that was relevant in C is irrelevant in C'. The *relevant* bag of hyperedges $rel(C, F)$ for a configuration C and a bag F of finished state nodes consists of those hyperedges whose non-action state node sources are contained in C and whose action state node sources have terminated, so are in F.

```
34.          var OnTL: set PendingTimeLimit; // new relevant timeouts
35.          var NewRelevant : bag HyperEdge;
36.          NewRelevant:=rel(newC,newF)-rel(C,F);
37.          foreach h ∈ NewRelevant do
38.             if (h.tl.notEmpty) then // there is a time out specified for h
39.                var ptl : PendingTimeLimit;
40.                if (h.tl.type=after) then // create a new pending time limit
                                             scheduled tl.limit time units from now
41.                   ptl:=new PendingTimeLimit(e,h.tl.limit+Clock.time);
42.                else ptl:=new PendingTimeLimit(h,h.tl.limit);
```

```
43.                    fi
44.                    OnTL:=OnTL + bag { ptl };
45.                    fi
46.                od
```

Next, the set $OnTL$ of new relevant scheduled time outs is computed. A time out becomes scheduled iff the hyperedge that the time out corresponds to was irrelevant in the old configuration but becomes relevant in the new configuration. For example, in Fig. 1, if the old configuration contains Send questionnaire and the activity *Send questionnaire* has terminated, then the new configuration contains WAIT-1 instead of Send questionnaire. Then time out after(2 weeks) becomes scheduled.

```
47.                TL:=TL-OffTL+OnTL;
48.                foreach t ∈ OffTL do delete t; od;
```

Finally, set TL is updated and the irrelevant scheduled time outs are deleted.

```
49.                foreach s ∈ entered(C,step) do
```

Each entered state node is checked in order to start new activities (4.3), generate completion events (4.4), and generate *in* change events (4.5).

4.3 Create new activities:

```
50.                if (s.oclIsTypeOf(ActionStateNode)) then // s is action state node
51.                    var ais:=new ActivityInstance(s.controls,s) ;
52.                    start(ais); // start this activity instance
```

For each action state node that is entered, a new activity instance is created and started.

4.4 Generate completion events:

```
53.                elsif (s.oclIsTypeOf(WaitStateNode)) then // s is wait state node
54.                    generate completion event for s and add it to Q
55.                fi
```

If a wait state node is entered, its completion event is generated and inserted into Q.

4.5 Generate change events for the *in* predicate:

```
56.                if there is a hyperedge h such that
                        (h.trigger.isEmpty) and (h.guard.condition contains in(s)) then
57.                    create change event for in(s) and add it to Q;
58.                fi
59.            od
```

If a state node s is entered that is mentioned as change event in(s) for some hyperedge, a change event for in(s) is generated.

4.6 Update F and C:

```
60.                F:=newF;
61.                C:=newC;
62.            fi
63.        fi
64.    od
```

Finally, the bag F of finished (terminated and completed) state nodes and the configuration C are updated. This cannot be done earlier since in lines 27, 36 and 49 we refer to the old values of C and F.

```
proc ComputeEnabled(C,event,F) ≡
1.    foreach h ∈ rel(C,F) do // for every relevant hyperedge
2.      if (h.trigger.notEmpty) then
3.        if (event.oclIsTypeOf(ExternalEvent)) then
4.          if (h.trigger.name=event.name) then
5.            compute the truth value of the guard;
6.              if the guard is true then enabled:=enabled + bag {h} fi
7.          fi
8.        elsif (event.oclIsTypeOf(TemporalEvent)) then
9.          if (h=event.edge) then
10.           compute the truth value of the guard;
11.             if the guard is true then enabled:=enabled + bag {h} fi
12.         fi
13.       fi
14.     else // (h.trigger.isEmpty)
15.       if (h.guard=true) then enabled:=enabled + bag {h}
16.       elsif (event.type=change) then
17.         if (h.guard.condition ⇒ event.guard.condition) then
18.           enabled:=enabled + bag {h }
19.         fi
20.       elsif (event.type=termination) then
21.         if (event.activityinstance.node ∈ hyperedge.source) then
22.           compute the truth value of the guard
23.             if the guard is true then enabled:=enabled + bag {h} fi
24.         fi
25.       fi
26.     fi
27.   od
```

Fig. 10. Procedure ComputeEnabled

Compute Enabled Hyperedges. The definition of procedure ComputeEnabled is given in Fig. 10. Each hyperedge in the bag of relevant hyperedges $rel(C, F)$ is tested whether it can become enabled. A hyperedge with a trigger event or temporal event becomes enabled iff its trigger event or temporal event occurs and the hyperedge's guard expression is true (2-13). Remember that we require that a hyperedge does not have both a trigger event and a temporal event. A hyperedge that has no trigger event becomes enabled iff its guard is true by definition (15), or if the current event is a change event that implies the hyperedge's guard condition (16-19), or if the current event is a termination event of one of the source state nodes of the hyperedge and the hyperedge's guard expression is true (20-24). Note that during guard evaluation the database may have to be accessed in order to find the current value of a variable (cf. Fig. 2).

Example. We give an example how a case of the Processing complaints workflow of Fig. 1 might be routed. Assume the current configuration contains action state nodes Register and Evaluate. Table 1 shows part of one possible execution

Table 1. Possible execution scenario for Processing Complaints (Fig. 1)

state	C	Q	router
1	{Register,Evaluate}		
2	{Register,Evaluate}		*Register*
3	{Register,Evaluate}	*Evaluate*	*Register*
4	{Send questionnaire, Evaluate}		*Evaluate*
5	{Send questionnaire, Evaluate}	*Send questionnaire*	*Evaluate*
6	{Send questionnaire, WAIT-3}	*Send questionnaire*	*WAIT-3*
7	{Send questionnaire, WAIT-3}		*Send questionnaire*
8	{WAIT-1,WAIT-3}		*WAIT-1*
9	{WAIT-1,WAIT-3}		
10	{WAIT-1,WAIT-3}		*questionnaire received*
11	{Process questionnaire, WAIT-3}		
12	{Process questionnaire, WAIT-3}		*Process questionnaire*
13	{WAIT-2,WAIT-3}	$in(WAIT\text{-}2)$	*WAIT-2*
14	{WAIT-2,WAIT-3}		$in(WAIT\text{-}2)$
15	{WAIT-2,Process complaint}		

scenario for this case by listing the consecutive states of the WFS. Due to space limitations we only show the first 15 states and we do not show the I and TL variables. We assume that the event manager puts events in I immediately in Q. All events, including completion and termination events, are written in *italic* font, while state nodes are listed in sans serif. If an event occurs and the router is not busy, we assume the router immediately starts processing this event (states 2, 10, and 12). We assume that completion events have priority over non-completion events.

5   Related Work

Although activity graphs are widely used for process modelling (see e.g. [5,13]), none of these references make any comments upon the semantics they attach to an activity graph.

The most important difference of our work with the OMG UML 1.3 semantics [14] is that in our semantics an activity is done in a state and by the environment, rather than in a transition by the system itself (see the introduction). UML CASE tools such as Rhapsody [10] implement the OMG semantics of activity graphs. Other formalisations of UML activity graphs [3,4] follow the OMG semantics very closely and they too map activities into transitions done by the system. Besides, these formalisations neither deal with real time nor treat events as objects.

Lilius and Paltor [12] have defined an execution algorithm for UML state machines. They only deal with named external events and do not treat temporal events. Moreover, they focus on run-to-completion steps, which are not relevant for activity graphs, since in activity graphs no call actions on transitions are used.

In [7] we presented a formal high-level semantics for activity graphs in which we assumed that routing does not take time. There, we did not give an execution algorithm but instead we defined a mathematical structure. Our present definition stays closer to both the original UML definition and the way WFSs are implemented in practice.

6 Conclusion

We presented an execution algorithm for UML activity graphs that is intended for workflow systems. Our algorithm stays close to the UML semantics of state machines but differs from it, in particular since run-to-completion is not relevant for activity graphs.

We are currently using this algorithm to verify activity graphs by model checking tools. With the execution algorithm the activity graph is mapped into a transition system which is the standard format for most model checkers. Next, we plan to investigate how object flows can be dealt with in the execution algorithm.

References

1. W.M.P. van der Aalst. The application of Petri nets to workflow management. *The Journal of Circuits, Systems and Computers*, 8(1):21–66, 1998.
2. W.M.P. van der Aalst, A.H.M. ter Hofstede, B. Kiepuszewski, and A.P. Barros. Advanced workflow patterns. In O. Etzion and P. Scheuermann, editors, *Proc. CoopIS 2000*, LNCS 1901. Springer, 2000.
3. C. Bolton and J. Davies. Activity graphs and processes. In W. Grieskamp, T. Santen, and B. Stoddart, editors, *Proc. IFM 2000*, LNCS 1945. Springer, 2000.
4. E. Börger, A. Cavarra, and E. Riccobene. An ASM Semantics for UML Activity Diagrams. In T. Rus, editor, *Proc. AMAST 2000*, LNCS 1826. Springer, 2000.
5. H.-E. Eriksson and M. Penker. *Business Modeling With UML: Business Patterns at Work*. Wiley Computer Publishing, 2000.
6. R. Eshuis and R. Wieringa. A formal semantics for UML activity diagrams. Technical Report TR-CTIT-01-04, University of Twente, 2001.
7. R. Eshuis and R. Wieringa. A real-time execution semantics for UML activity diagrams. In H. Hussmann, editor, *Proc. FASE 2001*, LNCS 2029. Springer, 2001.
8. P. Grefen and R. Remmerts de Vries. A reference architecture for workflow management systems. *Journal of Data & Knowledge Engineering*, 27(1):31–57, 1998.
9. D. Harel and A. Naamad. The STATEMATE Semantics of Statecharts. *ACM Transactions on Software Engineering and Methodology*, 5(4):293–333, 1996.
10. I-Logix. Rhapsody. http://www.ilogix.com.
11. F. Leymann and D. Roller. *Production Workflow: Concepts and Techniques*. Prentice Hall, 2000.
12. J. Lilius and I. Porres Paltor. Formalising UML state machines for model checking. In R. France and B. Rumpe, editors, *Proc. UML'99*, LNCS 1723. Springer, 1999.
13. B. Paech. On the role of activity diagrams in UML. In Jean Bézivin and Pierre-Alain Muller, editors, *Proc. UML'98*, LNCS 1618. Springer, 1999.
14. UML Revision Taskforce. *OMG UML Specification v. 1.3*. Object Management Group, 1999.
15. Workflow Management Coalition. The workflow reference model (WFMC-TC-1003), 1995. http://www.wfmc.org.

Timing Analysis of UML Activity Diagrams*

Li Xuandong, Cui Meng, Pei Yu, Zhao Jianhua, and Zheng Guoliang

Department of Computer Science and Technology
Nanjing University, Nanjing
Jiangsu, P.R.China 210093
lxd@nju.edu.cn

Abstract. UML activity diagrams can be used for modeling the dynamic aspects of systems and for constructing executable systems through forward and reverse engineering. They are very suitable for describing the model of program behaviour. In this paper, we extend UML activity diagrams by introducing timing constraints so that they can be used to model real-time software systems, and give the solution for timing analysis of UML activity diagrams. We give the solution for timing analysis of simple UML activity diagrams (containing no loop) by linear programming, and present an algorithm for checking UML activity diagrams using integer time verification techniques. This work forms a base for verification of real-time software systems.

1   Introduction

Software systems keep growing in size and complexity. Many large and complex software systems must guarantee certain critical functional, real-time, fault-tolerant, and performance properties. Verifying that such a system satisfies these kinds of properties can increase our confidence that it will operate correctly and reliably.

In recent years, model checking has received much attention as a software system verification method [1-4]. Model checking is a technique that relies on building a finite model of a system and checking that a desired property holds in that model [5]. Applying model checking to software requires that program source code be translated to a finite model which is described by a modeling language. This modeling language should be of sufficient expressive power to program behaviour.

UML Activity diagrams [6,7] can be used for modeling the dynamic aspects of systems and for constructing executable systems through forward and reverse engineering. Activity diagrams emphasize the flow of control from activity to activity. An activity is an ongoing non-atomic execution within a state machine. Activities ultimately result in some action, which is made up of executable atomic

---

* This work is supported by the National Natural Science Foundation of China under Grant 60073031 and Grant 69703009, Jiangsu Province Research Foundation, and by International Institute for Software Technology, The United Nations University (UNU/IIST).

M. Gogolla and C. Kobryn (Eds.): UML 2001, LNCS 2185, pp. 62–75, 2001.

computations that results in a change in state of the system or the return value. A activity diagram focuses on activities, chunks of process that may or may not correspond to methods or member functions, and the sequencing of these activities. In this sense it is like a flow chart. It differs, however, from a flow chart in that it explicitly supports parallel activities and their synchronization. So UML activity diagrams are very suitable for describing the model of program behaviour.

In this paper, we extend UML activity diagrams by introducing timing constraints so that they can be used to model real-time software systems, and give the solution for timing analysis of UML activity diagrams. The paper is organized as follows. In next section, we extend activity diagrams with timing constraints. Section 3 gives a formal definition of activity diagrams. In section 4, we give the solution for timing analysis of simple activity diagrams (containing no loop) by linear programming. In section 5, we present an algorithm for checking activity diagrams using integer time verification techniques, and improved the algorithm to avoid exhaustive path search. The last section discusses the related work and contains some conclusion.

2   UML Activity Diagrams with Timing Constraints

An activity diagram is a special form of state machine intended to model computations and workflows. The states of the activity diagram represent the states of executing the computation, not the states of an ordinary object.

An activity diagram contains activity states which represent the execution of a statement in a procedure or the performance of an activity in a workflow. Instead of waiting for an event, as in a normal wait state, an activity state waits for the completion of its computation. When the activity completes, then execution proceeds to the next activity state within the graph. A completion transition in an activity diagram fires when the preceding activity is complete.

An activity diagram may contain branches, as well as forking of control into concurrent threads. Concurrent threads represent activities that can be performed concurrently by different objects or persons in an organization.

In an activity diagram, an activity state is shown as a box with rounded ends containing a description of the activity; simple completion transitions are shown as arrows; branches are shown as guard conditions on transitions or as diamonds with multiple labeled exit arrows; fork or join of control is shown by multiple arrows entering or leaving a heavy synchronization bar. Figure 1 shows an activity diagram for processing an order by the box office.

For modeling real-time software systems, we introduce timing constraints in activity diagrams. Each activity state s in an activity diagram is associated with a time interval $[a, b]$. The times a and b are relative to the moment at which the activity state s starts. Assuming that s starts at time c, then s may complete only during the interval $[c + a, c + b]$ and must complete at the time $c + b$ at the latest, i.e. execution may proceed to the next activity state only during the interval $[c + a, c + b]$ and must proceed to the next activity state at the time $c + b$ at the latest. For example, in the activity diagram depicted in Figure 1, if the activity state for award bonus starts at time c, then it may complete only during the interval $[c+7, c+9]$ and must complete at the time $c+9$ at the latest, i.e. execution may proceed to the next activity state for mail packet only during the interval $[c+7, c+9]$ by firing the synchronization transition and must proceed to the activity state for mail packet at the time $c+9$ at the latest.

Without loss of generality, here we assume that any arrow leaving a synchronization bar must enter a activity state (it never enter another synchronization bar).

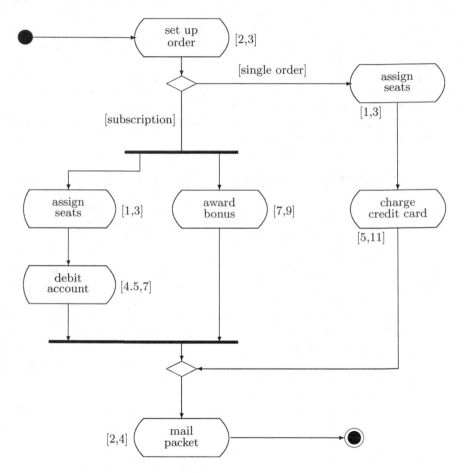

Fig. 1. An activity diagram

3   Formalizing UML Activity Diagrams

For analyzing activity diagrams, we formalize them as follows.

Definition 1. Let **N** be the set of natural numbers. An activity diagram $\mathcal{D}$ is a tuple, $\mathcal{D} = (A, T, F, Ect, Lct, a_I, a_F)$, where

- $A = \{a_1, a_2, \ldots, a_m\}$ is a finite set of *activity states*;
- $T = \{t_1, t_2, \ldots, t_n\}$ is a finite set of *completion transitions*;
- $F \subset (A \times T) \cup (T \times A)$ is the *flow relation*;
- $Ect, Lct : A \to \mathbf{N}$ are functions for the *earliest* and *latest completion* times of activity states, satisfying $Ect(a) \leq Lct(a)$ for $a \in A$;
- $a_I \in A$ is the *initial activity state*, and $a_F \in A$ is the *final activity state*; there is only one transition t such that $(a_I, t) \in F$, and $(t_1, a_I) \notin F$ and $(a_F, t_1) \notin F$ for any $t_1 \in T$; $Ect(a_I) = 0$ and $Lct(a_I) = 0$. □

Definition 2. Let $\mathcal{D} = (A, T, F, Ect, Lct, a_I, a_F)$ be an activity diagram. A *untimed state* μ of $\mathcal{D}$ is any subset of A. For any transition $t \in T$, let

$$^\bullet t = \{a \in A | (a, t) \in F\} \quad \text{and} \quad t^\bullet = \{a \in A | (t, a) \in F\},$$

which denote the *preset* and *postset* of t, respectively. A transition t is *enabled* in a untimed state μ if $^\bullet t \subseteq \mu$; otherwise, it is *disabled*. Let $enabled(\mu)$ be the set of transitions enabled in μ. □

Definition 3. Let $\mathcal{D} = (A, T, F, Ect, Lct, a_I, a_F)$ be an activity diagram. A *state* s of $\mathcal{D}$ is a pair $s = (\mu, c)$ where μ is a untimed state of $\mathcal{D}$, and c is called the *clock function* which maps each $a \in \mu$ to a nonnegative real number that indicates how long the activity state a has started. The *initial state* of $\mathcal{D}$ is $s_0 = (\{a_I\}, c_0)$ where $c_0(a_I) = 0$, and any $s = (\{a_F\}, c)$ is a *final state* of $\mathcal{D}$. □

For the firing of a transition to be possible at a certain time, four conditions must be satisfied.

Definition 4. Let $\mathcal{D} = (A, T, F, Ect, Lct, a_I, a_F)$ be an activity diagram. A transition $t \in T$ may fire from state $s = (\mu, c)$ after delay δ (δ is a nonnegative real number) if and only if

1. $t \in enabled(\mu)$,
2. $(\mu - {}^\bullet t) \cap t^\bullet = \emptyset$,
3. $Ect(a) \leq c(a) + \delta$ for any $a \in {}^\bullet t$, and
4. $c(a') + \delta \leq Lct(a')$ for any $a' \in \mu$. □

Not all enabled transitions can fire because of time constraints. The new state after a firing is calculated as follows.

Definition 5. Let $\mathcal{D} = (A, T, F, Ect, Lct, a_I, a_F)$ be an activity diagram. When a transition $t \in T$ fires after delay δ from the state $s = (\mu, c)$, the new state $s' = (\mu', c')$ is given as follows:

- $\mu' = (\mu - {}^\bullet t) \cup t^\bullet$, and
- for any $a \in \mu'$, $c'(a) = \begin{cases} 0 & \text{if } a \in \mu' - (\mu - {}^\bullet t), \\ c(a) + \delta & \text{else.} \end{cases}$

This is denoted by $s' = fire(s, (t, \delta))$. □

The untimed behaviour of an activity diagram is described in term of *untimed runs*.

Definition 6. Let $\mathcal{D} = (A, T, F, Ect, Lct, a_I, a_F)$ be an activity diagram. A *untimed run* σ of $\mathcal{D}$ is a sequence of untimed states and transitions

$$\sigma = \mu_0 \xrightarrow{t_0} \mu_1 \xrightarrow{t_1} \ldots \xrightarrow{t_{n-1}} \mu_n$$

where $\mu_0 = \{s_I\}$ and $\mu_n = \{s_F\}$, $t_i \in enabled(\mu_i)$ for any i ($i \geq 0$), and $\mu_i = (\mu_{i-1} - {}^\bullet t_{i-1}) \cup t_{i-1}{}^\bullet$ for any i ($i \geq 1$).   □

The behaviour of an activity diagram is described in term of *runs*.

Definition 7. Let $\mathcal{D} = (A, T, F, Ect, Lct, a_I, a_F)$ be an activity diagram. A *run* ρ of $\mathcal{D}$ is a sequence of states, transitions, and delays

$$\rho = s_0 \xrightarrow{(t_0, \delta_0)} s_1 \xrightarrow{(t_1, \delta_1)} \ldots \xrightarrow{(t_{n-1}, \delta_{n-1})} s_n$$

where s_0 is the initial state, s_n is a final state, and for every i ($1 \leq i \leq n$), s_i is obtained from s_{i-1} by firing a transition t_{i-1} after delay δ_{i-1} satisfying

$$s_i = fire(s_{i-1}, (t_{i-1}, \delta_{i-1})) \,.$$

A run is said to be *integral* if all the δ_is occurred in its combined steps are integers.   □

For a untimed run of an activity diagram, if all untimed states occurred in the untimed run are distinct, it is a *simple* untimed run. An activity diagram is *simple* if all its untimed runs are simple, that is, there is no loop in the activity diagram. In the following two sections, we first give the solution for timing analysis of simple activity diagrams by linear programming, then solve the problem for general activity diagrams using integer time verification techniques.

4   Checking Simple UML Activity Diagrams by Linear Programming Techniques

Now we consider timing analysis of simple activity diagrams. We know that for any simple activity diagram, all its untimed runs are simple. It follows that the number of untimed runs of a simple activity diagram is finite.

Let $\mathcal{D} = (A, T, F, Ect, Lct, a_I, a_F)$ be an activity diagram, and

$$\sigma = \mu_0 \xrightarrow{t_0} \mu_1 \xrightarrow{t_1} \ldots \xrightarrow{t_{n-1}} \mu_n \,,$$

be a untimed run of $\mathcal{D}$. For any untimed state μ_i ($0 \leq i < n$), for any activity state $a \in \mu_i$, let $last(\mu_i, a)$ be the last untimed state μ_j ($0 \leq j \leq i$) before the occurrence of t_i at which a starts, i.e. j satisfies that

- $a \in \mu_j$,
- if $j \neq 0$, then $a \in t_{j-1}{}^\bullet$, and
- for any k ($j \leq k < i$), $a \notin t_k{}^\bullet$.

For any activity diagram $\mathcal{D} = (A, T, F, Ect, Lct, a_I, a_F)$, for any untimed run σ of $\mathcal{D}$ which of the form

$$\sigma = \mu_0 \xrightarrow{t_0} \mu_1 \xrightarrow{t_1} \ldots \xrightarrow{t_{n-1}} \mu_n,$$

let $run(\sigma)$ be the set of runs of $\mathcal{D}$ which are of the form

$$(\mu_0, c_0) \xrightarrow{(t_0, \delta_0)} (\mu_1, c_1) \xrightarrow{(t_1, \delta_1)} \ldots \xrightarrow{(t_{n-1}, \delta_{n-1})} (\mu_n, c_n).$$

From the definitions in section 3, it follows that the delays $\delta_0, \delta_1, \ldots, \delta_{n-1}$ must satisfy that

- for each μ_i ($0 \leq i < n$), for each $a \in {}^\bullet t_i$ such that $last(\mu_i, a) = \mu_j$ ($0 \leq j \leq i$), $\delta_j + \delta_{j+1} \ldots + \delta_i \geq Ect(a)$, and
- for each μ_i ($0 \leq i < n$), for each $a' \in \mu_i$ such at $last(\mu_i, a') = \mu_k$ ($0 \leq k \leq i$), $\delta_k + \delta_{k+1} \ldots + \delta_i \leq Lct(a')$,

which form a group of linear inequalities on $\delta_0, \delta_1, \ldots, \delta_{n-1}$, denoted by $lp(\sigma)$.

The problems we concern in this paper are to check if any run of an activity diagram satisfies a given property, i.e. for any untimed run σ of an activity diagram, any run $\rho \in run(\sigma)$ satisfies a given property. In the following, we show that for simple activity diagrams, we can reduce some problems into linear programs.

The timing consistency problem for activity diagrams can be described as: for an activity diagram $\mathcal{D}$, is any untimed run σ of $\mathcal{D}$ such that $run(\sigma) \neq \emptyset$, i.e. is there at least one run of $\mathcal{D}$ corresponding to σ. Let

$$\sigma = \mu_0 \xrightarrow{t_0} \mu_1 \xrightarrow{t_1} \ldots \xrightarrow{t_{n-1}} \mu_n,$$

be a simple untimed run of an activity diagram. It follows that any run in $run(\sigma)$ is of the form

$$(\mu_0, c_0) \xrightarrow{(t_0, \delta_0)} (\mu_1, c_1) \xrightarrow{(t_1, \delta_1)} \ldots \xrightarrow{(t_{n-1}, \delta_{n-1})} (\mu_n, c_n).$$

Since $\delta_0, \delta_1, \ldots, \delta_{n-1}$ must satisfy $lp(\sigma)$, the problem of checking $run(\sigma) \neq \emptyset$ is equivalent to the problem of checking the linear inequality group $lp(\sigma)$ has no solution. The later is a linear programming problem. Since any simple activity diagram satisfies that any its untimed run is simple and that the number of its untimed runs is finite, we can solve the timing consistency problem for simple activity diagrams. In the same way, we can also solve the reachability problem for activity diagrams, which can be described as: for an activity diagram $\mathcal{D}$, for a untimed state μ, is there any run of $\mathcal{D}$ in which μ occurs.

For an activity diagram $\mathcal{D}$, the bounded delay timing analysis is to check if the separation in time between two given transitions in any run of $\mathcal{D}$ is not small than a given real number. For an activity diagram $\mathcal{D}$, given two transitions t, t' and a real number p, we denote a *delay constraint* by (t, t', p) which requires that for any run of $\mathcal{D}$

$$s_0 \xrightarrow{(t_0, \delta_0)} s_1 \xrightarrow{(t_1, \delta_1)} \ldots \xrightarrow{(t_{n-1}, \delta_{n-1})} s_n,$$

if there are t_i and t_j $(0 \leq i < j < n)$ such that $t = t_i$, $t' = t_j$ and that $t_k \neq t \wedge t_k \neq t'$ for any k $(i < k < j)$, then $p \leq \delta_{i+1} + \delta_{i+2} + \ldots + \delta_j$. For any activity diagram $\mathcal{D}$, the bounded delay timing analysis is to check if any run of $\mathcal{D}$ satisfies a given delay constraint.

Let σ be a simple untimed run of an activity diagram

$$\sigma = \mu_0 \xrightarrow{t_0} \mu_1 \xrightarrow{t_1} \ldots \xrightarrow{t_{n-1}} \mu_n .$$

It follows that any run in $run(\sigma)$ is of the form

$$(\mu_0, c_0) \xrightarrow{(t_0, \delta_0)} (\mu_1, c_1) \xrightarrow{(t_1, \delta_1)} \ldots \xrightarrow{(t_{n-1}, \delta_{n-1})} (\mu_n, c_n) .$$

Since $\delta_0, \delta_1, \ldots, \delta_{n-1}$ must satisfy $lp(\sigma)$, we can solve the problem of checking if any run in $run(\sigma)$ satisfies a delay constraint (t, t', p) as follows: for any t_i and t_j $(0 \leq i < j < n)$ such that $t = t_i$, $t' = t_j$ and that $t_k \neq t \wedge t_k \neq t'$ for any k $(i < k < j)$, find the minimum value of the linear function $\delta_{i+1} + \delta_{i+2} + \ldots + \delta_j$ subject to the linear constraint $lp(\sigma)$ and check whether it is not smaller than p, which can be solved by linear programming. Since any simple activity diagram satisfies that any its untimed run is simple and that the number of its untimed runs is finite, the bounded delay timing analysis can be solved for simple activity diagrams.

5   Checking UML Activity Diagrams Using Integer Time Verification Techniques

We have shown that for simple activity diagrams, some timing analysis problems can be reduced to linear programs. The solutions depend on that any simple activity diagram satisfies that any its untimed run is simple and that the number of its untimed runs is finite. We know that for a general activity diagram, its untimed run could be infinite and the number of its untimed run could be infinite because there could be loops in the activity diagram. Now we present an integer time verification approach to solving the problems. Here we assume that any time interval occurring in any activity diagram satisfies that its upper bounds are finite numbers, i.e. for any activity diagram $\mathcal{D} = (A, T, F, Ect, Lct, a_I, a_F)$, $Lct(a) \neq \infty$ for any $a \in A$.

For a run ρ of an activity diagram

$$s_0 \xrightarrow{(t_0, \delta_0)} s_1 \xrightarrow{(t_1, \delta_1)} \ldots \xrightarrow{(t_{n-1}, \delta_{n-1})} s_n ,$$

the total time which elapses on ρ is $\delta_0 + \delta_1 + \ldots \delta_{n-1}$, denoted by $delay(\rho)$. Now we consider the problem of checking if any run of an activity diagram satisfies that its total elapsing time is not small than a given real number. Actually this problem is a special case of the bound delay timing analysis. In the following, we show that this problem can be solved by the integer time verification techniques. The following theorem forms a base for the solution.

Theorem 1. For an activity diagram $\mathcal{D} = (A, T, F, Ect, Lct, a_I, a_F)$, for a real number p, any run ρ of $\mathcal{D}$ satisfies $delay(\rho) \geq p$ if and only if any integral run ρ' of $\mathcal{D}$ satisfies $delay(\rho') \geq p$. □

The proof of this theorem is presented in the appendix.

5.1   Basic Algorithm

Because of Theorem 1 we need only consider to check all integral runs of an activity diagram. For an activity diagram $\mathcal{D} = (A, T, F, Ect, Lct, a_I, a_F)$, a state (μ, c) of $\mathcal{D}$ is an *integral state* if $c(a)$ is an integer for any $a \in \mu$. It is clear that any state occurring in an integral run is an integral state. Since we assume that any activity diagram $\mathcal{D} = (A, T, F, Ect, Lct, a_I, a_F)$ satisfies that $Lct(a) \neq \infty$ for any $a \in A$, the number of the integral states in an activity diagram is finite. Therefore, for an activity diagram $\mathcal{D} = (A, T, F, Ect, Lct, a_I, a_F)$, we can construct a *reachability graph* $G = (V, E)$ as follows, where V is a set of nodes and E is a set of edges:

1. The initial state $(\{s_I\}, c_0)$ of $\mathcal{D}$ is in the set V, which is called *initial node*;
2. Let $s = (\mu, c)$ be in the set V, and κ is the minimal value of the set $\{Lct(a) \mid a \in \mu\}$. Then for any transition $t \in enabled(\mu)$, for any integer $\delta \geq 0$ such that $Ect(a') \leq c(a') + \delta \leq \kappa$ for any $a' \in {}^\bullet t$, $s' = fire(s, (t, \delta))$ is in V, and $s \xrightarrow{(t,\delta)} s'$ is in the set E.

For an activity diagram $\mathcal{D}$, a *path* in its reachability graph (V, E) is a sequence of states, transitions, and delays

$$s_0 \xrightarrow{(t_0, \delta_0)} s_1 \xrightarrow{(t_1, \delta_1)} \ldots \xrightarrow{(t_{n-1}, \delta_{n-1})} s_n$$

such that s_0 is the initial node, s_n is a final state of $\mathcal{D}$, $s_i \in V$ for every i ($0 \leq i \leq n$), and $s_i \xrightarrow{(t_i, \delta_i)} s_{i+1} \in E$ for every i ($0 \leq i < n$). It is clear that any run of an activity diagram $\mathcal{D}$ is a path in the reachability graph of $\mathcal{D}$. Thus, we can solve the problem based on depth-first traverse of the reachability graph of an activity diagram. The main idea is as follows. For a path ρ, if there is a repetition of the sequence ρ_1 in ρ, then we can get a path ρ' by removing any repetition of ρ_1 from ρ. It is clear that the total elapsing time of ρ' is not greater than the one of ρ. By applying the above elimination step repeatedly, we can finally get a path ρ'' which contains no repetition of any sequence, and ρ'' has the smallest total elapsing time in all paths which are constructed by applying the above elimination step. It follows that by investigating all the paths containing no repetition of any sequence (the number of such paths is finite), we can decide if any run of an activity diagram satisfies that its total elapsing time is not less than a given real number.

The detailed algorithm is depicted in Figure 2. The algorithm traverses the reachability graph of an activity diagram in a depth first manner starting from the initial node. The path in the reachability graph that we have so far traversed is stored in the variable *currentpath*. For each new node that we discover, we first check whether it is a final state of the activity diagram. If so, we check if the run corresponding path satisfies that its total elapsing time is not smaller than a given real number. If the node that we have found is in the current path, we have found a loop and need to backtrack.

$currentpath := \langle(\mu_0, c_0)\rangle;$
repeat
 $node :=$ the last node of $currentpath;$
 if $node$ has no new successive node
 then delete the last node of $currentpath$
 else begin
   $node :=$ a new successive node of $node;$
   if $node$ is a final state **then**
    begin
     check if the run corresponding path satisfies that its total elapsing time
     is not smaller than a given real number;
     if no **then return false;**
    end
   else if $node$ is not in $currentpath$ **then** append $node$ to $currentpath$
  end
until $currentpath = \langle\rangle;$
return true.

Fig. 2. Basic algorithm checking activity diagrams

5.2   Improved Algorithm

In the above, we give a basic algorithm in which all paths containing no repetition are searched. Since a node could be on many paths, a node could be searched for many times. In the following, we improve the algorithm so that each node is searched only once.

For an activity diagram $\mathcal{D}$, a *pre-run* ρ of $\mathcal{D}$ is a sequence of states, transitions, and delays

$$\rho = s_0 \xrightarrow{(t_0, \delta_0)} s_1 \xrightarrow{(t_1, \delta_1)} \ldots \xrightarrow{(t_{m-1}, \delta_{m-1})} s_m$$

where s_0 is the initial state, and for every i ($1 \leq i \leq m$), s_i is obtained from s_{i-1} by firing a transition t_{i-1} after delay δ_{i-1} satisfying

$$s_i = fire(s_{i-1}, (t_{i-1}, \delta_{i-1})).$$

It follows that any run of $\mathcal{D}$ is a pre-run of $\mathcal{D}$ whose last state is a final state. For any pre-run ρ of $\mathcal{D}$

$$\rho = s_0 \xrightarrow{(t_0, \delta_0)} s_1 \xrightarrow{(t_1, \delta_1)} \ldots \xrightarrow{(t_{m-1}, \delta_{m-1})} s_m,$$

an *extension* of ρ is a run of $\mathcal{D}$ which is of the form

$$s_0 \xrightarrow{(t_0, \delta_0)} s_1 \xrightarrow{(t_1, \delta_1)} \ldots \xrightarrow{(t_{m-1}, \delta_{m-1})} s_m \xrightarrow{(t_m, \delta_m)} \ldots \xrightarrow{(t_{n-1}, \delta_{n-1})} s_n.$$

It is clear that in the basic algorithm depicted in Figure 2, the purpose that we add a node into $currentpath$ is to check if all extensions of the pre-run corresponding to $currentpath$ satisfy that their total elapsing time are not smaller than a given real number.

Theorem 2. For an activity diagram $\mathcal{D}$, let ρ be a pre-run of $\mathcal{D}$ which is of the form

$$\rho = s_0 \xrightarrow{(t_0,\delta_0)} s_1 \xrightarrow{(t_1,\delta_1)} \dots \xrightarrow{(t_{m-1},\delta_{m-1})} s_m \,,$$

and d be the infimum of the set

$$\{delay(\rho_1) \mid \rho_1 \text{ is an extension of } \rho\} \,.$$

For any pre-run ρ' of $\mathcal{D}$ ending at s_m which is of the form

$$\rho' = s_0 \xrightarrow{(t'_0,\delta'_0)} s'_1 \xrightarrow{(t'_1,\delta'_1)} \dots \xrightarrow{(t'_{k-1},\delta'_{k-1})} s'_k \xrightarrow{(t'_k,\delta'_k)} s_m \,,$$

all runs which are an extension of ρ' satisfy that their total elapsing time are not smaller than a given real number p if and only if $delay(\rho') + d - delay(\rho) \geq p$. □

The proof of this theorem is presented in the appendix.

For an activity diagram $\mathcal{D}$, let ρ be the pre-run of $\mathcal{D}$ corresponding to *currentpath* in the algorithm depicted in Figure 2, which is of the form

$$\rho = s_0 \xrightarrow{(t_0,\delta_0)} s_1 \xrightarrow{(t_1,\delta_1)} \dots \xrightarrow{(t_{n-1},\delta_{n-1})} s_m \,,$$

where s_m is the node which will be moved from *currentpath*. Let d be the infimum of the set $\{delay(\rho_1) \mid \rho_1 \text{ is an extension of } \rho\}$. From Theorem 2, it follows that if we record $v = d - delay(\rho)$, then when we reach s_m again through another path whose corresponding pre-run is ρ'

$$\rho' = s_0 \xrightarrow{(t'_0,\delta'_0)} s'_1 \xrightarrow{(t'_1,\delta'_1)} \dots \xrightarrow{(t'_{k-1},\delta'_{k-1})} s'_k \xrightarrow{(t'_k,\delta'_k)} s_m \,,$$

we can check if all extensions of ρ' satisfy that their total elapsing time are not smaller than a given real number p by checking if $delay(\rho') + v \geq p$. But the problem is that we need to know what d is. Since the algorithm is based on depth-first search method, when s_m is moved from *currentpath*, we have searched all paths corresponding to all extensions of ρ. So, d should be the minimal total elapsing time for the runs reached during s_m being in *currentpath*.

Thus, we can improve the basic algorithm so that each node is searched only once as follows. We modify the data structure *currentpath* such that any node in *currentpath* is of the form (s, v), where s is a node in the reachability graph and v is the minimal total elapsing time for the runs reached since s is added into *currentpath* (we assume that the initial value of v is ∞ since no run is reached at the time s is added in *currentpath*). When a final state is reached, we replace v with the total elapsing time of the run corresponding to *currentpath* if v is greater than the total elapsing time. We define a new data structure *passedstates*, which is a set whose elements have the same form as the nodes in *currentpath*. When a node (s, v) is deleted from *currentpath*, we add $(s, v - delay(\rho))$ into *passedstates* where ρ is the pre-run corresponding to *currentpath*. So, before a new node (s, ∞) is added into *currentpath*, we check if there is a node (s', v') in *passedstates* such that $s = s'$. If yes, we do not need to add the node into *currentpath*. We just need to check if the pre-run ρ

$currentpath := \langle(s_0, \infty)\rangle;\ passedstates := \{\};$
repeat
    let (s, v) be the last node of $currentpath$ and ρ be pre-run corresponding to
    $currentpath$;
    $node := s$;
    if $node$ has no new successive node **then**
      begin
        delete the last node of $currentpath$;
        if $v \neq \infty$ **then**
          $passedstates := passedstate \cup \{(node, v - delay(\rho))\};$
      end
    else
      begin
        $node :=$ a new successive node of $node$;
        let ρ be pre-run corresponding to $currentpath$;
        if $node$ is a final state **then**
          begin
            check if the run corresponding path satisfies that its total elapsing time
            is not smaller than a given real number;
            if no **then return false**;
            for each node (s, v) in $currentpath$ **do**
              if $v > delay(\rho))$ **then** replace v with $delay(\rho)$;
          end
        else
          if $node$ is not in $currentpath$ **then**
            begin
             if there is $(s, v) \in passedstates$ such that $s = node$ **then**
              begin if $delay(\rho) + v < p$ **then return false; end**
             else
               append $(node, \infty)$ to $currentpath$;
            end;
      end
until $currentpath = \langle\rangle$;
return true.

Fig. 3. Improved algorithm checking activity diagrams

corresponding to $currentpath$ satisfies that $delay(\rho) + v'$ is not smaller than a given real number p. If no, the activity diagram does not satisfy that the total elapsing time of any run is not small than a given real number and we are done; otherwise we search the other nodes. The improved algorithm is depicted in Figure 3.

6   Conclusion

We have extended UML activity diagrams with timing constraints, and given the solution for timing analysis of UML activity diagrams. For simple UML activity diagrams (containing no loop), we have given the solution for timing analysis by linear programming. For general UML activity diagrams, we have presented an algorithm for checking them using integer time verification techniques, and improved the algorithm to avoid exhaustive path search. Since UML activity diagrams are very suitable for describing the model of program behaviour, this work forms a base for verification of real-time software systems.

To our knowledge, there has not been any literature on timing analysis of UML activity diagrams. UML activity diagrams can be interpreted as a global state automaton with a huge state space. Theoretically timing analysis of activity diagrams can thus be solved by checking a timied automaton [8], which is of very high complexity. UML activity diagrams and their formal definition we give are similar to Petri nets. However, from the consideration of describing timed program hehaviour, we put timing constraints on activity states instead of on transitions in activity diagrams. So we can not solve problems for activity diagrams by using directly the techniques for time Petri nets [9] in which the timing constraints are enforced on transitions. Also the existing techniques for time Petri nets are just for checking reachability, not for checking the delay properties discussed in this paper.

The solutions presented in this paper has been implemented in a tool for timing analysis of UML diagrams. Besides activity diagrams, the tool supports to analyze UML sequence diagrams with timing constraints described in [11,12]. The future work is to develop methods and tools for extracting activity diagrams from real-time software systems.

References

1. Jeannette M. Wing and Mandana Vaziri-Farahani. Model Checking Software Systems: A Case Study. In *Porc. SIGSOFT'95*, Washington, D.C., USA, 1995.
2. Gerard J. Holzmann and Margaret H. Smith. Software Model Checking: Extracting Verification Models from Source Code. In *Proceedings of 12th International Conference on Formal Description Techniques FORTE/PSTV'99*, Beijing, China, October 1999, Chapman & Hall.
3. David Y.W. Park, Ulrich Stern, Jens U. Skakebak, and David L. Dill. Java Model Checking. In *Proceedings of the First International Workshop on Automated Program Analysis, Testing, and Verification*, 2000.
4. Klaus Havelund and Thomas Pressburger. Model checking JAVA programs using JAVA PathFinder. In *International Journal on Software Tools for Technology Transfer*, (2000) 2: 366-381.
5. Edmund M. Clarke, Orna Grumberg, and Doron A. Peled. *Model Checking*, The MIT Press, 1999.
6. Grady Booch and James Rumbaugh and Ivar Jacobson. *The Unified Modeling Language User Guide*, Addison-Wesley, 1998.
7. J. Rumbaugh and I. Jacobson and G. Booch. *The Unified Modeling Language Reference Manual*, Addison-Wesley, 1999.

8. Rajeev Alur, David L. Dill. A theory of timed automata. In *Theoretical Computer Science*, 126(1994), pp.183-235.
9. B. Berthomieu and M. Diza. Modelling and verification of time dependent systems using time Petri nets. In *IEEE Transactions on Software Engineering*, 17(3):259-273, March 1991.
10. J. Seemann, J. WvG. Extension of UML Sequence Diagrams for Real-Time Systems. In *Proc. International UML Workshop*, Lecture Notes in Computer Science, Springer, 1998.
11. Xuandong Li, Johan Lilius. Timing Aanlysis of UML Sequence Diagrams. In Robert France, Bernhard Rumpe (Eds.), *UML'99 - The Unified Modeling Language*, Lecture Notes in Computer Science 1723, Springer, 1999, pp.661-674.
12. Xuandong Li, Johan Lilius. Checking UML Sequence Diagrams for Timing Inconsistency. In *Proceedings of 7th Asia Pacific Software Engineering Conference*, IEEE Computer Society Press, 2000, pp.154-161.

A   Proof of Theorems

Theorem 1. For an activity diagram $\mathcal{D} = (A, T, F, Ect, Lct, a_I, a_F)$, for a real number p, any run ρ of $\mathcal{D}$ satisfies $delay(\rho) \geq p$ if and only if any integral run ρ' of $\mathcal{D}$ satisfies $delay(\rho') \geq p$.

Proof. The theorem follows immediately from the following claim: for any run ρ of $\mathcal{D}$, there is an integral run ρ' of $\mathcal{D}$ such that $delay(\rho) \geq delay(\rho')$. This claim can be proved as follows. Let

$$\rho = s_0 \xrightarrow{(t_0, \delta_0)} s_1 \xrightarrow{(t_1, \delta_1)} \ldots \xrightarrow{(t_{n-1}, \delta_{n-1})} s_n$$

be a run of $\mathcal{D}$, where $s_i = (\mu_i, c_i)$ for each i ($0 \leq i \leq n$). For each i ($1 \leq i \leq n$), let $\tau_i = \delta_0 + \delta_1 + \ldots + \delta_{i-1}$. It is clear that if each τ_i ($1 \leq i \leq n$) is an integer, then ρ is an integral run. Let $frac(\rho)$ be the set containing all fractions of τ_i ($1 \leq i \leq n$), 0, and 1, i.e.

$$frac(\rho) = \left\{ \gamma_i \ \middle| \ \begin{array}{l} 0 \leq \gamma_i \leq 1, 1 \leq i \leq n, \\ \text{and } \tau_i - \gamma_i \text{ is an integer} \end{array} \right\} \cup \{0, 1\}.$$

Let $rank(\rho)$ be the number of the elements in $frac(\rho)$. Notice that if $rank(\rho) = 2$, then ρ is an integral run. In the following, we show that if $rank(\rho) > 2$, we can construct a run ρ_1 such that $rank(\rho_1) = rank(\rho) - 1$ and $delay(\rho_1) \leq delay(\rho)$. By applying this step repeatedly, we can get a run ρ' satisfying $rank(\rho') = 2$ and $delay(\rho') \leq delay(\rho)$ so that the claim is proved. Let $frac(\rho) = \{\gamma_0, \gamma_1, \ldots, \gamma_m\}$ ($\gamma_0 = 0, \gamma_m = 1, \gamma_i < \gamma_{i+1}$ ($0 \leq i \leq m - 1$)), and

$$index(\gamma_1) = \{i \mid 1 \leq i \leq n \text{ and } \tau_i - \gamma_1 \text{ is an integer}\}.$$

For each i ($1 \leq i \leq n$), let τ_i' be defined as

$$\tau_i' = \begin{cases} \tau_i - \gamma_1 & \text{if } i \in index(\gamma_1) \\ \tau_i & \text{if } i \notin index(\gamma_1) \end{cases}.$$

For each i ($0 \leq i \leq n-1$), let $\delta'_i = \tau'_{i+1} - \tau'_i$. Since for any $a \in A$, $Ect(a)$ and $Lct(a)$ are integers, there are states $s'_1, s'_2, \ldots, s'_n$ such that

$$\rho'_1 = s_0 \xrightarrow{(t_0, \delta'_0)} s'_1 \xrightarrow{(t_1, \delta'_1)} \ldots \xrightarrow{(t_{n-1}, \delta'_{n-1})} s'_n$$

is a runs of $\mathcal{D}$. It follows that $rank(\rho'_1) = rank(\rho) - 1$ Since $delay(\rho) = \tau_n$ and $delay(\rho'_1) = \tau'_n$, $delay(\rho) \geq delay(\rho'_1)$. By applying the above step repeatedly, the claim can be proved. $\qquad\square$

Theorem 2. For an activity diagram $\mathcal{D}$, let ρ be a pre-run of $\mathcal{D}$ which is of the form

$$\rho = s_0 \xrightarrow{(t_0, \delta_0)} s_1 \xrightarrow{(t_1, \delta_1)} \ldots \xrightarrow{(t_{m-1}, \delta_{m-1})} s_m,$$

and d be the infimum of the set

$$\{delay(\rho_1) \mid \rho_1 \text{ is an extension of } \rho\}.$$

For any pre-run ρ' of $\mathcal{D}$ ending at s_m which is of the form

$$\rho' = s_0 \xrightarrow{(t'_0, \delta'_0)} s'_1 \xrightarrow{(t'_1, \delta'_1)} \ldots \xrightarrow{(t'_{k-1}, \delta'_{k-1})} s'_k \xrightarrow{(t'_k, \delta'_k)} s_m,$$

all runs which are an extension of ρ' satisfy that their total elapsing time are not smaller than a given real number p if and only if $delay(\rho') + d - delay(\rho) \geq p$.

Proof. Since the infimum of the set

$$\{delay(\rho_2) \mid \rho_2 \text{ is an extension of } \rho'\}$$

is $delay(\rho') + d - delay(\rho)$, all runs which are an extension of ρ' satisfy that their total elapsing time are not smaller than a given real number p if and only if $delay(\rho') + d - delay(\rho) \geq p$. $\qquad\square$

UML Activity Diagrams as a Workflow Specification Language

Marlon Dumas and Arthur H.M. ter Hofstede

Cooperative Information Systems Research Centre
Queensland University of Technology
GPO Box 2434, Brisbane QLD 4001, Australia
{m.dumas, a.terhofstede}@qut.edu.au

Abstract. If UML activity diagrams are to succeed as a standard in the area of organisational process modeling, they need to compare well to alternative languages such as those provided by commercial Workflow Management Systems. This paper examines the expressiveness and the adequacy of activity diagrams for workflow specification, by systematically evaluating their ability to capture a collection of workflow patterns. This analysis provides insights into the relative strengths and weaknesses of activity diagrams. In particular, it is shown that, given an appropriate clarification of their semantics, activity diagrams are able to capture situations arising in practice, which cannot be captured by most commercial Workflow Management Systems. On the other hand, the study shows that activity diagrams fail to capture some useful situations, thereby suggesting directions for improvement.

1 Introduction

UML activity diagrams are intended to model both computational and organisational processes (i.e. workflows) [14,15]. However, if activity diagrams are to succeed as a standard in the area of organisational process modeling, they should compare favorably to the languages currently used for this purpose, that is, those supported by existing Workflow Management Systems (WFMS).

In this paper, we investigate the expressiveness and adequacy of the activity diagrams notation for workflow specification, by systematically confronting it with a set of *control-flow workflow patterns*, i.e. abstracted forms of recurring situations related to the ordering of activities in a workflow, and the flow of execution between them. Many of these patterns are documented in [3,4], and a comparison of several WFMS based on these patterns is provided in [4].

Our evaluation demonstrates that activity diagrams support the majority of the patterns considered, including some which are typically not supported by commercial WFMS. This is essentially due to the fact that activity diagrams integrate signal sending and processing at the conceptual level, whereas most commercial WFMS only support them as a low-level implementation mechanism.

While activity diagrams compare well to existing WFMS in this respect, they exhibit the major drawback that their syntax and semantics are not fully de-

M. Gogolla and C. Kobryn (Eds.): UML 2001, LNCS 2185, pp. 76–90, 2001.
© Springer-Verlag Berlin Heidelberg 2001

fined in the standard's documentation[1]. Indeed, while the features inherited from Harel's statecharts [9] have a formal operational semantics, the features specific to activity diagrams are only partially formalised in the standard (through OCL statements), and their description in natural language leaves room for some ambiguities that we point out throughout the paper. We hope that some of these ambiguities will be clarified in future releases of the standard.

The rest of the paper is structured as follows. Section 2 discusses some semantical issues of the activity diagrams notation, focusing on control-flow aspects. Sections 3, 4, and 5 evaluate the capabilities of activity diagrams against different families of workflow patterns. The patterns considered in sections 3 and 4 are extracted from [4], while those discussed in section 5 are variants of the well-known producer-consumer pattern. Finally, section 6 points to related work, and section 7 discusses directions for improving the activity diagrams notation.

2   Overview of Activity Diagrams

The aims of the following overview are (i) to discuss the semantics and properties of critical constructs used in the rest of the paper, (ii) to identify some ambiguities in the standard, and (iii) to explain how this paper deals with these ambiguities. It is not intended as an introductory overview. Readers not familiar with activity diagrams may refer to e.g. [8].

2.1   States and Transitions

UML activity diagrams are special cases of UML *state diagrams*, which in turn are graphical representations of *state machines*. The *state machine* formalism as defined in the UML, is a variant of Harel's statecharts [9].

State machines are transition systems whose arcs are labeled by ECA (Event-Condition-Action) rules. The occurrence of an event fires a transition if (i) the machine is in the source state of the transition, (ii) the type of the event occurrence matches the event description of the transition, and (iii) the condition of the transition holds. The event (also called trigger), condition (also called guard), and action parts of a transition are all optional. A transition without an event is said to be *triggerless*. Triggerless transitions are enabled when the action or activity attached to their source state is completed.

A state can contain an entire state machine within it, leading to the concept of *compound state*. Compound states come in two flavours: OR and AND. An OR-state contains a single statechart, while an AND-state contains several statecharts (separated by dashed lines) which are intended to be executed concurrently. Each of these statecharts is called a *concurrent region*. When a compound state is entered, its initial transition(s) are taken. The execution of a compound state is considered to be complete when it reaches (all) its final state(s). Initial states are denoted by filled circles, while final states are denoted by two concentric circles: one filled and one unfilled (see figure 1).

---

[1] When discussing the syntax and semantics of activity diagrams, we take as sole reference the final draft delivered by the UML Revision Task Force 1.4 [14].

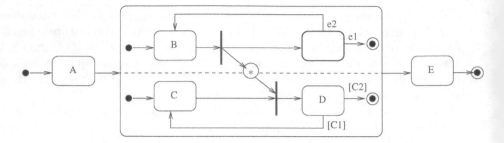

Fig. 1. An example of an activity diagram.

Actions or sequences of actions can be attached to basic (i.e. non-compound) states. In this respect, one can distinguish the following kinds of *basic* states:

- Wait state: no action or activity is performed. A state of this kind is exited when one of its outgoing transitions fires due to an event occurrence. The unlabeled state with a thick border in figure 1 is an example of a wait state.
- Action state: a single action is attached to a state. The execution of an action is non-interruptible, so that the transitions emanating from such a state cannot fire until the action is completed. The states labeled A through E in figure 1 are examples of action states (their labels are action names).
- Activity-in-state: an activity (expressed as a sequence of actions) is attached to the state. The execution of this activity can be aborted prior to its completion if one of the state's outgoing transitions fires. We found no definition of the term "activity abortion" in the standard, so it is not clear if an activity abortion means that no more actions in the sequence are executed (interruption semantics), or if it means that the system's state before the activity's commencement is restored (abortion semantics of ACID transactions).

A *subactivity state* is recursively defined as a compound state whose decomposition contains exclusively action and subactivity states. In [14] page 3-161, it is said that "an activity diagram is a special case of a state diagram in which all (or at least most) of the states are either action or subactivity states, and all (or at least most) of the transitions are [triggerless]". Unfortunately, no definition of "at least most" is given. Does it mean at least 50% of the states and transitions? In this paper, we assume that there is no quota on the percentage of action, subactivity states, and triggerless transitions, within an activity diagram. Indeed, wait states, activity-in-states, and transitions with triggers, are extremely useful features when it comes to model workflows, since they naturally capture exception handling and inter-process communication as pointed out in [16,1].

2.2 Forks and Joins

AND-states provide a means to express that a number of activities are intended to be executed concurrently. Still, activity diagrams also offer two other constructs for expressing concurrency, namely forks and joins. A fork (represented by a heavy bar as in figure 1) is a special transition with one source state and several target states. When this transition fires, the target states are all simultaneously entered, resulting in an increase in the number of concurrent *threads*. A join (represented by a heavy bar as well) is a transition with several source states and one target state, which reduces the number of concurrent threads.

An activity diagram with forks and joins must fulfill some *well-formedness* criteria. These criteria state that it must be possible to replace all forks and joins with AND-states. In particular, for every fork there should be a corresponding join, the delicate point being to define what is meant by "corresponding".

The well-formedness of activity diagrams is partially defined as OCL and natural language statements in the standard ([14] pp. 2-161 through 2-169). This definition however does not take into account the case where choice and junction vertices are used within the paths leading from a fork to a join, thereby permitting deadlocking situations which would not occur if forks and joins were replaced with AND-states. We argue that if activity diagrams are to be used as a workflow specification language, a precise definition of their well-formedness is crucial, as it prevents several kinds of deadlocks. In a different context than activity diagrams, [10] provides a formalisation of these well-formedness rules.

In this paper, we avoid the use of forks and joins, and use AND-states instead. Forks and joins are only used in conjunction with *synch state* as discussed below.

2.3   Synch States

A synch state is a synchronisation point between two threads. In its simplest form, a synch state has one incoming transition emanating from a fork in one thread, and one outgoing transition leading to a join in another thread. A fork (join) connected to a synch state is called a *synchronising fork (join)*.

Synch states differ from normal states in that they are not boolean. Using Petri net terminology, this means that a synch state may hold several tokens simultaneously. The number of tokens that a synch state can hold is constrained to be lower than, or equal to a given bound (the special symbol * denotes that there is no bound). Figure 1 shows an example of an unbounded synch state. In this diagram, one instance of activity D is executed each time that one instance of activity B *and* one instance of activity C are completed. This diagram shows that the use of synch states may lead to deadlocks. Indeed, in the given example, a deadlock occurs if B is performed only once, while C is performed twice.

2.4   Dynamic Invocations

Within an activity diagram, it is possible to specify that multiple *invocations* of an action or subactivity execute concurrently: a feature called *dynamic invocation*. The *dynamic multiplicity* of a state, is the maximum permitted number of invocations of its action or subactivity. It is indicated as a string on its upper right corner (a star indicates that there is no bound). At run time, the state receives a set of *dynamic arguments*, and performs one invocation of its action or subactivity for each of these arguments, up to the limit fixed by its multiplicity.

After a thorough search through [14], we found that there are no indications as to how multiple invocations of an action or activity synchronise once their execution is completed. Assuming that these invocations are not required to synchronise upon completion, inconsistencies may arise when a "dynamic" state is followed by a "non-dynamic" one. Consider for example the diagram in figure 2, where an action state A with dynamic multiplicity 2 is followed by an action state B with no dynamic multiplicity. Suppose that two invocations of A are made, and that the first invocation finishes before the second. If the two invocations are not required to synchronise, state B can be entered at this point. Now, what will happen when the second invocation of A finishes? Will it trigger activity B again (in which case two instances of B will run simultaneously)? Because of this semantical conflict, we consider in this paper that a dynamic state can only be exited when all its associated invocations are completed. In particular, if one invocation is aborted due to some external event, all the other invocations are aborted too. This is in line with the interpretation suggested in [8].

Fig. 2. An example of the use of dynamic invocation.

Another point regarding dynamic invocation which is left open by the standard, is whether each invocation runs in its own memory space, or if it shares the same memory space as the others. If two subactivities run in the same space, chances are that this could lead to write-write conflicts over shared variables.

3   Capturing Synchronisation Patterns

This and the following two sections, present a series of workflow patterns and their description using UML activity diagrams. For each pattern we provide:

- A description of the context, scope and intent of the pattern.
- A concrete example illustrating this description.
- A paragraph indicating to what extent the pattern is supported by WFMS.
- A discussion on how the pattern can be captured using activity diagrams.

The patterns in this section correspond to situations where one or several concurrent activities need to be completed before another activity is initiated.

3.1   The Discriminator[2]

Description. The discriminator is a point in a workflow that waits for one of its incoming branches to complete before activating the subsequent activity. From

---

[2] The term discriminator here, refers to a special kind of synchronisation. It should not be mistaken with the use of the term discriminator in UML class diagrams, where it refers to a "dimension of specialisation within a class hierarchy".

that moment on, it waits for the other branches to complete and "ignores" them. When the last incoming branch completes, the discriminator resets itself so that it can be triggered again (in case it is embedded in a loop).

Example. To improve query response time, a complex search is sent to two different databases over the Internet. As soon as the one of the databases comes up with a result, the execution flow proceeds. The second result is ignored.

Degree of support offered by commercial WFMS. In all but a few WFMS, the discriminator cannot be captured at the conceptual level [4]. A notable exception is Verve[3], which offers a specific construct for this pattern. In the SAP R/3 Workflow[4], for each AND-split/AND-join combination, it is possible to specify for how many of the parallel branches started by the split, does the join need to wait. One can be thus be tempted to capture the discriminator by specifying that the AND-join only needs to wait for one of the branches started by the AND-split. However, the branches that are still running when the first branch finishes, will be marked as "logically deleted" by the SAP R/3 Workflow, whereas in the discriminator pattern these branches should proceed normally.

A solution using UML activity diagrams. Figure 3 shows how to express the discriminator as a set of concurrent regions communicating through signals. Specifically, the incoming branches of the discriminator, as well as the outgoing branch, are placed in separate regions of a single subactivity state. When this subactivity state is entered, the regions corresponding to the incoming branches of the discriminator are executed, while the region corresponding to the outgoing branch "sits" in a wait state. When one of the incoming branches terminates, it produces a signal which causes the outgoing branch to start its execution.

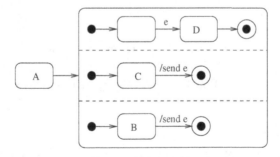

Fig. 3. Activity diagram capturing the discriminator pattern with 2 incoming branches.

This solution has a limitation when the discriminator is part of a loop. Consider for instance the situation depicted in figure 4(a), whose translation as an activity diagram is given in figure 4(b). This activity diagram forces an undesired synchronisation between activities B, C and D. Specifically, if B finishes before C, D is started immediately. Now, if D subsequently finishes before C, and con-

---

[3] http://www.verve.com or http://www.versata.com.
[4] http://www.sap.com.

dition cond holds, activity A cannot be started immediately: it has to wait for the completion of C. This is not in line with the semantics of the discriminator, which does not impose any synchronisation constraint besides the fact that one of its incoming transitions has to fire before firing the outgoing transition.

This example puts forward a limitation of activity diagrams inherited from statecharts. Unlike Petri nets whose places can hold several tokens, states in a statechart are boolean, in the sense that a state cannot be active several times simultaneously. In the example at hand, if A was started immediately after the completion of D, and if subsequently A finished before C, then the state labeled C would have to be entered (i.e. activated) again.

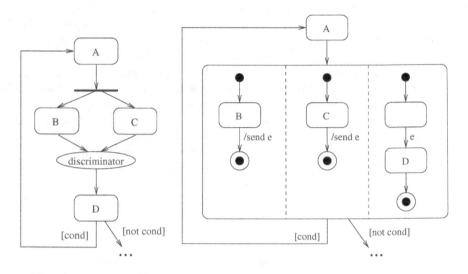

(a) Informal description   (b) Expressed as an UML activity diagram

Fig. 4. A discriminator within a loop

3.2   N-out-of-M Join

Description. The N-out-of-M Join is a point in a workflow where M parallel branches converge into one. The outgoing branch should be started once N incoming branches have completed. Completion of all remaining branches should be ignored. As with the discriminator, once all incoming branches have fired, the join resets itself. In fact, the discriminator is a 1-out-of-M join. The N-out-of-M join is identified in [6], where it is called *partial join*.

Example. A paper must be sent to three external reviewers. Upon receiving two reviews the paper can be processed. The third review can be ignored.

Degree of support offered by commercial WFMS. See previous pattern.

A solution using activity diagrams. This pattern can be treated in a similar way as the discriminator, except that a counter needs to be introduced, to keep track of the number of termination signals generated by the incoming branches of the N-out-of-M join. The execution of the outgoing branch is started when a new termination signal arrives while the value of the counter is N - 1.

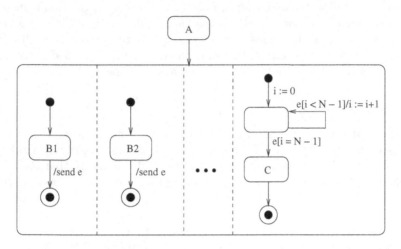

Fig. 5. Activity diagram corresponding to the N out of M pattern.

When the N-out-of-M join is part of a loop, the above solution has the same limitation as the solution of the discriminator pattern presented in figure 4(b).

3.3 Multiple Instances Requiring Synchronisation

Description. A point in a workflow where an activity A is enabled multiple times. The number of instances of A that need to be enabled is known only when the point is reached. After completing all the enabled instances of A, an instance of an activity B has to be executed.

Example. The requisition of 100 computers results in a number of (concurrent) deliveries. Once all deliveries are processed, the requisition has to be closed.

Degree of support offered by commercial WFMS. Many WFMS do not support the concept of "multiple instances of an activity" [4]. Systems that support multiple instances do not provide conceptual constructs to enforce the synchronisation of these instances. Interestingly, in UML the opposite holds : the synchronisation of multiple instances of an activity is imposed, so it is not possible to express (for example) that the activity B can be started as soon as one of the instances of A is completed (i.e. a discriminator-like synchronisation).

A solution using activity diagrams. Embed activity A within a subactivity state, and attach an unbounded dynamic multiplicity to it. Then, introduce a transition between this subactivity state and an action state labeled by B (as in figure 2). At run-time, provide one dynamic argument per required instance of activity A. Since UML does not provide a notation for passing dynamic arguments to a subactivity state, this has to be expressed in a programming language.

4   Capturing State-Based Patterns

In real workflows, where human and material resources are not always available, activities are more often in a waiting state than in a processing one [4]. This fact is central in the following two patterns, where a distinction is made between the moment when an activity is enabled, and that when it starts running. In the first pattern, the choice between two alternative enabled activities is delayed until an event occurs. In the second pattern, several enabled activities have to be processed, but at any point in time, at most one of them can be running.

4.1   Deferred Choice

Description. A point in a workflow where one among several branches is chosen based on some external information which is not necessarily available when this point is reached. This differs from the "normal" choice, in that the choice is not made explicitly (based on existing data) but several alternatives are offered to the environment, and the choice between them is delayed until an external signal is received. Using the WFMS terminology, this means that the alternative activities are placed in the worklist, but as soon as one of them starts its execution, the others are withdrawn. This pattern is called implicit XOR-split in [2].
Example. When a contract is finalised, it has to be signed either by the director, or by both the deputy director and the secretary, whoever is/are available first.
Degree of support offered by commercial WFMS. Although all WFMS provide a construct capturing the "normal" choice, few of them support the deferred choice. A notable exception is COSA[5]. In some WFMS, the deferred choice can be handled at the implementation level using cancellation messages (i.e. both A and B are enabled and one of them is cancelled when the other starts), but this solution will not always work due to concurrency problems.
A solution using activity diagrams. The deferred choice can be expressed as a normal state which waits for an event from the environment, and chooses one of its outgoing branches accordingly (see figure 6).

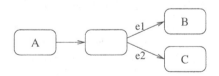

Fig. 6. Activity diagram corresponding to the deferred choice pattern.

4.2   Interleaved Parallel Routing

Description. A set of activities $\{A_1, A_2, \ldots, A_n\}$ need to be executed in an arbitrary order. Each activity in the set is executed exactly once. The order

---
[5] http://www.cosa.de and http://www.cosa.nl.

between the activities is decided at run-time: it is not until one activity is completed that the decision on what to do next is taken. In any case, no two activities among $A_1, \ldots, A_n$ can be active at the same time.

Example. The army requires every applicant to take 3 tests: an optical, a medical, and a mental. These tests can be conducted in any order but obviously not at the same time. When an applicant completes a test, the decision of which test to perform next is taken depending on the presence of the relevant doctors. If for example the doctor responsible for the optical test is present, while the doctor for the medical one is absent, the optical test is performed before the medical.

Degree of support offered by commercial WFMS. In many WFMS, this pattern cannot be expressed at the conceptual level. At the implementation level, it can be coded by introducing a resource shared by all activities $A_1, \ldots, A_n$. This shared resource acts as a semaphore, forcing a serialization of the activities.

Since this pattern can be expressed in terms of the deferred choice pattern (see below), it can be captured in those WFMS supporting the deferred choice [4].

Solutions using activity diagrams. This pattern can be expressed in terms of the deferred choice as follows. First, a deferred choice is made between n branches, such that the ith branch starts with activity A_i ($1 \leq i \leq n$). In the branch that leads to activity A_1, another deferred choice is made (after A_1 is executed) between n – 1 branches respectively starting with $A_2, \ldots, A_n$. A similar nested deferred choice is also made in all the other branches of the first deferred choice. This process of nesting deferred choices is recursively repeated, until all the permutations of $A_1, \ldots, A_n$ are enumerated. Clearly, for a large number of activities, this combinatorial explosion is undesirable.

A better alternative is to enforce the interleaving of activities by placing each activity in a separate concurrent region, and blocking their execution through synch states emanating from a single "blocking region" (this is the leftmost region in figure 7). A token is inserted into the synch state blocking an activity Ai, only after the processing of the event that enables the execution of Ai. When Ai starts its execution, the blocking region enters a state which defers the occurrences of events that may unblock the execution of other activities. For instance, in figure 7 events s1, s2 and s3 are used to indicate that activities A1, A2 and A3 respectively, can be executed. If one of these events occurs while one of the activities is being executed, the processing of this occurrence is deferred until the ongoing activity execution has completed.

5   Producer-Consumer Patterns

The patterns in this section are variants of the producer-consumer pattern found in distributed systems design. They correspond to situations where several instances of an activity A (the producer) are executed sequentially, and the termination of each of these instances triggers the execution of an instance of another activity B (the consumer). The instances of A and B execute concurrently, but some asymetric inter-dependencies link them (a "B" is caused by an "A").

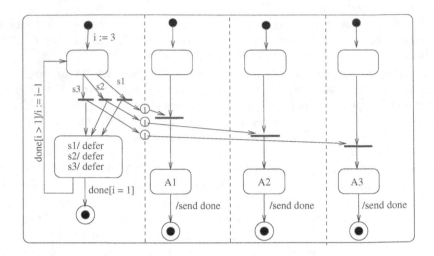

Fig. 7. Activity diagram for the interleaved parallel routing of 3 activities.

5.1   Producer-Consumer Pattern with Termination Activity

Description. This pattern involves three activities A, B and C. The process starts with the execution of an instance of A. When this execution completes, an instance of B is enabled. Concurrently, a second instance of A can be started. When this second instance of A completes, a second instance of B is enabled and a third instance of A can be started. This process continues in such a way that at any point in time, the following conditions hold: (i) at most one instance of A is running; (ii) the execution of the ith instance of B does not start before the ith instance of A is completed. When all the instances of A are completed, the system continues executing instances of B until the number of completed executions of B is equal to that of A. Finally, a terminating activity C is executed.

Example. A customer is shopping in a virtual mall aggregating several vendors. Every time that the customer orders an item, the system must trigger an activity which contacts the corresponding vendor to check the item's availability and expected delivery time. Once the customer states that (s)he does not want any other item, and once the availability of all the requested items is checked, a mail is sent to the customer with the list of available products and their delivery time.

Degree of support offered by commercial WFMS. We notice that in this pattern, an a priori unknown number of instances of B may run simultaneously, and these instances need to synchronise upon termination. Therefore, this pattern is not supported by those WFMS which do not support the pattern "Multiple instances with synchronisation". Now, if we restrict the description of the pattern to the case where at most one instance of B is executed at a time (i.e. the instances of B are executed sequentially), then it becomes possible to express this pattern using AND-splits, loops and counters. This is actually the approach that we adopt below to capture this pattern in UML activity diagrams.

Solution. The pattern is captured by the activity diagram shown in figure 8. Essentially, instances of activity A and B run in two concurrent regions of a compound state. Every time that an instance of activity A is completed, it puts a token in a synch state, and it increments a counter i. Each of the tokens generated by the completion of an instance of A, enables a transition leading to the execution of one instance of activity B. When the execution of an instance of activity B is completed, a token is put in a second synch state. Once all instances of A are completed, the tokens of this second synch state are "consumed" one after the other, and for each of these consumptions, the counter i is decremented. When the value of the counter is zero, it means that B was executed as many times as A was. The compound state is then exited and C is executed once.

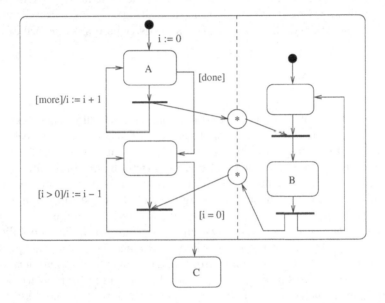

Fig. 8. Activity diagram for the producer-consumer pattern with termination activity.

This solution is such that at any point on time, at most one instance of B is running. Although we do not have a proof, we believe that the version of this pattern where multiple instances of B may run concurrently, cannot be expressed as an activity diagram. Indeed, this would require a dynamic invocation operator in which not all of the dynamic arguments are available at once, but rather arrive one by one. Given such an operator, it would be possible to express that an instance of B needs to be triggered each time that an instance of A terminates, even if the previously generated instances of B have not yet completed.

5.2   Producer-Consumer with Bounded Queue

Description. The description of this pattern is similar to that of section 5.1, except that at any time, the difference between the number of times that activity

A has been executed, and the number of times that activity B has been executed, is bounded by an integer called the *size of the queue*.

Example. To obtain an ID card, an applicant has to complete a form and present it to an officer for verification. Once the officer has checked the form, the applicant is sent to a photographer's room. However, the queue leading from the officer's counter to the photographer's room cannot contain more than 5 persons. Should the queue contain 5 persons, the officer would stop accepting applications until one of these persons enters the photographer's room.

Degree of support offered by commercial WFMS. See previous pattern.

Solution. The idea is to modify the diagram of figure 8, in such a way that two separate counters are kept: one counting the executions of A (na), and the other counting the executions of B (nb). Every time that activity A is completed, if the boolean variable "more" is true, a waiting state is entered, which is only exited when the condition $na - nb < s$ holds (where s is the size of the queue).

6   Related Work

The suitability of statechart-based notations for workflow specification has been recognised by many studies. For instance, [12] argues that statecharts are perceived by practitioners as being more intuitive and easier to learn than alternative formal notations such as Petri nets (whose suitability for workflow specification is advocated in e.g. [2]), yet have an equally rigorous semantics. More recently, [16] and [1] illustrate through selected case studies, the adequacy and limitations of activity diagrams for business process modeling. None of these references however undertakes a systematic evaluation of the capabilities of statecharts/activity diagrams for workflow specification as in the present paper. Interestingly, [16] agrees with us in saying that wait states and activity-in-states are crucial for workflow modeling, thereby sustaining our position that no restrictions on their use should be imposed as currently suggested by the standard.

The issue of defining a precise semantics of UML is the subject of intensive investigations, as evidenced by the number of projects, forums, and workshops in this area (see [13] for a list of links). Unfortunately, within this stream of research, activity diagrams have received relatively little attention, despite the fact that they are "one of the most unexpected parts of the UML" [8]. Ongoing efforts such as those reported in [5] and [7] are attempting to fill this gap. [5] defines an algebraic semantics of the core constructs of activity diagrams. It does not deal however with features such as synch states, dynamic invocation and deferred events. In this regard, the formalisation given in [7] is more complete. Based on the STATEMATE semantics of statecharts [9], this formalisation covers all activity diagrams constructs (except synch states and swimlanes), and considers issues such as data manipulation. The authors however do not formalise syntactical constraints such as the well-formedness rules linking forks with joins, which are essential to avoid some deadlocking situations. These syntactical constraints and some of their expressive power implications are studied in [10].

To summarise, we can state that the formalisation of the activity diagrams notation, and the evaluation of its suitability for workflow specification, are still open issues. It is expected that the ongoing OMG RFP "UML extensions for workflow process definition" [17] will provide an occasion to address them.

7   Conclusion

This paper presented an evaluation of UML activity diagrams against a set of workflow patterns involving control-flow aspects. Some of these patterns are extracted from [4], while others are variants of the producer-consumer pattern. Actually, we have confronted activity diagrams against the 22 control-flow patterns in [4], although for space reasons we have just presented some of them.

From this systematic evaluation, we conclude that in the context of workflow specification, the strong points of activity diagrams with respect to alternative languages provided by commercial WFMS are essentially the followings:

- They support signal sending and receiving at the conceptual level.
- They support both *waiting states* and *processing states*.
- They provide a seamless mechanism for decomposing an activity specification into subactivities. The combination of this decomposition capability with signal sending yields a powerful approach to handling activity interruptions.

However, activity diagrams exhibit the following drawbacks:

- Some of their constructs lack a precise syntax and semantics. For instance, the well-formedness rules linking forks with joins are not fully defined, nor are the concepts of dynamic invocation and deferred events, among others.
- They do not fully capture important kinds of synchronisation such as the discriminator and the N-out-of-M join (see section 3). Similarly, to the best of our knowledge, they do not fully support the producer-consumer pattern with termination activity (see section 5.1).

We encourage the participants of the OMG RFP "UML extensions for workflow definition" [17], to consider these two points in their proposals. Actually, [17] mentions the issue of capturing the N-out-of-N join, although it does not discuss what is the expected behaviour of this pattern when embedded in a loop.

In this paper, we focused on the *control-flow perspective*. However, workflows can also be viewed from a *data* and from a *resource* perspective [11]. The data perspective relates to the flow of information between activities, while the resource perspective defines human and device roles responsible for handling activities. The data and resource perspectives may be captured through *object flows* and *swimlanes* respectively. Assessing the suitability of these constructs against appropriate workflow patterns is a perspective to our work.

Another perspective is to study how the concepts and constructs of UML activity diagrams compare to those of the Workflow Management Coalition's Reference Model [18]. Such an effort could trace the road towards defining mappings from activity diagrams into vendor-specific workflow specification languages.

References

1. J.Ø. Aagedal and Z. Milosevic. ODP enterprise language: An UML perspective. In *Proc. of The 3rd International Conference on Enterprise Distributed Object Computing*, Mannheim, Germany, 1999. IEEE Press.
2. W.M.P. van der Aalst. The application of Petri nets to workflow management. *The Journal of Circuits, Systems and Computers*, 8(1):21–66, 1998.
3. W.M.P. van der Aalst, A.P. Barros, A.H.M. ter Hofstede, and B. Kiepuszewski. Advanced workflow patterns. In *Proc. of the 5th IFCIS Int. Conference on Cooperative Information Systems*, Eilat, Israel, September 2000. Springer Verlag.
4. W.M.P. van der Aalst, A.H.M ter Hofstede, B. Kiepuszewski, and A. Barros. Workflow patterns. Technical Report WP 47, BETA Research Institute, 2000. Accessed March 2001 from `http://tmitwww.tm.tue.nl/research/patterns`.
5. E. Börger, A. Cavarra, and E. Riccobene. An ASM semantics for UML activity diagrams. In *Proc. of the International Conference on Algebraic Methodology and Software Technology (AMAST)*, Iowa City, IO, USA, May 2000. Springer Verlag.
6. F. Casati, S. Ceri, B. Pernici, and G. Pozzi. Conceptual modeling of workflows. In *Proc. of the 14th International Object-Oriented and Entity-Relationship Modelling Conference (OOER'95)*, pages 341–354. Springer Verlag, December 1995.
7. R. Eshuis and R. Wieringa. A formal semantics for UML activity diagrams – Formalising workflow models. Technical Report CTIT-01-04, University of Twente, Department of Computer Science, 2001.
8. M. Fowler and K. Scott. *UML Distilled: A Brief Guide to the Standard Object Modeling Language (Second Edition)*. Addison Wesley, Readings MA, USA, 2000.
9. D. Harel and A. Naamad. The STATEMATE semantics of statecharts. *ACM Transactions on Software Engineering and Methodology*, 5(4):293–333, October 1996.
10. B. Kiepuszewski, A.H.M. ter Hofstede, and C. Bussler. On structured workflow modelling. In *Proc. of the Int. Conference on Advanced Information Systems Engineering (CAiSE)*, Stockholm, Sweden, June 2000. Springer Verlag.
11. F. Leymann and D. Roller. *Production Workflow: Concepts and Techniques*. Prentice Hall, Upper Saddle River, NJ, USA, 2000.
12. P. Muth, D. Wodtke, J. Weissenfels, A.K. Dittrich, and G. Weikum. From centralized workflow specification to distributed workflow execution. *Journal of Intelligent Information Systems*, 10(2), March 1998.
13. The precise UML group. Home page. `http://www.cs.york.ac.uk/puml/`.
14. UML Revision Task Force. *OMG Unified Modeling Language Specification, Version 1.4 (final draft)*. February 2001.
15. J. Rumbaugh, I. Jacobson, and G. Booch. *The Unified Modeling Language Reference Manual*. Addison-Wesley, 1999.
16. M. Schader and A. Korthaus. Modeling business processes as part of the BOOSTER approach to business object-oriented systems development based on UML. In *Proc. of The Second International Enterprise Distributed Object Computing Workshop (EDOC)*. IEEE Press, 1998.
17. The Object Management Group. UML Extensions for Workflow Process Definition, RFP-bom/2000-12-11. Accessed on June 2001 from `ftp://ftp.omg.org/pub/docs/bom/00-12-11.pdf`.
18. The Workflow Management Coalition. The Workflow Reference Model. `http://www.aiim.org/wfmc/standards/docs/tc003v11.pdf`, accessed on January 2001.

On Querying UML Data Models with OCL

D.H. Akehurst and B. Bordbar

University of Kent at Canterbury,
Canterbury, Kent, CT2 7NF
{D.H.Akehurst, B.Bordbar}@ukc.ac.uk

Abstract. UML is the de-facto standard language for Object-Oriented analysis and design of information systems. Persistent storage and extraction of data in such systems is supported by databases and query languages. UML sustains many aspects of software engineering; however, it does not provide explicit facility for writing queries. It is crucial for any such query language to have, at least, the expressive power of Relational Algebra, which serves as a benchmark for evaluating its expressiveness. The combination of UML and OCL can form queries with the required expressive power. However, certain extensions to OCL are essential if it is to be used effectively as a Query Language. The adoption of the ideas presented in this paper will enable query expressions to be written using OCL, that are elegant and ideally suited for use in conjunction with UML data models. This technique is illustrated by expressing the UML equivalent of an example Relational data model and associated query expressions.

1 Introduction

There is a long-standing approach to data modelling, based on the mathematical concept of relations. This approach is supported by Entity Relationship diagrams [6] [21] as a specification language; by relational databases [9] as a means to provide persistence; and the Standard Query Language (SQL [17]) for querying the data.

More recently the Object-Oriented approach to data modelling has been developed. Similarly, this is supported by the Unified Modelling Language (UML [1]), OO-databases [3] [10] and the Object Query Language (OQL [5]).

UML is the OMG's standard for object oriented modelling and has quickly become the de facto standard for specifying OO systems. A UML diagram (such as a Class Diagram) is typically not sufficient to define all aspects of the specification. Therefore, UML provides a textual Object Constraint Language (OCL [1] [23]), which can be used to express detailed aspects about the modelled system.

OCL was originally designed specifically for expressing constraints about a UML model. However, its ability to navigate the model and form collections of objects has lead to attempts to use it as query language [18] [19] [14] [16].
It is well known that in the case of relational databases, in order for a query language to be useful, it must have the expressive power of a relational algebra [9] [22]. Hence, it follows that the same must be true for OO databases and their respective query languages. In this respect, the authors of [16] discuss the expressive power of OCL, and infer that OCL in isolation is not as expressive as a relational algebra.

M. Gogolla and C. Kobryn (Eds.): UML 2001, LNCS 2185, pp. 91-103, 2001.
© Springer-Verlag Berlin Heidelberg 2001

Building upon their approach, this paper makes use of the detailed semantics of UML and OCL to present an indirect method of forming query expressions. We show that this method leads to a technique for forming expressions that are as expressive as those formed using a relational algebra.

The proposed method requires extra UML classes to be added to the model; this can be cumbersome and resource consuming. Since the UML reference model is currently undergoing a major revision [2] [8], the final part of the paper takes the opportunity to propose extensions to OCL, which enable OCL to be used as an ideal Object-Oriented Query Language.

The rest of this paper is organised as follows: Section 2 discusses the relational approach to data modelling and provides a definition of a relational algebra (RA). Section 3 defines the example used throughout the paper. Section 4 discusses the problems of constructing queries using OCL. Section 5 illustrates a method by which UML and OCL in conjunction can provide all the functionality required by a query language. Section 6 proposes some extensions to the OCL core that would enable OCL query expression to be much more easily formed. Finally, the paper concludes in section 7 by summarising the work presented.

2 Relational Data Modelling

A long standing technique for modelling data in information systems is to represent data using a set of *tables* and relationships between tables. This approach is supported using Relational Database Management Systems (RDBMS), which manage computerised implementation of the data, tables and relationships.

One of the major features of an RDMBS is the provision of extensive support for the manipulation of data. The standard language for expressing the required manipulations (or queries) is called SQL [17]. The principle behind such query languages, giving them a sound mathematical foundation, is called Relational Algebra [9] [22].

A relational algebra (RA) is a set of operators that take relations as their operands and return a relation as their result. There are eight main operators (defined in [9]), called: *Select*; *Project*; *Intersect*; *Difference*; *Join*; *Divide*; *Union*; and *Product*. However, these eight are not independent and three (Intersect, Join and Divide) can be defined in terms of the other five, which are called primitive operators (see [9]). Consequently, in order for a query language to be considered fully expressive, it must support as a minimum, the primitive operators [7]: Union, Difference; Product; Project; and Select. A definition of a relation and these five operators (taken from [9]) is given below:

Relation: Is a mathematical term for table, which is a set of tuples; a relation with arity k is a set of k-tuples.

Union: Returns a relation containing all tuples that appear in either or both of two specified relations.

Difference: Returns a relation containing all tuples that appear in the first and not the second of two specified relations.

Product: Returns a relation containing all possible tuples that are a combination of two tuples, one from each of two specified relations.

Project: Returns a relation containing all (sub) tuples that remain in a specified relation after specified attributes have been removed.

Select: Returns a relation containing all tuples from a specified relation that
               satisfy a specified condition.

The interested reader is referred to [9] and [22] for further details on relational
algebras.

3 Example

As an example, we use through out the paper a data-model that could form part of a
database used by an educational institution. The model records information regarding
students, courses and teachers, and additionally it relates each student to the courses
they study and each course to the teachers who teach the courses. The model can be
specified in UML as shown in Fig. 1.

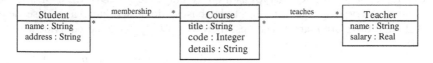

Fig. 1. Example specified in UML

The data-model shown in Fig. 1 can be mapped to a Relational Database (RDB)
using the technique suggested in [3]. The mapping is formed such that each Class and
each Association forms a Table definition and the tables are related by including the
appropriate foreign keys, as shown in Fig. 2. The keys for each of the tables Student,
Course, and Teacher are respectively named stu_id, crs_id and tch_id.

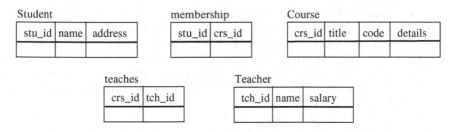

Fig. 2. Example expressed as an RDB

Using this model, assume that there is a requirement to provide a list that shows
which students are taught by which teachers, irrespective of which course.

With respect to the RDB definition, the required list of teachers and students can
be generated using an SQL statement as follows:

```
SELECT DISTINCT s.name, t.name                                        (1)
    FROM Student s, Teachers t, membership m, teaches ts
    WHERE t.tch_id = ts.tch_id
    AND   ts.crs_id = m.crs_id
    AND   m.stu_id = s.stu_id;
```

This Query produces a table showing the names of each teacher and student pair. If we subsequently required more information regarding either the teacher or student in any particular pairing, the SQL statement would need to be changed to include the additional information.

Ideally, we would like the list to contain the pairs of teacher and student objects, rather than just a list containing pairs of their names. Thus, any requirement for additional information (about teachers or students) can be navigated to, from the results of the query, rather than having to alter the specification of the query to return the additional information.

4 OCL as a Query Language (QL)

Integrating OO models of data into RDBMS is state of the art in software development. While SQL serves as a query language in RDBMS, OQL [5], the most famous query language for object databases, does not have a precise semantics. Although there are many variations, there is no fully accepted equivalent to SQL for querying an OO data model.

Blaha and Premerlani [3] introduce the Object Navigation Notation (ONN) for navigation of OMT [20] models (a predecessor to UML). UML has instead OCL, which in addition to being useful as a navigation and constraint language poses a natural choice for use in making queries on the model.

Work such as [11] shows how OCL, when used to specify integrity constraints (well-formedness rules) on the model, can be mapped to the equivalent SQL for the specification of integrity constraints on the tables of an RDB. Their work shows how each OCL language construct can be mapped to an equivalent declarative SQL statement. Their continuing work in [12] discusses the provision of tool support for their approach.

In order for OCL to be considered a fully expressive QL, we must be able to translate any SQL statement into an equivalent OCL expression.

The authors of [14] point out certain obstacles regarding the use of OCL as a QL. In particular they recognise that most Object-Oriented modelling environments that include a QL, provide as a basic type a facility for structured aggregation (such as a tuple or "struct") and give as examples [4], [13] and [15]. As it stands, OCL does not provide such a feature.

Mandel and Cengarle's work [16] explicitly addresses the expressiveness of OCL in the context of its use as a query language. They conclude that OCL is not expressive enough to define all of the operations required by a relational algebra and hence it does not form an adequate query language.

As it stands, OCL supports three out of the five required RA operations. Union, Difference, and Select are all supported directly by operations defined on the OCL collection types. However, the operations Product (or Cartesian Product) and Project are not supported, and cannot be supported as they directly require a facility for structured aggregation or a notion of tuples (see [14]).

5 UML and OCL as a Query Language

Based on the semantics of UML, in this section we demonstrate the UML and OCL together *can* form expressions with the functionality of the RA operators. The key is to provide the concept of a tuple.

The following subsections start by explaining a way of supporting the notion of an n-tuple using the UML concept of AssociationClass and n-ary Association. This is followed by an explanation of how to use the concept to provide the functionality of the Product and Project operations. The section concludes by illustrating that the approach enables the expression of our example query.

5.1 LinkObjects as Tuples

As illustrated by an extract of the UML meta-model [1] shown in Fig. 3. An instance of an Association is called a *Link* and is defined by the UML standard to be a *tuple of object references*. Dually, the instance of an AssociationClass is called a *LinkObject*. The object references are modelled within the UML meta-model as *LinkEnds* and each Link contains an *ordered* list of LinkEnds.

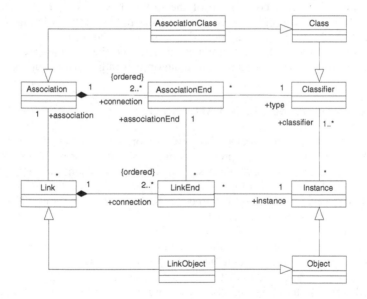

Fig. 3. Extract from the UML meta-model showing AssociationClass and LinkObject

Given this definition of the meta-model, the concept of a LinkObject can be used to represent a tuple of other objects. The relationship between the elements (coordinates) of the tuple is expressed by the Link and the object representing the tuple, is the connected LinkObject. Fig. 4a illustrates an object diagram showing three objects – a, b and c – that are involved in the tuple (a,b,c).

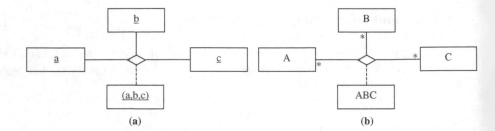

(a)   (b)

Fig. 4. Class and instance specification of a tuple.

The appropriate class specification defining a type for the tuple object can be given using an AssociationClass as shown in Fig. 4b. The multiplicity of the AssociationEnds is defined as '*' to allow each involved object to partake in any number of tuples.

The above describes support for 3-tuples; the approach is extensible, supporting n-tuples with n-ary associations for any n.

An issue to consider at this point, is how to determine the ordering of a tuple; for example, is the first co-ordinate of the tuple of type A, B or C? There is nothing within the notation for n-ary associations that indicates the ordering of its ends, even though the UML meta-model does define that the ends are ordered. Generally, this is not a problem as each end is uniquely named and these names are used within OCL expressions to navigate to the co-ordinate objects rather than an index number.

5.2 Cartesian Product Using UML and OCL

The above approach describes how to support tuples using the UML concept of a Link. In this subsection, we present an indirect method for providing the functionality of the Product operator over three sets. In a similar way, one can support the operation over n sets for any value of n.

By definition, the product of three sets S, T and U is the set of all tuples (s,t,u) such that s is in S, t is in T and u is in U.

Since OCL is a side effect free language an OCL expression cannot create new objects. Thus, the result of the Product operation must be formed by selecting appropriate tuples from a set in which they already exist.

The only way to ensure that such a set exists is to constrain the model as a whole. For the model shown in Fig. 4b, containing classes A, B, C and ABC, the following constraint is sufficient:

```
context ABC inv:
```
(2)
```
ABC.allInstances->size = A.allInstances->size *
                         B.allInstances->size *
                         C.allInstances->size
```

Strictly speaking, this constraint could be placed anywhere inside the UML model, it constrains the instantiation of the model as a whole, rather than specifically constraining the class ABC; however, we use class ABC as a convenient placeholder. It should be noted that, since we are dealing with models of data, at any fixed point in time there are a finite number of instances of each class, and hence the numerical values in constraint (2) are finite.

The semantics of UML and this constraint result in a model definition, for which the instances of class ABC correspond to the Cartesian Product of the instances of A, B and C; i.e.:

```
ABC.allInstances = A.allInstances x                                    (3)
                   B.allInstances x
                   C.allinstances
```

To see this, notice that the Left Hand Side (LHS) of (3) is a subset of its Right Hand Side (RHS). Each ABC object is a LinkObject connecting A, B and C objects and we have proposed (in the previous subsection) that a Link Object is equivalent to a tuple, so it follows that the LHS $\subset$ RHS.

The UML standard [1, p2-94] states that "There are not two Links of the same Association which connects the same set of Instances in the same way." Due to constraint (2) the LHS and RHS have the same finite number of elements. Since there cannot be two identical instances of ABC the LHS = RHS in equation (3).

A Cartesian Product between two arbitrary Sets of objects can be formed by selecting appropriate instances from the Set of allInstances of an AssociationClass defined in this way.

5.3 Project Using UML and OCL

The previous section explained our method for the creation of Cartesian Products. We now build on this to define a method of support for the Project operation. Again, we explain our approach for three classes and projection over 3-tuples, but it is extensible to the general case for n-tuples.

As defined in [16], for a Binary Association (Pair or 2-tuple), the project function must return either the first or second co-ordinates, by simple navigation. The difficult issue with Project occurs when we consider tuples with more than two co-ordinates.

Consider three classes A, B, C and the Cartesian Product of their instances as represented by AssociationClass ABC (Fig. 4b). Formally, a projection, $proj_{1,3}$ maps a tuple (a,b,c) into a 2-tuple (a,c). To implement the operation $proj_{1,3}$ there are two issues to address:

1. The AssociationClass that provides a type for the tuple (a,c), and whose instances represent the Cartesian Product of A and C.
2. The specification of the function that maps (a,b,c) onto (a,c).

Following the method defined in the previous section, we must add the AssociaitonClass AC to the model, relating classes A and C, as shown in Fig. 5.

The project operation can be subsequently defined as follows:

```
context tuple : ABC                                                    (4)

tuple->project_a_c : AC
pre: OclType.allInstances->exists( t | t = AC )
post: result = AC.allInstances->select( tup |
               tup.a = tuple.a and tup.c = tuple.c ) )
```

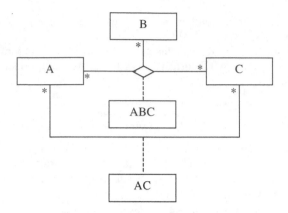

Fig. 5. Extended class specification

The pre condition of the operation ensures that the class AC has been defined. The post condition defines the result to be the tuple of type AC that has its co-ordinates 'a' and 'c' equal to the 'a' and 'c' co-ordinates of this tuple. (Remember that the elements of a LinkObject, the tuple, are navigated to via the rolenames of the Association, rather than by their index value.)

This explains a method for indirectly supporting a project function that maps 3-tuples of type ABC onto 2-tuples consisting of the first and third co-ordinates. In a similar way, we can support creation of $proj_{2,3}$ and $proj_{1,2}$, which involve associating B to C and A to B respectively.

There are also project functions, $proj_1$, $proj_2$ and $proj_3$, which project a tuple to its individual co-ordinates. These do not require the creation of new links and are supported simply by the navigation semantics of the OCL '.' operator.

Performing a project operation over a set of tuples can be easily supported by making use of the *collect* operation defined for OCL collections.

5.4 Solution to the Example Problem

Our example of section 3 requires an expression that results in a list, relating teachers to their pupils. In this subsection, we use our method to specify the query expression corresponding to the SQL statement (1).

To achieve such an expression, we first modify the original data model (Fig. 1) to include a new class, TeacherxStudent, as shown in Fig. 6.

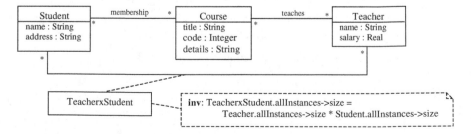

Fig. 6. Extensions to example data model

This AssociationClass specifies a class for tuples of teacher and student objects and defines each member of the Cartesian Product of Student and Teacher objects.

The required list of (teacher, student) pairs can be subsequently specified using an OCL expression as follows:

```
Teacher.allInstances->collect( t |                              (5)
   t.course.student->collect(s |
      TeacherxStudent.allInstances->select( ts |
         ts.teacher = t and
         ts.student = s ) ) )->asSet
```

The expression defines two nested *collect* operations, which iterate over each required pair of teacher and student objects. These are used to select the appropriate tuple object from the instances of TeacherxStudent.

This OCL query provides a collection (list) of student and teacher pairs, rather than the pairing of name strings provided by the SQL statement defined earlier. Although it has some complexity, it is functionally similar to the SQL, and we do not need to explicitly state how the data items are joined.

However, the complexity of the model rises as a result of defining additional classes within the UML specification. Ideally, a mechanism should be provided which enables queries to be specified that do not require additional model elements to be defined. The following section proposes essential extensions to the OCL language and pre-defined types that will enable such query expressions to be formed.

6 Extending OCL to Be a Fully Expressive Query Language

In the previous section, we presented our indirect method for using OCL as a query language. However the method requires new components to be added to the original data model; this is cumbersome and undesirable. The approach relies heavily on the use of the *allInstances* operation, which is expensive to implement and controversial with respect to its use on classes such as String and Integer.

To be able to form OCL query expressions that are more seamlessly useable within the context of a UML model, a Tuple type needs to be added to the pre-defined types of the OCL language. This can be easily achieved in a similar manner to the Collection classes.

The following subsections define an appropriate Tuple type and show how instances can be defined as part of an OCL expression. This is in line with the current language semantics, which does allow new instances of collection classes to be specified.

Based on this new OCL Tuple type, the operations Product and Project are defined as operations on (respectively) the Collection and Tuple types. Finally, we show how the provision of this type enables the example query to be easily written as an OCL expression.

6.1 Creating Tuples in OCL

A generic type for tuple objects can be provided using a ParameterisedClass, in a very similar way to the Collection types (Set, Sequence and Bag) already defined. A simple Tuple Class could be defined such that its co-ordinate members are all of the root type OclAny; all tuples would thus belong to the set of *allInstances* of that class.

It would be useful to enable a distinction to be made between tuples of different sizes and between tuples with co-ordinate members of differing types. The concept of a ParameterisedClass can be used to provide a type for tuples that enables this distinction to be made. Fig. 7 illustrates a UML definition of this Tuple Class.

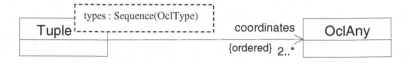

Fig. 7. Definition of a Generic Tuple Class

To support the Project and Product operators, it is necessary to be able to create tuple objects within an OCL expression. Unfortunately, this directly contravenes the OCL policy of no side effects. However, an OCL expression can include the explicit creation of a Collection object. This is not only described as possible in the UML version 1.3 standard, it is also used as part of the definition of the OCL collection classes, for example, as taken from the definition of subSequence :

```
Sequence{lower..upper}->forAll( index | ...
```
(6)

Thus, we propose that the semantics should support the creation of Tuple objects in a similar manner, as follows:

```
Tuple { a, b, c }
```
(7)

Semantically, the types for each of the co-ordinate members of a Tuple created in this way, can be deduced from the types of the objects used to instantiate it. Thus, the tuple instantiated in equation (7) can be deduced to be an instance of a specific tuple type Tuple(Sequence(A,B,C)), assuming that objects a, b and c are instances of classes A, B and C.

6.2 Definition of a Product Operation

Given the provision of this Tuple type, providing a Product operation is an easy addition to the Collection classes, defined as follows:

```
context c1:Collection(T1)
```
(8)
```
c1->product(c2:Collection(T2))
      : Collection( Tuple(Sequence{T1,T2}) )
post: result = c1->collect( t1 |
              c2-> collect( t2 |
                Tuple {t1,t2} ) )
```

The Cartesian Product between more than two sets can be formed from multiple nested products of two sets. Semantically, an extension to the *product* operation could be defined, which flattens out nested 2-Tuples into appropriate n-Tuples. For example, given three sets S, T and U, the product:

$$S.product(T).product(U) \tag{9}$$

gives 3-tuples of the form ((s,t), u). The extension proposes that this be flattened to a tuple of the form (s, t, u).

6.3 Definition of a Project Operation

The Project operator can be supported by providing appropriate operations on the Tuple class itself. The Project operation extracts specific elements from its target tuple. Extraction of single elements should result in that element and extraction of multiple elements should result in another tuple, containing the required elements.

This functionality is provided as two separate project operations, defined as follows:

```
context tuple : Tuple( types : Sequence(OclType) )

tuple->project( index : Integer) : types->at(index)
post: result = tuple.coordinates.at(index)

tuple->project( indices: Sequence(Integer) )
        : Tuple( indices->collect(i|types.at(i)) )
pre: indices->size > 1
post: result =
    Tuple { indices->collect( i| tuple.project(i) ) }
```
(10)

The first of these operations takes a single index value as a parameter and returns the object contained at the co-ordinate position of the requested index. The second takes a sequence of indices as a parameter and returns a new Tuple that is formed from the combination of objects at the co-ordinate position of each index in the parameter.

6.4 Ideal Solution for Example Problem

If we provide OCL with the above extension, adding the concept of tuple and the related operation definitions of *product* and *project*, then we can easily write powerful and concise OCL query expressions.

For example, considering the example of section 3, the required collection of pairs indicating which students are taught by which teachers, can be formed using the following OCL expression:

```
Teacher.allInstances->collect( t |
    (Set{t}).product( t.course.student ) )
```
(11)

The resulting collection contains the set of tuples formed by collecting the union[1], for each teacher, of all products of a teacher and the student objects navigable to from it.

---

[1] Due to the flattening semantics of collect.

This gives the ideal solution of pairs of student and teacher objects. An expression equivalent to the SQL, giving a collection of pairs of teacher and student names is specified as follows:

```
Teacher.allInstances->collect( t |                                    (12)
    (Set{t.name}).product( t.course.student.name ) )
```

7 Conclusion

In this paper, we have shown that for OCL to be effectively and elegantly used as a Query Language, certain extensions are required – primarily the addition of a Tuple type.

Using as a benchmark the five primitive operators of Relational Algebra, this paper has shown that the combination of UML and OCL are expressive enough to form expressions functionally equivalent to those formed using Relational Algebra.

However, since OCL was not originally designed to be a query language, it lacks certain technical concepts required for writing query expressions, which can be provided by extending the underlying UML model.

Adding extra components to the underlying model is cumbersome and undesirable in the context of a query language. To avoid such measures, this paper has proposed and demonstrated the use of some extensions to OCL that are essential, if it is to be effectively used as a query language.

These extensions, which are in line with the existing semantics of OCL, enable us to write concise queries without modifying the underlying UML model.

Acknowledgement. We would like to thank Stuart Kent and Nigel Dalgliesh for their valuable comments. The second author wishes to acknowledge the generous support of the EPSRC project (GR/M69500).

References

1.   Object Management Group; *Unified Modelling Language Specification, version 1.3*; OMG ad/99-06-08 (June 1999); http://www.omg.org.
2.   Object Management Group; *UML 2.0 RFI*; OMG Document ad/99-08-08 (August 1999); http://www.omg.org.
3.   M.Blaha, W.Premerlani; *Object-Oriented Modeling and Design for Database Applications*; Prentice Hall Inc., ISBN: 0-13-123829-9 (1998).
4.   P. Butterworth, A. Otis, J. Stein; *The GemStone Object Database Management System*; Communications of the ACM, 34(10) (1991) pp 64 - 77.
5.   R. G. G. Cattell; *The Object Database Standard: ODMG 2.0*; Morgan Kaufmann Publishers, Inc. (1997).
6.   P. P. Chen; *The Entity-Relationship Model - Toward a Unified View of Data*; ACM Transactions on Database Systems, 1(1) (1976).
7.   E. F. Code; *Relational completeness of database sub-languages*; In Data Base Systems, R.Rustin, Ed., Prentice Hall, Englewood Cliffs (1972) pp 65 - 98.
8.   S. Cook, A. Kleppe, R.Mitchell, B.Rumpe, J.Warmer, A.Wills; *The Amsterdam Manifesto on OCL*; (December 1999); http://www.trireme.com/amsterdam/.

9.   C. J. Date; *An Introduction to Database Systems (Introduction to Database Systems, 7th Ed)*; Addison Wesley Publishing Company, ISBN: 0201385902 (August 1999).
10. C. J. Date, H. Darwin; *Foundation for Object/Relational Databases: The Third Manifesto*; Addison Wesley Publishing Company, ISBN: 0201309785 (June 1998).
11. B. Demuth, H. Hussmann; *Using UML/OCL Constraints for Relational Database Design*; Proceedings of «UML» '99 - The Unified Modelling Language: Beyond the Standard (October 1999) pp 598 - 613.
12. H. Hussmann, B. Demuth, F. Finger; *Modular Architecture for a Toolset Supporting OCL*; Proceedings of «UML» 2000 – The Unified Modeling Language: Advancing the Standard (October 2000) pp 278 - 293.
13. O. Deux; *The O2 System*; Communications of the ACM, 34(10) (1991) pp 34-48.
14. M.Gogolla, M.Richters; *On Constraints and Queries in UML*; Proc. UML'97 Workshop `The Unified Modeling Language - Technical Aspects and Applications' (1997).
15. C. Lamb, G. Landis, J. Orenstein, D. Weinreib; *The ObjectStore Database System*. Communications of the ACM, 34(10) (1991) pp 50 - 63.
16. L. Mandel, M. V. Cengarle; *On the Expressive Power of OCL*; FM'99 - Formal Methods, World Congress on Formal Methods in the Development of Computing Systems, Toulouse, France, Springer LNCS 1708 (September 1999) pp 854 - 874.
17. J. Melton, A. R. Simon; *Understanding the New SQL: A Complete Guide*; Morgan Kaufmann Publishers, Inc., ISBN: 1558602453 (1994).
18. Jan Nordén; *Bold Executable Model Architecture*; (June 2000); http://www.boldsoft.com/products/whitepapers/index.htm.
19. ModelRun; *Boldsoft modelling tool*; http://www.boldsoft.com/products/modelrun/.
20. J. Rumbaugh, M. Blaha, W. Premerlani, F. Eddy, W. Lorensen; *Object-oriented Modeling and Design*; Prentice Hall International Paperback Editions, ISBN: 0136300545 (March 1991).
21. B. Thalheim; *Fundamentals of Entity-relationship Modeling*; Springer-Verlag Berlin and Heidelberg GmbH & Co. KG, ISBN: 3540654704 (December 1999).
22. J. D. Ullman; *Principles of Database Systems*; Pitman Publishing Ltd, ISBN: 0273084763 (1980).
23. J. B. Warmer, A. G. Kleppe; *The Object Constraint Language: Precise Modeling With Uml (Addison-Wesley Object Technology Series)*; Addison Wesley Publishing Company; ISBN: 0201379406 (October 1998).

OCL as a Specification Language for Business Rules in Database Applications

Birgit Demuth, Heinrich Hussmann, and Sten Loecher

Dresden University of Technology, Department of Computer Science

Abstract. Business rules are often specified only implicitly by applications to express user-defined constraints. OCL provides the chance to explicitly and automatically deal with business rules when building object-oriented applications. We investigate how OCL constraints can be handled in database applications as one of the most important kind of business applications. Based on our OCL toolset prototype and earlier research work we particularly experiment with various strategies for the evaluation of OCL constraints in object-oriented applications which use relational databases. For this work, a flexible SQL code generator is needed which can be used and adapted for different relational database systems and different object-to-table mappings. We implement such a database tool as an additional module for our OCL toolset using XML techniques.

1 Introduction

Business rules are not a new approach to define or constrain some aspects of the business. They represent business knowledge and govern how the business processes should execute [7]. There are many definitions at different abstraction levels of what business rules are. Within the context of data-intensive applications we only consider a subset of business rules: integrity constraints which are supported by database management systems (DBMS). We explicitly aim at non-trivial integrity constraints which may affect in relational DBMS tuples of several tables.

Business rules are often specified only implicitly by applications to express user-defined constraints. Facing this problem, an ECOOP'98 Workshop [12] discussed and listed requirements for tools and environments for business rules. Some of these requirements such as the use of a declarative language to express business rules or the support for maintaining software integrity are fullfilled by the UML Object Constraint Language (OCL) [14]. OCL provides the chance to explicitly and automatically deal with business rules when building UML-based object-oriented applications. Several authors already investigated the use of OCL for expressing business rules (e.g. [24] [7] [5]). Some OCL tools have also been built to allow experiments with formally specified business rules [18] [10], [14]. In first applications of OCL, these tools were particularly used during the software development itself such as for simulation, code generation and test automation

M. Gogolla and C. Kobryn (Eds.): UML 2001, LNCS 2185, pp. 104–117, 2001.
© Springer-Verlag Berlin Heidelberg 2001

[10]. Using OCL as a language for business rule specification, extended investigations can be carried out which aim at maintaining the software integrity by checking business rules during the execution of a business process. This check can be done by two basic strategies:

- The theoretically best way is the *immediate constraint check*: The OCL expressions are immediately evaluated when objects are changed. In databases, the unit of consistency is the transaction. In object-oriented applications, check points are more difficult to find because most runtime systems like the Java Virtual Machine do not provide transaction support. In [25], this problem is addressed.
- A more realistic way in many cases is an *independent constraint check*: The OCL expression is only checked at selected points to achieve a trade-off between consistency maintenance and efficiency. As a consequence, inconsistent states of objects respectively of the database are possible.

According to the classification in [9] we basically distinguish active and passive constraints. Whereas *active integrity constraints* maintain consistency by executing actions, *passive integrity constraints* only prevent data manipulation operations which violate the consistency. Furthermore, there are two primary methods by which integrity constraints can be specified, applied and enforced in database applications [11]:

- through the application programs (*application enforced* constraints).
- through the DBMS itself (*database enforced* constraints)

Both methods are controversial [23], [13], [3]. Apriori we focus on database-enforced constraints because then we can exploit all advantages of the database technology [5]. The OMG proposal for a Data Modeling UML profile [19] includes constraints as stereotyped operations in a relational manner like <<check>> representing passive constraints and <<trigger>> representing active constraints. Based on this UML profile, an object-to-table mapping is given in [20]. In [5], we discussed the mapping of UML objects including OCL constraints to a relational database schema in a very similar way. However, we found many limitations both in the object-to-table mapping supported by most environments and in the maturity of current DBMS. In this paper, we address these problems and present some ideas to make object-to-table and OCL-to-SQL mappings more flexible and practicable.

Section 2 discusses an advanced approach for supporting OCL in object-relational applications by application- and database-enforced constraints. The basic idea is applying an independent constraint check by the evaluation of a database view representing invalid tuples. In Section 3 we describe a prototype implementation of an SQL tool including code generation for OCL constraints and its integration into our OCL toolset and CASE tools like Argo/UML. Finally, section 4 summarizes our results and gives an outlook for further research and tool development.

2   Approaches Supporting OCL Constraints in Object-Relational Applications

2.1   Discussion of Different Approaches

Up to now a number of different approaches and suggestions for the implementation of OCL specified business rules using the current database technology have been made. All these approaches support the immediate constraint check and share the problem of being not efficient for runtime evaluation or not practicable on current database systems.

The implementation of the OCL-to-SQL patterns from [5] shows that to the best of our knowledge no current relational DBMS supports the Full SQL92 level [11] as far as automatic integrity checks are concerned. The required check clause is provided by all advanced DBMS, but only for Intermediate SQL. That means that the search condition contained in the check clause shall not contain a subquery. Furthermore, standalone integrity constraints including an arbitrary number of tables (SQL92 assertions) are not supported at all. Therewith, only simple one-tuple related constraints can be checked in real DBMS.

In [22], procedural mapping patterns were investigated to translate an OCL expression into code executable on relational database systems. The resulting code of such a translation was a (proprietary) procedure such as a Sybase' Transact SQL stored procedure. The evaluation of the constraint can be done by calling this procedure. The right moment for doing this is at the end of a transaction that is before the transaction commit. One drawback of this approach is the dependence of database integrity from the applications instead of being part of the database constraints.

Another way to implement passive as well as active integrity constraints is to apply triggers to check respectively maintain the integrity after each data manipulation statement. One problem is that triggers are standardized foremost by SQL-99 [6], but are already implemented by different dialects.

2.2   The VIEW Approach

Driven by our implementation experience and motivated by database literature [21], [17] we propose an approach to realize either an independent or an immediate constraint check for an SQL based implementation of OCL specified business rules. The basic element of our approach are SQL *views* generated from OCL invariants. Each single OCL invariant is translated into a separate view definition. The result of a view evaluation is a set of tuples from the constrained table respectively the object which violate the specified business rule. This approach yields a number of advantages:

- The usage of SQL features available in most database systems makes the usage of OCL in database design practicable. A view allows to evaluate a complex search condition which is part of an integrity constraint. In this sense, a view can substitute the evaluation of the not supported assertions respectively "multiple table" check constraints in current DBMS.

- The generation of views from OCL invariants is basically not different from generating SQL92 assertions. For this reason we can use our already developed technique for SQL code generation.
- The views are based on declarative SQL code and, therefore, are subject of query optimization of the DBMS.
- The generation of declarative SQL code from OCL invariant specifications is simpler than the generation of procedural DBMS code.
- The views can be integrated into different constraint evaluation strategies. Then it can be decided when to evaluate the constraint and what to do if some constraint is violated.

The last mentioned item should be discussed in detail. Most real world applications have their own requirements according to performance, integrity, and other design issues. Some applications may prefer performance over integrity, others may demand full integrity at each database state[1]. For this reason, it is not realistic to always apply the typical immediate constraint check for any kind of application. Another question arises with respect to the handling of faulty data. Some applications may prefer to get notified about all constraint violations, others may prefer the handling of faulty data by the database system. The proposed view approach can be used to support various kinds of requirements. We consider the following three variations:

Application driven view evaluation. The evaluation of a view is not coupled to any database integrity mechanism like assertions or triggers. Instead, it is evaluated by an application. In the given context, the evaluation of the view representing invalid tuples can be seen as an independent constraint check. Furthermore, it is a hybrid method of checking application- and database-enforced constraints. For example, to access to a database, an object-relational middleware with an own transaction approach is often used. The middleware can evaluate the views just before the transaction commit is executed. If one of the views returns any tuples, the middleware is able to rollback the current transaction or do some treatment for the faulty data. This approach has the disadvantage of taking the integrity control away from the database system, but allows the middleware or the application itself to decide on the moment of constraint evaluation and thus leaves some space for the treatment of performance problems. Another possible way to use "integrity views" are database monitor applications which support database administrators to maintain huge data stores and keep them clean from faulty data.

Assertion replacement. The views can be used by triggers which evaluate the constraints after each critical data manipulation operation. When any constraint violation is found, the trigger should rollback the current transaction and send an appropriate error message to the invoking application. This approach can be used as a replacement for SQL92 assertions, if the database system does not support such a feature.

---

[1] In [17] these kinds of integrity are called *qualified* respectively *absolute* integrity.

ECA trigger template. To support the idea of active database systems a trigger template can be generated which must be edited by the application or database developer respectively. The template should support the ECA (Event-Condition-Action) rule paradigm [1]. Such a trigger is evaluated after each critical data manipulation operation (the *event*). If the *condition* holds, for instance a constraint is violated, the *action* part is executed. This way, faulty data can be treated before storing them in the database.

For a better understanding of how our concept works, we give a simple example. Suppose there is a class called PERSON with two attributes: the age of a person and a Boolean flag which indicates whether this person isMarried or not. In our case, this class is mapped to a single table with the according columns AGE and ISMARRIED respectively. A simple business rule is that all persons which are married should be at least 18 years of age. The respective OCL expression is given below:

```
context Person
inv ageOfMarriage: (isMarried = true) implies (age>=18)
```

The first step is the translation of this invariant into a corresponding SQL view evaluating all tuples of the table PERSON which violate the specified business rule. We use an adapted version of the OCL INVARIANT pattern from [5]:

```
create view AGEOFMARRIAGE as
(select * from PERSON SELF
where not (not (ISMARRIED = true) or (AGE>=18)))
```

According to the three approaches for the use of integrity views, the evaluation of the given business rule is as follows:

Application driven view evaluation. Invoking the evaluation of views by an application can be done in various ways. Using Java and JDBC to access to the database, the following code can be used:

```
ResultSet rs = theStatement.executeQuery(
  "select nvl(count(*),0) from AGEOFMARRIAGE "
);
if (rs.next().getInt(0) > 0) {
  // integrity error handling
}
```

Note that nvl() is an Oracle specific function which, in the above example, returns 0 if count(*) is null, otherwise it returns the number of selected tuples.

Assertion replacement. The trigger template for the assertion replacement would look like this:

```
create trigger TR_AGEOFMARRIAGE
after insert or update or delete on PERSON
begin
  if (select nvl(count(*),0) from AGEOFMARRIAGE) > 0 then
    raise_application_error("Integrity error !", 20900);
  end if;
end;
```

ECA trigger template. If the treatment of faulty data is necessary, the use of the according trigger template should be preferred. In this example, the action code would be implemented directly by the trigger body:

```
create trigger TR_AGEOFMARRIAGE
after insert or update or delete on PERSON
begin
  if (select nvl(count(*),0) from AGEOFMARRIAGE) > 0 then
    // todo: add action code here
  end if;
end;
```

Due to the simplicity of the example, an important fact is not shown which must be considered in more detail. If an integrity view uses more than one table of the database to evaluate a business rule, the constraint evaluation must be done after manipulation of all of these tables.

For instance, a view can be generated from an OCL expression which uses navigation to express constraints on a model. Suppose we add a second class to our example stated above. This class is called Car and is also mapped to a single table. Between class Person and class Car exists an one-to-many association which describes the ownership between persons and cars. This association will be mapped by inserting the primary key of the PERSON table (PID) to the CAR table. A constraint is that each person can be the owner of at most two cars:

```
context Person
inv maxCars: self.car->size <= 2
```

This OCL expression is mapped using the NAVIGATION pattern from [5] into the following view:

```
create view MAXCARS as
(select * from PERSON SELF
where not ((select count(CID)
            from CAR
            where PID = self.PID) <= 2)
```

As one can see, the view uses both the table PERSON and the table CAR to evaluate the constraint. It is important to evaluate the view if any of the two tables is modified. If the view MAXCARS is integrated into any trigger evaluation mechanism, this means that a trigger must be created for each table to evaluate the according view.

3   Extended OCL Toolset

The implementation of the OCL constraint translation to SQL (called the **OCL2SQL tool**) follows the above explained VIEW approach and is done by a modular extension of the OCL toolset [10]. Our toolset has already proven to be a stable and flexible environment for the development of OCL tools [25]. In the following subsections, we describe the design and outline the implementation of the OCL2SQL tool based on a first prototype implementation.

3.1   Experience with the OCL-to-SQL Pattern Catalogue

We use the OCL-to-SQL pattern catalogue from [5] to translate OCL invariants to SQL code. Our first prototype implementation of an SQL code generator implementing these patterns has shown the following problems:

Object-relational mapping. The translation of OCL expressions to SQL code is dependent from the underlying object-to-table mapping. Therefore, one requirement for the SQL code generator should be a flexible interface that allows the integration of different object-to-table mappings. Unfortunately, the patterns are described only based on the commonly used one-object-to-one-tuple mapping.

Metadata. The mapping of operations on metadata is not considered and thus should be added by new patterns.

Full SQL92 level. The mapping patterns take advantage of the SQL92 full level specification. Assertions over any number of tables, and derived tables in the from clause of select statements are important SQL features for the patterns. How explained above, current database systems lack the support for these features, especially the first one.

The iterate problem and sequences. The iterate operator and OCL sequences are two features which have to be discussed in more detail.

3.2   Design

The current version of the OCL2SQL tool takes a static UML model and a number of OCL invariants as input and generates an according DDL script including a database schema as well as view definitions and trigger templates representing the constraints as output. It consists of the following components:

Model repository. As stated above, the OCL2SQL tool needs information about the used static UML model and the number of OCL invariants specified on this model. Since we aim at the integration of the OCL2SQL tool into different environments like UML CASE tools, it is mandatory to provide appropriate interfaces which can be implemented for different use cases. A more loose integration is the use of XMI files [26] for static UML model information. The OCL toolset already provides the necessary component to use this technology. For a tight integration as it has been realized for Argo/UML, the "model interfaces" must be implemented by a CASE tool integration component accessing whose repository.

SQL code generator. The core component is the SQL code generator which generates the SQL code for an OCL invariant based on the parsed, type-checked and normalized OCL expression given as an abstract syntax tree. The "SQL code" generated by this component is a view definition such as the AGEOFMARRIAGE example in subsection 2.2. The implementation of the SQL code generator is explained in the following subsections in more detail. To make such a SQL code generator work, we need some additional information about the underlying object-to-table mapping. Since there exists a great number of different object-to-table mappings, an interface is provided for the integration of various strategies.

Schema generator. The first idea was to integrate the SQL code generator with the database schema generation functions available by most UML-CASE tools. Unfortunately, we recognized that the quality of the generated schemas does not match flexible requirements. Therefore, we had to implement an own object-to-table mapping and to provide an interface for later CASE tool integration efforts.

Trigger template generator. In contrast to the SQL code generator, the trigger template generator is rather simple. It takes the output of the SQL code generator and produces a number of triggers according to the view specifications and user requirements.

3.3   XML Coded Pattern Refinement

The implementation of the eight rather general OCL-to-SQL patterns requires a further refinement of the patterns to make them applicable in code generation. Beyond the refinement, a flexible specification of the patterns is needed to adapt them to different SQL dialects for their practical use in DBMS. We decided to use XML [27] to describe the refined patterns because of the following reasons:

– The XML files can be comfortably edited by XML editors and thus are easily adaptable to a certain SQL dialect.
– An XML file containing a set of refined patterns can be directly interpreted by the SQL code generator written in Java.
– XML technology supports well defined structures of documents.

The structure of an XML document is specified by a Document Type Definition (DTD). An adequate DTD called **CODEGEN** describing OCL-to-SQL patterns is shown in fig. 1. According to this DTD, the XML file is structured as a catalogue which consists of a description and an arbitrary number of patterns. Each pattern is associated to an OCL grammar rule. For example, the patterns that

```
<?xml version="1.0" encoding="UTF-8"?>
<!ELEMENT  catalog         (description?, pattern*)>

<!ATTLIST  catalog name CDATA #REQUIRED>
<!ELEMENT  description  (#PCDATA)>
<!ELEMENT  pattern         (template)*>
<!ATTLIST  pattern rule ID #REQUIRED>
<!ELEMENT  template     (li)+>
<!ATTLIST  template        spec CDATA #REQUIRED
                           rem  CDATA #IMPLIED>
<!ELEMENT  li              (#PCDATA | param)*>
<!ATTLIST  li connector (true|false) "false">
<!ELEMENT  param           EMPTY>
<!ATTLIST  param name    CDATA #REQUIRED>
```

Fig. 1. The CODEGEN DTD

describe the mapping of OCL features like operations over collections are associated to the `featureCall` grammar rule. Since a single pattern usually consists of several mapping descriptions, a pattern consists of at least one SQL code template. Each SQL code template again is described by lines of code. The templates are identified by the `spec` parameter to distinguish them from each other. Let us consider for example the OCL grammar rule `featureCall`. There are several mapping templates for collection operators like `collect`, `select`, `reject`, and `forAll`. The templates can contain parameters respectivly placeholders which must be replaced by further templates. One example for such a pattern rule is represented in fig. 2. The example shows the template which maps the OCL

```
<?xml version="1.0">
<!DOCTYPE catalogue SYSTEM "CODEGEN.dtd">
<catalog name="EntrySQL">
  ...
  <pattern rule="feature_call">
    ...
    <template spec="collect" rem="QUERY">
      <li>select <param name="column"></li>
      <li>from <param name="table"></li>
    </template>
    ...
  </pattern>
  ...
</catalogue>
```

Fig. 2. Example of the *feature call* pattern rule

operator `collect` to an SQL query block and refines the general QUERY pattern [5] (indicated by the `rem` parameter). As explained above, from a translation point of view, the template belongs to the grammar rule `featureCall` and needs two further templates for the complete code generation. That is, the parameters `column` and `table` must be replaced with appropriate SQL code.

3.4   SQL Code Generator

In our first prototype implementation based on the OCL-to-SQL92 patterns we already got some experience with the implementation of an SQL code generator. The recent SQL code generator represents the adapted prototype and realizes the generation of view definitions. The design of the SQL code generator is done under consideration of two primary aspects:

- The SQL code generator should be completely based on the OCL toolset because the toolset provides a quite reliable platform for syntactical analysis, typechecking and normalisation of OCL expressions.
- The XML based approach for the translation of OCL expressions to SQL statements has been proven and therefore should be used.

For the integration of different code generators like for Java or SQL, the OCL toolset provides two interfaces [8]. At first a code generator must implement the interface `CodeGenerator`. Such a code generator produces a certain number of code fragments. These code fragments are stored in objects of classes which implement the interface `CodeFragment` (see fig. 3).

The patterns described in [5] aim at the generation of declarative SQL code only. As already described in the preceeding subsection, each pattern was designed to encapsulate one OCL language concept. The equivalent SQL code allows the nesting of SQL expressions according to the structure of the given OCL expression. To implement this concept, we chose a general syntax driven approach.

The feature of being rather general than specific to SQL code generation led to the following design decision. The core functionality of the strategy is encapsulated in a separate class called `DeclarativeCodeGenerator` since the strategy seems to be suitable for the generation of declarative target code preferably. Subclasses of this class generate code fragments that will be stored in objects of the class `DeclarativeCodeFragment`.

The actual generation of SQL code is realized by the class `SQLCodeGenerator` which implements only features specific to the SQL code generation problem. The `SQLCodeGenerator` uses an XML file based on the CODEGEN DTD. The `CodeAgent` parses the XML file and fetches the appropriate code template for the code generator. Therefore it is prepared with a number of parameters which are supposed to replace the placeholders in the templates. Then the `getCode()` method is called with the pattern rule ID for the requested OCL grammar rule and the accurate template specification (`spec` parameter). The placeholders allow an arbitrary nesting of templates. Then the `getCode()` method returns a prepared SQL code template which can be further handled by the SQL code generator.

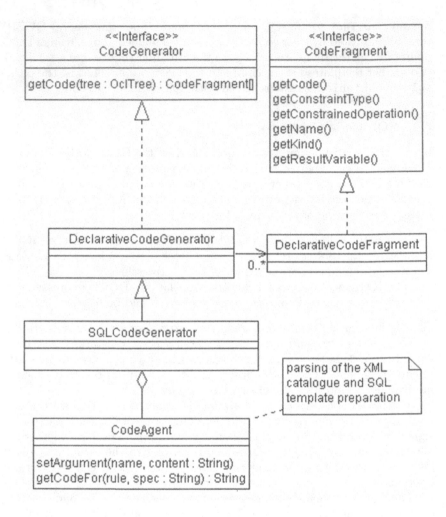

Fig. 3. SQL code generator

Experiments with the first SQL code generator prototype have already shown the applicability of the XML based approach for code generation. We used two XML coded pattern catalogues, one for an "ideal" DBMS supporting SQL92 full level and another one for Oracle 8i. Oracle8i is an example for an advanced DBMS where we could demonstrate our mapping approach and its limitations on current database management systems. Now, we reuse the code generator prototype for the implementation of the above described OCL2SQL tool.

3.5   CASE Tool Integration

An important requirement of tools supporting OCL is the tight integration with UML-CASE tools. As explained in the preceding subsections, our OCL2SQL tool has a number of well defined interfaces which allow the integration of the tool into different environments. A new module of the OCL toolset is a comfortable OCL editor which includes besides editing of constraints features like a toolbar and adequate error messages. The according user interface is designed to integrate the OCL editor not into a specific CASE tool, but into various environments. Currently it is tested with the Open Source CASE Tool Argo/UML and also serves as test environment for the OCL2SQL tool. The screenshot in fig. 4 gives an impression of the new OCL editor integrated into Argo/UML.

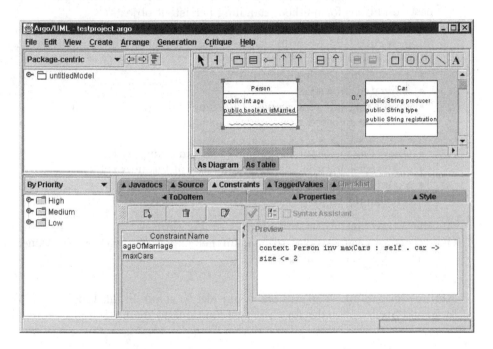

Fig. 4. OCL editor integrated into Argo/UML

4   Conclusion

In this paper, we reported on our recent research results using OCL constraints as business rules in object-relational database applications [5] as well as extending the OCL toolset [10] for SQL code generation. The automatic translation of complex OCL expressions to database integrity constraints specified by SQL rises some serious problems which we try to solve by trigger-based techniques or, especially if performance plays an important role, by an unusual approach which we call independent constraint check. All these techniques use an integrity view which is defined as the set of tuples from the constrained tables respectively objects violating the according OCL invariant. We design an SQL tool extending the OCL toolset which supports in a flexible way both different constraint evaluation strategies and different SQL dialects of the DBMS vendors. Furthermore, different object-to-table mappings can be handled by the design of flexible interfaces.

Our plans for further practical and theoretical investigations as well as OCL toolset development are the following:

- So far we only considered the use of OCL invariants for the specification of business rules in database applications. However, which role play pre and post conditions for methods handling persistent objects?
- The OCL toolset should realize important requirements for the handling of business rules [12]. According these requirements it seems desirable to extend the OCL toolset by modules such as
  - a repository for business rules
  - dedicated browsers
  - supporting different scopes of business rules (application and database enforced constraints) including different constraint evaluation strategies
  - adaptable for changing, refining and removing existing rules
  - a debugger for systems containing lots of business rules
  - a conflict detection
  - a reasoning engine

For the future, an important objective of our work is the practical use of the OCL toolset in case studies to gain further experience with application- and database-enforced constraints.

Acknowledgment. The authors would like to thank Frank Finger, Ralf Wiebicke and Steffen Zschaler for their contributions to the OCL toolset.

References

1. ACT-NET Consortium, The Active Database Management System Manifesto: A Rulebase of ADBMS Features. SIGMOD Record 25(1996)3:40-49
2. Argo/UML Page, http://www.ArgoUML.com
3. Blaha, M., Premerlani, W.: Object-Oriented Modeling and Design for Database Applications. Prentice Hall, 1998
4. Booch, G., Rumbaugh, J., Jacobson, I.: The Unified Modeling Language User Guide. Addison-Wesley, 1999
5. Demuth, B., Hussmann, H.: Using OCL Constraints for Relational Database Design. in: UML'99 The Unified Modeling Language, Second Int. Conference Fort Collins, CO, USA, October 1999, Springer, 1999
6. Eisenberg, A., Melton, J.: SQL: 1999, formerly known as SQL-3. ACM SIGMOD Record, 22(1999)1, 131-138
7. Eriksson, H.-E., Penker, M. Business Modeling with UML. Business Patterns at Work, John Wiley & Sons, Inc., New York, 2000

8. Finger, F., Design and Implementation of a Modular OCL Compiler. diploma thesis, Dresden University of Technology, 2000

9. Herbst, H. et al, The specification of business rules: a comparison of selected methodologies. in: Methods and Associated Tools for the Information System Life Cycle. Elsevier, Amsterdam, 1994

10. Hussmann, H., Demuth, B., Finger, F.: Modular Architecture for a Toolset Supporting OCL. in: UML'2000 - The Unified Modeling Language. Advancing the Standard, Third Int. Conference York, UK, October 2000, Springer, 2000

11. Melton, J., Simon, A.: Understanding the New SQL: A Complete Guide. Morgan Kaufmann, 1993

12. Mens, K. et al, Workshop Report - ECOOP'98 Workshop 7 Tools and Environments for Business Rules. in: Object oriented technology: ECOOP'98 Workshop Reader. Springer, 1998

13. O'Neil, P., Database - principles, programming, performance. Morgan Kaufmann, 1994

14. OCL Center, Klasse Objecten, http://www.klasse.nl/ocl/index.htm

15. OCL Page, Dresden University of Technology, http://dresden-ocl.sourceforge.net/

16. OMG UML v. 1.3 specification, http://www.omg.org/cgi-bin/doc?ad/99-06-08

17. Motro, A., Integrity= validity + completeness. ACM Transactions on Database Systems, 14(1989)4,480-502

18. Richters, M., Gogolla, M., Validating UML Models and OCL Constraints. in: UML'2000 - The Unified Modeling Language. Advancing the Standard, Third Int. Conference York, UK, October 2000, Springer, 2000

19. Rational. The UML and Data Modeling. Whitepaper TP-180, 2000, http://www.rational.com

20. Rational. Mapping Objects to Data Models with the UML. Whitepaper TP-185, 2000, http://www.rational.com

21. Ross, K., Srivastava, D., Sudarshan, S., Materialized view maintenance and integrity constraint checking: Trading space for time. in: Proc. of the ACM SIGMOD Int. Conference on Management of Data, Montreal, Canada, 1996, ACM Press, 1996

22. Schmidt, A.: Untersuchungen zur Abbildung von OCL-Ausdruecken auf SQL. Dresden University of Technology, diploma thesis, 1998

23. Spencer, B., Business Rules vs. Database Rules. A Position Statement. in: Object oriented technology: ECOOP'98 Workshop Reader. Springer, 1998

24. Warmer, J., Kleppe, A.: The Object Constraint Language. Precise Modeling with UML. Addison-Wesley, 1999

25. Wiebicke, R., Utility Support for Checking OCL Business Rules in Java Programs. diploma thesis, Dresden University of Technology, 2001

26. OMG, XMI SMIF Revised Submission (ad/98-10-06). http://www.omg.org

27. W3C, Extensible Markup Language (XML). http://www.w3.org

A Formal Semantics for OCL 1.4

María Victoria Cengarle* and Alexander Knapp

Ludwig–Maximilians–Universität München
{cengarle,knapp}@informatik.uni-muenchen.de

Abstract. The OCL 1.4 specification introduces `let`-declarations for adding auxiliary class features in static structures of the UML. We provide a type inference system and a big-step operational semantics for the OCL 1.4 that treat UML static structures and UML object models abstractly and accommodate for additional declarations; the operational semantics satisfies a subject reduction property with respect to the type inference system. We also discuss an alternative, non-operational interpretation of `let`-declarations as constraints.

1 Introduction

The "Object Constraint Language" (OCL) allows to define constraints, like invariants and pre- and post-conditions, for models of the "Unified Modeling Language" (UML). The language has been extensively employed in the specification of the UML meta-model itself throughout UML 1.1. However, the meta-model constraints rely on the possibility of declaring auxiliary (meta-)class features, which was not provided for explicitly in OCL up to version 1.3. For example [12, p. 2-66], two additional features `parent` and `allParents` are declared for the meta-class `GeneralizableElement` in order to express the constraint that the inheritance relationship of a UML model must be acyclic. The OCL 1.4 specification [12, Ch. 6] defines the `let`-construct to introduce so-called pseudo-features for (meta-)classes, such that the acyclicity constraint could now be recast as:

```
context GeneralizableElement inv:
  let parent : Set(GeneralizableElement) =
        self.generalization.parent
  let allParents : Set(GeneralizableElement) =
        self.parent->union(self.parent.allParents)
  in not self.allParents->includes(self)
```

Though this `let`-construct is rather different from its conventional usage in functional languages like SML [10], the OCL specification does not provide a precise semantics, let alone for the whole language. In particular, it is not clear how `let`-declarations interfere with inheritance and whether arbitrary recursive defining expressions are allowed (cf. a comparable requirement on recursive post-conditions [12, p. 6-59]). Moreover [13], are additional features like `allParents` to be interpreted operationally (leading to non-termination when evaluated over a cyclic inheritance relationship) or should declarations of auxiliary features be regarded as a constraint?

---

* Current affiliation: Fraunhofer Institute for Experimental Software Engineering.

M. Gogolla and C. Kobryn (Eds.): UML 2001, LNCS 2185, pp. 118–133, 2001.

Several formal semantics for OCL have already been presented, in particular by Bickford and Guaspari [2], Hamie, Howse, and Kent [7], and Richters and Gogolla [14,16] for OCL 1.1 and by Clark [4] and the authors [3] for OCL 1.3. The let-construct of the previous OCL versions is neglected by all these semantics, with the exception of [3] where it is treated as an SML-style declaration. Moreover, these semantics show deficiencies in handling the OCL types OclAny and OclType [14,7], the OCL flattening rules [2,7], empty collections [14,4], undefined values [7,4], non-determinism [2,7,14], and overridden properties [2,7,14, 4]. Also, several OCL implementations have been provided, most noteworthy the Bremen USE tool [15], the Dresden OCL tool [8], and the pUML "Meta-Modelling Tool" (MMT [9]). These differ e.g. in their handling of collections and oclAsType; the USE tool does not include let, the Dresden tool and MMT also seem to handle the let-construct as an SML-style declaration.

We provide an improved and more comprehensive formal semantics of the OCL 1.4 including its main novelty, the possibility of declaring pseudo-features. We axiomatise UML static structures and UML object models such that the semantics is parametric in the treatment of declarations. We introduce a type inference and annotation system for OCL terms (Sect. 2) and define a big-step operational semantics that evaluates annotated terms (Sect. 3); the operational semantics satisfies a subject reduction property with respect to the type inference system. Finally, we discuss an alternative, non-operational interpretation of declarations as model constraints (Sect. 4). We conclude with some remarks on future work.

We assume a working knowledge of the OCL syntax and informal semantics. The concrete syntax of the OCL sub-language that we consider can be found in Table 1; in particular, we omit navigation to association classes and through qualified associations, templates, package pathnames, enumerations, the types OclExpression and OclState, the functions that can be defined by iterate, pre- and in-fix syntax, and pre- and post-conditions.

Table 1. OCL syntax fragment

$$
\begin{aligned}
\textit{Term} &::= \textit{Constr} \mid \textit{Inv} \mid \textit{Decl} \mid \textit{Expr} \\
\textit{Constr} &::= \textbf{context } \textit{Type } \textbf{inv: } \textit{Inv} \{\textbf{inv: } \textit{Inv}\} \\
\textit{Inv} &::= [\textit{Decl}\{\textit{Decl}\} \textbf{ in}] \textit{Expr} \\
\textit{Decl} &::= \textbf{let } \textit{Name} [(\textit{Var} : \textit{Type} \{ , \textit{Var} : \textit{Type} \})] : \textit{Type} = \textit{Expr} \\
\textit{Expr} &::= \textit{Literal} \mid \textbf{self} \mid \textit{Var} \mid \textit{Type} \mid \\
&\quad\ (\textbf{Set} \mid \textbf{Bag} \mid \textbf{Sequence}) \{ [\textit{Expr} \{ , \textit{Expr} \}] \} \mid \\
&\quad\ \textbf{if } \textit{Expr} \textbf{ then } \textit{Expr} \textbf{ else } \textit{Expr} \textbf{ endif} \mid \\
&\quad\ \textit{Expr} \text{->}\, \textbf{iterate} (\textit{Var} : \textit{Type} ; \textit{Var} : \textit{Type} = \textit{Expr} \mid \textit{Expr}) \mid \\
&\quad\ \textit{Expr} \,.\, \textbf{oclAsType} (\textit{Type}) \mid \textit{Type} \,.\, \textbf{allInstances} ( ) \mid \\
&\quad\ \textit{Expr} \,.\, \textbf{and} (\textit{Expr}) \mid \textit{Expr} \,.\, \textbf{or} (\textit{Expr}) \mid \\
&\quad\ \textit{Expr} \,.\, \textit{Name} [([\textit{Expr} \{ , \textit{Expr} \}])] \mid \textit{Expr} \text{->} \textit{Name} ([\textit{Expr} \{ , \textit{Expr} \}]) \\
\textit{Literal} &::= \textit{IntegerLiteral} \mid \textit{RealLiteral} \mid \textit{BooleanLiteral} \mid \textit{StringLiteral} \\
\textit{Type} &::= \textit{Name} \mid (\textbf{Set} \mid \textbf{Bag} \mid \textbf{Sequence} \mid \textbf{Collection}) (\textit{Name}) \\
\textit{Var} &::= \textit{Name}
\end{aligned}
$$

2   Type System

The type of an OCL term depends on information from an underlying UML static structure, its classifiers, structural and query behavioural features, generalisation relationship, opposite association ends, &c., and the built-in OCL types and properties. We abstractly axiomatise this information as a static basis which is parametric in the classifiers and the generalisation relationship and provides an extension mechanism by pseudo-features; the axiomatisation also captures the declaration retrieval of (overloaded) features and properties that is only vaguely described in the UML specification by full-descriptors [12, p. 2-75]. We present a type inference system for OCL terms over such a static basis that also annotates the terms for later evaluation of overloaded features and properties and pseudo-features; the type system entails unique annotations and types.

2.1   Static Bases

A *static basis* Ω defines types, a type hierarchy, functions for declaration retrieval, and an extension mechanism for declarations.

Types. The *(compile-time) types* T_Ω of a static basis Ω are defined as follows:

$$
\begin{aligned}
T_\Omega &::= \overline{A}_\Omega \mid \overline{S}\,(\overline{A}_\Omega\,) & B &::= \texttt{Integer} \mid \texttt{Real} \mid \texttt{Boolean} \mid \texttt{String} \\
\overline{A}_\Omega &::= A_\Omega \mid \texttt{OclType} & \overline{S} &::= S \mid \texttt{Collection} \\
A_\Omega &::= \texttt{Void} \mid B \mid C_\Omega \mid \texttt{OclAny} & S &::= \texttt{Set} \mid \texttt{Bag} \mid \texttt{Sequence}
\end{aligned}
$$

where the set parameter C_Ω represents a set of *classifiers*, that does not contain $\texttt{Integer}$, $\texttt{Real}$, $\texttt{Boolean}$, $\texttt{String}$, $\texttt{Void}$, $\texttt{OclAny}$, and $\texttt{OclType}$.

The set B contains all built-in simple OCL types, the *basic types*. The type $\texttt{Void}$ is not required by the OCL specification; it denotes the empty type. The set A_Ω comprises $\texttt{Void}$, the basic types, the *classifier types*, and $\texttt{OclAny}$, which is the common super-type of all basic and classifier types. The type $\texttt{OclType}$ is the type of all types (as used in impredicative polymorphism [11]). Finally, the set S defines the concrete collection type functions yielding, when applied to a type parameter, a concrete *collection type*; $\overline{S}$ adds the abstract collection type function $\texttt{Collection}$ that yields the abstract collection type.

Each *Literal l* has a type, written as *type(l)*, such that *type(n)* = $\texttt{Integer}$ if n is an *IntegerLiteral*, &c. The type parameter of a collection type $\overline{\sigma}(\tau)$ may be recovered by $base(\overline{\sigma}(\tau)) = \tau$; for simplicity, we set $base(\tau) = \tau$ if τ is not a collection type.

Type hierarchy. The *subtype relation* $\leq_\Omega$ of a static basis Ω is defined as the least partial order that satisfies the following axioms:

1. for all $\tau \in T_\Omega$, $\texttt{Void} \leq_\Omega \tau$
2. for all $\alpha \in A_\Omega$, $\alpha \leq_\Omega \texttt{OclAny}$
3. $\texttt{Integer} \leq_\Omega \texttt{Real}$

4. for all $\zeta_1, \zeta_2 \in C_\Omega$, if $\zeta_1 \leq_{C_\Omega} \zeta_2$, then $\zeta_1 \leq_\Omega \zeta_2$
5. for all $\sigma \in S$ and $\overline{\alpha} \in \overline{A}_\Omega$, $\sigma(\overline{\alpha}) \leq_\Omega$ Collection($\overline{\alpha}$)
6. for all $\overline{\sigma} \in \overline{S}$ and $\overline{\alpha}_1, \overline{\alpha}_2 \in \overline{A}_\Omega$, if $\overline{\alpha}_1 \leq_\Omega \overline{\alpha}_2$, then $\overline{\sigma}(\overline{\alpha}_1) \leq_\Omega \overline{\sigma}(\overline{\alpha}_2)$

where the partial order parameter $\leq_{C_\Omega}$ denotes the *generalisation hierarchy* on the classifier types C_Ω.

In particular, OclType $\not\leq_\Omega$ OclAny (in contrast to [9]) and $\sigma(\tau) \not\leq_\Omega$ OclAny. According to [12, p. 6-54] collection types are basic types, following [12, pp. 6-75f.] these types are *not* basic types (cf. [1]). We choose the second definition (in contrast to [14]), avoiding the Russell paradox that could arise from Set(OclAny) $\leq_\Omega$ OclAny (see [2]); however, note, that thus none of the properties of OclAny, like inequality or oclIsKindOf, is immediately available for collections. Moreover, $\tau \leq_\Omega base(\tau)$ if, and only if $\tau \in \overline{A}_\Omega$.

We denote by $\bigsqcup_\Omega\{\tau_1, \dots, \tau_n\}$ the least upper bound of types $\tau_1, \dots, \tau_n$ with respect to $\leq_\Omega$; simultaneously, when writing $\bigsqcup_\Omega\{\tau_1, \dots, \tau_n\}$ we assume this least upper bound to exist (which may not be the case in the presence of multiple inheritance). Note that $\bigsqcup_\Omega \emptyset = $ Void.

Declaration retrieval. The retrieval of (overridden) properties, features, pseudo-features, and opposite association ends in a static basis Ω is defined by two suitably axiomatised maps yielding *declarations* in

$$D_\Omega ::= T_\Omega \cdot Name : T_\Omega \mid T_\Omega \cdot Name : T_\Omega^* \to T_\Omega \ .$$

Given a name a and a type τ, the partial function $fd_\Omega : Name \times T_\Omega \rightharpoonup D_\Omega$ yields, when defined, a declaration $\tau'.a : \tau''$ such that $\tau \leq_\Omega \tau'$. The type τ' represents a type that shows a structural (pseudo-)feature or an opposite association end with name a of type τ''. If $fd_\Omega(a, \tau)$ is defined, then $fd_\Omega(a, \tau')$ is defined for all $\tau' \leq_\Omega \tau$, i.e., a is inherited to all subtypes of τ.

Analogously, given a name o, a type τ, and a sequence of types $(\tau_i)_{1 \leq i \leq n}$ the partial function $fd_\Omega : Name \times T_\Omega \times T_\Omega^* \rightharpoonup D_\Omega$ yields, when defined, a declaration $\tau'.o : (\tau_i')_{1 \leq i \leq n} \to \tau_0'$ such that $\tau \leq_\Omega \tau'$ and $\tau_i \leq_\Omega \tau_i'$ for all $1 \leq i \leq n$. The type τ' represents a type that shows a query behavioural (pseudo-)feature or a property with name o, parameter types $\tau_1', \dots, \tau_n'$, and return type τ_0'. If $fd_\Omega(o, \tau, (\tau_i)_{1 \leq i \leq n})$ is defined, then $fd_\Omega(o, \tau', (\tau_i)_{1 \leq i \leq n})$ is defined for all $\tau' \leq_\Omega \tau$.

Table 2 shows some sample axioms for OCL properties, where $\alpha, \alpha' \in A_\Omega$ and $\overline{\alpha}, \overline{\alpha}' \in \overline{A}_\Omega$; all other OCL properties [12, Sect. 6.8] may be added analogously. We require these axioms for all static bases Ω.

Extensions. We require that a static basis Ω be *extendable* by a declaration of a structural pseudo-feature $\zeta.a : \tau$ with $\zeta \in C_\Omega$, if $fd_\Omega(a, \zeta)$ is undefined, and by a declaration of a behavioural pseudo-feature $\zeta.o : (\tau_i)_{1 \leq i \leq n} \to \tau_0$ with $\zeta \in C_\Omega$, if $fd_\Omega(o, \zeta, (\tau_i)_{1 \leq i \leq n})$ is undefined. Such an extension Ω' of Ω must again be a static basis. For the extension by a declaration $\delta = \zeta.a : \tau$ we require that $fd_{\Omega'}(a, \zeta) = \delta$ and that $fd_{\Omega'}(a', \zeta')$ is the same as $fd_\Omega(a', \zeta')$ if $a' \neq a$; and by a declaration $\delta = \zeta.o : (\tau_i)_{1 \leq i \leq n} \to \tau_0$ that $fd_{\Omega'}(o, \zeta, (\tau_i)_{1 \leq i \leq n}) = \delta$ and that

Table 2. Typing of sample built-in OCL properties

$fd_\Omega(=, \alpha, \alpha') = \alpha.= : \alpha' \to \texttt{Boolean}$

$fd_\Omega(\texttt{oclIsKindOf}, \alpha, \texttt{OclType}) = \alpha.\texttt{oclIsKindOf} : \texttt{OclType} \to \texttt{Boolean}$

$fd_\Omega(\texttt{first}, \texttt{Sequence}(\overline{\alpha})) = \texttt{Sequence}(\overline{\alpha}).\texttt{first} : \to \overline{\alpha}$

$fd_\Omega(\texttt{including}, \sigma(\overline{\alpha}), \overline{\alpha}') = \sigma(\overline{\alpha}).\texttt{including} : \overline{\alpha}' \to \sigma(\bigsqcup_\Omega\{\overline{\alpha}, \overline{\alpha}'\})$

$fd_\Omega(\texttt{union}, \sigma(\overline{\alpha}), \sigma(\overline{\alpha}')) = \sigma(\overline{\alpha}).\texttt{union} : \sigma(\overline{\alpha}') \to \sigma(\bigsqcup_\Omega\{\overline{\alpha}, \overline{\alpha}'\})$

$fd_{\Omega'}(o', \zeta', (\tau_i')_{1 \le i \le n})$ is the same as $fd_\Omega(o', \zeta', (\tau_i')_{1 \le i \le n})$ if $o' \neq o$. Moreover, we must have $T_{\Omega'} = T_\Omega$ and $\le_{\Omega'} = \le_\Omega$.

These requirements only weakly characterise possible extension mechanisms for declarations. We assume that some scheme of extending static bases is fixed and we write Ω, δ for the extension of a static basis Ω by the declaration δ according to the chosen scheme.

2.2   Type Inference

The type inference system on the one hand allows to deduce the type of a given OCL term over a given static basis. On the other hand, the inference system produces a normalised and annotated OCL term adding type information on declarations and overridden properties for later evaluation.

The grammar for *annotated* OCL terms transforms the grammar in Table 1 by consistently replacing *Term*, *Constr*, *Inv*, *Decl*, and *Expr* by *A-Term*, *A-Constr*, *A-Inv*, *A-Decl*, and *A-Expr*, respectively; furthermore, the original clauses

> **let** *Name* [(*Var* : *Type* {, *Var* : *Type*})] : *Type* = *Expr*
> *Expr* . *Name* [([*Expr* {, *Expr*}])] | *Expr* -> *Name* ([*Expr* {, *Expr*}])

are replaced by

> **let** *Name Type* [(*Var* : *Type* {, *Var* : *Type*})] : *Type* = *A-Expr*
> *A-Expr* . *Name Type* [([*A-Expr* {, *A-Expr*}])] |
> *A-Expr* -> *Name Type* ([*A-Expr* {, *A-Expr*}])

The annotations by *Type* for **let** and $\tilde{e}.a$ record the defining class, the annotations for $\tilde{e}.o(\dots)$ and $\tilde{e}$->$o(\dots)$ the expected return type. Annotations are written as subscripts.

A *type environment* over a static basis Ω is a finite sequence Γ of variable typings of the form $x_1 : \tau_1, \dots, x_n : \tau_n$ with $x_i \in \mathit{Var} \cup \{\texttt{self}\}$ and $\tau_i \in T_\Omega$ for all $1 \le i \le n$; we denote $\{x_1, \dots, x_n\}$ by $\mathrm{dom}(\Gamma)$, and τ_i by $\Gamma(x_i)$ if $x_j \neq x_i$ for all $i < j \le n$. The empty type environment is denoted by $\emptyset$, concatenation of type environments Γ and Γ' by Γ, Γ'.

The type inference system consists of judgements of the form $\Omega; \Gamma \vdash t \rhd \tilde{t} : \theta$ where Ω is a static basis, Γ is a type environment over Ω, t is a *Term*, $\tilde{t}$ is an *A-Term*, and $\theta \in T_\Omega \cup D_\Omega$. When writing such a judgement, we assume that `self`, `oclAsType`, `allInstances`, `and`, and `or` are reserved names and that *Var* and $T_\Omega \subseteq$ *Type* are disjoint. The empty type environment may be omitted.

The judgement relation $\vdash$ is defined by the rules in Tables 3–4; a rule may only be applied if all its constituents are well-defined. The meta-variables that are used in the rules and which may be variously decorated range as follows: $l \in$ *Literal*; $\alpha \in A_\Omega$, $\overline{\alpha} \in \overline{A}_\Omega$, $\zeta \in C_\Omega$, $\sigma \in S$, $\overline{\sigma} \in \overline{S}$, $\tau \in T_\Omega$, $\delta \in D_\Omega$; $x \in$ *Var*; $a, o \in$ *Name*; $e \in$ *Expr*, $\tilde{e} \in$ *A-Expr*, $d \in$ *Decl*, $\tilde{d} \in$ *A-Decl*, $p \in$ *Inv*, $\tilde{p} \in$ *A-Inv*.

The rules follow the OCL specification [12, Ch. 6] as closely as possible. The (Inv^τ) and $(\text{Decl}_1^\tau – \text{Decl}_2^\tau)$ rules in Table 3 treat `let`-declarations as being simultaneous; dependent declarations may be easily introduced (cf. [10]). The rule (Coll^τ) provides a unique type for the empty concrete collections (in contrast to [4]) and for "flattening" nested collections; for a motivation see [12, p. 6-67], though the least upper bound is not directly justified by the specification (in particular, Schürr [17] suggests to employ union-types instead; [4,15] require homogenous collections; the typing rules of [8] depend on the expression order; [9] shows no flattening). The type of a conditional expression, as given by the (Cond^τ) rule, differs from what is stated in [12, p. 6-83]: there, independently of the type of e_2, the (evaluation) type of e_1 is assumed to be the type of the whole expression ([14] requires comparable types, [4] a single type). For the casting rule (Cast^τ) see [12, pp. 6-56, 6-63f., 6-77] ([14] requires that the new type is smaller than the original type; not present in [7,4]); note, however, that this rule does not allow for arbitrary expressions resulting in a type as the argument for `oclAsType`, since this would imply term-dependent types as, for example, in

   `5.oclAsType(if 1.=(2) then Real else Integer endif)` .

By the same argument, (Inst^τ) does not allow `allInstances` to be called on arbitrary expressions, but only type literals. The annotation in (Feat_1^τ) in Table 4 accounts for the retrieval of an overridden structural feature or opposite association end [12, pp. 6-63f.] (not present in [14,4]); the annotations in (Feat_2^τ) and (Prop^τ) are necessary, since we do not require any return type restrictions for query behavioural features and properties (in contrast to [4]). The rules $(\text{Sing}_1^\tau – \text{Sing}_2^\tau)$ in Table 4 are the so-called "singleton" rules, see [12, pp. 6-60f.], allowing to apply collection properties to non-collection expressions (not present in [14, 4]). The $(\text{Short}_1^\tau – \text{Short}_2^\tau)$ rules define the shorthand notation for features on members of collections [12, p. 6-71] combined with flattening [12, p. 6-67] (not present in [2,7,14,4]). There is no subsumption rule; such a rule would interfere with the overriding of properties and features (cf. e.g. [5]).

The type inference system entails unique annotations and types:

Proposition 1. *Let Ω be a static basis, Γ a type environment, and t a Term. If $\Omega; \Gamma \vdash t \triangleright \tilde{t} : \tau$ and $\Omega; \Gamma \vdash t \triangleright \tilde{t}' : \tau'$ for some A-Term's $\tilde{t}$ and $\tilde{t}'$ and types τ and τ', then $\tilde{t} = \tilde{t}'$ and $\tau = \tau'$.*

Proof. By induction on the term t. $\qquad$

We also write $\Omega; \Gamma \vdash \tilde{t} : \tau$ if $\Omega; \Gamma \vdash t \triangleright \tilde{t} : \tau$ where $t \in$ *Term* is obtained from $\tilde{t} \in$ *A-Term* by erasing the annotations; t and $\tilde{t}$ are called *well-typed*.

Table 3. Type inference system I

(Ctxt^τ)
$$\frac{(\Omega; \Gamma, \mathtt{self} : \zeta \vdash p_i \triangleright \tilde{p}_i : \mathtt{Boolean})_{1 \leq i \leq n}}{\Omega; \Gamma \vdash \mathtt{context}\ \zeta\ (\mathtt{inv:}\ p_i)_{1 \leq i \leq n} \triangleright}$$
$$\mathtt{context}\ \zeta\ (\mathtt{inv:}\ \tilde{p}_i)_{1 \leq i \leq n} : \mathtt{Boolean}$$

(Inv^τ)
$$\frac{(\Omega, (\delta_j)_{1 \leq j \leq n}; \Gamma \vdash d_i \triangleright \tilde{d}_i : \delta_i)_{1 \leq i \leq n} \quad \Omega, (\delta_j)_{1 \leq j \leq n}; \Gamma \vdash e \triangleright \tilde{e} : \tau}{\Omega; \Gamma \vdash (d_i)_{1 \leq i \leq n}\ \mathtt{in}\ e \triangleright (\tilde{d}_i)_{1 \leq i \leq n}\ \mathtt{in}\ \tilde{e} : \tau}$$

(Decl_1^τ)
$$\frac{\Omega; \Gamma \vdash e \triangleright \tilde{e} : \tau'}{\Omega; \Gamma \vdash \mathtt{let}\ x : \tau = e \triangleright \mathtt{let}\ x_\zeta : \tau = \tilde{e} : \zeta.x : \tau}$$
if $\tau' \leq_\Omega \tau$ and where $\zeta = \Gamma(\mathtt{self})$

(Decl_2^τ)
$$\frac{\Omega; \Gamma, (x_i : \tau_i)_{1 \leq i \leq n} \vdash e \triangleright \tilde{e} : \tau'}{\Omega; \Gamma \vdash \mathtt{let}\ x(x_1 : \tau_1, \ldots, x_n : \tau_n) : \tau = e \triangleright}$$
$$\mathtt{let}\ x_\zeta(x_1 : \tau_1, \ldots, x_n : \tau_n) : \tau = \tilde{e} : \zeta.x : (\tau_i)_{1 \leq i \leq n} \rightarrow \tau$$
if $\tau' \leq_\Omega \tau$ and where $\zeta = \Gamma(\mathtt{self})$

(Lit^τ) $\quad \Omega; \Gamma \vdash l \triangleright l : type(l)$ $\qquad\qquad$ (Self^τ) $\quad \Omega; \Gamma \vdash \mathtt{self} \triangleright \mathtt{self} : \Gamma(\mathtt{self})$

(Var^τ) $\quad \Omega; \Gamma \vdash x \triangleright x : \Gamma(x)$ $\qquad\qquad$ (Type^τ) $\quad \Omega; \Gamma \vdash \tau \triangleright \tau : \mathtt{OclType}$

(Coll^τ)
$$\frac{(\Omega; \Gamma \vdash e_i \triangleright \tilde{e}_i : \tau_i)_{1 \leq i \leq n}}{\Omega; \Gamma \vdash \sigma\{e_1, \ldots, e_n\} \triangleright} \qquad \text{where } \alpha = \bigsqcup_\Omega \{base(\tau_i) \mid 1 \leq i \leq n\}$$
$$\sigma\{\tilde{e}_1, \ldots, \tilde{e}_n\} : \sigma(\alpha)$$

(Cond^τ)
$$\frac{\Omega; \Gamma \vdash e \triangleright \tilde{e} : \mathtt{Boolean} \quad (\Omega; \Gamma \vdash e_i \triangleright \tilde{e}_i : \tau_i)_{1 \leq i \leq 2}}{\Omega; \Gamma \vdash \mathtt{if}\ e\ \mathtt{then}\ e_1\ \mathtt{else}\ e_2\ \mathtt{endif} \triangleright} \qquad \text{where } \tau = \bigsqcup_\Omega \{\tau_1, \tau_2\}$$
$$\mathtt{if}\ \tilde{e}\ \mathtt{then}\ \tilde{e}_1\ \mathtt{else}\ \tilde{e}_2\ \mathtt{endif} : \tau$$

(Iter^τ)
$$\frac{\Omega; \Gamma \vdash e \triangleright \tilde{e} : \overline{\sigma}(\overline{\alpha}') \quad \Omega; \Gamma \vdash e' \triangleright \tilde{e}' : \tau' \quad \Omega; \Gamma, x : \overline{\alpha}, x' : \tau \vdash e'' \triangleright \tilde{e}'' : \tau''}{\Omega; \Gamma \vdash e\mathtt{->iterate}(x : \overline{\alpha}; x' : \tau = e' \mid e'') \triangleright} \quad \begin{array}{l} \text{if } \overline{\alpha}' \leq_\Omega \overline{\alpha} \text{ and} \\ \tau', \tau'' \leq_\Omega \tau \end{array}$$
$$\tilde{e}\mathtt{->iterate}(x : \overline{\alpha}; x' : \tau = \tilde{e}' \mid \tilde{e}'') : \tau$$

(Cast^τ)
$$\frac{\Omega; \Gamma \vdash e \triangleright \tilde{e} : \tau}{\Omega; \Gamma \vdash e.\mathtt{oclAsType}(\tau') \triangleright \tilde{e}.\mathtt{oclAsType}(\tau') : \tau'} \quad \text{if } \tau \leq_\Omega \tau' \text{ or } \tau' \leq_\Omega \tau$$

(Inst^τ) $\quad \Omega; \Gamma \vdash \tau.\mathtt{allInstances}() \triangleright \tau.\mathtt{allInstances}() : \mathtt{Set}(base(\tau))$

(And^τ)
$$\frac{(\Omega; \Gamma \vdash e_i \triangleright \tilde{e}_i : \mathtt{Boolean})_{1 \leq i \leq 2}}{\Omega; \Gamma \vdash e_1.\mathtt{and}(e_2) \triangleright} \qquad (\text{Or}^\tau) \quad \frac{(\Omega; \Gamma \vdash e_i \triangleright \tilde{e}_i : \mathtt{Boolean})_{1 \leq i \leq 2}}{\Omega; \Gamma \vdash e_1.\mathtt{or}(e_2) \triangleright}$$
$$\tilde{e}_1.\mathtt{and}(\tilde{e}_2) : \mathtt{Boolean} \qquad\qquad\qquad \tilde{e}_1.\mathtt{or}(\tilde{e}_2) : \mathtt{Boolean}$$

Table 4. Type inference system II

$$(\text{Feat}_1^\tau) \quad \frac{\Omega;\Gamma \vdash e \triangleright \tilde{e} : \tau}{\Omega;\Gamma \vdash e.a \triangleright \tilde{e}.a_{\tau'} : \tau''} \quad \text{if } fd_\Omega(a,\tau) = \tau'.a : \tau''$$

$$(\text{Feat}_2^\tau) \quad \frac{\begin{array}{c}\Omega;\Gamma \vdash e \triangleright \tilde{e} : \tau \\ (\Omega;\Gamma \vdash e_i \triangleright \tilde{e}_i : \tau_i)_{1 \le i \le n}\end{array}}{\begin{array}{c}\Omega;\Gamma \vdash e.o(e_1, \ldots, e_n) \triangleright \\ \tilde{e}.o_{\tau_0'}(\tilde{e}_1, \ldots, \tilde{e}_n) : \tau_0'\end{array}} \quad \begin{array}{l}\text{if } fd_\Omega(o, \tau, (\tau_i)_{1 \le i \le n}) = \\ \tau'.o : (\tau_i')_{1 \le i \le n} \to \tau_0'\end{array}$$

$$(\text{Prop}^\tau) \quad \frac{\begin{array}{c}\Omega;\Gamma \vdash e \triangleright \tilde{e} : \overline{\sigma}(\overline{\alpha}) \\ (\Omega;\Gamma \vdash e_i \triangleright \tilde{e}_i : \tau_i)_{1 \le i \le n}\end{array}}{\begin{array}{c}\Omega;\Gamma \vdash e\texttt{->}o(e_1, \ldots, e_n) \triangleright \\ \tilde{e}\texttt{->}o_{\tau_0'}(\tilde{e}_1, \ldots, \tilde{e}_n) : \tau_0'\end{array}} \quad \begin{array}{l}\text{if } fd_\Omega(o, \overline{\sigma}(\overline{\alpha}), (\tau_i)_{1 \le i \le n}) = \\ \tau'.o : (\tau_i')_{1 \le i \le n} \to \tau_0'\end{array}$$

$$(\text{Sing}_1^\tau) \quad \frac{\begin{array}{cc}\Omega;\Gamma \vdash e \triangleright \tilde{e} : \overline{\alpha}' & \Omega;\Gamma \vdash e' \triangleright \tilde{e}' : \tau' \\ \Omega;\Gamma, x : \overline{\alpha}, x' : \tau \vdash e'' \triangleright \tilde{e}'' : \tau''\end{array}}{\begin{array}{c}\Omega;\Gamma \vdash e\texttt{->iterate}(x : \overline{\alpha}; x' : \tau = e' \mid e'') \triangleright \\ \texttt{Set\{}\tilde{e}\texttt{\}->iterate}(x : \overline{\alpha}; x' : \tau = \tilde{e}' \mid \tilde{e}'') : \tau\end{array}} \quad \begin{array}{l}\text{if } \overline{\alpha}' \le_\Omega \overline{\alpha} \text{ and} \\ \tau', \tau'' \le_\Omega \tau\end{array}$$

$$(\text{Sing}_2^\tau) \quad \frac{\begin{array}{c}\Omega;\Gamma \vdash e \triangleright \tilde{e} : \overline{\alpha} \\ (\Omega;\Gamma \vdash e_i \triangleright \tilde{e}_i : \tau_i)_{1 \le i \le n}\end{array}}{\begin{array}{c}\Omega;\Gamma \vdash e\texttt{->}o(e_1, \ldots, e_n) \triangleright \\ \texttt{Set\{}\tilde{e}\texttt{\}->}o_{\tau_0'}(\tilde{e}_1, \ldots, \tilde{e}_n) : \tau_0'\end{array}} \quad \begin{array}{l}\text{if } fd_\Omega(o, \texttt{Set}(\overline{\alpha}), (\tau_i)_{1 \le i \le n}) = \\ \tau'.o : (\tau_i')_{1 \le i \le n} \to \tau_0'\end{array}$$

$$(\text{Short}_1^\tau) \quad \frac{\Omega;\Gamma \vdash e \triangleright \tilde{e} : \overline{\sigma}(\overline{\alpha})}{\begin{array}{c}\Omega;\Gamma \vdash e.a \triangleright \tilde{e}\texttt{->iterate}(i : \overline{\alpha}; a : \sigma(\overline{\alpha}') = \sigma\{\} \mid \\ a\texttt{->union}_{\sigma(\overline{\alpha}')}(\sigma\{i.a_\tau\})) : \sigma(\overline{\alpha}')\end{array}}$$

$$\begin{array}{l}\text{if } fd_\Omega(a, \overline{\alpha}) = \tau.a : \overline{\alpha}' \text{ and} \\ (\overline{\sigma} \ne \texttt{Sequence}, \sigma = \texttt{Bag}) \text{ or } (\sigma = \overline{\sigma} = \texttt{Sequence}) \\ \text{or } fd_\Omega(a, \overline{\alpha}) = \tau.a : \sigma(\overline{\alpha}')\end{array}$$

$$(\text{Short}_2^\tau) \quad \frac{\begin{array}{cc}\Omega;\Gamma \vdash e \triangleright \tilde{e} : \overline{\sigma}(\overline{\alpha}) & (\Omega;\Gamma \vdash e_i \triangleright \tilde{e}_i : \tau_i)_{1 \le i \le n}\end{array}}{\begin{array}{c}\Omega;\Gamma \vdash e.o(e_1, \ldots, e_n) \triangleright \\ \tilde{e}\texttt{->iterate}(i : \overline{\alpha}; a : \sigma(\overline{\alpha}') = \sigma\{\} \mid \\ a\texttt{->union}_{\sigma(\overline{\alpha}')}(\sigma\{i.o_{\tau_0'}(\tilde{e}_1, \ldots, \tilde{e}_n)\})) : \sigma(\overline{\alpha}')\end{array}}$$

$$\begin{array}{l}\text{if } fd_\Omega(o, \overline{\alpha}, (\tau_i)_{1 \le i \le n}) = \tau.o : (\tau_i')_{1 \le i \le n} \to \overline{\alpha}' = \tau_0' \text{ and} \\ (\overline{\sigma} \ne \texttt{Sequence and } \sigma = \texttt{Bag}) \text{ or } (\sigma = \overline{\sigma} = \texttt{Sequence}) \\ \text{or } fd_\Omega(a, \overline{\alpha}, (\tau_i)_{1 \le i \le n}) = \tau.o : (\tau_i')_{1 \le i \le n} \to \sigma(\overline{\alpha}') = \tau_0'\end{array}$$

3   Operational Semantics

The result of an OCL term depends on information from an underlying UML object model, the instances and their types, the values of structural features, and the implementations of query behavioural features of instances, as well as the implementations of the built-in OCL properties. We abstractly summarise this information in a dynamic basis which is the dynamic counterpart of static bases and is axiomatised analogously. We define a big-step operational semantics for annotated OCL terms and a conformance relation between static and dynamic bases, such that the semantics satisfies a subject reduction property with respect to the type system of the previous section.

3.1   Dynamic Bases

A *dynamic basis* ω defines values, results, a typing relation, implementation retrieval functions, and an extension mechanism for implementations.

Values and results. The values V_ω and results R_ω of a dynamic basis ω are defined as follows:

$$R_\omega ::= V_\omega \mid \bot$$
$$V_\omega ::= N_\omega \mid (\textsf{Set} \mid \textsf{Bag} \mid \textsf{Sequence})\,\{\,[N_\omega\,\{\,,\,N_\omega\}]\,\}$$
$$N_\omega ::= \textit{Literal} \mid T_\omega \mid O_\omega$$

The *(run-time) types* T_ω are defined as T_Ω for a static basis Ω in Sect. 2.1, but replacing C_Ω by a set parameter C_ω, again representing classifiers. The finite set parameter O_ω represents the *instances* in a model, disjoint from *Literal* and T_ω.

The result $\bot$ represents "undefined". Values of the form $\sigma\{\ldots\}$ with $\sigma \in S = \{\textsf{Set}, \textsf{Bag}, \textsf{Sequence}\}$ are *collection values*, the values in N_ω are *simple values*. We assume suitably axiomatised arithmetical, boolean, &c. functions and relations on values such that, e.g., $1 + 1 = 2$, $\textsf{false} \wedge \textsf{true} = \textsf{false}$, $\textsf{Set}\{\,1,\,2\,\} = \textsf{Set}\{\,2,\,1,\,1\,\}$, $1 \leq 2$, &c.

For collection values, we use a function $\textit{flatten}_\omega : V_\omega \to N_\omega^*$ to sequences of simple values, stipulating that $\textit{flatten}_\omega(\sigma\{v_1, \ldots, v_n\}) = v_1 \cdots v_n$ and that $\textit{flatten}_\omega(v) = v$, if $v \in N_\omega$. Collection values are constructed by a map $\textit{make}_\omega : S \times V_\omega^* \to V_\omega$ such that $\textit{make}_\omega(\sigma, v_1 \cdots v_n) = \sigma\{v_1, \ldots, v_n\}$ if $\sigma \in S$ and $v_i \in N_\omega$ for all $1 \leq i \leq n$, and, if $v_i \in V_\omega \setminus N_\omega$ for some $1 \leq i \leq n$ then $\textit{make}_\omega(\sigma, v_1 \cdots v_n) = \textit{make}_\omega(\sigma, \textit{flatten}_\omega(v_1) \cdots \textit{flatten}_\omega(v_n))$; if $\sigma = \textsf{Set}$, repetitions in $\textit{flatten}_\omega(v_1) \cdots \textit{flatten}_\omega(v_n)$ are discarded, such that only the leftmost occurrence of a value remains. If $n = 0$, we write $\textit{make}_\omega(\sigma, \emptyset)$; more generally, for a set $M = \{v_1, \ldots, v_n\}$, we let $\textit{make}_\omega(\sigma, M)$ denote $\textit{make}_\omega(\sigma, v_1 \cdots v_n)$.

A collection value $v = \sigma\{v_1, \ldots, v_n\}$ has a *sequence value representation* v', written as $v \rightsquigarrow v'$, if $\textit{make}_\omega(\textsf{Sequence}, \textit{flatten}_\omega(\textit{make}_\omega(\sigma, \textit{flatten}_\omega(v'')))) = v'$ for some $v'' = v$. In general, a collection value has several different sequence value representations; e.g. $\textsf{Set}\{1,\,2\} \rightsquigarrow \textsf{Sequence}\{1,\,2\}$ and also $\textsf{Set}\{1,\,2\} \rightsquigarrow \textsf{Sequence}\{2,\,1\}$; but not $\textsf{Set}\{1,\,2\} \rightsquigarrow \textsf{Sequence}\{1,\,1,\,2\}$.

Typing relation. We require a relation $:_\omega \subseteq V_\omega \times T_\omega$ between values and types defined by the least left-total relation satisfying the following axioms:

1. For $v \in Literal$, $v :_\omega type(v)$
2. For $v \in T_\omega$, $v :_\omega \texttt{OclType}$
3. For $v \in O_\omega$, if $v :_{O_\omega} \tau$ then $v :_\omega \tau$
4. $\sigma\{\} :_\omega \sigma(\texttt{Void})$
5. If $v :_\omega \texttt{Integer}$ then $v :_\omega \texttt{Real}$
6. If $v_i :_\omega \overline{\alpha} \in \overline{A}_\omega$ for $1 \le i \le n$, then $\sigma\{v_1, \ldots, v_n\} :_\omega \sigma(\overline{\alpha})$
7. If $v :_\omega \sigma(\overline{\alpha})$ then $v :_\omega \texttt{Collection}(\overline{\alpha})$
8. If $v :_\omega \alpha \in A_\omega$ then $v :_\omega \texttt{OclAny}$

where the left-total relation parameter $:_{O_\omega} \subseteq O_\omega \times C_\omega$ denotes the *typing relation* between instances and classifiers.

In particular, by rule (6), we have that if $v :_\omega \tau$ and $flatten_\omega(v) = v_1 \cdots v_n$ then $v_i :_\Omega base(\tau)$ for all $1 \le i \le n$. Note, however, that there is no $v \in V_\omega$ with $v :_\omega \texttt{Void}$ and no type $\tau \in T_\omega$ such that $\texttt{Set\{1, Boolean\}} :_\omega \tau$.

We write $\tau \le_\omega \tau'$ if, and only if $v :_\omega \tau$ implies $v :_\omega \tau'$ for all $v \in V_\omega$. Given a type $\tau \in C_\omega \cup \{\texttt{Void}, \texttt{Boolean}, \texttt{OclType}\}$ we denote the finite set $\{v \in V_\omega \mid v :_\omega \tau\}$ by $\omega(\tau)$; for all other types τ, $\omega(\tau)$ is undefined.

Implementation retrieval. The retrieval of implementations of (overridden) properties, features, pseudo-features, and opposite association ends in a dynamic basis ω is defined by two partial maps yielding *implementations* in

$$I_\omega ::= T_\omega \,.\, Name \equiv (A\text{-}Expr \mid R_\omega) \mid T_\omega \,.\, Name(\,Var^*) \equiv (A\text{-}Expr \mid R_\omega) : T_\omega \;.$$

Given a name a, a type τ (the annotation), and a value v, the partial function $impl_\omega : Name \times T_\omega \times V_\omega \rightharpoonup I_\omega$ yields, when defined, an implementation $\tau.a \equiv \psi$ with $v :_\omega \tau$, representing the implementation of a structural (pseudo-)feature or an opposite association end with name a, defined in τ, as required by the annotation. If $\psi \in A\text{-}Expr \setminus R_\omega$, then $\tau \in C_\omega$, accounting for class pseudo-features. If $impl_\omega(a, \tau, v)$ is defined, then $impl_\omega(a, \tau, v')$ is defined for all v' such that $v :_\omega \tau'$ implies $v' :_\omega \tau'$, i.e., a is present for all values with the same types as v.

Analogously, given a name o, a type τ (the annotation), a value v, and a sequence of values $(v_i)_{1 \le i \le n}$, the partial function $impl_\omega : Name \times T_\omega \times V_\omega \times V_\Omega^* \rightharpoonup I_\omega$ yields, when defined, an implementation $\tau'.o((x_i)_{1 \le i \le n}) \equiv \psi : \tau$ with $v :_\omega \tau'$, representing the implementation of a query behavioural (pseudo-)feature or a property with name o, defined with a return type as required by the annotation. If $\psi \in A\text{-}Expr \setminus R_\omega$, then $\tau' \in C_\omega$. If $impl_\omega(o, \tau, v, (v_i)_{1 \le i \le n})$ is defined, then $impl_\omega(o, \tau, v', (v_i)_{1 \le i \le n})$ is defined for all v' such that $v :_\omega \tau'$ implies $v' :_\omega \tau'$.

Table 5 contains some sample axioms for the retrieval of the implementation of built-in OCL properties. Generally, we write the types for $impl_\omega$ as subscripts and omit the types and name for implementations that do not show an annotated expression.

Extensions. We require that a dynamic basis ω be *extendable* by an implementation $\zeta.a \equiv \psi$ with $\zeta \in C_\omega$, if $impl_\omega(a_\zeta, v)$ is undefined for all $v :_\omega \zeta$, and by an implementation $\zeta.o((x_i)_{1 \le i \le n}) = \psi : \tau$ if $impl_\omega(o_\tau, v, (v_i)_{1 \le i \le n})$ is undefined for all $v :_\omega \zeta$ and all $v_1, \ldots, v_n \in V_\omega$. Such an extension ω' of ω must again

Table 5. Semantics of sample built-in OCL properties

$$impl_\Omega^\omega(=_{\texttt{Boolean}}, v, v') = (v = v')$$

$$impl_\Omega^\omega(\texttt{oclIsKindOf}_{\texttt{Boolean}}, v, \tau) = v :_\omega \tau$$

$$impl_\Omega^\omega(\texttt{first}_{\texttt{Sequence}(\overline{\alpha})}, \texttt{Sequence}\{v_1, \ldots, v_n\}) = v_1$$

$$impl_\Omega^\omega(\texttt{including}_{\sigma(\overline{\alpha})}, v, v') = make_\omega(\sigma, v\ v')$$

$$impl_\Omega^\omega(\texttt{union}_{\sigma(\overline{\alpha})}, v, v') = make_\omega(\sigma, v\ v')$$

be a dynamic basis. For the extension by an implementation $\iota = \zeta.a \equiv \psi$ we require that $impl_{\omega'}(a_\zeta, v) = \iota$ for all $v :_\omega \zeta$ and that $impl_{\omega'}(a_{\zeta'}', v)$ is the same as $impl_\omega(a_{\zeta'}', v)$ if $a' \neq a$; and by an implementation $\iota = \zeta.o((x_i)_{1 \leq i \leq n}) \equiv \psi : \tau$ that $impl_{\omega'}(o_\tau, v, (v_i)_{1 \leq i \leq n}) = \iota$ for all $v :_\omega \zeta$ and some $v_1, \ldots, v_n \in V_\omega$ and that $impl_{\omega'}(o_{\tau'}', v', (v_i)_{1 \leq i \leq n})$ is the same as $impl_\omega(o_{\tau'}', v', (v_i)_{1 \leq i \leq n})$ if $o' \neq o$. Moreover, we must have $T_{\omega'} = T_\omega$ and $:_{\omega'} = :_\omega$.

As the requirements for extensions of static bases, the constraints on extensions of dynamic bases only weakly characterise possible extension mechanisms for implementations. We assume that some scheme of extending dynamic bases is fixed and we write ω, ι for the extension of a dynamic basis ω by the implementation ι according to this scheme.

3.2   Operational Rules

The operational semantics evaluates annotated OCL terms in the context of a dynamic bases and some variable assignments.

A *variable environment* over a dynamic basis ω is a finite sequence γ of variable assignments of the form $x_1 \mapsto v_1, \ldots, x_n \mapsto v_n$ with $x_i \in Var \cup \{\texttt{self}\}$ and $v_i \in V_\omega$ for all $1 \leq i \leq n$; we denote $\{x_1, \ldots, x_n\}$ by $\mathrm{dom}(\gamma)$ and v_i by $\gamma(x_i)$ if $x_i \neq x_j$ for all $i < j \leq n$. The empty variable environment is denoted by $\emptyset$, concatenation of variable environments γ and γ' by γ, γ'.

The operational semantics consists of judgements of the form $\omega; \gamma \vdash \tilde{t} \downarrow \rho$ where ω is a dynamic basis, γ is a variable environment over ω, $\tilde{t}$ is an *A-Term*, and $\rho \in R_\omega \cup I_\omega$. The empty variable environment may be omitted.

The judgement relation $\vdash$ is defined by the rules in Tables 6–7; a rule may only be applied if all its constituents are well-defined. The meta-variables range as follows: $l \in Literal$; $\alpha \in A_\omega$, $\zeta \in C_\omega$, $\sigma \in S$, $\tau \in T_\omega$, $\iota \in I_\Omega$; $x \in Var$; $a, o \in Name$; $v \in V_\omega$, $\overline{v} \in R_\omega$; $\tilde{e} \in A\text{-}Expr$, $\tilde{d} \in A\text{-}Decl$, $\tilde{p} \in A\text{-}Inv$.

We additionally adopt the following general *strictness convention* that applies to all rules with the single exception of the rules $(\text{And}_1^\downarrow\text{–And}_3^\downarrow)$ and $(\text{Or}_1^\downarrow\text{–Or}_3^\downarrow)$ in Table 6: if $\perp$ occurs as a result in a judgement of a premise of some rule, the whole term evaluates to $\perp$.

The operational rules are presented in close correspondence to the typing rules in Tables 3–4. All rules, except the rules $(\text{And}_2^\downarrow\text{–And}_3^\downarrow)$ and $(\text{Or}_2^\downarrow\text{–Or}_3^\downarrow)$ in Table 6 require of all sub-terms to be fully evaluated and to result in a value

Table 6. Operational semantics I

$(\text{Ctxt}^{\downarrow})$
$$\frac{(\omega; \gamma, \textbf{self} \mapsto v \vdash \tilde{p}_i \downarrow v_{i,v})_{1 \leq i \leq n, v \in \omega(\varsigma)}}{\omega; \gamma \vdash \textbf{context } \varsigma \text{ (inv: } \tilde{p}_i)_{1 \leq i \leq n} \downarrow \bigwedge_{i,v} v_{i,v}}$$

$(\text{Inv}^{\downarrow})$
$$\frac{\begin{array}{c}(\omega; \gamma \vdash \tilde{d}_i \downarrow \iota_i)_{1 \leq i \leq n} \\ \omega, (\iota_i)_{1 \leq i \leq n}; \gamma \vdash \tilde{e} \downarrow v\end{array}}{\omega; \gamma \vdash (d_i)_{1 \leq i \leq n} \textbf{ in } \tilde{e} \downarrow v}$$

$(\text{Decl}_1^{\downarrow})$ $\omega; \gamma \vdash \textbf{let } x_\varsigma : \tau = \tilde{e} \downarrow \varsigma.x = \tilde{e}$

$(\text{Decl}_2^{\downarrow})$ $\omega; \gamma \vdash \textbf{let } x_\varsigma(x_1 : \tau_1, \ldots, x_n : \tau_n) : \tau = \tilde{e} \downarrow \varsigma.x((x_i)_{1 \leq i \leq n}) = \tilde{e} : \tau$

$(\text{Lit}^{\downarrow})$ $\omega; \gamma \vdash l \downarrow l$ $(\text{Self}^{\downarrow})$ $\omega; \gamma \vdash \textbf{self} \downarrow \gamma(\textbf{self})$

$(\text{Var}^{\downarrow})$ $\omega; \gamma \vdash x \downarrow \gamma(x)$ $(\text{Type}^{\downarrow})$ $\omega; \gamma \vdash \tau \downarrow \tau$

$(\text{Coll}^{\downarrow})$
$$\frac{(\omega; \gamma \vdash \tilde{e}_i \downarrow v_i)_{1 \leq i \leq n}}{\omega; \gamma \vdash \sigma\{\tilde{e}_1, \ldots, \tilde{e}_n\} \downarrow make_\omega(\sigma, v_1 \cdots v_n)}$$

$(\text{Cond}^{\downarrow})$
$$\frac{\begin{array}{c}\omega; \gamma \vdash \tilde{e} \downarrow v \\ (\omega; \gamma \vdash \tilde{e}_i \downarrow v_i)_{1 \leq i \leq 2}\end{array}}{\omega; \gamma \vdash \textbf{if } \tilde{e} \textbf{ then } \tilde{e}_1 \textbf{ else } \tilde{e}_2 \textbf{ endif} \downarrow v'} \quad \begin{array}{l}\text{if } v = \textbf{true} \text{ and } v' = v_1 \text{ or} \\ v = \textbf{false} \text{ and } v' = v_2\end{array}$$

$(\text{Iter}^{\downarrow})$
$$\frac{\begin{array}{cc}\omega; \gamma \vdash \tilde{e} \downarrow v & \omega; \gamma \vdash \tilde{e}' \downarrow v_0' \\ (\omega; \gamma, x \mapsto v_i, x' \mapsto v_{i-1}' \vdash \tilde{e}'' \downarrow v_i')_{1 \leq i \leq n}\end{array}}{\omega; \gamma \vdash \tilde{e}\text{->iterate}(x : \alpha; x' : \tau = \tilde{e}' \mid \tilde{e}'') \downarrow v_n'}$$
$$\text{if } v \rightsquigarrow \texttt{Sequence}\{v_1, \ldots, v_n\}$$

$(\text{Cast}^{\downarrow})$
$$\frac{\omega; \gamma \vdash \tilde{e} \downarrow v}{\omega; \gamma \vdash \tilde{e}.\texttt{oclAsType}(\tau) \downarrow \overline{v}} \quad \begin{array}{l}\text{if } v :_\Omega \tau \text{ and } \overline{v} = v \text{ or} \\ v \not\mathrel{/}_\Omega \tau \text{ and } \overline{v} = \bot\end{array}$$

(Inst^τ) $\omega; \gamma \vdash \tau.\texttt{allInstances}() \downarrow make_\omega(\textbf{Set}, \omega(base(\tau)))$

$(\text{And}_1^{\downarrow})$
$$\frac{(\omega; \gamma \vdash \tilde{e}_i \downarrow v_i)_{1 \leq i \leq 2}}{\omega; \gamma \vdash \tilde{e}_1.\texttt{and}(\tilde{e}_2) \downarrow v_1 \wedge v_2}$$
$(\text{Or}_1^{\downarrow})$
$$\frac{(\omega; \gamma \vdash \tilde{e}_i \downarrow v_i)_{1 \leq i \leq 2}}{\omega; \gamma \vdash \tilde{e}_1.\texttt{or}(\tilde{e}_2) \downarrow v_1 \vee v_2}$$

$(\text{And}_2^{\downarrow})$
$$\frac{\omega; \gamma \vdash \tilde{e}_i \downarrow \textbf{false}}{\omega; \gamma \vdash \tilde{e}_1.\texttt{and}(\tilde{e}_2) \downarrow \textbf{false}}$$
$$\text{where } i = 1 \text{ or } i = 2$$
$(\text{Or}_2^{\downarrow})$
$$\frac{\omega; \gamma \vdash \tilde{e}_i \downarrow \textbf{true}}{\omega; \gamma \vdash \tilde{e}_1.\texttt{or}(\tilde{e}_2) \downarrow \textbf{true}}$$
$$\text{where } i = 1 \text{ or } i = 2$$

$(\text{And}_3^{\downarrow})$
$$\frac{(\omega; \gamma \vdash \tilde{e}_i \downarrow \overline{v}_i)_{1 \leq i \leq 2}}{\omega; \gamma \vdash \tilde{e}_1.\texttt{and}(\tilde{e}_2) \downarrow \bot}$$
$$\begin{array}{l}\text{if } \overline{v}_1 \neq \textbf{false} \text{ and } \overline{v}_2 = \bot \text{ or} \\ \overline{v}_1 = \bot \text{ and } \overline{v}_2 \neq \textbf{false}\end{array}$$
$(\text{Or}_3^{\downarrow})$
$$\frac{(\omega; \gamma \vdash \tilde{e}_i \downarrow \overline{v}_i)_{1 \leq i \leq 2}}{\omega; \gamma \vdash \tilde{e}_1.\texttt{or}(\tilde{e}_2) \downarrow \bot}$$
$$\begin{array}{l}\text{if } \overline{v}_1 \neq \textbf{true} \text{ and } \overline{v}_2 = \bot \text{ or} \\ \overline{v}_1 = \bot \text{ and } \overline{v}_2 \neq \textbf{true}\end{array}$$

Table 7. Operational semantics II

$$(\text{Feat}_1^\downarrow) \quad \frac{\omega;\gamma \vdash \tilde{e} \downarrow v}{\omega;\gamma \vdash \tilde{e}.a_\tau \downarrow \overline{v}'} \qquad (\text{Feat}_2^\downarrow) \quad \frac{\omega;\gamma \vdash \tilde{e} \downarrow v \quad \omega;\gamma, \mathbf{self} \mapsto v \vdash \tilde{e}' \downarrow \overline{v}'}{\omega;\gamma \vdash \tilde{e}.a_\tau \downarrow \overline{v}'}$$
$$\text{if } impl_\omega(a_\tau, v) = \overline{v}' \qquad\qquad\qquad \text{if } impl_\omega(a_\tau, v) = \zeta.a \equiv \tilde{e}'$$

$$(\text{Feat}_3^\downarrow) \quad \frac{\omega;\gamma \vdash \tilde{e} \downarrow v \quad (\omega;\gamma \vdash \tilde{e}_i \downarrow v_i)_{1 \le i \le n}}{\omega;\gamma \vdash \tilde{e}.o_\tau(\tilde{e}_1, \ldots, \tilde{e}_n) \downarrow \overline{v}'} \qquad \text{if } impl_\omega(o_\tau, v, (v_i)_{1 \le i \le n}) = \overline{v}'$$

$$(\text{Feat}_4^\downarrow) \quad \frac{\omega;\gamma \vdash \tilde{e} \downarrow v \quad (\omega;\gamma \vdash \tilde{e}_i \downarrow v_i)_{1 \le i \le n}}{\omega;\gamma, \mathbf{self} \mapsto v, (x_i \mapsto v_i)_{1 \le i \le n} \vdash \tilde{e}' \downarrow \overline{v}'} \quad \begin{array}{l} \text{if } impl_\omega(o_\tau, v, (v_i)_{1 \le i \le n}) = \\ \zeta.o((x_i)_{1 \le i \le n}) \equiv \tilde{e}' : \tau \end{array}$$
$$\frac{}{\omega;\gamma \vdash \tilde{e}.o_\tau(\tilde{e}_1, \ldots, \tilde{e}_n) \downarrow \overline{v}'}$$

$$(\text{Prop}^\downarrow) \quad \frac{\omega;\gamma \vdash \tilde{e} \downarrow v \quad (\omega;\gamma \vdash \tilde{e}_i \downarrow v_i)_{1 \le i \le n}}{\omega;\gamma \vdash \tilde{e}\text{->}o_\tau(\tilde{e}_1, \ldots, \tilde{e}_n) \downarrow \overline{v}'} \qquad \text{if } impl_\omega(o_\tau, v, (v_i)_{1 \le i \le n}) = \overline{v}'$$

in V_ω in order to deliver a result for a term. In particular, this makes for a strict conditional; on the other hand, the (And$^\downarrow$) and (Or$^\downarrow$) rules yield parallel **Boolean** properties **and** and **or**; see [12, Sect. 6.4.10] (not treated in [2,14,4]). The only rules that introduce the undefined result $\bot$ are the (Cast$^\downarrow$) rule in Table 6 (cf. [12, p. 6-56]) and, possibly, (Feat$_1^\downarrow$), (Feat$_3^\downarrow$), and (Prop$^\downarrow$) in Table 7. The (Iter$^\downarrow$) allows for considerable non-determinism if applied to a collection value that is not a sequence (in contrast to [14,16]; not present in [2]).

3.3   Subject Reduction

We define a relation between dynamic and static bases ensuring that, on the one hand, the compile-time and run-time types and type hierarchies are compatible and, on the other hand, that implementations respect declarations. A dynamic basis ω *conforms* to a static basis Ω if $T_\Omega = T_\omega$ and $\le_\Omega = \le_\omega$ and

1. for every $a \in Name$ such that $fd_\Omega(a, \tau) = \tau'.a : \tau''$, $impl_\omega(a_{\tau'}, v)$ is defined for all $v \in V_\omega$ with $v :_\omega \tau$. If $impl_\omega(a_{\tau'}, v)$ is $\tau'.a \equiv v'$ with $v' \in V_\omega$ then $v' :_\omega \tau''$; if $impl_\omega(a_{\tau'}, v)$ is $\tau'.a \equiv \tilde{e}$ then $\Omega; \mathbf{self} : \tau' \vdash \tilde{e} : \tau'''$ with $\tau''' \le_\Omega \tau''$.
2. for every $o \in Name$ such that $fd_\Omega(o, \tau, (\tau_i)_{1 \le i \le n}) = \tau'.o : (\tau'_i)_{1 \le i \le n} \to \tau'_0$, $impl_\omega(o_{\tau'_0}, v, (v_i)_{1 \le i \le n})$ is defined for all $v, v_1, \ldots, v_n \in V_\omega$ with $v :_\omega \tau$ and $v_i :_\omega \tau_i$ for all $1 \le i \le n$. If $impl_\omega(o_{\tau'_0}, v, (v_i)_{1 \le i \le n})$ is $\tau''.o((x_i)_{1 \le i \le n}) \equiv v' : \tau'_0$ with $v' \in V_\omega$ then $v' :_\Omega \tau'_0$; if $impl_\omega(o_{\tau'_0}, v, (v_i)_{1 \le i \le n})$ is $\tau''.o((x_i)_{1 \le i \le n}) \equiv \tilde{e} : \tau'_0$ then $\tau'' \le_\Omega \tau'$ and $\Omega; \mathbf{self} : \tau', (x_i : \tau'_i)_{1 \le i \le n} \vdash \tilde{e} : \tau''_0$ with $\tau''_0 \le_\Omega \tau'_0$.

Even when typing and annotating an OCL term over a static basis and evaluating the annotated term over a dynamic basis that conforms to the static basis, the operational semantics turns out to be not type sound in the strict sense, i.e., converging well-typed terms do not always yield a result of the expected type. For example,

```
Set{1, 1.2}->iterate(i : OclAny;
                     a : Sequence(OclAny) = Sequence{} |
                     a->including(i))->first.oclAsType(Integer)
```

may evaluate (after annotation) to 1, if `Set{1, 1.2}` is chosen to be represented by `Sequence{1, 1.2}`; or it may evaluate to $\bot$, if `Set{1, 1.2}` is represented by `Sequence{1.2, 1}`.

However, if the operational semantics reduces an OCL term of inferred type τ to some value then this value is indeed of type τ, i.e., the operational semantics in Sect. 3.2 satisfies the subject reduction property with respect to the type inference system in Sect. 2.2. In order to state and prove this result, we say that a variable environment γ over ω *conforms* to a type environment Γ over Ω if $\mathrm{dom}(\gamma) \supseteq \mathrm{dom}(\Gamma)$ and $\gamma(x) :_\omega \Gamma(x)$ for all $x \in \mathrm{dom}(\gamma)$.

Proposition 2. *Let Ω be a static basis and ω a dynamic basis conforming to Ω; let Γ be a type environment over Ω and γ a variable environment over ω conforming to Γ; let t be a Term and $\tilde{t}$ an A-Term; let $\tau \in T_\Omega$ and $v \in V_\omega$. If $\Omega; \Gamma \vdash t \triangleright \tilde{t} : \tau$ and $\omega; \gamma \vdash \tilde{t} \downarrow v$, then $v :_\omega \tau$.*

Proof. By induction on the proof tree for $\Omega; \Gamma \vdash t \triangleright \tilde{t} : \tau$.

4 Constraint Semantics

The operational semantics, as detailed in the previous section, suggests that an (annotated) OCL constraint $\tilde{c} = \mathtt{context}\ \zeta\ (\mathtt{inv}\colon \tilde{p})_{1 \le i \le n}$ over a static basis Ω is *satisfied* by a dynamic basis ω conforming to Ω if, and only if $\omega; \vdash \tilde{c} \downarrow \mathtt{true}$; and thus, that $\tilde{c}$ is not satisfied by ω if either $\omega; \vdash \tilde{c} \downarrow \mathtt{false}$, or $\omega; \vdash \tilde{c} \downarrow \bot$, or when the operational evaluation of $\tilde{c}$ over ω does not terminate.

The possibility of non-termination can be tracked down to the introduction of recursive pseudo-features in OCL 1.4: When the operational evaluation of a constraint $\tilde{c}$ does not involve applications of rules $(\mathrm{Feat}_2^\downarrow)$ or $(\mathrm{Feat}_4^\downarrow)$, the evaluation will always terminate and yield a result. In fact, it may even be shown [3], that *expressions* of either OCL 1.3 or OCL 1.4 over empty UML static structures, that is, where no additional features other than built-in OCL properties are available, represent exactly all primitive recursive functions. Thus, when evaluated operationally, the declaration of pseudo-features increases the expressive power of OCL 1.4 over OCL 1.3 considerably.

Non-termination is illustrated by the acyclicity constraint on the generalisation relationship stated in the introduction: Assuming two classes A and B, such that A is the parent of B and, vice versa, B is the parent of A, the operational evaluation of `allParents` on A or B will loop. However, declarations may be interpreted differently, when taking the acyclicity constraint to be read as

```
context GeneralizableElement inv:
    self.parent = self.generalization.parent
and self.allParents = self.parent->union(self.parent.allParents)
and not self.allParents->includes(self)
```

over an extended static and dynamic basis, where `GeneralizableElement` shows the features `parent` and `allParents`. This reading would only require *constraints* on the implementation of `parent` and `allParents`. For the cyclic generalisation relation above `parent` of A must yield B, `parent` of B must yield A; the implementations of `allParents` for A and B are only required to result in a fix-point, e.g., both could yield `Set{A, B}` or both could yield $\bot$.

More generally, we call a dynamic basis ω a *result dynamic basis* if all implementation retrieval functions $impl_\omega$ yield only implementations showing a result in R_ω. Given an annotated declaration of a structural pseudo-feature `let` $a_\zeta : \tau = \tilde{e}$ we say that a result dynamic basis ω has a *fix-point* for a_ζ if

$$\omega; \mathtt{self} \mapsto v \vdash \tilde{e} \downarrow impl_\omega(a_\zeta, v)$$

for all $v \in \omega(\zeta)$; and likewise for an annotated declaration of a query behavioural pseudo-feature `let` $o_\zeta(x_1 : \tau_1, \ldots, x_n : \tau_n) : \tau = \tilde{e}$.

The *constraint semantics* interprets a constraint over result dynamic bases showing fix-points for all declarations occurring in the given constraint: Let $\tilde{c} = \mathtt{context}\ \zeta\ \mathtt{inv:}\ (\tilde{d}_i)_{1 \le i \le n}\ \mathtt{in}\ \tilde{e}$ be a constraint annotated and typed over a static basis Ω such that $\Omega'; \mathtt{self} : \zeta \vdash \tilde{d}_i : \delta_i$ for all $1 \le i \le n$ for the static basis Ω' extending Ω. Then $\tilde{c}$ *holds* in a dynamic basis ω conforming to Ω with respect to the constraint semantics if, and only if $\omega'; \mathtt{self} \mapsto v \vdash \tilde{e} \downarrow \mathtt{true}$ for all result dynamic bases ω' conforming to Ω', which extend ω and show fix-points for all declarations $\tilde{d}_i$ with $1 \le i \le n$, and all $v \in \omega'(\zeta)$.

This constraint semantics employs all fix-point dynamic bases; it may be desirable to restrict attention only to *least* fix-points.

5 Conclusions

We have presented a type inference system and a big-step operational semantics for the OCL 1.4 including the possibility of declaring additional pseudo-features; the operational semantics satisfies a subject reduction with respect to the type inference system. The corrections and additions to previous formal approaches to OCL 1.1/3 are pervasive. We have also discussed an alternative, non-operational interpretation of the declaration of pseudo-features as model constraints.

On the one hand, the semantics may form a new, more comprehensive basis for the treatment of OCL pre- and post-conditions, cf. Richters and Gogolla [16]; global pseudo-feature declarations using the `def:` stereotype may be easily incorporated. On the other hand, we have abstractly axiomatised UML static structures and UML object models, stating only some sufficient conditions such that OCL terms can be typed uniquely and evaluated type-safely. In particular, we have not treated the more complex UML template types, which have been investigated by Clark [4] though making additional assumptions on the inheritance relationship and contra-variance. However, this axiomatisation may contribute to the necessary clarification of the overall UML type system.

Acknowledgements. We thank Hubert Baumeister for pointing out the constraint interpretation of `let`-declarations and careful proof-reading.

References

1. T. Baar and R. Hähnle. An Integrated Metamodel for OCL Types. In R. France, editor, *Proc. OOPSLA'2000 Wsh. Refactoring the UML: In Search of the Core*, Minneapolis, 2000.
2. M. Bickford and D. Guaspari. Lightweight Analysis of UML. Draft NAS1-20335/10, Odyssey Research Assoc., 1998. http://cgi.omg.org/cgi-bin/doc?ad/98-10-01.
3. M. V. Cengarle and A. Knapp. On the Expressive Power of Pure OCL. Technical Report 0101, Ludwig–Maximilians–Universität München, 2001.
4. T. Clark. Type Checking UML Static Diagrams. In R. B. France and B. Rumpe, editors, *Proc. 2nd Int. Conf. UML*, volume 1723 of *Lect. Notes Comp. Sci.*, pages 503–517. Springer, Berlin, 1999.
5. S. Drossopoulou and S. Eisenbach. Describing the Semantics of Java and Proving Typing Soundness. In J. Alves-Foss, editor, *Formal Syntax and Semantics of Java*, volume 1523 of *Lect. Notes Comp. Sci.*, pages 41–82. Springer, Berlin, 1999.
6. A. Evans, S. Kent, and B. Selic, editors. *Proc. 3nd Int. Conf. UML*, volume 1939 of *Lect. Notes Comp. Sci.* Springer, Berlin, 2000.
7. A. Hami, J. Howse, and S. Kent. Interpreting the Object Constraint Language. In *Proc. Asia Pacific Conf. Software Engineering*. IEEE Press, 1998.
8. H. Hußmann, B. Demuth, and F. Finger. Modular Architecture for a Toolset Supporting OCL. In Evans et al. [6], pages 278–293.
9. http://www.cs.york.ac.uk/puml/mmf/mmt.zip.
10. R. Milner, M. Tofte, R. Harper, and D. MacQueen. *The Definition of Standard ML (Revised)*. MIT Press, Cambridge, Mass., 1997.
11. J. C. Mitchell. *Foundations for Programming Languages*. Foundations of Computing. MIT Press, Cambridge, Mass.–London, England, 1996.
12. Object Management Group. Unified Modeling Language Specification, Version 1.4. Draft, OMG, 2001. http://cgi.omg.org/cgi-bin/doc?ad/01-02-14.
13. http://www.cs.york.ac.uk/puml/puml-list-archive.
14. M. Richters and M. Gogolla. On Formalizing the UML Object Constraint Language OCL. In T. W. Ling, S. Ram, and M. L. Lee, editors, *Proc. 17th Int. Conf. Conceptual Modeling*, volume 1507 of *Lect. Notes Comp. Sci.*, pages 449–464. Springer, Berlin, 1998.
15. M. Richters and M. Gogolla. Validating UML Models and OCL Constraints. In Evans et al. [6], pages 265–277.
16. M. Richters and M. Gogolla. OCL — Syntax, Semantics and Tools. In T. Clark and J. Warmer, editors, *Advances in Object Modelling with the OCL*, Lect. Notes Comp. Sci., pages 38–63. Springer, Berlin, 2001.
17. A. Schürr. New Type Checking Rules for OCL (Collection) Expressions. In T. Clark and J. Warmer, editors, *Proc. UML'2000 Wsh. UML 2.0 — The Future of OCL*, York, 2000.

Refactoring UML Models

Gerson Sunyé, Damien Pollet, Yves Le Traon, and Jean-Marc Jézéquel

IRISA, Campus de Beaulieu, F-35042 Rennes Cedex, France
sunye,dpollet,yletraon,jezequel@irisa.fr

Abstract. Software developers spend most of their time modifying and maintaining existing products. This is because systems, and consequently their design, are in perpetual evolution before they die. Nevertheless, dealing with this evolution is a complex task. Before evolving a system, structural modifications are often required. The goal of this kind of modification is to make certain elements more extensible, permitting the addition of new features. However, designers are seldom able to evaluate the impact, on the whole model, of a single modification. That is, they cannot precisely verify if a change modifies the behavior of the modeled system. A possible solution for this problem is to provide designers with a set of basic transformations, which can ensure behavior preservation. These transformations, also known as refactorings, can then be used, step by step, to improve the design of the system. In this paper we present a set of refactorings and explain how they can be designed so as to preserve the behavior of a UML model. Some of these refactorings are illustrated with examples.

1 Introduction

The activity of software design is not limited to the creation of new applications from scratch. Very often software designers start from an existing application and have to modify its behavior and functionality. In recent years, it has been widely acknowledged as a good practice to divide this evolution into two distinct steps:

1. Without introducing any new behavior on the conceptual level, re-structure the software design to improve quality factors such as maintainability, efficiency, etc.
2. Taking advantage of this "better" design, modify the software behavior.

This first step has been called *refactoring* [12], and is now seen as an essential activity during software development and maintenance.

By definition, refactorings should be behavior-preserving transformations of an application. But one of the problems faced by designers is that it is often hard to measure the actual impact of modifications on the various design views, as well as on the implementation code.

This is particularly true for the Unified Modeling Language, with its various structural and dynamic views, which can share many modeling elements. For

M. Gogolla and C. Kobryn (Eds.): UML 2001, LNCS 2185, pp. 134–148, 2001.

instance, when a method is removed from a class diagram, it is often difficult to establish, at first glance, what is the impact on sequence and activities diagrams, collaborations, statecharts, OCL constraints, etc.

Still, the UML also has a primordial advantage in comparison with other design languages: its syntax is precisely defined by a metamodel, where the integration of the different views is given meaning. Therefore, the metamodel can be used to control the impact of a modification, which is essential when it should preserve the initial behavior an application.

The contribution of this paper is to show that refactorings can be defined for UML in such a way that their behavior-preserving properties are guaranteed, based on OCL constraints at the meta-model level. In Section 2 we first recall the motivation for such behavior-preserving transformations for the UML, and then give two concrete examples of refactorings, along with an empirical justification of their behavior-preserving properties. We then try to go further by formalizing refactorings using the OCL at the meta-model level to specify behavior-preserving transformations. For the sake of conciseness, we restrict the scope of this article to the refactoring of class diagrams (Sect. 3) and statecharts (Sect. 4). Finally, we conclude on the perspectives of this approach, most notably tool support that is prototyped in the context of our UML general purpose transformation framework called Umlaut.

2   Refactoring in a Nutshell

2.1   Motivation

Brant and Roberts [4] present refactorings as an essential tool for handling software evolution. They point out that "traditional" development methods, based on the waterfall life cycle, consider the maintenance of a software as the last phase of its life cycle and do not take into account the evolution of software. They also remark that some other methods, usually based on the spiral life cycle, such as Rapid Prototyping, Joint Application Development and more recently Extreme Programming [2], have better support for software evolution, and therefore for refactorings. These methods encourage the use of fourth generation languages and integrated developing environments, and thus are more appropriate for refactorings. Since UML seems to be closer to the first family of methods and tools than to the second one, one could expect the integration of refactorings in UML not to be worthwhile.

Despite this apparent methodological incompatibility, we still believe that refactorings can be integrated into UML tools. Methods have changed since the first observations of Fred Brooks [5], and the boundary between these two families of methods and tools is now less distinct. Recent methods, e.g. Catalysis [8] which uses UML as a notation language, take into account software evolution and thus design evolution. Additionally, since some UML tools, e.g. Rose, have some facilities for creating design models from application source code, refactorings could be used to modify this code and improve the design of existing applications.

The forthcoming Action Semantics [1] (AS) is an important issue for the integration of refactorings into UML tools. More precisely, the AS will allow UML to fully represent application behavior. Once UML tools could control the impact of modifications, they could propose a set of small behavior-preserving transformations, which could be combined to accomplish important design refactorings, as for instance, apply design patterns [7,14,15]. These transformations could be performed inside a *behavior-preservation* mode, where designers could graphically perform design improvements without generating unexpected results on the various UML views. One may accurately argue that OCL constraints may also be used to specify behavior of applications. Whilst this is true, the use the OCL is also more complex, since the integration of the OCL syntax into the UML metamodel is not yet precisely defined.

Before presenting these transformations in details and to better explain our motivation, we introduce 2 examples where refactorings are used to improve the design of existing applications.

2.2   Class Diagram Example

The class diagram given in Fig. 1 is a simple model of a graphical hierarchy for a vector graphics program. Graphics are constituted of geometric Primitives and subgraphs; they have a method to be displayed. Primitives have a matrix attribute representing how they are scaled, rotated or translated in the global coordinate system.

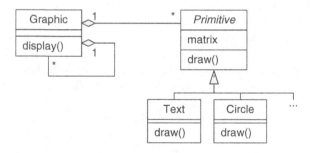

Fig. 1. Initial class diagram.

This model has some design flaws; for instance, as Primitives have no inheritance relation with Graphics, they must be treated differently, thus making the code unnecessarily complex. Fortunately, the *Composite* design pattern adresses this type of problem, where a structure is composed of basic objects that can be recursively grouped in a part-whole hierarchy. We will therefore introduce this pattern in the model through the following steps, leading to the diagram presented in Fig. 2:

1. Renaming the Graphic class to Group;
2. Adding an abstract superclass named Graphic to Group.
3. Making the class Primitive a subclass of Graphic.
4. Merging the Group-Group and Group-Primitive aggregations into Group-Graphic.
5. Finally, we can move relevant methods and attributes up to Graphic.

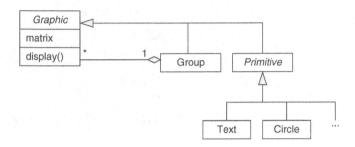

Fig. 2. Restructured class diagram.

We need to justify why the behavior preservation condition holds for these model transformations:

– Renaming of a model element does not change anything to the model behavior, provided the new name is legal (i.e. it does not already exist in the model).
– The added abstract superclass has no attributes or methods. It is an "empty" model element; its addition has no effect on the model.
– Creating a generalization between two classes does not introduce new behavior, provided no conflict (due to multiple inheritance, for instance) is introduced; in our case, Primitive had no superclass and Graphic is empty.
– Merging two associations is only allowed when these two associations are disjoint (they do not own the same objects), when the methods invoked through these associations have the same signature, and when the invocation through an association is always followed by an invocation through the other.
– Finally, moved methods or attributes to the superclass will simply be inherited afterwards (overriding is not modelled).

While most of these transformations – namely element renaming and the addition of a superclass – do not have an impact on other views, the merge of two associations may require changes on collaborations and object diagrams.

2.3   Statechart Example

Refactorings can also be used to improve the design of statecharts. However, as state diagrams do not simply model the system structure but its behavior, their transformation raises some difficulties. Figure 3 shows a state diagram for a simple telephone object. It is quite messy: since one can hang up at any time during communication, transitions have been drawn to the Idle state from every other state in the diagram.

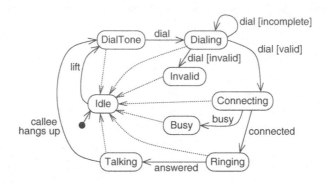

Fig. 3. Initial phone state diagram (dotted transitions are triggered when the caller hangs up).

In order to improve understandability, we group the states modeling the behavior of the phone when it is in use into a composite state, thus segregating the Idle state and allowing the use of high-level transitions.

To obtain the result shown in Fig. 4, four refactoring steps are needed:

1. Create a composite superstate, named Active, surrounding the whole current diagram.
2. Move Idle and the initial pseudostate out of Active.
3. Merge the "hang up" transitions into a transition leaving the boundary of Active.
4. Finally, split the "lift" transition into a transition from Idle to the boundary of Active and a default pseudostate/transition targeting DialTone.

These are the justifications for the previous transformations:

- Creating a surrounding state is trivially behavior-preserving.
- Moving the Idle state out is legal here: Active has no entry or exit actions, and so the execution order of existing actions is unchanged.
- Transitions exiting Active can be folded to a toplevel transition since they are equivalent (they hold the same label and target the same state).
- The replacement of the "lift" transition by a toplevel one is possible given that there is no other toplevel transition entering Active.

3   Refactoring Class Diagrams

The refactorings presented by W. Opdyke in his PhD thesis [12], which were later perfected and implemented by D. Roberts [13], as well as the restructuring

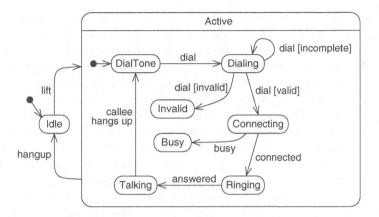

Fig. 4. Final phone state diagram.

transformations presented by other research efforts [6,9,10,3] apply essentially to three concepts: class, method and variable. Therefore, when we started the transpositions of existing refactorings to UML, we began with class diagrams.

The refactorings presented here can be summarized in five basic operations: *addition, removal, move, generalization* and *specialization* of modeling elements. The two last actions use the generalization relationship to transfer elements up and down a class hierarchy.

Most part of the modeling elements composing the class diagram may have a direct connection to the elements of other views. Therefore, some of the refactorings that apply to class diagrams may have an impact on different UML views.

3.1   Add, Remove, and Move

The *Addition* of features (attributes and methods) and associations to a class can be done when the new feature (or association) does not have the same signature as any other features owned by the class or by its parents. The *Removal* of associations and features can only be done when these elements are not referenced in the whole model. A method, for instance, may be referenced inside an interaction diagram (linked to messages and stimuli) and statecharts (linked to actions and events).

Adding and removing classes can be particularly interesting when the inheritance hierarchy is taken into account. The *Insert Generalizable Element* refactoring replaces a generalization between two elements with two other generalizations, having a new element between them. The inserted element must have the same type as the two initial elements and must not introduce new behavior. The *Remove Generalizable Element* does the contrary, it removes an element whithout defined behavior and links its subclasses directly to its superclasses. The element must not be referenced directly and indirectly (by the way of instances, features, etc.) in other diagrams.

The *Move* is used to transfer a method from a class to another, and create a forwarder method in the former. The constraints required by this transformation are rather complex. Initially, it implies the existence of an association, possibly inherited, between both classes. This association must be binary and its association ends must be both navigable, instance-level and have a multiplicity of 1. These constraints are different from those defined by D. Roberts [13] for a similar refactoring, where the association was not needed (and could not be identified since Smalltalk is dynamically typed). In his transformation the the transfered method gets an additional parameter, an instance of the original classifier. However, this additional parameter is not needed for a 1:1 multiplicity.

Although this transfer could be applied to any operation, some other constraints must be specified, in order to keep it coherent. The body of the concerned operation must not make references to attributes and only navigate through an association to the target classifier. After the transformation, messages that are sent to *self* are replaced by messages sent through an association. The references to the target classifier are replaced by references to self. This transformation requires the use of the Action Semantics, which can be used to find out which attributes and methods are used inside the body of the operation.

3.2   Generalization and Specialization

The *Generalization* refactoring can be applied to elements owned by classes, such as attributes, methods, operations, association ends and statecharts. It consists in the integration of two or more elements into a single one which is transfered to a common superclass. Since private features are not accessible within the subclasses, they can not be moved.

This transformation implies that all direct subclasses of the superclass own an equivalent element. Whilst the equivalence of attributes, association ends and operations can be verified by a structural comparison, the one of methods and statecharts is rather complex.

The *Specialization* refactoring is the exact opposite of *Generalization*, it consists in sending an element to all direct subclasses of its owner. In an informal way, the behavior is preserved if its owner class is not its *reference context*. The reference context is the class of the object to which a message or an attribute read/write is sent. In a general manner the reference context is the class, or any of its subclasses, that owns the attribute or the method. For instance, the reference context for the display() method (2) is potentially instances of Graphic or of any of its subclasses. If somewhere in the whole model a message calling this method is sent to an instance of Graphic, then the present refactoring can not be applied.

The reference context of attributes is obtained inside object diagrams (if the body of methods is expressed with the Action Semantics, it can be obtained by an analysis of read and write attribute actions). Object diagrams and collaborations can be used to obtain the reference context of association ends. The reference context of methods may be obtained inside interaction diagrams and statecharts.

Since multiple-inheritance is allowed in UML, we must verify whether the classes that would receive the feature do not have common subclasses (i.e. if a repeated-inheritance exists). If a common subclass exists, this means that after the transformation it would inherit two equivalent features, which would be a conceptual error.

4   Refactoring Statecharts

Statecharts make the behavior of classifiers and methods explicit and provide an interesting context for refactorings. Since this kind of refactorings is not considered in the research efforts previously cited, we will detail the constraints that must be satisfied before and after each transformation to ensure behavior preservation. Since our approach concerns the UML, we use the OCL [11], at the metamodel level, to specify these constraints

For the sake of simplicity, we will not enter into the details of how each refactoring accomplishes its intent (by the creation of objects and links), but only describe with the OCL what should be verified before and after the transformation. Indeed, the understanding of these meta-level OCL constraints requires some knowledge of the UML metamodel.

Most of the complexity encountered when defining these transformations comes from the activation of actions attached to states, such as *do*, *entry* and *exit* actions. The first one is executed while its state is active. The *entry* action is executed when a state is activated. In the particular case of a composite, its entry action is executed before the entry action of its substates. However, this action is only executed when a transition crosses the border of the composite. The *exit* action is executed when a state is exited. In the particular case of a composite, its exit action is executed after the exit action of its substates.

4.1   State

Fold Incoming/Outgoing Actions. These transformations replace a set of actions attached to Transitions, leaving from or leading to a state, by an exit or entry action attached to this state. They imply that an equivalent action is attached to all incoming or outgoing Transitions. Moreover, the source and the target state of each transition must have the same container, i.e. the transition must not cross the boundary of a composite, which could fire an entry or an exit action. Essentially, two actions are equivalent when they call the same operation, instantiate the same class, send the same signal, etc. In the case of action sequences, they are equivalent when they are composed of a basic equivalent actions.

Moreover, the concerned state must not own an entry or an exit action. The pre and post conditions of the *Fold Incoming Actions* transformation are presented below. Since the *Fold Outgoing Actions* is quite similar, it is not presented here.

Fold Incoming Actions

State :: foldIncoming
pre:
    self .entry→**isEmpty**() **and**
    self .incoming. effect →**forAll**(a,b:Action|
        a <>b **implies** a.isEquivalentTo(b)) **and**
    self .incoming.source→**forAll**(s:State| s.container = self .container)
post:
    self .entry→**notEmpty**() **and** self.incoming.effect→**isEmpty**() **and**
    self .incoming. effect @pre→**forAll**(a :Action| a.isEquivalentTo(self.entry))

OCL pre and post conditions of subsequent transformations are listed in the appendices of the paper, starting at p. 145.

Unfold Entry/Exit Action. These transformations are symmetrical to the previous ones. They replace an entry or an exit action attached to a state by a set of actions attached to all transitions incoming from or outgoing to this state. The concerned transitions must have no actions attached to them and must not cross the boundary of a composite.

These transformations, as well as those presented above, could be performed on transitions between states having different containers. In these cases, all composite states that are crossed by the transition should not have an exit action (if the transition leaves the composite) or an entry action (if the transition enters the composite).

Group States. Groups states into a new composite state. The transformation applies to a set of at least one state, belonging to the same *container*. It takes a name as parameter. The *container* is always a composite state, since according to the UML well-formedness rules for statecharts, the top of any state machine is always a single composite state. The container should not contain a state having the same name as the new composite.

Once this transformation is performed, the state machine contains a new composite state, which contains all states of the collection. This new state must not have incoming, outgoing nor internal transitions, nor any do, entry, or exit actions. This is the refactoring we used during the first step in the phone example (Sect. 2.3).

4.2   Composite State

Fold Outgoing Transitions. This transformations replaces a set of transitions, leaving from components of a composite state (one transition for each component) and going to the same state, by a single transition leaving from the composite state and going to this state, as was done in step 3 of the phone example. The actions attached to the transitions must be equivalent. The concerned target state must be specified.

Unfold Outgoing Transition. Replaces a transition, leaving from a composite state, by a set of transitions, leaving from all substates (one transition for each substate) going to the same target. All these transitions must own a equivalent action and event. In any case, the order of (entry/exit/transition) actions execution is not changed.

Move State into Composite. The insertion of a state into a composite state is a rather complex transformation. Several constraints must be verified before and after its execution. Since the transformation must not add new transitions to the state, for each outgoing transition leaving the composite, the state must have an equivalent one. transitions incoming from other states are indirectly bound to a substate, and thus do not affect the state. The transformation must ensure that the state will not have two equivalent transitions leaving from it. If the composite has a *do* action, then the state must have an equivalent one. After the transformation, the action contained by the state must be removed.

If some of the incoming transition to the state comes from the composite outside, the composite must not have an entry action. But, if the composite has an entry action, then the transitions of the state going to the sub-states must not have an attached action. After the transformation, these transitions receive a copy of the entry action.

If a target of a transition coming from the state is not a substate, then the composite must not have an exit action. If the composite has an exit action, then the transitions of the state coming from sub-states must not have an attached action. After the transformation, these transitions receive a copy of the exit action.

Move State out of Composite. Moving a substate out of its composite is also a complex task that is worth some clarification. This refactoring was used in a simple situation with the Idle in the phone example. The substate may have *inner* and *outer* transitions, i.e. transitions with states that are inside or outside the same composite, respectively.

Inner transitions are a problem when the composite has exit and entry actions, since these actions are not activated by this kind of transition and will be activated when the substate is extracted from the composite. In these cases, the extraction can only be done if the inner transitions own an action, which is equivalent to the exit (for incoming) or to the entry action (for outgoing). After the transformation, the actions attached to these transitions must be removed.

The existence of entry and exit actions is also a problem for outer transitions, which cross the composite border and activate these actions, because they will no longer occur after the transformation. The solution used in these cases is simple, a new action is attached to each outer transition. These actions are equivalent to the entry or exit actions, for incoming and outgoing transitions, respectively.

If the substate is linked to the initial pseudostate of the composite — which means that the composite incoming transitions are actually incoming transitions of the substate — then, after the transformation, these transitions must be transferred to the extracted state.

5   Conclusion

We have presented an initial set of design refactorings, which are transformations used to improve the design of object-oriented applications, without adding new functionalities. Adapting code refactorings to the design level as expressed in UML has proved itself a very interesting endeavor, far more complex than we thought initially. The search for some UML specific refactorings has been somehow frustrating, specially when we wanted transformations to have an impact on different UML views.

For instance, we wanted the activity diagram to be used as the starting place for the *Move Operation* refactoring. Indeed, this diagram, which is used to represent the behavior of a particular functionality, can be split into several *swimlanes* which seem to represent different classes. Thus, moving an activity from a swimlane to another could be interpreted as a *Move Operation*. Unfortunately, this is not possible, since the current syntax does not allow swimlanes to be directly linked to classes: swimlanes are just labels in the underlying model.

Moreover, the abstract syntax of the OCL is not yet precisely specified. Consequently, we are not able to define some OCL-based refactorings, neither to analyze the contents of a constraint and use this information to improve the definition of some refactorings. This might change in the future since an abstract syntax is curently proposed for normalization at the OMG.

As a perspective to this work, we foresee an extensive use of the action Semantics to make design models more precise, which would pave the way for more secure (i.e. proven) refactorings, that would also be, too a large extent, programming language independent. Our initial set of refactorings could then be widely expanded, and directly supported in standard UML tools.

References

1. Updated joint initial submission against the action semantics for uml rfp.
2. Kent Beck. *Extreme Programming Explained: Embracing Change*. Addison-Wesley, 1999.
3. Paul Bergstein. Maintainance of object-oriented systems during structural schema evolution. *TAPOS*, 3(3):185–212, 1997.
4. John Brant and Don Roberts. Refactoring techniques and tools (Plenary talk). In *Smalltalk Solutions*, New York, NY, 1999.
5. F. P. Brooks. *The Mitical Man-Month: Essays on Software Engineering*. Addison-Wesley, Reading, Mass, 1982.
6. Eduardo Casais. *Managing Evolutuin in Object Oriented Environments: An Algorithmic Approach*. Phd thesis, University of Geneva, 1991.

7. Mel Cinnéide and Paddy Nixon. A methodology for the automated introduction of design patterns. In *International Conference on Software Maintenance*, Oxford, 1999.

8. Desmond D'Souza and Alan Wills. *Objects, Components and Frameworks With UML: The Catalysis Approach*. Addison-Wesley, 1998.

9. W. Griswold. Program restructuring as an aid to software maintenance, 1991.

10. Walter Hursch. *Maintaining Consistency and Behavior of Object-Oriented Systems during Evolution*. Phd thesis, Northeastern University, June 1995.

11. Anneke Kleppe, Jos Warmer, and Steve Cook. Informal formality? the Object Constraint Language and its application in the UML metamodel. In Jean Bézivin and Pierre-Alain Muller, editors, *The Unified Modeling Language, UML'98 - Beyond the Notation. First International Workshop, Mulhouse, France, June 1998*, pages 127–136, 1998.

12. William F. Opdyke. *Refactoring Object-Oriented Frameworks*. PhD thesis, University of Illinois, Urbana-Champaign, 1992. Tech. Report UIUCDCS-R-92-1759.

13. Donald Roberts. *Practical Analysis for Refactoring*. PhD thesis, University of Illinois, 1999.

14. Donald Roberts, J. Brant, and Ralph Johnson. A refactoring tool for smalltalk. *Theory and Practice of Object Systems*, 3(4), 1997.

15. G. Sunyé, A. Le Guennec, and J.-M. Jézéquel. Design pattern application in UML. In E. Bertino, editor, *ECOOP'2000 proceedings*, number 1850, pages 44–62. Lecture Notes in Computer Science, Springer Verlag, June 2000.

A   Appendix: Statechart Refactorings

A.1   Unfold Exit Action

```
State :: unfoldExit
pre:
    self . exit→notEmpty() and self.outgoing.effect→isEmpty()
    self . outgoing.target→forAll(s:State| s .container = self .container)
post:
    self . exit→isEmpty() and
    self . outgoing. effect →forAll(a:Action| a.isEquivalentTo( self . exit @pre))
```

The *Unfold Entry Action* refactoring is very similar to this one, so its OCL constraints are not detailed here.

A.2   Group States

```
Collection→groupStates(name : Name)
pre:
    self →notEmpty() and
    self →forAll(each | each.oclIsKindOf(State)) and
    let coll = self→container→asSet() in coll →size = 1 and
        coll →first (). subvertex→select(each:State|each.name=name)→isEmpty()
post:
    let coll = self .container→asSet() in ( coll →size = 1 and
    let compositeState = coll→first ()  in ( compositeState.oclIsNew and
    -- no internal actions
    compositeState.exit→isEmpty() and compositeState.entry→isEmpty() and
    compositeState.do→isEmpty() and
    -- no transitions
```

compositeState.internal→**isEmpty**() and compositeState.incoming→**isEmpty**() and
compositeState.outgoing→**isEmpty**() and compositeState.subVertex = self **and**
-- *the container is the same*
self .container@**pre**→**forAll**(each:CompositeState| each = compositeState.container)))

A.3   Fold Outgoing Transition

CompositeState::foldOutgoing
pre:
    let possible = self .subvertex.outgoing→**select**(a,b:Transition|
      a < >b **implies** (a.target = b.target **and**
        a. effect .isEquivalentTo(b. effect) **and**
        a. trigger .isEquivalentTo(b.trigger))) **in** (
    self .subvertex→**forAll**(s:State| s.outgoing→**intersection**(possible)→**size**() = 1)
post:
    possible→**isEmpty**() **and**
    self .outgoing→**select**(t:Transition | possible@**pre**→**forAll**(each:Transition|
      each.target = t.target **and**
        each. effect .isEquivalentTo(t. effect) **and**
        each. trigger .isEquivalentTo(t. trigger)))→**size**() = 1

For the sake of clarity, we have used the *possible* expression, defined in the
preconditions, inside the postcondition. Actually, this is not possible, the *let*
expression should be rewritten.

A.4   Unfold Outgoing Transition

Transition :: unfoldOutgoing
pre:
    let cs = self .source **in** (cs.**oclIsKindOf**(CompositeState) **and**
    cs.subvertex→**notEmpty**())
post:
    let cs = self@**pre**.source **in** (cs.subvertex→**forAll**(s:State| s.outgoing→
      select(t:Transition| t.target = self@**pre**.target **and**
        t. effect .isEquivalentTo(self@**pre**.effect) **and**
        t. trigger .isEquivalentTo(self@**pre**.trigger))→**size**() = 1) **and**
    -- *the transition is no longer referenced:*
    self .source→**isEmpty** and self.target→**isEmpty** and
    self . trigger →**isEmpty** and self.effect→**isEmpty**

A.5   Move State into Composite

State :: moveInto(cs:CompositeState)
pre:
    let substates = cs.subvertex **in**
    substates→**excludes**(s) **and**
    cs .container = self .container **and**
    not cs.isConcurrent **and**
    -- *outgoing transitions*
    cs.outgoing→**forAll**(each:Transition | self .outgoing→**exists**(t:Transition|
      t.sameLabel(each) **and** t.target = each.target)) **and**
    -- *do action*
    cs.do→**notEmpty implies** cs.do.sameLabel(self.do) **and**
    -- *entry action*
    cs.entry→**notEmpty implies** (substates→**includesAll**(self.incoming.source) **and**
      self .outgoing→**select**(t:Transition | substates→ **includes**(t.target))→
        collect(effect)→**isEmpty**()) **and**

```
    -- exit action
    cs.exit→notEmpty implies (substates→includesAll(self.outgoing.target) and
        self.incoming→select(t:Transition | substates→includes(t.source))→
            collect( effect )→isEmpty())
post:
    let substates = cs.subvertex in
    substates→includes(s) and
    cs.outgoing→forAll(each:Transition | self.outgoing→select(t:Transition|
        t.sameLabel(each) and t.target = each.target))→isEmpty() and
    cs.do→notEmpty implies cs.do→isEmpty() and
    cs.entry→notEmpty implies self.outgoing→ select(t:Transition | substates→
        includes(t.target))→forAll(t:Transition | cs.entry.sameLabel(t.effect )) and
    cs.exit→notEmpty implies self.incoming→ select(t:Transition | substates→
        includes(t.source))→forAll(t:Transition | cs.exit.sameLabel(t.effect ))
```

To compare two transitions, an operation named *Same Label* was defined and is presented p. 148.

A.6   Move State out of Composite

```
State :: moveOutOf
pre:
    -- inner transitions
    self.container.exit→notEmpty() implies
        self.incoming→select(t:Transition| t.source <> self and
            self.container.allSubvertex()→includes(t.source))→
        forAll(t:Transition|t.effect .isEquivalentTo( self.container.exit )) and
    self.container.entry→notEmpty() implies
        self.outgoing→select(t:Transition| t.target <> self and
            self.container.allSubvertex()→includes(t.target))→
        forAll(t:Transition|t.effect .isEquivalentTo( self.container.entry )) and
    -- outer transitions
    self.container.exit→notEmpty() implies self.outgoing→select(t:Transition|
        self.container.allSubVertex()→excludes(t.target))→forAll(t:Transition|
        t.effect →isEmpty) and
    self.container.entry→notEmpty() implies self.incoming→select(t:Transition|
        self.container.allSubVertex()→excludes(t.source))→forAll(t:Transition|
        t.effect →isEmpty) and
    self.container.do→notEmpty() implies self.do→isEmpty()
post:
    let cs = self.container→select(s:State| s = self@pre.container)→first() in (
    cs→notEmpty and
    -- composite outgoing transitions
    cs.outgoing→forAll(t:Transition | self.outgoing→
        exists(ot:Transition| ot.target = t.target and ot.sameLabel(t))) and
    -- initial pseudo substate
    self@pre.incoming.source→exists(s:State| s.oclIsKind(Pseudostate) and
        s.kind = #initial) implies (cs.incoming→isEmpty() and not cs.subvertex→
            exists(s:State| s.oclIsKind(Pseudostate) and s.kind = #initial) and
                self@pre.container.incoming→forAll(t:Transition| self.incoming→
                    exists(ot:Transition| ot.source = t.source and ot.sameLabel(t)))) and
    -- ex inner incoming/outgoing
    cs.exit→notEmpty() implies self.incoming→select(t:Transition| cs.allSubVertex→
        includes(t.source)).effect →isEmpty() and
    cs.entry→notEmpty() implies self.outgoing→select(t:Transition| cs.allSubVertex→
        includes(t.target )).effect →isEmpty() and
    -- ex outer incoming/outgoing
    cs.exit→notEmpty() implies self.outgoing→select(t:Transition| cs.allSubVertex→
        exludes(t.target )).effect →forAll(a:Action| a.isEquivalentTo(cs.exit )) and
    cs.entry→notEmpty() implies self.incoming→select(t:Transition| cs.allSubVertex→
        exludes(t.source )).effect →forAll(a:Action| a.isEquivalentTo(cs.entry )) and
    cs.do→notEmpty() implies self.do.isEquivalentTo(cs.do))
```

A.7 Same Label

Transition :: sameLabel(t:Transition)
post:
result = self . effect .isEquivalentTo(t. effect) **and**
    self . trigger .isEquivalentTo(t. trigger) **and**
    self .guard.isEquivalentTo(t.guard)

UML Support for Designing Software Systems as a Composition of Design Patterns

Sherif M. Yacoub[1] and Hany H. Ammar[2]

[1] Hewlett-Packard Labs, 1501 Page Mill, MS 1L-15,
Palo Alto, CA 94304, USA
`sherif_yacoub@hp.com`
[2] Computer Science and Electrical Engineering Department, West Virginia University
Morgantown, WV 26506, USA
`hammar@wvu.edu`

Abstract. Much of the research work on design patterns has primarily focused on discovering and documenting patterns. Design patterns promise early reuse benefits at the design stage. To reap the benefits of deploying these proven design solutions, we need to develop techniques to construct applications using patterns. These techniques should define a composition mechanism by which patterns can be integrated and deployed in the design of software applications. Versatile design models should be used to model the patterns themselves as well as their composition. In this paper, we describe an approach called *Pattern-Oriented Analysis and Design* (POAD) that utilizes UML modeling capabilities to compose design patterns at various levels of abstractions. In POAD, the internal details of the pattern structure are hidden at high design levels (pattern views) and are revealed at lower design levels (class views). We define three hierarchical traceable logical views based on UML models for developing pattern-oriented designs; namely the *Pattern-Level* view, the *Pattern Interfaces* view, and the *Detailed Pattern-Level* view. The discussion is illustrated by a case study of building a framework for feedback control systems.

Keywords: Pattern-Oriented Design, Design Patterns, and Pattern Composition.

1 Introduction

Patterns are reusable good-quality design practices that have proven useful in the design of software applications [2,11]. Patterns can help in leveraging reuse to the design level because they provide a common vocabulary of designs and they are proven design units from which more complex applications can be built. Much work has focused on documenting patterns [e.g. 2,11,12,16]. Other work is concerned with applying these reusable designs in constructing applications [e.g. 3,10,14,15]. We can generally classify design approaches that utilize patterns as:

1. Adhoc. A design pattern records a solution and forces and consequences of applying this solution. However, this is not usually sufficient to systematically develop

M. Gogolla and C. Kobryn (Eds.): UML 2001, LNCS 2185, pp. 149-165, 2001.

applications using patterns. For instance, the coincidental use of a *Strategy* pattern [2] in the implementation of a control application is not a systematic approach to deploy patterns. This is simply because there is no process to guide the development and to integrate the pattern with other design artifacts.

2. *Systematic*. A systematic approach to design with patterns goes further beyond just applying a certain pattern. Systematic approaches can be classified as:

a) *Pattern Languages*. A pattern language provides a set of patterns that solve problems in a specific domain. Pattern languages not only document the patterns themselves but also the relationships between these patterns. They imply the process to apply the language to completely solve a specific set of design problems.

b) *Development processes*. A systematic development process defines a pattern composition approach, analysis and design steps, design models, and tools to auto-mate the development steps. Such development process produces consistent designs each time the process steps are conducted.

We are concerned here with systematic development processes because they are the way to repeatable software design practice. To improve the practice of *systematically* deploying design patterns, we need to define methodologies to construct applications using patterns and support these methodologies with appropriate modeling languages. In this paper, we discuss a process to develop pattern-oriented applications using UML modeling capabilities. Specifically, we discuss using UML in the Pattern-Oriented Analysis and Design (POAD) process [10,17,31]. POAD uses design patterns as building blocks. The design of an application is built by gluing together these con-struction fragments and defining dependencies and collaboration between participating patterns. To make this approach availing, we need to define modeling artifacts that support its automation. Applications developed using this approach are object-oriented in nature. Thus, the Unified Modeling Language [1,13] is used in each step.

In this paper, we discuss UML support for modeling design patterns and developing pattern-oriented designs. We show how to use UML modeling capabilities and the POAD process to develop logical design views that capture relationship between pat-terns while hiding details not utilized directly in the design. We then show how to use these views to overlap participants of patterns to produce a denser and a more pro-found class diagram. To illustrate the application of the proposed models and process, we use a case study of building a framework for feedback control systems.

2   Stringing versus Overlapping Patterns

"It is possible to make buildings by stringing together patterns in a rather loose way. A building made like this, is an assembly of patterns. It is not dense. It is not profound. But it is also possible to put patterns together in such a way that many patterns overlap in the same physical space: the building is very dense; it has many meanings captured in small space; and through this density, it becomes profound."[7]

In the field of civil engineering, Alexander *et.al.* discuss techniques for composing patterns as they experienced in making buildings. They compare two approaches: stringing and overlapping patterns. Many of these principles apply to the design of software systems as well. Inspired by Alexander's approaches to make buildings, consider the two approaches to build software applications using design patterns:

1)   *Stringing patterns.* In this design approach, patterns are glued together to compose an application design. The glue here could simply be UML relationships between patterns as packages (for example dependency between packages) or UML relationships between participants of the patterns (for example UML association, dependency, etc. between classes of one pattern and classes of another pattern). The design is a loose assembly of patterns because it is made by simply stringing patterns and using all the internal participants of a pattern as independent design constructs. The design is neither dense nor profound. It is not dense because we end up with a design that has a large population of classes. It is not profound because many classes have trivial responsibilities. The reason is that the design of many of these patterns has several classes that are only responsible for forwarding to other classes, acting as an interface to the internal design of the pattern, or representing a class that is intended to be part of the external system design not the internal design of the pattern (i.e. a client class of a pattern).

2)   *Overlapping patterns.* This approach advocates that many patterns should overlap in the same logical design. Overlapping means that a class, as a participant in one pattern, could be at the same time a participant of another pattern in the same application design. For instance, consider gluing together the *Strategy* and the *Observer* patterns [2]. Overlapping these two patterns could mean that the abstract `Strategy` class of the *Strategy* pattern plays the role of abstract `Subject` class in the *Observer* pattern. The designer will use one application class to play the role of both participants. As a result, the design is dense and it becomes more profound. It is dense because we end up having fewer classes in the application design than the total number of classes in the patterns used to develop that design. It is profound because each class carries out several responsibilities.

With the overlapping patterns approach, we gain the advantage of having less number of classes in the application design than the one produced by stringing patterns. However, there is one salient disadvantage. The pattern boundary is lost and patterns become hard to trace. With stringing patterns, we can always identify the pattern by circling the classes that implement it. When circling the classes of a pattern in the overlapping pattern design, we end up with so many intersecting circles.

As an example, consider an application in which the designer has decided to use the *Reactor* pattern [8] and the *Composite* pattern [2]. We will use these two patterns in the sequel to illustrate the difference between the overlapping and stringing approaches. The class diagram model for each of the two patterns is shown in Figure 1.

The *Reactor* pattern is a robust design for a system that receives events, manages a set of event handlers, and dispatches the event to the appropriate handler. It consists of: the abstract `EventHandler` class which is the interface that all the concrete event handlers have to comply with; the `Reactor` class which is the class responsible for scheduling events and dispatching them to event handlers according to the type of the event; and finally the `ConcreteEventHandler` classes which implement the `EventHandler` interface.

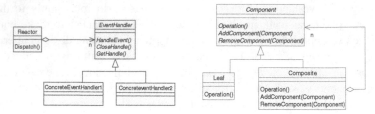

Fig. 1. The class diagram for a) *Reactor* pattern, and b) *Composite* pattern

The *Composite* pattern is a robust design for a system that provides a unique interface to a complex structure of objects that could be simple or composites. It is composed of: the `Component` class which is the interface for the structure; the `Leaf` class which implements the `Component` interface but does not contain other objects of type `Component`; and finally the `Composite` class that implements the `Component` interface and consists of other components that it manages.

Consider the case where we want to use these two patterns in designing a reactive system. When using a *Reactor* pattern, we might find that the handlers for the application specific events are not simple objects; instead, they could be complex objects containing other objects that react as well to the events. Hence, we decide to use a *Composite* pattern for the handlers. Now, how do we glue these two pattern?

The first solution is to string the two patterns together by establishing a relationship between the `Component` class of the *Composite* pattern and the `EventHandler` class of the *Reactor* pattern. By stringing the two patterns, we develop the design shown in Figure 2, which contains all the classes of the two patterns.

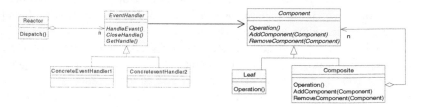

Fig. 2. Stringing the Reactor and Composite patterns

The design in Figure 2 is not profound because it assumes that the handlers use or reference composite components while in reality the handlers *are* the composite components.

The second solution is to overlap the two patterns. We overlap the `EventHandler` of the *Reactor* pattern and the `Component` class of the *Composite* pattern and both roles are integrated in one class call it `EventHandlerComponent`. This class will have the methods from both classes. Consequently, the concrete event handlers become concrete classes derived from the `EventHandlerComponent` class. The design of the overlapped pattern design is shown in Figure 3.

The question that rises here is: are these two approaches independent? Must we construct a design that is either a sparse assembly or a condensed overlap of patterns? Can we use both?

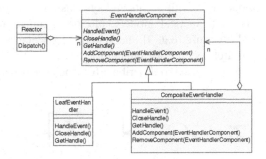

Fig. 3. Overlapping the *Reactor* and *Composite* patterns

Clearly, the first approach, assembling and stringing patterns, is avoided by many designers. This can be attributed to the perceivable disadvantages of simply assembling patterns to produce designs. It is, however, an easy approach to practice. The stringing pattern approach provides good traceability from high-level designs, in terms of patterns, to lower-level designs, in terms of classes. We can simply encapsulate the classes of a pattern in one package or a template package [5], which will become the high level view and use the pattern classes in the class diagram model which will become the low level design.

The Pattern-Oriented Analysis and Design (POAD) approach reaps benefits from both worlds; the stringing and overlapping patterns worlds. It makes use of the simplicity and traceability of the stringing-patterns approach and the density and profoundness of the overlapping-patterns approach. In POAD, the two approaches are not independent and in fact they could be integrated in one process. POAD starts by assembling patterns at a higher level of abstraction using the stringing approach, provides models to trace the patterns to lower levels of abstraction, and then allows the designer to integrate lower level classes to produce dense and profound designs.

3   Pattern-Oriented Analysis and Design with UML

In this section, we discuss a pattern oriented analysis and design process that utilizes UML modeling capabilities at various development steps. The following subsections describe each step with application to the development of a feedback control framework. Feedback systems are commonly modeled using block diagrams. The design framework that we develop in this paper is based on design patterns as building constructs. The framework is documented at various design levels using UML models and is reusable as an initial phase in designing feedback control applications.

3.1 Analysis

The purpose of this step is to analyze the application requirements and decide on the set of design patterns that will be used in designing the system. To design a feedback control system, the specification and description of the system configuration and its components must be put into a form amenable for analysis and design. Three basic representations (models) of components and systems are used extensively in the study of control systems: mathematical models, block diagrams, and signal-flow graphs. Referring to control literature [e.g. 9], the generic block diagram of feedback systems represents an initial architecture documentation to start with. Figure 4 illustrates the block diagram that is often used to describe a feedback control system.

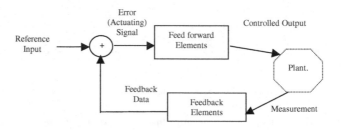

Fig. 4. Block diagram for a feedback control system

The portion of a system to be controlled is usually called the *Plant*. An output variable is adjusted as required by the error signal. This error signal is the difference between the system response as measured by the feedback element and the reference signal, which represent the desired system response. Generally, a controller is required to process the error signal such that a certain control strategy will be applied. Using the generic block diagram of a closed loop control system, the system is decomposed into: a *feedforward* component that processes the error data and applies a control algorithm to the plant; a *feedback* component that measures data from the plant, processes it, and provides the feedback data; an *error calculation* component that compares the input and feedback data and produces the error; and the *plant* that is an external component on which control is applied and from which measurements are taken.

3.2 Pattern Selection

We analyze the responsibilities and the functionalities of each component and identify candidate patterns that could provide a design solution for each component. In doing so, we have considered the design problem that we want to solve and match it to the solution provided by general purpose design patterns [e.g. 2, 11, 12]:

1. The *feedforward* component implements some sort of a control strategy. The change in the control strategy should be flexible and hidden from any calls and invocations form any other component. For example, the *feedforward* component should provide the same interface to the rest of the components in the system while the framework can provide the flexibility to plug in and plug out different control strategies. If we consider this as the design problem that we want to solve

and search for patterns whose intent is to solve similar problems, we find that a *Strategy* pattern [2, pp315] is a good candidate for this task.

2. The *feedback* component receives measurements and applies a feedback control strategy. It feeds the result to the error calculation component. The measurement unit observes and measures data from the plant and feeds it to the feedback branch. Thus, measurement observations can be communicated to the feedback controller using the *Observer* pattern [2, pp293]. Thus we can use the *Observer* pattern to loosen the dependency between the objects doing the plant observation and those actually doing the feedback control. The measured data is fed to the feedback control strategy, which - similar to the *feedforward* component- should provide flexibility to plug in and plug out different feedback control strategies. This can be implemented using another *Strategy* pattern [2, pp315].

3. In the *error calculation* component, the feedback controller notifies the error calculation unit with the feedback data. The feedback controller can be viewed as the subject that notifies the error calculator with changes in the feedback data. Error calculation is done whenever feedback data becomes available, at that moment, this data is compared with the persistent input data. Thus, an *Observer* pattern [2, pp293] can implement this behavior.

4. If we examine the data manipulated in the feedback system, we find that the system handles: measurement data that is measured from the plant; feedback data that is the result of processing the measured data by the feedback element; and finally the error data that is the result of processing the feedback data and the input data. Data of different types need to be exchanged between the framework components. We can use a *Blackboard* pattern (a modified version of the blackboard patterns in [24, 11]) for managing the system repository.

In choosing these patterns, we consider how the pattern solves the design problem and the intent of the pattern. In summary, a *Strategy* pattern is selected for the *feedforward* component, an *Observer* and a *Strategy* pattern are selected for the *feedback* component, an *Observer* pattern is selected for the *error calculation* component, and a *Blackboard* pattern is selected as the system repository. In this small example, it was obvious which patterns could be used. In other complex example, the analyst could use UML use cases and sequence diagrams to understand the functionality required by each component.

3.3 Constructing *Pattern-Level* Diagrams

In this step, we create instances of the selected patterns and identify the relationships between these instances. As a result, a *Pattern-Level* diagram of the system is developed.

First, we create pattern instances. In the previous step, we have selected to use two *Strategy* patterns one in the *feedforward* component and the other in the *feedback* component. Thus, we use the instances *FeedforwardStrategy* and *FeedbackStrategy* of type *Strategy* pattern in the design of the *feedforward* and *feedback* components respectively. We have also selected to use two *Observer* patterns one for the *feedback* component and the other for the *error calculation* component. Thus, we use a *FeedbackObserver* instance of type *Observer* pattern to observe and measure data from the plant and an *ErrorObserver* instance of type *Observer* pattern to calculate the error. We use a *Blackboard* of type *Blackboard* pattern to manage the system data repository. This is just giving domain specific names to abstract patterns types (templates).

Second, we define dependency relationships between pattern instances. The *FeedbackObserver* uses the *FeedbackStrategy* to apply a feedback control algorithm, which in-turn, uses the *ErrorObserver* to calculate the error. The *ErrorObserver* uses the *FeedforwardStrategy* to apply a forward control algorithm. The *Blackboard* is used by all patterns to store and retrieve data.

Finally, we use the pattern instances and their relationships to construct the *Pattern-Level* diagram as shown in Figure 5. We use UML stereotypes to show the type of the pattern instance.

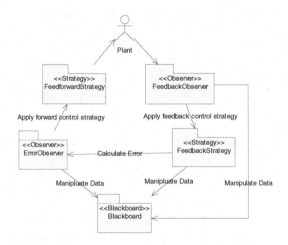

Fig. 5. A *Pattern-Level* diagram for feedback control systems

The product of this process is the *Pattern-Level* diagram of the framework. It describes the architecture of a feedback system using design patterns, which explains why the names "*Pattern-Oriented Analysis and Design*" is used. During the design or design refinement phases we could discover that a selected pattern has limitations or impacts on other design aspects. In this case, the designer would revisit this design level to choose another pattern, replace previous choices, or create a new pattern dependency or a new uses relationship.

3.4 Constructing *Pattern-Level with Interfaces* Diagram

In this step, the dependency relationship between patterns in the *Pattern-Level* view is further traced to lower level design relationships between pattern interfaces.

First, we declare interfaces for the patterns used in each *Pattern-Level* diagram (only one diagram for the feedback system). The *Strategy* pattern has the class `Context` as the interface to the encapsulated control strategy. The *Observer* has two interfaces that allow coordinating the subject observed with its observer. These interfaces are implemented by the `notify()` interface in the subject and the `update()` interface in the observer. The *Blackboard* pattern has the interfaces to get and store data in the repository, these interfaces are implemented by the getData() and setData() methods. Then, we identify the relationship between pattern interfaces by translating all dependency relationships between patterns in a *Pattern-Level* diagram to relationships between interface classes and/or interface operations. The product of this process is the *Pattern-Level with Interfaces* diagram. Figure 6 illustrates the *Pattern-Level with Interface* diagram for the feedback control framework.

As an example consider the relationship between the *FeedbackObserver* and the *FeedbackStrategy* pattern instances in the *Pattern-Level* view. The relationship between these two patterns at the *Pattern-Level* view is that the *FeedbackObserver* uses the *FeedbackStrategy* to apply a feedback control strategy whenever the measurement data is ready. The interfaces of the *FeedbackObserver* are the Update() and the notify() interface methods. The interface of the *FeedbackStrategy* is the Context interface class. Thus the relationship between these two patterns is translated to a relationship between the Update() interface of the earlier and the Context interface of the latter. Similarly, all pattern relationships of Figure 5 are translated to relationships between the pattern interfaces in Figure 6.

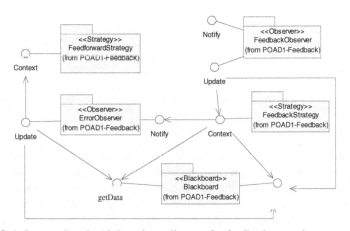

Fig. 6. A *Pattern-Level with Interfaces* diagram for feedback control systems

3.5 Constructing *Detailed Pattern-Level* Diagrams

To construct the *Detailed Pattern-Level* diagram, we express the internals (i.e. participants) of each instantiated pattern in the *Pattern-Level with Interfaces* diagram. Since we have used pervasive design patterns in developing the feedback control framework, their structure can be found in the literature. For example, the class diagram model for the *Strategy* and *Observer* patterns is documented in [2]. Figure 7 illustrates the *Detailed Pattern-Level* diagram for the feedback pattern-oriented framework. Note that we do not take any additional design decisions in this step. With the appropriate tool support Figure 7 is a direct generation from the *Pattern-Level with Interfaces* diagram by simply retrieving the class diagram model from a pattern database.

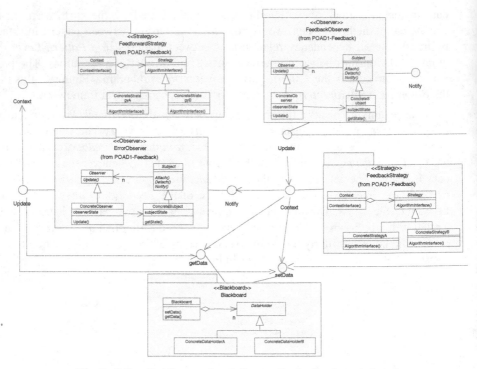

Fig. 7. A *Detailed Pattern-Level* diagram for feedback control systems

3.6 Instantiating Pattern Internals

In this step, we add domain specific nature to the *Detailed Pattern-Level* diagrams by renaming internal pattern classes according to the application domain, choosing names for pattern participants that are meaningful in the application context, and defining domain specific names for operations in the patterns. Due to space limitation, we will illustrate few examples only in the sequel.

Instantiating the *ErrorObserver* Pattern

The error calculation component consists of the *ErrorObserver* pattern, which is composed of:

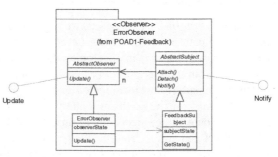

Fig. 8. Instantiating the *ErrorObserver* pattern

- **AbstractObserver.** An updating interface for objects that are notified of changes in the subject.
- **AbstractSubject.** An interface for attaching and detaching observers. It knows about its observers that ought to be notified of a subject's change.
- **ErrorObserver.** It is a concrete observer that maintains a reference to the FeedbackSubject, reads the feedback data after being processed by the feedback strategy, analyzes the feedback data with respect to the reference input data, and stores the error in the blackboard. It implements AbstractObserver update interface.
- **FeedbackSubject.** It is a concrete subject that sends notification to the concrete observers of new data received from the feedback component.

Instantiating the *FeedbackObserver* Pattern

The *FeedbackObserver* is used in the feedback component and is composed of:

- **AbstractObserver** and **AbstractSubject.** They play an interface role similar to that of the **ErrorObserver** pattern.
- **MeasurementSubject.** It receives measurement notifications from the plant and notifies its observer **FeedbackObserver** that a measurement is ready.
- **FeedbackObserver.** When notified by changes in the plant (through the MeasurementSubject), it pulls the data identifier from the subject (using the pull mode of the *Observer* pattern) and invokes the feedback controller to process the measured data.

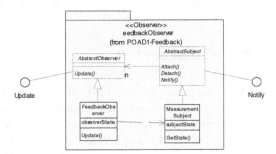

Fig. 9. Instantiating the *FeedbackObserver* pattern

Instantiating the *FeedbackStrategy* Pattern

The *FeedbackStrategy* pattern is composed of:

- **Feedback.** It is the context of the feedback control strategy. It is configured with a feedback control strategy object through a reference to an FBAbstractController.
- **FBAbstractController:** It is the interface for all feedback control strategies. The Feedback uses this interface to call the feedback concrete algorithm.
- **FBControlStrategyA,** and **FBControlStrategyB.** They represent concrete implementations for feedback control strategies.

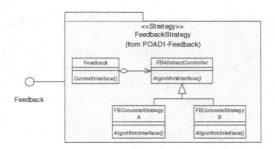

Fig. 10. Instantiating the *FeedbackStrategy* pattern

The `FeedbackObserver` invokes the control routine of the `Feedback` that applies the feedback control strategy required from the component. The `Feedback` class interacts with the `FeedbackSubject` of the observer pattern in the error calculation component and invokes its `notify()` procedure. This establishes the link between the feedback component and the error calculation component.

Two features can help the designer keep track of the patterns. First, the three models *Pattern-Level* diagram, the *Pattern-Level with Interfaces* diagram, and the *Detailed Pattern-Level* diagram provide a documentation of the framework as a composition of patterns. Second, with the appropriate tool support, the *renaming* process is not an *editing* process. In editing we simply change the names and the old names are lost. But in the renaming process of a class, the tool support for POAD should provide a system with memory to keep the history of the changed name specifically in pattern instantiation.

3.7 Developing an Initial Class Diagram

From the *Detailed Pattern-Level* diagram, we use pattern interfaces and the instantiated details of pattern internals to construct a UML class diagram. The class diagram that is developed at this phase is an initial step to develop the static design model of the pattern-oriented framework. Figure 11 illustrates the class diagram for the framework. It can be recognized that the patterns are still notable in the class diagram as shown by the dotted boxes around the classes. As part of POAD, all the models in Figure 6 through Figure 11 are saved as analysis and design models. It is the role of a tool support to preserve these models and provide the necessary traceability.

The class diagram obtained from gluing patterns together at the high-level design is neither dense nor profound because we just stringed the patterns together. It has many replicated abstract classes due to the fact that we used multiple instances of the same pattern. For example we used the *FeedbackStrategy* and the *FeedforwardStrategy* instances of type *Strategy* pattern. It also has many classes with trivial responsibilities because many classes are just doing forwarding of messages to internal participants of the pattern. In the following step we use reduction and grouping mechanisms to optimize the UML design diagrams obtained initially in the previous step.

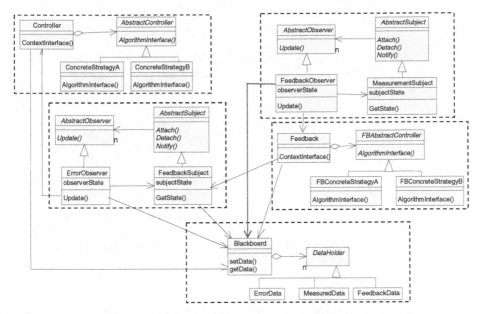

Fig. 11. The initial class diagram of the feedback design framework

3.8 Design Refinement

The complexity of the framework can be reduced by eliminating replicated abstract classes. A pattern has one or more abstract classes. Since the same pattern type is used in more than one instance, we expect to find similar abstract classes. For example, the *Observer* pattern is used in the feedback component and in the error component. The classes `AbstractObserver` and `AbstractSubject` are replicated. Similarly, the abstract class `AbstractController` of the strategy pattern used in the *feedforward* and *feedback* components. Therefore, the replicated classes are eliminated and only one common version of the abstract classes is used. This step is not usually applicable to all designs because the interfaces offered by abstract classes may substantially differ and hence we might not be able to merge these two abstract classes. For the feedback control system this was possible. In general, this is an activity that the designer might consider doing as part of the development process.

More optimization in class usage can be achieved by merging concrete classes together depending on their interaction and responsibilities. This step mainly depends on the framework designer skills. From Figure 11, we find that the classes `FeedbackObserver`, `FeedbackSubject` and `Feedback` perform highly related functions, which are summarized as receiving measurement notification, applying control strategy, and notifying the error component that the feedback data is ready. Instead of implementing a primitive function in each class, the three classes are merged into one class `FeedbackSubjectObserver`, which carries out the responsibilities of the three classes. Figure 12 illustrates the refined class diagram of the framework

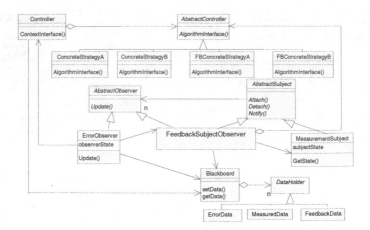

Fig. 12. The refined class diagram for the feedback design framework

It could become difficult to identify the patterns at this level because at this level we are using domain specific classes. This problem has always been recognized in many techniques that directly use patterns at the class diagram level without developing higher level design models: patterns are lost and are not traceacble [25,26]. POAD has one particular advantage. When applying POAD, we keep all the models developed through out the development lifecycle. These models are traceable bottom-up from the class level to the pattern level and top-down from the pattern level to the class level.

As an example of top-down traceability, we can identify the pattern participants in the above class diagram. For example, *FeedforwardStrategy:Strategy,* is composed of the classes `Controller`, `AbstractController`, `ControlStrategyA`, `ControlStrategyB`. Another example is *ErrorObserver:Observer,* which is composed of the classes `AbstractSubject`, `AbstractObser-ver`, `FeedbackSubjectObserver` (a concrete subject) , and `ErrorObserver` (a concrete observer). As an example of bottom-up traceability, we find that the class `FeedbackSubjectObserver` is a common participant in multiple patterns. It is the observer for `MeasurementSubject` in the `FeedbackObserver`. It acts as a controller in the `FeedbackStrategy` that invokes a concrete control strategy to be applied on the `FeedbackData`. It acts as a subject for the `ErrorObserver`.

4   Related Work

Several successful experiences have reported on the advantages of using patterns in designing applications [15, 27]. These experiences do not follow a systematic method to develop applications using patterns. Systematic development using patterns utilizes a composition mechanism to glue patterns together at the design level.

Generally, we categorize composition mechanisms as behavioral and structural compositions. Behavioral composition approaches are concerned with objects as elements that play several roles in various patterns. These approaches are also known in the OO literature as interaction-oriented or responsibility-driven design [28]. Reenskaug [29,30] developed the Object Oriented Role Analysis and Software Synthesis method (OORASS, later called OOram). The method uses a role model that abstracts the traditional object model. Riehle [18] uses role diagrams for pattern composition. Riehle focuses mainly on developing composite patterns, which are compositions of patterns whose integration shows a synergy that makes the composition more than just the sum of its parts. The approach by Jan Bosch [26] uses design patterns and frameworks as architectural fragments. Each fragment is composed of roles and components that are merged with other roles to produce application designs. Lauder et. al. [20] take a visual specification approach to design patterns. They utilize constraint diagrams that are developed by Kent [19] together with UML diagrams.

Structural composition approaches build a design by gluing pattern structures that are modeled as class diagrams. Structural composition focuses more on the actual realization of the design rather than abstractions as role models. Behavioral composition techniques such as roles [30,18] leave several choices to the designer with less guidelines on how to continue to the class design phase. Keller and Schauer [21,22] address the problem of software composition at the design level using design components. Their approach and ours share the same objective of creating software designs that are based on well-defined and proven design patterns packaged into tangible, customizable, and composable design components. Larsen [23] takes a structural approach to glue patterns by mapping the participants of a pattern into implementation components. POAD shares the same concept of defining interfaces for patterns.

Xavier Castellani and Stephan Y. Liao [4] propose an application development process that focuses on the reuse of object-oriented application design. D'Souze et. al. [5,6] define a component-based approach to develop software that is heavily based on interfaces at both the design and implementation level. D'Souza's approach is general in addressing software development issues such as composing physical components, distribution of components, and business driven solutions, etc. Modeling patterns as template packages is similar to the pattern level view developed in earlier development models used in POAD.

5 Conclusion and Future Work

The work in this paper stems from the need to develop systematic approaches to glue patterns in the development of software applications and to develop pervasive pattern-level views that document a design as a composition of patterns. Patterns tend to be lost and blurred at the implementation and low-level design phases. The proposed POAD process and the associated UML models provide a solution for this problem. We discuss the support of the Unified Modeling Language to model pattern-oriented designs. We illustrate the use of UML modeling capabilities to develop three logical views, *Pattern-Level*, *Pattern-Level with Interfaces*, and *Detailed Pattern-Level* to facilitate the process of designing with patterns. The three views are based on the principle of pattern interfaces and support hierarchical traceable designs where high-level views of collaborating patterns are traced to lower level views of collaborating classes. One challenge to the POAD approach is how to analyze the user requirements for the purpose of selecting patterns. Moreover, we did not address the problem of how patterns can be combined with parts of design that are not expressed as patterns. Several applications may include application classes or frameworks as building blocks. Since we are using UML models, we expect that other modeling construct could be directly integrated with POAD models.

References

1.   Booch, G., Rumbaugh, J., Jacobson, I.: The Unified Modeling Language User Guide. Addison-Wesley, 1999.
2.   Gamma, E., Helm, R., Johnson, R., Vlissides, J.: Design Patterns: Elements of Object-Oriented Software. Addison-Wesley, 1995.
3.   Vlissides, J.: Pattern Hatching, Design Patterns Applied. Addison-Wesley, 1998.
4.   Castellani, X., and S. Y. Liao, "Development Process for the Creation and Reuse of Object-Oriented Generic Applications and Components", *Journal of Object Oriented Programming*, June 1998, Vol 11, No.3, pp24-31
5.   D'Souze, D., and A. Wills. Objects, Components, and Frameworks with UML. Addison Wesley 1999.
6.   D'Souza, D. "Interface Specification, Refinement, and Design with UML/Catalysis", *Journal of Object Oriented Programming, June 1998, pp12-18*
7.   Alexander, C., S. Inshikawa, M. Silverstiein, M. Jacobson, I. Fiksdahl-king, and S. Angel, "A Pattern Language", Oxford University Press, New York, 1977
8.   Schmidt, D. : Reactor: An Object Behavioral Pattern for Concurrent Event Demultiplexing and Event Handler Dispatching. In Pattern Languages of Program Design, Coplien, J. and Schmidt, D. (eds.), 1995, Chapter 29, pp529-545.
9.   Distefano, J., A. Stubberud, and I. Williams, "Feedback and Control Systems", McGraw-Hill, 1990
10.   Yacoub, S., Ammar, H.: Towards Pattern Oriented Frameworks. The Journal of Object Oriented Programming, JOOP, January 2000.
11.   Buschmann, F., Meunier, R., Rohnert, H., Sommerlad, P., Stal, M.: Pattern-Oriented Software Architecture - A System of Patterns. Addison-Wesley, 1996.
12.   Martin, R., Riehle, D., Buschmann, F. (eds.): Pattern Language of Program Design 3. Addison-Wesley, 1998.
13.   The Unified Modeling Language homepage. http://www.omg.com/technology/uml
14.   Pree, W.: Design Patterns for Object-Oriented Software Development. Addison-Wesley 1995.
15.   Garlow, J., Holmes, C., Mowbary, T.: Applying Design Patterns in UML. Rose Architect, Vol 1, No. 2, Winter 1999
16.   Fowler, M.: Analysis Patterns. Addison Wesley, 1997.
17.   Yacoub, S. and H. Ammar. Pattern-Oriented Analysis and Design. Addison Wesley, to appear 2002.
18.   Riehle, D. Composite Design Patterns. *Proceedings of Object-Oriented Programming, Systems, Languages and Applications*, OOPSLA'97, pp218-228, Atlanta, October 1997.
19.   Kent, S. Constraint Diagrams: Visualizing Invariants in Object-Oriented Models. *Proceedings of Object-Oriented Programming, Systems, Languages and Applications*, OOPSLA'97, Atlanta Georgia USA, October 1997.

20. Lauder, A., and S. Kent. Precise Visual Specification of Design Patterns. *Proceedings of the 12th European Conference on Object Oriented Programming*, ECOOP'98, pp114-134, Brussels, Belgium, July 1998.

21. Keller, R., and R. Schauer. Design Components: Towards Software Composition at the Design Level. *Proceedings of 20th International Conference on Software Engineering*, ICSE'98, pp302-311, Kyoto, Japan, April 19-25, 1998.

22. Schauer, R., and R. Keller. Pattern Visualization for Software Comprehension. *Proceedings of the 6th International Workshop on Program Comprehension*, (IWPC'98), pages 4-12, Ischia, Italy, June 1998.

23. Larsen, G. Designing Component-Based Frameworks using Patterns in the UML. *Communications of the ACM*, 42(10):38:45, October 1999.

24. Rogers, G., "Framework-Based Software Development in C++", Prentice Hall 1997

25. Soukup, J.. Implementing Patterns. Chapter 20, pp395-415, in *Pattern Language of Program Design*, Addison-Wesley, 1995.

26. Bosch, J. Specifying Frameworks and Design Patterns as Architecture Fragments. *Proceedings of Technology of Object-Oriented Languages and Systems*, China, Sept. 22-25 1998.

27. Srinivasan, S., and J. Vergo. Object-Oriented Reuse: Experience in Developing a Framework for Speech Recognition Applications. *Proceedings of 20th International Conference on Software Engineering*, ICSE'98, pp322-330, Kyoto, Japan, April 19-25, 1998.

28. Wirfs-Brock, R., and B. Wilkerson. Object-Oriented Design: A Responsibility-Driven Approach. *Proceedings of Object-Oriented Programming, Systems, Languages and Applications*, OOPSLA'89, pp71-75, October 1989.

29. Reenskaug, T.OORASS: Seamless Support for the Creation and Maintenance of Object Oriented Systems. *Journal of Object Oriented Programming*, 5(6):27-41, October 1992.

30. Reenskaug, T.. Working with Objects: The OOram Software Engineering Method. Manning Publishing Co., ISBN 1-884777-10-4, 1996.

31. Yacoub S., and H. Ammar, "UML Support for Constructional Design Patterns", in the special issue of *The Object* journal on Object Modeling, Hermes Science Publications, B. Henderson-Sellers and F. Barbier (eds.) 2000.

Integrating the ConcernBASE Approach with SADL

Valentin Crettaz, Mohamed Mancona Kandé, Shane Sendall, and Alfred Strohmeier

Swiss Federal Institute of Technology Lausanne (EPFL)
Software Engineering Laboratory
1015 Lausanne EPFL, Switzerland
{Valentin.Crettaz, Mohamed.Kande, Shane.Sendall, Alfred.Strohmeier}@epfl.ch

Abstract. We describe ConcernBASE, a UML-based approach that is an instantiation of the IEEE's Conceptual Framework (Std 1471) for describing software architectures. We show how the approach supports advanced separation of concerns in software architecture by allowing one to identify and define multiple viewpoints, concern spaces and views of an architecture. Our work focuses on integrating the ConcernBASE approach with the Structural Architecture Description Language (SADL) in order to make the verification capabilities of SADL available to those who develop in UML. The result is a UML profile for structural description of software architecture. The paper also presents a prototype tool that supports this UML profile.

Keywords: Software Architecture, Unified Modeling Language, UML, Structural Architecture Description, SADL, Advanced Separation of Concerns.

1 Introduction

The fact that numerous software systems are becoming increasingly complex, distributed, and deployed in heterogeneous environments leads us to think that modeling the software architecture of a system is a very important part of the development life cycle. But, software architecture modeling should not be seen as a separate activity that is limited to a particular "phase" of the software life cycle, as one might deduce from the limited scope of existing architecture description languages (ADLs) [7][8][9]. ADLs have the advantage of being mathematically defined and deeply rooted in formal methods, but also the disadvantage of lacking the flexibility for modeling systems from various viewpoints. In addition, due to their formal nature they can be hard to understand and to use [2].

Unlike ADLs, the Unified Modeling Language (UML) is a widely used general-purpose language, which provides a large number of well-known techniques and concepts for modeling various kinds of software artifacts from different perspectives. Unfortunately, UML, in its current state, is not sufficient for an explicit software architecture description [2][10][11]. To gain the benefit of software architecture description with UML, the core UML needs to natively define some key ADL-concepts as first-class modeling elements, such as connectors and styles.

In previous work, we proposed a UML-based approach to software architecture descriptions, which focused on extending the UML by incorporating key abstractions found in most existing ADLs into a profile [2].

This work has been integrated into a new approach called ConcernBASE[1]. ConcernBASE is centered around the principle of *multi-dimensional separation of concerns*

---

1. ConcernBASE stands for **Concern-B**ased and **A**rchitecture-centered **S**oftware **E**ngineering

M. Gogolla and C. Kobryn (Eds.): UML 2001, LNCS 2185, pp. 166–181, 2001.

(MDSOC). MDSOC is an advanced form of separation of concerns that allows one to identify and simultaneously separate multiple kinds of software concerns, including principles for composition and decomposition of those concerns [6]. However, unlike other approaches based on MDSOC [12], ConcernBASE uses the standard UML notation and addresses some fundamental limitations of UML for supporting software architecture descriptions.

The Structural Architecture Description Language (SADL) [4] has been developed to support the specification of structural aspects of complex software systems. Unlike other ADLs, e.g. Wright [13], it also focuses on the refinement of high-level system structures. In addition, SADL provides an assortment of tools that support both refinement and verification of different structural aspects of complex software.

This paper discusses how to map ConcernBASE architectural descriptions, written in UML, to SADL architectural descriptions, making available the verification capabilities of SADL tools for ConcernBASE. In addition, we present a UML-based tool that supports the ConcernBASE approach and its integration with SADL, and implements the UML profile for structural architectural descriptions.

The paper is organized as follows: section 2 briefly presents the ConcernBASE approach. Section 3 illustrates the application of the ConcernBASE approach on a compiler example, which is based on the reference model for compiler construction. Section 4 briefly presents the key concepts of SADL. Section 5 presents a method for translating ConcernBASE models to SADL specifications. Section 6 gives a concise overview of the tool that fully supports the ConcernBASE approach. Finally, section 7 summarizes the paper and discusses future work.

2 The ConcernBASE Approach

ConcernBASE is a software architecture approach that aims at providing support for software (component) development and software (system) construction, by combining the capabilities of both MDSOC and UML. It addresses techniques for developing individual software components and particularly focuses on understanding, reasoning and specifying mechanisms for gluing those components together.

ConcernBASE is a UML-based instantiation of the IEEE's Recommended Practice for Architectural Description (Std 1471) [1], that is augmented with support for advanced separation of concerns [3]. Thus, it supports mechanisms to produce software architecture descriptions in a flexible and incremental way, allowing one to identify, separate, modularize and integrate different software artifacts based on various kinds of concerns. According to the IEEE Std 1471, *Concerns* are those interests which pertain to the system development, its operation or any other aspects that are critical or otherwise important to one or more stakeholders. Concerns include system considerations such as performance, reliability, security, distribution, and evolvability [1].

Throughout the approach, we take the premise that *software architecture is multidimensional*. That is, when constructing complex software, an architect represents the system in many different ways in order to be able to understand, communicate and reason about its high-level properties, from different perspectives or viewpoints. Each way of representing the system may be considered as a different view of the architecture of the system, that takes into account *multiple dimensions* of concern (i.e., different kinds of architectural concerns).

In the IEEE's conceptual framework for architectural description (IEEE Std-147), a *viewpoint* is a specification of the conventions for constructing and using a view. While this is an important and precise definition that helps understand how to separate different concerns, it does say how those concerns can be identified, encapsulated and represented in architectural views. In ConcernBASE, viewpoints are characterized by two essential architectural abstractions that we refer to as concern space and projection. *Concern space* represents a conceptual repository that contains all relevant concerns related to a particular viewpoint. It allows us to structure different concerns into different categories (dimensions), to specify the relationships between these categories and maintain changes in the concern structure. Thus, a concern space can be considered as a "multi-dimensional model of system considerations" that pertains to a software architect from a particular perspective. A *projection* defines the relationship between a viewpoint, a concern space and a view. It is an architectural abstraction that specifies how to transform a set of concerns (sub-concern space) into a specific representation (view) relative to a particular perspective (viewpoint). Different projections along different dimensions of concern result in different views. A *view* of the software architecture of a system is a partial architecture description of that system that may consist of one or architectural models. Finally, the *architecture description* of the whole system may be considered as a set of different architectural views.

Without the notion of concern space, the definition of a viewpoint language, as proposed by the IEEE Std-1471, can be very difficult, since it becomes quickly unclear what the viewpoint language should define. Once we have the notion of concern space, one can use some UML extensions mechanisms to define a UML profile that represents the viewpoint language. In this case, the concrete syntax and semantics of the concern space will be fixed by the UML profile.

To discuss the mapping between ConcernBASE and SADL, we briefly present a ConcernBASE structural viewpoint and SADL, then we describe the mapping between them. Finally, we discuss some issues related the tool support.

2.1 Structural Viewpoint

The structural viewpoint is a particular ConcernBASE viewpoint that specifies the rules for constructing and using some structural views of the architecture of system. In addition, it defines a structural concern space, a UML Profile for structural architecture description and specifies three kinds architectural projections: a static structure projection, a behavioral projection and a configuration projection. These projections allows one to create three corresponding views, which together build the architecture description of the system.

2.2 Structural Concern Space

The structural concern space is the most abstract representation of all significant concerns that are relative to the structural viewpoint. It focuses on what kind of architectural components, connectors, constraints and styles are needed to understand and reason about the system's structure. The structural concern space abstracts from many details of the system components and connectors and does not provide any information on how the communication among the architectural components is implemented or on the internal structure of those elements. A component represents a particular UML subsystem. Its type is defined by the UML stereotype <<archComponent>> that inherits properties of both a UML Class and a UML Package. In contrast, a connector represents a special kind of UML Collaboration, in which participant components are omitted. Instead, they are represented by connection points (their interactions points belong to the connector)[2].

2.3 Static View

The static view describes the static models of the components and connectors composing the system. *Computational components* represent subsystems, system-level reusable modules with well-defined interfaces, or plug-in capabilities[2]. A computational component is a locus of definition of some computation and data concerns, which usually do not crosscut the boundaries of a single subsystem or module. Some components may have internal structures that can be represented at subsystem or lower levels using a number of representation units. Thus, the representation units that compose a specific component must pertain to those computation and data concerns, which are modularized by the same component.

The UML Profile for SADL defined for ConcernBASE supports the specification of computation components by using a class-like notation. To visually distinguish computational components from other components, such as classes, the keyword <<computational>> or the computational icon (placed in the upper right hand corner of the class name compartment) are used. LexicalAnalyzer, shown in figure 3 is an example of a computational component.

The interface of a component is specified as a collection of several interface element types, each of which defines a logical interaction point between the component and its environment. The interface elements of a component can be of three different types: operational, signal or stream. An <<operational>> interface element type of a component describes a set of operations that can be required by or provided to other components, whereas a <<signal>> interface element type specifies a set of signals that can be sent to or received from other components. A <<stream>> interface element type enumerates a collection of streams that can be consumed by or produced to other components, as well as a set of quality of services to be guaranteed by those streams. There is a composition association between a component type and its interface element types.

A connector is a locus of modularization for component interconnections and communication protocols. Basically, the static structure of a connector consists of connection points and a connection role. A *connection point* describes a point at which a component can join a connector to communicate with other components. Thus, it represents an element of the connector interface through which the participation of a component in an interconnection can be defined. A *connection role* is an abstract representation of the channel between compatible connection points. It also specifies the protocol of interactions between connection points.

2.4 Behavioral View

The behavioral view describes the dynamic (or behavioral) properties of all architecturally significant elements of the system under development. The behavior of a computational component is specified by the component interface protocol (CIP). A CIP defines the temporal ordering of data flows, call events, and signal events that can be received or sent by the component. It is defined by composing the protocol statemachines of all interface elements. Composition is defined by "anding" all statemachines

---

2. As described later, dynamically attaching and detaching connection points to components, as defined in system configurations, enable our component model to describe plug-in capabilities.

of the interface, i.e. the statemachine of each interface element runs concurrently to all the others.

The behavior of a connector type is defined by specifying the protocol of interactions for each connection role and the behavior associated to the connection points. Both of these are described using UML protocol statemachines.

2.5 Configuration View

The configuration view describes the organization of the system in terms of component and connector type instances. An instance of a connector type has two categories of elements: dynamic ports and links between these ports. The *dynamic ports* are instantiations of connection points, whereas the links are instantiations of connection roles. Similarly, when a component type is instantiated, its interface element types are instantiated as *static ports* that are parts of the boundary of the component instance. Two or more component instances can be then interconnected to define a configuration of the system by attaching dynamic ports of the connector instance(s) to the component instances. Before a dynamic port is attached to a component, we have to check that its contract is fulfilled.

3 Compiler Example

This section presents an example that illustrates the benefits of the ConcernBASE approach by applying its techniques to a well known compiler example. Figure 1 depicts an informal representation of a Level-3 Compiler architecture taken from [4], which uses the reference model for compiler construction.

Despite the box-and-arrow architecture representation, figure 1 shows that the compiler has a batch-sequential architectural style. The main component coordinates the correct execution sequence of the components composing the compiler system. First, it transfers the control to the LexicalAnalyzer, then to the Parser, then to the AnalyzerOptimizer, and finally, to the CodeGenerator. The rounded-edge components, SymbolTable and Tree, are shared-memory components. The former holds binding information and makes them available to the LexicalAnalyzer and AnalyzerOptimizer. The latter keeps abstract syntax trees and is accessed by the Parser, AnalyzerOptimizer and CodeGenerator. Note that some components have read and write access, while others are only granted read or write access. The Parser component is directly receiving tokens from the LexicalAnalyzer via the unidirectional pipe relating them and not through shared-memory components.

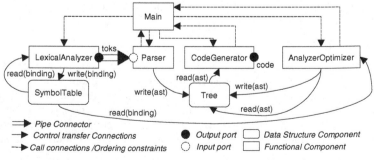

Fig. 1. Compiler Architecture: taken from [3]

Figure 2 depicts the set of significant concerns that define the structural concern space of the compiler system. It contains six components: LexicalAnalyzer, Parser, AnalyzerOptimizer, CodeGenerator, SymbolTable and Tree, which are connected together by a complex connector, named CompilerConnector. As shown below, the connector plays a central role in this example. It mediates different kinds of communications between the components of the system and encapsulates all the communication paths. The CompilerConnector also coordinates the interactions among participant components. Therefore, it may enforce a particular communication protocol among the components.

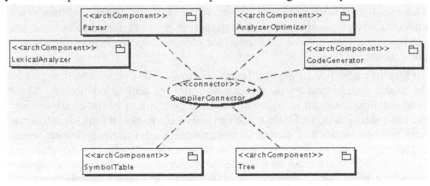

Fig. 2. Structural Concern Space Model of the Compiler System

Figure 3 illustrates the static structure of the LexicalAnalyzer component. Its component interface is composed of five interface elements, where each element defines a logical interaction point between the component and its environment. The ExecutionControl interface element provides the operation start with the meaning that another component can activate the LexicalAnalyzer, i.e. starts it by implementing this interface. The MemoryAccessControl interface element requires two operations: read and write. This means that the LexicalAnalyzer requires these operations to be provided by another component. The ControlFlowSignaling interface element declares incoming and outgoing signals necessary to control the execution of the LexicalAnalyzer, while the MemoryFlowSignaling interface element enumerates signals needed for the communication with the shared-memory components.

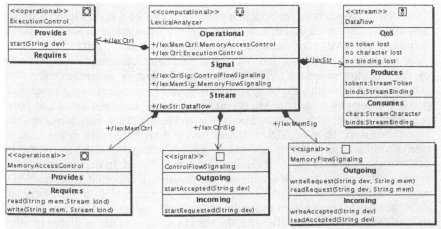

Fig. 3. Static Structure of the LexicalAnalyzer

Lastly, the Dataflow interface element defines two streams produced by the LexicalAnalyzer, namely a stream of tokens and a stream of bindings, as well as two consumed streams conveying characters and bindings. It is important to remark that bindings are both produced and consumed by the component, showing the similarity with figure 2, where the LexicalAnalyzer component reads and writes bindings, i.e. produces and consumes them. As shown below, all these interface elements are involved in a composition relationship with the component that realizes them. Furthermore, the interface elements are externally visible parts of the component.

The use of communication-specific interface elements clearly exhibits separation of concerns when defining specialized interaction points (referred to as static ports in the configuration view), since each interface element type is responsible for a particular communication type.

To illustrate a portion of the configuration view of the compiler system, we instantiate the LexicalAnalyzer and Parser components and the simple connectors. The resulting configuration is shown in figure 4, which depicts a part of the configuration view of the compiler system. In figure 4, we can see one instance of the LexicalAnalyzer component and one instance of the Parser component. Each interface element owned by the component is shown as a static port on its boundary. We distinguish three connectors instances, which are used to mediate the communication between components. One connector links the <<operational>> static ports of ExecutionControl together, another relates the <<stream>> Dataflow ports, and another the <<signal>> ControlFlowSignaling ports.

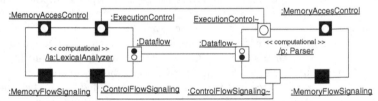

Fig. 4. Configuration View of the Compiler System

4 Overview of SADL

This section gives a brief introduction to the concepts of SADL. Figure 5 shows a portion of the architecture description of the compiler_L1 example in SADL. The top-most section of an SADL architectural description is called ARCHITECTURE; it encloses other lower-level SADL section. We can see that an architecture section is referenced by the identifier compiler_L1. The architecture description given after the ARCHITECTURE keyword includes exchanged data with its environment using input and output ports. The compiler_L1 has an input port, named char_iport, and an output port, called code_oport. char_iport receives a sequence of characters (SEQ(character)), and code_oport sends code data. To use SADL to definitions that are externally defined, an architecture description must first import them. This is achieved by the using the keyword IMPORTING, indicating where the definitions can be found. In our example, IMPORTING Function FROM Functional_Style tells us that Function is imported from an SADL style named Functional_Style. In order to be imported into an SADL architecture, an SADL definition has to be exported using the EXPORTING statement. For instance, the declaration EXPORTING start specifies that the start function is made available to other architectures wanting to utilize that function.

An SADL architecture description contains three different sections dealing with various aspects of its software architecture, namely COMPONENTS, CONNECTORS and CONFIGURATION. The first and the second sections contain the declaration of the components and connectors, respectively, whereas the third section defines constraints on the configuration of the architectural elements defined in the first and second sections.

```
IMPORTING Function FROM Functional_Style
...
compiler_L1 : ARCHITECTURE [ chars_iport : Finite_Stream(Character) -> code_oport : Finite_Stream(code)]
BEGIN
   COMPONENTS
      lexicalAnalyzerModule : ARCHITECTURE
         [chars_iport : Finite_Stream(Token), bind_iport: Finite_Stream(Binding) ->
         bind_oport: Finite_Stream(Binding), token_oport : Finite_Stream(Token)]
      BEGIN
         COMPONENTS
            lexicalAnalyzer : Function
                  [chars_iport : Finite_Stream(Token), bind_iport: Finite_Stream(Binding) ->
                  bind_oport: Finite_Stream(Binding), token_oport : Finite_Stream(Token)]
            characterVariable : Variable(Character)
            tokenVariable : Variable(Token)
            bindingVariable : Variable(Binding)
         CONNECTORS
            ...
         CONFIGURATION
            token_read  : CONSTRAINT = Reads(lexicalAnalyzer, tokenVariable)
            token_write : CONSTRAINT = Writes(lexicalAnalyzer, tokenVariable)
            ...
      END
      ...
   CONNECTORS
      tokenPipe : Pipe[Finite_Stream(Token)]
      ...
   CONFIGURATION
      tokenFlow : CONNECTION = Connects(tokenPipe,lexicalAnalyzerModule!token_oport,parserModule!token_iport)
      ...
END
```

Fig. 5. Extract of the Level-3 Compiler SADL Specification

The COMPONENTS section contains mainly elements like ARCHITECTURE, Function, Variable and Operation. In SADL, all of those elements are considered as being components. The ARCHITECTURE section allows us to define sub-architectures that can be contained in a higher-level architecture. For instance, in figure 5, lexicalAnalyzerModule is a sub-architecture contained in the compiler_L1 architecture. Note that through this feature, SADL provides a support for modularization.

Functionality of architectures can be expressed through the definition of Function components. As an architecture element, a Function component may have input and output ports through which data can be received or sent. In figure 5, the sub-architecture lexicalAnalyzerModule contains a function called lexicalAnalyzer representing the main functionality of the sub-architecture.

Operation and Function components have similar meanings. The difference between them lies in the fact that the input ports of an Operation are seen as the parameters and the output port as the return value of the operation. However, the number of output ports of an Operation component is limited to one.

Variable components are used to hold different types of data and make them available to other components in the sense of shared-memory, which is local to a sub-architecture. One component is only able to keep a single type of data, which means that we need different Variable components for different types of data. For instance, the lexicalAnalyzerModule contains three different Variable components (character-, token- and bindingVariable), the only three that are used by the sub-architecture.

The CONNECTORS section contains the definitions of connectors, these are, e.g., kind Pipe and Enabling_Signal. Connectors enable communication among components. A Pipe connector carries data from an output port of one component to an input port of another. The transmitted data must be of the same type supported by the related output and input ports. An Enabling_Signal connector mediates signal communication that is likely to occur between two components.

The CONFIGURATION section defines the configuration constraints on the previously defined components and connectors. These constraints may state, for instance, which Function or Operation component has read/write access to a Variable component, which component sends a signal, which component receives it, the direction of the data flow between two components, and from which component an Operation is called. We use two different types of statements, namely CONNECTION and CONSTRAINT. The former defines data flow connections and the latter specifies all other kinds of constraints.

5 Mapping ConcernBASE to SADL

This section presents our approach for translating a ConcernBASE architectural description written in UML into a textual form written in SADL.

The mapping consists of 5 steps. The first step identifies all data types utilized in the ConcernBASE architectural description and map them to SADL. The second step requires that all the architectural components be found and mapped to SADL. The third step requires that all the interface elements of each architectural component be found and mapped to SADL. The fourth step identifies data flow connections and maps them to SADL. And finally, the fifth step puts the pieces together.

5.1 Mapping Data Types

To perform this task, we use an SADL feature that allows SADL styles to be defined anytime [4]. Figure 6 shows an SADL style which defines the data types used in the level-3 compiler (see section 4).

Basically, we define a new style that consists of all data types contained in the current architectural description. To do this, we have to look at every stream interface in the static view of all the components and connectors. Then, we build up the data types list by gathering every data type supported by the different streams. Then, we simply define a new style having the name of the current architecture appended with the suffix Types in a file having the name of the style with the extension ".sadl".

5.2 Mapping Architectural Components

Before mapping ConcernBASE components to SADL, we have to look at the structural concern space and identify the architectural components that are contained in the system. It is possible that other UML artifacts (for instance, high-level connectors) might have to be modeled as components. Such artifacts will be discovered during the next steps.

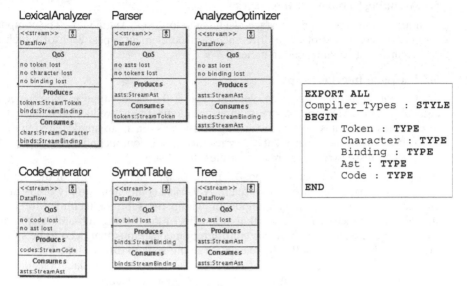

Fig. 6. Compiler_Types.sadl

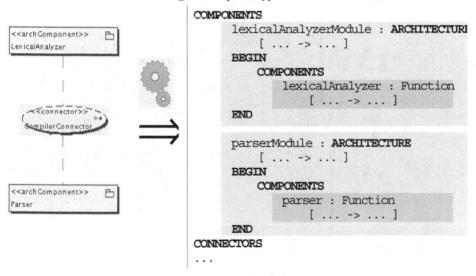

Fig. 7. Translating Architectural Components

We translate every architectural component (subsystems) as an SADL sub-architecture with the suffix Module and declare them in the COMPONENTS section of the main architecture. We then declare a Function component with the same name as the component and the same input and output ports. The Function represents the main functionality of the sub-architecture and will be referred to as the sub-architecture's main component. Figure 7 shows how the structural concern space is translated to SADL.

5.3 Mapping Component Interfaces

To translate the component interface, we have to look at its static view. The component interface is composed of three different interface element types, each of which supports a different communication pattern.

5.3.1 Stream Interface Type

Clearly, the <<stream>> interface element type is the easiest type to map, since it is equivalent to a SADL port. A stream interface element may produce and consume different kinds of streams, e.g., video and audio streams. Each stream declared in the Produces and Consumes compartments are translated into an output and an input port of the component, respectively. Figure 8 illustrates this idea.

Also, we to declare a Variable component in the COMPONENTS section of the sub-architecture for every different type of stream. A Variable component simply holds the data and acts as a shared-memory component within the sub-architecture. Moreover, it should only be accessed by internal components of the owning sub-architecture using Reads/Writes predicates. These are configuration constraints that need to be specified in the sub-architecture itself. The reason for doing so is to differentiate between functional and data-holding concerns of components. In this way, all data consumed by a component is directly stocked into a Variable component dealing with the corresponding data type.

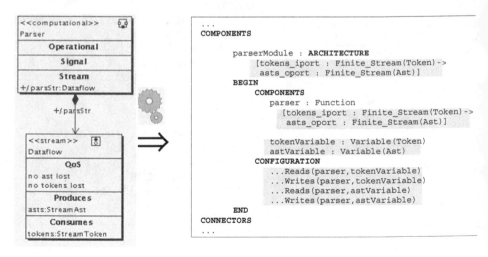

Fig. 8. Translating stream interface type

5.3.2 Operational and Signal Interface Types

SADL lacks precise formalism for the definition of operational connectors, i.e. connectors that mediate operation calls between two components. However, the SADL style, Procedural_Style, contains the definition of the Called_From predicate taking the invoked Operation and the calling COMPONENT as parameters. For instance, Called_From(B!start,A) means that the component A calls the operation start implemented by component B. Note that start is declared as an Operation in the COMPONENTS section of the sub-architecture B.

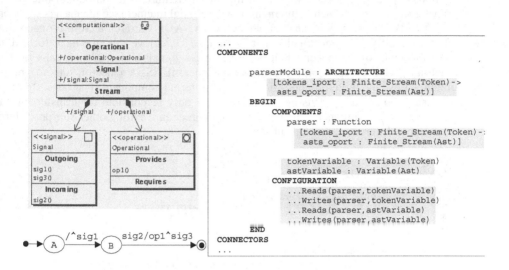

Fig. 9. Translating Behavioral Aspects

The Outgoing compartments of the <<signal>> interfaces of a component allow us to identify the set of signals defined by that component. We therefore declare the signals in the CONNECTORS section of the sub-architecture representing the architectural component. To retain the behavior, we have to translate the ordering constraints on the signals. To do this we analyze the behavioral view, which provides all information we need to get the correct sequencing of signals. Figure 9 shows the translation of the behavior of a component into SADL with respect to the mediation of signal and operational communication. The static view is helpful for identifying operations and signals, while the behavioral view helps discover the temporal ordering of signals and operation calls.

Furthermore, C1 sends the signal sig1 and enters state B. The component C2 (not shown in the figure) receives sig1 and immediately sends sig2, which is in turn received by C1. Upon reception of sig2, C1 calls the operation op1 and sends the signal sig3. The ordering is translated by means of SADL predicates (Sender, Receiver, Called_From) indicating the kind of relationship existing between the predicate's arguments. For instance, Sender(c1Module!sig1,c1Module) means that c1Module is the sender of the signal sig1. Outgoing signals are declared within the sub-architecture. The constraints that specify the correct sequencing of the signals are declared in the CONFIGURATION section of the main architecture.

Another very important thing that has to be taken into account in order to retain the semantics of the source model is to translate the behavior of connectors. ConcernBASE and SADL differ on the fact that connectors may have behavior, too. We cannot specify the behavior of a connector in SADL. In section 5.2, we have mentioned that we may have to create an additional SADL component to represent a ConcernBASE connector with behavior. For instance, in the level-3 compiler, the CompilerConnector is responsible for controlling the execution flow of the components being part of the compiler system. In SADL, we would model this feature as a component that would transfer the control to each component in a sequential manner (see the main component in figure 1). This simply means that we create an SADL sub-architecture for each simple ConcernBASE connector that has behavior. To achieve this, we have to find all state machines of a connector that do not transfer signals and operation calls further. Such an SADL component, standing for a ConcernBASE connector, has no precise functionality, and therefore, does not own any internal component (Functions, Operation or Variable component). This new component is only responsible for transferring the control to other components, much like a main procedure calling other sub-procedures to delegate different sequential sub-tasks.

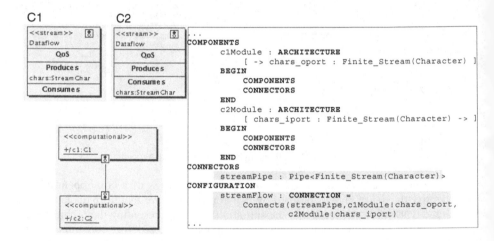

Fig. 10. Translating Data Connections

5.4 Mapping Connections

In the SADL formalism, a connection represents a data link between two components. It is further specified as being a CONNECTION constraint relating an output port of a component with an input port of another component via a data connector (e.g., a Pipe).

We have shown how to identify SADL ports in section 5.3.1, and now, we show how to relate those ports together to allow data exchange between two components. The only thing we have to do is to look at the configuration view and identify the simple stream connectors between any two components. Figure 10 illustrates this concept by showing that C1 produces a finite stream of characters, C2 consumes this stream, and the connector between the <<stream>> static ports carries it. The connector and the connection are respectively declared in the CONNECTOR and the CONFIGURATION sections of the main architecture.

5.5 Putting It All Together

The last thing to do is to add IMPORTING and EXPORTING statements before the declaration of the main architecture as depicted in figure 11. An IMPORTING statement allows the use of architectural elements defined in other specifications and makes them available for the definition of the current architecture and sub-architectures. An EXPORTING statement allows an architecture to make its elements available to other architectural descriptions.

```
IMPORTING Character,Binding,Ast,Token,Code FROM Compiler_Types
IMPORTING Function FROM Functional_Style
IMPORTING Operation,Called_From FROM Procedural_Style
IMPORTING Sender,Receiver,Before,Enabling_Signal FROM Control_Transfer_Style
IMPORTING Pipe,Finite_Stream FROM Process_Pipeline_Style
IMPORTING Variable,Reads,Writes FROM Shared_Memory_Style
compilerL3 : ARCHITECTURE [ ... -> ... ]
BEGIN
COMPONENTS
      lexicalAnalyzerModule : ARCHITECTURE   [ ... -> ... ]
      BEGIN
          COMPONENTS
              lexicalAnalyzer : Function [ ... -> ... ]
              start : Operation [ ... -> ... ]
              tokenVariable : Variable(Token)
              ...
      END
CONNECTORS
...
```

Fig. 11. Putting everything together

6 Tool Support

The ConcernBASE Modeler is an integrated tool for developing architectural descriptions using the ConcernBASE approach (described in section 2). The tool allows one to translate UML architectural models into SADL descriptions, providing at the same time a new and elegant way to supply verification support for UML models using the existing SADL tools. Tool proactiveness supports the developer in modeling because it actively manages the consistency between different overlapping views. For instance, when the user wants to instantiate a component type in the configuration view, the tool proposes a list of components that have been defined in the structural concern space. When the user is modeling the behavior of architectural elements by means of state machines, the trigger and call event lists are populated with signals and operations that already exist, i.e. that have been defined in the corresponding interface elements. These features reduce user accidents and errors.

The software is single project-based, which means that it only allows one architecture to be modeled at a given time. One project may contain several model files depicting the architecture. The structural concern space is depicted by one model; each architectural element declared in the structural concern space model has its own static and behavioral view models in the same file; finally, the configuration view is defined by one model. All models are saved on disk using the standard XMI file format.

The graphical user interface is simple, usable and intuitive. It has a menu bar that provides different options, a tool bar containing frequently-used functions, a left pane displaying a structured view of the architecture, a right pane allowing one to graphically and easily modify architectural diagrams, and a message pane keeping the user informed of what is going on within the system. The interface is completely event-driven and all resources, i.e. labels, texts, messages, images, etc., are internationalized; this means that the aspect of the interface can be changed and localized without having to rebuild the system. Finally, a complete built-in help system offers information on the system itself, its functionalities, and its application domain (ConcernBASE and SADL).

7 Conclusion and Future Work

In this paper, we have presented the ConcernBASE approach and a method for translating ConcernBASE models into SADL specifications. The mapping discussed in this work enabled us to make use of SADL verification tools, and integrate them with the ConcernBASE Modeler tool. The ConcernBASE approach and the tool supporting it are young. Both are undergoing refinement and improvement, but they are already being applied. Although the tool is not yet complete, one can already develop models, translate them to SADL, edit and syntax-check the resulting SADL descriptions and save the models to disk. Support for dynamic reconfiguration, an important feature that allows one to dynamically change the configuration of a system, is planned as future work.

Acknowledgement. This work was partially supported by the Defense Advanced Projects Research Agency (DARPA) under contract F30602-00-C-0087. Valentin Crettaz would also like to thank the SRI System Design Laboratory and in particular Robert Riemenschneider for their support.

References

[1] The Institute of Electrical and Electronics Engineers (IEEE) Standards Board. *Recommended Practice for Architectural Description of Software-Intensive Systems (IEEE-Std-1471-2000)*. September 2000.

[2] M. Kande and A. Strohmeier. *Towards an UML Profile for Software Architecture Descriptions*. UML'2000 - The Unified Modeling Language: Advancing the Standard, Third International Conference, York, UK, October 2-6, 2000, S. Kent, A. Evans, B. Selic (Ed.), LNCS (Lecture Notes in Computer Science)

[3] M. Kande and A. Strohmeier. *On The Role of Multi-Dimensional Separation of Concerns in Software Architecture*. Position paper for the OOPSLA'2000 Workshop on Advanced Separation of Concerns. (Online at http://lglwww.epfl.ch/~kande/Publications/role-of-mdsoc-in-swa.pdf)

[4] M. Moriconi and R. Riemenschneider. *Introduction to SADL 1.0*. SRI Computer Science Laboratory, Technical Report SRI-CSL-97-01, March 1997.

[5] OMG Unified Modeling Language Revision Task Force. *OMG Unified Modeling Language Specification*. Version 1.4 draft, February 2001. http://www.celigent.com/omg/uml-rtf/

[6] P.Tarr, H. Ossher, W. Harrison, and S. Sutton Jr. *N Degrees of Separation: Multi-Dimensional Separation of Concerns*. Proceedings of the International Conference on Software Engineering - ICSE'99 (May 1999).

[7] D. Garlan, R. T. Monroe and D. Wile. *ACME: An Architecture Description Interchange Language*. Proceedings of CASCON '97 (1997).

[8] N. Medvidovic and R. N. Taylor. *A Classification and Comparison Framework for Software Architecture Description Languages*. IEEE Transactions on Software Engineering, Vol. 26, No.1, January 2000.

[9] P. Clements. *A Survey of Architecture Description Languages*. 8th International Workshop on Software Specification and Design, Germany, March, 1996.

[10] D. Garlan and A. Kompanek. *Reconciling the Needs of Architectural Description with Object-Modeling Notations*. In UML 2000 - The Unified Modeling Language: Advancing the Standard, Third International Conference, S. Kent and A. Evans (Ed.), LNCS, York, UK, October 2-6, 2000.

[11] O. Weigert (moderator). *Panel: Modeling of Architectures with UML*. In UML 2000 - The Unified Modeling Language: Advancing the Standard, Third International Conference, S. Kent and A. Evans (Ed.), LNCS, York, UK, October 2-6, 2000.

[12] P. Tarr and H. Ossher. *Multi-Dimensional Separation of Concerns and The Hyperspace Approach*. In Proceedings of the Symposium on Software Architectures and Component Technology: The State of the Art in Software Devel-opment. Kluwer, 2000. (To appear.)

[13] Allen R. *A Formal Approach to Software Architecture*. Ph.D. Thesis, Carnegie Mellon University, School of Com-puter Science, available as TR# CMU-CS-97-144, May (1997).

The Message Paradigm in Object-Oriented Analysis

Frank Devos and Eric Steegmans

Software Development Methodology Research Group
Department of Computer Science
K.U. Leuven, Belgium
frank.devos@cs.kuleuven.ac.be

Abstract. The message paradigm is one of the most specific concepts of object orientation. This paradigm works well as long as one object is involved. When more than one object is involved, a choice has to be made with which type the message will be associated. In our opinion, this choice has to be postponed during object-oriented analysis. We propose to extend the concept of the message paradigm to messages with more than one implicit argument. Postponing the choice results in one model for one reality. Another problem rises when no object is involved. In our opinion this issue can best be tackled by introducing a domain layer and a functionality layer.

1 Introduction

Object-oriented software development is now generally accepted as the most promising approach for the construction of complex software systems. As for other areas of engineering, the development of a software system is split into a number of activities, namely analysis, design, implementation and verification or testing. The development of a software system is considered to be an incremental process.

The major purpose of object-oriented analysis is to establish the requirements for the software system to be developed. In view of the object-oriented paradigm, a conceptual model of relevant objects is developed including a specification of their characteristics and their behaviour. The conceptual model is also referred to as the business model or domain model of the external world. This model describes the problem context in all its facets. The model will therefore be as close as possible to the facts, as they can be observed in the external world. We are using UML and OCL as modelling technique in this paper [12][13].

Object-oriented analysis is a relative young research area and its concepts are derived from object-oriented programming. This can explain why many conceptual models are oriented towards system implementation and a lot of design decisions are already taken. As a result, the border between object-oriented analysis and design is vague. We are convinced that we have to rethink and extend object-oriented concepts used at the level of analysis in order to add a surplus value.

It's a very blind assumption that techniques that are convenient in some object-oriented programming languages are valid also for analysis.

During object-oriented design we transform the conceptual model into an operational model. Software quality factors will dominate the transformation. In the

M. Gogolla and C. Kobryn (Eds.): UML 2001, LNCS 2185, pp. 182-193, 2001.

design phase we describe how a conceptual model can be implemented in terms of software. Any decision that adds nothing new to the conceptual model of the observed world is a design decision.

One of the most specific concepts in object orientation, aside inheritance, is that one can send messages to an object. This principle is know as the message paradigm. The receiving object is the sole responsible for responding to the message. This message has access to the characteristics of the object. In order to respond to a message, a proper method will be selected. The receiving object may appeal to other objects by sending them messages in turn. The receiving object is the implicit argument for the underlying method. The message paradigm forces the software engineer to associate a message with a type. This leads to a more consistent structure of the software system.

The message paradigm in object-oriented analysis works well as long as one object is involved. Problems arise when none or more than one object is involved in a message. These topics are described in the following sections.

2 Messages with One and with More than One Object Involved

As an introduction we briefly discuss messages with one object involved. As an example consider figure 1. If we want to know the total amount of money we can withdraw from a specific account, we send the message "moneyToWithdraw()" to this account

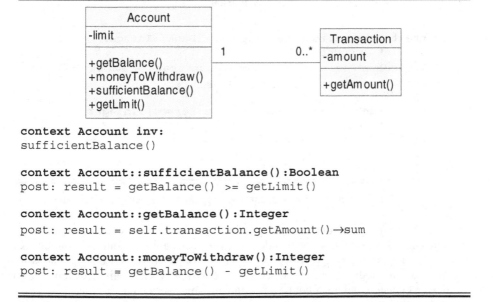

```
context Account inv:
sufficientBalance()

context Account::sufficientBalance():Boolean
post: result = getBalance() >= getLimit()

context Account::getBalance():Integer
post: result = self.transaction.getAmount()→sum

context Account::moneyToWithdraw():Integer
post: result = getBalance() - getLimit()
```

Fig. 1. A message with one implicit argument

This message in turn will send the message "getBalance()" to the same account. The getBalance() sends the message "getAmount()" to all the transactions linked to this account. For each of these messages only one object is involved.

The message paradigm simulates the way people interact with all kinds of things in their surroundings. When turning on a television, a signal (message) is sent by means of a remote control. In responding, the television will sent proper messages to some of its components. It is a natural way of communicating.

Aside the natural way of communication the message paradigm permits us also to encapsulate the characteristics of objects of a class. Encapsulation is again a faithful reproduction of the way human beings deal with objects in their surrounding. When driving a car or watching television, internal details are completely irrelevant for a model user. Technicians and more advanced users need more information, resulting in a gradual presentation of internal details.

When more than one object is involved in a message, the question rises with which type we will associate the message. Consider the example in figure 2. We want to model a message returning the total balance of all the accounts of a specific person at a specific bank. The message "totalBalance()" could be attached to the type Person or to the type Bank. The answer to the above question will be rather arbitrary. Also looking at the different specification of the postconditions will not help: the specifications are each other's mirror image.

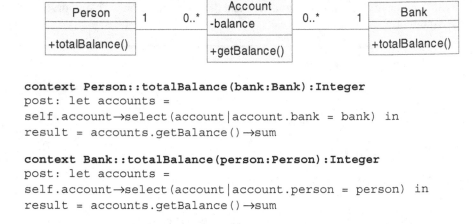

```
context Person::totalBalance(bank:Bank):Integer
post: let accounts =
self.account→select(account|account.bank = bank) in
result = accounts.getBalance()→sum

context Bank::totalBalance(person:Person):Integer
post: let accounts =
self.account→select(account|account.person = person) in
result = accounts.getBalance()→sum
```

Fig. 2. A message with one implicit argument and one explicit argument

In this case two solutions are possible, modelling the same external world. In analysis we strive at only one model for the same reality. In our opinion, the decision to which type a message with more than one object involved belongs, adds nothing new to our model about the facts in the external world. This decision is clearly a design decision and must not be taken during object-oriented analysis.

For that reason we propose to introduce messages with more than one implicit argument. We call these messages binary or more general n-ary messages. These message have access to the characteristics of the implicit arguments. Binary messages in conceptuals models are illustrated for the bank case in figure 3. As a result we have only one possible model for the requirements of the domain.

Graphically these kinds of messages are modelled in all context types adding the other types before the name of the message. Remember that in UML the returning value is given at the end of the message.

Instead of one context type, we now have two context types. The implicit arguments are referenced by "self" followed by the name of the type. If more than one object of the same type is involved the implicit arguments are numerated with self1Type, self2Type and so on. If no other classes are involved we could abbreviate to self1, self2 and so on. When calling the message the involved objects are separated through a comma.

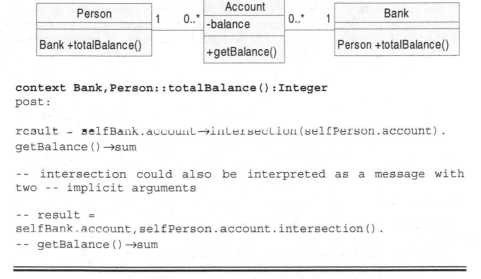

```
context Bank,Person::totalBalance():Integer
post:

result - selfBank.account→intersection(selfPerson.account).
getBalance()→sum

-- intersection could also be interpreted as a message with
two -- implicit arguments

-- result =
selfBank.account,selfPerson.account.intersection().
-- getBalance()→sum
```

Fig. 3. A message with more than one implicit argument

More important is that also the specification for the postcondition is changed. Instead of starting with one object and navigating through the model, the postcondition in figure 3 has two starting objects. This way of modelling is more declarative and abstract in the sense that it doesn't suggest an implementation strategy.

Notice that also the intersection could be interpreted as a message with two implicit arguments. This specification is worked out in the comment. The specifications in figure 2 and figure 3 could be interchanged, in our opinion however the specifications in figure 3 reveal better "the way of thinking".

A typical application of this concept is the linking of two or more objects. Consider the relationship among persons and cars. How should the acquisition of a car by a given person be reflected in term of messages?[1] Should there be a message applicable to a person, to a car or both? When using n-ary messages the answer is already given.

---

[1] Is a person buying a car? Or is a car bought by a person?

One could argue that we don't have to make this choice if we use a characteristic instead of an object as an argument. In our example one could have associated a message totalBalance(nameOfTheBank:String) to the type Person, assuming that the name of the bank is unique. In the next section the answer is given why this is not a valid option.

3   Messages with No Objects Involved

Another problem with the message paradigm arises when no specific object is involved. This is the case when an object or a set of objects has to be searched among a collection of objects based on a certain characteristic. This is also the case when new objects have to be created. For that purpose class-scoped operations are introduced in UML. These kinds of operations are underlined. Two examples are illustrated in figure 4. The name of the bank is assumed to be unique for each bank. This is not formally modelled[2].

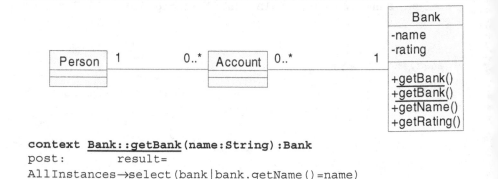

```
context Bank::getBank(name:String):Bank
post:          result=
AllInstances→select(bank|bank.getName()=name)

context Bank::getBank(rating:String):set of Bank
post:                                          result=
AllInstances→select(bank|bank.getRating()=rating)
```

Fig. 4. Class-scoped operations

A problem with class-scoped operations is that they easily could be misused: object-scoped operations could be modelled as class-scoped operations. This is frequently observed in practice. The use of class-scoped operations could, in an extreme way, lead to functional decomposition or structured design. In functional decomposition the system function is organised as a hierarchy of functional procedures, and the development consists of elaborating this hierarchy from the top downwards [9].

---

[2] We could have modelled these constraints as object-scoped constraints or as class-scoped constraints.

As an example consider figure 5. We have modelled our object-scoped operation totalBalance() of section 2 as a class-scoped operation. The two explicit arguments are objects, they could be replaced by characteristics identifying the person and the bank.

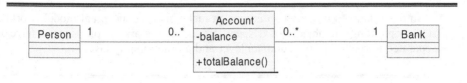

```
context Account::totalBalance(person:Person,bank:Bank):Integer
post : result = AllInstances→select(account|account.person =
person and account.bank = bank).balance→sum
```

Fig. 5. TotalBalance() as a class-scoped operation

Another, more object-oriented way to select objects is to introduce a new type. In our banking example, one could introduce the type "BankAssociation". A bank is then always linked with one bankassociation. The messages for selecting banks are associated with this new type. Consider as an example figure 6. This approach also has a lot of disadvantages:

1. The first is that we introduce an artificial type not belonging to the domain context. In fact the only reason why we introduce this type is that it permits us to model a message for the selection of objects. This is a technical reason. In our opinion only types that play an important role in the domain context of our system must to be modelled.

2. Further we assume that there is only one bankassociation object. Only then is it possible to select all the banks with a specific characteristic. We also postpone our problem. How could we select our bankassociation object ? By introducing a new type? Or by introducing a class-scoped operation "getBankAssociation()"?

3. If we adopt this approach we have to introduce new singleton types for every type without an existential dependency constraint[3]. In our problem we had to introduce a new artificial type for messages selecting persons.

4. A next problem is that, if we want to select objects of types with an existencial dependency constraint we may have to make a choice between more than one type to attach this kind of messages. In our example, if we want to select accounts on creation date we could use the type Bank or the type Person for it. The choice is rather arbitrary in object-oriented analysis.

---

[3] A type with an existential dependency constraint means that an object of this type can't exist without other objects of a certain type.

5. A last problem is that this approach leads to long navigation expressions. Suppose we want to select all transactions on accounts for a certain date. We could attach this message to the type "BankAssociation". From bankassociation we are navigating to all the banks, and from there to all the accounts and at last to all the transactions on accounts.

In our point of view the two important tasks of our conceptual model, working on sets, containing all objects of a specific type and working on objects, have to be separated into two layers: a domain layer and a functionality layer.

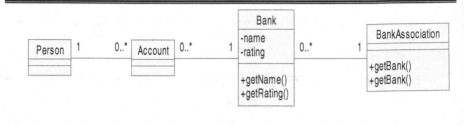

```
context BankAssociation::getBank(name:String):Bank
post :          result = self.bank→select(getName()=name)

context BankAssociation::getBank(rating:String):set of Bank
post :          result = self.bank→select(getRating()=rating)
```

Fig. 6. Introducing a new type for selecting objects

The functionality layer, which works on sets of objects, has several responsibilities: operations on sets of objects, like the conversion of characteristics in involved objects or counting the number of elements in a set, the selection of the right accessible messages of the domain layer to be send to the involved objects and operations on basic types converting the input or output. The basic types in OCL are Integer, Real, String and Boolean. In the domain layer, which works with objects, most[4] of the relevant facts about the real world are modelled.

Consider our example in figure 7. We assume that the name of the bank is a unique characteristic and that we can select one person on the basis of his name and address. These uniqueness constraints are not modelled[5]. The main task of the functionality layer in our example is the selection of the right person and bank and sending the right message, totalBalance(), to these two involved objects.

---

[4] Further research has to be done on which layer class-scoped constraints have to be modelled. If they are modelled in the functional layer some domain knowledge is modelled in the top layer. If these constraints are modelled in domain layer, we have messages with no objects involved.

[5] We could have modelled these constraints as object-scoped constraints or as class-scoped constraints.

The functionality layer is built as a set of input and output services, offering the desired information functionality to the users of the model. In this sense we see the functionality layer as a more formal approach of use cases [14]. We could use the functionality layer as a way to control whether all the necessary domain knowledge and all user requirements have been modelled.

By separating functional requirements and domain knowledge we are able to focus in a first phase on our domain layer. Users tend to mix these specifications, together with technical requirements. Like Jackson we are convinced that a great part of the complexity of a system is caused by the complexity of the real world [9]. Jackson suggests first modeling reality and in a later step considering functionality. We agree on this, from a theoretical point of view. In practice this process will be iterative.

The functionality layer may send accessible messages of the domain layer. The domain layer has no access to the functionality layer. In this way we want to stimulate maintainability of our model. We consider the domain layer as more stable as the functionality layer. Types that exist in the domain layer are quite stable. The functional requirements tend to change more often. This ensures that modifications in the functionality layer have no or little effect on the domain layer. Technically this means that we can only use the OCL-expression AllInstances in the functionality layer.

We explicitly haven't modelled the messages of the functionality layer as part of one or more types to underline that this layer has other responsibilities than the domain layer. Further research has to be done on how to structure the messages of this layer.

One could argue that even with these two layers it is possible to model the message totalBalance() as in figure 5. This is true, but the idea is to work as early as possible with objects and to send as soon as possible accessible messages of the domain layer to these objects. So when respecting these rules this way of modelling is not an option anymore.

One could argue that we don't need this functionality layer. We could agree with this argument to a certain extent but never the less we are convinced that we better model our domain layer not only on the basis of facts about the real world but with the combined knowledge of the real world and the knowledge of the functional requirements. It makes no sense to model reality without having any functionality in mind. We strive for formalisation of this functionality.

As an example consider that we could model a mutator as a type. The functional layer helps us to decide how to model it. Also the decision on which types, message, characteristics, constraints, ... are relevant is influenced by the functional layer. We already described that we use the functional layer as a way to control completeness of the domain layer.

One could argue that using and defining characteristics as key attributes has to be done at the design phase. In fact this has nothing to do with the uniqueness or non-uniqueness of a characteristic. On the functionality layer one could also select a set of involved objects. In our example we could have selected a set of banks by the rating characteristic modelling not the totalBalance() of one specific person by one specific bank but by a specific set of banks.

Functionality Layer

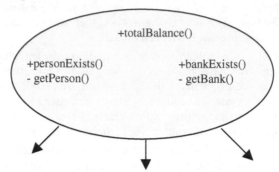

Domain Layer

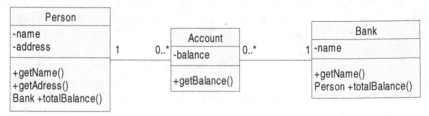

personExists(name: String,address:String):Boolean
post: result = getPerson(name,adress)→size = 1

getPerson(name:String,address:String):set of Person
post: result = Person.AllInstances→select(getName()= name and
getAddress()= address)

bankExists(name:String):Boolean
post: result = getBank(name)→size = 1

getBank(name: String):set of Bank
post: result = Bank.AllInstances→select(getName() = name)

totalBalance(namePerson:String,address:String,nameBank:String):
Integer
pre: personExists(namePerson,adress)
       BankExists(nameBank)
post:
let
       person = getPerson(namePerson,address)
       bank = getBank(nameBank)
in
result = person,bank.totalBalance()

Fig. 7. Modelling with the functionality layer and domain layer

One could argue that instead of modelling a functional layer, we could have modelled this by a type user, in our case, for example the fiscal authority. In other words there is always a context for a message. Every message of the functional layer is attached to this type. The advantages are that we don't use another concept and we don't have problems anymore modelling the class-scoped constraints. So a constraint about the average rating of all banks is associated with the type FiscalAuthority. The singleton constraint for the type User could be modelled as object-scoped[6]. The disadvantages are that this type is still, in our view, artificial. Every person and bank is linked to the fiscal authority. In reality this is not the case. A more fundamental disadvantage is that all of the messages of the functional layer are associated with this type. This type is a receptacle of different kinds of messages without structure. This is certainly true if more types without existence dependency constraint are added to the model.

The link with the user is made by this user type, without explicitly specifying this. Also the responsibilities for this user type and the other types are not clear. It is just a type like another. The disadvantages mentioned by figure 6 are here still valid: long navigations and choice in navigation.

We underline that not the notation, in our case a rectangle or an oval, is important but the method, the segregation of responsibilities in hierarchical layers and the intention to further structure the functional layer.

4   Conclusion

In traditional object-oriented analysis one has to make a choice as to which object will be the implicit argument and which object(s) will be the explicit argument(s) when more than one object is involved in a message. This choice is an arbitrary one during object-oriented analysis. By making all the involved objects implicit arguments we can postpone this decision. This results in one model for one reality. The specification of the message is also changed: instead of writing the specification starting from one point, we write the specification in view of more than one starting point. This leads to specifications with a more intuitive character.

By introducing a functional layer we bridge the gap between the domain layer and the user. The main responsibilities of the functional layer are the selection of the involved objects and messages and the preparation of the input or output for the user. The functional layer is helping the analyst to control the completeness of the domain layer and the user requirements.

Segregation of responsibilities leads to a large degree of independence between the two layers. The formal specification of the functionality layer, in contrast with use cases, makes ,in combination with the domain layer, rigorous and tool-based verification possible. The conceptual model is not only structured by its types but also hierarchical structured by its layers. This should improve maintainability, especially for larger systems.

---

[6] **context User,User inv** :
      singleton()

context User,User :: singleton() : Boolean
post: result = self1 = self2

5 Further Research

When combining inheritance, the other fundamental concept in object orientation, and n-ary messages ambiguity is possible. Consider the figure below. Two binary messages m() with different contexts are modelled. If we send the message m() to the involved objects a1 of type A1 and b1 of type B1 the selection of one of the binary messages is arbitrarily. Some possible solutions are proposed here. The simplest one is to forbid ambiguity. Another one could be the obligation to introduce a binary message m() with contexts A1 and B1. A more complex one is to combine the postconditions of both messages through the logical operator and.

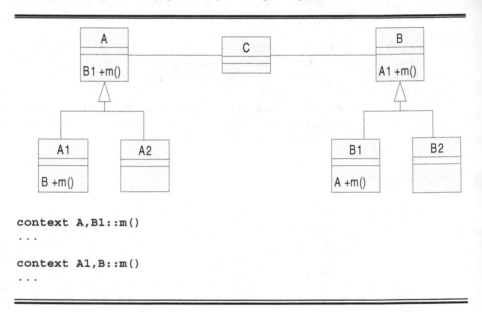

```
context A,B1::m()
...

context A1,B::m()
...
```

Fig. 8. Combining inheritance and n-ary messages

Further research has to be done on how to structure the messages in the functionality layer. A possible way is to group messages that are using the same set of all objects of a type. Another interesting question to be resolved is: is it desirable to have sets of objects as implicit arguments? We think that it isn't, because it's in our view another way of modelling static messages.

A strict separation of responsibilities between the two layers is needed. Although we already draw a strict line between the two layers some issues are still open. Class-scoped constraints are an example of such an issue. Another one is how far we could go in transformation, or conversion of objects in the functional layer.

As an example consider as input for the model the number of an account. For this account we want to know the totalBalance() of the owner of this account by the bank of this account. Two solutions are possible: either we query the person and the bank of this account and then send the already modelled binary message totalBalance() to person and bank or, we model a new objectmessage totalBalance() with as context the type Account.

References

[1] BODART F., PIGNEUR Y., Conception assistée des systèmes d'information, 1989, Masson, 302 p.

[2] BOOCH G., Object-Oriented Analysis and Design, 1994, The Benjamin/Cummings Publishing Company, 589 p.

[3] COOK S., DANIELS J., Designing Object Systems: Let's get formal, 1994, The Journal of Object Oriented Programming, Vol. 7, p. 22 - 24.

[4] D'SOUZA D., WILLS A., Catalysis Book, 1998, 684 p.

[5] ERIKSSON H.E., PENKER M., Business Modelling with UML, 2000, Wiley Computer Publishing, 459 p.

[6] FOWLER M., SCOTT K., UML Distilled, Applying the Standaard Object Modeling Language, 1997, Addison-Wesley, 179 p.

[7] FOWLER M., Analysis Patterns, 1997, Addison-Wesly, 357 p.

[8] RUMBAUGH J., Object-Oriented Modeling and Design, 1991, Prentice Hall, 500 p.

[9] JACKSON M., System Development, 1983, Prentice Hall, 418 p.

[10] SNOECK M., DEDENE G., VERHELST M., DEPUYDT A., Object-Oriented Entreprise Modelling with Merode, 1999, Unversitaire Pers Leuven, 227 blz.

[11] STEEGMANS, E., LEWI, J., DE BACKER, S., DOCKX, J., SWENNEN, B., AND VAN BAELEN, S., EROOS Reference Manual Version 1.1, Department of Computer Science, K.U.Leuven, Leuven, B, 1995, 173 p.

[12] OBJECT MANAGEMENT GROUP, Unified Modeling Language Specification, 1999, 808 p.

[13] WARMER J., KLEPPE A., The Object Constraint Language, Precise Modeling with UML, 1999, Addison-Wesley, 112 p.

[14] WARMER J., KLEPPE A., Praktisch UML, 1999, Addison-Wesley, 252 p.

A UML-Based Approach to System Testing

Lionel Briand and Yvan Labiche

Software Quality Engineering Laboratory
Systems and Computer Engineering Department, Carleton University,
1125 Colonel By Drive, Ottawa, Canada, K1S 5B6
{briand, labiche}@sce.carleton.ca

Abstract. System testing is concerned with testing an entire system based on its specifications. In the context of object-oriented, UML development, this means that system test requirements are derived from UML analysis artifacts such as use cases, their corresponding sequence and collaboration diagrams, class diagrams, and possibly the use of the Object Constraint Language across all these artifacts. Our goal is to support the derivation of test requirements, which will be transformed into test cases, test oracles, and test drivers once we have detailed design information.

Another important issue we address is the one of testability. Testability requirements (or rules) need to be imposed on UML artifacts so as to be able to support system testing efficiently. Those testability requirements result from a trade-off between analysis and design overhead and improved testability. The potential for automation is also an overriding concern all across our work as the ultimate goal is to fully support testing activities with high-capability tools.

1. Introduction

System testing is concerned with testing an entire system based on its functional and non-functional specifications, the latter being the focus of this paper. In other words, the implementation under test is compared to its intended specification. In the context of object-oriented, UML development, this means that we use UML analysis artifacts to derive system test requirements. For example, use cases, their corresponding sequence or collaboration diagrams, and class diagrams can be used as a source of relevant information for testing purposes.

However, UML analysis artifacts vary from one development method to another. As there is no well-accepted standard method for object-oriented development, some variability in the analysis artifacts' content and structure is unavoidable. However, most methods assume that Analysis produces use case diagrams, use case descriptions in some standard format, sequence and/or collaboration diagrams associated with each use case, a class diagram including application domain classes, and possibly a set of contracts for each operation (pre- and post- conditions) and each class (class invariant). With the exception of use cases, this description is, for example, similar to what the Fusion method [6] proposed before UML became a standard.

Based on such analysis artifacts, our goal is to support the derivation of test requirements. At a later point in the development process, using test requirements and detailed design information, test cases, test oracles, and test drivers can be developed.

M. Gogolla and C. Kobryn (Eds.): UML 2001, LNCS 2185, pp. 194-208, 2001.
© Springer-Verlag Berlin Heidelberg 2001

Test requirements can be generated early, after analysis artifacts are completed. This is very important as it helps devising a system test plan, size the system test task, and plan appropriate resources early in the life cycle. Once the low level design is complete, when detailed information is available regarding both application domain and solution domain classes, then test requirements can be used to derive test cases, test oracles, and test drivers. The work presented here is part of a larger scale project named TOTEM, which stands for Testing Object-orienTed systEms with the unified Modeling language.

One important issue is the one of *testability* [3]. Since the use of the UML notation is not constrained by any particular, precise method, one can find a great variability in terms of the content and form of UML artifacts, whether at the analysis or design stages. However, the way UML is used determines the testability of the produced UML artifacts. It is therefore important to determine what are the testability requirements we need to impose on UML artifacts –and therefore on any development methodology– to be able to support our system test methodology efficiently.

Another important aspect is *automation*. Large systems are inherently complex to test and require, regardless of the test strategy, large numbers of test cases. If a system testing method requires the tester to perform frequent, complex manual tasks, then such a method is not likely to be usable in a context where time to market is tight and qualified personnel is scarce. Therefore, the potential for automation of a test methodology is an important criterion to consider. This paper, however, focuses on methodological aspects. Automation and testability, though important, are partially addressed here, and will be the main focus of subsequent papers.

The paper starts by providing an overview of our methodology for system testing. Section 3 then gets into the core of the paper, describing the procedure we use to derive test requirements, using a system analysis example. Section 4 summarizes the testability requirements of our approach and justifies the decisions and trade-offs that were made. Section 5 then concludes and outline future work.

2. Overview of the TOTEM System Test Methodology

The TOTEM system test methodology, as far as deriving test requirements is concerned, is based on the artifacts produced at the end of the Analysis development stage. These artifacts include: use case diagram, use case descriptions, sequence or collaboration diagrams for each use case, class diagrams composed of application domain classes, and a data dictionary that describes each class, method, and attribute.

In addition, as discussed further in Section 4, we assume each class is characterized by a class invariant expressed with the Object Constraint Language (OCL) and each operation is described by a contract in OCL, detailing pre- and post-conditions.

Those artifacts are similar, though we use a different terminology, to what is proposed by Fusion [6]. Furthermore, as discussed in detail in Section 3, use cases have sequential constraints that have to be specified. Such constraints are the direct result of the logic of the business process the system purports to support[1]. In other words, use case scenarios are usually not executed in arbitrary orders. Some use case scenarios need to be executed before others. Think, for example of a library system

---

[1] Even this aspect bears some similarity with the notion of *life-cycle model* in Fusion.

where a user needs to register before being able to borrow a book. Registering and borrowing correspond to different use cases and, for a given library user, one has to be performed before the other. Therefore, in addition to the artifacts above, we will see that one of our testability requirements is to specify such sequential constraints, for example under the form of an activity diagram.

Figure 1 summarizes the steps of the TOTEM system test methodology. In this paper, we will focus on activities A2, A3, and A5. A1 is the first step where we check that the provided UML diagrams are complete and fulfill our testability requirements – it is partially addressed in Section 4. A4 is not addressed here though it is an important contribution to test requirements [3] and is to be addressed by future work. However, activities A2, A3, and A5 constitute by themselves a self-contained methodology and the fact that A4 is missing will not affect the validity and usefulness of what we present in this paper.

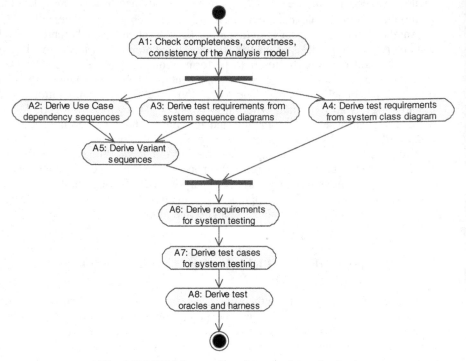

Fig. 1. TOTEM System Test Steps (activity diagram)

Once TOTEM's testability requirements are ensured (A1), we move on to derive test requirements from the different artifacts (from A2 to A5). Then these requirements are merged into one set of test requirements, thus avoiding redundancy and combining test requirements into one test plan (A6). A7 and A8 are concerned with generating the test cases and oracles, and embedding them into executable test drivers. These steps are typically performed at a later stage once detailed design information is available and they will not be discussed here. One important objective of TOTEM is to provide a systematic methodology to perform the activities presented above and to automate them to the maximum extent possible, thus allowing the development of a test support environment.

Note that test requirements, which are the focus of this paper, will not only be used to help generate test cases and harness (drivers, stubs), but also to make our testing goals explicit and to help planning testing early on, after the completion of Analysis. Regardless of the methodology followed to generate them, test requirements are a very good source of information to size the testing task and, therefore, to help determine required testing resources early on.

3. Generating System Test Requirements at the Completion of Analysis

This section covers the steps A2, A3, and A5 of the TOTEM system test methodology. We proceed with steps in chronological order. The interested reader can find far more detailed descriptions of these steps (algorithms, diagrams, ...) in [4].

3.1   Generating Use Case Sequences

Use cases are a first good source for deriving system test requirements. After all they represent the high level functionalities provided by the system to the user. But they are usually not independent. Not only they may have <<extend>> and <<include>> dependencies but they may also have *sequential* dependencies. In other words, based on the logic of the business process the system supports, some use cases need to be executed before others. For example, in a library system[2], a user needs to register before being able to borrow a book. When planning test cases for use cases, we need to identify *possible* execution sequences of use cases. Possible sequences of use cases may be also seen as a model of the user business process while using the system. We aim at "covering" use case sequences as they may trigger different failures. Coverage strategies have to be developed but a first step is to generate a model of possible use case sequences. As described below, we will generate regular expressions to model this (their alphabet will be the use cases themselves), and those regular expressions will constitute one component of the system test requirements.

We first represent sequential dependencies between use cases by the means of an activity diagramfor each actor in the system. Such a representation will facilitate the identification of these dependencies by application domain experts as activity diagrams are easy to interpret.

In such a diagram, the vertices are use cases and the edges are sequential dependencies between the use cases. The use cases are grouped into *swimlanes* with respect to their responsibilities in terms of manipulated objects (application domain classes). Edges may have *guard conditions* attached to them (represented with OCL) that determine whether a transition from one use case to the other is enabled. An example[3], from our library system, can be found in Figure 2 (use cases are identified

---

[2] We use this example system as a running example throughout the paper. See [4] for details.

[3] For the sake of better readability, note that no OCL guard condition but one (which is an illustrative example) is shown.

by their name and also, for brevity, by a capital letter from A to K). This activity diagram is built for the Librarian (actor) and, in general, one diagram should be provided for each actor. Note that a detailed analysis model is provided in [4] and cannot be provided here due to space constraints. Since the library system example is rather simple and intuitive, this will not hinder the reader to understand our examples at the required level of detail.

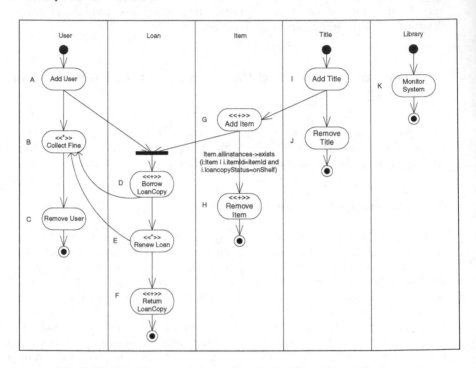

Fig. 2. Use Case Sequential Constraints for the Librarian (activity diagram)

We defined two stereotypes (<<*>> and <<+>>) that apply to the use cases in this activity diagram. They specify that use cases can be executed several times (0 to n times and 1 to n times, respectively). Note that, from a general standpoint, we may also need stereotypes in order to specify that a use case is optional (executed 0 or 1 time), is (always) executed several times (say 3 times for instance), or is executed several times within a range (between 2 and 4 times). In our example, the two abovementioned stereotypes are used to specify that, for example, a loan can be renewed several times (0 to n times), and at least one item is created for a particular title (1 to n items).

If not related by cross-swimlanes sequential dependencies or synchronizations, use cases from different swimlanes are independent, and thus can occur independently, in any order (concept of *interleaving* in [6]). Each swimlane represents the life cycle of objects from their creation in the system, through all the functions being performed on them, to their destruction.

Within our test support environment, in order to support the automated derivation of test requirements, this UML diagram will be represented as a weighted graph that is amenable to graph analysis (i.e., the generation of regular expressions).

An algorithm has been defined to produce (augmented) regular expressions that model possible paths in the graph. It is based on the principles presented in [2] and accounts for possible synchronizations. The result for our example, is four regular expressions, including one with interleaving (denoted $||$): K, $I.J$, $I.G^+.H^+$, $(I.G^+||A).D+.E^*.(F|B^*.C)$.

As we said previously, swimlanes are independent (except in case of cross-swimlanes dependencies) and then can occur in any order, i.e., they are interleaved. Moreover, the swimlanes are not mandatory: for instance, it is not necessary to execute the MonitorSystem use case (use case K) each time the other use cases are executed. Then the resulting regular expression of the algorithm is an interleaving of the previous regular expressions, each of them being optional. It can be formalized as the following regular expression:

$$(K|\varnothing)||(I.J|\varnothing)||(I.G^+.H^+|\varnothing)||(((I.G^+||A).D+.E^*.(F|B^*.C))|\varnothing)$$

It is easy from such an expression to then derive actual paths to be covered. We pick a use case from each interleaved term and instantiate every iteration symbol, if any, using a strategy similar to what is used to test loops in code. For example, we can make sure that each iteration is set to 0 (for * only), 1, a legal number above 1 (say 2), and the maximum number of iterations. The latter, in some cases, may be determined by the guard condition on the reflexive sequential dependency driving the iteration. Using our example, such a coverage strategy would include, for example, the following two paths, which are both legal based on the expression above: (1) $I.G.A.G.D.F$, (2) $I.G.H.J$.

3.2   Identifying Use Case Scenarios

To each use case corresponds an interaction model, i.e., either a collaboration or a sequence diagram. They represent one interaction model describing alternative object interactions, each of them realizing one possible scenario of the use case. In many cases, an interaction diagram models one *nominal* scenario and a number of error / exceptional scenarios, where the system has to react appropriately.

Interaction diagrams are also, like the use case dependency activity diagram in Figure 2, a form of weighted graphs. For interaction diagrams, vertices are objects and edges are messages. Edges may be reflexive and may be characterized by a guard condition, in addition to specifying the target object operation to be triggered by the message. They can, therefore, as far as our needs are concerned, be also modeled as a regular expression in order to derive test paths. In this case the alphabet of the regular expressions is composed of the set of public operations in application domain classes.

In the previous section, we have seen how to derive use case sequences that should be part of the test plan. Now, using the interaction diagrams associated with use cases, we have to go one more level down into details, and derive sequences of use case *scenarios* to be tested.

Let us illustrate the procedure we propose using an example and then summarize the procedure. Figure 3 presents a sequence diagram for the use case `Remove Title`.

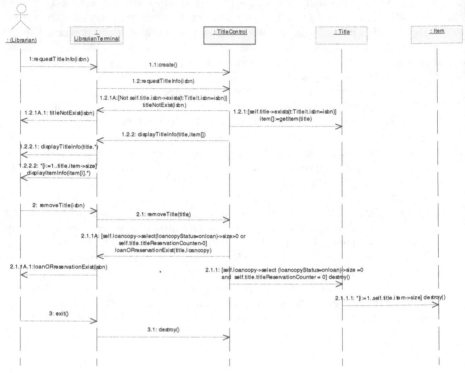

Fig. 3. Analysis Sequence Diagram for `Remove Title`, after merging it with *included* use cases.

3.2.1   Expressing Sequence Diagrams as Regular Expressions

In order to represent them in an analyzable and compact form, the sequence diagrams may be re-expressed as regular expressions whose alphabet is the public methods of the objects playing a role in sequence diagrams. So, for example, for `Remove Title` this would yield the following regular expression where we use the notation $Operation_{Class}$ to denote which operation is executed and to which class it belongs:

```
Remove Title ->
RequestTitleInfo_LibrarianTerminal . create_TitleControl . requestTitleInfo_TitleControl .
(
    getItem_Title . displayTitleInfo_LibrarianTerminal .
    displayTitleInfo_Librarian . displayItemInfo_Librarian* . removeTitle_LibrarianTerminal .
    removeTitle_TitleControl .
    (destroy_Title . destroy_Item* + loanORreservationExist_LibrarianTerminal) +
    titleNotExist_LibrarianTerminal . titleNotExist_Librarian
) . exit_LibrarianTerminal . destroy_TitleControl
```

The next step, in order to be able to identify scenarios, is to re-express the regular expression above in a *sum-of-products* form (here 3 *product terms* separated by "+"):

RequestTitleInfo$_{\text{LibrarianTerminal}}$.create$_{\text{TitleControl}}$.requestTitleInfo$_{\text{TitleControl}}$.
getItem$_{\text{Title}}$.displayTitleInfo$_{\text{LibrarianTerminal}}$.
displayTitleInfo$_{\text{Librarian}}$.displayItemInfo$_{\text{Librarian}}^{*}$.removeTitle$_{\text{LibrarianTerminal}}$.
removeTitle$_{\text{TitleControl}}$.
destroy$_{\text{Title}}$.destroy$_{\text{Item}}^{*}$.exit$_{\text{LibrarianTerminal}}$.destroy$_{\text{TitleControl}}$
+
RequestTitleInfo$_{\text{LibrarianTerminal}}$.create$_{\text{TitleControl}}$.requestTitleInfo$_{\text{TitleControl}}$.
getItem$_{\text{Title}}$.displayTitleInfo$_{\text{LibrarianTerminal}}$.
displayTitleInfo$_{\text{Librarian}}$.displayItemInfo$_{\text{Librarian}}^{*}$.removeTitle$_{\text{LibrarianTerminal}}$.
removeTitle$_{\text{TitleControl}}$.
loanORreservationExist$_{\text{LibrarianTerminal}}$.loanORreservationExist$_{\text{Librarian}}$.
exit$_{\text{LibrarianTerminal}}$.destroy$_{\text{TitleControl}}$
+
RequestTitleInfo$_{\text{LibrarianTerminal}}$.create$_{\text{TitleControl}}$.requestTitleInfo$_{\text{TitleControl}}$.
titleNotExist$_{\text{LibrarianTerminal}}$.titleNotExist$_{\text{Librarian}}$.exit$_{\text{LibrarianTerminal}}$.
destroy$_{\text{TitleControl}}$

3.2.2   Identifying Path Realization Conditions for Product Terms

From the procedure above, we obtain a regular expression with three product terms (referred to below as Term 1, 2, and 3), each having a number of conditions associated with their executions. Indeed, associated with each path within a sequence/collaboration diagram, one can derive from the guard conditions associated with these paths, the conjunction of conditions that must be fulfilled for that path to be enabled. Recall we require that these conditions be expressed in OCL so as to be unambiguous. As an example, the *path realization condition* for Term 2 above is:

```
Term2, path realization condition:
self.titleControl.title ->exists(t:Title | t.isbn=isbn) and
(self.titleControl.loancopy->select(loancopyStatus=onloan)->size>0 or
self.titleControl.title.titleReservationCounter>0)
```

Note that OCL guard conditions, which compose the conjunctives of path realization conditions such as the one above, have to be re-expressed as they assume different *contexts*[4] in the interaction diagrams. The transformation should ensure that every guard condition in the path realization condition uses the same context. It is convenient to assume, as a general rule, that the *boundary class* [5] corresponding to the use case executed (e.g., LibrarianTerminal in our example) be used as a common context.

The terms that are not part of navigation expressions, e.g., isbn in "...=isbn ..." above, can either be parameters of the use case [3] or strings matching enumeration types, e.g., onloan.

Because Term 2's path realization condition contains a disjunction, it can be satisfied in three ways[5]:

```
Term2, Condition 1:
self.titleControl.title ->exists(t:Title | t.isbn=isbn) and
(self.titleControl.loancopy->select(loancopyStatus=onloan)->size>0
and self.titleControl.title.titleReservationCounter>0)
```

---

[4] We use the OCL definition of *context* here. The context of an OCL expression is always a specific element of a UML model (e.g., a class in the case of an invariant).

[5] Changes from the path realization condition for Term 2 are underlined.

```
Term2, Condition 2:
self.titleControl.title ->exists(t:Title | t.isbn=isbn) and
(self.titleControl.loancopy->select(loancopyStatus=onloan)->size>0
and self.titleControl.title.titleReservationCounter=0)
```

```
Term2, Condition 3:
self.titleControl.title ->exists(t:Title | t.isbn=isbn) and
(self.titleControl.loancopy->select(loancopyStatus=onloan)->size=0
and self.titleControl.title.titleReservationCounter>0)
```

It is important that all three conditions be tested as the implementation may not implement one or more cases correctly and not testing one of them could lead to the non-detection of a fault in the implementation of the path realization condition of Term 2. This issue is related to the literature on testing logic expressions [3]. Complex conditions need to be tested by exercising operation sequences under several alternative conditions. These alternatives correspond to the different combinations of truth values of logical clauses in a path realization condition such that this condition holds true.

3.2.3   Specifying Operation Sequences

Having identified the test conditions under which each term is going to be executed and therefore tested, we need to identify the precise operation sequences to be executed for each term. Since product terms may contain iteration symbols (*, +), precise sequences to be tested need to be defined by giving those iteration symbols actual values. We can use a strategy which is similar to what we did earlier to cover use case variant sequences: the iteration is bypassed (for * only), performed once, an intermediary number of times (possibly a statistical median if available), and a maximum M number of times. Let us take Term 2 as an example. Sequence 4 of Term 2, where $displayItemInfo_{Librarian}$ is executed a maximum M number of times, is as follows:

$RequestTitleInfo_{LibrarianTerminal} . create_{TitleControl} . requestTitleInfo_{TitleControl} .$
$getItem_{Title} . displayTitleInfo_{LibrarianTerminal} .$
$displayTitleInfo_{Librarian} . displayItemInfo_{Librarian}^{M} . removeTitle_{LibrarianTerminal} .$
$removeTitle_{TitleControl} .$
$loanORreservationExist_{LibrarianTerminal} . exit_{LibrarianTerminal} . destroy_{TitleControl}$

The maximum number of iterations M represents the number of items corresponding to a title, modeled in OCL by title.item->size in the UML interaction diagram. The specific number of items depends on how the initial object configuration of the system is set by the test driver. In other words this is a parameter to be set by the test driver and it can be of any value as long as it is above the intermediary value (e.g., 2 above) selected. One strategy is to try to estimate a practical maximum based on a thorough understanding of the application domain and the context in which the system will be used. Those scale limitations will then be specified as the limits of testing for a given version of the system. The other operation sequences for Term 2 and other product terms are presented in [4].

3.2.4   Identifying Test Oracles

Now assuming we have defined the operation sequences to be executed and tested, we need to derive test oracles for each tested sequence. It is crucial to address efficiently the oracle problem in order to make automated testing possible. These oracles, if defined precisely, can then be easily used at a later stage to instrument the test driver code using a system to instrument code with assertions, such as the ones that exist for Java [7]. The main source for deriving a test oracle is the post-condition of operations in a sequence, which are defined using OCL. Let us consider Sequence 4 in Term 1.

RequestTitleInfo$_{LibrarianTerminal}$.create$_{TitleControl}$.requestTitleinfo$_{TitleControl}$.
getItem$_{Title}$.displayTitleInfo$_{LibrarianTerminal}$.
displayTitleInfo$_{Librarian}$.displayItemInfo$_{Librarian}^{M}$.removeTitle$_{LibrarianTerminal}$.re
moveTitle$_{TitleControl}$.
destroy$_{Title}$.destroy$_{Item}^{M}$.exit$_{LibrarianTerminal}$.destroy$_{TitleControl}$

We note that only the two removeTitle operations have a non-trivial post-condition. The removeTitle$_{LibrarianTerminal}$ operation merely delegates to removeTitle$_{TitleControl}$ (see sequence diagram in Figure 3) and they, therefore, have the same post-conditions (but defined using a different context, as expected). From the data dictionary, where all model elements are defined and where pre- and post-conditions are assumed to be provided, we can extract:

```
TitleControl::removeTitle(title, loancopy):void
post:self.title=self.title@pre-set{title} and
     item.allinstances.title->select(isbn = title.isbn)->size=0
```

This expression's context is a titleControl object, created to control the execution of the Remove Title use case. This object has, however, disappeared by completion of the use case as the last message triggers its destruction and cannot be used as a context object in the test oracle expression[6]. The oracle that needs to be checked by the test driver, after the use case of operations has been executed, is:

```
Title.allInstances= Title.allInstances@pre-set{title} and
Item.allInstances.title->select(isbn = title.isbn)->size=0
```

We therefore need, in general, to transform the post-conditions to make them usable as test driver oracles[7]. A general transformation rule is that self should be removed in the post-condition and allInstances should be used to refer to the instances of the class following self in the navigation expression (Title here). Then select may be used, if necessary, to select the appropriate instances and check the required condition. It is, however, not necessary in the above example as all Title instances are of interest.

The case above is rather simple as, as mentioned above, only two operations have a non-trivial and identical post-condition. In the general case, the conjunction of post-conditions in the sequence of operations has to be used to determine the test oracle. This may lead to complex cases where, for example, one subsequent operation's post-condition clause cancels out a former post-condition term. This issue will be addressed by future work.

An alternative that does not require complex OCL expression analysis and transformations, but that requires more code instrumentation, is to systematically

---

[6] It is typical [5] to instantiate a control object during a use case's initiation and then to dispose of it when its corresponding use case is completed.

[7] OCL oracle expressions have then to be transformed into executable assertions in the test driver. But this interesting issue is not addressed here. Assertion tools, such as [7], can be used to support this.

execute postconditions and class invariants at the exit of each operation and raise an exception when they are violated. This was recently presented as an oracle solution in [1] but still needs further investigation.

3.2.5   Constructing Decision Tables

Once we have, for a given use case, identified the operation sequences to be tested, their initial conditions and oracles, we can formalize all this in a decision table that will be used as a formal set of test requirements, which will be part of the test plan. For `RemoveTitle`, the corresponding decision table is provided in Table 1.

Table 1. Decision Table for RemoveTitle (use case J)

Variants (use case J)	Condition Section					Action Section			
						Messages to Actor			State Change
	A	B	C	D	E	I	II	III	
j_1	Yes	No	No	No	No	No	No	Yes	Yes
j_2	No	Yes	No	No	No	No	Yes	Yes	Yes
j_3	No	No	Yes	No	No	No	Yes	Yes	No
j_4	No	No	No	Yes	No	No	Yes	Yes	No
j_5	No	No	No	No	Yes	Yes	No	No	No

Each row in Table 1 is what is commonly called in testing terminology a *variant* [3]. Test cases should cover all variants, at least once. Due to the fact that a product term (Section 3.2.2) is tested instantiating iteration symbols into several operation sequences (Section 3.2.3), each variant will be covered by several test cases, one for each tested operation sequence. The columns model the *initial conditions* in which test cases must be run, the actions that are taken as a result of running the test cases. Namely, this corresponds to *system state changes* and *output messages* being sent to actors. Further details describing the columns of Table 1 are provided below[8].

Initial Conditions:

```
A:  self.titleControl.title ->exists(t:Title | t.isbn=isbn) and
    self.titleControl.loancopy->select(loancopyStatus=onloan)->size=0
    and self.titleControl.title.titleReservationCounter=0

B:  self.titleControl.title ->exists(t:Title | t.isbn=isbn) and
    self.titleControl.loancopy->select(loancopyStatus=onloan)->size>0
    and self.titleControl.title.titleReservationCounter>0

C:  self.titleControl.title ->exists(t:Title | t.isbn=isbn) and
    self.titleControl.loancopy->select(loancopyStatus=onloan)->size>0
    and self.titleControl.title.titleReservationCounter=0

D:  self.titleControl.title ->exists(t:Title | t.isbn=isbn) and
    self.titleControl.loancopy->select(loancopyStatus=onloan)->size=0
    and self.titleControl.title.titleReservationCounter>0

E:  Not self.titleControl.title->exists(t:Title | t.isbn=isbn)
```

---

[8] The context of OCL expressions is the boundary class for the corresponding use case, i.e., `LibrarianTerminal`.

The three Messages to actor `Librarian` are: `titleNotExist` (`I`), `loanReservationExist` (`II`), `displayTitleInfo.displayItemInfo*` (`III`). A * appended to a message indicates that the message may be sent several times. This number of iterations is determined by the operation sequence, as discussed in Section 3.2.3, which is being executed.

State Changes:

```
Title.allInstances= Title.allInstances@pre-set{title} and
Item.allInstances.title.select(isbn = title.isbn)->size=0
```

In this example, there is only one possible state change or no state change at all. But in general, we have to expect that some alternative state changes will be possible.

Based on the example above, we can now summarize the steps of the procedure used to extract a decision table for each use case. Our source of information is an Analysis model described in UML, which is complying with our testability requirements (discussed in Section 4).

1. For each use case, model possible operation sequences in a *regular expression* having a *sum-of-product terms* form, where the alphabet is the public operations of the objects involved in the use case sequence diagram.
2. For each product term, which models a set of possible operation sequences, determine the *initial conditions* that must be set up by the test driver to be able to execute any of the sequences matching the term.
3. Specify precisely the *operation sequences* that match the term to be executed and tested. We use a strategy similar to boundary analysis but in a different context.
4. Identify *test oracles* by making use of the operation *post-conditions* specified in the Analysis model (data dictionary).
5. Formalize all the information above into *decision tables* that follow the format proposed above, which is similar to what is described in [3].

3.3   Generating Variant Sequences

If we assume that for each use case, we have a decision table such as the one presented above, we need to go further and devise a sequence of operations to be tested over an entire *use case sequence* (as defined in Section 3.1). In other words, we need to go from use case sequences to use case *variant* sequences, using use case *decision tables*. Assuming we would have a use case sequence of three use cases A.B.C, having respectively a number of variants |A|, |B|, and |C|, the maximum number of variant sequences would then be |A| * |B| * |C|. As described in Section 3.2.5 above, one variant corresponds to a possible path realization condition for one of the product terms in the interaction diagram regular expression. A variant may require several test cases as iterations may be present in the corresponding product term (up to four if we use the sequence test strategy presented in Section 3.2.3).

Let us take as an example the use case sequence I.G.H.J, which is a possible sequence based on the use case sequential constraints (Figure 2). The use cases I, G, H, and J have, respectively, 2, 2, 3, and 5 variants. One possible variant sequence, which happens to be a *nominal* sequence in our example, is the case where a title is added, one corresponding items is added, and then the item and title are subsequently removed. This would correspond to the variant sequence $i_1.g_1.h_1.j_1$, that is the first (nominal) variant in each of the decision tables.

Note that, at the beginning of a variant sequence, the system is in its initial state. Then assuming we are still testing I.G.H.J, a practical problem arises. Some use case variant sequences, though legal based on their sequential constraints, may be *incomplete*. That is, some variants may have initial conditions that, in order to be fulfilled, require additional use case variants to be executed. Let us look at the following simple example, using the same use case variant notation as above and '*' in the subscript to denote any variant of a use case. Any sequence of the type $i_2.g_*.h_*.j_*$ requires that I be executed twice, with the same isbn, as i_2 implies to add a title that already exists. This would yield a sequence of type $i_1.i_2.g_*.h_*.j_*$. So, executing some legal variant sequences require that additional variants be executed in order to create the required conditions to run all the variants in the sequence. We are currently investigating how to support this by, for example, augmenting the decision tables to indicate relationships between initial conditions and use case post-conditions. In other words, we need to provide support to generate *complete* use case variant sequences from use case sequences and decision tables.

In practice another issue may arise. Some variant sequences may turn out to be impossible as some of the variants are not *compatible*. A variant b_i of B is incompatible with a variant a_j of A if the state of the system after the execution of a_j is contradicting (a part of) the initial condition of b_i. This is an issue that needs to be addressed in the future as the detection of impossible variant sequences needs to be supported to help generate clean, concise test requirements.

4. Testability Issues

Since the application of the UML notation is not constrained by any particular, precise development method, one can find a great variability in terms of the content and form of UML artifacts, whether at the analysis or design stages. However, the way UML is used determines the *testability* of the UML artifacts. That is the ease with which they can be used to support testing activities and the derivation of test artifacts (test requirements, cases, oracles, drivers)[9]. Moreover, since we are concerned with the degree to which our testing methodology can be automated, our methodology and its associated algorithms have precise requirements regarding the information to be contained in UML artifacts. Thus, in the previous sections, we made a number of assumptions regarding the way a UML analysis model is to be developed. Those assumptions were carefully thought out and are referred to as *testability requirements*. We discuss and justify them in this section.

The very first of those testability requirements concerns the sequential constraints between use cases, in addition to the other dependencies shown in the use case diagram. We decided to build one activity diagram per actor in the system to model such dependencies (see Section 3.1 and Figure 2). These activity diagrams capture the

---

[9] Note that testability can also be seen as probability of failure occurrence due to the existence of a fault [8]. Orthogonal but complementary definitions of testability exist in the literature.

sequential dependencies between the use cases related to the actors, and the sequences may have guard conditions (expressed in OCL), that determine whether a sequence from one use case to the other is enabled.

Then each use case is described using an interaction model, which in UML is either an interaction diagram or a collaboration diagram. We supposed that these diagrams use OCL for the description of the alternative object interactions (guard conditions), thus making them unambiguous and linking precisely to the system class diagram (see Figure 3). In addition, we are defining and using *extended* use cases (as described in [3]) that specify, among other things, information about the parameters that determine the behavior to be exhibited. For example, we show in Section 3.2.2, that isbn is a parameter for the Remove Title use case. We further show that the value of this parameter needs to be carefully chosen to execute some of the variant sequences (Section 3.3).

Finally, the data dictionary is assumed to provide (in OCL), in addition to an informal description of classes, attributes, and operations–the contracts (pre- and post-conditions for the operations) and class invariant when they are warranted. We presented such a post-condition in Section 3.2.4, for method removeTitle in class TitleControl. It describes that at the end of method removeTitle, the set of titles contains one element less and that all the items for that title are destroyed.

```
TitleControl::removeTitle(title, loancopy):void
post:self.title=self.title@pre-set{title} and
     item.allinstances.title->select(isbn = title.isbn)->size=0
```

Testability requirements are a trade-off between testability and the effort overhead they entail. We believe that having a description of the business model supported by the system (captured by the use case sequential constraints), as well as precise definitions for operations and classes (contracts), is not only relevant for testing but also for sound Analysis. This view is supported by numerous articles and books [3, 6]. The argument is similar regarding the sequence diagrams, with precise OCL guard conditions, for each use case. In this light, our testability requirements do not seem unrealistic, though they are to be investigated further.

5. Conclusion and Future Work

This paper has presented the TOTEM (Testing Object-orienTed systEms with the unified Modeling language) system test methodology [4]. We derive test requirements from early artifacts produced at the end of the analysis development stage, namely use case diagram, use case description, interaction diagram (sequence or collaboration) associated with each use case, and class diagram (composed of application domain classes and their contracts). This early use of analysis artifacts is very important as it helps devising a system test plan, size the system test task, and plan appropriate resources early in the life cycle. Once the low level design is complete, when detailed information is available regarding both application domain and solution domain classes, then test requirements can be used to derive test cases, test oracles, and test drivers.

We emphasized here the fundamental principles of our methodology, which is based on part on published material [2, 3]. We first showed how activity diagrams can be used to capture sequential dependencies between use cases and allow the specification of use case sequences to be tested. For each use case involved in a particular sequence, the key issues regarding the selection of use case scenarios to undergo testing were then addressed, i.e., what paths to cover in the corresponding sequence diagrams. The derivation of key information for determining the initial system conditions for testing scenarios and their corresponding test oracles was also addressed. Our methodological decisions were justified in terms of their potential for automation and their implications in terms of testability.

Ongoing and future work include:

1. How these test requirements (derived from use case dependencies and from sequence diagrams) are used together with test requirements derived from the system class diagram (A4 in Fig. 1) in order to produce *complete* test requirements for system testing.
2. How system test requirements are used at a later stage to produce the test harness.
3. Precise algorithms to support automation (some are already provided in [4]).
4. We need to provide effective automation to help people achieve good testability (i.e., consistency and completeness checks).
5. Last but not least, our methodology needs to be carefully experimented with, within control settings and through industrial case studies.
6. How non-functional aspects of system testing, such as performance testing, can be integrated in the TOTEM approach.

Acknowledgements. Lionel Briand and Yvan Labiche were in part supported by NSERC operational grants. This work was further supported by the CSER consortium and Mitel Networks. We are also grateful to Michelle Wang for her support.

References

[1]   B. Baudry, Y. Le Traon and J. M. Jezequel, "Robustness and Diagnosability of OO Systems Designed by Contracts," *Proc. 7th International Software Metrics Symposium*, London, England, pp. 272-283, 4-6 April 2001.
[2]   B. Beizer, *Software Testing Techniques*, Van Nostrand Reinhold, New York, 2nd Ed., 1990.
[3]   R. V. Binder, *Testing Object-Oriented Systems - Models, Patterns, and Tools*, Addison-Wesley, 1999.
[4]   L. Briand and Y. Labiche, "A UML-Based approach to system testing," Carleton University, Technical Report SCE-01-01, 2001,
      http://www.sce.carleton.ca/Squall/Articles/TR_SCE-01-01.pdf.
[5]   B. Bruegge and A. H. Dutoit, *Object-Oriented Software Engineering - Conquering Complex and Chalenging Systems*, Prentice Hall, 2000.
[6]   D. Coleman, P. Arnold, S. Bodoff, C. Dollin, H. GilChrist, F. Hayes and P. Jeremaes, *Object-Oriented Development - The Fusion Method*, Prentice Hall Ed., 1994.
[7]   iContract, http://www.reliable-systems.com/,
[8]   J. M. Voas, "Object-Oriented Software Testability," *Proc. International Conference on Achieving Quality in Software*, pp. 279-2901996.

UML Modelling and Performance Analysis
of Mobile Software Architectures

Vincenzo Grassi and Raffaela Mirandola

Dipartimento di Informatica, Sistemi e Produzione
Università di Roma "Tor vergata"
via di Tor Vergata, 00133 Roma, Italy
{grassi, mirandola}@info.uniroma2.it

Abstract. Modern distributed software applications generally operate in complex and heterogeneous computing environments (like the World Wide Web). Different paradigms (client-server, mobility based, etc.) have been suggested and adopted to cope with the complexity of designing the software architecture of distributed applications for such environments, and deciding the "best" paradigm is a typical choice to be made in the very early software design phases. Several factors should drive this choice, one of them being the impact of the adopted paradigm on the application performance. Within this framework, the contribute of this paper is twofold: we suggest an extension of UML to best modeling the possible adoption of mobility-based paradigms in the software architecture of an application; we introduce a complete methodology that, starting from a software architecture described using this extended notation, generates a performance model (namely a Markov Reward or Decision Process) that allows the designer to evaluate the convenience of introducing logical mobility into a software application.

Keywords. Distributed systems, Architecture modelling, Extensions, Performance analysis, Mobile components

1 Introduction

Distributed software systems operate in large scale computing environments (like the World Wide Web), where the computing sites are both geographically and logically distributed, and some of them may be even physically mobile. Because of the complexity of such systems, it is widely recognized that decisions taken in the first phases of the software lifecycle may have a strong impact on the quality of the final product, thus suggesting the need of an early assessment of non functional quality requirements, like performance. Some of theseearly decisions concern the architectural organization of the software system, that is its organization in terms of components and patterns of interaction among them [3]. The *client-server*interaction paradigm represents a well established solution in this sense, typically based on the assumption that components are bound to a given site, and may be even unaware of their respective locations during their interactions. However, it has grown the concern that such a "location unaware" perspective could not be appropriate to a context where interactions among components may have very different characteristics and

M. Gogolla and C. Kobryn (Eds.): UML 2001, LNCS 2185, pp. 209-224, 2001.

constraints, depending on components location. For this reason, there is a growing consensus about the idea of introducing the concept of "location"already at the design stage. As a consequence,"location aware" interaction paradigms have emerged in recent years, based on the notion of *code mobility* [7], where components of an application may (autonomously, or upon request) decide to move themselves to different locations, during the application lifetime. Modern software technologies (e.g. Java) provide the tools to implement these paradigms. Among the arguments in favor of these new paradigms there is the consideration that in a large scale distributedenvironment it may be convenient to move components close to their current partners, with the goal of transforming non local interactions into local ones. The rationale behind this idea is that local interactions are more efficient, and hence code mobility could improve the system efficiency. However, moving components does not come at no cost, so it is also recognized that the arguments in favor of code mobility are not valid in general, and hence the choice between location unaware interaction paradigms like client-server, and location aware ones like code mobility should be performed on a case-by-case basis [7].

As a consequence, our aim is to provide tools that support the designer of complex distributed software systems, in making the architectural choices that are more promising for the software system under development. To this purpose, the methodology we present in this paper gives insights about the impact of the two above mentioned interaction paradigms on some performance-related quality attributes. To reach this goal, the methodology exploits information extracted from design artifacts to build a model of the system dynamics. The model generation procedure lends itself to automation, to minimize the effort required to the designer to use this methodology. To guarantee a wide applicability of this methodology, we assume that the design artifacts are expressed in a UML-based notation, since this formalism represents a *de facto* standard in the field of industrial software design. The model we derive from the application description expressed in UML is a Markov decisional process (MDP), since we intend to exploit its stochastic-decisional features to model both the uncertainty about the system dynamics and the (possiblyoptimal) design choices that can be adopted, and that can have different impacts on the system performance.

The paper is organized as follows. In section 2, we briefly introduce the current UML approach to mobility modeling, as outlined in [4], and then describe our extensions to this formalism to express the possible use of mobile code paradigms in the design of a software system. In section 3, we present some basic notions about MDPs. In section 4 we briefly discuss how we exploits the features of this kind of model in our framework, and then present an algorithm to derive a suitable MDP from a software system description expressed in the notation defined in section 2. Related work is reviewed in section 5. Throughout the paper we use a simple example of network management application [1] to show the use of our methodology. Finally, section 6 concludes the paper.

2   UML and Mobility

As remarked in the introduction, code mobility is not only a technology popularized by the success of technologies like Java, but also represents a design paradigm that can give a new perspective in the way the software architecture of distributed applications is conceived and deployed [7, 18]. From an architectural viewpoint, one of the main impacts of this paradigm is on thedesign of components interaction, since it can turn non local interactions into local ones. To express and analyze this new paradigm, we need a suitable notation. In the next two subsections, we show the standard UML approach to mobility modeling, and oursuggested modification.

2.1 UML Standard Approach

The need of a notation for components mobility in a UML framework has already emerged, so that UML already provides some mechanisms with this goal. They are mainly based on the use of a tagged value `location` within a component to express its location, and of the `copy` and `becomes` stereotypes to express the location change of a component, where the former can be used to specify the creation of an independent component copy at a new location (like in the *code on demand* and *remote evaluation*paradigms), and the latter to specify a location change of a component that preserves its identity (like in the *mobile agent* paradigm) [7]. In [4] these mechanisms are applied to a collaboration diagram (CD). As an example of this modeling approach, figure 1 shows a network management scenario, where a network manager n periodically collects informations about the state of some remote devices. In this example, nstarts a migrating agent cthat moves from node to node collecting information, eventually delivering the collected information to n, for further elaboration. At each node, the collecting agent engages a sequence of N message exchanges with a local `DEVICE` component to collect information.

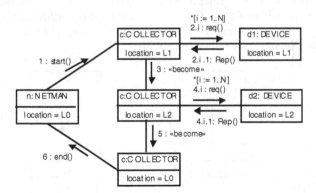

Fig. 1. Network management example, with a migrating agent

However, this modeling approach presents some drawbacks, since it mixes together two different views, one concerning the interaction *style* (e.g. the fact that a component behaves as a mobile agent), and the other one concerning the actual sequence of messages exchanged between components during a particular interaction. Moreover, this approach leads to a proliferation of objects in a CD, that actually represent the same object at different locations. While acceptable when the number of locations and mobile components is very small, this approach quickly leads to hardly read diagrams when the number of components and/or locations grows.

For these reasons we suggest a different approach to model components mobility in a UML framework, as shown in the next subsection.

2.2 Suggested Extension

Our approach is based on the use of both collaboration and sequence diagrams (SD), with a separation of concerns between them, similarly to (Petriu, in [24]). In our case the SD describes the actual sequence of interactions between components, which is basically independent of the adopted style and obeys only to the intrinsic logic of the application, while the CD only shows who interacts with whom and how (i.e. according to which style), without showing the actual sequence of exchanged messages, thus avoiding object proliferation.

In this new approach, we describe the SDs using the standard UML notation, while we suggest an extension of the UML semantics for the associated CD. Indeed, we are interested in distinguishing a style where components are unaware of their respective locations during interactions, and hence do not change them (e.g. client-server style), and a style where they do change location with the goal of turning non local interactions into local ones. To this purpose we introduce a new stereotype moveTo that applies to messages in the CD, and that, when present, indicates that the source component moves to the location of its target before starting a sequence of consecutive interactions with it. If no other information is present, this style applies to each sequence of interactions shown in the associated SD, between the source and target components of the moveTo message; otherwise a condition can be added to restrict this style to a subset of the interactions between two components. Figures 2.a and 2.b show two CD fragments, for the two styles described above: figure 2.a models a style where neither Ci nor Cj change their location during any interaction between them, while figure 2.b models a style where Ci moves to the location of Cj, before starting any sequence of interactions with it.

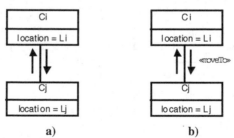

a)   b)

Fig. 2. a) Interaction style without mobility, b) Interaction style with mobility

Note that in the definition of the moveTo semantics there is no indication about whether the moving decision is autonomously taken by the source component (as in a *mobile agent* style) or forced in some way by another component (as in *code on demand* or *remote evaluation* styles), neither about the role of the source component in the interaction (e.g. whether it starts interaction or not). This does not means that in a more complete modeling environment this information is not necessary, but we believe that the adopted notation is sufficient to illustrate the approach we are suggesting.

According to our modeling framework, the application described in figure 1 can be modeled as shown in figures 3 and 4. Figure 3 shows a SD that describes in detail the "logic" of the interaction, i.e. the sequence of messages exchanged among the components. In this diagram no information is present about the adopted style, that is whether or not some component changes location during the interactions. This style information is provided by the CDs in figures 4.a and 4.b. The CD in figure 4.a models a style where component mobility is not considered, and each component is bound to a given location. In particular, this diagram shows that n and c are colocated, and hence c interacts remotely with the devices. On the other hand, for the same application, the CD in figure 4.b corresponds to the case where a mobile style is adopted. More precisely, the diagram shows that only c can change location, and according to the moveTo semantics presented above, it moves to the location of n, d1 or d2 before interacting with them. Hence, the location change of c can occur at the beginning of each of the four interaction sequences enclosed by a dashed line, shown in figure 5, if at that time c and its partner do not have the same location.

Note that in figure 4.b the location of c is left unspecified, since it can dynamically change. In general, we could also give it a specified value in the diagram, that would show the "initial" location of the mobile object in an initial deployment configuration.

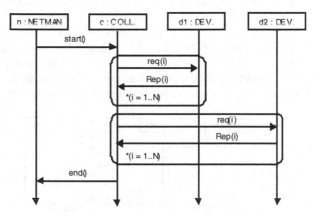

Fig. 3. SD modeling the interaction "logic"

As outlined in the introduction, there is no guarantee that the adoption of a mobile style is always advantageous from a performance viewpoint. Hence, at the early design stage where the above diagrams can be drawn, there can be uncertainty about the opportunity of adopting this style. We suggest that it is worth modeling also this uncertainty within the framework described above; then, in the next section, we will show how we can extract information (including the uncertainty about mobility) to build a system behavior model whose solution provides insights about the opportunity of adopting mobility.

To model uncertainty about mobility of components, we propose a new stereotype moveTo?, that extends thesemantics of the moveTo stereotype described above. When a message between two components in a CD is labeled with moveTo?, this means that the source component "could" move to the location of its target at the be-

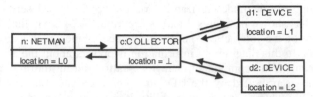

Fig. 4.a. CD modeling an interaction style without mobility

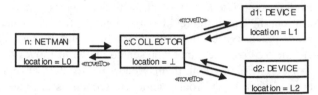

Fig. 4.b. CD modeling an interaction style with mobility

ginning of a sequence of interactions with it. In a sense, this means that, based on the information the designer has at that stage, he considers acceptable both types of behaviors. Hence, the general framework we are suggesting to model the interaction style in a distributed software system, consists of a CD where some messages are unlabeled, some can be labeled with the moveTo stereotype, and some with the moveTo? stereotype. The former two cases correspond to a situation where the designer feels confident enough to decide about the best interaction style, while the latter to a situation where the designer lacks such a confidence. Figure 6 shows the CD for the same example used before, but modeling the case where the designer is uncertain about the effectiveness of designing c as a mobile agent.

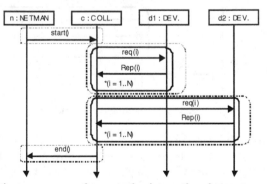

Fig. 5. Distinct sequences of consecutive interactions between components

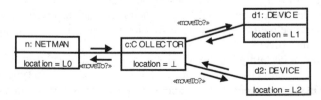

Fig. 6. CD modeling uncertainty about interaction style with mobility

As a final remark, we would like to point out that our proposal does not simplify the overall complexity of the application description, since it basically splits into two diagrams types the information included in one diagram, as in the standard UML notation. Our goal, from the notation viewpoint, is rather to make clearer the model description, thanks to the separation of concerns between the two diagram types.

3 MRP and MDP Models

Our goal is to build a stochastic model that describes the system dynamics, whose evaluation provides information about the performance we can expect by adopting one of the interaction styles described in the previous section. We focus on performance measures that can be expressed as function of the number and types of interactions among components. To this purpose, we assumethat the diagrams described in the previous section are augmented with appropriate annotations expressing the "cost" of each interaction, with respect to a given performance measure [24]. For example, if the measure we are interested in is the generated network traffic, the corresponding cost of each interaction is the number of bytes sent over a network link. This cost may be, in general, location dependent.

The stochastic model we build is a Markov Reward Process (MRP) [17] when the CDs modeling the interaction style only use the moveTo stereotype, and a Markov Decision Process (MDP) [17] when the CDs modeling the interaction style also use the moveTo? stereotype. In the following, we briefly review these two models.

In general, a MRP models a state transition system, where the next state is selected according to a transition probability that only depends on the current state. Moreover, each time a state is visited or a transition occurs, a *reward* is accumulated, that depends on the involved state or transition. Typical measures that we can derive from such a model are the reward accumulated in a given time interval, or the reward accumulation rate in the long period.

A MDP extends the MRP model by associating to each state a set of alternative *decisions*, where both the rewards and the transitions associated to that state are decision dependent. A *policy* for a MDP consists in a selection, for each state, of one of the associated decisions, that will be taken each time that state is visited. Hence, different policies lead to different system behaviors, and to different accumulated rewards. In other words, a MDP defines a family of MRPs, one for each different policy that can be determined. Methodologies exist to determine the optimal policy with respect to some optimality criterion (e.g. minimization of the accumulated reward).

4 Performance Model Generation from UML Diagrams

In this section we show how we can derive a suitable MRP or MDP based on information extracted from the SD and CD that defines the interactions and interaction style among components. For the sake of simplicity, the methodology is defined in terms of a single CD and a single SD, where only sequential or iterative interactions are considered. In case of multiple SDs or conditional selection of interactions within a SD, the methodology should be appropriately extended, by weighting the contribution of different SDs or alternative interactions within a SD. However, this extension appears quite straightforward, and we feel that the case considered here is enough to give the flavour of our methodology.

In our modeling framework, a system state corresponds to a possible configuration of the components location, while a state transition models the occurrence of an interaction between components or a location change, and the associated reward is the cost of that interaction. Hence we use MRPs or MDPs where the reward is associated to transitions only. In case of MDP, the decisions associated to states model the alternative choices of mobility or nomobility as interaction style between some components, for those components that are the source of a moveTo? message.

Since a MRP can be considered as a special case of MDP (obtained when no moveTo? message is present) we show only the general methodology for the derivation of a MDP. We first define some elementary generation rules, and then use these rules to define the MDP generation algorithm.

4.1 Elementary Rules

Let Ci, Cj be two components in the CD that models the interaction style, and let (La, Lb) denote any system state where the location of Ci and Cj are La and Lb, respectively, with La≠Lb, while let (Lb, Lb) denote any state where their locations are the same. Moreover, in case of transition from (La, Lb) to (Lb, Lb), we mean that (Lb, Lb) only differs in the shown state component from (La, Lb), while all the other state components maintain the same value as in (La, Lb).The general idea behind the following rules is that the frequency of the interactions between Ci and Cj can be derived from the SD as the ratio between the number of interactions between Ci and Cj and the total number of interactions that can be counted in the SD [23], including in this number also "interactions" corresponding to the location change of components. Similarly, the average cost of an interaction between Ci and Cj is derived as the sum of the cost of all the interactions between Ci and Cj divided by their number. All the costs must be considered location dependent, i.e. they depend on La and Lb, in general.

Since a state models a possible configuration of component locations, a transition from a state to itself models a normal[1]interaction between components, while a transition to a different state models a location change.

Rule A: if Ci and Cj are source and target of a non labeled message, then a transition exists from any state (La, Lb) or (Lb, Lb) to itself, with frequency and reward given by, respectively:

$$\text{freq}((La,Lb)\text{-->}(La,Lb)) = \text{freq}((Lb,Lb)\text{-->}(Lb,Lb))$$

$$= \frac{\text{total number of "normal" interactions between Ci and Cj}}{\text{total number of interactions}} \quad (1)$$

---

[1] In the following, we call "normal" any interaction different from a location change.

$rew((La,Lb)\text{-->}(La,Lb)) = rew((La,La)\text{-->}(La,La))$

$$= \frac{\sum_{\substack{\text{all the interactions} \\ \text{between Ci and Cj}}} \text{cost of an interaction}}{\text{total number of interactions between Ci and Cj}} \qquad (2)$$

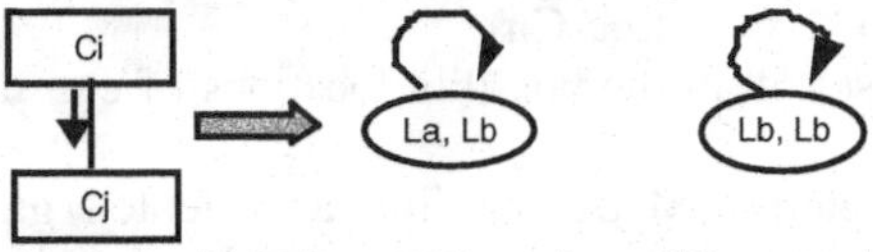

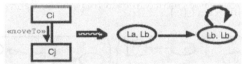

Fig. 7. Derivation of MDP transitions from CD, according to rule *A*

Rule B: if Ci and Cj are source and target of a message labeled with the `moveTo` stereotype, then a transition exists from any state (Lb, Lb) to itself, with frequency and rewards given by (1) and (2) respectively; moreover, a transition exists from any state (La, Lb) to (Lb, Lb), with frequency and reward given by, respectively:

$freq((La,Lb)\text{-->}(Lb,Lb))$

$$= \frac{\text{total number of "move to" interactions from Ci to Cj}}{\text{total number of interactions}} \qquad (3)$$

$rew((La,Lb)\text{-->}(Lb,Lb)) = \text{migration cost of Ci from La to Lb} \qquad (4)$

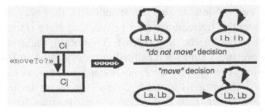

Fig. 8. Derivation of MDP transitions from CD, according to rule*B*

Rule C: if Ci and Cj are source and target of a message labeled with the `moveTo?` stereotype, then a transition exists from any state (Lb, Lb) to itself, with frequency and reward given by (1) and (2), respectively.

On the other hand, in any state (La, Lb) two alternative decisions can be taken: Ci moves or does not move from La to Lb. In the former case a transition occurs from (La, Lb) to (Lb, Lb), while in the latter no state change occurs; the corresponding transition frequencies and rewards are:

- decision "Ci moves to Lb": frequencies and rewards of the transition from any state (La, Lb) to (Lb, Lb) are given by (3) and (4), respectively;

- decision "Ci does not move to Lb": frequencies and rewards of the transition from any state (La, Lb) to itself are given by (1) and (2), respectively

Fig. 9. Derivation of MDP transitions from CD, according to rule *C*

4.2 State Space Generation

Let C1, C2, ..., Cn be the system components. The set S of all the possible system states can be defined as:

S = Loc(C1)xLoc(C2)x ...xLoc(Cn)

where Loc(Ci) is the set of all the possible locations of component Ci, because of its mobility.

Loc(Ci) can be determined by building an oriented graph G (not necessarily connected) obtained from the CD that models the interaction style among components. The nodes of G correspond to the components in CD, plus additional "pit" nodes, one for each different `location` value reported in the CD. Oriented arcs in G correspond to messages labeled with the `moveTo` or `moveTo?` stereotypes in the CD; moreover, for each component Ci in CD that has a defined `location` value Li, an oriented arc exists in G from the node corresponding to Ci and the pit node corresponding to Li. Loc(Ci) is the set of all the pit nodes that can be reached in G starting from the node corresponding to Ci. Figures 10.a and 10.b show the graphs corresponding to the CDs in figure 4.a and 4.b (or 6), respectively, where the pit nodes correspond to square nodes. For example, from the graph in figure 10.b, considering the components ordered as n, c, d1, d2, we get S = {(L0, L0, L1, L2), (L0, L1, L1, L2), (L0, L2, L1, L2)}. For simplicity, since only the location of c can change, in the following we will consider as system state the location of this component only, with S = {L0, L1, L2}.

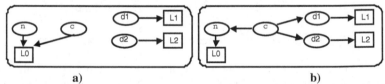

a)   b)

Fig. 10. Graphs of reachable locations for each component. a) for the CD in fig. 4.a, b) for the CDs in figs. 4.b and 6

4.3 MDP Generation

Once we have built the process state space, we can complete the MDP generation. The generation algorithm is presented in appendix 1. In this section we briefly comment the algorithm and then apply it to the network management example.

The core of the algorithm consists of the application of rules *A*, *B* and *C* shown in section 4.1 to each pair of interactingcomponents. In this way we obtain, for each pair, its contribution to the frequencies and rewards of state transitions (construction of the F(s) and D(s) sets in the algorithm). To obtain the overall transition rate between two states, we must sum each contribution obtained in this way, concerning the two states. Similarly, to get the average reward associated to that transition, we must sum the reward coming from each considered contribution, weighted by its relative frequency. Moreover, rule *C* generates contributions to state transitions and rewards that depend on alternative decisions concerning the interaction style between two components. The set of the possible combinations of such decisions concerning any pair of interacting components represents the set of possible "global" decisions in a state (construction of the DecVec(s) set in the algorithm); each of these decisions is associated with a corresponding set of transition frequencies and rewards.

Let us apply this procedure to the considered example. The performance measure we are interested in is the generated network traffic. Hence, the cost associated to each interaction is the corresponding number of bytes sent over network links, derived from opportune annotations in SD. Let us define:

s : size in bytes of a start() message;
r : size in bytes of a req() message;
R : size in bytes of a Rep() message;
e : size in bytes of a end() message;
m : size in bytes of a c component during a location change.

The cost of any interaction is equal to the size of the corresponding message, given above, when the interacting components are not colocated, and zero otherwise.

Now, let us apply the algorithm. As shown in appendix 1, we must first calculate its input. For each pair of interacting components, we get from the SD in figure 5:

- pair (n, c):   number of normal interactions: $Ni(n, c) = 2$
       number of "move to" interactions: $Nm(n, c) = 2$
       cost of a normal interaction: $Ci(n, c) = (s+e)/2$
       cost of a "move to" interaction: $Cm(n, c) = m$
- pair (d1, c):   number of normal interactions: $Ni(d1, c) = 2N$
       number of "move to" interactions: $Nm(d1, c) = 1$
       cost of a normal interaction: $Ci(d1, c) = (r+R)/2$
       cost of a "move to" interaction: $Cm(d1, c) = m$
- pair (d2, c):   number of normal interactions: $Ni(d2, c) = 2N$
       number of "move to" interactions: $Nm(d2, c) = 1$
       cost of a normal interaction: $Ci(d2, c) = (r+R)/2$
       cost of a "move to"interaction: $Cm(d2, c) = m$

From these values, we get the total number of interactions $Ntot = 4N + 6$.

Now, let us apply rules A, B, and C to each state in the set S = {L0, L1, L2}, considering any possible pair of interacting components. In this way, we obtain the sets F(s) and D(s) of transition frequencies and rewards (possibly associated to alternative decisions), each concerning a particular pair of components. Then, we have to appropriately combine the elements of these sets, to get the overall (decision dependent) state transition frequencies and rewards.

As an example, let us consider state L0. In this state, the possible decisions concern whether component c moves to the location of d1 and d2 when interacts with them. Then, the set DecVec(L0) consists of the following four alternative global decision vectors:

decision 1: [c does not move to d1, c does not move to d2]
decision 2:[c moves to d1, c does not move to d2]
decision 3: [c does not move to d1, c moves to d2]
decision 4: [c moves to d1, c moves to d2].

For each decision, we must calculate the corresponding overall transition frequencies and rewards (note that the cost of an interaction between colocated components is zero). For the sake of conciseness, we only show the results obtained for state L0, limited to decision 2:

$$\text{freq(L0-->L0)} = \frac{N_i(n,c) + N_i(d2,c)}{N_{tot}} = \frac{2 + 2N}{4N + 6}$$

$$\text{rew(L0-->L0)} = \frac{N_i(n,c)\cdot 0 + N_i(d2,c)C_i(d2,c)}{N_i(n,c) + N_i(d2,c)} = \frac{N(r+R)}{2 + 2N}$$

$$\text{freq(L0-->L1)} = \frac{N_m(d1,c)}{N_{tot}} = \frac{1}{4N + 6}$$

$$\text{rew(L0-->L1)} = \frac{N_m(d1,c)C_m(d1,c)}{N_m(d1,c)} = m$$

$$\text{freq(L0-->L2)} = 0$$
$$\text{rew(L0-->L2)} = 0$$

As outlined in section 3, the resulting MDP, obtained from the algorithm, defines a family of MRPs, each corresponding to a different policy. For the considered example, figure 11 shows the transition diagrams of two possible MRPs belonging to this family. For simplicity, the figure only shows the possible transitions, without the associated rates and rewards. Figure 11.a shows the transition diagram corresponding to a policy where component c changes location only at the beginning of interactions with m and d1, while it does not change location for interactions with d2. On the other hand, the diagram in figure 11.b corresponds to a "full mobility" policy, where c always moves to the location of its partner.

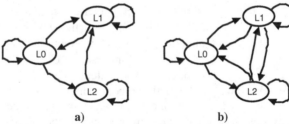

a)   b)

Fig. 11. MRP transition diagrams for two possible policies. a): a "partial mobility" policy; b): "full mobility" policy

Once we have generated the MDP, we can solve it to determine the optimal policy, that is the selection of a decision in each state that optimizes the reward accumulated in the corresponding MRP. In our example, the optimality criterion could correspond to the minimization of the reward accumulation rate, that is the minimization of the network traffic per unit time. Of course, the optimal policy depends on the values given to the system parameters (in our example, the size of the messages andof the possibly mobile component c). Different values for these parameters model different scenarios. If, for example, the optimal policy for a given set a parameter values corresponds to the diagram of figure 11.b, this suggest that the optimal design decision for that scenario is the definition of c as a mobile agent that visits all the locations of its partners.

5 Related Work

In this section we present a short survey of the existing work on performance modeling generation starting from UML based software models by identifying two main areas: "static"architectures, where no kind of mobility is present, and "mobile"architectures.

In the former area, several papers have presented methodologies for the generation of performance evaluation models starting from UML diagrams, possibly augmented with opportune performance annotations [6, 8, 9, 11, 12, 13, 14, 24]. These papers consider different target models, spanning simulation models, Petri nets and queueing networks. Recently, the growing interest in software architectures has brought to extending performance model generation to also encompass the software architecture concept, with particular emphasis given to the impact on performance of the software organization into components and patterns of interaction [2, 15, 21, 24]. In all these papers the target performance model is a queueing network.

On the other hand, in the latter area of mobile architectures, no methodology has been presented for the generation of performance models starting from suitable UML diagrams, to the best of our knowledge. Some papers have been presented, that analyze different forms of code mobility in "isolation" [16, 22], independently of their utilization within particular applications, thus providing some form of general guidelines that can help in taking decisions during the design of an application. Other papers consider particular applications that exploit code mobility [1, 10, 19, 20], and evaluate their performance using "ad hoc" models. [5] presents the definition of a general methodology that can be used as a support for the designer during the early phases of the development of a specific software application, providing insights about the consequences of architectural choices that can be taken during those phases. However, this paper uses an *ad hoc* designed formal language for the software description.

6 Conclusions

With respect to the existing literature, the main contributions of this paper can be synthesized as follows. We have suggested an extension of UML to model the possible adoption of mobility based paradigms in software architecures. The extension allows a clear distinction between the interaction style and the actual interactions among components. Moreover, we have provided a methodology that, starting form aset of (extended) UML diagrams, derives a performance model that allows the designer, early in the design phase, to evaluate the convenience of introducing logical mobility into a software application. Finally, the definition of algorithms whithin the methodology is a step ahead towards automatic generation of software performance models.

Future work includes the extension of the methodology to include a wider range of Sequence Diagrams, a refinement of mobility modeling, to model more precisely different mobile code paradigms, and the inclusion of physical device mobility. Different types of performance models (e.g. queueing networks) should also be considered.

Acknowledgements. Work partially supported by MURST project „SALADIN: Software architectures and languages to coordinate distributed mobile components".

References

1. M. Baldi, G.P. Picco "Evaluating the tradeoffs of mobile code design paradigms in network management applications" in Proc. *20th Int. Conf. on Software Engineering* (ICSE 98), (R. Kemmerer and K. Futatsugi eds.), Kyoto, Japan, Apr. 1998.
2. S. Balsamo, P. Inverardi, C. Mangano "An Approach to Performance Evaluation of Software Architectures", Proc. of *First Int. Workshop on Software and Performance* (WOSP 1998), September 1998, SantaFe, USA, 1998.
3. L. Bass, P. Clements, R. Kazman, *Software Architectures in Practice*, Addison-Wesley, New York, NY, 1998.
4. G. Booch, J. Rumbaugh, I. Jacobson, *The Unified Modeling Language User Guide*, Addison Wesley, 1999.
5. V. Cortellessa, V. Grassi "Performance Evaluation of Mobility-based Software Architectures" Proc. of the *2nd Int. Workshop on Software and Performance*, WOSP2000, Ottawa, Canada, Sept. 2000
6. V. Cortellessa, G. Iazeolla,, R. Mirandola "'Early Performance Verification for Object-Oriented Software Systems", *IEE Proceedings on Software*, July 2000. .
7. A. Fuggetta, G.P. Picco, G. Vigna "Understanding code mobility" *IEEE Trans. on Software Engineering*, vol. 24, no. 5, May 1998, pp. 342-361.
8. Kahkipuro P. "UML based Performance Modeling Framework for Object-Oriented Distributed Systems'", Proc. of *2nd Int. Conf. on the Unified Modeling Language*, October 28-30, 1999, USA, LNCS, Springer Verlag, vol.1723, 1999.
9. King, P. and Pooley, R. "Using UML to Derive Stochastic Petri Net Models", Proc. of the *15th UK Performance Engineering Workshop*, Dept. of Computer Science, The University of Bristol, N. Davies and J. Bradley editors, UKPEW '99 July 1999.
10. D. Kotz, G. Jiang, R. Gray, G. Cybenko, R.A. Peterson "Performance analysis of mobile agents for filtering data streams on wireless networks " in *3rd Int. Workshop on Modeling, Analysis and Simulation of Wireless and Mobile Systems*(MSWiM 2000), Aug. 2000.
11. Merseguer, J., Campos, J. and Mena E. "Performance Evaluation for the design of Agent-based Systems: A Petri Net Approach", Proc. of *Software Engineering and Petri Nets* (SEPN 2000), June 2000, Aarhus, Denmark, 2000.
12. Mirandola R. and Cortellessa, V. "UML based Performance Modeling of Distributed Systems" Proc. of *3rd International Conference on the Unified Modeling Language*, October 2-6, 2000, York, UK, LNCS, Springer Verlag, 2000.
13. Petriu, D. Shousha, C., Jalnapurkar, A. "Architecture based Performance Analysis Applied to a Telecommunication System", *IEEE Trans. on Software Engineering*, Nov. 2000.
14. Pooley, R. and King, P. "The Unified Modeling Language and Performance Engineering", *IEE Proceedings Software*, vol.146, no.1, pp. 2-10, February 1999.
15. Williams, L.G. and Smith, C.U. "Performance Evaluation of Software Architecture", Proc. of *1st Int. Workshop on Software and Performance*, WOSP1998, Sept. 1998, SantaFe, USA.
16. A. Puliafito, S. Riccobene, M. Scarpa "An analytical comparison of the client-server, remote evaluation and mobile agent paradigms" in *1st Int. Symp. on Agent Systems and Applications and 3rd Int. Symp. on Mobile Agents* (ASA/MA 99), Oct. 1999.
17. M.L. Puterman, *Markov Decision Processes*, J. Wiley & Sons, 1994.
18. G.C. Roman, G.P. Picco, A.L. Murphy "Software enginering for mobility: a roadmap" in *The future of SW engineering* (A. Finkelstein ed.), ACM Press, 2000, pp. 241-258.

19. G. Samaras, M.D. Dikaiakos, C. Spyrou, A. Liverdos "Mobile agent platforms for Web databases: a qualitative and quantitative assessment" in *1st Int. Symp. on Agent Systems and Applications and 3rd Int. Symp. on Mobile Agents* (ASA/MA 99), Oct. 1999.
20. T. Spalink, J.H. Hartman, G. Gibson "The effects of a mobile agent on file service " in *1st Int. Symp. on Agent Systems and Applications and 3rd Int. Symp. on Mobile Agents*(ASA/MA 99), Oct. 1999.
21. B. Spitznagel, D. Garlan "Architecture-based performance analysis" in Proc. 1998 Conference on Software Engineering and Knowledge Engineering, June 1998.
22. M. Strasser, M. Schwehm "A performance model for mobile agent system" in *Int. Conference on Parallel and Distributed Processing Techniques and Applications* (PDPTA 97), vol. II, (H.R. Arabnia ed.), Las Vegas 1997, pp. 1132-1140.
23. S.M.Yacoub, B. Cukic, H.H. Ammar "Sceario-based reliability analysis of component-based software" in Proc. of *ISSRE'99*, 1-4 Nov. 1999, Boca Raton, Florida.
24. *WOSP2000*, Proc. of the *2nd Int. Workshop on Software and Performance*, Ottawa, Canada, Sept. 2000

Appendix

In this appendix we present more formally the MDP generation algorithm, outlined in section 4.3.

For each state $s \in S$, let us define:

$F(s) = \{[succ_j, f_j, c_j]\}$ $(j = 1, \ldots, \#F(s))$ a sequence of 3-tuples, where $succ_j \in S$ is a destination state, f_j is a transition rate, and c_j is a transition cost;

$$D(s) = \left\{ \left[\{d_{j1}, d_{j2}\}, \{succ_{j1}, succ_{j2}\}, \{f_{j1}, f_{j2}\}, \{c_{j1}, c_{j2}\} \right] \right\} (j = 1, \ldots, \#D(s)?)$$

a sequence of 4-tuples, where each element of the 4-tuple consists of a pair; in particular d_{j1} expresses the selection of the no-mobility option as interaction style between two components (source and target of a moveTo? message) and d_{j2} expresses the selection of the alternative mobility option for the same pair of components; then, $succ_{jr} \in S$, f_{jr}, and c_{jr} $(r = 1, 2)$ are the corresponding destination state, transition rate, and transition cost.

Input:
   - the state set S (see section 4.2);
   - the set $P = \{[C_h, C_k]\}$ of pairs of interacting components, obtained from CD (each $[C_h, C_k]$ is a pair of components in CD that are source and target, respectively, of a message);
   - for each pair in P, the number N_i of normal interactions, obtained from SD;
   - for each pair in P, where the two components are the source and target, respectively, of a moveTo or moveTo? message, the number N_m of possible location changes, obtained from SD and CD (equal to number of consecutive interactions sequences between the pair of components that can be isolated in SD);
   - for each pair in P, the average cost C_i of a normal interaction, obtained from annotations in SD (equal to the sum of all the costs that characterize the interactions between the pair of components, divided by the corresponding N_i);
   - for each pair in P, where the two components are the source and target, respectively, of a moveTo or moveTo? message, the average cost C_m of a location change for the source component;

- the total number of interactions $N\text{tot} = \sum\limits_{\substack{\text{all the pairs} \\ \text{in P}}} (Ni + Nm)$.

Output:
for each state s ?S, the set of alternative decisions concerning components mobility in that state, and the associated transition rates and transition rewards.

Algorithm:
for each state s ?S:

$F(s) := ?;$
$D(s) := ?;$
for each pair [Ch, Ck] ?P:
$F(s) := F(s)$?{3-tuples generated by rules A, and B};
if (Ch and Ck are colocated in state s)
then $F(s) := F(s)$? {3-tuple generated by rule C}
else $D(s) := D(s)$? {4-tuples generated by rule C}
/* the application of rules A, B, and C requires the use of the Ni, Nm, Ci, Cm, and $N\text{tot}$ quantities provided as input */
endfor;

build the set $\text{DecVec}(s) := \prod\limits_{j=1}^{|D(s)|} \{dj1, dj2\};$

/* DecVec(s) is the set of all decision vectors concerning components mobility in state s; the cardinality of DecVec(s) is $?D(s)?^2$; each element of DecVec(s) is a vector V with $?D(s)?$ components, where the j-th component V[j] takes as value one of the two decisions {dj1,

for each $V \in \text{DecVec}(s)$:
for each state $s' \in S$:

$$\text{freq}(s\text{-->}s') := \sum\limits_{\substack{j=1 \\ \text{s.t. } \text{succ}_j = s'}}^{|F(s)|} f_j \; + \; \sum\limits_{\substack{j=1 \\ \text{s.t. } V[j]=d_{jr} \\ \text{and } \text{succ}_{jr} = s'}}^{|D(s)|} f_{jr}$$

$$\text{rew}(s\text{-->}s') := \frac{\sum\limits_{\substack{j=1 \\ \text{s.t. } \text{succ}_j = s'}}^{|F(s)|} c_j \cdot f_j \; + \; \sum\limits_{\substack{j=1 \\ \text{s.t. } V[j]=d_{jr} \\ \text{and } \text{succ}_{jr}=s'}}^{|D(s)|} c_{jr} \cdot f_{jr}}{\text{freq}(s\text{-->}s')}$$

endfor
endfor
endfor
dj2} */

Extending UML for Object-Relational Database Design

E. Marcos, B. Vela, and J.M. Cavero

Kybele Research Group
Rey Juan Carlos University
Madrid (Spain)
{cuca, b.vela, j.m.cavero}@escet.urjc.es

Abstract. The most common way of designing databases is using de E/R model without taking into account other views of the system. However, new object-oriented design languages, such as UML (Unified Modelling Language), permit modelling the full system, including the database schema, in a uniform way. Besides, as UML is an extensible language, it allows introducing new stereotypes for specific applications if it is needed. There are some proposals to extend UML with stereotypes for database design but, unfortunately, they are focused on relational databases. However, new applications require representing complex objects related with complex relationships and object-relational databases are more appropriated to support the new application requirements. The framework of this paper is an Object-Relational Database Design Methodology. The methodology defines new UML stereotypes for Object-Relational Database Design and proposes some guidelines to translate an UML schema into an object-relational one. The guidelines are based on the SQL:1999 object-relational model and on Oracle8*i* as an example of product. In this paper we focus on the UML extensions required for object-relational database design.

Keywords: UML extensions, Stereotypes, Database Design, Object-Relational Databases, Design Methodology, UML, SQL:1999, Oracle8*i*

1 Introduction

In spite of the impact of relational databases over the last decades, this kind of databases has some limitations for supporting data persistence required by present day applications. Due to recent hardware improvements more sophisticated applications have emerged such as CAD/CAM (Computer-Aided Design/Computer-Aided Manufacturing), CASE (Computer-Aided Software Engineering), GIS (Geographic Information System), etc. These applications can be characterised as consisting of complex objects related by complex relationships. Representing such objects and relationships in the relational model implies that the objects must be decomposed into a large number of tuples. Thus, a considerable number of joins is necessary to retrieve an object and, when tables are too deeply nested, performance is significantly reduced [3]. A new generation of databases has appeared to solve these problems: the object-oriented database generation, which include the object–relational [23] and object databases [4]. This new technology is well suited for storing and retrieving complex

M. Gogolla and C. Kobryn (Eds.): UML 2001, LNCS 2185, pp. 225–239, 2001.
© Springer-Verlag Berlin Heidelberg 2001

data because it supports complex data types and relationships, multimedia data, inheritance, etc.

Nonetheless, good technology is not enough to support complex objects and applications. It is necessary to define methodologies that guide designers in the object database design task, in the same way as it has been done traditionally with relational databases. Over the last years some approaches to object-oriented database design have appeared [5,12,18,22,24]. Unfortunately, none of these proposals can be considered as "the method", neither for object-relational nor for object databases. On the one hand, they do not consider the latest versions of the representative standards for both technologies: ODMG 3.0 for object databases [8] and SQL:1999 for object-relational databases [10]. And, on the other hand, some of them are based on old techniques as OMT [5] or, even, on the E/R model [24]. As a result they have to be updated considering UML, SQL:1999 and ODMG 3.0 as their reference models. In this paper we give a brief description of a methodology for object-relational database design which is based on UML extended with the required stereotypes. We will focus on object-relational databases, although the UML proposed extensions could also be fitted for object database design.

UML [6], as a Unified Modelling Language, is becoming increasingly more accepted. It also presents the advantage of being able to model the full system, including the database view, in a uniform way. Besides, as UML is an extendable language, it is possible to define the required stereotypes, tagged values and/or constraints, for each specific application. Therefore, the aforesaid methodology proposes to use the UML class diagram as the conceptual modelling notation.

The methodology provides some guidelines for translating a conceptual schema (in UML notation) into a logical schema. As the logical model we use the SQL:1999 object-relational model so that the guidelines were not dependent on the different implementations of object-relational products. We use Oracle8i as an implementation example.

Traditionally, methodologies provided graphical techniques to represent a relational schema, such as Data Structured Diagrams (DSD), relational "graph", etc. In the same way, an object-relational schema can be represented either in SQL (SQL:1999 or Oracle8i) or using some graphical notation. As the graphical notation to represent the logical schema we also propose to use the UML class diagram extended with the required stereotypes, tagged values and/or constraints.

We have applied the methodology and the UML's extensions in an internal project of our research group: the computer classroom reservation for the *Rey Juan Carlos* University. Now we are starting to apply it to a real development (together with INTESYS, a Spanish Company) in the framework of the MIDAS[1] project.

We want to outline the importance of providing methodological guidelines for database design using UML for data intensive applications. *"Generic lifecycle methodologies for object-oriented development have, to date, not given serious consideration to the need for persistence; either in terms of storage of objects in a relational database or in an objectbase"* [7]. Information systems and, of course,

---

[1]   MIDAS is partially financed by the Spanish Government and the European Community (reference number: 2FD97-2163)

Web information systems, have to manage a lot of data that need to be persistent. A good design of persistent data will improve its use and its maintenance. Currently, the main mechanism of persistence is still the database. As it is stated in [13], the IDC market research firm reported global 1999 sales revenue of $11.1 billion for relational and object-relational databases and $211 million for object databases. Through to 2004, IDC predicts annual growth rates of 18.2 percent for relational and object-relational databases and 12.5 percent for object databases. Therefore, databases will still be the kernel of almost every information system for a long time.

The rest of the paper is organised as follows: section 2 summarises the current UML extensions for database design. Section 3 proposes new UML extensions for relational-database design based on SQL:1999 and Oracle8*i* object-relational models. Section 4 sums up the methodology showing some examples, which use the proposed extensions. Finally, section 5 summarises the main conclusions and future work.

2 Previous Concepts

The UML extension mechanism permits you to extend the language in controlled ways. This mechanism includes stereotypes, tagged values and constraints [6].

* Stereotype: *a stereotype extends the vocabulary of the UML, allowing us to create new kinds of building blocks that are derived from existing ones but that are specific to a problem. This new block has its own special properties (each stereotype may provide its own set of tagged values), semantics (each stereotype may provide its own constraints, and notation (each stereotype may provide its own icon). A stereotype is rendered as a name enclosed by guillemets (<<name>>) and placed above the name of another element. It is also possible to define an icon for the stereotype.*
* Tagged value: *a tagged value extends the properties of a UML building block, allowing us to create new information in that element's specification. With stereotypes we can add new things to the UML; with tagged values, we can add new properties. A tagged value is rendered as a string enclosed by brackets and placed below the name of another element.*
* Constraint: *A constraint extends the semantics of a UML building block, allowing us to add new rules or modify existing ones. A constraint specifies conditions that must be held true for the model to be well- formed. A constraint is rendered as a string enclosed by braces and placed near the associated element.*

For applications that are very common (such as Web applications, DB applications, etc.) it would be desirable to provide a standard extension that could be used by every developer. So, Conallen has proposed a UML's extension for Web applications [9] and there are also some extensions for database design [1, 6, 19] (see Table 1).

We can notice that table 1 considers the relational model including stereotypes to represent the primary key, the foreign key, etc. Nevertheless, it does not provide specific stereotypes for an object model such as stereotypes for collection types, REF types, methods, etc.). The next section introduces the new required extensions (stereotypes, tagged values and/or constraints) for object-relational database design.

Table 1. Stereotypes for database design.

DB Element	UML Element	Stereotype	Icon
Database	Component	<<Database>>	
Schema	Package	<<Schema>>	
Tablespace	Component	<<Tablespace>>	
Table	Class	<<Table>>	
View	Class	<<View>>	
Index	Class	<<Index>>	
Column	Attributes	<<Column>>	
Primary Key	Attributes	<<PK>>	
Foreign Key	Attributes	<<FK>>	
Multivalued Attribute	Attribute	<<AM>>	
Calculated Attribute	Attribute	<<AD>>	
Composed Attribute	Attribute	<<AC>>	
NOT NULL Restriction	Attributes	<<NOT NULL>>	
Unique Restriction	Attributes	<<Unique>>	
Trigger	Restriction	<<Trigger>>	
Restriction	Restriction	<<Check>>	
Stored Procedure	Class	<<Stored Procedure>>	

3 UML Extensions for Object-Relational Database Design

Before explaining the UML extensions for object-relational database design we have to introduce the main constructors of the object-relational model. As we have explained in section 1, we have considered the SQL:1999 and Oracle8*i* models. The first one, because it is the current standard for object-relational databases and the second one as an example of product implementation. SQL:1999 data model extends the relational data model with some new constructors to support objects. Most of the latest versions of relational products include some object extensions. However, because in general these products have appeared in the market before the standard approval, current versions of object-relational products do not totally adjust to the SQL:1999 model.

3.1. The Object-Relational Model: SQL:1999 and Oracle8*i*

SQL:1999 Object-Relational Model

SQL:1999 [10,14] is the current standard for object-relational databases. Its data model tries to integrate the relational model with the object model. In addition to the object extensions, SQL:1999 provides other extensions to the SQL-92, such as triggers, OLAP extensions, new data types for multimedia data storage, etc. One of the main differences between the relational and the object-relational model is that the First Normal Form (1NF), the basic rule of a relational schema, has been removed from the object-relational model. So a column of an object table can contain a collection data type.

SQL:1999 allows the user to define new structured data types according to the required data types for each application. Structured data types provide SQL:1999 the main characteristics of the object model. It supports the concept of strongly typed language, behaviour, encapsulation, substitutability, polymorphism and dynamic binding.

Structured types can be used as the type of a table or as the type of a column. A structured type used as the base type in the definition of a column permits the representation of complex attributes; in this case, structured types represent value types. A structured type used as the base type in the definition of a table corresponds to the definition of an object type (or a class); the table being the extension of the type. In SQL:1999 these kinds of tables are called typed tables. An object in SQL:1999 is a row of a typed table. When a typed table is defined, the system adds a new column representing the OID (Object IDentifier) of each object of the table. The value of this attribute is system generated, it is unique for each object and the user cannot modify it. Figure 1 shows an example of a structured type defined in SQL:1999; in (a) the structured type is used as a value type (as the type of a column of a table) whereas in (b) it is used as an object type (as the type of a table).

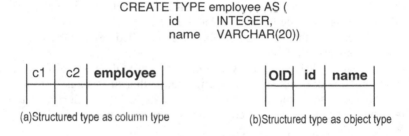

```
CREATE TYPE employee AS (
      id        INTEGER,
      name      VARCHAR(20))
```

c1	c2	**employee**

(a)Structured type as column type

OID	**id**	**name**

(b)Structured type as object type

Fig. 1. Structured types used as value and object types [14].

A structured type can include associated methods representing its behaviour. A method is a SQL function, whose signature is defined next to the definition of the structured type. The body specification is defined separately from the signature of the method.

SQL:1999 supports simple inheritance for structured types and for typed tables. A subtype inherits the attributes and the behaviour of the supertype. A subtable inherits the columns, restrictions, triggers and methods of the supertable.

A row of a typed table is an object and differs from the rest of objects by its OID. The value of the OID is generated by the system when a new object is inserted in the table. The type of this column is a reference type (REF). Therefore, each typed table has a column that contains the OID value. There are different REF types, one for each object type; that is, the REF type is a constructor of types rather than a type itself. An attribute defined as reference type holds the OID of the referred object. So, the REF type permits the implementation of relationships without using foreign keys.

SQL:1999 supports another structured type: the ROW type. The ROW type is a structured type defined by the user. It has neither extension nor OID; so, it cannot be used as an object type.

SQL:1999 only supports a collection type: ARRAY. The ARRAY can be used whenever another type can be placed (as the type of an attribute of a structured type, as the type of a column, etc.). The ARRAY type allows the representation of multivalued attributes not forcing tables to be in 1NF.

Oracle8*i* Object-Relational Model

As well as SQL:1999, Oracle8*i* [20,21] supports structured data types that can be defined by the user (although, with a different syntax). A structured type can be used, as in SQL:1999, as a column type or as a type of a table. A structured type used as a column type represents a value type and a structured type used as the type of a table represents an object type; the table being the extension of the type. Each row of this kind of tables is an object and, in the same way as in SQL:1999, they have a special column of reference type (REF) that allows the identification of each object (OID). It is also possible to define an attribute as a reference to an object type. Oracle8*i* allows the association behaviour to object types, defining the signature of the methods as part of the type definition. The body of the method is defined separately.

Oracle8*i* supports two kinds of collections: VARRAYS, equivalent to the SQL:1999 ARRAY and the nested table. A nested table is a table that is embedded in another table. It is possible to define a table data type and to use this type as a column type in a table. Therefore, this column contains a table (called nested table) with a collection of values, objects or references.

One of the main differences between Oracle8*i* and SQL:1999 object-relational model is that Oracle8*i* does not support inheritance, neither of types nor of tables. There do exist, however, some relational products, such as, Universal Server of Informix [11], that support the inheritance concept in a similar way as the standard.

3.2. Object-Relational Extension for UML

If we want UML to be used as the standard modelling language for designing databases, we have to modify it so it allows us to represent object-relational schema. In this way, it would be able to represent the constructors defined above such as the ARRAY, the NESTED TABLE or the REF type.

One possible solution could be to modify the meta-model of UML but this may seem like a drastic solution. However, UML has been designed to be extended in a controllable way. To accommodate this need for flexibility UML provides an extension mechanism that we have explained in section 2. This mechanism enables us to create new types of building blocks by means of stereotypes, tagged values and constraints.

According with [9] an UML's extension should contain: a brief description of the extension; the list and description of the stereotypes, tagged values and constraints; and a set of well-formedness-rules that are used to determine whether a model is semantically consistent. For each stereotype we have to specify the common properties and semantics that go beyond the basic element being stereotyped by defining a set of tagged values and constraints for the stereotype [6]. If we want these stereotype elements to have a distinctive visual cue, we have to define a new icon for the stereotype [6]. Table 2 summarises the UML's extension proposed for object-relational database design.

Table 2. UML Extension for object-relational database design.

Description
This extension to UML defines a set of stereotypes, tagged values and constraints that enable us to model applications that work with object-relational databases. The extensions are defined for certain components that are specific to object-relational models allowing us to represent them in the same diagram that describes the rest of the system. The extension is based on SQL:1999 and Oracle8*i* object-relational models. Each element of the object-relational model has to have a UML representation. To choose the stereotyped element we used the following criteria: • For SQL:1999 we have considered *structured types* and *typed tables* as stereotyped classes because they are explicitly defined in the SQL schema. The rest of the types (REF, ROW and ARRAY) are considered as stereotyped attributes. • For Oracle8*i* we have considered *object types*, *object tables* and *nested tables* as stereotyped classes for the same reason as in SQL:1999. The REF type has been considered as a stereotyped attribute because it cannot be defined explicitly in the SQL schema. As the VARRAY can be, or cannot be, defined explicitly in the schema we will allow the two possibilities: to define it as stereotyped attributes or as stereotyped classes. We will use the stereotyped class when the VARRAY type was defined explicitly in the schema. In this way, the UML schema with stereotypes for Oracle8*i* will help the developer in the compilation process (compiling these schemas in Oracle8*i* is tedious because types have to be recompiled, so this technique can be helpful for the user).

Prerequisite Extensions
We consider that the required extension for the relational mode has already been defined [1, 19].

SQL:1999 Stereotypes	

Structured Type
Metamodel class: Class
Description: A <<*udt*>> allows the representation of new User defined Data Types.
 	
Icon: None
Constraints: It can only be used to define value types
Tagged values: None
	Typed Table
	Metamodel class: Class
	Description: It is defined as <<*persistent*>>. It represents a class of the database schema, that should be defined as a table of a structured data type.
	
	`<<udt>>`
	`<<persistent>>`
	Icon:
	Constraints: A typed table implies the definition of a structured type, which is the type of the table.
	Tagged values: None

Composes Metamodel class: Association Description: A <<*composes*>> association is a special relationship that joins a user defined data type <<*udt*>> with the class that uses it. It is a uni-directional relationship. The direction of the association is represented by an arrow at the end of the class, which use the user defined type. Icon: None Constraints: It only can be used to join a <<*persistent*>> class with a <<*udt*>> class Tagged values: None	**REF Type** Metamodel class: Attribute Description: A <<*ref*>> represents a link to some <<*persistent*>> class. Icon: ●▶ Constraints: A <<*ref*>> attribute can only refer to a <<*persistent*>> class Tagged values: The <<*persistent*>> class to which it refers

ARRAY	**ROW Type**
Metamodel class: Attribute	Metamodel class: Attribute
Description: An <<*array*>> represents an indexed and bounded collection type.	Description: A <<*row*>> type represents a composed attribute with a fixed number of elements, each of them can be of different data type
Icon: ▭▭▭	
Constraints: The elements of an <<*array*>> can be of any data type except the <<*array*>> type	Icon: ▤
Tagged values: The basic types of the array The number of elements	Constraints: It does not have methods
	Tagged values: The name for each element and its data type
Redefined Method	**Deferred Method**
Metamodel class: Method	Metamodel class: Method
Description: A <<*redef*>> method is a inherited method that is implemented again by the child class.	Description: A <<*def*>> method is a method that defers its implementation to its child classes.
Icon: None	Icon: None
Constraints: None	Constraints: It has to be defined in a class with children
Tagged values: The list of parameters of the method with their data types. The data type returned by the method.	Tagged values: The list of parameters of the method with their data types. The data type returned by the method.
Oracle8*i* Stereotypes	
Object Type	**Object Table**
Metamodel class: Class	Metamodel class: Class
Description: A <<*udt*>> allows the representation of new user defined data types. It corresponds to the structured type in SQL:1999.	Description: It is define as <<*persistent*>>. It represents a class of the database schema, that should be defined as a table of an object type. It corresponds to the typed table in SQL:1999.
Icon: None	Icon: <<*udt*>> <<*persistent*>>
Constraints: It can only be used to define value types	Constraints: A typed table implies the definition of a structured type, which is the type of the table.
Tagged values: None	Tagged values: None
Composes	**REF Type**
Metamodel class: Association	Metamodel class: Attribute
Description: A <<*composes*>> association is a special relationship that joins a user defined data type (<<*udt*>>, <<*array*>> or <<*nt*>>) with the class that uses it. It is an uni-directional relationship. The direction of the association is represented by an arrow at the end of the class, which uses the data type.	Description: A <<*ref*>> represents a link to some <<persistent>> class.
Icon: None	Icon: ●▶
Constraints: It only can be used to join a <<*persistent*>> class with a <<*udt*>> class	Constraints: A <<*ref*>> attribute can only refer to a <<*persistent*>> class
Tagged values: None	Tagged values: The <<*persistent*>> class to which it refers

VARRAY	Nested Table
Metamodel class: Attribute/Class	Metamodel class: Class
Description: A <<*array*>> represents an indexed and bounded collection type. It corresponds to the array type in SQL:1999.	Description: A <<nt>> represents an non-indexed and unbounded collection type.
Icon: ▭▭▭▭	Icon: ▥
Constraints: The elements of an <<*array*>> can be of any data type except another collection type (<<*array*>> or <<*nt*>>)	Constraints: The elements of a <<nt>> can be of any data type except another collection type (<<array>> or <<nt>>).
Tagged values: The basic types of the array The number of elements	Tagged values: The basic type of the nested table

Well-Formedness Rules

Each <<*udt*>>, <<*array*>> or <<*nt*>> class has to be joined by a <<*composes*>> association with any class.
A <<*ref*>> attribute in a <<*persistent*>> class implies an association with another class.
A <<*persistent*>> class that contains a collection attribute whose elements were objects of a <<*persistent*>> class of <<*ref*>> to these objects implies an association between both classes.
Each <<*persistent*>> class corresponds in SQL:1999 to a structured type with its corresponding extension. The extension is the typed table. Each <<*persistent*>> class in Oracle8*i* corresponds to an object type with its corresponding extension. The extension is the table of object type. That is to say: the object type and its extension are represented in the UML extension just as a <<*persistent*>> class.

Comments

This extension considers the object-relational model of SQL:1999 and Oracle8*i*. It should be modified according to the new versions of both object-relational models. Moreover, if we want to use other products this extension has to be adapted. For example, for Informix, we will have to introduce new extensions for the set, multiset and list collection types.

4 Integrating the UML Extension in a Methodology for Object-Relational Database Design

In this section we show an example of object-relational database design using the extension for UML proposed in the previous section. This example is made in the framework of a methodology for object-relational database design. This methodology is based on the proposal of [3] for object-oriented database design and on the proposal of [15]. Figure 2 summarises the main steps of the methodology.

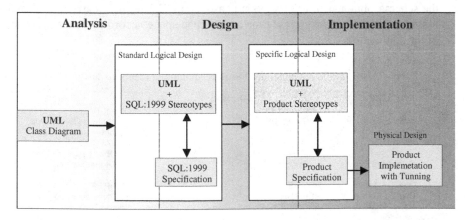

Fig. 2. Object-Relational Database Design Methodology

The methodology proposes three phases: analysis, design and implementation. Nonetheless, as it is shown in figure 5, differences between analysis, design and implementation phases are not as strong as in structured design.

At the **analysis** phase, we propose to use the UML class diagram to design the conceptual schema instead of the Extended E/R Model (commonly used for relational databases), because UML is the standard language for object-oriented system design. Unlike E/R, UML has the advantage that it allows the design of the entire system making the integration between different system views easier.

The **design** phase is divided into two steps:

- Standard design, that is, a logical design independent of any product.
- Specific design, that is, the design for a specific product (Oracle8*i*, Informix, etc.) without considering tuning or optimisation tasks.

Standard design is especially important in object-relational database design because each product implements a different object-relational model. This phase provides an object-relational specification independent of the product improving the database maintainability as well as making migration between products easier. As it is shown in figure 2, we propose two alternative techniques for this phase: defining the schema in SQL:1999, because it does not depend on any specific product; and/or using a graphical notation describing a standard object-relational model (the SQL:1999 model). This graphical notation corresponds with the relational graph that represents the logical design of a relational database [2]. As graphical notation we propose to use the UML extensions defined in section 3 for the SQL:1999 object-relational model.

For the specific design (intermediate stage between design and implementation), we have to specify the schema in the SQL (language) of the chosen product. We use, as an example, Oracle8*i*. Besides, we also propose to make optional use of a graphical technique to improve the documentation and the understandability of the generated SQL code. Moreover, this technique makes the compilation of the database schema easier by showing the correct order in which we have to compile each new user defined type and each table. The graphical notation is also UML substituting the SQL:1999 stereotypes with the specific stereotypes for the selected product.

Finally, the **implementation** phase includes the physical design tasks. In this phase the schema obtained in the previous phase should be refined, carrying out making a tuning to improve the response time and storage space according to the specific needs of the application.

Table 3. Guidelines for object-relational database design.

UML	SQL:1999	Oracle8*i*
Class	Structured Type	Object Type
Class Extension	Typed Table	Table of Object Type
Attribute	Attribute	Attribute
Multivalued	ARRAY	VARRAY
Composed	ROW / Structured Type in column	Object Type in column
Calculated	Trigger/Method	Trigger/Method
Association		
One-To-One	REF/REF	REF/REF
One-To-Many	REF/ARRAY	REF/Nested Table
Many-To-Many	ARRAY/ARRAY	Nested Table/Nested Table
Aggregation	ARRAY	Nested Table
Generalisation	Types/Typed Tables	Oracle cannot directly represent the generalisation concept

Relational database methodologies propose some rules to transform a conceptual schema into a standard logical schema. In the same way, our methodology also proposes a technique that allows the transformation of a schema from one phase to the next. This technique suggests some rules that should be considered only as guidelines. These rules are summarised in table 3 and are detailed in [16, 17].

4.1. Example

As we have explained in the introduction, we have used the described methodology and the UML's extensions in an internal project of our research group. The application resolves the problem of the computer reserves in our university. The application has been developed for a Web environment using XML and Oracle8*i*.

In this section we describe part of the application. to show an example of how to use the defined stereotypes for object-relational database design. Teachers can reserve computer-classrooms to impart their practical classes. A classroom is composed of a set of computers. The students can only reserve computers if a teacher or another student have not previously reserved them. To develop the application we have applied the mentioned methodology following the phases shown in figure 2.

Analysis phase: Figure 3 shows the UML class diagram used to design the conceptual schema.

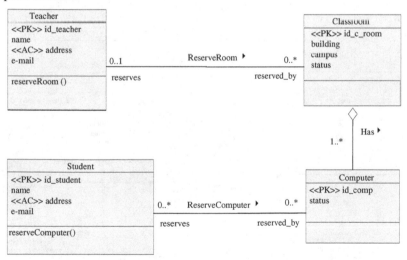

Fig. 3. Conceptual Design in UML

Analysis-Design phase: Figure 4 shows the standard design with the proposed graphical notation, consisting in the defined UML extensions for the SQL:1999 object-relational model.

Design-Implementation phase: Figure 5 shows the specific design (intermediate stage between design and implementation phases), with the proposed graphical notation. The graphical notation is also UML substituting the SQL:1999 stereotypes with the specific stereotypes for the selected product. We have also specified the obtained schema in the SQL (language) of the chosen product, Oracle8*i*, as figure 6 shows.

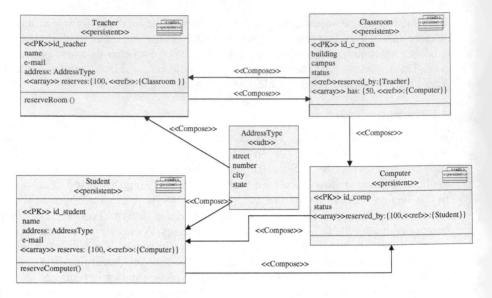

Fig. 4. Logical Design in SQL:1999

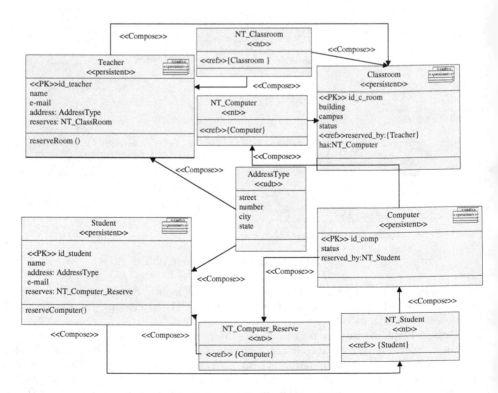

Fig. 5. Logical Design in Oracle8*i*

```
CREATE OR REPLACE TYPE AddressType AS OBJECT
( street VARCHAR(20)
, num NUMBER
, city   VARCHAR(20)
, state  VARCHAR(10))
/
CREATE OR REPLACE TYPE Computer AS OBJECT
(id_comp VARCHAR(5)
, status   VARCHAR(2)
, reserved_by NT_Student)
/
CREATE OR REPLACE TYPE NT_Computer
AS TABLE OF REF Computer
/
CREATE OR REPLACE TYPE NT_Computer_Reserve
AS TABLE OF REF Computer
/
CREATE OR REPLACE TYPE Student AS OBJECT
( id_student VARCHAR(5)
, name VARCHAR(50)
, address AddressType
, e_mail VARCHAR(100)
, reserves NT_Computer_Reserve)
/
CREATE OR REPLACE TYPE NT_Student
AS TABLE OF REF Student
/
CREATE OR REPLACE TYPE Teacher AS OBJECT
( id_teacher VARCHAR(5)
, name VARCHAR(50)
, e_mail VARCHAR(100)
, address AddressType
, reserves NT_ClassRoom)
/
CREATE OR REPLACE TYPE Classroom AS OBJECT
(id_c_room VARCHAR(5)
, building VARCHAR(50)
, campus VARCHAR(10)
, status VARCHAR(2)
, reserved_by REF Teacher
, has NT_Computer)
/
```

```
CREATE OR REPLACE TYPE NT_ClassRoom
AS TABLE OF Ref Classroom
/

/* Recompilation */
CREATE OR REPLACE TYPE Computer AS OBJECT
(id_comp VARCHAR(5)
, status  VARCHAR(2)
, reserved_by NT_Student)
/
CREATE OR REPLACE TYPE Teacher AS OBJECT
( id_teacher VARCHAR(5)
, name VARCHAR(50)
, e_mail VARCHAR(100)
, address AddressType
, reserves NT_ClassRoom)
/

/* Table Creation*/
CREATE TABLE TClassroom OF Classroom
(PRIMARY KEY (id_c_room))
NESTED TABLE has STORE AS table_computer_cr;

CREATE TABLE TComputer OF Computer
(PRIMARY KEY (id_comp))
NESTED TABLE reserved_by STORE AS table_student;

CREATE TABLE TStudent OF Student
(PRIMARY KEY (id_student))
NESTED TABLE reserves STORE AS table_computer_s;

CREATE TABLE TTeacher OF Teacher
(PRIMARY KEY (id_teacher))
NESTED TABLE reserves STORE AS table_classroom;
```

Fig. 6. Oracle8*i* Code

6 Conclusions and Future Work

Object-relational databases will be become increasingly each day more extended because they provide a better support than relational technology for complex data and relationships. As a result, new methodologies for object-relational database design are emerging. In this paper we have summarised a methodology for object-relational database design, which is based on UML extended with the required stereotypes. We have focused on object-relational databases, although the UML's proposed extensions could also be fitted for object database design.

The methodology proposes three phases: analysis, design and implementation. As conceptual modelling technique we have chosen the UML class diagram. As the logical model we have used the SQL:1999 object-relational model, so that the guidelines are not dependent on the implementations of object-relational products. As a product example we have used Oracle8*i*.

Traditionally, methodologies provided graphical techniques to represent a relational schema, such as Data Structured Diagrams (DSD), relational "graph", etc. In the same way, an object-relational schema can be represented either in SQL (SQL:1999 or Oracle8*i*) or using some graphical notation. As graphical notation to represent the logical schema we have proposed using the UML class diagram extended with the required stereotypes, tagged values and/or constraints. This paper has been focused on the UML's extensions required for object-relational design in both models, SQL:1999 and Oracle8*i*. We have summarised the stereotypes, tagged values and constraints. We have also explained a part of an application that we have developed using the UML extension: the computer classroom reservation for the *Rey Juan Carlos* University. Now we are starting to apply it to a real development in the framework of the MIDAS project. The development has been carried out together with INTESYS, a Spanish Company that participates in the MIDAS project.

Acknowledgments. This work is being carried out as part of the MIDAS project. MIDAS is partially financed by the Spanish Government and the European Community (reference number: 2FD97-2163).

References

1. Ambler (1999), *Persistence Modelling in the UML*. In:
    http://www.sdmagazine.com/articles/1999/0008/0008q/0008q.htm
2. Atzeni, Ceri, Paraboschi and Torlone (1999). *Database Systems. Concepts, Languages and Architectures*. McGraw-Hill.
3. Bertino and Marcos (2000), "Object Oriented Database Systems". In *Advanced Databases: Technology and Design*, O. Díaz and M. Piattini (Eds.). Artech House.
4. Bertino and Martino (1993), *Object-Oriented Database Systems. Concepts and Architectures*. Addison-Wesley.
5. Blaha and Premerlani (1998), *Object-Oriented Modeling and Design for Database Applications*. Prentice Hall.
6. Booch, Rumbaugh and Jacobson (1999), *The Unified Modelling Language User Guide*. Addison Wesley.
7. T. Case, B. Henderson-Sellers and G.C. Low (1996). A generic object-oriented design methodology incorporating database considerations. *Annals of Software Engineering*. Vol. 2, pag. 5-24.
8. Cattell and Barry (2000), *The Object Data Standard: ODMG 3.0*. Morgan Kaufmann.
9. J. Conallen (2000), *Building Web Application with UML*. Addison-Wesley.
10. Eisenberg and Melton (1999), "SQL:1999, formerly known as SQL3". *ACM SIGMOD Record*, Vol. 28, No. 1, pp. 131-138, March 1999.
11. Informix Corporation (1999), *Informix Guide to SQL: Reference*. Electronic Documentation, Informix Press.
12. C. Kovács and P. Van Bommel (1998), "Conceptual modelling-based design of object-oriented databases". *Information and Software Technology*, Vol. 40, No. 1, pp. 1-14.
13. Leavit, N. (2000), "Whatever Happened to Object-Oriented Databases?". *Computer*, pp. 16-19, August 2000.
14. Mattos, N. M (1999), *SQL:1999, SQL/MM and SQLJ: An Overview of the SQL Standards*. Tutorial, IBM Database Common Technology.
15. Marcos, E. and Cáceres, P. (2001), "Object Oriented Database Design". In: *Developing Quality Complex Database Systems: Practices, Techniques, and Technologies*. Ed. Shirley Becker. Idea Group (accepted to publish in 2001).
16. E. Marcos, B. Vela and J. M. Cavero (2001), A Methodology for Object-Relational Database Design Using UML (submitted to 12th International Conference and Workshop on Database and Expert Systems and Applications, DEXA 2001).

17. E. Marcos, B. Vela and J. M. Cavero (2001), Aggregation and Composition in Object-Relational Database Design (submitted to Fifth East European Conference on Advances in Databases and Information Systems, ABDIS'2001).

18. Muller (1999), *Database Design for Smarties*. Morgan Kaufmann.

19. Naiburg, E. (2000), "Database Modeling and Design Using Rational Rose 2000e". *Rose Architect* Vol. 2, Issue 3, pp. 48-51.

20. Oracle Corporation (1998), "Objects and SQL in Oracle8". Oracle Technical White paper. In: *Extended DataBase Technology conference (EDBT'98)*. Valencia (Madrid).

21. Oracle Corporation (2000), Oracle8*i*. *SQL Reference. Release 3 (8.1.7)*. In: www.oracle.com.

22. Silva and Carlson (1995), "MOODD, a method for object-oriented database design." *Data & Knowledge Engineering*, Vol. 17, pp.159-181.

23. Stonebraker and Brown (1999). *Object-Relational DBMSs. Traking the Next Great Wave.* Morgan Kauffman.

24. Ullman and Widom (1997), *A First Course in Database Systems*. Prentice-Hall.

Understanding UML – Pains and Rewards

Werner Damm

OFFIS, Germany

Abstract. UML is there – it's accepted, it's booming, and even more: it's a standard. From telecom to train systems to avionics: using UML to capture the system is "in".
But do we really understand what we model?
This talk takes for granted, that models are alive, are executable, are used to explore the design space, are used to communicate design decisions, and ultimately are evolving to target code. And it asks plenty of nasty questions about the meaning of all these diagrams, which are so intuitive, but which require clarification if viewed from the most rigorous possible perspective – that of a formal semantics.
Formal Semantics are to modeling languages what X rays are to the human body: they bring to the surface problem spots not typically seen – and this process is painful. It shows, that what we see, is possibly far from what we expect: it highlights design decisions in giving a rigorous semantics to UML, which could have significant impact on e.g. meeting timeliness requirements.
But it also shows the rewards derivable from this painful exercise: giving a rigorous semantics offers the floor for powerful analysis techniques allowing to boost the quality of models.

Acknowledgments. This paper benefits from substantial discussions with David Harel and Amir Pnueli from the Weizmann Institute of Sciences, Israel.

A Formal Semantics of UML State Machines Based on Structured Graph Transformation⋆

Sabine Kuske

University of Bremen, Department of Computer Science
P.O. Box 330 440, D-28334 Bremen, Germany
kuske@informatik.uni-bremen.de
http://www.uni-bremen.de/~kuske

Abstract. UML state machines are quite popular and useful to specify dynamic components of software systems. They have a formal static semantics but their execution semantics is described only informally. Graph transformation, on the other hand, constitutes a well-studied area with many theoretical results and practical application domains. In this paper, an operational semantics for a subset of UML state machines is proposed which is based on graph transformation. In more detail, a UML state machine is described as a structured graph transformation system in such a way that the wellformedness rules of UML state machines are satisfied and the firing of a (maximum) set of enabled non-conflicting transitions corresponds to the application of a graph transformation rule. The presented approach uses the concept of transformation units, a recently developed modularization concept for graph transformation systems.

1 Introduction

UML state machines are widely used to model the dynamic behaviour of components in object oriented systems (see e.g. [BRJ98,RJB98,OMG99]). Whereas the static semantics of a state machine is precisely defined, the execution semantics is only given informally in natural language.

Graph transformation, on the other hand, is a thoroughly studied area with many potential application domains such as pattern recognition, theorem proving, functional programming languages, database systems, abstract data types, specification of distributed systems, etc. (see [Roz97,EEKR99,EKMR99] for an overview). The main idea of graph transformation consists of the local manipulation of graphs via the application of a rule. There exist various tools that implement graph transformation and may be used to specify visual languages or to generate diagram editors.

Since UML diagrams can be represented as graphs in a straightforward way, graph transformation rules can be employed to specify transformations of or

---

⋆ This work has been supported by the *Deutsche Forschungsgemeinschaft*, the ESPRIT Working Group Applications of Graph Transformation (APPLIGRAPH) and the EC TMR Network GETGRATS (General Theory of Graph Transformation Systems).

M. Gogolla and C. Kobryn (Eds.): UML 2001, LNCS 2185, pp. 241–256, 2001.

translations between UML diagrams (cf. [GP98,EHHS00,Gog00,PS00,TE00]). Hence, graph transformation seems to be a suitable means to formalize UML semantics and to check the consistency between different UML diagrams. Moreover, existing graph transformation tools can be used to obtain an implementation of UML semantics that is based on the theory of graph transformation. For the case of state machines this means that state configurations can be represented as graphs and the firing of transitions can be modelled via the application of graph transformation rules.

The main emphasis of this paper is to illustrate how graph transformation can be employed to model the dymnamic semantics of systems using the UML metamodel notation. Moreover, it is meant as a contribution to the modelization of UML diagrams with graph transformation with the overall aim to describe the interconnections between different types of UML diagrams in a uniform way. Concretely, this paper presents a formalization of a subset of UML state machines with graph transformation systems. The state configurations of state machines are represented as instances of the UML metamodel for state machines, and the application of a graph transformation rule to an instance corresponds to the firing of a maximum set of enabled non-conflicting transitions. It can be shown that the presented modelization satisfies the wellformedness rules of UML state machines. In order to obtain a structured and manageable representation of state machines (and not a flat system consisting of a set of rules only), we employ the concept of transformation units [KK99] which is a modularization concept for graph transformation systems.

The paper is organized as follows. Section 2 presents a short introduction to UML state machines. In Section 3 graph transformation systems are introduced. Section 4, the main part of the paper, gives a formalization of state machines based on structured graph transformation. Section 5 contains some concluding remarks. For reasons of space limitations, proofs are omitted.

2   State Machines

In this section, we briefly review the basic concepts of UML state machines. For further details see e.g. [BRJ98,RJB98,OMG99].

A state machine consists of a tree of distinctly named states. In general, states may contain several internal components, like entry and exit actions, activities, deferred events, etc. A state may be composite or simple. A composite state is either concurrent or sequential. Moreover, there may exist final states, synch states, pseudo states (i.e. initial states, history states, joins, forks, etc.), and stub states. States are connected by transitions which are labelled with a guard, an event, and an action. For reasons of space limitations, we do not consider internal components of states, actions, guards, synch states, and history states.[1] Nevertheless, we believe that at least history and synch states can be incorporated in our model without trouble.

---

[1] According to [RACH00] entry and exit actions and internal transitions can be eliminated by replacing them by equivalent other constructs.

States are depicted as boxes with rounded corners. Transitions are graphically represented as directed event-labelled arcs. Initial states are drawn as filled circles, and final states as circles surrounding a small filled circle. Fig. 1 shows an example of a state machine consisting of the states T, U, V, W, $A, \ldots, F$, a final state, some initial states, and the transitions $t_1, \ldots, t_9$ which are labelled with event a, b, or c.[2]

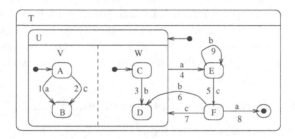

Fig. 1. A state machine

The execution semantics of a state machine comprises an *event queue* for storing incoming events, an *event dispatcher mechanism* for selecting and removing events from the event queue, and an *event processor* for performing so-called run-to-completion steps. Such a step transforms a state configuration of a state machine into another one, where a state configuration can be represented as a tree of states. In more detail, a run-to-completion step consists of the selection of a maximum set of enabled non-conflicting transitions such that a special priority rule is obeyed, and the firing of all selected transitions, in any order. A transition is enabled if its event corresponds to the currently dispatched event, its source state belongs to the leaves of the current state configuration, and its guard is true. Two enabled transitions are conflicting if their sources overlap in a certain form. The priority rule says that for two enabled conflicting transitions t and t', the transition t has a higher priority than t' if the source of t is a substate of the source of t'. As an example consider the state machine of Fig. 1, which is in the states A and C in the beginning. If event b is triggered t_3 is the only enabled transition, and after firing t_3 the machine is in the states D and A. If afterwards a is triggered, t_1 and t_4 are enabled and conflicting. The conflict is resolved in favour of t_1.

3 Graph Transformation

Graph transformation originated about thirty years ago as a generalization of the well-known Chomsky grammars to graphs. The basic operation of graph transformation consists of the local manipulation of graphs via the application

---

[2] Note that the names $1, \ldots, 9$ are written beside the transitions in order to distinguish them properly later on.

of a rule. In the field of graph transformation there are several co-existing approaches (cf. [Roz97]). For our purposes we choose the so-called double-pushout approach [CEH+97], the basic definitions of which are recalled in this section. Moreover, we introduce the modularization concept of transformation units that will be used to model state machines.

As underlying class of graphs we consider labelled directed graphs. In order to define graph transformation rules and rule application we also need the concepts of subgraph and graph morphism. Intuitively, a graph G is a subgraph of a graph G' if G is a part of G', and a graph morphism from a graph G to a graph G' relates G to an image of G in G' (which is structurally equivalent to G). Two graphs which are structurally equivalent (i.e. equal up to names of nodes and edges) are called isomorphic.

Definition 1 (Graph, subgraph, graph morphism).

1. A *graph* over a labelling alphabet $\mathcal{L}$ is a system $G = (V, E, s, t, l, m)$ where V is a finite set of *nodes*, E is a finite set of *edges*, $s, t: E \to V$ assign to every edge e its *source* $s(e)$ and its *target* $t(e)$, $l: V \to \mathcal{L}$ assigns to every node its *label*, and $m: E \to \mathcal{L}$ assigns a label to every edge. The components of G are also denoted by V_G, E_G, s_G, t_G, l_G, m_G, respectively. The set of all graphs will be denoted by $\mathcal{G}$.
2. A graph G is a *subgraph* of a graph G', denoted by $G \subseteq G'$, if $V_G \subseteq V_{G'}$, $E_G \subseteq E_{G'}$, $s_G = s_G|E_G$, $t_G = t_{G'}|E_G$, $l_G = l_{G'}|V_G$, and $m_G = m_{G'}|E_G$.[3]
3. A *graph morphism* g from a graph G to a graph G' consists of two mappings $g_V: V_G \to V_{G'}$, $g_E: E_G \to E_{G'}$ such that labels, sources, and targets are preserved, i.e. $l_G = l_{G'} \circ g_V$, $m_G = m_{G'} \circ g_E$, $g_V \circ s_G = s_{G'} \circ g_E$, and $g_V \circ t_G = t_{G'} \circ g_E$. The image of G in G' is also called an *occurrence* of G in G' and will be denoted by $g(G)$. The graphs G and G' are called *isomorphic* if g_V and g_E are bijective.

A graph transformation rule r consists of three graphs L, K, and R, called *left-hand side*, *gluing graph*, and *right-hand side*, respectively. It will be graphically represented as $L \to R$. The gluing graph is not depicted explicitly and consists of all nodes and edges which have the same label and position in L and R.

Definition 2 (Rule). A *rule* is a triple $r = (L, K, R)$ where L, K, and R are graphs and $L \supseteq K \subseteq R$.

A rule can be applied to a graph G if there exists a graph morphism from L to G which satisfies a certain requirement called gluing condition. In this case the application of r to G yields a graph G' which is obtained by replacing the occurrence $g(L)$ by R such that the gluing graph K is kept. The gluing graph K can be regarded as an interface between the part of G that is rewritten and the part of G that is not changed. Formally, a rule application, also called a direct derivation, corresponds to the construction of two pushouts in the category

---

[3] For a mapping $f: A \to B$ and a set $C \subseteq A$, $f|C$ denotes the restriction of f to C.

of graphs (see [CEH+97] for more details). Here we give a more algorithmic definition of rule application.

Definition 3 (Derivation). A graph G *directly derives* a graph G' via a rule $r = (L, K, R)$ according to the following steps. (1) *Choose* a graph morphism g from L to G. (If there is no morphism, the rule cannot be applied.) (2) *Check* the gluing condition: If the image of a node v in L contacts some edge not in the image of L, then v must be a node of K (contact condition). If different items x and y (nodes or edges) of L are identified in the image of L, then x and y must be in K (identification condition). (3) *Remove* $g(L) - g(K)$ from G. (4) *Add* the right-hand side R disjointly to the resulting graph D. (5) *Glue* D and R together by identifying the nodes and edges of K with their images.

A direct derivation from G to G' via r is denoted by $G \Rightarrow_r G'$. Instead of $G \Rightarrow_r G'$ we may also write $(G, G') \in \Rightarrow_r$. In this sense $\Rightarrow_r$ defines a binary relation on graphs. For a set R of rules, $\Rightarrow_R$ will denote the union of $\Rightarrow_r$ for all $r \in R$, and $\Rightarrow_R^*$ will denote the reflexive transitive closure of $\Rightarrow_R$.

In order to model state machines in a structured way, we employ the concept of transformation units (see [KK99]). A transformation unit contains a set of rules, a control condition, initial and terminal graph class expressions, and it can import other units. Roughly speaking, its semantics consists of all pairs (G, G') of graphs which can be obtained by interleaving rule applications with the semantics of imported transformation units, such that the control condition is obeyed, G is an initial graph, and G' is a terminal graph. In this paper, we consider transformation units with an acyclic import structure. Transformation units with cyclic imports are studied in [KKS97]. Note that originally, transformation units are approach independent, i.e. they are not bound to the double-pushout approach to graph transformation.

Definition 4 (Transformation unit). A *transformation unit* is a system $tu = (I, U, R, C, T)$ where I and T are *graph class expressions* each of which specifies a set of graphs, i.e. $SEM(I) \subseteq \mathcal{G}$ and $SEM(T) \subseteq \mathcal{G}$; U is a set of names referring to other transformation units; R is a set of rules; C is a *control condition* which specifies a binary relation $SEM(C)$ on graphs.[4] The *semantics* of tu is recursively given as follows: If $U = \emptyset$, $SEM(tu) = SEM(I) \times SEM(T) \cap \Rightarrow_R^* \cap SEM(C)$. Otherwise, assume that for every $t \in U$, $SEM(t)$ is defined, i.e. $SEM(t) \subseteq \mathcal{G} \times \mathcal{G}$. Then $SEM(tu) = SEM(I) \times SEM(T) \cap (\Rightarrow_R \cup SEM(U))^* \cap SEM(C)$. If $SEM(I) = \{G_0\}$, the set of all *generated graphs* of tu is defined as

$$generate(tu) = \{G \in \mathcal{G} \mid (G_0, G) \in SEM(tu)\}.$$

Here we give a few examples of graph class expressions and control conditions which will be used later on. (A detailed study of control conditions can be found in [Kus00].) A single graph G may be used as a graph class expression

---

[4] Please note that for technical simplicity we have slightly simplified the semantics of control conditions in this paper.

which specifies itself, i.e. $SEM(G) = \{G\}$. Moreover, given a set R of rules, the expression $reduced(R)$ specifies the set of all graphs to which no rule in R is applicable. As control conditions, regular expressions over rule names and names of imported units may be used. Since every such control condition C specifies a language L, a pair (G, G') is in $SEM(C)$ if there exists a word $x_1 \cdots x_n \in L$ such that G' can be obtained from G by applying successively x_1 to x_n.

4   Formalization of UML State Machines

The state hierarchy of a state machine can be modelled by a tree-like object diagram which is an instance of the UML metamodel for state machines. In more detail, every state is an object of type *CompositeState*, *SimpleState*, or *FinalState*. In the first case the value of the attribute *isConcurrent* indicates whether the state is concurrent or sequential. The substate relation is modelled by compositions. For example, the state hierarchy of the state machine in Fig. 1 is the lower right graph of Fig. 3 where the types *CompositeState*, *SimpleState*, *FinalState*, and *StateMachine* are abbreviated by CS, SST, FS, and STM, respectively. The attribute *isConcurrent* and the role names *container* and *subvertex* are abbreviated by *isC*, *c*, and *s*, respectively.

In the following, we assume that every state s is contained in an arbitrary but fixed state set $\mathcal{S}$ and has an arity $arity(s) \in \mathbb{N}$. All states with arity zero represent simple states; if a state has arity one, it is a composite sequential state; and a state with arity $n \geq 2$ is a concurrent state with n regions (cf. also [LP99]). For $i \in \mathbb{N}$ let $\mathcal{S}_i$ denote the set of all states in $\mathcal{S}$ with $arity(s) = i$. Moreover, let $\bullet \notin \mathcal{S}$ be the *final state*.[5]

The set of all state hierarchies over $\mathcal{S}$ are generated with the transformation unit *statehierarchy*($\mathcal{S}$) in Definition 5. The initial graph of *statehierarchy*($\mathcal{S}$) consists of a node for an object of type *StateMachine*, a round node labelled with *cs* and a composition connecting the two nodes. The role of the object is *container* and the role of the round node is *subvertex*. The *cs*-labelled node can be viewed as a placeholder for the rest of the hierarchy; it is refined using the rules of the unit.

With the rule r_1 of *statehierarchy*($\mathcal{S}$) (which more precisely is a rule set consisting of a rule for every $s \in \mathcal{S}_n$, $n > 1$) a *cs*-labelled node can be replaced by a concurrent state with n regions. For every region, a *cs*-labelled node is inserted which can be refined to an arbitrary state hierarchy (but not to a simple state) via further rule applications. The rule r_2 replaces a *cs*-node by a sequential state. The inserted *SorC*-labelled node can be refined to an arbitrary state hierarchy (by applying first r_6, afterwards r_1 or r_2, etc.) or to a simple state with r_4 or r_5. The rule r_3 serves to add substates to sequential states.

Note that in order to guarantee technical soundness of our approach, a composition in a state hierarchy is formally represented by a diamond-labelled node and two labelled edges connecting the diamond-node with object nodes. In the

---

[5] Note that every UML state machine with multiple final states can be transformed into an equivalent one with one final state (cf. [GP98,RACH00]).

case where the composed object is a state, the first edge is labelled with c and goes from the composed object to the diamond. The second edge is labelled with s and goes from the diamond to the part this object is composed of. In the case where the composed object is of type *StateMachine* the first edge is labelled with $*$ (standing for *unlabelled*) and the second is labelled with *top*. Moreover, every label x of an object node v is internally modelled with an x-labelled loop attached to v.

The control condition of *statehierarchy*($\mathcal{S}$) requires that any rule in r_1, r_2, r_4, and r_5 be applied at most once in order to assure that every state occurs at most once in the generated state hierarchy. Moreover, the terminal expression requires that neither r_1 nor r_4 be applicable to a state hierarchy. Hence, the generated graphs do not contain nodes that are labelled with cs or $SorC$. Fig. 3 shows the generation of the state hierarchy of the state machine in Fig. 1 using the transformation unit *statehierarchy*($\mathcal{S}$).

Definition 5 (State hierarchy). The set of all *state hierarchies* over $\mathcal{S}$ are generated by the transformation unit in Fig. 2.

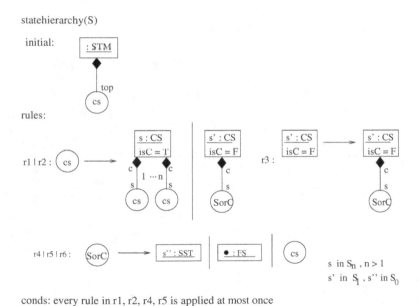

conds: every rule in r1, r2, r4, r5 is applied at most once
terminal: reduced(r1,r2)

Fig. 2. The transformation unit *statehierarchy*($\mathcal{S}$)

Every label which occurs in an object node of a state hierarchy G is called a *state* of G. The set of states of G is denoted by $States_G$. The top state of G is denoted by top_G. For every state s of G $container_G(s)$ denotes its containing state. In the case where $s = top_G$ its container is equal to the state machine.

A *path* of *length* n ($n \geq 0$) from a node v_0 to a node v_n in a state hierarchy G is a sequence $v_0, e_1, v_1, e_2, \ldots, v_{n-1}, e_n, v_n$ where $v_1, \ldots, v_n \in V_G$, $e_1, \ldots, e_n \in E_G$, $s_G(e_1) = v_0$, $t_G(e_n) = v_n$, and for $i = 1, \ldots, n-1$ $t_G(e_i) = s_G(e_{i+1}) = v_i$. In this case we say that $e_1, \ldots, e_n$ and $v_0, \ldots, v_n$ are *reachable* from v_0. Moreover, the *subgraph* $ind_G(v_0)$ *of* G *induced by* v_0 consists of all nodes and edges which are reachable from v_0. Analogously, for every state $s \in States_G$, $ind_G(s)$ is equal to $ind_G(v)$ where v is the (only) node in G labelled with s.

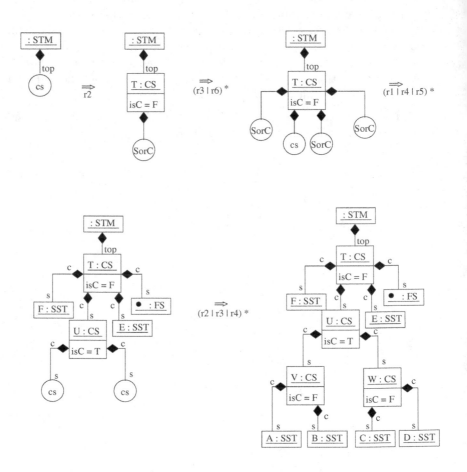

Fig. 3. Generation of a state hierarchy

The current active states of a UML state machine are represented as state configurations which are (isomorphic to) subgraphs of state hierarchies. More precisely, a state configuration is a state hierarchy where every non-concurrent object node has exactly one subvertex (a state machine cannot be in more than one substate of a sequential state at the same time).

Definition 6 (State configuration). The set of *state configurations over* S consists of all graphs generated by the transformation unit *config*(S) which is obtained from *statehierarchy*(S) by removing the rule r_3. For a state hierarchy G over S the set *Conf*(G) of *state configurations of* G consists of all state configurations over S which are isomorphic to some subgraph of G. The set of *final state configurations* of G, denoted by *Final*(G), consists of all state configurations with five nodes v_1, v_2, v_3, v_4, v_5 where v_1 is labelled with : STM, v_2 and v_4 are diamonds, v_3 represents the top state of G, and v_5 is the final state of G. Moreover, v_1 is composed of v_3 which in turn is composed of v_5. This means that an unlabelled edge goes from v_1 to v_2, a *top*-labelled edge connects v_2 with v_3, a c-labelled edge goes from v_3 to v_4, and an s-labelled edge from v_4 to v_5.

The firing of a transition of a UML state machine corresponds to the application of a graph transformation rule to a state configuration. The definition of such graph transformation rules is based on the notion of state term graphs which can be regarded as a special kind of term graphs. The transformation unit *term*(S) in Definition 7 generates state term graphs. It has no control condition and no terminal expression. This means that the rules of *term*(S) can be applied arbitrary often and in any order, and all graphs are accepted as terminal ones.

Definition 7 (State term graph). The set of all *state term graphs over* S are generated with the transformation unit *term*(S) given in Fig. 4.

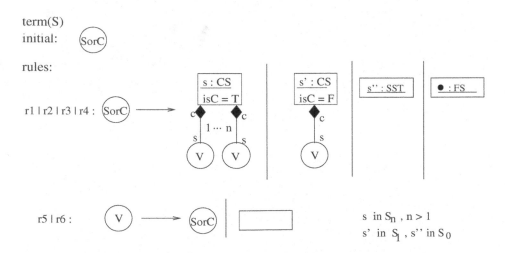

Fig. 4. The transformation unit *term*(S)

For a state hierarchy G over S the set of *state term graphs of* G consists of all state term graphs over S which are isomorphic to some subgraph of G.

For every state term graph G, $root_G$ denotes the topmost node of G and top_G denotes its label. Moreover, every unlabelled node v of G is called a *variable*. The set of all variables of G are denoted by Var_G. A node of G is called a *composite source* of G if all its subvertices are variables. For every node $v \in V_G$, let $depth_G(v)$ denote the length of the path from $root_G$ to v. Then a composite source v is called a *most nested source* if for all composite sources v' of G $depth_G(v') \leq depth_G(v)$.

It follows easily from the definitions that every state term graph G' of G without variable nodes has exactly one occurrence in G. This occurrence will be denoted by $occ(G', G)$. Moreover, every state term graph G' of G has at most one occurrence in a state configuration G'' of G. If it exists it will be denoted by $occ(G', G'')$.

Every transition of a state machine is represented as a graph transformation rule that contains the source states of the transition in its left-hand side, and the target states in its right-hand side. More precisely, the left-hand side consists of a state term graph, and the right-hand side consists of the variable nodes of the left-hand side plus a state term graph the root of which is equal to the root of the left-hand side. The gluing graph is composed of the root and the variable nodes of the left-hand side. Fig. 5 shows the graph transformation rules which correspond to transitions 1, 4, and 7 of Fig. 1.

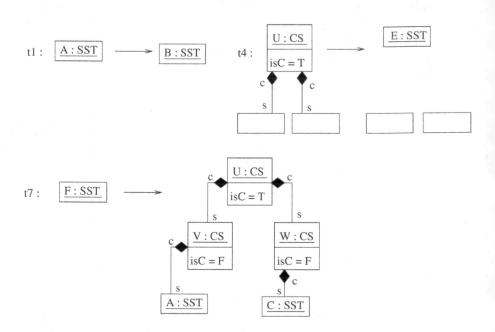

Fig. 5. Some transitions.

Definition 8 (Transition). Let G be a state hierarchy over $\mathcal{S}$. A *transition* of G is a graph transformation rule (L, K, R) such that L is a state term graph of G, $ind_G(top_L)$ contains no final state, K is composed of $root_L$ and Var_L, and R is composed of R' and Var_L where R' is a state term graph of G with $Var_{R'} = \emptyset$, $root_L = root_{R'}$, $container_G(top_{occ(R',G)}) = container_G(top_{occ(L,G)})$, and: $top_L \neq top_R$, or top_L is concurrent or $\#V_L = 1$.

For all transitions of Fig. 5 the top states of the left-and right-hand sides are different. Transitions with $\#V_L = 1$ and $top_L = top_R$ represent self-transitions, and transitions where top_L is concurrent and $top_L = top_R$ can be used to model transitions that leave and enter all regions of a concurrent state, as e.g. a compound transition leaving a substate of each region of a concurrent state s and entering the state s again.

A state machine consists of a state hierarchy, an initial state configuration, and a set of labelled transitions. For defining the labels of transitions we assume the existence of an arbitrary but fixed set *Events* of events that contains the symbol *comp* denoting the *completion event*.

Definition 9 (State machine). A *state machine* is a system $S = (G, I, T, ev)$ where G is a state hierarchy, I is a state configuration of G called the *initial state configuration*, T is a finite set of transitions of G, and $ev. T \rightarrow Events$ is a mapping that assigns an event to every transition in T.

It can be shown that state machines are *well-formed*, i.e. they satisfy the wellformedness rules of [OMG99].[6]

Observation 1 State machines are well-formed.

As in term graph rewriting, the application of a transition to a state configuration may produce garbage. For example, the application of t_4 of Fig. 5 produces as garbage the subgraphs which are connected to the images of the two variables in the right-hand side. (Note that every transition that contains variables produces garbage.) The garbage produced by the application of a transition to a state configuration can be collected with a following transformation unit, called *garbage(S)* which due to lack of space is omitted here.

It follows from the definitions that the application of a transition to a state configuration yields again a state configuration (up to garbage).

Observation 2 Let $S = (G, I, T, ev)$ be a state machine. Let $G' \in Conf(G)$, and let $G' \Rightarrow_T G''$. Then G'' is a state configuration of G (up to garbage).

A transition is enabled with respect to a state configuration G and an event e if it is applicable to G and if its label is equal to e.

---

[6] For reasons of space limitations we cannot present the wellformedness rules explicitly. Please note also that only a subset of the wellformedness rules is applicable to our state machines because we do not consider all components (e.g. history and synch states etc.).

Definition 10 (Enabled transition). Let $S = (G, I, T, ev)$ be a state machine. Let $G' \in Conf(G)$, and let $e \in Events$. Then a transition $(L, K, R) \in T$ is *enabled with respect to e and G'* if $ev((L, K, R)) = e$ and there is an occurrence of L in G'.

Two transitions r_1 and r_2 enabled with respect to a state configuration G' are in conflict if their left-hand sides have common states. Moreover, r_1 and r_2 are in conflict with respect to G' if r_2 modifies the garbage produced by r_1. If the left-hand side of r_1 has a unique most nested source and r_2 is applied to the garbage below this source, the source of the UML transition corresponding to r_2 is a substate of the source of the UML transition corresponding to r_1. Hence, according to [OMG99], r_2 has a higher priority than r_1 in the latter case.

Definition 11 (Conflict, priority). Let $S = (G, I, T, ev)$ be a state machine. Let $G' \in Conf(G)$, and let $r_1 = (L_1, K_1, R_1)$ and $r_2 = (L_2, K_2, R_2)$ be two transitions that are enabled with respect to G' and an event $e \in Events$. Then r_1 and r_2 are *in conflict with respect to G'* if $States_{L_1} \cap States_{L_2} \neq \emptyset$, or $occ(L_2, G') \subseteq ind_{G'}(v)$where v is the image of some variable v' of L_1. In the case where $container_{L_1}(v')$ is the unique most nested source of L_1, r_2 has a *higher priority* than r_1, denoted by $r_1 <_{G'} r_2$.

The semantics of UML state machines is based on so-called run-to-completion steps that correspond to the firing of a maximum set of non-conflicting enabled transitions. Such a maximum set can be computed based on the following definition.

Definition 12 (Maximum set). Let $S = (G, I, T, ev)$ be a state machine, let $G' \in Conf(G)$, and let $e \in Events$. Then a non-empty set $max(e, G') \subseteq T$ is a *maximum set of non-conflicting enabled transitions for e and G'* if the following holds. (1) Every $r \in max(e, G)$ is enabled with respect to e and G'. (2) For all $r_1, r_2 \in max(e, G')$, r_1 and r_2 are not in conflict with respect to G'. (3) For every $r \in T - max(e, G')$ with $ev(r) = e$, r is in conflict with some $r' \in max(e, G')$. (4) There is no $r \in T - max(e, G')$ with $ev(r) = e$ and $r' <_{G'} r$ for some $r' \in max(e, G')$.

The firing of a maximum set of non-conflicting transitions can be modelled with a single direct derivation. For this purpose, its rules are combined via parallel composition.

Definition 13 (Parallel composition of transitions). The *parallel composition* of two transitions $r_1 = (L_1, K_1, R_1)$ and $r_2 = (L_2, K_2, R_2)$ is defined as $r_1 + r_2 = (L_1 + L_2, K_1 + K_2, R_1 + R_2)$.[7] For a set $T = \{r_1, \ldots, r_n\}$ of transitions, the parallel composition of its rules is denoted by $par(T)$, i.e. $par(T) = r_1 + \cdots + r_n$.

---

[7] $+$ denotes the disjoint union of graphs.

The next observation states that the application of a parallel transition to a state configuration yields again a state configuration. The proof makes use of the parallelism theorem of graph transformation [CEH$^+$97] which states that there is a derivation $G \Rightarrow_{r_1+r_2} G$ if and only if there are derivations $G \Rightarrow_{r_1} M_1 \Rightarrow_{r_2} G'$ and $G \Rightarrow_{r_2} M_2 \Rightarrow_{r_1} G'$.

Observation 3 Let $S = (G, I, T, ev)$ be a state machine. Let $G' \in Conf(G)$ such that $G' \Rightarrow_{par(A)} G''$ for some $A \subseteq T$. Then G'' is a state configuration (up to garbage).

In the following we assume the existence of a set $Queue$ of event queues represented as graphs together with graph transformation rules $remove(e)$ and $insert(e)$ that dequeue and enqueue events from a queue. Then every configuration of a state machine can be represented as a *configuration graph* which consists of an event queue and a state configuration. The firing of a maximal set of non-conflicting transitions is defined with the transformation unit $fire(e, G')$ given in Definition 14. The initial graph is a configuration graph the state configuration of which is equal to G'. If there is no transition enabled for G' and e, the unit applies the rule $remove(e)$. Otherwise, it imports the unit $garbage(S)$ and the rule set consists of $remove(e)$ and all parallel rules constructed from a maximum set of enabled non-conflicting transitions for e and G'. The rule $remove(e)$ is first applied, afterwards one of the parallel rules, and finally the unit $garbage(S)$.

Definition 14 (Firing). Let $S = (G, I, T, ev)$ be a state machine, let $e \in Events$ and let $G' \in Conf(G)$. Moreover, let $MAX(e, G') = \{max(e, G')_1, \dots, max(e, G')_{n(e,G')}\}$ be the set of maximum sets of enabled non-conflicting transitions for e and G'. Then the *firing* of a set of transitions in $MAX(e, G')$ is given by the transformation unit $fire(e, G')$ defined as follows. If $MAX(e, G') = \{\}$, $fire(e, G') = (\{G'\} + Queue, \emptyset, \{remove(e)\}, remove(e), all)$ where $SEM(all) = \mathcal{G}$. Otherwise, if $e \neq comp$,

$fire(e, G')$

initial:	$\{G'\} + Queue$
uses:	$garbage(S)$
rules:	$\{remove(e)\} \cup \{par(max(e, G')_1), \dots, par(max(e, G)_{n(e,G')})\}$
conds:	$remove(e)\,;\,(par(max(e, G')_1) \mid \cdots \mid par(max(e, G')_{n(e,G')}))\,;$
	$garbage(S)$

Otherwise, $fire(comp, G')$ is obtained from $fire(e, G')$ above by removing $remove(e)$ from the rule set and the control condition.

The next observation follows immediately from the definitions and from Observation 3.

Observation 4 Let $S = (G, I, T, ev)$ be a state machine, let $e \in Events$ and let G' be a state configuration of G. Then $(G_1, G_2) \in SEM(fire(e, G'))$ iff G_2 is a configuration graph obtained from G_1 by firing a maximum set of non-conflicting enabled transitions.

To define the execution semantics of a state machine we assume that there is a transformation unit *eventhandler* that receives events and puts them into the event queue. The execution semantics can now be defined as follows.

Definition 15 (Execution semantics). Let $S = (G, I, T, ev)$ be a state machine. Then the *execution semantics* of S is given by

$exec(G, I, T, ev)$
   initial: $\{I\} + Queue$
   uses: $\{fire(e, G') \mid e \in Events, G' \in Conf(G)\} \cup \{eventhandler\}$
   terminal: $Final(G) + Queue$

5   Conclusion

In this paper, we presented an operational semantics for a subset of UML state machines which is based on structured graph transformation. The state hierarchy of a state machine was represented with an acyclic graph and the transitions with graph transformation rules. The firing of a maximum set of enabled non-conflicting transitions was modelled with a graph transformation rule composed of the rules corresponding to the transitions in the set. In the literature one encounters a series of formalizations of UML state machines. There exist a short comparison of our approach with the modelizations of state machines in [MP94, GP98,LMM99,LP99,EHHS00,Kwo00,RACH00,BP01] which, for reasons of space limitations, could not be included in this paper. There remain some topics to be worked out in the future:

- The presented approach should be extended to history and synch states, actions, guards, etc. and to an explicit representation of object interaction.
- The presented modelization can be used as an internal representation of the execution semantics of UML state machines. For this purpose it should be implemented in a graph transformation based language. In order to obtain a realistic implementation, it should be worked out how a system of communicating state machnines can be implemented with graph transformation.
- An interesting question concerning UML diagrams addresses the interrelations and consistency between distinct diagram types. Hence diagrams other than state machines should be specified with graph transformation systems and it should be investigated if structured graph transformation can serve as a basis for formalizing the interrelations and consistency conditions between UML diagrams (cf. also [PS00,TE00]).
- One main feature of the presented approach is the use of transformation units which allow to modularize graph transformation systems. For verification purposes, transformation units have the advantage that proofs of "large problems" can be splitted into smaller ones. It should be worked out in which way transformation units are useful for verification purposes in the context of UML diagrams.

Acknowledgement. I would like to thank the anonymous referees for their helpful comments.

References

[BP01]   Luciano Baresi and Mauro Pezzè. On formalizing UML with high-level
            Petri Nets. In G. Agha and F. De Cindio, editors, *Proc. Concurrent
            Object-Oriented Programming and Petri Nets*, volume 2001 of *Lecture
            Notes in Computer Science*, pages 271–300, 2001.

[BRJ98]   Grady Booch, James Rumbaugh, and Ivar Jacobson. *The Unified Mod-
            eling Language User Guide*. Addison-Wesley, 1998.

[CEH⁺97]   Andrea Corradini, Hartmut Ehrig, Reiko Heckel, Michael Löwe, Ugo
            Montanari, and Francesca Rossi. Algebraic approaches to graph transfor-
            mation part I: Basic concepts and double pushout approach. In Rozen-
            berg [Roz97].

[EEKR99]   Hartmut Ehrig, Gregor Engels, Hans-Jörg Kreowski, and Grzegorz
            Rozenberg, editors. *Handbook of Graph Grammars and Computing by
            Graph Transformation, Vol. 2: Applications, Languages and Tools*. World
            Scientific, Singapore, 1999.

[EHHS00]   Gregor Engels, Jan Hendrik Hausmann, Reiko Heckel, and Stefan Sauer.
            Dynamic meta modeling: A graphical approach to the operational se-
            mantics of behavioral diagrams in UML. In Andy Evans, Stuart Kent,
            and Bran Selic, editors, *UML 2000 – The Unified Modeling Language.
            Advancing the Standard*, volume 1939 of *Lecture Notes in Computer Sci-
            ence*, pages 323–337, 2000.

[EKMR99]   Hartmut Ehrig, Hans-Jörg Kreowski, Ugo Montanari, and Grzegorz
            Rozenberg, editors. *Handbook of Graph Grammars and Computing by
            Graph Transformation, Vol. 3: Concurrency, Parallelism, and Distribu-
            tion*. World Scientific, Singapore, 1999.

[Gog00]   Martin Gogolla. Graph transformations on the UML metamodel. In
            Andrea Corradini and Reiko Heckel, editors, *Proc. ICALP Workshop on
            Graph Transformation and Visual Modeling Techniques*, 2000.

[GP98]   Martin Gogolla and Francesco Parisi-Presicce. State diagrams in UML:
            A formal semantics using graph transformations. In Manfred Broy, Derek
            Coleman, Tom Maibaum, and Bernhard Rumpe, editors, *Proc. ICSE'98
            Workshop Precise Semantics of Modeling Techniques*, Technical Report
            TUM-I9803, pages 55–72, 1998.

[KK99]   Hans-Jörg Kreowski and Sabine Kuske. Graph transformation units with
            interleaving semantics. *Formal Aspects of Computing*, 11(6):690–723,
            1999.

[KKS97]   Hans-Jörg Kreowski, Sabine Kuske, and Andy Schürr. Nested graph
            transformation units. *International Journal on Software Engineering
            and Knowledge Engineering*, 7(4):479–502, 1997.

[Kus00]   Sabine Kuske. More about control conditions for transformation units.
            In Hartmut Ehrig, Gregor Engels, Hans-Jörg Kreowski, and Grzegorz
            Rozenberg, editors, *Proc. Theory and Application of Graph Transforma-
            tions*, volume 1764 of *Lecture Notes in Computer Science*, pages 323–337,
            2000.

[Kwo00]   Gihwon Kwon. Rewrite rules and operational semantics for model checking UML statecharts. In Andy Evans, Stuart Kent, and Bran Selic, editors, *Proc. UML 2000 – The Unified Modeling Language. Advancing the Standard*, volume 1939 of *Lecture Notes in Computer Science*, pages 528–540, 2000.

[LMM99]   Diego Latella, Istvan Majzik, and Mieke Massink. Towards a formal operational semantics of UML statechart diagrams. In *Proc. FMOODS'99, IFIP TC6/WG6.1 Third International Conference on Formal Methods for Open Object-Based Distributed Systems, Florence, Italy, February 15-18, 1999*. Kluwer, 1999.

[LP99]   Johan Lilius and Ivan Porres Paltor. Formalising UML state machines for model checking. In Robert France and Bernhard Rumpe, editors, *Proc. UML'99 – The Unified Modeling Language. Beyond the Standard*, volume 1723 of *Lecture Notes in Computer Science*, pages 430–445, 1999.

[MP94]   Andrea Maggiolo-Schettini and Adriano Peron. Semantics of full statecharts based on graph rewriting. In Hans-Jürgen Schneider and Hartmut Ehrig, editors, *Proc. Graph Transformation in Computer Science*, volume 776 of *Lecture Notes in Computer Science*, pages 265–279, 1994.

[OMG99]   OMG. UML 1.3 documentation, 1999.
            Available at http://www.rational.com/uml/resources/documentation.

[PS00]   Dorina C. Petriu and Yimei Sun. Consistent behaviour representation in activity and sequence diagrams. In Andy Evans, Stuart Kent, and Bran Selic, editors, *Proc. UML 2000 – The Unified Modeling Language. Advancing the Standard*, volume 1939 of *Lecture Notes in Computer Science*, pages 359–368, 2000.

[RACH00]   Gianna Reggio, Egidio Astesiano, Christine Choppy, and Heinrich Hussmann. Analysing UML active classes and associated state machines – A lightweight formal approach. In Tom Maibaum, editor, *Proc. Fundamental Approaches to Software Engineering (FASE 2000), Berlin, Germany*, volume 1783 of *Lecture Notes in Computer Science*, 2000.

[RJB98]   James Rumbaugh, Ivar Jacobson, and Grady Booch. *The Unified Modeling Language Reference Manual*. Addison-Wesley, 1998.

[Roz97]   Grzegorz Rozenberg, editor. *Handbook of Graph Grammars and Computing by Graph Transformation, Vol. 1: Foundations*. World Scientific, Singapore, 1997.

[TE00]   Aliki Tsiolakis and Hartmut Ehrig. Consistency analysis of UML class and sequence diagrams using attributed graph grammars. In Hartmut Ehrig and Gabriele taentzer, editors, *Proc. Joint APPLIGRAPH and GETGRATS Workshop on Graph Transformation Systems*, Report Nr. 2000-2, Technical University of Berlin, pages 77–86, 2000.

A Visualization of OCL Using Collaborations*

Paolo Bottoni[1], Manuel Koch[2], Francesco Parisi-Presicce[1], and
Gabriele Taentzer[3]

[1] Università di Roma "La Sapienza" Italy
[2] - PSI Berlin -
[3] Technical University of Berlin

Abstract. We propose a visualization of OCL within the context of the
UML meta model, so that OCL expressions are represented by extending
collaboration diagrams. We exploit the OCL meta model introduced in
[9] and further elaborated on in [1] and base the description of properties
of objects on collaborations, while classifier and association roles are
used to describe navigation paths. Operations computing properties are
described by interactions consisting of messages between classifier roles.
The introduction of new graphical core elements is kept to a minimum.
New notation mainly concerns the predefined operations in OCL and
provides more convenient visual forms for the notation by interactions
here. The proposed visualization is described in detail and is illustrated
with examples taken from an industrial project under development.

1 Introduction

Although UML is gaining acceptance as a standard for designing and documenting software and systems, there are still wide differences as to the use of
its components. In particular, OCL is still of limited use even in organizations
which extensively employ some form of UML diagrams. The reasons for this
are various, but they can often be traced back to the difficulty of integrating a
purely textual language like OCL into diagrams. Recommendations have been
issued towards the formulation of a diagrammatic version of OCL [3] and some
proposals have been advanced in order to provide a visual counterpart of OCL
by exploiting visualizations with a set-theoretic semantics [5]. The disadvantage
of such proposals is that the diagrams look quite different from others in UML
and thus, force the user to learn yet another visual language. Moreover, such
new visualizations are often not well integrated in the meta model of UML.

The work presented in this paper aims at achieving a visualization of OCL
within the context of the UML meta model while departing as little as possible
from the use of graphical elements already belonging to the UML notation.
Where a new notation is adopted, it is easily recognizable as derived from the
UML core notation, or it is simply employed as a shortcut to an equivalent more
complex visualization. Additional meaning is attached to some specific notation
and to a selected set of spatial relations and aspectual features of the notation.

---

* Partially supported by the EC under Esprit Working Group APPLIGRAPH.

M. Gogolla and C. Kobryn (Eds.): UML 2001, LNCS 2185, pp. 257–271, 2001.
© Springer-Verlag Berlin Heidelberg 2001

This visualization adapts the notation for UML core elements. Furthermore, we follow the recommendations of the standards, by avoiding the use of colors or special typography to express meaning. Throughout the paper, we illustrate the principles behind our choices for the proposed visualization and expand on how these principles led to specific choices. A prominent principle is to limit the introduction of new graphical elements. This responds to two main motivations. On the one hand, it limits the cognitive effort of the user, thus facilitating diagram understanding. On the other hand, the use of elements already in the UML syntax facilitates the checking of model diagrams against the constraints expressed by our OCL diagrams. Another principle aimed at better understanding is to limit the size of the diagram. In particular, no two occurrences of a sub-diagram need be present in the same diagram. Moreover, visual shortcuts for predefined operations support a compact notation of OCL constraints.

In [2] we proposed to use graph rewriting with rule expressions to provide a semantics for OCL, exploiting graph rewriting mechanisms for checking the consistency of model diagrams with respect to constraints. The use of a graph-based formalism opened the way to a visualization of OCL constraints and an extension of the UML meta model was defined to this effect by introducing two new classes. Now, we proceed towards a full description of a visualized OCL, by defining a meta model for OCL which combines the proposal in [9] with the UML meta model for collaborations. Hence, OCL constraints can be expressed in a more visual way, reducing the need for additional text.

The rest of the paper is structured as follows: the following subsection introduces the running example taken from an industrial project and used to illustrate the visualization of OCL constraints throughout the paper. Sections 2, 3 and 4 present the visualization proposed for OCL, showing sample OCL constraints in textual and visual form. In Section 5, we adapt the OCL meta model proposed in [9] and further elaborated in [1] to the visualization proposed. Finally, Sections 6 and 7 discuss related work and conclusions.

1.1   The Running Example

Our example is taken from an 'eGovernment' project in Berlin on which one of the authors has worked. The project objective is to replace the existing software system used in the residents' registration office in Berlin by a new software system that supports and facilitates both the business processes within one or among several authorities and the business processes between the authority and the citizen by exploiting Internet technologies. The main responsibilities of the residents' registration office are the registration of inhabitants, the maintenance and preparation of the inhabitants data for other authorities like police or fire department, and the certification of passports and ID cards.

The client requires explicitly the use of object-oriented technologies. UML is used, as it is the standard object-oriented notation also accepted by the client. However, whereas class diagrams, collaboration and sequence diagrams are techniques widely used in discussions about specifications between the client and the designer, OCL does not attract interest at all despite its appropriateness. Constraints, if any, are expressed in natural language.

The experience acquired in this project and in other big OO-projects in the author's company point to a simple conclusion: OCL is too difficult not only for the client but also for the designer and does not facilitate the transition from the intended requirements to a precise and legible presentation. Natural language formulations are preferred, though their ambiguity might often cause misunderstanding later in the project.

In the sequel, we present some of the constraints occurring in the project. Fig. 1 shows a (very small) part of the business object model of the project for which constraints have been defined. We give a brief explanation of the parts that are not self-explanatory.

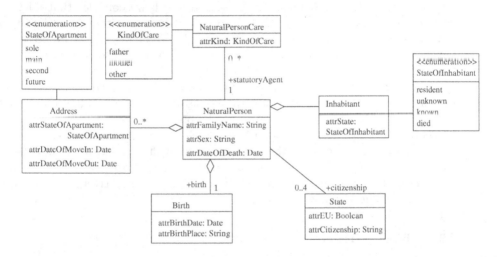

Fig. 1. Business Object Model.

The Class **NaturalPerson** describes natural persons (as opposed to legal persons). These are persons currently registered in Berlin or previously registered (e.g. moved outside Berlin or dead) or non resident members of the family. The class **Address** contains addresses of natural persons. The possible attribute values of the attribute **attrStateOfAppartment** are: <u>sole</u> apartment, <u>main</u> apartment, <u>second</u> apartment, <u>future</u> apartment (to which the inhabitant will move), and the <u>apartment</u> (to which the inhabitant has moved). The class **NaturalPersonCare** contains the custody, care or custodianship, as a statutory agent, of a natural person. By default, the mother becomes the statutory agent of a child. Additionally, the father becomes the statutory agent of a child if the father's family name is the child's family name. The values for the attribute **attrKind** are: child's <u>father</u>, child's <u>mother</u>, and <u>other</u>. The class **Inhabitant** contains data of natural persons who are inhabitants. For instance, non resident or dead natural persons are not inhabitants. The values of the attribute `attrState` are: <u>resident</u> natural person, non resident natural person with <u>unknown</u> address, non resident natural person with <u>known</u> address, and natural person who <u>died</u> in Berlin.

2   Constraints on Properties of Objects Based on Collaborations

One of the main ingredients of OCL are navigation expressions to object properties. The visualization of navigation paths helps the developer to maintain an overview without forcing a reformulation of an object structure, given in some static structure diagram, in a completely different syntax. Thus, the idea is to base object navigation on collaboration diagrams.

Conforming to the meta model presented in [9], we consider that all OCL expressions produce a value. The type of this value can either be a data type or a classifier type of some instance. Expressions producing values are presented within an enclosing frame where the value is in a precise position with respect to the frame. If the value is of type Boolean, the explicit mention of the value can be omitted, provided that no other reference to it is needed. Hence a framed diagram without an external return value maps to a Boolean value. If the OCL expression produces an instance, or a collection of instances, the corresponding object or multi-object is double-bordered. Such an element must be reachable by navigating the diagram from the instance defining the context of the expression (usually named by 'self'). The kind of constraint is indicated by shortcuts 'inv', 'pre' or 'post' (for invariants, pre- or postconditions, respectively) in the upper left corner of the visualized constraint.

2.1   Object Attributes

The following is a simple OCL constraint stating that the birth date of a natural person comes before the date of moving into an apartment; the constraint is stated textually in the usual OCL syntax.

```
context NaturalPerson inv:
self.birth.attrBirthDate < self.address.attrDateOfMoveIn
```

The visualized form of this constraint, in Figure 2, contains three classifier roles, two with attributes. The attribute values, x and y, are compared in a simple Boolean constraint in the bottom compartment.

2.2   Operations and Methods

In OCL, operations and methods may be used if they are queries, i.e. they are free from side-effects.

Although in the project constraints for operations and methods have not been explicitly formulated using OCL syntax, such constraints are known to the

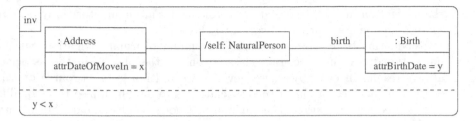

Fig. 2. The birth date comes before the date of moving into an apartment.

designers. For instance, we have constraints for the range of the possible values of the attributes. Consider Figure 3 for the visualization of a constraint saying that the date of birth has to be earlier than today. Similar constraints are necessary also for the other dates occurring in the business model.

context `NaturalPersonCare` inv:
self.birth.attrDateOfBirth < currentDate()

This constraint is visualized by an instance of the self classifier role. A method call may be depicted as an interaction with this instance as the target. Its return value can be used to formulate a constraint. As a shortcut, the method compartment can contain the constraint, as shown in Figure 3.

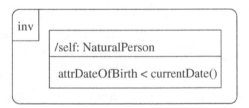

Fig. 3. The date of birth has to be earlier than today.

2.3   Navigation through Associations

This part of an OCL constraint is the most interesting one to be visualized. Navigation through an object structure is much easier if the path can be visualized directly. Consider again the example in Figure 2. The constraint visualization shows three classifier roles, with two association roles in between, where a role name is attached to one. A more complex navigation is shown in Figure 8.

If the multiplicity of the association end has a maximum of 1, the target is an object, otherwise a multi-object. Examples for navigation to multi-objects will be shown in Section 3, where the target is a collection. When describing the navigation in this visualized form, role names are mandatory only if there is more than one association between two classes.

Navigation from association classes is similar to usual navigation. Since the navigation from an association class to one of the objects in the association always results in one object, we never have multi-objects as source or target objects of the association. If the associations are qualified, also these qualifiers can be used for navigation. The qualifier is denoted via the usual UML notation.

3   Collections and Operations on Collections

OCL supports three different types of collections: sets, bags and sequences. They are given in the UML_OCL package in an abstract way, i.e. element types are left open. For their concrete usage, the abstract element type has to be instantiated. The visualization may stick to the usual representation of classifier roles but may also use special notions to support the three predefined collection types.

These special notions of sets corresponds directly to the layout of multi objects in UML, and the correspondence extends to the semantical level as well. We call this visual form *set box*. The other types of collections are represented by adorning the set box with details recalling the collection type. Hence, a *sequence* is represented by connecting the corners of the shifted rectangles with dots recalling a series, and a *bag* is represented by placing a semi circle, recalling a handle, over the upper rectangle of the collection element (see Figure 4). The concrete element type of a collection occurs inside the rectangle in front.

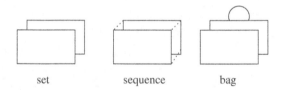

set   sequence   bag

Fig. 4. Visualization of collection types

3.1   Query Operations

Collections offer a variety of query operations which support the computation of projections based on boolean expressions. Applying such a projective query operation to a collection results in a new collection (or in a scalar).

So far, we described the application of an operation by an interaction. This is possible for query operations, too, but these predefined operations can be visualized more adequately based on set boxes.

In the following, we take the `select` operation to describe how query operations and their application can be visualized. If the selecting expression is simple, i.e. a constraint on attributes, this constraint may be included into the constrained classifier role as a shortcut. Usually, the selecting expression is framed by a set box. Such a representation is employed on the left of Figure 5 to select all the addresses of a natural person who is a resident or a non-resident with a known address. The number of addresses has to be greater than 0. The expression **#n** inside the dotted box produces a name for the cardinality of the selected collection. Moreover, the iterating variable may be depicted on the right side of the set box (here 'a'). This visualization of a query is very flexible, since there might be a complex expression visualized within the set box. The visualization becomes difficult if the set of addresses might be used in other queries as well. In this case, there is a preference for the visualization on the right of Figure 5. Here, a special *isIn* edge is introduced which expresses the fact that the addresses in the selecting expression belong to the set of addresses of a natural person. Moreover, the natural person is repeated in the selecting expression, as depicted by an id-connection. The corresponding textual OCL constraint looks like:

context NaturalPerson inv:
self.address→select(naturalPerson.inhabitant.attrState = #resident or
naturalPerson.inhabitant.attrState = #known)→ size > 0

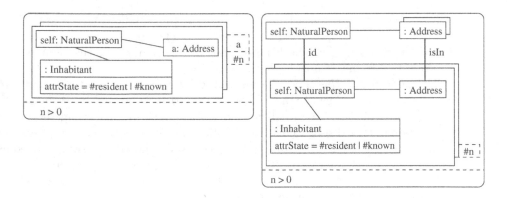

Fig. 5. A select statement with two variants

The use of the alternative operator (|) in the figures is a shortcut for a disjunction involving duplication of the classifier role to present the possible alternative values.

An overview of all visualized query operations for collections is given in Figure 6. For a better understanding, we show the visualization of the *collect* operation together with the conversion to a certain collection type. Actually, the conversion to a bag is not necessary, since the resulting collection is always a bag. The *iterate* operation is slightly more complicated, since it contains the specification of an iterator *elem* and an accumulator *acc*. These are variable declarations depicted on the right side. The accumulator gets an initial value which is depicted by *init* in the left upper corner. Please remember these visual notations are meant as shortcuts for pure collaboration diagrams with queries being interactions.

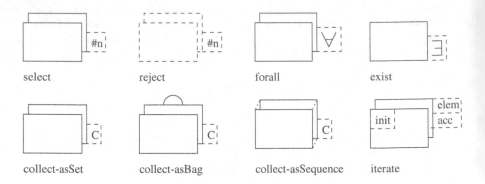

Fig. 6. Visualization of query operations

3.2   Further Operations on Collections

OCL predefines many operations on collections. In the following, we briefly discuss the shortcuts proposed for the main ones. The operation *size* has already been used, visualized by a hash mark and a variable name at the right border of a collection frame. (Consider Figure 5.)

The operation *includes* can be visualized by an arrow from the element to the set which has to include this element. The arrow is labeled by *includes*.

The visualization of the predicate *isEmpty* is done by presenting the tested collection in a dashed style. This visualization should stress the non-existence of any instance. For the same reason, all adjacent links should be drawn dashed as well. In general, negated parts of a diagram are drawn with dashed lines.

Due to space limitations, we do not discuss shortcuts for all predefined operations of collections. They follow the same design principles as the ones we discussed.

4   Visualized Logical Expressions

Logical expressions can occur at two different levels: 1) Expressions on simple data types, denoted textually in the usual OCL syntax; 2) Logical expressions on object navigation, represented by object interaction or more adequately by several sorts of frames and dashed diagram parts for negation.

As an example of the first type, the textual requirement "There are no instances of class `Address` for natural persons without a state of inhabitation", when formulated in natural language, is ambiguous. The intended meaning is that the attribute `attrState` has the value "unknown" or "died", but it could also be interpreted to mean that the attribute has no value at all. The OCL syntax, in this case, helps disambiguate the request:

```
context NaturalPerson inv:
    self.inhabitant.attrState = #unknown or self.inhabitant.attrState = #died
implies
        self.address→isEmpty
```

The conclusion contains some redundancy, since it repeats the classifier role "self: NaturalPerson" which is needed to formulate the conclusion. The visual constraint is depicted in Figure 7.

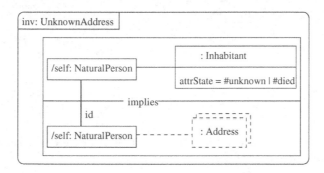

Fig. 7. There are no instances of class Address for natural persons without a state of inhabitant.

As an example of the second type, the visualization for "If the statutory agent is *mother*, the birth date of the statutory agent must be earlier than the birth date of the child" is shown in Figure 8.

```
context NaturalPerson inv:
    (self.naturalPersonCare.attrKind = #mother)
implies self.birth.attrBirthDate <
        self.naturalPersonCare.statutoryAgent.birth.attrBirthDate
```

For the formulation of the constraint "The citizenships of a person are different", "we need a "for all" query: Its visualization is depicted in Figure 9.

```
context NaturalPerson inv:
self.citizenship− >forall(x, y : state| x.attrCitizenship = y.attrCitizenship
implies x = y)
```

The use of identical classifier roles allows a form of factorization, or of abstraction, used in several places in our visualization. In fact, in a UML expression, elements can be referenced several times. This can occur explicitly as in

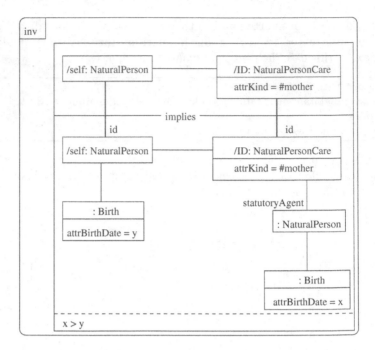

Fig. 8. If the statutory agent is *mother*, the birth date of the statutory agent must precede the birth date of the child.

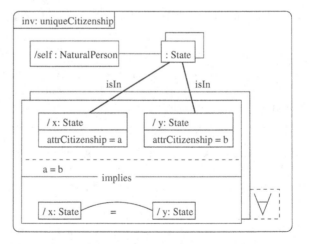

Fig. 9. The citizenships of a person are different.

let expressions, or implicitly if a navigation expression is textually replicated in different parts of a textual constraint. In the latter case, an element corresponding to the longest common prefix of a set of navigation expressions can be identified. In any case, we present only one model element and produce another box connected to the original element for each reference to it in the diagram. If a named element, e.g. an instance of a classifier, is replicated, then identity may alternatively be expressed by the use of the same name.

A similar mechanism can be used to decompose a diagram into subdiagrams, via a hierarchical view of the expression. Boxes in a high level diagram can represent whole subdiagrams. In this case, the box can be named and expanded in different subdiagrams. This can be used whenever a complex expression is used several times. An example is shown in Fig. 10 which contains the conjunction of the constraints shown in Fig. 7 and 9.

Fig. 10. A composed constraint.

Boolean predefined operations are represented by associations labeled by the name of the operation. Boolean connectives are represented by combining appearance of graphical elements with their enclosing and nesting.

In particular, negation, disjunction and conjunction are treated. We elaborate on the convention of Peircean graphs [4] which represent conjunction by copresence in the diagram and negation by enclosing the negated elements in a contour. On the contrary, we represent negation by modifying the appearance of the elements (using dashed lines) and use confinement within contours to express both conjunction and disjunction. In particular, an odd value of the nesting level indicates that the expressions within a same frame are taken in conjunction and an even value indicates that the expressions are taken in disjunction.

More precisely, we assume that the logical expressions are organized as *AND / OR* trees, with an *AND* connective at the root. Each subtree is enclosed within a frame and its depth determines whether it has to be interpreted as a conjunction or as a disjunction. Expressions within a frame at an *AND* level of nesting are taken as conjuncts, while expressions within a frame at an *OR* level of nesting are taken as disjuncts. In case the original OCL formula had disjunctions at the top level, a new fictitious top node is first inserted to constitute the *AND*-labeled root, and then the translation process is started. In this case, the first UML element can be found at the second layer of nesting at least. A dashed frame indicates that the whole expression within it must be negated, while dashed individual elements indicate that they enter the expression in a negated form.

If-then-else expressions can be depicted by frames with different compartments. The *if* compartment is above the *then* compartment on the left, and the *else* compartment on the right. A sample constraint like "there is a date of death if the person has died" looks as shown in Figure 11.

context **Inhabitant** inv:
if self.attrState = #died then

  not(isUndefined(self.naturalPerson.attrDateOfDeath))
else

  isUndefined(self.naturalPerson.attrDateOfDeath)

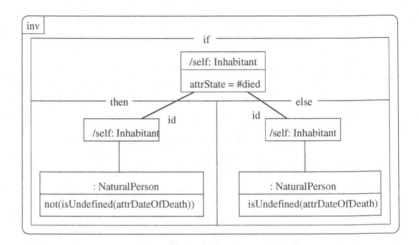

Fig. 11. There is a date of death if the person has died.

5 Adaptation of the OCL Meta Model

Basing the visualization of OCL on collaborations, the OCL meta model introduced in [9] and further elaborated in [1] has to be adapted to the meta model for collaborations. The idea is to use collaborations to describe properties of objects. In this sense, roughly speaking, the sub-meta model for a property operation is replaced by a section of the meta model for collaborations.

The description of object properties is based on classifier and association roles which are used to describe navigation paths. Here, the existence of navigation paths is expressed by the usual collaborations whereas non-existence can be expressed by negated classifier and association roles. A special classifier role is the self classifier role. The dynamic aspects of collaboration diagrams are exploited to represent the calling of methods to determine properties. Method calls are described by interactions consisting of messages between two classifier roles. These messages are actions, possibly with parameters.

Attribute expressions can be described by collaborations too, since classifier roles might contain attributes with instantiation. The proper constraint is expressed by a Boolean expression attached to the property operation.

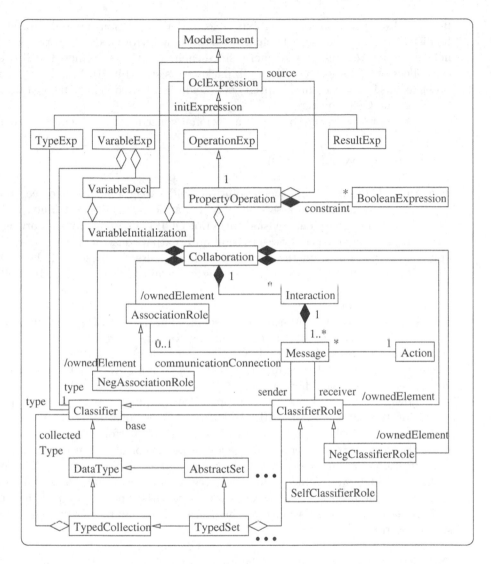

Fig. 12. Meta model for Visual OCL

As in [1], a special package UML_OCL contains basic data types and collections. Abstract collections are thought to be incorporated in this package as data types. They have to be instantiated by concrete element types, which is done in a special profile which introduces typed collections with a link back to classifiers to capture the collected type.

Operation expressions are property operations in any case. If they consist of constraints only, simple Boolean expressions are formed as constraints. Special OCL operations are integrated by offering special data types in the UML_OCL package as described above. As already presented in [9], OCL expressions may be variables, operations or result expressions. Self expressions no longer need to be distinguished, since self classifier roles are now introduced. Moreover, we do not need query expressions anymore, since their operations are now handled by the collection types in the UML_OCL package, as stated in [1]. Finally, type expressions, as introduced in [1], specify types which are needed in some operations based on the OCLAny type.

We do not have space to discuss additional constraints on the meta model.

6   Related Work

Constraint diagrams [7] and their evolution, spider diagrams [5], have been proposed as a way to express a set-theoretic semantics of OCL constraints. However, they do not represent a visualization of OCL expressions by supporting a structural correspondence between visual and textual constructs. Moreover, the approach is not based on the graphical elements already present in the UML core. The difficulty of immediately relating constraint diagrams to UML model diagrams suggested the combination of annotating such diagrams with fragments of textual OCL constraints defining the context of the evaluation, the environment defined by a let expression, or specific operations [8]. Such an approach suffers from the typical difficulties of parsing together diagrams and text, that we overcome by providing suitable visualizations for all the structural elements where [8] needs textual constraints, and by constraining the use of text in well defined positions in the diagram.

Following the OCL meta model proposed in [9], in [10] an approach is proposed for the validation of UML models and OCL constraints based on the animation of model diagrams. Static checks can be performed automatically, while the designer can interactively generate prototypical instances of a model in the form of diagram snapshots, to be compared against the specification. Although providing an interactive form of integration between diagrams and OCL constraints, the proposal is based on a purely textual syntax, obtained through a translation of UML to a textual representation and adding "wrapping" constructs on top of OCL syntax.

Discussing the general requirements for the construction of tools supporting OCL, Hussmann *et al.*, advocate the use of normal forms, such as the reduction of `forall` and `exists` constructs to `iterate` [6]. The existence of normal forms would facilitate the choice of alternative representations for constraints with the same models, e.g. `size = 0` and `isEmpty`. In this paper we have maintained adherence to the original syntax rather than to the semantics, as in Figure 6.

7   Conclusion

The paper has presented an approach to the visualization of OCL constraints based on collaborations, aiming at the formulation of complete constraining expressions on UML models in the same visual language as the model. The proposed visualization is based on a number of principles which favor a greater readability and amenability to OCL constraints. The proposal conforms to the UML meta model and adapts recent proposals for a meta model for OCL. The proposed visualization introduces a limited amount of new core notation, but offers a variety of visual shortcuts for convenient visual notation. They exploit spatial relations between model elements and their appearance properties in a consistent way. In particular, spatial relations are used in the form of frames with nesting to represent the tree structure of a Boolean expression.

As to appearance properties, we use different kinds of line thickness, replication for representing collections, adornments to qualify collections, and connecting lines or names, to express references to elements.

As future work, two mapping algorithms, commuting between textual and visual OCL notations, are desirable once the discussions on the OCL meta model have converged. In this case, the textual and the visual notations could be considered as two concrete syntaxes of one and the same abstract syntax.

References

1. M. Bodenmüller. The OCL Metamodel and the UML-OCL package. Proc. of OCL Workshop, Satellite Event of UML 2000, York, October 2000, 2000.
2. P. Bottoni, M. Koch, F. Parisi Presicce, and G. Taentzer. Automatic Consistency Checking and Visualization of OCL Constraints. In *UML 2000*, pages 294–308. Springer LNCS 1939, 2000.
3. S. Cook, A. Kleppe, R. Mitchell, B. Rumpe, J. Warmer, and Wills A. The Amsterdam Manifesto on OCL. Technical Report tum-19925. Technical report, Tecnische Universität München, 1999.
4. E. Hammer. Peircean graphs for propositional logic. In G. Allwein and J. Barwise, editors, *Logical Reasoning with Diagrams*, pages 129–147. Oxford University Press, 1996.
5. J. Howse, F. Molina, J. Taylor, S. Kent, and J. Gil. Spider diagrams: A diagrammatic reasoning system. *Journal of Visual Languages and Computing*, pages 299–324, 2001.
6. M. Hussmannn, B. Demuth, and F. Finger. Modular architecture for a toolset supporting OCL. In A. Evans, S. Kent, and Selic B., editors, *UML 2000*, pages 278 – 293. Springer LNCS 1939, 2000.
7. S. Kent. Constraint diagrams: Visualising invariants in object oriented models. In *Proceedings of OOPSLA'97*. ACM Press, 1997.
8. S. Kent and J. Howse. Mixing visual and textual constraint languages. In R. France and B. Rumpe, editors, *UML'99*, pages 384 – 398. Springer LNCS 1723, 1999.
9. M. Richters and M. Gogolla. A metamodel for OCL. In R. France and B. Rumpe, editors, *UML'99*, pages 156 – 171. Springer LNCS 1723, 1999.
10. M. Richters and M. Gogolla. Validating UML models and OCL constraints. In A. Evans, S. Kent, and B. Selic, editors, *UML 2000*, pages 265 – 277. Springer LNCS 1939, 2000.

Rule-Based Specification of Behavioral Consistency Based on the UML Meta-model

Gregor Engels, Reiko Heckel, and Jochen Malte Küster

University of Paderborn, Dept. of Mathematics and Computer Science
D-33095 Paderborn, Germany
reiko|jkuester@upb.de

Abstract. Object-oriented modeling favors the modeling of object behavior from different viewpoints and at different levels of abstraction. This gives rise to consistency problems between overlapping or semantically related submodels. The absence of a formal semantics for the UML and the numerous ways of employing the language within the development process lead to a number of different consistency notions. Therefore, general meta-level techniques are required for specifying, analyzing, and communicating consistency constraints. In this paper, we discuss the issue of consistency of behavioral models in the UML and present techniques for specifying and analyzing consistency. Using meta-model rules we transform elements of UML models into a semantic domain. Then, consistency constraints can by specified and validated using the language and the tools of the semantic domain. This general methodology is exemplified by the problem of protocol statechart inheritance.

Keywords: meta modeling, model verification, behavioral consistency

1 Introduction

A model in the UML usually consists of several diagrams specifying different viewpoints of the system at different levels of abstraction. However, these viewpoints are often not disjoint and models produced at different stages in the development process are semantically related. As a consequence, the handling of (in)consistency between diagrams or, more generally, between submodels, is an issue of major importance.

As the term *(in)consistency management* suggests, we do not expect consistency between all submodels and throughout the development process [10,11]. Nevertheless, it is important to be able to specify consistency constraints and to verify them, e.g., when certain milestones are reached or the model is completed. Thus, as a prerequisite for (in)consistency management, techniques are required for the specification and verification of consistency constraints. Although several approaches to consistency in formal specifications exist [2], a general approach to consistency for the UML is still missing [5]. In particular, no general techniques have been proposed to deal with the consistency of behavioral diagrams.

M. Gogolla and C. Kobryn (Eds.): UML 2001, LNCS 2185, pp. 272–286, 2001.
© Springer-Verlag Berlin Heidelberg 2001

Abstractly speaking, consistency means that the requirements expressed in different parts of a model do not contradict each other. Thus it is ensured that there exists an implementation satisfying all requirements. Consistency problems arise from the overlap between submodels within certain aspects. For example, both sequence and statechart diagrams express different views of the behavior of objects.

In general, we may distinguish between *syntactic* and *semantic consistency*. In the context of the UML, syntactic consistency is concerned with the structural well-formedness of the abstract syntax as specified in the meta model [20] by means of class diagrams and the object constraint language. For example, identifier names used in one submodel must be properly defined in another submodel.

Semantic consistency is concerned, for example, with the compatibility of the specified behavior. A typical example is the compatibility between sequence diagrams modeling test scenarios and statechart diagrams describing the implementation of classes. In contrast to syntactic consistency, there exists no general techniques for specifying semantic (and, in particular, behavioral) consistency constraints. In this paper, we propose such a technique and exemplify its application by the well-known problem of *statechart inheritance* [4,22,13].

An "ideal approach" to semantic consistency would build on a complete formal definition of the UML semantics, e.g., as a mapping $M : UML \to D$ which associates every model $m \in UML$ with an element $M(m)$ of a (mathematically founded) semantic domain D, representing the "meaning" of m. Then, the semantic relation between submodels m_1 and m_2 could be deduced by studying their images $M(m_1)$ and $M(m_2)$ in the semantic domain, and consistency constraints could be expressed by requiring a certain relation. However, a complete formalization of the UML semantics is presently beyond hope. Moreover, as a general-purpose modeling language, the UML even lacks precise *conceptual* guidelines of how to use certain diagrams in the development process. As a consequence, the semantic relation between different diagrams or submodels cannot be fixed once and for all.

In order to meet the requirements of particular application domains, the UML provides extension mechanisms to define domain or project-specific specializations and dialects, called *profiles* [19]. Since each of these may come with its own methodology, in general, semantic consistency constraints should be part of a profile definition. To make this feasible, meta-level techniques are needed in order to support the specification and verification of behavioral consistency constraints. Such specifications have to be *flexible* in order to support changes in the methodology (and revisions of the language) and *local* in order to provide the possibility of a partial specification for only those parts of the UML that are well enough understood.

In this paper, we outline a general approach to the *specification and verification* of constraints for the UML. The approach consists of the following steps.

1. **Identifying the consistency requirements.** In order to formalize consistency requirements, first they have to be stated informally. Such a description

should include the development context (the method employed and the localization of the problem), the model elements of interest, and the conceptual rules which describe the relation between these model elements in this context.

2. **Choosing a semantic domain.** To support the formalization of constraints, a semantic domain must be chosen which provides a mathematical model for the consistency requirements identified before. Furthermore, the semantic domain should provide both a language for specifying constraints and analysis techniques for verifying them. Note, that the semantic domain is not supposed to provide a semantics of the UML in general. Thus, it can be specifically tailored towards the aspect of interest.

3. **Defining a partial semantic mapping.** Those aspects of the model that contribute to the consistency requirements identified in Step 1 have to be mapped onto the semantic domain chosen in Step 2. This mapping is the most subtle part of the overall process because it requires to establish a correspondence between the concepts of the semantic domain and the UML.

4. **Specification of consistency constraints.** The consistency requirements are formalized in terms of the semantic representations of the model elements identified in Step 1 as defined by the mapping defined in Step 3. The constraints are given using the language of the semantic domain.

5. **Verification of consistency constraints.** Using the analysis techniques of the semantic domain the validity of the previously formulated consistency constraints can be analyzed w.r.t. the individual models. Therefore, the relevant aspects of a model are translated into the language of the semantic domain and the corresponding verification techniques are used to establish the constraints.

In particular, Step 3 and 4 above are complicated by the fact that UML models have a graphical abstract syntax while most programming or specification languages (which provide the most interesting semantic domains) are textual and abstractly based on trees or terms. Thus, techniques for the translation of graphical into textual languages are required in order to simplify the formulation of these mappings. In this paper we use a hybrid, rule-based notation [6] which combines textual rules in the style of attribute grammars with meta model queries expressed as visual patterns.

This generic approach is instantiated as follows. In the next section (Sect. 2), we review the consistency problem of statechart inheritance, which involves both statechart and class diagrams, and introduce two running examples. Then, Sect. 3 gives a brief introduction to CSP [14] which is our semantic domain for behavioral consistency and shows a rule-based mapping of (a subset of) statechart and class diagrams into this domain. In Sect. 4 we formulate the actual behavioral constraints by means of CSP refinement relations and discuss the automated verification of such constraints.

2   UML Protocol Statecharts and Inheritance

Following the roadmap outlined in the Introduction, in this section we identify (informally) the consistency requirements, discuss the development context and specify the relevant model elements in the UML meta model.

In the UML, a statechart can be associated to a class in order to specify the *object life cycle*, i.e., the order of operations called upon an object of this class during its life-time. Given a class A and a subclass B of A, the behavioral conformity of the associated statecharts gives rise to the problem of *statechart inheritance*. In the literature, different notions are proposed (see, e.g., [4,13,22, 23]). In this paper, we will restrict ourselves to *protocol statechart*, i.e., statecharts without actions which are used, for example, in the Unified Process [15]. Even in this simplified case, (at least) two different notions of consistency can be defined which are related to two dual interpretations of statecharts as specifying *invocable or observable behavior*.

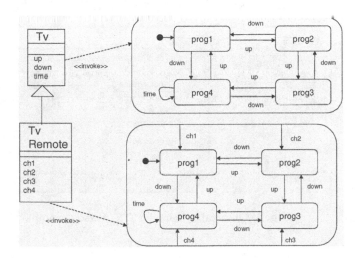

Fig. 1. Invocable behavior: The Tv example

Invocable behavior. In this view, which has its origin in object-oriented programming and is thus typical for behavioral descriptions at the design or implementation level, a statechart is seen as a *contract* between a class and its clients about the possible sequences of method calls whose implementation should be guaranteed. Thus, it specifies a lower bound to the behavior offered by a class. The corresponding notion of behavior inheritance is based on the *substitution principle* requiring that an object of class B can be used where an object of class A is required. This means, any sequence of operations invocable on the superclass can also be invoked on the subclass [4].

In Fig. 1, a class Tv for a simple television set is introduced. The behavior is specified in the statechart as follows: The television only has four programs and switching between these programs can only be done by calling up and down methods. The class TvRemote extends the Tv class and models a more sophisticated television set. It introduces additional methods for directly switching to a particular channel. For a client of the Tv class who is used to the simpler interface, it is important that the more elaborate device can still be used in the same way. In fact, any sequence of operations invocable on a Tv object can also be invoked on a TvRemote object, as the statechart of the former is completely included in the statechart of the latter.

In order to associate a statechart to a class, we use a stereotyped dependency from the class to the statechart. In this case, the stereotype invoke expresses that the statechart models the invocable behavior of the class.

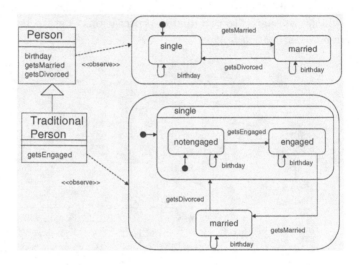

Fig. 2. Observable behavior: The Person example

Observable behavior. At the earlier stage of development, a statechart is often used to describe all sequences of method calls that could be observed by the clients of an object. Thus, it specifies an upper bound to the behavior. In this case, the notion of inheritance reflects the idea that an object of the subclass should always behave like an object of the superclass if viewed only according to the superclass description. Hence, each sequence observable with respect to a subclass must result (under projection to the methods known) in an observable sequence of its superclass [4].

In Fig. 2, a statechart is introduced modeling the behavior of persons with respect to marriage: A Person may be either single or married, switching between the two states by means of methods getsMarried and getsDivorced. The class TraditionalPerson extends this behavior by the new method getsEngaged. A traditional person always gets engaged before getting married. This is modeled in the corresponding statechart by refining the state single and changing the behavior accordingly. In any state of a person, a birthday event may occur modeling that the person has grown one year older.

From the point of view of an observer who does not care about engagement, the behavior of both classes coincides because, by filtering out the getsEngaged method, the sequences of methods of TraditionalPerson objects can be projected onto that of Person objects. Following similar conventions as above, we use an observe stereotype to express that the statechart models the observable behavior of the class.

Meta model. In order to identify more precisely the model elements involved in the consistency problem, in Fig. 3 we present the relevant fragments of the UML meta model [20]. It covers a (simplified) notion of statechart diagrams and their association with classes by stereotyped dependencies. Note that the actual stereotypes visible in the examples are only defined at the model level, e.g., as part of a profile [19]. In addition, Generalization (between classes) is modeled. The presentation conforms to the UML meta model but for the flattening of some inheritance relations and the introduction of one derived attribute events which shall contain the set of all events attached to the transitions internal to a State. All meta classes contain a meta attribute name:string which is not shown in the figure. (In the UML meta model this is inherited from the super class ModelElement).

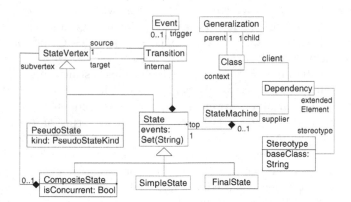

Fig. 3. UML meta model fragment integrating statecharts, generalization of classes, and stereotypes

In Sect. 4, we shall formalize the two notions of behavior consistency discussed in this section by means of a mapping of meta model instances into CSP, which is defined below. The meta model fragment in Fig. 3 identifies the domain of definition of this partial semantic mapping.

3   Mapping Protocol Statecharts to CSP

In this section, we exemplify steps 2 and 3 of our general methodology. First, we give a brief introduction to CSP as semantic domain for behavioral consistency. Then, we describe, by means of meta model-based mapping rules, a translation of statecharts into CSP.

CSP as semantic domain. Communicating Sequential Processes (CSP) [14] provide a mathematical model for concurrency based on a simple programming notation and supported by tools [8]. In fact, the existence of *language* and *tool support* are most important to our aim of *specifying* and *verifying* consistency constraints, despite the existence of more expressive mathematical models. Next, we briefly review the syntax and semantics of the CSP processes we are using.

Given a set $\mathcal{A}$ of actions and a set of process names $\mathcal{N}$, the syntax of CSP is given by

$$P ::= \text{STOP} \mid \text{SKIP} \mid a \to P \mid P \sqcap P \mid P \,\square\, P \mid P \setminus a \mid pn$$

where $a \in \mathcal{A}$, $A \subseteq \mathcal{A}$, and $pn \in \mathcal{N}$. Process names are used for defining recursive processes using equations $pn = P$. The interpretation of the operations is as follows. The processes STOP and SKIP represent, respectively, deadlock and successful termination. The prefix processes $a \to P$ performs action a and continues like P. The processes $P \sqcap Q$ and $P \,\square\, Q$ represent internal and external choice between P and Q, respectively. That means, while $P \sqcap Q$ performs an internal (τ-)action when evolving into P or into Q, for $P \,\square\, Q$ this requires an observable action of either P or Q. For example, $(a \to P) \sqcap (b \to Q)$ performs τ in order to become either $a \to P$ or $b \to Q$. Instead, $(a \to P) \,\square\, (b \to Q)$ must perform a or b and evolves into P or Q, respectively. This distinction shall be relevant for the translation of statechart diagrams below. Finally, the process $P \setminus a$ behaves like P except that all occurrences of action a are hidden.

The semantics of CSP is usually defined in terms of *traces*, *failures*, and *divergences* [14]. A trace is just a finite sequences $s \in \mathcal{A}^*$ of actions which may be observed when a process is executing. A failure (s, A) provides, in addition, the set A of actions that can be refused by the process after executing s. Divergences are traces that, when executed, are followed by an infinite internal computation.

Together with these semantic models come several notions of process refinement. We write $P \sqsubseteq_T Q$ if $\mathcal{T}(Q) \subseteq \mathcal{T}(P)$, i.e., every trace of Q is also a trace of P. Analogously, refinement relations based on failures and divergences are defined. In general, the idea is that Q is a refinement of P if Q is more deterministic (more completely specified) than P. These refinement relations shall be used to express behavioral consistency constraints.

Mapping rules for statecharts. As discussed in the introduction, the translation of graphical into textual languages is supported by a hybrid, rule-based notation which combines textual grammar rules with graphical patterns. Each rule consists of three parts: a meta model pattern, its concrete syntax, and a CSP

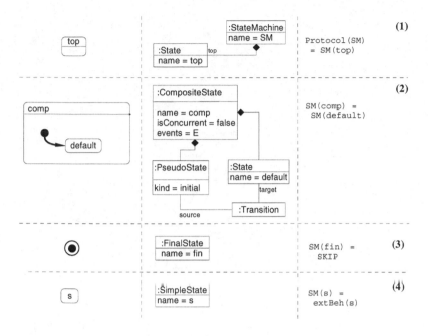

Fig. 4. Mapping rules for states

expression. Consider, for example, rule (2) in Fig. 4 which defines the semantics of a composite (OR) state in terms of the semantics of its default state. In the center, this is represented by a meta model pattern showing the abstract syntax of the source language UML. On the right, the corresponding expression in the target language CSP is shown. It is parameterized over the names of the UML model elements and contains non-terminals like extBeh which are to be replaced by application of other rules. On the left, the corresponding concrete UML syntax is shown.

The translation of (a simplified version of) statecharts into CSP processes is described by the rules in Fig. 4 and 5. In a top-down fashion, following the hierarchical decomposition of states, the rules (1) and (2) in Fig. 4 generate for each composite state an equation synthesizing its behavior from the behavior of its substates. The final state translates into the process SKIP (cf. rule (3)) representing successful termination (instead of a deadlock). A simple state is defined by rule (4) in terms of its *external behavior* which captures both the transitions directly starting from the state as well as the transitions from all (direct and transitive) superstates.

This bottom-up computation of external behavior is specified in Fig. 5. If the state in question is already the top state of the state machine, its external behavior is empty (cf. rule (5)). In general, the external behavior of a state consists of an external choice between its direct behavior and the external behavior of its super state (cf. rule (6)). The difference between external and internal non-determinism ($\Box$ and $\sqcap$) becomes obvious when looking at rules (7) and (8),

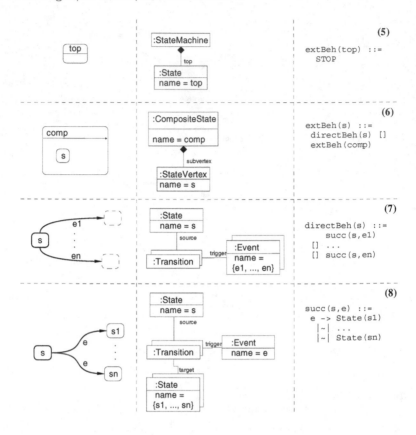

Fig. 5. Mapping rules for external behavior

respectively. In rule (7), the use of external choice formalizes the idea that the next event to be processed is determined by the environment of the statechart represented, e.g., by the client objects and the event queue. In contrast, once an event e is chosen, the choice between two transitions with the same trigger e is performed internally.

The translation creates a system of (mutually recursive) equations, one for the overall state machine (using rule (1)) and one for every instance of meta class State (using rules (2–4)). Then, the rules (5–8) in Fig. 5 are used to replace all occurrence of the auxiliary (non-terminal) process names *extBeh, directBeh*, and *succ* by their corresponding process definitions. Notice that we have used the machine-readable version of the CSP notation where [] and |˜| denote □ and ⊓, respectively.

Observe that the rules (7) and (8) contain multi-objects (denoted by shaded borders) which represent maximal sets of concrete objects. As a consequence, their attributes represent sets of values. For example in rule (7), the multi-object of class Transition matches all instances of this meta class connected via their source link to the state named s. Moreover, the multi-object of class Event matches all events connected to these transitions. The names of these events $\{e1, \ldots, en\}$ are listed in the name attribute of the multi-object.

Next, the application of these rules to the statechart for the class Tradition-alPerson is shown. (Assume that TP is the name of the state machine associated to the TraditionalPerson class.) In order to simplify the following derivation, we shall make use of the following equivalence (*)

$$extBeh(single) = directBeh(single) \square extBeh(top) = extBeh(top) = STOP$$

which follows by rule (5,6,7) and the CSP axiom $p \square STOP = p$. Intuitively, the external behavior of the top state (which is not visible in the concrete syntax and does not have outgoing transitions or super-states) is empty, and the same holds for state *single* which does not have outgoing transitions either.

In the derivation below, the semantics of state *single* is defined to be that of its default state *notengaged*. As *notengaged* is a SimpleState, rules (4) and (6) are applied. After dropping the super-state component using (*), we just collect the outgoing transitions using rules (7) and (8). The semantics of *engaged* and *married* is computed in a similar way.

$$
\begin{array}{lll}
Protocol(TP) & = TP(top) & (1) \\
TP(top) & = TP(single) & (2) \\
TP(single) & = TP(notengaged) & (2) \\
TP(notengaged) & = extBeh(notengaged) & (4) \\
& = directBeh(notengaged) \square extBeh(single) & (6) \\
& = directBeh(notengaged) & (*) \\
& = succ(notengaged, birthday) \sqcup succ(notengaged, getsEngaged) & (7) \\
& = birthday \rightarrow TP(notengaged) \square getsEngaged \rightarrow TP(engaged) & (8) \\
TP(engaged) & = extBeh(engaged) & (4) \\
& = directBeh(engaged) & (6, *) \\
& = getsMarried \rightarrow TP(married) \square birthday \rightarrow TP(engaged) & (7, 8) \\
TP(married) & = directBeh(married) & (4, 6, *) \\
& = getsDivorced \rightarrow TP(notengaged) \square birthday \rightarrow TP(married) & (7, 8)
\end{array}
$$

As shown in this example, our mapping rules support not only the visual description of model translators based on the concrete and abstract syntax of the language, but they can also be used as a formal calculus to reason about such mappings.

4   Specifying and Analyzing Behavioral Constraints

As outlined by steps 4 and 5 of our roadmap, in this section formal consistency constraints for the two notions of statechart inheritance discussed in Sect. 2 shall be formulated based on the mapping of statecharts into CSP. Then, their verification w.r.t. the sample models shall be discussed.

Specification. Consistency constraints are specified by identifying a model pattern which gives rise to a consistency problem (like a generalization between two classes with associated statecharts), and formulating the consistency constraint in the language of the semantic domain (e.g., as an assertion of trace refinement between two CSP expressions). The visual specification of these consistency constraints uses the same kind of mapping rules as in the previous section: In the center, the (meta) model pattern of is shown with the corresponding concrete syntax on the left, and the (textual specification of) the consistency constraint on the right.

The upper part of Fig. 6 shows the constraint for *invocation consistency* which asserts that each trace of the (processes derived from the) superclass' statechart should also be contained in the set of traces of the statechart for the subclass. By definition of trace refinement $P \sqsubseteq_T Q$ iff $T(Q) \subseteq T(P)$, this translates into a refinement in the opposite direction. Note that we use the notation supported by the FDR tool [8] where [T= denotes trace refinement $\sqsubseteq_T$.

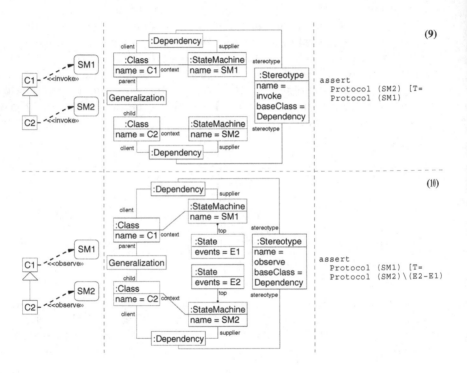

Fig. 6. Behavioral constraints for statechart inheritance

The constraint specifying *observation consistency*, where the superclass' statechart specifies an upper bound to the behavior of the subclasses, is shown in the lower part of Fig. 6. The assertion states that, after hiding (with $\backslash (E_2 - E_1)$) all new events, the subclass' statechart is a trace refinement of the superclass' statechart.

Analysis. In order to verify the consistency of an individual model, for each occurrence of a model pattern representing a consistency problem we derive a corresponding assertion as specified by rule (9) or (10). The assertions make reference to the CSP expressions derived by the mapping rules (1) to (8). Thus, in the case of the Person example in Fig. 2, we obtain the following assertion.

```
assert
    Protocol(P) [T= Protocol(TP) \ getsEngaged
```

Analogously, the Tv example in Fig. 1 yields

```
assert
    Protocol(TvRemote) [T= Protocol(Tv)
```

The different assertions derived in the two examples result from the use of different stereotypes observe and invoke, respectively, and they formalize different requirements for consistency in both cases.

Using the FDR tool, both assertions can be verified automatically. In the Person example, representing observation consistency, this means that all traces of TraditionalPerson are included in the set of traces of Person if we hide all occurrences of the getsEngaged operation, which is not defined for Person. For the Tv example, representing invocation consistency, the assertion implies that any sequence of operations invoked on a Tv object is also invocable on a TvRemote object.

On the contrary, observe that the two examples do not satisfy the respective dual notions of consistency. (This does not contradict the consistency of the models because the corresponding assertions are not produced by the rules in Fig. 6.) With respect to invocable behavior, Protocol(TP) is not a consistent refinement of Protocol(P) because the trace getsMarried is not invocable on instances of TraditionalPerson. Similarly, TvRemote is not observation consistent with Tv because the restriction of trace up ch4 time up invocable on TvRemote yields the trace up time up which is not a trace of Tv.

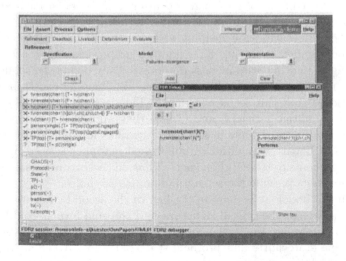

Fig. 7. A screenshot of the FDR tool showing a counterexample

Figure 7 shows a screenshot of the FDR tool with this example. The tool is essentially a model checker verifying refinements between CSP expressions. If this relation does not hold, a trace or failure is produced as a counterexample. It is evident that, in order to make our approach usable in practice, an interface will be required which presents such counterexamples in UML notation. This could either be done via sequence diagrams representing the error trace, through animations of the respective submodels, or by back-annotating consistency errors in UML diagrams. Thus, ordinary modelers would not have to deal with formal notations such as CSP.

5   Conclusion

In this paper, we have proposed a methodology for specifying and analyzing behavioral constraints in the UML based on a mapping of models into a semantic domain with language and tool support. It was not our aim to provide a full denotational semantics for the UML (or even a reasonable sublanguage of it). On the contrary, the mapping can be defined locally for the language features of interest, even if the semantics of other model elements is not yet clarified.

This methodology generalizes ideas from different approaches to the formalization and analysis of object-oriented models. Some of them are based on a complete formalization of the modeling language. For example, [18,3] translate object-oriented models to LOTOS specifications which can be analyzed for consistency using tools for state exploration and concurrency analysis. Thus, in this case LOTOS provides the semantic domain for specifying and checking consistency properties, with support for both data type and behavioral aspects. The design of a general-purpose semantic framework, which capture most aspects of object-oriented modeling through a combination of transition systems, algebraic specifications, and transformation rules is the objective of [12].

Other approaches are dealing with one particular consistency problem in isolation. Fradet et al. [9], for example, propose an approach to consistency checking of multiplicities in class diagrams. They define the semantics of a class diagram to be the set of all its instances fulfilling the constraints. Consistency then means that this set is not empty. This is checked by solving a system of linear inequalities derived from the class diagram. A similar example is [17] who analyze timing constraints in sequence diagrams for their consistency by solving systems of linear inequalities. A rule-based mapping is used in [1] to translate UML fragments to (timed) Petri nets. Thus, in these examples, linear inequalities and Petri nets provide the semantic domains of choice.

Our methodology is more in the line of the second category of "partial solutions", although the overall structure and the rule format could also support a complete mapping. In [7], the approach is applied to the problem of consistency of capsule statecharts and protocol statecharts in UML-RT, while [16] follows a similar idea for analyzing the consistency of timing constraints in sequence diagrams by calculating the worst-case execution times of statecharts.

In order to be able to modify the notion of consistency (when the development process evolves or a new profile is created), it is important that the semantic mapping is defined in a *flexible* and *extensible* way. We think, that the rule-based notation used in Sect. 3, which was first used in [6] for describing JAVA code generation and is originally motivated by pair grammars [21], provides a good starting point. However, it has to be supported by a tool which is able to generate a model compiler from such a rule-based description. Currently, we are investigating the use of XSL transformations for this purpose.

References

1. L. Baresi and M. Pezzè. Improving UML with Petri nets. In A. Corradini and M. Bauderon, editors, *Proc. ETAPS 2001 Workshop on Uniform Approaches to Graphical Process Specification Techniques (UniGra 2001), Genova, Italy*, Electronic Notes in TCS 51. Elsevier Science, 2001.
2. E. Boiten, H. Bowman, J. Derrick, and M. Steen. Viewpoint consistency in Z and LOTOS: A case study. In J. Fitzgerald, C. B. Jones, and P. Lucas, editors, *Proc. 4th Intl. Symposium of Formal Methods Europe, Graz, Austria*, LNCS 1313, pages 644–664. Springer-Verlag, 1997.
3. B. Cheng, L. Campbell, and E. Wang. Enabling automated analysis through the formalization of object-oriented modeling diagrams. In *Proc. IEEE Intl. Conference on Dependable Systems and Networks*. IEEE Computer Society, 2000.
4. J. Ebert and G. Engels. Structural and behavioral views of OMT-classes. In E. Bertino and S. Urban, editors, *Proc. Object-Oriented Methodologies and Systems*, LNCS 858, pages 142–157. Springer-Verlag, 1994.
5. G. Engels and L. Groenewegen. Object-oriented modeling: A roadmap. In A. Finkelstein, editor, *Future Of Software Engineering 2000*, pages 105–116. ACM, 2000.
6. G. Engels, R. Hücking, St. Sauer, and A. Wagner. UML collaboration diagrams and their transformation to Java. In R. France and B. Rumpe, editors, *Proc. UML'99, Fort Collins, CO, USA*, LNCS 1723, pages 473–488. Springer-Verlag, 1999.
7. G. Engels, J.M. Küster, L. Groenewegen, and R. Heckel. A methodology for specifying and analyzing consistency of object-oriented behavioral models. In V. Gruhn, editor, *Proc. European Software Engineering Conference (ESEC/FSE 2001), Vienna, Austria*. To appear.
8. Formal Systems Europe (Ltd). *Failures-Divergence-Refinement: FDR2 User Manual*, 1997.
9. P. Fradet, D. Le Métayer, and M. Périn. Consistency checking for multiple view software architectures. In O. Nierstrasz and M. Lemoine, editors, *Proc. European Software Engineering Conference (ESEC/FSE 1999)*, LNCS 1687, pages 410–428. Springer-Verlag / ACM Press, 1999.
10. C. Ghezzi and B. A. Nuseibeh. Special Issue on Managing Inconsistency in Software Development (1). *IEEE Transactions on Software Engineering*, 24(11), November 1998.
11. C. Ghezzi and B. A. Nuseibeh. Special Issue on Managing Inconsistency in Software Development (2). *IEEE Transactions on Software Engineering*, 25(11), November 1999.
12. M. Große-Rhode. Algebra transformation systems and their compositions. In *Proc. Fundamental Approaches to Software Engineering (FASE 1998)*, LNCS 1382, pages 107–122. Springer-Verlag, 1998.
13. D. Harel and O. Kupferman. On the Inheritance of State-Based Object Behavior. Technical Report MCS99-12, Weizmann Institute of Science, Faculty of Mathematics and Computer Science, June 1999.

14. C. A. R. Hoare. *Communcating Sequential Processes.* Prentice Hall, 1985.
15. I. Jacobson, G. Booch, and J. Rumbaugh. *The Unified Software Development Process.* Addison Wesley, 1999.
16. J. M. Küster and J. Stroop. Consistent design of embedded real-time systems with UML-RT. In *Proc. 4th IEEE International Symposium on Object-Oriented Real-Time Distributed Computing (ISORC'2001)*, 2001.
17. X. Li and J. Lilius. Timing analysis of UML sequence diagrams. In R. France and B. Rumpe, editors, *Proc. UML'99, Fort Collins, CO, USA*, LNCS 1723, pages 661–674. Springer-Verlag, 1999.
18. A. Moreira and R. Clark. Combining object-oriented modeling and formal description techniques. In M. Tokoro and R. Pareschi, editors, *Proc. 8th European Conference on Object-Oriented Programming (ECOOP'94)*, LNCS 821, pages 344 – 364. Springer-Verlag, 1994.
19. Object Management Group. Analysis and design platform task force – white paper on the profile mechanism, April 1999.
    http://www.omg.org/pub/docs/ad/99-04-07.pdf.
20. Object Management Group. UML specification version 1.4, 2001.
    http://www.omg.org.
21. T. W. Pratt. Pair grammars, graph languages and string-to-graph translations. *Journal of Computer and System Sciences*, 5:560–595, 1971.
22. Jean Louis Sourrouille. UML behavior: Inheritance and implementation in current object-oriented languages. In R. France and B. Rumpe, editors, *Proc. UML'99, Fort Collins, CO, USA*, LNCS 1723, pages 457–472. Springer-Verlag, 1999.
23. Markus Stumptner and Michael Schrefl. Behavior consistent inheritance in UML. In A.H.F. Laender, S.W. Liddle, and V.C. Storey, editors, *Proc. 19th International Conference on Conceptual Modeling, Salt Lake City, Utah, USA*, LNCS 1920. pages 527–542. Springer-Verlag, 2000.

A New UML Profile for Real-Time System Formal Design and Validation

L. Apvrille[1,2,3], P. de Saqui-Sannes[1,2], C. Lohr[2], P. Sénac[1,2], and J.-P. Courtiat[2]

[1] ENSICA, 1 place Emile Blouin, 31056 Toulouse Cedex 05, France
{apvrille, desaqui, senac}@ensica.fr
[2] LAAS-CNRS, 7 avenue du Colonel Roche, 31077 Toulouse Cedex 04, France
{lohr, courtiat}@laas.fr
[3] Alcatel Space Industries, 26 avenue J.-F. Champollion, B.P. 1187,
31037 Toulouse Cedex 01, France

Abstract. UML solutions in competition on the real-time system market share three common drawbacks: an incomplete formal semantics, temporal operators with limited expression and analysis power, and implementation-oriented tools with limited verification capabilities. To overcome these limitations, the paper proposes a UML profile designed with real-time system validation in mind. Extended class diagrams with associations attributed by composition operators give an explicit semantics to associations between classes. Enhanced activity diagrams with a deterministic delay, a non deterministic delay and a time-limited offering make it possible to work with temporal intervals in lieu of timers with fixed duration. The UML profile is given a precise semantics via its translation into the Formal Description Technique RT-LOTOS. A RT-LOTOS validation tool generates simulation chronograms and reachability graphs for RT-LOTOS specifications derived from UML class and activity diagrams. A coffee machine serves as example. The proposed profile is under evaluation on a satellite-based software reconfiguration system.

1. Introduction

The Unified Modeling Language [17] has received increasing attention from industrial practitioners who develop real-time systems, and several proprietary "Real-time UML" solutions have been marketed by tool manufacturers [1, 4, 11, 12, 22]. Meanwhile, Real-Time UML has stimulated research work on integrating UML and a Formal Description Technique [1, 12, 19]. A FDT has a formal semantics, which enables a priori validation. UML models that are given a precise semantics can be checked against inconsistencies, such as deadlocks or timing errors. This significantly increases the interest of UML notation for life-critical and time-constrained system design.

The paper proposes a UML profile specifically designed with real-time constraint validation in mind. Main ideas behind the definition of the profile are as follows. First, a formal semantics is given to associations between classes. Second, temporal operators with non deterministic delay and time-limited offering are introduced in behavior descriptions. Third, classes and their behavior descriptions are translated into a formal description written in RT-LOTOS [10], a timed process algebra

M. Gogolla and C. Kobryn (Eds.): UML 2001, LNCS 2185, pp. 287-301, 2001.

supported by a validation tool. An important issue is that RT-LOTOS syntax remains transparent to UML users. The latter can validate UML diagrams without learning RT-LOTOS. The profile is named TURTLE, an acronym for *Timed UML and RT-Lotos Environment*.

The paper is organized as follows. Section 2 surveys related work. Section 3 introduces RT-LOTOS. Section 4 defines the TURTLE profile. Section 5 gives an example: a coffee machine. Section 6 concludes the paper and discusses future work.

2. Related Work

With the support of the Object Management Group, the UML notation has received increasing attention from real-time system designers. In practice, not one but several real-time UMLs in competition exist to meet the needs stated by the OMG's Request For Proposal [18].

- UML-RT is supported by Rose RT; it includes ROOM language concepts in UML [22];
- RT-UML is supported by Rhapsody; it uses as much as possible native UML 1.3 constructs [11];
- UML paired with SDL is proposed by Telelogic with the TAU suite [5];
- Artisan Software Real-Time Studio [4].

Beyond their differences, the solutions implemented by these industrial tools have strict limitations in terms of temporal constraint expression. First, temporal operators are limited to timers with a fixed duration. Second, the lack of operator to handle time intervals makes it impossible to describe jitter and asynchronism in multimedia network systems [23]. Last but not least, UML misses an operator to express a time-limited offering.

The limitations above are currently overcome by using system primitives that do not have any formal semantics, which makes it impossible to validate UML models against temporal requirements. Therefore, concerted actions have been carried out to provide UML with a precise semantics [7, 8, 13]. Much work has been done on joint use of UML and a formal method: Labeled Transition Systems [14, 16], Petri Nets [19], Z [12, 16], synchronous languages [1, 12], PVS [24] and E-LOTOS [25].

3. RT-LOTOS

LOTOS [15] is an ISO-based Formal Description Technique for distributed processing system specification and design. A LOTOS specification, itself a process, is structured into processes. A LOTOS process is a black box which communicates with its environment through gates using a multiple rendezvous offer. Values can be exchanged at synchronization time. That exchange can be mono- or bi-directional.

Parallelism and synchronization between processes are expressed by composition operators. The latter include process sequencing, synchronization on all communication gates, synchronization on some gates, non deterministic choice and interleaving (parallel composition with no synchronization). Composition operators are identified by their symbols (Table 1).

Table 1. LOTOS operators

Operator	Description	Example
[]	Choice.	P[a,b,c,d] = P1[a,b] [] P2[c,d]
III	Parallel composition with no synchronization.	P[a,b,c,d] = P1[a,b] III P2[c,d]
I[b]I I[b,c,d]I	Parallel composition with synchronization on gate b. Parallel composition with synchronization on several gates (b,c,d).	P[a,b,c] = P1[a,b] I[b]I P2[b,c] P[a,b,c,d,e] = P1[a,b,c,d] I[b,c,d]I P2[b,c,d,e]
hide b in I[b]I	Parallel composition with synchronization on gate b, moreover where gate b is hidden.	P[a,c] = hide b in P1[a,b] I[b]I P2[b,c]
>>	Sequential composition.	P[a,b,c,d] = P1[a,b] >> P2[c,d]
[>	Disrupt.	P[a,b,c,d] = P1[a,b] [> P2[c,d]
;	Process prefixing by action a.	a; P
stop	Process which cannot communicate with any other process.	
exit	Process which can terminate and then transforms itself into stop.	

RT-LOTOS extends LOTOS with three temporal operators (Table 2). The combination of a deterministic and a non deterministic delay makes it possible to handle time intervals. The extended language keeps the control part of LOTOS, but replaces algebraic data types by implementations in C++ or Java [10].

Table 2. RT-LOTOS temporal operators

Temporal operator	Description
a{T}	Time limited offering.
delay(t1)	Deterministic delay.
latency(t2)	Non deterministic delay.

4. TURTLE: A Real-Time UML Profile

A UML profile specializes the UML meta-model into a specific meta-model dedicated to a given application domain [9]. A profile may contain selected elements of the reference meta-model, extension mechanisms, a description of the profile semantics, additional notations, and rules for model translation, validation and presentation.

The TURTLE profile aims to give a better description of inter- and intra-class logical and real-time control. At the class diagram level, inter-class control is addressed by adding one stereotype[1] to the UML meta-model. At the activity diagram level, three temporal operators are introduced for better expressiveness in intra-class control.

In TURTLE, a class diagram contains "normal" classes and classes stereotyped as *Tclass*. Four relationships (use, aggregation, composition and generalization) permit to establish links between classes. As in UML, TURTLE classes can be active or passive. An active class is a class whose instances own a process or a thread and can initiate control activity.

4.1. *Gate* Abstract Type

Besides usual communication via operations, *Tclasses* are given the possibility to communicate via gates, a concept for which we introduce a *Gate* abstract type (Fig. 1a) and distinguish between *InGate* and *OutGate* (Fig. 1b). *Gate* has no attribute nor operation. In the rest of the paper, we use "a *Tclass* performs an action on *Gate* g" to express that the *Tclass* wants to communicate on *Gate* g.

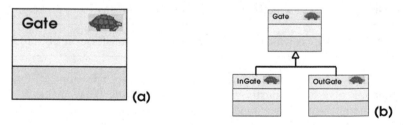

Fig. 1. *Gate* stereotype and differentiation between *InGate* and *OutGate*

4.2. *Tclass* Stereotype

Fig.2 depicts the structure of a *Tclass* stereotype. A *Tclass* is a UML class in which *Gates* are separated from other attributes. Main properties of a *Tclass* are listed below.

---

[1] A stereotype is an indirect add to the meta-model. The TURTLE stereotype and abstract types are graphically identified by a "turtle symbol" in the upper right corner of the class.

- *Prop1*: All the attributes but the *Gate* ones must be declared as private (-) or protected (#).
- *Prop2*: All the operations but the constructors must be declared as private (-) or protected (#). Constructors can be declared as public (+).
- *Prop3*: A *Tclass* is not complete without its behavior description given in the form of an activity diagram[2]. The latter can use the *Tclass* operations and attributes, as well as inherited operations and attributes.
- *Prop4*: Communications (data exchanges) between two *Tclasses* are necessarily performed using *Gates*. Synchronous communications via *Gates* are the only ones taken into account for validation. A *Tclass* may communicate with a non *Tclass* class by operation call, signal or attribute modification; these communications are not taken into account for validation.
- *Prop5*: All classes may have *Gate* attributes. Nevertheless, *Tclasses* are the only classes allowed to communicate via *Gates*.
- *Prop6*: A *Tclass* T can inherit from a class C iff C and its ascendants satisfy properties *Prop1* and *Prop2*.
- *Prop7*: Use, composition and generalization relationships between two classes are taken into account for validation iff the two classes are *Tclasses*.
- *Prop8*: There exists at most one relationship between two *Tclasses*. If that relationship is an association, it must be attributed with a *Composer*.
- *Prop9*. A class or a *Tclass* can be composed of *Tclasses* and classes.
- *Prop10*: Aggregation relationships between two *Tclasses* are not supported.
- *Prop11*: Let us assume that *Tclass* T1 is composed of *Tclass* T2 and that T1 has a public *Gate* g1 and T2 has a public *Gate* g2. Then a *Tclass* T3 which wants to communicate with T2 has two solutions: (i) to communicate directly with T2 on *Gate* g2 or (ii) to communicate with T1 on *Gate* g1 at the condition that an OCL formula associates g1 and g2 (that formula is attached to the association between T1 and T2; it takes the form of *{T1.g1=T2.g2}*).

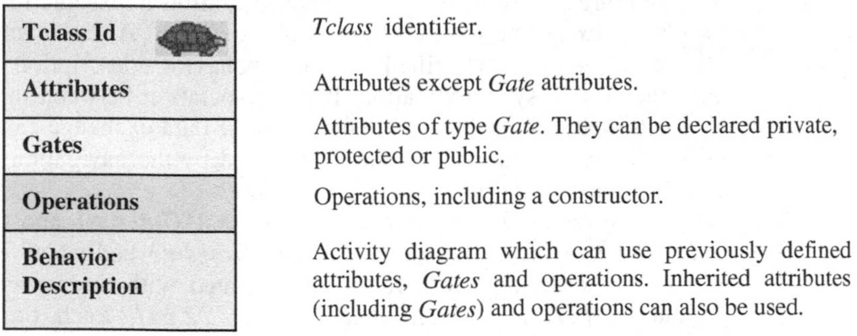

Tclass Id 🐢	*Tclass* identifier.
Attributes	Attributes except *Gate* attributes.
Gates	Attributes of type *Gate*. They can be declared private, protected or public.
Operations	Operations, including a constructor.
Behavior Description	Activity diagram which can use previously defined attributes, *Gates* and operations. Inherited attributes (including *Gates*) and operations can also be used.

Fig. 2. *Tclass* component

---

[2] Only activity diagrams are considered in the paper. State machines are left for future work.

4.3. *Composer* Abstract Type

A UML class diagram graphically defines a set of classes interconnected by relationships, such as associations. In the TURTLE context, we offer the possibility to give an association a precise semantics. The *Composer* abstract type is introduced to support that idea. Note that *Composer* is not used directly; associations are attributed with associative classes (*Parallel, Synchro, Invocation, Sequence, Preemption*) that inherit from *Composer*. Two inherited classes of *Composer* are presented in Fig. 3.

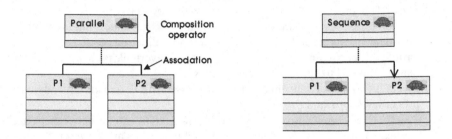

Fig. 3. Use of two inherited classes of the *Composer* abstract type

For each association between two *Tclasses,* there exists one and only one meaning, and therefore one *Composer*. The following classes inherit from *Composer*.

Parallel   The two *Tclasses* related by an association to which this operator is assigned are executed in parallel and without any synchronization. The two *Tclasses* should be active classes.

Synchro   The two *Tclasses* related by an association to which this operator is assigned, are synchronized. This synchronization is executed by the two *Tclasses* in two distinct threads of execution. A data exchange whose format is described in the behavior description may accompany this synchronization. If the association between the two *Tclasses* includes a navigation indication, the data exchange can only take place in the same direction as indicated by the navigation. Two *Tclasses* may synchronize on different *Gates*
an OCL formula. For example, suppose that *Gates* g1 and g2 of *Tclass* T1 synchronize respectively with *Gates* g3 and g4 of *Tclass* T2; in that case, the OCL formula associated with the association should be *{T1.g1 = T2.g3 and T1.g2 = T2.g4}*. Each time T1 performs an action on g1, it must wait for T2 to perform an action on g3, and reciprocally.

Invocation   Let us consider two *Tclasses* T1 and T2 linked by an association directed from T1 to T2 and attributed by the *Invocation* associative class. T2 can be activated by T1. Both T1 and T2 must have a *Gate* involved in the invocation. For example, let us consider that g1 (resp. g2) is a T1 (resp. T2) *Gate* and that the following OCL formula is · added to the association: *{T1.g1 = T2.g2}*. Then, when T1 performs an action on g1, it must wait for T2 to perform an action on g2. When T2 performs an action on g2, data can only be exchanged as indicated by the navigation. T1 is then blocked on g1 until T2 performs again an action on g2. The second data exchange can only be performed in an opposite direction to navigation. *Invocation* is similar to an operation call in the object oriented paradigm. Therefore, T2's invoked code is performed in the same thread of execution as T1.

Sequence   The two *Tclasses* related by an association to which this operator is associated, are triggered one after the other in the same navigation direction as the association. Note that in (T1 *Sequence* T2) T1 must terminate[3] before T2 starts. The two *Tclasses* classes.

Preemption   The *Tclass*, designated by the navigation of the association relating two *Tclasses*, whose operator is *Preemption* interrupt the other *Tclass*. Note that in (T2 *Preemption* T1), T2 may interrupt T1 until the termination of T1. The two *Tclasses* should be active classes.

4.4. *Tclass* Behavior Description

Table 3 illustrates for all graphic constructions of the activity diagrams [10], those to which specific semantics are given via a translation into LOTOS. Let AD denote a TURTLE activity diagram, and τ(AD) the RT-LOTOS process corresponding to the translation of AD.

Table 3. Non temporal TURTLE operators

TURTLE activity diagram	*Description*	*LOTOS translation*
AD	Beginning of the activity diagram. Therefore, beginning of the translation.	τ(AD)
g / AD	Synchronization on *Gate* **g**. AD is subsequently interpreted.	g ; τ(AD)
g ?x / AD	Synchronization on *Gate* **g** with value reception. AD is subsequently interpreted.	g ?x:nat ; τ(AD)
g !x / AD	Synchronization on *Gate* **g** with value emission. AD is subsequently interpreted.	g !x ; τ(AD)

---

[3] A *Tclass* terminates when all its activities have reached their termination points.

g !x ?y AD	Synchronization on *Gate* **g** with value emission and reception. AD is subsequently interpreted.	g !x ?y:nat ; $\tau(AD)$
y := x*2 AD	Assignation of a value to an attribute. AD is subsequently interpreted.	let y : YType = x*2 in $\tau(AD)$
operation(x, y) AD	Operation call. AD is subsequently interpreted.	$\tau(AD)$ (operation call not translated)
AD or AD	Loop structure. AD is interpreted each time the loop is entered.	process LabelX[g1,...gn] : noexit := $\tau(AD)$ >>LabelX[g1,...gn] end proc;
AD1 AD2 ... ADn	Parallelism between n sub-activities described by AD1, AD2, ..., ADn. For documentation purposes, sub-activities can be separated by swimlanes.	$\tau(AD1)$ ||| $\tau(AD2)$ ||| ... ||| $\tau(ADn)$ (swinlanes not translated)
[g1, ..., gm] AD1 AD2 ... ADn	Synchronization on *Gates* g1,...gm between n sub-activities described by AD1, AD2, ..., ADn.	$\tau(AD1)$ |[g1,...gm]| $\tau(AD2)$ |[g1,...gm]| ... |[g1,...gm]| $\tau(ADn)$
AD1 AD2 ... ADn	Selecting the first ready-to-execute activity among n activities described by AD1, AD2, ... , ADn.	$\tau(AD1)$ [] $\tau(AD2)$ [] ... [] $\tau(ADn)$
c1] [c2] [cn] AD1 AD2 ... ADn	AD1, AD2, ..., ADn sub-activities for which conditions are true can be selected. The first ready-to-execute activity whose guard is true is executed.	[c1] -> $\tau(AD1)$ [] [c2] -> $\tau(AD2)$ [] ... [] [cn] -> $\tau(ADn)$
AD1 AD2 ... ADn AD'1 AD'2 ... AD'm	Once terminated the n sub-activities described by AD1, AD2, ..., ADn are followed by the execution of the m sub-activities described by AD'1, AD'2, ..., AD'm. The latter are executed in parallel (interleaving)[4].	($\tau(AD1)$ ||| $\tau(AD2)$ ||| ... $\tau(ADn)$) >> ($\tau(AD'1)$ ||| $\tau(AD'2)$ ||| ... $\tau(AD'm)$)

---

[4] If ADi cardinal is 1 and AD'j cardinal is also 1, then a simple arrow is used between AD1 and AD'1.

	The n sub-activities described by AD1, AD2, ..., ADn are followed by the execution of the m sub-activities described by AD'1, AD'2,..., AD'm. The latter are executed with synchronization on k *Gates* g1, g2, ..., gk.	$(\tau(AD1) \,\|\|\, \tau(AD2) \,\|\|\, ...$ $\tau(ADn)\,) >>$ $(\tau(AD'1) \,\|[g1, \,...gk]\|$ $\tau(AD'2) \,\|[g1, \,...gk]\| \,...$ $\tau(AD'm)\,)$
	Termination of an activity.	exit

Table 4 presents the pictograms adopted for temporal operators. The third operator applies to a time interval. It is equivalent to two operators put in sequence: first, a fix duration delay equal to the interval's lower bound, and second, a latency equal to the difference between the interval's upper and lower bounds. The translation into RT-LOTOS for each operator is provided.

Table 4. TURTLE temporal operators

TURTLE operator	Description	RT-LOTOS translation
	Deterministic delay. AD is interpreted after d time units.	**delay**(d) τ(AD)
	Non deterministic delay. AD is interpreted at most after t time units.	**latency**(t) τ(AD)
	Non deterministic delay between dmin and dmax. AD is interpreted at least after dmin and at most after dmax time units.	**delay**(dmin,dmax) τ(AD)
	Time-limited offering. Action **a** is offered during a period which is less or equal to **t**. If the offer happens, AD1 is interpreted. Otherwise, AD2 is interpreted.	**a**{t, τ(AD2)}; τ(AD1)
	Time-limited offering. Action **a** is offered during a period which is less or equal to **t**. Note that latency and time-limited offering start at the same time. If the offer happens, AD1 is interpreted. Otherwise, AD2 is interpreted.	**latency**(l) **a**{t, τ(AD2)}; τ(AD1)

4.5. Validation Process

The validation process developed for the TURTLE profile is organized as follows. TURTLE classes and their relationships are extracted from the class diagram. The resulting diagram is saved under the XMI format and converted into RT-LOTOS code. The reachability graph obtained for that RT-LOTOS code can then be analyzed. As usually, the reachability graph is generated iff the system is finite. Otherwise, analysis is limited to partial exploration using simulation techniques.

TURTLE models can be diagrammed with an UML 1.3 tool [21].

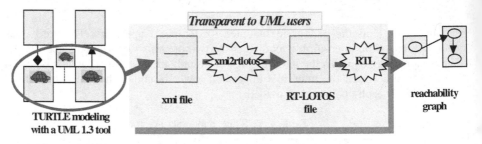

Fig. 4. From a TURTLE model to validation

5. Application

To make it easier to understand, we will use an example recognized by all: a coffee machine. Despite its simplicity, this example allows us to illustrate the *Tclass* stereotype, the abstract types and the three temporal operators added to UML.

5.1. Class Diagram

We consider a coffee machine which distributes tea or coffee after inserting two identical coins (Fig. 5). Excessive delay in inserting the second coin or in choosing the drink will result in the coins already inserted being reimbursed. Both these situations are modeled by time limited offerings (*coinDelay* and *buttonDelay*). Delays are used to physically represent the response time of the button and the minimum preparation time for a drink. This preparation time may vary, thus explaining the presence of latency operators. Lastly, note the constraints added to the associations between classes to show the *Gates* involved in each synchronization.

5.2. Generating RT-LOTOS Code

Fig. 6 proposes an extract from the RT-LOTOS code derived from the class diagram in Fig. 5. The RT-LOTOS description is itself a process structured in processes (behavior) whose internal behaviors are described in the *where* section.

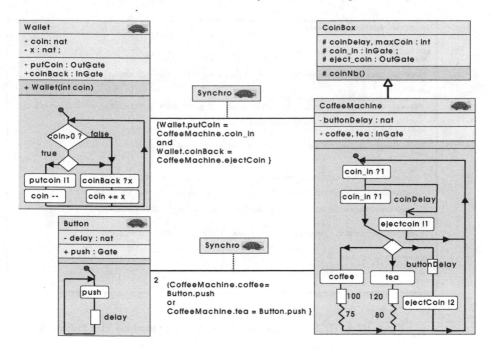

Fig. 5. Coffee machine class diagram #1

5.3. Validating with the RTL Tool

Validation consists in verifying that the system under design conforms to its expected behavior. This analysis is carried out by generating a reachability graph of the system under design. This graph helps identifying sink states and the different states reachable from a logical and temporal viewpoint. From the graph generated from the model in Fig. 5, let us consider the sequence of action which corresponds to a user wishing to have a tea. Assume the user inserts two coins and waits too long. The synchronization offer on *tea* or *coffee* expires, which means that both coins are ejected. The user pushes the button *tea* (*Button* class, *push Gate*) just afterwards. The synchronization offer can no longer take place. The user takes his coins back thinking the machine is out of order. Another user wishing to have a coffee arrives and inserts two coins. As the synchronization offer on *tea* has not expired (unlimited offer), he or she is instantly served a tea.

To overcome this problem, we modified the diagram as in Fig. 7. An additional synchronization enables the machine to activate buttons which can only be activated for a limited period of time (*push* offer limited to 40). This button activation implies a processing time in the machine (delay of 50).

```
specification VendingMachine : noexit :=
......
behaviour
hide putCoin, coinBack, coffee, tea, ejectCoin in
  Wallet[putCoin, coinBack](10)
  |[putCoin, coinBack]|
  ( Button[tea]  |[tea]|  ( CoffeeMachine[putCoin, coffee, tea, coinBack](150, 200)  |[coffee]|  Button[coffee] ) )

where
  process Wallet[putCoin, coinBack](amount:nat) : noexit :=
    [amount > 0] -> ( (putCoin!1; Wallet[putCoin, coinBack](amount - 1))  []  (coinBack?x:nat; Wallet[putCoin, coinBack](amount + x)) )
    []
    [amount == 0] -> ( coinBack?x:nat; Wallet[putCoin, coinBack](amount + x) )
  endproc

  process CoffeeMachine[coin_in, coffee, tea, ejectCoin](coinDelay:nat, buttonDelay:nat) : noexit :=
    coin_in!1;
    (
      coin_in{coinDelay}!1;
      ( coffee{buttonDelay}; delay(100, 175) CoffeeMachine[coin_in, coffee, tea, ejectCoin](coinDelay, buttonDelay) )
      []
      ( tea{buttonDelay}; delay(120, 200) CoffeeMachine[coin_in, coffee, tea, ejectCoin](coinDelay, buttonDelay) )
      []
      ( delay(buttonDelay) ejectCoin!2; CoffeeMachine[coin_in, coffee, tea, ejectCoin](coinDelay, buttonDelay) )
    )
    []
    ( delay(coinDelay) ejectCoin!1; CoffeeMachine[coin_in, coffee, tea, ejectCoin](coinDelay, buttonDelay) )
  endproc

  process Button[push] : noexit :=
    push; delay(100) Button[push]
  endproc
endspec
```

Fig. 6. RT-LOTOS code generated from the coffee machine TURTLE model

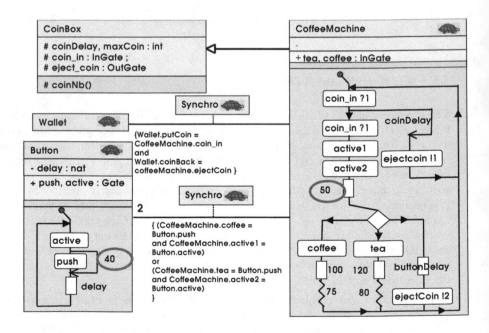

Fig. 7. Coffee machine class diagram # 2

It is now necessary to validate the coffee machine again. For readability reasons, Fig. 8a presents the reachability graph for the coffee machine in Fig. 7 reduced to distributing tea. For each logical state (rectangle), several classes of temporal states (circles) may coexist. Conditions for leaving a state are as follows: either time has elapsed (transition *t*) or a synchronization has occurred. Let us take examples from the reachability graph in Fig. 8a. Moving from the initial state (state 0) demands a synchronization on *Gate putCoin*. In state 21, no synchronization can occur in the first two sub-states; a state change corresponds to a time progression exclusively (transition *t*). When the offer on *Gate tea* or *coffee* expires (delay *buttonDelay*), then a synchronization on *coinBack* makes it possible to move from State 21 to State 7; a value equal to two is exchanged at that occasion.

The graph in Fig. 8.a highlights that it is impossible for a user to get either tea or coffee. In fact, the button activation delay (*push*) expires before the machine is ready to deliver coffee or tea. If this delay is increased from 40 to 60 (Fig. 8.b), it becomes possible to get tea: the transition from state 21 is now *tea*.

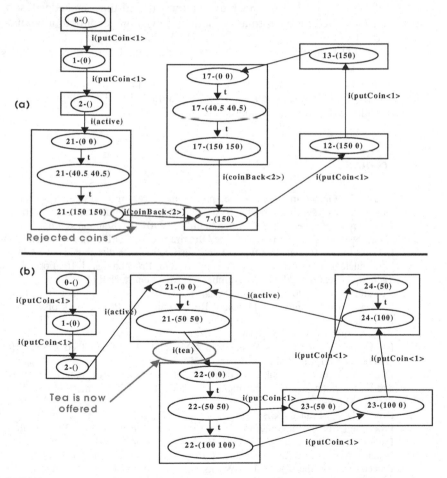

Fig. 8. Coffee machine # 2 reachability graph. (a): case where the offer on the button is limited to 40. (b): case where the offer is limited to 60

6. Conclusions and Future Work

The paper defines TURTLE, a UML profile for real-time system design and validation. Class diagrams are extended with a stereotype (*Tclass*) and two abstract types (*Gate* and *Composer*). A precise semantics is given to associations between classes (see the *Parallel, Synchro, Invocation, Sequence* and *Preemption* classes). The behavior of a *Tclass* is described by an enhanced activity diagram with three temporal operators: a deterministic delay, a non deterministic delay and a time-limited offering. Last but not least, TURTLE models can be translated into RT-LOTOS, a formal description technique supported by a validation tool. RT-LOTOS specifications derived from TURTLE diagrams can be simulated and verified using reachability analysis techniques. The objective is to keep RT-LOTOS hidden to the system designer.

The TURTLE profile is under evaluation on real-time embedded software. In particular, it is used for the formal validation of dynamic reconfiguration of embedded software [3].

The TURTLE profile will be extended in the near future. State machines will be used in lieu of activity diagrams. New associative classes will be introduced to extend association semantics (resume/suspend, interrupt) [20]. The latter will allow us to perform schedulability analysis on TURTLE models [2]. The integration of TURTLE profile with UML 2.0 is also under study.

References

1.   André, C. : Object and synchronous paradigms in real-time systems (in French). Journée Objets Temps Réel du Club SEE Systèmes Informatiques de Confiance, Paris, 18 January 2001. http://www.cert.fr/francais/deri/seguin/SEE/01.01.18/annonce.html
2.   Andriantsiferana L., Courtiat J.-P., de Oliveira R.C., Picci L.: An experiment in using RT-LOTOS for the formal specification and verification of a distributed scheduling algorithm in a nuclear power plant monitoring system Proceedings IFIP Formal Description Techniques X, Osaka, Japan, November 97, Chapman & Hall (1997)
3.   Apvrille L., de Saqui-Sannes P., Sénac P., Diaz M.: Formal Modeling of Space-Based Software in the Context of Dynamic Reconfiguration, Proceedings of DAta Systems In Aerospace (DASIA), 28 May - 1st June, 2001, Nice, France (2001)
4.   Artisan Software Tools: http://www.artisan-software.com (1999)
5.   Bjorkander M.: Real-Time Systems in UML and SDL, Embedded System Engineering, October/November 2000 (http://www.telelogic.com)
6.   Dupuy S., Ledru Y., Chabre-Peccoud M. : Towards a useful integration of semi-formal and formal notations: an experiment with UML and Z (in French), Vol.6, No.1, Hermès, Paris (2000) 9-32
7.   Bruel, J.-M. France R.B.: Transforming UML Models to Formal Specifications, Proceedings of the International Conference on Object Oriented Programming Systems Language and Applications (OOPSLA'98), Vancouver, Canada (1998)
8.   Bruel J.-M.: Integrating Formal and Informal Specification Techniques. Why? How?, Proceedings of the 2nd IEEE Workshop on Industrial-Strength Formal Specification Techniques (WIFT'98), Boca Raton, Florida, USA, IEEE Computer Press (1999) 50-57
9.   Terrier, F, Gérard, S: Real Time System Modeling with UML: Current Status and Some Prospects, Proceedings of the 2nd Workshop of the SDL Forum society on SDL and MSC, SAM 2000, Grenoble, France (2000)

10. Courtiat J.-P., Santos C.A.S., Lohr C., Outtaj B.: Experience with RT-LOTOS, a Temporal Extension of the LOTOS Formal Description Technique, Computer Communications, Vol. 23, No. 12 (2000) 1104-1123
11. Douglass B.P.: Doing Hard Time: Developing Real-Time Systems with UML, Objects, Frameworks and Patterns, Addison-Wesley Longman (1999) (http://www.ilogix.com)
12. Dupuy S., du Bouquet L.: A Multi-formalism Approach for the Validation of UML Models, Formal Aspects of Computing, No.12 (2001) p.228-230
13. Evans A.S., Cook S., Mellor S., Warmer J., Wills A.: Advanced Methods and Tools for a Precise UML, Proceedings of the 2nd International Conference on the Unified Modeling Language, UML'99, Colorado, USA, LNCS 1723 (1999)
14. Le Guennec, A.: Formal Methods with UML Modeling, Validation and Test Generation, Proceedings of CFIP'2000", Toulouse, October 2000, Hermès, p.151-166 (2000) (in French)
15. Bolognesi T, Brinksma E.: Introduction to the ISO specification Language LOTOS, Computer Networks and ISDN Systems, vol 14, No1 (1987)
16. Jard C., Jézéquel J.-M., Pennaneac'h F. : Towards Using Protocol Validation Tools in UML, Technique et Science Informatiques, Vol. 17, N°9, Hermès, Paris, p. 1083-1098 (1998) (in French)
17. OMG Unified Modeling Language Specification. Version 1.3, Object Management Group http://www.omg.org/technology/uml/index.htm (1999)
18. Object Management Group, UML Profile for Scheduling, Performance, and Time, Request for Proposal (1999) ftp://ftp.omg.org/pub/docs/ad/99-03-13.doc
19. Delatour J. Paludetto M.: UML/PNO, a way to merge UML and Petri net objects for the analysis of real-time systems, OO Technology and Real Time Systems Workshop (ECOOP'98), Bruxelles, Belgium (1998)
20. Hernalsteen C., Specification, Validation and Verification of Real-Time Systems in ET-LOTOS, Ph.D. dissertation, Université Libre de Bruxelles, Belgium (1998)
21. de Saqui-Sannes P., "Diagramming TURTLE classes using Rhapsody", ENSICA internal report (2001)
22. Selic B., Rumbaugh J.: Using UML for Modeling Complex Real-Time Systems, http://www.rational.com (1998)
23. Sénac P., Diaz M., de Saqui-Sannes P., Léger A.: Modeling Logical and Temporal Synchronization in Hypermedia Systems", IEEE Journal on Selected Areas in Communication, special issue on multimedia synchronization (1996)
24. Traoré I.: An Outline of PVS Semantics for UML Statecharts, Journal of Universal Computer Science, Vol. 6, No. 11 '2000) 1088-1108
25. Clarck, R.G., Moreira, A.M.D.: Use of E-LOTOS in Adding Formality to UML, Journal of Universal Computer Science, vol.6, no 11, p. 1071-1087 (2000)

Representing Embedded System Sequence Diagrams as a Formal Language

Elizabeth Latronico and Philip Koopman

Carnegie Mellon University
Electrical and Computer Engineering Department
D-202 Hamerschlag Hall, 5000 Forbes Avenue
Pittsburgh, PA 15213
beth@cmu.edu, koopman@cmu.edu

Abstract. Sequence Diagrams (SDs) have proven useful for describing transaction-oriented systems, and can form a basis for creating statecharts. However, distributed embedded systems require special support for branching, state information, and composing SDs. Actors must traverse many SDs when using a complex embedded system. Current techniques are insufficiently rich to represent the behavior of real systems, such as elevators, without augmentation, and cannot identify the correct SD to execute next from any given state of the system. We propose the application of formal language theory to ensure that SDs (which can be thought of as specifying a grammar) have sufficient information to create statecharts (which implement the automata that recognize that grammar). A promising approach for SD to statechart synthesis then involves 'compiling' SDs represented in an LL(1) grammar into statecharts, and permits us to bring the wealth of formal language and compiler theory to bear on this problem area.

1 Introduction

One of a designer's toughest challenges is attaining the appropriate level of abstraction. Include too little information, and a design is under-specified, often resulting in an incorrect or incomplete implementation. Include too much information, and the design is overly constrained or exceeds time-to-market allowances. Distributed, embedded systems present particularly onerous design challenges, combining complex behavior with a need for quick development cycles.

The Unified Modeling Language (UML) supplies an approach to express requirements and design decisions at various stages in the product development life cycle. The ideal level of abstraction provides the minimum sufficient amount of information required to create a set of correct, cohesive diagrams. UML offers two main diagrams for modeling system behavior: sequence diagrams and statecharts. While related, these diagrams often originate separately and serve diverse purposes. Sequence diagrams (SDs) are easier for people to generate and discuss, while statecharts provide a more powerful and thorough description of the behavior of a system. We present an algorithm to ensure that sequence diagrams contain sufficient information to be translated into statecharts. Specifically, this algorithm determines whether or not a set of sequence diagrams produces deterministic statecharts. This

M. Gogolla and C. Kobryn (Eds.): UML 2001, LNCS 2185, pp. 302-316, 2001.
© Springer-Verlag Berlin Heidelberg 2001

allows a designer to start with a skeletal structure and add information only when necessary. If automated, this technique could relieve a large burden of manual consistency-checking.

UML can be used to model a wide range of systems. To ensure that our results are applicable to actual embedded systems, the problem space needs to be carefully defined. Embedded systems may differ from the traditional transaction processing paradigm. Three major differences include:

- *Multiple initial conditions*
  Distributed, embedded systems typically run continuously and handle many user requests concurrently. Therefore, the system may not necessarily be in the same initial state for each user. Additionally, users may have disjoint objectives and responsibilities, so a second user may finish what a first user started.
- *Same user action evokes different system response*
  In transaction processing systems, there tends to be a one-to-one mapping from a user request to a system response. Embedded systems often have a limited user interface, so interface component functionality may depend on context.
- *Timing sensitivity*
  Embedded system functionality may depend on temporal properties such as duration, latency, and absolute time.

Sequence diagrams may contain information besides objects and messages. Three categories of additional information are presented, to show the scalability of the method and to provide examples of situations where supplemental information is required.

- *State*
  System history may affect present behavior. One example is a toggle power switch. The switch turns the system on or off, depending on current system state. Systems typically have a finite number of states.
- *Data*
  System behavior may depend on the current value of a variable with effectively infinite range. For example, in many elevators, selecting a floor will cause the doors to close, unless the user selects the current floor - then the doors will open.
- *Timing*
  Properties such as latency, duration, and absolute time may affect system response. One example is a car radio, where buttons are held to set the station.

In this paper, we explore how to use UML sequence diagrams to support the needs of embedded systems designers. Section 2 reviews methods for composing sequence diagrams that support flexible embedded systems modeling. Section 3 shows how determining required information content can be represented as a grammar parsing problem to guarantee correct, cohesive diagrams. A generic approach is described, with supporting embedded systems examples incorporating state, data, and timing information. Finally, the more commonly discussed transaction processing model is revisited to illustrate system differences. Section 4 summarizes conclusions.

2   Terminology and Related Work

2.1   Scenarios

2.1.1   Sequence Diagrams and Message Sequence Charts

A scenario describes a way to use a system to accomplish some function [5]. UML supports two main ways of expressing scenarios: collaboration diagrams and sequence diagrams. Sequence diagrams emphasize temporal ordering of events, whereas collaboration diagrams focus on the structure of interactions between objects [7]. Khriss et al. show how each may be readily translated into the other [7].

We concentrate on sequence diagrams because they elucidate temporal and object relation properties. As defined in the UML standard 1.3, a sequence diagram models temporal and object relationships using two dimensions, vertical for time and horizontal for objects [14]. Activity diagrams may also specify temporal properties, but typically do not include objects. As statecharts are usually defined per object, sequence diagrams are a more natural candidate for synthesis. The notation of sequence diagrams is based on, and is highly similar to, the Message Sequence Chart standard [6].

2.1.2   Composition of Scenarios

A crucial challenge in describing distributed embedded systems is the composition of scenarios. In order to be adequately expressive, sequence diagrams must reflect the structures of the programs they represent. In this paper, we survey approaches to modeling execution structures and transfer of control, and select a method that lends itself to embedded systems.

Our first objective is to refine a model that utilizes sequential, conditional, iterative, and concurrent execution. As many ideas exist, our task is to determine which are appropriate for embedded systems. Hsia et al. [5] discuss a process for scenario analysis that includes conditional branching. Somé et al. [12] present three ways of composing scenarios: sequential, alternative, and parallel. Glinz [2]   includes iteration as well. Koskimies et al. [8] and Systä [13] present a tool that handles "algorithmic scenario diagrams" - sequence diagrams with sequential, iterative, conditional and concurrent behavior. We use elements of each, for a combined model that allows sequential, conditional, iterative, and concurrent behavior.

Our second objective is to model transfer of control through sequence diagram composition. The main concern is where to annotate control information. One approach is to include composition information in individual diagrams. Hitz and Kappel [4] examine sequence diagram generation from use cases, and discuss the probe concept - the insertion of a small scenario into a larger one at a specified juncture. Koskimies et al. [8] present a similar method using sub-scenarios. A second approach is to use a separate hierarchical diagram, instead of embedding control information in the constituent diagrams. The Message Sequence Chart (MSC) standard specifies a separate diagram to organize sub-diagrams [6]. Leue et al. [9] explore the usage of base MSCs and high-level MSCs. The high-level MSC graph describes how to compose base MSC graphs to obtain sequential, conditional, iterative, and concurrent execution. Li and Lilius [10] present an additional example of a high-level MSC graph, and apply this method to UML sequence diagrams to assess timing inconsistency. We use the hierarchical diagram approach.

2.1.3 Finite State Machines and Statecharts

Finite state automata describe the possible *states* of a system and *transitions* between these states. Unfortunately, properties of complex systems such as concurrent execution of components lead to extremely large state machines that challenge human comprehension. Statecharts were proposed by Harel [3] to control state explosion problems with finite state machines by introducing the concepts of hierarchy and orthogonal execution, and are the basis for UML statecharts [14].

2.1.4 Statechart Synthesis

The second challenge in describing distributed embedded systems is ensuring there is sufficient information for correct, cohesive diagrams. Sequence diagrams are often constructed first in the design life cycle; therefore, we addresses synthesis of statecharts from sequence diagrams.

Existing work has two shortcomings. First, sufficiency of information for generating statecharts is not checked. Additional information is either absent or applied globally. Our goal is to provide an approach by which a designer can include a minimum amount of information, thereby reducing design time and guaranteeing a correct set of statecharts. We present a methodology to verify sufficiency, by applying well-established parsing theory.

Second, systems with all three embedded system qualities of multiple initial conditions, mapping identical user actions to different system responses, and timing dependencies have not been scrutinized. Systems that lack one of these three qualities generally do not require additional information to produce correct statecharts; therefore, the sufficiency question seems to not have arisen.

We present three embedded systems and show, by applying grammar parsing techniques, that these embedded systems do require additional information to produce correct statecharts. Additionally, we examine a transaction processing system, to illustrate that additional information is not required.

Prior work contains a number of suggestions as to what information sequence diagrams should include to enable statechart synthesis. Information is used for various purposes, but deterministic translation to statecharts has not been emphasized, and information is globally annotated. Hsia et al. [5] give a regular grammar for scenarios in order to construct a deterministic finite state machine. This grammar is similar to ours, but information sufficiency is assumed, not proven. Other work has proposed additional information, comprising three categories: state, data, and timing information. Douglass [1] advocates incorporating state symbols to represent object state. Somé et al. [12] use data pre-conditions and post-conditions to define possible scenario execution ordering. Whittle and Schumann [15] discuss implications of repeated user actions as a motivation for incorporating data pre-conditions and post-conditions. Koskimies et al. [8] annotate sequence diagrams with assertions on data variables. Timing intervals between messages are included by Li and Lilius [10]. Our examples examine these three categories, exposing situations where additional information is needed for statechart synthesis, and situations where it is not.

A number of different systems have been explored and documented; however, these systems lack the combination of multiple initial conditions, same user action evoking different system responses, and timing criteria. Systems without one of these characteristics often fail to manifest sufficiency issues.

A library checkout system is explored by Glinz [2] and by Khriss et al. [7]. In [2], scenarios have differing initial conditions, and system response depends on data attributes. However, statecharts are constructed directly from an informal textual description, not sequence diagrams. [7] synthesizes statecharts from UML collaboration diagrams, but these diagrams have identical initial conditions, one-to-one response mapping, and no timing criteria.

The Automated Teller Machine (ATM) system is a common example, discussed by Somé et al. [12], Whittle and Schumann [15], and Koskimies et al. [8]. [12] permits timeouts and global timed transitions, but all scenarios share a single initial condition, and user actions are mapped one-to-one with system responses (aside from time-influenced transitions). Scenarios in [15] can have a one-to-many action-response mapping, but have identical initial conditions and no timing restrictions. [8] approaches the problem iteratively, generating partial statecharts from sequence diagrams and vice versa. Different subscenarios may handle the same user request; however, there is a single initial condition and timing information is not discussed. The methodology in [8] is extended by Systä [13] for a File Dialog application with the same properties.

We examine three embedded systems to provoke sufficiency questions, then apply our methodology to a traditional transaction processing system to show that these systems do not require additional information for sufficiency.

2.2 Sequence Diagram Composition

The hierarchical graph approach used by the Message Sequence Chart community [6, 9, 10] explicitly represents composition information not shown in standard UML sequence diagrams. Figure 1 shows a set of sequence diagrams for a television power switch. TV_1 and TV_2 are regular sequence diagrams. The system has two objects - the user and the TV. The user can send one message, power. The TV can send two messages, turn_on and turn_off. TV_{main} expresses the relationships between TV_1 and TV_2. The triangle indicates a possible initial condition - the system may start out in

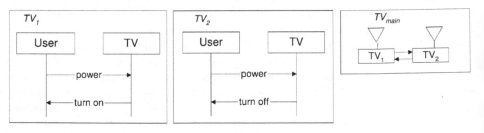

Fig. 1. Sequence diagrams for a television power switch

TV_1 or TV_2. Arrows indicate legal compositions. TV_1 and TV_2 must alternate - the sequence TV_1 TV_1 is not allowed. Without TV_{main}, composition information is absent.

Embedded system statechart synthesis typically requires more information than solely the messages an object receives. Three cases will be examined where sequence diagrams can be extended using state, data, and timing information to generate a deterministic grammar. Customary representations include state symbols, pre-conditions and post-conditions, and timing marks. Finally, the widely used ATM example will be reviewed to show that the ATM sequence diagrams generate a deterministic grammar without additional information regarding state, data, or timing.

3 Diagram Content

3.1 Deterministic Grammar

The main challenge in statechart synthesis is generating correct statecharts from a set of sequence diagrams with minimum sufficient information. The statecharts do not necessarily need to be complete, but they should give an unambiguous representation of the system. Rather than attempt an exhaustive annotation, a more achievable goal is to include the minimum sufficient amount of information.

Correct statechart synthesis from sequence diagrams with minimal annotation can be posed as a context-free grammar parsing problem. A similar approach was used by Hsia et al. [5] for text-based scenarios. To identify information gaps, we locate sequence diagram messages that translate into non-deterministic transitions in statecharts, as non-deterministic transitions often indicate information deficiencies. Standard methods for removing non-determinism, such as left factoring [11], and for implementing non-determinism, such as backtracking [11], cannot always be applied to embedded system sequence charts because messages may have global side effects on the external environment. Therefore, the only guaranteed correct approach is to ensure that sequence diagrams form an LL(1) grammar without left factoring or backtracking.

The context-free grammar for a sequence diagram may be defined as a set of message-response pairs. Given a message or set of messages, an object must produce a unique response or set of responses. An SD can be defined as a series of message-response events:

$$SD \rightarrow message \ \textbf{response} \ SD \mid \varepsilon \tag{1}$$

where ε indicates the absence of a message or response. The goal is to construct an SD with a context-free grammar of the form

$$message \ \textbf{response} \rightarrow \alpha \ \textbf{ResponseA} \mid \beta \ \textbf{ResponseB} \mid \chi \ \textbf{ResponseC} \ldots \tag{2}$$

where α, β and χ are distinct sequences of messages. A grammar of the form

$$message \ \textbf{response} \rightarrow \alpha \ \textbf{ResponseA} \mid \alpha \ \textbf{ResponseB} \tag{3}$$

does not produce a deterministic state machine. Upon receipt of α, the object does not know whether to execute `ResponseA` or `ResponseB`. The sequence diagram set for this grammar is shown in Figure 2. The system may start in either Seq_1 or Seq_2, and execute any combination of Seq_1 and Seq_2.

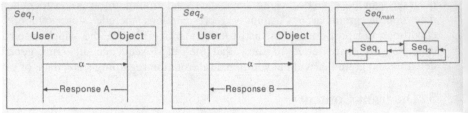

Fig. 2. Sequence diagrams for a generic non-deterministic grammar

Left factoring transforms the grammar in (3) to

$$\text{message } \textbf{response} \rightarrow \alpha\, A' \qquad\qquad (4)$$
$$A' \rightarrow \textbf{ResponseA} \mid \textbf{ResponseB}$$

This is equivalent to the sequence diagram set given in Figure 3. The sequence diagram Seq_{factor} is executed, followed by either Seq_1 or Seq_2. However, this only changes the composition of the diagrams. The problem of whether to execute `ResponseA` or `ResponseB` after the receipt of α remains.

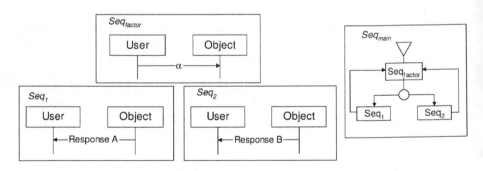

Fig. 3. Left-factored sequence diagrams for a generic non-deterministic grammar

The backtracking method picks a random response to be executed, and backtracks if the incorrect response was selected. Say the grammar is

$$\text{message } \textbf{response} \rightarrow \alpha\, \textbf{ResponseA}\ \delta \mid \alpha\, \textbf{ResponseB}\ \phi \qquad (5)$$

Upon receipt of α, it is unclear whether `ResponseA` or `ResponseB` is the correct behavior. Suppose `ResponseA` is randomly selected. The next message is ϕ. `ResponseA` was clearly incorrect, so the system backtracks and chooses `ResponseB` instead. However, in many real-time embedded systems, responses cannot be undone. For example, a microwave oven cannot undo burning popcorn, and an airbag cannot undo triggering its pyrotechnic charge. A greater difficulty emerges in scenarios where it is impossible to select a correct response based on messages alone. For instance, if α is the only message the user can generate, no amplifying information can be acquired; thus, the correct choice will never be known without querying existing system state.

3.2 State Information

A system may require state information to generate a deterministic set of statecharts. State symbols, advocated by Douglass [1], provide a succinct annotation. (Pre-conditions and post-conditions may alternatively be used, and are discussed in the next section). Figure 1 shows the sequence diagram set for a television with a power button. The television either turns on or off in response to the power message. Two initial conditions are possible – the television may be on or off when the user enters the room.

The grammar for the television is

$$\text{SD} \rightarrow \text{message } \textbf{response } \text{SD} \mid \varepsilon \tag{6}$$
$$\text{message } \textbf{response} \rightarrow \text{power } \textbf{turn\_on} \mid \text{power } \textbf{turn\_off}$$

This is of the form

$$\text{message } \textbf{response} \rightarrow \alpha \textbf{ turn\_on} \mid \alpha \textbf{ turn\_off} \tag{7}$$

and therefore non-deterministic, per the discussion in section 3.1

Adding state information can solve this non-determinism. The problem is that the state of the television is not represented in either sequence diagram, so the response to the power message is ambiguous. The television can be in two states, *on* or *off*. Appending this information to the sequence diagrams yields Figure 4.

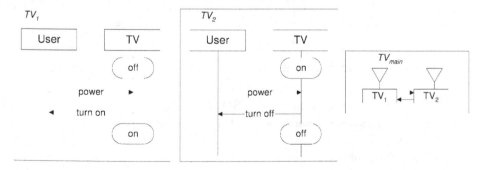

Fig. 4. Sequence diagrams for a television power switch, including state information

The new state information can be incorporated into the grammar. The template for constructing the grammar is now

$$\text{SD} \rightarrow state \text{ message } \textbf{response } \text{SD} \mid \epsilon \tag{8}$$

$$state \text{ message } \textbf{response } \rightarrow off \text{ power } \textbf{turn\_on} \mid on \text{ power } \textbf{turn\_off}$$

This is of the form

$$\text{message } \textbf{response} \rightarrow \alpha \textbf{ turn\_on} \mid \beta \textbf{ turn\_off} \tag{9}$$

and is therefore deterministic.

3.3 Data

Execution may depend on the value of a stored piece of data that is not directly modeled as a state or transition. Pre-conditions/post-conditions and assertions have been used to represent this additional information (e.g, [8, 13, 15]). Statements are annotated, usually in a formal language, that specify interesting properties of variables.

As an example, consider an elevator. The elevator contains a set of numbered car buttons, one per floor, that passengers use to select a destination floor. While inside the car, if a passenger pushes the button for the floor the elevator is already on, the doors will open. This is required to allow passengers inside an idle elevator to disembark at the current floor. If the passenger pushes the button for a floor other than the current floor, the doors will close. This is a common, although not universal, set of elevator behaviors. The sequence diagram set for car button behavior is shown in Figure 5.

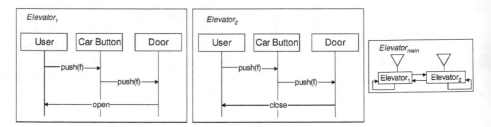

Fig. 5. Sequence diagrams for an elevator

The grammar for this example is

$$\text{SD} \rightarrow \text{message } \textbf{response } \text{SD} \mid \epsilon \tag{10}$$

$$\text{message } \textbf{response} \rightarrow \text{push(f) } \textbf{close} \mid \text{push(f) } \textbf{open}$$

This is of the form

$$\text{message } \textbf{response} \rightarrow \alpha \textbf{ close} \mid \alpha \textbf{ open} \tag{11}$$

and therefore non-deterministic.

Pre-conditions for the messages can be added to make this example deterministic, as shown in Figure 6. The crucial piece of missing information is that the response of the elevator depends on the value of (f) in push(f) compared to the current state. The value of (f) in push(f) can be either the same as the current floor or other than the current floor.

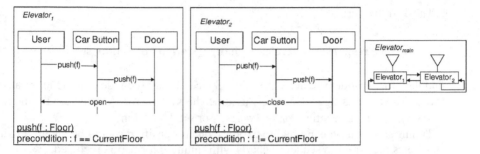

Fig. 6. Sequence diagrams for an elevator, including pre-conditions

The template for constructing the grammar with pre-conditions is

$$SD \rightarrow pre\text{-}condition \text{ message } \textbf{response } SD \mid \varepsilon \qquad (12)$$
$$pre\text{-}condition \text{ } message \textbf{ response} \rightarrow$$

$$(f == currentFloor) \text{ push(f) } \textbf{open} \mid (f \mathrel{!=} currentFloor) \text{ push(f) } \textbf{close}$$

This is of the form

$$\text{message } \textbf{response} \rightarrow \alpha \textbf{ close} \mid \beta \textbf{ open} \qquad (13)$$

and is deterministic.

3.4 Timing Information

The response of an embedded system may depend on timing information, such as the duration of the stimulus. Consider a car radio with a set of buttons to allow users to save and switch to preferred stations. If the button is held for a short time, the radio will change stations to the button's preset station when the button is released. If the button is held longer, the radio will save the current station as the value of the button. The basic sequence charts for this system are given in Figure 7.

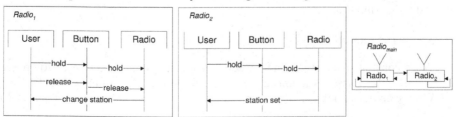

Fig. 7. Sequence diagrams for a radio

The grammar for the car radio is

SD → message **response** SD | ε   (14)
message **response** → hold release **change_station** | hold **station_set**

This is of the form

message **response** → α release **change_station** | α **station_set**   (15)

and therefore non-deterministic. At first glance, it may seem deterministic because of the `release` message. However, assume the system receives the `hold` message. Does it do nothing (waiting for `release`), or set the station?

Timing information is needed to express which transition should be taken. Figure 8 illustrates the car radio sequence charts with timing information included.

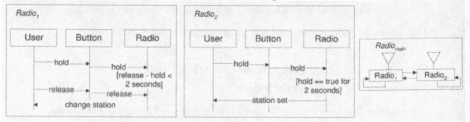

Fig. 8. Sequence diagrams for a radio, including timing information

The template for constructing the grammar with timing information is

SD → message *duration* **response** SD | ε   (16)
message *duration* **response** →
    hold *(holdDuration < 2 seconds)* release **change_station** |
    hold *(holdDuration reaches 2 seconds)* **station_set**

This is of the form

message **response** → α release **change_station** | β **station_set**   (17)

and is deterministic.

3.5   ATM Example

To demonstrate the distinction between embedded systems and transaction processing systems, the classic Automated Teller Machine (ATM) example will be analyzed. Whittle and Schumann [15] synthesize statecharts from a set of four scenarios for the

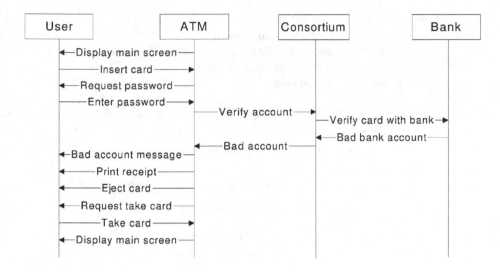

Fig. 9. Interaction with an ATM (from Whittle and Schumann [15])

ATM system. Figure 9 is the sequence diagram for the first scenario. (The complete set of SDs can be found in [15]). Four objects exchange messages : the user, the ATM, the consortium, and the bank. In this example, statecharts are generated for the ATM object only. The scenarios share the same initial condition. We constructed grammar descriptions for the set of diagrams, given in formulas 18-21. We will apply grammar parsing to locate any non-determinism present.

SD → message **response** SD | ε
message **response** → **Display_main_screen** | (18)
Insert_card **Request_password** | Enter_password **Verify_account** |
Bad_account **Bad_account_message Eject_card Request_take_card** |
Take_card **Display_main_screen**

SD → message **response** SD | ε   (19)
message **response** → **Display_main_screen** |
Insert_card **Request_password** | Enter_password **Verify_account** |
Bad_password **Request_password** |
Cancel **Canceled_message Eject_card** | Take_card **Display_main_screen**

SD → message **response** SD | ε   (20)
message **response** → **Display_main_screen** |
Insert_card **Request_password** |
Cancel **Canceled_message Eject_card Request_take_card** |
Take_card **Display_main_screen**

SD → message **response** SD | ε   (21)
message **response** → **Display_main_screen** |
Insert_card **Request_password** | Enter_password **Verify_account** |
Cancel **Canceled_message Eject_card Request_take_card** |
Take_card **Display_main_screen**

Table 1 lists all the message-response pairs observed in the grammar for the sequence diagram set.

Table 1. Message-response pairs for the ATM system

Message	ATM Response	Used in SD#
ε	Display main screen	All
Insert card	Request password	All
Bad account	Bad account message Print receipt Eject card Request take card	SD_1
Bad password	Canceled message Eject card	SD_2
Cancel	Canceled message Eject card	SD_2
Cancel	Canceled message Eject card Request take card	SD_3, SD_4
Take card	Display main screen	All

Note that each incoming message produces a unique set of system responses, with the exception of `Cancel`. In the second SD grammar (19), `Cancel` evokes `Canceled_message` and `Eject_card`. In the third and fourth SD grammars, (20) and (21), `Cancel` evokes `Canceled_message`, `Eject_card`, and `Request_take_card`. Upon reflection, this is likely an omission in the second sequence diagram, not a design decision.

The `Display_main_screen` message occurs before the receipt of any user messages, but does not cause non-determinism because the ATM has a single initial condition. If multiple initial conditions existed, this would pose a problem. Whittle and Schumann [15] discuss a permutation of SD_1, where `Insert_card` is repeated.

message **response** → Insert_card ε | Insert_card **Request_Password**   (22)

This is non-deterministic and would mandate additional information for constructing statecharts (which the authors provided).

4 Conclusions

We have presented a methodology that guarantees *sufficient* sequence diagram information to generate correct statecharts. We convert sequence diagrams to a context-free grammar and apply parsing theory to locate non-deterministic behavior. When state, data, and timing information are included in a grammar, being LL(1) seems to be sufficient to guarantee determinism for the embedded systems we discussed. We showed how this approach identified additional information needed to attain deterministic behavior, and provided examples incorporating state, data, and timing information. Finally, we discussed a transaction processing example to show that transaction processing systems commonly used as examples tend to be more deterministic than embedded control systems.

We have also examined diagram composition and information content to assess adequacy for embedded systems. We advocate hierarchical diagrams [6, 9, 10] as the preferred format for sequence diagram composition for designing embedded systems. Hierarchical diagrams work well for expressing sequential, conditional, iterative, and concurrent execution of sequence diagrams common in embedded systems. Further, they support multiple initial conditions, one-to-many action-response mapping and timing dependencies.

Acknowledgements. This research is supported by the General Motors Satellite Research Lab at Carnegie Mellon University, Intel and the United States Department of Defense (NDSEG/ONR). Additionally, this paper would not have been possible without the scrutiny and guidance of John DeVale.

References

[1] Douglass, B. Doing Hard Time. Addison-Wesley, 1999.

[2] Glinz, M. An Integrated Formal Model of Scenarios Based on Statecharts. In Proceedings of the 5th European Software Engineering Conference (ESEC 95), Sitges, Spain, 1995, pp. 254-271.

[3] Harel, D. Statecharts: A Visual Formalism for Complex Systems. *Science of Computer Programming*, vol.8, no.3, 1987, pp. 231-274.

[4] Hitz, M., and G. Kappel. Developing with UML - Some Pitfalls and Workarounds. *UML '98 - The Unified Modeling Language*, Lecture Notes in Computer Science 1618, Springer-Verlag, 1999, pp. 9-20.

[5] Hsia, P. et al. Formal Approach to Scenario Analysis. *IEEE Software*, vol.11,   no.2, 1994, pp. 33-41.

[6] ITU-T. Recommendation Z.120. ITU - Telecommunication Standardization Sector, Geneva, Switzerland, May 1996.

[7] Khriss, I., M. Elkoutbi, and R. Keller. Automating the Synthesis of UML StateChart Diagrams from Multiple Collaboration Diagrams. *UML '98 - The Unified Modeling Language,* Lecture Notes in Computer Science 1618, Springer-Verlag, 1999, pp. 132-147.

[8] Koskimies, K., T. Systä, J. Tuomi, and T. Männistö. Automated Support for Modeling OO Software. *IEEE Software*, vol.15, no.1, 1998, pp. 87-94.

[9] Leue, S., L. Mehrmann, and M. Rezai. Synthesizing Software Architecture Descriptions from Message Sequence Chart Specifications. In *Proceedings of the 13th IEEE International Conference on Automated Software Engineering*, Honolulu, Hawaii, 1998, pp. 192-195.

[10] Li, X. and J. Lilius.   Checking Compositions of UML Sequence Diagrams for Timing Inconsistency.   In *Proceedings of the Seventh Asia-Pacific Software Engineering Conference (APSEC 2000)*, Singapore, 2000, pp. 154-161.

[11] Louden, K. Compiler Construction : Principles and Practice. PWS Publishing Company, 1997.

[12] Somé, S., R. Dssouli, and J. Vaucher.   From Scenarios to Timed Automata: Building Specifications from User Requirements. In *Proceedings of the 1995 Asia-Pacific Software Engineering Conference*, Australia, 1995, pp. 48-57.

[13] Systä, T. Incremental Construction of Dynamic Models for Object-Oriented Software Systems. *Journal of Object-Oriented Programming*, vol.13, no.5, 2000, pp. 18-27.

[14] Unified Modeling Language Specification, Version 1.3, 1999. Available from the Object Management Group. http://www.omg.com.

[15] Whittle, J., and J. Schumann.   Generating Statechart Designs from Scenarios.   In *Proceedings of the 2000 International Conference on Software Engineering (ICSE 2000)*, Limerick, Ireland, 2000, pp. 314.

Scenario-Based Monitoring and Testing of Real-Time UML Models

Marc Lettrari[1] and Jochen Klose[2]

[1] OFFIS, Escherweg 2, D-26111 Oldenburg
[2] University of Oldenburg – Department of Computer Science
P.O.Box 2503, D-26111 Oldenburg, Germany
e-mail:{lettrari,klose}@informatik.uni-oldenburg.de

Abstract. In this paper it is shown how Sequence Diagrams can be used both for monitoring and testing functional and real-time requirements of an executable UML design. We show how this testing approach can be integrated in an UML-based development process. In addition, we will present how a prototype which implements the described monitoring and testing methods is integrated in a well known UML design tool.

1   Introduction

Distributed real-time computer systems are very complex and intrinsically difficult to specify and implement correctly. One cause is the lack of adequate methods and tools to deal with this complexity. The use of UML for developing such systems is gaining more and more attention both from research and industry. A major goal in developing such systems is a validation that the design fulfills certain properties. Besides functional conformity several real-time properties are important for real-time systems. Although there are some approaches with the goal of a formal proof of the correctness of a design [11,3,10], testing still plays a dominant role in validating functional and real-time behavior. The reasons are the limited applicability of the methods which strive for a formal proof:

- Fully automatic methods (model checking) can only be applied to small designs and simple properties.
- Semi-automatic (with the help of theorem provers) or manual proofs are often very difficult and require significant knowledge and experience.

Furthermore all correctness proofs are based on a formal semantics of the design language. When transforming a design into an implementation, the behavior on the machine level can be significantly different from the behavior on the design level. Therefore even a formal proof does not supersede testing the implementation.

Besides these difficulties to formally prove the correctness of a design a main problem is a methodological one. The typical UML development process (e.g. Rational Unified Process (RUP) [8] or Rapid Object-oriented Process for Embedded Systems (ROPES) [6]) is iterative, starting with an early fairly abstract

M. Gogolla and C. Kobryn (Eds.): UML 2001, LNCS 2185, pp. 317–328, 2001.

version and progressing to more and more concrete prototypes. The first version will often be incomplete having some classes which are already well developed and others which are just empty shells, i.e. the classes exist together with their (incomplete) set of events and methods which are not implemented yet. An appropriate validation technique has to support such a development process which is often not the case.

Therefore we propose in this paper an approach which supports validation during the whole development process. We use Sequence Diagrams as a graphical language to describe certain functional and real-time properties. We believe that Sequence Diagrams are well suited for such a testing process because of several reasons, e.g

- SDs are used early in the development process to capture the relevant use cases of the desired system. Therefore the testing process can run in parallel with the development process which allows early detection of functional or timing errors.
- The graphical fashion of SDs eases the communication between users and developers. Therefore the acceptance of the developed systems will increase.
- Most of the common real-time properties (e.g. response times) can be expressed using SDs.

For SDs we present an automata-based semantics which is used to automatically generate test drivers and monitors for an UML design. By means of an example the applicability of our testing approach is shown, and we present an implementation for an UML design tool which supports this testing approach.

1.1   Related Work

[7] propose a merge of (Highlevel-)MSCs and SDs to define test cases for UML models; the resulting notation is called HyperMSCs. These HyperMSCs form a graphical front-end for TTCN (Tree and Tabular Combined Notation) test cases. Their approach is therefore focused on testing the implementation whereas we want to test the model while it is still under design. They consequently also do not consider testing incomplete systems (stubbing).

Telelogic is offering a product which also generates TTCN test suites from a UML model, although they apply an intermediate step, transforming the UML model into SDL (Specification and Description Language) where additionally MSCs can be used to derive test cases. It is also possible to test an executable (SDL/MSC) model, but stubbing is not supported.

[1] use Collaboration Diagrams to derive static and dynamic checks for software, not necessarily UML models. Their dynamic checks are close in spirit to our approach, insofar as they require an executable model or software system. But they put two restrictions on the collaboration diagrams which we do not enforce, namely

- one collaboration diagram is triggered by exactly one operation and contains only the body of this operation

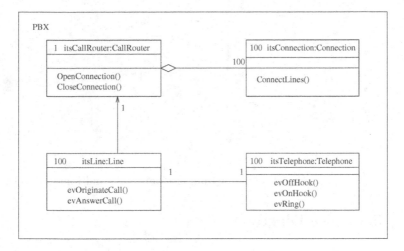

Fig. 1. Class diagram of PBX system

- the message sequence triggered by an operation has to be complete, i.e. every
  message of the body has to be included in the collaboration diagram

1.2   Structure

The paper is organized as follows: In Sect. 2 we introduce a running example, an
UML design of a telephone system (PBX). The variant of Sequence Diagrams
we use is presented in Sect. 3. Then in Sect. 4 we describe certain properties of
the design with SDs at different levels of the design and show how we use them
for monitoring and testing. Before we conclude the implementation of the tool
is explained in Sect. 5.

2   The PBX System

We will demonstrate our testing approach by introducing a small example, the
PBX telephone system. The overall structure of the system can be seen in figure 1. The PBX consists of 4 different classes: Telephone, Line, Connection and
CallRouter. The multiplicities of the classes indicate that it contains 100 Telephones, Lines and Connections and one CallRouter. Each telephone is connected
to one line. The central CallRouter establishes connections between two lines (c.f.
figure 2).
This design need not to be the final one, it can also be an arbitrary intermediate
design. For example, in a later design step fig. 2 can be changed in a way that
one connection can contain more than only two lines thus allowing some kind of
conference call, or we can enhance the functionality of the telephones.
    Before we explain how we monitor and test the PBX system we briefly de-
scribe the variant of Sequence Diagrams we use.

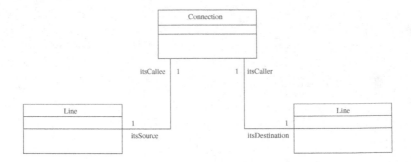

Fig. 2. Class diagram of Connection and Lines

3   Sequence Diagrams

The Sequence Diagrams we are considering here do not completely conform to the ones presented in the UML Specification [12]. We disregard one SD feature which is part of the UML standard and also add some new features which we feel are needed to use SDs for the testing of UML models. The standard feature which we do not consider is the description of concurrent scenarios in one diagram, i.e. we do not allow to specify conditional sending of more than message at one point in time. This means that situations like: "If $x > 0$ then send message $foo(x)$ to object $O2$ else send message $bar(x)$ to object $O3$" are not allowed. In order to express this we require the user to draw two scenarios.

In the context of monitoring and driving an UML design we need more expressiveness than that provided by the UML standard. For this reason we have added a feature which we feel is essential for this application area: the capability to specify when a scenario described in a SD should be activated, i.e. when should we start to monitor the system or generate certain inputs? The simplest possibility would be to only consider *initial* SDs, i.e. those which are activated at system start. This is clearly too restrictive, since we also want to be able to use scenarios which are active more than once. We therefore introduce the concept of *activation mode* which can be either *initial* or *iterative*, where the second choice indicates that the SD can be activated several times, whenever the activation condition is true during a run of the system and the SD is not already active. For the iterative case another feature is needed, which allows us to specify when exactly the SD should be activated. Here we use an *activation condition*, a Boolean expression which characterizes the state of the UML design when the scenario should start. Both the activation mode and condition we have adopted from *Live Sequence Charts* (LSCs) [4], [5]. Conforming to the LSC approach we also allow conditions (Boolean expressions) within the SD, a feature which is also not covered in the UML standard.

The semantics for our SDs is given by an automaton which represents all the communication sequences allowed by the SD from which it is constructed. The algorithm for deriving this automaton from an SD is again taken from the LSC world (see [9] for a detailed description). Roughly, the principle behind

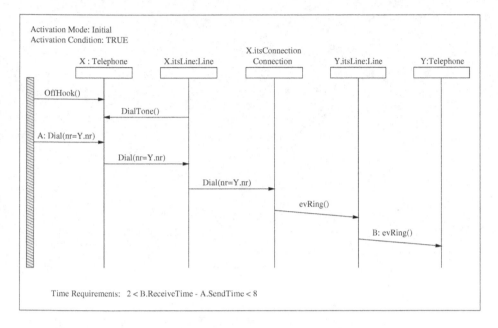

Fig. 3. Sequence diagram example SD1

the algorithm is to walk through the LSC from top to bottom while respecting the partial order. The algorithm uses *cuts* to step through the LSC, where a cut contains exactly one location of each instance line. Each cut corresponds to a state in the automaton generated by the algorithm and transitions in the automaton represent the successor relation among the cuts. We use Timed Büchi Automata (TBA) [13] [2] as our automata format.

We support the full capabilities of real-time features offered by the UML standard, i.e. we allow the usage of (textual) constraints talking about the sending and receiving time of messages as well as the graphical interval notation. These timing constraints are represented in the TBA of an LSC by setting clocks and adding clock constraints to the appropriate states of the TBA. Consider the example in figure 3. The scenario depicted there shows the simple protocol for the set up of the connection between two telephones. The caller takes the handle off the hook, waits for the dial tone and dials the number of the telephone he wants to reach. The dialed number is propagated to the line of the caller's phone and on to the connection which lets the callee's phone ring (via its line). Note that the scenario specification is generic, since the names of both telephone objects are parameters (X and Y) and not concrete object IDs. The timing requirement we want to associate with this protocol in this example is that the delay between dialing the number and the ringing of the callee's phone is more than 2 and less than 8 time units. We do not characterize the time base for the real-time annotations further, because this is highly dependent on the system being monitored/tested. Whatever metric this system supports can be used in the real-time constraints in the SD.

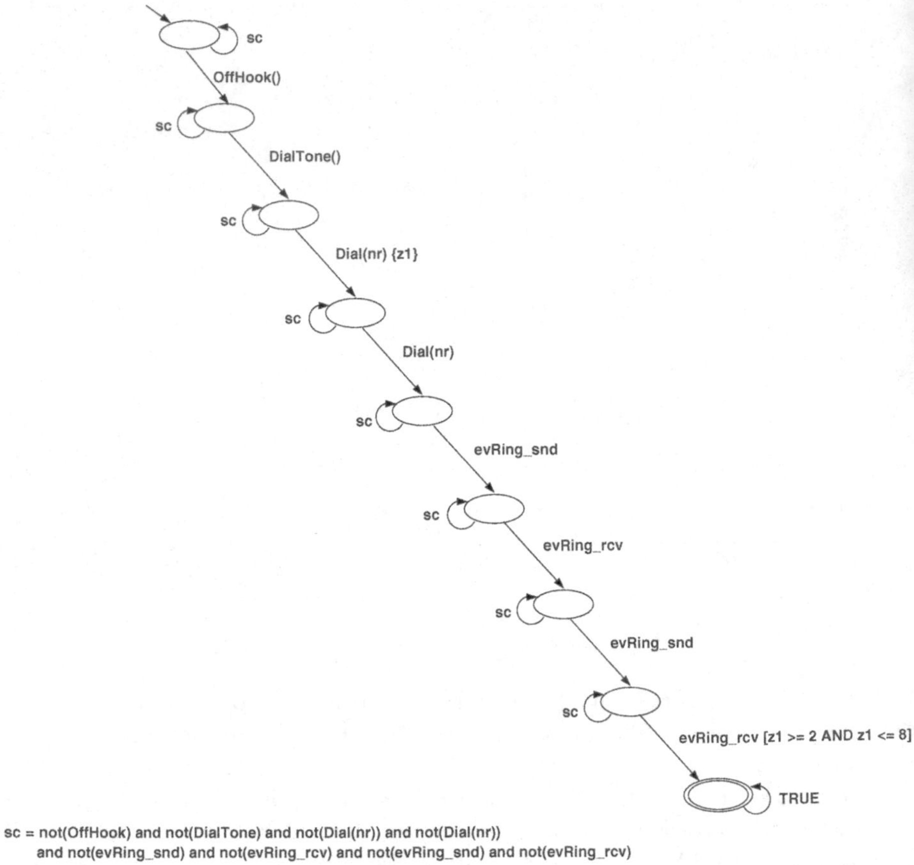
sc
OffHook()
sc
DialTone()
sc
Dial(nr) {z1}
sc
Dial(nr)
sc
evRing_snd
sc
evRing_rcv
sc
evRing_snd
sc
evRing_rcv [z1 >= 2 AND z1 <= 8]
TRUE
sc = not(OffHook) and not(DialTone) and not(Dial(nr)) and not(Dial(nr))
and not(evRing_snd) and not(evRing_rcv) and not(evRing_snd) and not(evRing_rcv)

Fig. 4. Automaton representation for SD1

The TBA generated from this LSC is shown in figure 4. In this simple example we have a total ordering of the messages in the SD, which consequently leads to a linear TBA with only one possible path. In practice the size and complexity of LSCs and TBAs may be significantly greater than shown here. The only accepting state in this example (denoted by a double border) is the last state, i.e. it has to be reached in order for the LSC to be fulfilled. Each state is annotated with a *stable condition*, which has to be fulfilled in order for the TBA to stay in this state. This is represented by adding a self loop to each state of the TBA and annotating it with the stable condition. This condition corresponds to conjunction of the negation of all messages appearing in the SD, i.e. the messages must be observed or generated only at those points in time which correspond to the order defined by the SD. This entails in particular that a message that appears only once in a SD may not occur more than once while the SD is active. In figure 4 the stable condition is abbreviated by `sc`; the full definition of `sc` is shown in the lower left-hand corner. Note that the activation mode and condition are not treated explicitly in the TBA; they are passed on to the test tool in textual form.

Timing requirements are represented in the TBA by clocks and constraints on these clocks. For each timing requirement we introduce an unique clock which is reset to zero when the message corresponding to the starting point of the constraint is observed. When the message which indicates the end point of the timing requirement occurs, it is constrained by a clock condition which represents the specified requirement. In our example the clock $z1$ is reset to zero (denoted by the clock name in curly braces, $\{z1\}$) when the first Dial message is observed. Note that since this message is synchronous we do not distinguish between the send and receive time. The TBA transition which corresponds to the receipt of the second evRing message is annotated by the appropriate clock constraint.

4   Monitoring and Testing

We show the application of our testing approach at three typical stages in the development process where we have an early prototype, a first full implemented design and an enhanced design. Although during a real project often more than the following three development phases can be distinguished, they illustrate the applicability of the SD based approach.

4.1   Early Prototype

Suppose we have a system under construction where we want to test the already implemented classes. This is possible by designating the incomplete classes as *stubs* in the SD(s) and letting the test tool take over their behavior. Consider for example the situation where the class Telephone from our PBX system is not yet implemented, but we want use the SD in figure 3 to test the Lines and the Connection. We would therefore designate both telephones as stubs (shaded instances in figure 5). The class Telephone has to provide at least those interface objects which appear in the SD, in our example it would need to have the methods OffHook(), DialTone() and Dial() and the event evRing defined but the method bodies may be empty and the class does not need to be able to consume the event. The difference between monitoring and testing a SD is the way the environment is treated. If we want to monitor a SD, then we only observe if all described events and method calls occur in the right order and within the right time intervals. If we want to test a SD, then the events coming from the environment (and the ones from stubbed instances) are generated automatically at the appropriate points in time, and all other messages are monitored. In our example the test tool would generate the method call Dial() to the line of telephone X after the method call Dial() has been received by X from the environment.

Even for this early design we can also monitor and test elementary behavior. For example, simple properties of the type "Whenever X happens, Y must occur" can also be tested at this level of the design.

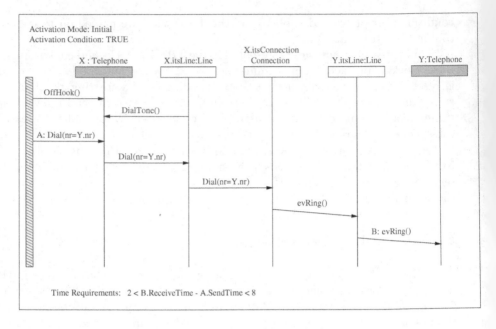

Fig. 5. SD1 with stubbed telephones

4.2   First Full Implementation

In later iterations as the design becomes more and more complete the stubbed SD instances can be transformed into regular ones as the underlying class becomes more complete. In general, SDs which have been specified in earlier iterations can be used for regression testing in the later phases, thereby becoming invariants of the model. For example, suppose that the class Telephone is now completely implemented. To check if the Telephones behave properly we can use the SD in fig. 3 which is the same as the SD in fig. 5 but without stubbed instances, so we can simply reuse SDs from earlier design stages. Another important aspect of reusing SDs is the possibility to parameterize them. By using parameters such as "X" and "Y" (c.f. Fig. 3) it can be used to test all pairs of Telephones. If we want to use this SD for monitoring or testing, we have to instantiate the parameters with concrete objects of the system.

Fig. 6 shows one dialog of our testing tool (which will be described later in section 5) which allows the definition of tests. Each test can consist of arbitrary many SD-instances, which are SDs with instantiated parameters. The activation of the SD-instances can be controlled either implicitly by their activation mode and activation condition or explicitly by an ordering given by the user. For example, the test shown in fig. 6 consists of 6 SD-instances of the SD "X_calls_Y" (which describes the scenario of making a call from Telephone X to Telephone Y) and 4 instances of the SD "Receive_X" (which describes the scenario that Telephone X receives a call). All SD-instances are drivers, and we ordered them in a way that first Telephone 1 calls sequentially Telephone 2, 3 and 4 and after that Telephone

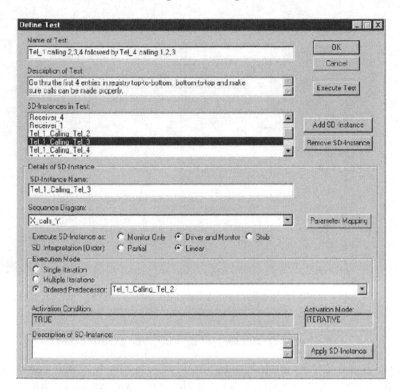

Fig. 6. Dialog to define tests

4 calls Telephone 1, 2 and 3. As an alternative we could also not prescribe any order for the calls from Telephone 1 and Telephone 4, which would yield a test where calls were made in parallel.

4.3   Adding Functionality

In each new iteration new SDs can be added which specifically test those features which have been introduced in this iteration cycle. Suppose we have enhanced the Telephones with a "NoDisturb" function, which puts the telephone automatically in a busy state. If we have added such a new feature, we want to test it specifically. Therefore we can introduce a new SD (c.f. Fig. 7).
If we use this SD for testing, we first turn on the NoDisturb function on one Telephone and then try to call this telephone from another telephone, which should as a result receive a busy tone from its line. When inserting new functionality in a design, other functions should not be affected. To test this, we can use the SDs from the previous iterations for regression testing.

5   Implementation

We have developed a prototypic implementation of our tool which can monitor and test implementations of Rhapsody UML models. A prerequisite of testing

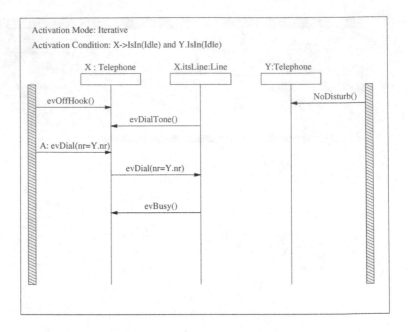

Fig. 7. SD for testing the NoDisturb function

is the possibility to interact with the system under test. For our approach it is important that the tester is informed about every event and method call which is described in the considered SDs. Furthermore the tester must have the possibility to send events to the system under test. These capabilities can be realized in different ways (e.g. code instrumentation, model executor etc.). Figure 8 shows how our prototype interacts with a system under test.

Rhapsody generates instrumented code, which communicates with a simulation interface during runtime. Whenever relevant things occur with regard to the considered SDs, the simulation interface informs the testing tool about them. Based on these notifications the testing tool detects possible errors or generates events automatically which can be sent back to the implementation through the simulation interface. In addition, every notification has a time-stamp which indicates the point in time where the appropriate message occurred in the implementation. We use these time-stamps to check if the real-time constraints expressed in the SDs are fulfilled by the implementation.

We have integrated the whole test environment directly in Rhapsody. For each project the user can define an arbitrary number of tests which are automatically stored together with the project files. For each test it can be specified which SDs it should contain, how the parameters should be instantiated and which SDs should run in parallel or sequentially. During the execution of the test the user is informed about which parts of the test behave as expected and which not. If an error was detected, a SD is generated automatically to visualize the error.

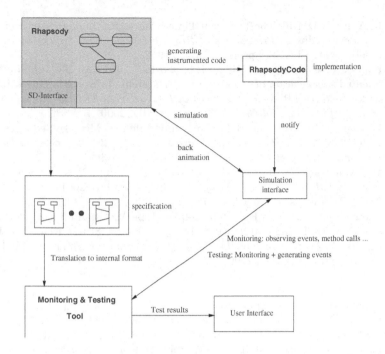

Fig. 8. Communication between testing tool and implementation

6   Conclusion

We consider our scenario-based testing approach as a suitable way to support testing through the whole development process of object-oriented real-time systems. The availability of SDs in early design phases and the possibility to define stubs allows early testing, and detected errors can be corrected early before design changes become too expensive. Furthermore these SDs can be used for regression testing in the later design steps. A limitation of our approach is the fact that we cannot instantiate parameters of generic SDs automatically at the moment. One goal for the future is to enhance our testing approach in a way that we can extract the necessary information to instantiate parameters in generic SDs directly out of UML models.

Acknowledgements. The authors thank the members of our group for fruitful discussions on the subject of this paper. We also want to thank Uwe Higgen for implementing large parts of our prototype.

References

1. Aynur Abdurazik and Jeff Offutt. Using UML Collaboration Diagrams for Static Checking and Test Generation. In Andy Evans, Stuart Kent, and Bran Selic, editors, *Proceedings of the UML2000 - Advancing the Standard*, number 1939 in LNCS. Springer Verlag, 2000.

2. R. Alur and D. Dill. The Theory of Timed Automata. In de Bakker, Henzinger, and de Roever, editors, *Proceedings of Rex 1991: Real Time in Theory and Practice*, number 600 in LNCS. Springer Verlag, 1992.
3. Paulo J.F. Carreira and Miguel E.F. Costa. Automatically verifying an object-oriented specification of the steam-boiler system. In Stefania Gnesi, Ina Schieferdecker, and Axel Rennoch, editors, *5th International ERCIM Workshop on Formal Methods for Industrial Critical Systems*. GMD, 2000.
4. W. Damm and D. Harel. LSCs: Breathing Life into Message Sequence Charts. In *FMOODS'99 IFIP TC6/WG6.1 Third International Conference on Formal Methods for Open Object-Based Distributed Systems*, 1999.
5. W. Damm and D. Harel. LSCs: Breathing Life into Message Sequence Charts. *Formal Methods in System Design*, 19(1):45 – 80, July 2001.
6. Bruce P. Douglass. *Doing Hard Time*. Addison-Wesley, 1999.
7. Peter Graubmann and Ekkart Rudolph. HyperMSCs and Sequence Diagrams for Use Case Modelling and Testing. In Andy Evans, Stuart Kent, and Bran Selic, editors, *Proceedings of the UML2000 - Advancing the Standard*, number 1939 in LNCS. Springer Verlag, 2000.
8. I. Jacobsen, G. Booch, and J. Rumbaugh. *The Unified Software Development Process*. Addison-Wesley, 1999.
9. Jochen Klose and Hartmut Wittke. An Automata Based Representation of Live Sequence Charts. In Tiziana Margaria and Wang Yi, editors, *Proceedings of TACAS 2001*, number 2031 in LNCS. Springer Verlag, 2001.
10. Diego Latella, Istvan Maijzik, and Mieke Massink. Towards a formal operational semantics of uml statechart diagrams. In *3rd International Conference on Formal Methods for Open Object-Oriented Distributed Systems*, Lecture Notes in Computer Science. Kluwer Academic Publishers, 1999.
11. Johan Lilius and Ivan Porres Paltor. Formalising uml state machines for model checking. In R. France and B. Rumpe, editors, *UML'99 - The Unified Modeling Language: Beyond the Standard*, number 1723 in Lecture Notes in Computer Science. Springer-Verlag, 1999.
12. OMG. *Unified Modeling Language Specification, Version 1.3*. OMG, 1999. http://www.rational.com/uml/resources/documentation.
13. Wolfgang Thomas. Automata on Infinite Objects. In J. van Leeuwen, editor, *Handbook of Theoretical Computer Science, Vol. B*. Elsevier, 1990.

Semantics of the Minimum Multiplicity in Ternary Associations in UML

Gonzalo Génova, Juan Llorens, and Paloma Martínez

Computer Science Department, Carlos III University of Madrid,
Avda. Universidad 30, 28911 Leganés (Madrid), Spain
{ggenova, llorens, pmf}@inf.uc3m.es
http://www.inf.uc3m.es/

Abstract. The concept of multiplicity in UML derives from that of cardinality in entity-relationship modeling techniques. The UML documentation defines this concept but at the same time acknowledges some lack of obviousness in the specification of multiplicities for n-ary associations. This paper shows an ambiguity in the definition given by UML documentation and proposes a clarification to this definition, as well as a simple extension to the current notation to represent other multiplicity constraints, such as participation constraints, that are equally valuable in understanding n-ary associations.

Introduction

The entity-relationship model [4] has been widely used in structured analysis and conceptual modeling, and it has evolved into object oriented class diagrams such as those of the Unified Modeling Language [29]. This approach is easy to understand, powerful to model real-world problems and readily translated into a database schema, although other forms of implementation, such as object-oriented programming languages, are not so simple and straight [23]. Both in entity-relationship diagrams and in class diagrams the main constructs are the entity and the relationship among entities (class and association, in UML terminology). In this sense, important authors strongly reject the entity-relationship approach, since they consider that the very distinction between entity and relationship suffers of lack of precision [6, 7].

For many analysts, one of the most problematic aspects of systems modeling is the correct understanding of ternary associations and, in general, n-ary associations (we use this term, as usual, to refer to associations with three or more roles). Ternary associations represent often a complex situation which modelers find specially difficult to understand, regarding both structural and behavioral modeling. From the structural point of view, these difficulties are very often interlinked with the fourth and fifth normal form issue [13]. From the behavioral point of view, atomic interactions that involve more than two objects are another source of conceptual complexity (these interactions are denoted by some authors as "joint actions" or "atomic multiway synchronous interactions" [12]).

The cardinality of a relationship (multiplicity of an association, in UML terminology) is considered by some experts as the most structural property of a model [17]. However, the multiplicity values typically specified for n-ary associations

M. Gogolla and C. Kobryn (Eds.): UML 2001, LNCS 2185, pp. 329-341, 2001.

provide only partial understanding of the object structure. Additional conditions may be included within written descriptions that accompany the models, but a better integration, as far as it is possible, is always desirable. Worst of all, often the very meaning of the multiplicities is badly understood. As we will see, the multiplicity of binary associations is rather simple to specify and understand in UML, but, unfortunately, this is not the case for n-ary associations, for which UML has defined incomplete and unclear multiplicities.

The purpose of this paper is, on the one hand, to clarify the meaning of n-ary multiplicity values, which is acknowledged by UML to be not very obvious [29, p. 3-73], and on the other hand to propose an extension to the notation of UML n-ary multiplicities, one extension that provides more complete and precise definitions for n-ary associations with the smallest notational burden. Although our main concern is UML, the core of our exposition is general enough to be useful in other methods based on the entity-relationship approach. This work forms part of a more general research that is aimed towards a better understanding of the concept of "association" among classes. We hope that this better understanding will improve the models constructed both by novel and expert analysts.

The remainder of this paper is organized as follows. Section 1 recalls some definitions from UML: multiplicity, association, and multiplicity for binary and n-ary associations. Section 2 searches the roots of these definitions in data modeling techniques that derive mainly from the entity-relationship approach of Chen. Section 3 reveals an ambiguity, or at least uncertainty, in the definition of UML minimum multiplicity for n-ary associations; three alternative interpretations are presented, each one with its own problems and unexpected consequences. Finally, section 4 tries to understand the root of these problems by paying more attention to the participation constraint; a notation compatible with the three alternative interpretations of section 3 is proposed to recover a place for this constraint in n-ary associations in UML, and its semantics is carefully explained.

1   Definition of Multiplicity in UML

The Unified Modeling Language defines "multiplicity" as the range of allowable cardinalities that a set may assume [29, p. 3-68], where "cardinality" is the number of elements in a set [29, p. B-4]. A cardinality is a specific value, whereas multiplicity is the range of possible cardinalities a set may hold [22, p. 182]. Multiplicity specifications are given mostly for association ends, but they are used also for other purposes like repetitions of messages, etc. An "association" is the semantic relationship between two or more classes that involves connections (links) among their instances [22, p. 152; 29, p. 2-19]. These are the definitions within UML, although many authors, probably coming from the field of entity-relationship modeling, will use the term cardinality to mean multiplicity, and the term relationship to mean association. In this paper we use one terminology or the other depending on the context.

A binary association is drawn in UML as a solid path connecting two class symbols. The multiplicity of a binary association, placed on an association end (the target end), specifies the number of target instances that may be associated with a single source instance across the given association, in other words, how many objects of one class (the target class) may be associated with a given single object from the other class (the source class) [22, p. 348; 29, p. 2-22].

The classical example in Figure 1 illustrates binary multiplicity. Each instance of Person may work for none or one instance of Company (0..1), while each company may be linked to one or more persons (1..*). For those readers less familiarized with UML notation, the symbol (*) stands for "many" (unbounded number), and the ranges (1..1) and (0..*) may be abbreviated respectively as (1) and (*).

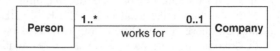

Fig. 1. A classical example of binary association with the expression of multiplicities

(Note that this association is intended to mean only the present situation: "a person *is working* for 0..1 companies", but not "a person *has worked or works* for 0..1 companies". In this paper we are going to avoid all issues of history, since this concern would depart us from our main objective.)

An n-ary association is an association among three or more classes, shown as a diamond with a path from the diamond to each participant class. *Each instance of the association is an n-tuple of values from the respective classes* (a 3-tuple or triplet, in the case of ternary associations). Multiplicity for n-ary associations may be specified, but is less obvious than binary multiplicity. The multiplicity on an association end represents *the potential number of values at the end, when the values at the other n-1 ends are fixed* [29, p. 3-73]. This definition is compatible with binary multiplicity [22, p. 350].

The example in Figure 2, taken from the UML Reference Manual [22, p. 351] and the UML Standard [29, p. 3-74], shows the record of a team in each season with a particular goalkeeper. It is assumed that the goalkeeper might be traded during the season and can appear with different teams. That is, for a given player and year, there may be many teams, and so on for the other multiplicities stated in the diagram.

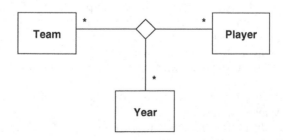

Fig. 2. Ternary association with many-many-many multiplicities

However, as we shall see, a subtle paradox hides behind the apparent clearness of these multiplicity specifications.

2   Definition of Cardinality in Entity-Relationship Models

The definition of multiplicity of an association in UML follows that of OMT [24], which is generally acknowledged [2, 20] to derive from the definition of cardinality of a relationship in the entity-relationship model [4]. In fact, Chen does not use the term "cardinality" in his proposal: he uses the expressions "1:1 mapping", "1:n mapping" and "m:n mapping", and he explains the meaning of each one, but he does not give any formal definition of the concept of "type of mapping". Moreover, he draws an example of an M:N:P ternary relationship SUPPLIER-PROJECT-PART, but he does not explain at all how these "cardinalities" are to be understood. Note, too, that he deals only with "maximum cardinality", in a close relation to the concept of "functional dependency".

Many data modeling techniques have followed, formalized and extended the Chen style of cardinality values [8, 10, 18, 21, 28]. Others, following the French method Merise [27], invert the placement of cardinality values [1, 3, 5]. It has been well established that the semantics of both conventions are equivalent for binary relationships, but differ substantially when they are applied to relationships of higher degree [2, 19, 20, 26]. This issue will be dealt with more detail in section 4.

In some of these methods we find the explicit and useful distinction between the concepts of a cardinality constraint and a participation constraint [10, 18, 26]:

- A *cardinality constraint* specifies the number of relationship instances in which an entity can participate. They are in the form of 1:1, 1:N, or M:N, to express the two constraints in a binary relationship, and 1:1:1, 1:1:N, 1:N:M, or M:N:P, to express the three constraints in a ternary relationship. These constraints correspond to *maximum* cardinality constraints in some notations. In the Chen style, the entity with a cardinality constraint of 1 is *functionally dependent* on the other entity (or entities, in an n-ary relationship). In the example in Figure 1, Company is functionally dependent on Person.

- A *participation constraint* specifies whether an entity instance can exist without participating in a relationship with another entity. This constraint corresponds to *minimum* cardinality constraints in some notations. Total and partial participation are the two types of participation, also denoted as *mandatory* and *optional* participation. Mandatory participation exists when an entity instance cannot exist without participating in a relationship with another entity instance. Optional participation exists when the entity instance can exist without participating in a relationship with another entity instance. In the example in Figure 1, Company has mandatory participation, while Person has optional participation.

Other authors define in a more general way a *co-occurrence constraint*, which specifies how many objects (or n-tuples of objects) may co-occur in a relationship with another object (or m-tuple of objects) [11]: for example, how many pairs *product-prize* may co-occur with a particular pair *seller-buyer* in the 4-ary relationship *sale*. This generalized concept of cardinality is studied more deeply in section 4.

Some methods combine cardinality and participation constraints and represent them using minimum and maximum constraints in the form of *(min, max)* notation. This is the case of UML. However, the concept of minimum multiplicity is not equivalent to the concept of participation constraint. For example, a minimum multiplicity of 2 implies mandatory participation, but mandatory participation implies only a minimum multiplicity of 1. Moreover, the potential multiplicities in UML extend to any subset of nonnegative integers [22, p. 346], not only a single interval as (2..*), not even to a comma-separated list of integer intervals as (1..3, 7..10, 15, 19..*): specifications of multiplicity like {prime numbers} or {squares of positive integers} are also valid, although there is no standard notation for them. Nevertheless, in UML as in other modeling techniques, the most usual multiplicities are (0..1), (1..*), (0..*) and (1..*). We are going to restrict our analysis to these combinations of multiplicity values.

3   Paradoxes and Ambiguities of Ternary Multiplicities

Let's recall the definition of UML multiplicity in an n-ary association: "the multiplicity on an association end represents the potential number of values at the end, when the values at the other n-1 ends are fixed". Now consider the ternary association "A works in B using C", which is a classical example in the literature [20], defined among employees, projects and skills: an employee works in a certain project using a certain skill. Table 1 illustrates possible sets of instances for the three classes, while Table 2 illustrates a possible set of instances (triplets) for the association.

Table 1. Three possible sets of instances for the three classes Employee, Project, Skill

Employee	Project	Skill
Albert	Kitchen	Welding
Benedict	Laboratory	Painting
Claire	Basement	Foreman

Table 2. Possible set of instances for the ternary association "works-in-using"

— works in — using —		
Employee	**Project**	**Skill**
Albert	Kitchen	Welding
Albert	Laboratory	Welding
Benedict	Kitchen	Foreman
Benedict	Basement	Foreman
Claire	Kitchen	Painting

Figure 3 shows a diagram for this ternary association, with multiplicity constraints that, according to the definition given above, are consistent with the values in Tables 1 and 2:

- Multiplicity for class Project in association "works-in-using" is 0..*, since an n-tuple of instances of Employee-Skill may be linked to a minimum of 0 and an unbounded maximum of instances of Project: tuple Albert-Welding is linked to two different instances of Project, Kitchen and Laboratory, and the same for Benedict-Foreman.
- Multiplicity for class Employee, also 0..*, is consistent as well: although there is no pair Project-Skill linked to two different instances of Employee, the diagram

states that a tuple such as Claire-Laboratory-Welding, which would duplicate the pair Laboratory-Welding, may be added to the existing set of tuples.

- Finally, multiplicity for class Skill, in this case 0..1, states that for each pair Employee-Project there may be none or one skill: that is, an employee uses at most one skill in each project, which is consistent with the given values, but the constraint also forbids adding a tuple such as Claire-Kitchen-Welding unless the tuple Claire-Kitchen-Painting is deleted first. In other words, Skill is functionally dependent on Employee-Project.

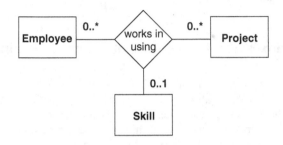

Fig. 3. The ternary association "works-in-using", according to the interpretation of *potential tuples*

Now, everything seems working well... but that's not that easy. So far, in applying the definition to this example we have considered only maximum multiplicity. Let's concentrate now on minimum multiplicity, and we will see that there is some ambiguity in its definition. We are going to propose and examine three different interpretations of the phrase "each pair Employee-Project", inviting the reader to check which one he or she has accepted until now, probably in an unconscious manner. We will show that each one of these interpretations has also its own problems and unexpected consequences. As far as we know, nobody has made this point beforehand.

First interpretation (actual tuples). "Each pair Employee-Project" may be understood as an "actually existing pair", or an *actual pair*, that is, a pair of instances that are linked by some ternary link within the ternary association. Pairs Albert-Kitchen and Benedict-Basement are actual pairs, since there are in fact some triplets that contain them, while pairs Albert-Basement and Claire-Laboratory are not.

This interpretation of the rule seems rather intuitive, but... note that for an actual pair Employee-Project there *must* be always at least one Skill: if it is an actual pair, there is an actual triplet that contains it, therefore there is an instance of Skill that is also in the triplet. There cannot be an actual pair that is not connected to a third element, because a ternary link is by definition a triplet of values from the respective classes; a ternary link has three "legs", and none of them may be empty: "limping" links are not allowed.

So, in this interpretation, *the minimum multiplicity is always at least 1*, since the value 0 has no sense. This "zero-forbidden effect" is not consistent with the frequent assigning of minimum multiplicity 0 in ternary associations (and, first of all, with UML documentation, as in the example in Figure 2). In fact, the diagram in Figure 3 would be incorrect, although it could be substituted by the one in Figure 4.

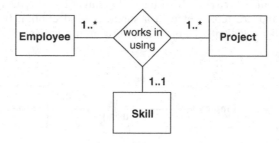

Fig. 4. The ternary association "works-in-using", according to the interpretation of *actual tuples*

Second interpretation (potential tuples). "For each pair Employee-Project" may be understood as a "merely possible pair", or a *potential pair*, that is, a pair of instances that belongs to the Cartesian product of Employee and Project. There are three employees and three projects, so there are nine potential pairs. For some of these pairs, like Benedict-Basement or Claire-Kitchen, there is a related skill; for some others, like Albert-Basement or Claire-Laboratory, there is none. So, minimum multiplicity 0 is allowed in Tables 1 and 2, and the diagram in Figure 3 would be correct and consistent with them.

But, what would be the meaning of minimum multiplicity 1? Consider multiplicity 1..1 assigned to class Skill, as in Figure 4. It would mean that, for each potential pair Employee-Product, there might be one Skill, *but not zero*; that is, any potential pair not linked to a skill would be forbidden. In other words, any potential pair must be linked to at least one skill, and therefore any potential pair Employee-Product must exist at least once within one triplet in the association: every employee *must* be linked to every project at least once. This rule and the diagram in Figure 4 would not be consistent with the values in Tables 1 and 2, since we would need the full Cartesian product Employee-Product to be present in Table 2 (in fact, we should have *exactly* nine lines and no more, due to maximum multiplicity 1 of Skill).

So, in this interpretation, *a minimum multiplicity 1 assigned to one class forces all potential pairs of instances of the remaining classes to actually exist within some triplet.* This would be a "bouncing effect of the one" that is probably unexpected by most modelers. Nevertheless, this interpretation seems valid, as it is implicitly in agreement with UML documentation and some works on the formalization of multiplicities [20].

Third interpretation (limping links). We could try an entirely different kind of interpretation, by means of allowing the existence of *limping links*, that is, ternary links that link only two instances and leave a blank for the third one. Thus, we would read the multiplicity for class Skill in Figure 3 as "each actual pair Employee-Project may be linked to none or one instance of Skill", that is, each link would be actually either a pair Employee-Project (belonging to a hidden binary association) or a triplet Employee-Project-Skill (belonging to the true ternary association). On the contrary, if multiplicity were 1..1, then limping links would not be allowed on the side of class Skill: every actual combination of employee and project should have a skill linked to it. Within this interpretation, the diagram in Figure 3 would be equivalent to the one in Figure 5, in which the limping links have been removed from the ternary association, and are represented in a superimposed explicit binary association (this could be further done with the other two zero-multiplicities).

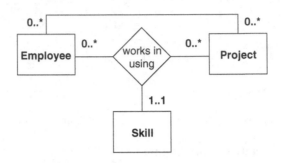

Fig. 5. The ternary association "works-in-using", according to the interpretation of *limping links*, in which the limping links on the side of Skill are shown as an explicit binary association

In this interpretation, *the ternary association symbol is used as an abbreviated form to represent a genuine ternary association together with a hidden binary association.* Probably many modelers use the ternary symbol as if it were to mean this, but, in general, the procedure of merging a binary association with a ternary association by using limping links is not advisable. On the other hand, UML states that each instance of an n-ary association is an n-tuple of values from the respective classes (recall section 1 of this paper).

The limping links interpretation for incomplete associations is a variation of the actual pairs interpretation, in which minimum multiplicity 0 means that a lack of information is allowed. Nevertheless, there are some difficulties left: How many legs may be lacking in an n-ary link? One, two, up to n-2? How is the maximum multiplicity constraint to be interpreted when a leg is lacking on an opposite end?

So, this interpretation may seem simple and useful at first glance, but there are still some points that are not at all clear, first of all the very definition of n-ary association in UML. These unsolved semantic difficulties are enough, in our opinion, to discard the concept of a limping link as a misleading one, in spite of its apparent advantages, in favor of the more rigorous approach of the potential pairs interpretation. In consequence, in the rest of this paper we adopt this interpretation for clearness, although the issues addressed are up to a point independent of this choice.

4   A Place for the Participation Constraint

We have seen three different interpretations that could solve the ambiguity in the definition of minimum multiplicity of n-ary associations in UML. The first one, *actual pairs*, implies that minimum multiplicity must be always 1, which is not consistent with documentation and practice; the second one, *potential pairs*, seems correct but has a strange effect when the value is 1; the third one, *limping links*, is semantically weak and contradicts the definition of n-ary association. Why is minimum multiplicity in n-ary associations so elusive?

McAllister offers a good formalization of the concept of cardinality (or multiplicity, in UML terminology) [20]. Being a and b two non-null, non-overlapping sets of roles in an n-ary relationship R, the cardinality $C(a, b)=(min, max)$ specifies that any given set of entity instances of a must be associated by R with between min and max unique sets of entity instances for b (for simplicity, we restrict ourselves to the simplest form of cardinality, a single integer interval, although this does not affect the reasoning). Note that this corresponds to the *co-occurrence constraint* defined above. In the example of Figure 3, if a = {Employee, Skill} and b = {Project}, then $C(a, b)$ = (0..*). McAllister demonstrates that the total number of cardinality values that may be defined in a relationship with N roles is given by $3^N - 2^{N+1} + 1$, and applies this calculation for N from 2 to 5, giving the results in Table 3.

Table 3. Total number of cardinality values that may be defined in a relationship with N roles

N = number of roles in R	number of C(a, b) for R
2	2
3	12
4	50
5	180

As N increases, there is a rapid increase in the number of cardinality values that should be analyzed if the nature of the relationship is to be fully understood. This may be one factor why many data modeling practitioners encounter difficulties in dealing with n-ary relationships, especially if only a small number of the applicable cardinalities are considered for each such relationship.

For N = 3, a ternary relationship such as "works-for-using", the twelve values to be considered are: the three Chen/UML style values, the three Merise values, and six values for the three embedded (that is, implicit) binary relationships Employee-Project, Employee-Skill and Project-Skill (remember they are not truly independent relationships). McAllister further defines a set of rules for consistency checking, since these values are not completely independent [20]. To fully understand the structure of an n-ary relationship, the modeler should specify all these *co-occurrence constraints*, but most of times it is enough with the N Chen values and the N Merise values (the others being usually many-to-many [15]). When these values are specified as simple *(min, max)* intervals, consistency between Chen and Merise values is determined by ensuring that each *min* or *max* Chen value is less than or equal to the *min* or *max* Merise values of the other classes [20]. This rule may be checked against the example in Figure 6, which shows both sets of values: *minChen* for Skill is 0, which is equal to *minMerise* for Employee (0) and less than *minMerise* for Project (1); *maxChen* for Skill is 1, which is less than *maxMerise* for Employee (*) and *maxMerise* for Project (*). If, besides Chen and Merise values, the other values are also important, McAllister's tabular representation for relationship cardinality is a good choice; these cardinality constraints that are difficult to express in traditional entity-relationship models are also very naturally expressed using assertions [17] ("assertions" are declarative specifications of what has to be true in the "stable state" of the system, that is, outside of atomic operations; they are also referred to as "invariants").

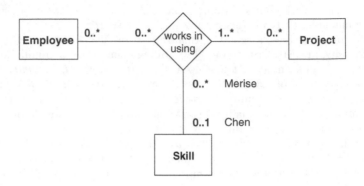

Fig. 6. The ternary association "works-in-using", showing both Chen and Merise multiplicity values

We can better understand now the semantic problems of minimum multiplicity considered above. Minimum multiplicity is associated with the *participation constraint*, but in the case of a ternary association, in the Chen style, it does not mean the participation of the class, but the participation of a pair of the other two classes. A value 0 for Skill does not mean optional participation for Skill in the association, but optional participation for instance pairs of Employee-Project in the association with an instance of Skill. If this goes against intuition, all the more reason to be clarified. In fact, the participation of each individual class remains unexpressed in the Chen style, while the Merise style represents it adequately. On the other side, the *functional dependencies* remain unexpressed in the Merise style, while they are represented by maximum multiplicity 1 in the Chen style. This is probably the reason why OMT and UML have chosen Chen instead of Merise, although functional dependency is not inherently more important than participation.

Both Chen and Merise styles are correct and can describe the same association, but they state different facts about the nature of the association. The facts represented by each style are not specified when using the other, nor can they be derived from the other (except in the case of binary associations, where they simply interchange their placement). Therefore, if the two styles provide useful information to understand the association, why not represent both in the same diagram? Figure 6 repeats the example of Figure 3, but adding a set of Merise values close to the association diamond. This values are consistent with the values in Tables 1 and 2, and add new and useful semantics to the association: we note especially that class Project is the only one that has mandatory participation (*minMerise* for Project is 1), that is, a project cannot exist without being linked to a pair employee-skill, although there may be many (potential) pairs employee-skill not linked to any project (*minChen* for Project is 0); and we note also that class Skill may participate in multiple association instances (*maxMerise* for Class is *), that is, a certain skill may be linked to many different pairs employee-skill, although for each pair at most one skill can be used (*maxChen* for Class is 1).

This notation may seem similar to that of replacing the ternary association by a new entity and three binary associations that simulate the ternary association, as shown in Figure 7. This new entity is usually referred to as *intersection entity* or *associative entity* or *gerund* [26]. We note that the Merise values of multiplicity are preserved in this transformation, and placed again close to the associative entity, but all Chen values have been replaced by 1..1, since every instance of Work is linked to one and only one instance of the other classes (this is the same as saying that every ternary link has "three legs"). In other words, the semantics of functional dependencies expressed by the ternary association are lost when simulating it with a gerund, but the semantics of participation are preserved. There are other differences between binary and ternary associations and, in general, binary representations of ternary associations are not functional-dependency preserving [14, 16, 25].

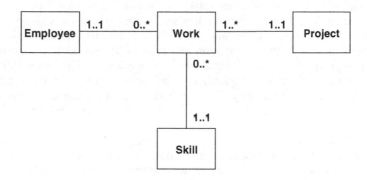

Fig. 7. The ternary association "works-in-using" substituted by the associative entity "Work". Only Merise multiplicity values are preserved in the transformation

Conclusions

In this paper we have considered some semantic problems of minimum multiplicity in n-ary associations, as it is currently expressed in UML; nevertheless, our ideas are general enough to be applicable to other modeling techniques more or less based on the entity-relationship approach. Minimum multiplicity is closely related to the participation constraint, although in the case of n-ary associations it does not mean the participation of the class in the association, but the participation of tuples of the other n-1 classes. Moreover, we discovered that this latter participation is defined with uncertainty, allowing three conflictive interpretations: participation of actual tuples, participation of potential tuples, and participation with limping links.

The second interpretation seems more probable, as it is implicitly in agreement with UML documentation, in spite of the bouncing effect of minimum multiplicity 1. The Standard should clarify this question, without resigning itself to a lack of obviousness in the definition. Besides, if this second interpretation were chosen, the Standard should also warn, since this result is not at all intuitive, that a minimum multiplicity 1 or greater assigned to one class forces all potential tuples of instances of the remaining classes to actually exist within some n-tuple; therefore, minimum multiplicity would be 0 in nearly every n-ary association.

The third interpretation, which is a variation of the first one, seems intuitive and has also some pragmatic advantages, although it is in contradiction with the definition of n-ary association in UML (maybe more with the letter than with the spirit). In addition, it has some unsolved semantic difficulties that have lead us to discard it, at least for the time being.

The eventual clarification of this point leaves another problem unresolved: the participation of each class remains unexpressed in the Chen style of representing multiplicities (which is also the UML style), while the Merise style shows it adequately. Both Chen and Merise styles are correct, but they describe different characteristics of the same association, which cannot be derived from each other in the n-ary case, although they are related by a simple consistency rule.

Being both styles useful to understand the nature of associations, we propose a simple extension to the notation of UML n-ary multiplicities that enables the representation of both participation and functional dependency (that is, Merise and Chen styles). Since this notation is compatible with the three alternative interpretations of Chen multiplicities, its use does not avoid by itself the ambiguity of the definition of multiplicity: they are independent problems. If this notation were accepted, the Standard should also modify the metamodel accordingly, since it foresees only one multiplicity specification in the AssociationEnd metaclass. If this were not the case, it could be at least recognized that Chen multiplicities are not the only sensible co-occurrence constraints that may be defined in an n-ary association.

Understanding n-ary associations is a difficult problem in itself. If the rules of the language used to represent them are not clear, this task may become inaccessible. If the interpretation of n-ary associations is uncertain, straight communication among modelers becomes impossible. If the semantic implications of a model are ambiguous, implementers will have to take decisions that do not correspond to them, and possibly wrong decisions. These reasons are more than enough to expect a more precise definition of UML on this topics.

Acknowledgements. The authors would like to thank Vicente Palacios and José Miguel Fuentes for his frequent conversations on the issues discussed in this paper; Jorge Morato for his stylistic corrections on the first draft; Ana María Iglesias, Elena Castro and Dolores Cuadra for the useful bibliographic material provided for this research, and criticism on the first draft; and Guy Genilloud for his many suggestions to improve this paper.

References

1. Batini, C., Ceri, S., Navathe, S.B.: *Conceptual Database Design: an Entity-Relationship Approach*. Benjamin-Cummings (1992)
2. Castellani, X., Habrias, H., Perrin, Ph.: "A Synthesis on the Definitions and Notations of Cardinalities of Relationships", *Journal of Object Oriented Programming*, 13(6):32-35 (2000)
3. Ceri, S., Fraternali, P.: *Designing Database Applications with Objects and Rules: the IDEA Methodology*. Addison-Wesley (1997)
4. Chen, P.P.: "The Entity-Relationship Model", *ACM Transactions on Database Systems*, 1(1):9-36 (1976)
5. Coad, P., Yourdon, E.: *Object-Oriented Analysis*, 2nd ed. Prentice-Hall (1991)

6. Codd, E.F.: *The Relational Model for Database Managament: Version 2.* Addison-Wesley (1990)
7. Date, C.J.: *An Introduction to Database Systems*, 6th ed. Addison-Wesley (1995)
8. De Miguel, A., Piattini, M., Marcos, E.: *Diseño de bases de datos relacionales.* Ra-Ma, Madrid (1999)
9. Dullea, J., Song, I.-Y.: "An Analysis of Structural Validity of Ternary Relationships in Entity-Relationship Modeling", *Proceedings of the 7th International Conference on Information and Knowledge Management*, 331-339, Washington, D.C., Nov. 3-7 (1998)
10. Elmasri, R., Navathe, S.B.: *Fundamentals of Database Systems*, 2nd ed. Benjamin-Cummings (1994)
11. Embley, D.W.: *Object Database Development: Concepts and Principles.* Addison-Wesley (1998)
12. Genilloud, G.: "Common Domain Objects in the RM-ODP Viewpoints", *Computer Standards and Interfaces*, 19(7):361-374 (1998)
13. Hitchman, S.: "Ternary Relationships--To Three or not to Three, Is there a Question?" *European Journal of Information Systems*, 8:224-231 (1999)
14. Jones, T.H., Song, I.-Y.: "Binary Representations of Ternary Relationships in ER Conceptual Modeling", *14th International Conference on Object-oriented and Entity-Relationship Approach*, pp. 216-225, Gold Coast, Australia, Dec. 12-15 (1995)
15. Jones, T.H., Song, I.-Y.: "Analysis of Binary/Ternary Cardinality Combinations in Entity-Relationship Modeling", *Data & Knowledge Engineering*, 19(1):39-64 (1996)
16. Jones, T.H., Song, I.-Y.: "Binary Equivalents of Ternary Relationships in Entity-Relationship Modeling: a Logical Decomposition Approach", *Journal of Database Management*, April-June:12-19 (2000)
17. Kilov, H., Ross, J.: *Information Modeling: An Object-Oriented Approach.* Prentice Hall (1994)
18. Martin, J., Odell, J.: *Object-Oriented Methods: A Foundation.* Prentice Hall (1995)
19. Martínez, P., Nieto, C., Cuadra, D., De Miguel, A.: "Profundizando en la semántica de las cardinalidades en el modelo E/R extendido", *IV Jornadas de Ingeniería del Software y Bases de Datos,* pp. 53-54, Cáceres, Spain, Nov. 24-26 (1999)
20. McAllister, A.: "Modeling N-ary Data Relationships in CASE Environments", *Proceedings of the 7th International Workshop on Computer Aided Software Engineering*, pp. 132-140, Toronto, Canada (1995)
21. *Metodología de planificación y desarrollo de sistemas de información, METRICA versión 2. Tomo 3: Guía de técnicas.* Instituto Nacional de Administración Pública, España. Madrid (1993)
22. Rumbaugh, J., Jacobson, I., Booch, G.: *The Unified Modeling Language Reference Manual.* Addison-Wesley (1998)
23. Rumbaugh, J.: "Relations as Semantic Constructs in an Object-Oriented Language", *Proceedings of the ACM Conference on Object-Oriented Programming: Systems, Languages and Applications*, pp. 466-481, Orlando, Florida (1987)
24. Rumbaugh, J., Blaha, M., Premerlani, W., Eddy, F., Lorensen, W.: *Object-Oriented Modeling and Design.* Prentice-Hall International (1991)
25. Song, I.-Y., Jones, T.H.: "Analysis of binary relationships within ternary relationships in ER Modeling", *Proceedings of the 12th International Conference on Entity-Relationship Approach*, pp. 265-276, Dallas, Texas, Dec. 15-17 (1993)
26. Song, I.-Y., Evans, M., Park, E.K.: "A Comparative Analysis of Entity-Relationship Diagrams", *Journal of Computer and Software Engineering*, 3(4):427-459 (1995)
27. Tardieu, H., Rochfeld, A., Coletti, R.: *La méthode MERISE. Tome 1: Principles et outils.* Les Editions d'Organisation, Paris (1983, 1985)
28. Teorey, T.J.: *Database Modeling and Design*, 3rd ed, Morgan Kaufmann Publishers (1999)
29. Object Management Group: *Unified Modeling Language Specification*, Version 1-3, (June 1999)

Extending UML to Support Ontology Engineering for the Semantic Web

Kenneth Baclawski[2], Mieczyslaw K. Kokar[2], Paul A. Kogut[1], Lewis Hart[5],
Jeffrey Smith[3], William S. Holmes III[1], Jerzy Letkowski[4], and
Michael L. Aronson[1]

[1] Lockheed Martin Management and Data Systems
[2] Northeastern University
[3] Mercury Computer
[4] Western New England College
[5] GRC International

Abstract. There is rapidly growing momentum for web enabled agents that reason about and dynamically integrate the appropriate knowledge and services at run-time. The World Wide Web Consortium and the DARPA Agent Markup Language (DAML) program have been actively involved in furthering this trend. The dynamic integration of knowledge and services depends on the existence of explicit declarative semantic models (ontologies). DAML is an emerging language for specifying machine-readable ontologies on the web. DAML was designed to support tractable reasoning.

We have been developing tools for developing ontologies in the Unified Modeling Language (UML) and generating DAML. This allows the many mature UML tools, models and expertise to be applied to knowledge representation systems, not only for visualizing complex ontologies but also for managing the ontology development process. Furthermore, UML has many features, such as profiles, global modularity and extension mechanisms that have yet to be considered in DAML.

Our paper identifies the similarities and differences (with examples) between UML and DAML. To reconcile these differences, we propose a modest extension to the UML infrastructure for one of the most problematic differences. This is the DAML concept of property which is a first-class modeling element in DAML, while UML associations are not. For example, a DAML property can have more than one domain class. Our proposal is backward-compatible with existing UML models while enhancing its viability for ontology modeling.

While we have focused on DAML in our research and development activities, the same issues apply to many of the knowledge representation languages. This is especially the case for semantic network and concept graph approaches to knowledge representations.

M. Gogolla and C. Kobryn (Eds.): UML 2001, LNCS 2185, pp. 342–360, 2001.
© Springer-Verlag Berlin Heidelberg 2001

1 Introduction and Motivation

Representing knowledge is an important part of any knowledge-based system. In particular, all artificial intelligence systems must support some kind of knowledge representation (KR). Because of this, many KR languages have been developed. For an excellent introduction to knowledge representations and ontologies see [20].

Expressing knowledge in machine-readable form requires that it be represented as data. Therefore it is not surprising that KR languages and data languages have much in common, and both kinds of language have borrowed ideas and concepts from each other. Inheritance in object-oriented programming and data languages was derived to a large extent from the corresponding notion in KR languages.

KR languages can be given a rough classification into three categories:

- Logical languages. These languages express knowledge as logical statements. One of the best-known examples of such a KR language is the Knowledge Interchange Format (KIF) [6].
- Frame-based languages. These languages are similar to object-oriented database languages.
- Graph-based languages. These include semantic networks and conceptual graphs. Knowledge is represented using nodes and links between the nodes. Sowa's conceptual graph language is a good example of this [20].

Unlike most data modeling languages, KR languages do not have a rigid separation between meta-levels. While one normally does maintain such a separation to aid in understanding, the languages do not force one to do so. In effect, all of the statements in the languages are in a single space of statements, including relationships such as "instanceOf" that go between metalevels. In DAML, as in many other KR languages, `Class` is an entity whose instances are classes. A class can have instances, and those instances may also be classes. A chain of "instanceOf" links may be of any length. The `Class` entity, in particular, is an instance of itself. As a result, KR languages incorporate not only modeling capabilities, but at the same time they include meta-modeling, meta-meta-modeling, etc.

On the other hand, DAML and most other KR languages do not have profiles, packages or other modularity mechanisms. DAML does make use of XML namespaces, but only for disambiguating names, not as a package mechanism.

The analogy between hypertext and semantic networks is compelling. If one identifies semantic network nodes with Web resources (specified by Universal Resource Identifiers or URIs) and semantic network links with hypertext links, then the result forms a basis for expressing knowledge representations that could span the entire World Wide Web. This is the essence of the Resource Description Framework (RDF) [14]. RDF is a recommendation within the XML suite of standards, developed under the auspices of the World Wide Web Consortium. RDF is developing quickly [5]. There is now an RDF Schema language, and there are many tools and products that can process RDF and RDF Schema.

The DARPA Agent Markup Language (DAML) [16,10] is an extension of RDF and RDF Schema that will be able to express a much richer variety of constraints as well as support logical inference.

As in any data language, KR languages have the ability to express schemas that define the structure and constraints of data (instances or objects) conforming to the schema. A schema in a KR language is called an *ontology* [8,9,12]. An ontology is an explicit, formal semantic model. Data conforming to an ontology is often referred to as an *annotation*, since it typically abstracts or annotates some natural language text (or more generally a hypertext document). An ontology may include vocabulary terms, taxonomies, relations, rules/assertions. An ontology should not include instances/annotations.

The increasing interest in ontologies is driven by the large volumes of information now available as well as by the increasing complexity and diversity of this information. These trends have also increased interest in automating many activities that were traditionally performed manually. Web-enabled agents represent one technology for addressing this need [11]. These agents can reason about knowledge and can dynamically integrate services at run-time. Formal ontologies are the basis for such agents. DAML is designed to support agent communication and reasoning. We have been developing tools for developing and testing DAML ontologies and knowledge representations.

RDF and DAML, which currently do not have any standard graphical form, could leverage the UML graphical representation. In addition, RDF and DAML are relatively recent languages, so there is not as many tools or as much experience as there is for UML. We are currently engaged in projects that have realized benefits in productivity and clarity by utilizing UML class diagrams to develop and to display complex DAML ontologies. Cranefield [4] has also been promoting ontology development using UML and has been translating UML to RDF. Although their purposes are different, UML and DAML have many characteristics in common. For example, both have a notion of a *class* which can have *instances*, and the DAML notion of *subClassOf* is essentially the same as the UML notion of specialization/generalization. Table 2 lists our best attempt to capture the similarities between the two languages.

Our paper discusses the similarities and differences between UML and DAML and they might be reconciled. We are proposing a modest extension to the UML infrastructure to deal with the DAML concept of *property*, which represents one of the most problematic differences. The DAML concept of *property* was recently split into the notions of *ObjectProperty* and *DatatypeProperty*. A DAML ObjectProperty, at a first glance, appears to be the same as a UML association, and a DAML DatatypeProperty appears to be the same as a UML attribute. This is misleading, since the DAML notion of ObjectProperty is a first-class modeling element, while UML associations are not. More precisely, in DAML, an ObjectProperty can exist without specifying any classes that it might relate, i.e., it can exist independently of any classes. In UML, on the other hand, an association is defined in terms of *association ends*, which must be related to classifiers. Similar remarks apply to DAML DatatypeProperties versus UML attributes. This difference between UML and most other KR languages has also been noted by Cranefield [4].

After analyzing the differences between the two modeling languages, we came to the conclusion that it would not take too much to close the gap in the expressibility of UML while remaining backward-compatible with existing UML models. Future work will highlight other proposals that would enhance its viability for ontology modeling. Eventually, this work will culminate in a contribution to UML and MOF [7], in the form of a Profile or Infrastructure and UML 2.0/MOF 2.0 recommendation, to lead to more general acceptance of UML as a development environment for ontologies based on DAML and other KR languages. The recommended changes to UML would have some effect on existing tools, but the changes are not any more significant than other changes that being considered for UML 2.0 which would also have an impact on existing tools.

2   DAML Background

The aim of the DAML program is to achieve "semantic interoperability between Web pages, databases, programs, and sensors." An integration contractor and sixteen technology development teams are working to realize the DAML vision of "providing a set of tools for programmers to build broad concepts into their Web pages ... and allowing the bottom-up design of meaning while allowing higher-level concepts to be shared." The problem DAML addresses is how to build a monolithic set of ontologies upon agreed-upon domain models to share in a military grid. The solution is to develop usable interoperability technologies, similar to those that enable the web to function. Towards this end, DAML will enable annotating information on the web to make knowledge about the document machine-readable so that software agents can interpret and reason with the meaning of web information. The only mechanism currently generally available for such annotations on the Web is metadata in the head element of an HTML file. DAML enriches and formalizes metadata annotations (see Figure 1).

DAML is only part of the *Semantic Web* vision [2,13] of the automation or enabling of things that are currently difficult to do: locating content, collating and cross-relating content, drawing conclusions from information found in two or more separate sources. DAML's part is to serve as a markup language for network agents to provide a mechanism for advertising and reusing specifications. The software tools for creating these agents will be accomplished through the TASK (Taskable Agent Software Kit) Program to reduce the per agent development cost. The third part of the Semantic Web vision addresses the middleware layer as a continuation of the CoABS (Control of Agent Based Systems) investment to bring systems, sensors, models, etc. into the prototype "agent grid" as an infrastructure for the run-time integration of heterogeneous multi-agent and legacy systems.

DAML's applications will be far-reaching, extending to both the military and commercial markets. Its machine-to-machine language capabilities might be instrumental in realizing the application-specific functionality, independent of

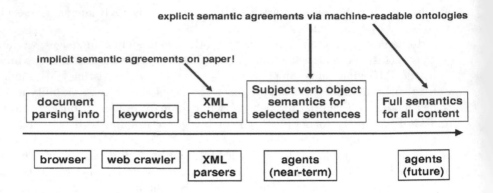

Fig. 1. The Evolution of Metadata

human control. DAML will also enhance the efficiency and selectivity of search engines and other automated document processing tools. Such engines and tools will be able to scan multiple Web pages and conceptually relate content that currently might seem unrelated because of variations or imprecision in the language programmers used to identify that content. A number of DAML tools have been built or are in progress, including an ontology library, parser/serializer, ontology editor/analyzer, DAML crawler and viewer, etc. Trial government (e.g. Intelink at the Center for Army Lessons Learned) and commercial (in e-commerce and information retrieval) applications have been planned and built.

The latest specification of the DAML ontology language (called DAML+OIL) was released in March, 2001. A description of the language specifications and documentation can been seen at [21]. For a good discussion of the design rationale see [15]. Also a variant called DAML-L (logic) is in progress for rule representation and reasoning. DAML+OIL is the basic representation language (analogous to the UML basic diagrams), while DAML-L will provide for logical assertion (analogous to the Object Constraint Language (OCL) of UML).

3   Properties of Mappings

Because of the increasing number of modeling languages, it is becoming more important to introduce systematic techniques for constructing mappings (or *transformations*) between modeling languages and proving that the mappings are correct [17,18,19]. In this section we discuss in general terms some of the issues that arise when constructing mappings between modeling languages. When constructing mappings between modeling languages, it is important to understand the goals and purpose of the mappings. A precise statement of goals and purpose is essential for dealing with the many mapping issues, such as the following:

- Is the mapping required to preserve semantics? Ideally, the two languages should have well-defined notions of semantics. In practice, they will not, so the best one could hope for is to have some reasonably precise and convincing argument that the semantics are preserved.

- Is the mapping required to be defined on the entire modeling language? In many cases, it may suffice to define the mapping on a subset of the modeling language. The purpose of the mapping can be used to answer this question. If the language is simply a means (or "front-end") for constructing models of the second language, then it is reasonable to use only those constructs of the first language that are needed for the second.
- Is the mapping simply a one-way mapping from one language to the other or should it be defined in both directions? If the mapping is defined in both directions, then it is called a *two-way* mapping.
- If the mapping is a two-way mapping, should the two directions be inverses of each other? Having inverse mappings is generally only possible when the languages are very similar to one another. This is not the case for UML and DAML.

To make the discussion of mapping properties more precise, we need to introduce some concepts. We presume that each modeling language has notion of *semantic equivalence*. The precise meaning of this notion will depend on the language, but it usually takes a form such as the following: Two models M_1 and M_2 are *semantically equivalent* if there is a one-to-one correspondence between the instances of M_1 and the instances of M_2 that preserves relationships between instances. Semantic equivalence of two models should mean that the models differ from each other only in inessential ways, such as renaming, reordering or adding redundancy.

We also presume that each model of a language can be serialized in a unique way. For example, one can serialize a UML model using the XMI format, while DAML is defined in terms of RDF which has a standard XML representation. For a model M in a language L, the *size* of M is the size of its serialization (in whatever unit is appropriate for the serialization, such as the number of characters). The size of M is written $\#M$.

Now suppose that L_1 and L_2 are two modeling languages. A *mapping* f from L_1 to L_2 is a function from the models of L_1 to the models of L_2 which preserves semantic equivalence. In other words, if M_1 and M_2 are two semantically equivalent models in L_1, then $f(M_1)$ is semantically equivalent to $f(M_2)$. In the case of UML and DAML, the mapping is defined only on those UML models that are necessary for expressing DAML ontologies, so it is only a partial mapping.

A *two-way mapping* from L_1 to L_2 is a pair of mappings, the first f_1 from L_1 to L_2 and the second f_2 from L_2 to L_1, such that if f_1 is defined on M, then f_2 is defined on $f_1(M)$, and vice versa for f_2 and f_1. By assumption, two-way mappings preserve semantics in both directions

In general, two-way mappings are not inverses, even for the models on which they are defined. The best one can hope for is that applying the two mappings successively will stabilize, but even this is hard to achieve. To be more precise, we say that a two-way mapping is *stable* if for any model M on which f_1 is defined, $f_1(f_2(f_1(M))) = f_1(M)$, and similarly for models of L_2. While stability is much easier to achieve than invertibility, it is still a strong property of mappings. Let (f_1, f_2) be a stable two-way mapping. For any model M on which f_1 is defined,

$f_2(f_1(M))$ forms a kind of "canonical form" for M in the sense that f_1 and f_2 are inverses of each other on the canonical forms. Put another way, stable two-way mappings furnish canonicalizations for the two languages as well as invertible mappings between canonical forms.

While stability is clearly desirable, it may not be necessary. A more realistic goal is for the two-way mapping to settle down eventually. To be more precise, a two-way mapping (f_1, f_2) is *bounded* if for any model M on which f_1 is defined, the sequence $\#f_1(M), \#f_2(f_1(M)), \#f_1(f_2(f_1(M))), \ldots$ is bounded.

While it is desirable for mappings to be bounded, this can conflict with the desire to keep the mapping simple. Consider, for example, a mapping from UML that maps each association to a DAML class and each association end to a DAML property. This is certainly necessary for association classes and nonbinary associations. Using the same mapping uniformly for all associations is certainly simpler than treating binary associations that are not association classes in a different manner. However, doing so is unbounded. A binary association will map to a class and two properties, which map back to a class and two associations, these then map to three classes and four properties, and so on. This example illustrates how keeping the mapping simple can result in unbounded mappings. We intend to propose mappings that are bounded, even though this may make them somewhat more complex.

4   UML to DAML Mapping

In order to discuss the similarities between UML and DAML an initial incomplete mapping between the languages has been created. Table 1 presents a high-level mapping of concepts from UML and DAML, and serves as an overview of the overall strategy applied to the mapping.

Table 1. High-Level Mapping of UML and DAML Concepts

DAML Concept	Similar UML Concepts
Ontology	Package
Class	Class
As Sets (disjoint, union)	Difficult to represent
Hierarchy	Class Generalization Relations
Property	Aspects of Attributes, Associations and Classes
Hierarchy	None for Attributes, limited Generalization for Associations, Class Generalization Relations
Restriction	Constrains Association Ends, including multiplicity and roles. Implicitly as class containing the attribute
Data Types	Data Types
Instances and Values	Object Instances and Attribute Values

Table 2 elaborates on the high-level concepts and expresses some of the specific extensions necessary for the initial mapping between the languages. This proposed mapping is made with the assumption that UML class diagrams are created specifically for the purpose of designing DAML ontologies. Legacy class diagrams that were not originally intended for DAML applications would be usable for DAML purposes but would need modification in order to make full use of DAML capabilities.

Table 2. Mapping Between UML and DAML

UML	DAML
class	Class
instanceOf	type
type of ModelElement	type
attribute	ObjectProperty or DatatypeProperty
binary association	ObjectProperty
generalization	subClassOf
≪subPropertyOf≫ stereotyped dependency between 2 associations	subPropertyOf
generalization between stereotyped classes	subPropertyOf
note	comment
name	label
"seeAlso" tagged value on a class and association	seeAlso
"isDefinedBy" tagged value on a class and association	isDefinedBy
class containing the attribute	"subClassOf" a property restriction
source class of an association	"subClassOf" a property restriction
attribute type	"toClass" on a property restriction
target class of an association	"toClass" on a property restriction
≪equivalentTo≫ stereotyped dependency	equivalentTo
≪sameClassAs≫ stereotyped dependency between two classes	sameClassAs
≪samePropertyAs≫ stereotyped dependency between two associations	samePropertyAs
≪Ontology≫ stereotyped package	Ontology
"versionInfo" tagged value on a package	versionInfo
import (dependency stereotype)	imports
multiplicity	cardinality
multiplicity range Y..Z	Y = minCardinality, Z = maxCardinality
association target with end multiplicity = 0..1 or 1	UniqueProperty
association source with end multiplicity = 0..1 or 1	UnambiguousProperty
≪inverseOf≫ stereotyped dependency between two associations	inverseOf
≪TransitiveProperty≫ stereotype on an association	TransitiveProperty

4.1   Representing DAML Properties

Individual elements of this mapping can be illustrated to further explain the principles used to create the mapping. Figure 2 depicts the "mother" relationship that exists between the class Person and the class Woman. In UML this is represented as a labeled association between the two classes. In DAML the property "mother" exists independently of the two classes and is not given significance until a restriction is placed on the source class of the relationship.

In Figure 2, this is represented as a restriction for class Person, on property "mother", to class Woman.

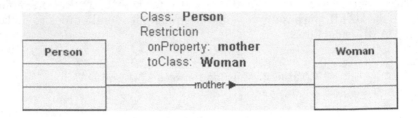

Fig. 2. DAML Property Restriction

By applying the proposed DAML to UML mapping, a DAML translation can be generated. Listing 3 represents a section of an ontology that has been constructed from Figure 2

```
<daml:Class rdf:ID="Person">
  <daml:label>Person</daml:label>
  <daml:subClassOf>
    <daml:Restriction>
      <daml:onProperty rdf:resource="#mother"/>
      <daml:toClass rdf:resource="#Woman"/>
    </daml:Restriction>
  </daml:subClassOf>
</daml:Class>
<daml:Class rdf:ID="Woman">
  <daml:label>Woman</daml:label>
</daml:Class>
<daml:Property rdf:ID="mother"/>
```

Fig. 3. DAML Translation of Figure 2

Another concept of the mapping can be seen in Figure 4, which shows one of the UML representations of a DAML Sub-Property. In the figure, the property that represents a person as being the "father of" another person is a refinement of the property of a person being the "parent of" another person.

4.2   Representing DAML Instances

Figure 5 illustrates the concept of an instantiated class in UML. In a similar fashion, this would described in DAML as an element identified as "Tommy", with type identified as Person and the value "9" assigned to the property "age".

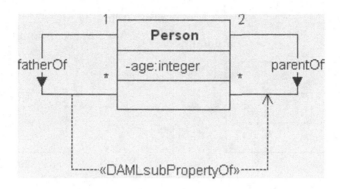

Fig. 4. Example of a Sub-Property

Fig. 5. DAML type property

4.3   Representing Facets of Properties

To demonstrate the mapping between UML multiplicity and DAML cardinality, Figure 6 depicts the correlation between the multiplicity of an association end and the corresponding cardinality in DAML. In the figure, an association end that contains a single value would map to a specific cardinality value for the property restriction. An association end that contains a range of values would map to the minimum and maximum cardinality allowed for the corresponding property restriction.

Figure 7 and Figure 8 depict special cases of DAML properties with predefined cardinality restrictions. The first of these is called an Unambiguous Property and is depicted in Figure 7. An Unambiguous Property is defined in DAML as a relation that, given a specified target element, will always originate from the same source element.

Figure 8 represents the UML notation for the DAML concept of a Transitive Property. A Transitive Property is defined in the terms of three or more elements. To be considered transitive, a property that holds true for the first and second elements and holds true for the second and third elements must also hold true for the first and third elements. For example, given that Tom is the ancestor

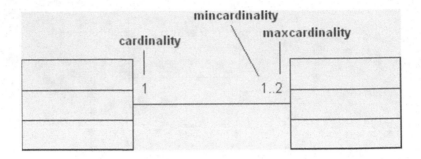

Fig. 6. DAML Cardinality

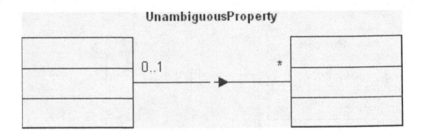

Fig. 7. Example of an Unambiguous Property

of Jack, and Jack is the ancestor of Robert, then Tom is also the ancestor of Robert.

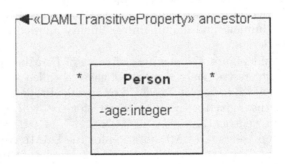

Fig. 8. Example of a Transitive Property

5   Incompatibilities between UML and DAML

While there are many similarities between UML and DAML, there are also many differences. Reconciling these differences has been one of the major problems of our project. We now discuss the major incompatibilities between UML and DAML.

5.1   Containers and Lists

RDF has a number of container notions: *Bag*, *Seq* and *Alt*. The semantics of these notions are not very clear, and DAML has largely replaced them with the notion of a *List*. UML does have containers (in OCL), and it also has ordered associations which implicitly define a list within the context of the association. For a particular modeling task, one can often use either one (e.g., a design using an explicit list structure could be redesigned to use an ordered association instead). However, lists and ordered associations have different interfaces, and it is difficult to map one to the other in an automated fashion.

5.2   Universal Classes

RDFS and DAML have "universal" classes. The *Resource* class has every object as an instance, and the *Literal* has every literal as an instance. DAML adds the *Thing* class that has every object, including both objects and literals (and presumably anything else as well). No such universal classes exist in UML. One can certainly add such classes to a UML model, but it is not compatible with the spirit of UML modeling.

5.3   Constraints

DAML imposes a constraint by specifying that a class is a subclass of a restriction class. The semantics of each kind of restriction constraint is specified by the DAML axioms. UML can specify constraints using a variety of graphical mechanisms, and one can also specify constraints using OCL. The graphical constraint mechanisms (e.g., multiplicity constraints) are specified by OCL, so ultimately all constraints get imposed, directly or indirectly, in OCL.

5.4   Property

As we have noted in Section 1 above, the DAML notion of property is a first-class modeling element, while the UML notion of an association is not. Furthermore, a UML binary association always has just one domain class and one range class, but a DAML property can have many domain classes, although it can only have one range class.

A UML nonbinary association cannot be directly represented as a single DAML property, and it must be reified as a DAML class with as many properties as the arity of the UML association. In other words, a UML nonbinary association must be *reified*. Of course, binary associations can also be reified. Whether to reify an association is a design choice. Ontology developers refer to such design choices as *ontological commitment*. Reification is a useful design technique, but it has the disadvantage that the design is more complex, and the design units that make up the reification are no longer explicitly related to one another. In addition, if one uses reification in an automated mapping from one language to another (e.g., from DAML to UML), then the resulting mapping is unbounded, as the example at the end of Section 3 illustrates.

Another significant difference between UML and DAML is that the relation between UML classes and associations is not exactly the same as between DAML classes and properties. In UML, multiplicity constraints on associations can affect membership of objects in the classes related through the association; this is because multiplicity constraints constrain the number of objects that can be instantiated for these classes. Classes in UML do not directly affect associations. In DAML, constraints on properties are imposed somewhat indirectly by specifying that a class is a subtype of a class called a *restriction*. Doing this may limit the scope of the properties being constrained by the restriction class.

Finally, another important difference between UML and DAML is that descriptions of both classes and properties in DAML can be distributed over various locations. This is not in the spirit of UML.

The differences identified above have their own advantages and disadvantages. The idea of distribution of descriptions, for instance, goes against the principle of modularization, an accepted principle in software engineering, but it does help to support reuse. Similarly, the idea of a property being associated with multiple classes is more flexible and might foster reuse, but it clashes with modularity. Consider, for example, the notion of a `location`. This is a property that occurs frequently in models, often several times within the same model. In UML, such occurrences are different associations, while in DAML, they would all be the same property.

For instance, the property of `location` could associate `Faculty` with `University`. Each link of this association would give the University affiliation of a faculty member. In UML it would be modeled as an association. The same property might also be used for associating a `Building` with its `Address`. In UML, this would be modeled as a second association, whether or not the associations use the same name, because the associations are in different namespaces.

In RDF and DAML (as well as many other knowledge representation languages), properties are first class. A property need not have any domain or range specifications at all, but when it does it may have multiple domains and only one range. Furthermore, properties may have values that are literals as well as objects, so that properties subsume both the association and the attribute concepts in UML.

On the other hand, UML allows associations that are nonbinary, while properties can only be binary. There are well-known techniques for dealing with nonbinary relationships, but it is much harder to deal with the fact that UML associations and attributes cannot be first class.

Although two UML associations may have the same name, they are still different associations because the names are in different namespaces. If one chooses to map two UML associations having the same name to the same RDFS property, then this could violate the requirement that an RDFS property have only one range. If one maps each association to a different RDFS property, then RDFS properties having multiple domains will not be expressible in UML.

To deal with the problem of first class properties, we recommend that a new type of model element be added to UML for representing properties. Since RDF properties are unidirectional, it would be incorrect to view a property as a grouping of associations. The correct interpretation is to define a property to be an aggregation of associations ends from different associations. This is discussed in more detail in Section 7.

5.5   Cardinality Constraints

UML multiplicity constraints on an association end correspond relatively accurately to the UML cardinality constraints. The only incompatibility has to do with the fact that properties are first class model elements and that properties are one-directional. The first class feature of properties means that one can specify a cardinality constraint for every domain of a property all at once. In UML one must specify this separately for each association (end) belonging to the property, while in DAML it is only necessary to specify it once. On the other hand, UML allows one to specify cardinality constraints on all of the ends of an association. In DAML, one must introduce an inverse property in order to specify a cardinality constraint on the domain of a property.

5.6   Transitivity

DAML has the capability of imposing constraints on properties. From the point of view of UML, this means that one can impose a constraint on a number of associations all at once. This is a useful modularization technique related to current work on aspect-oriented programming. The only constraint of this kind that is explicitly supported at the moment is transitivity, but other constraints may be added later.

5.7   Subproperties

RDF allows one property to be a subproperty of another. UML has the ability to specify that one association is a specialization of another, though this construct is rarely used. In our recommendation, *Property* is a specialization of *Classifier*, so that a property can be a specialization of another. Of course, OCL constraints must be added to ensure that one does not have meaningless specializations, such as properties that are specializations of associations, and the semantics of property specialization must be specified carefully.

5.8   Namespaces

While it is reasonable to define a mapping from UML to DAML by specifying how each construct is to be mapped, one must also consider how the constructs are related to one another. In other words, in addition to the major constructs one must also consider the "glue" that ties them together.

Constructs in DAML are linked together either through the use of URIs or by using the hierarchical containment relationship of XML. DAML objects need not be explicitly named (i.e., they can be anonymous), and such objects can be related to other objects using XML containment.

UML uses a very different kind of "glue" to link its objects to each other. Instead of URIs, it uses names in a large number of namespaces. For example, each class has its own namespace for its attributes and associations. This is further enriched by the ability to specify private, protected and public scopes. RDF also has namespaces (from XML), but XML namespaces are a very different notion. RDF lacks any kind of name scoping mechanism. In addition, one cannot specify navigability constraints for RDF properties. While RDF properties are unidirectional, this is only a mechanism for distinguishing the roles of objects being related. It does not limit accessibility.

Any mapping from UML to DAML or the reverse must have a mechanism for ensuring that names are properly distinguished. However, there are known methods for dealing with this problem, and no new UML features are needed to deal with this.

UML also uses graphical proximity to specify relationships, and these are the only way that unnamed objects can be linked with other objects. Graphical relationships are more complex than hierarchical containment, and one would expect that graphical interfaces would be more general than hierarchical containment. However, this is not quite true. The XML serialization form of RDF can specify sequence information very easily while it is awkward to specify a sequential order for graphical objects. Indeed, serializations impose a sequence ordering on every relationship even when it is irrelevant.

When specifying a mapping from UML to DAML, one should also address the issue of how relationships between model elements are to be mapped. The most important issue is the mapping of names, but other issues are also significant.

6   Semantics of Constraints

One overriding distinction between UML and DAML is the semantics of constraints. In UML a constraint is a requirement that restricts the instantiations that are possible for a given model. In DAML and other logic-based KR languages, constraints are axioms from which one can perform logical inference. To understand the distinction, suppose that in a UML class diagram one has **Student** and **Department** classes, and one has an association **major** that specifies the department in which a student is majoring. Assume that there is a cardinality constraint on **major** that constrains a student to major in at most one department. Now suppose that a particular student is majoring both in **Computer Science** and **Chemistry**. In UML this would violate the cardinality constraint. In DAML, on the other hand, one can conclude that **Computer Science** and **Chemistry** must be the same department.

7   Recommendations

DAML is similar to many other KR languages that are based on the mathematical notion of a graph or network (consisting of a set of vertices and edges). Conceptual graphs and semantic networks are examples of commonly used KR languages of this kind. Natural Language Processing (NLP) systems are well suited to this kind of knowledge representation because an edge from one vertex to another corresponds to a predicate linking a subject to an object. Parts of speech in general map reasonably well to modeling constructs in KR systems (see, for example, [1]). In DAML a predicate is represented by a property. However, the DAML notion of a property is defined independently of any context in which it might be used. Whether properties should be *decontextualized* in this manner is a hotly debated philosophical issue.

We do not take any particular stand on whether decontextualized properties are appropriate for modeling activities. Rather we feel that this decision should be left to the modeler. Furthermore, the knowledge representation community is a large and growing community, and it makes sense to support their modeling techniques if it is convenient to do so and it does not break any existing models. We argue here that by adding a few additional model elements to the UML metamodel one can make UML compatible with knowledge representation languages.

To close the gap in the expressibility of UML, we propose to extend UML by adding two meta-model elements called *Property* and *Restriction*. The MOF diagram for this extension is shown in Figure 9. As can be seen from the diagram, *Property* is an aggregation of a number of association ends. The notion of Association End does not need to be changed. The notion of *Property* serves as a means of grouping various association ends. This capability is not present in the current UML. The fact that *Property* is a first-class concept is shown by the fact that *Property* can exist without being associated with any classes. This is imposed by setting the multiplicity constraint on the aggregation to 0..*. A property can be constrained by zero or more *Restrictions*, as is the case in DAML. The *Restriction* is a Classifier. It is also related to at least one class.

It is tempting to deal with the issue of first-class properties by simply reifying them. Classes are first-class modeling elements, so this appears to solve the problem. For example, instead of attempting to model `location` as an association, one could model it as a class `Location`. However, this has several disadvantages. It can result in complex, unnatural ontologies, and it puts the burden on the ontology developer to deal with this incompatibility issue. Furthermore, if this is used as a mechanism for mapping between DAML and UML, then the resulting mapping is unbounded, as has been discussed in Section 5.4.

7.1   Property Semantics

A property is a grouping of association ends. Properties "cross-cut" the Association concept. In particular, no property can have more than one of the association ends of an association. To express this in OCL one uses `allConnections`, the set of all Association Ends of an Association, and we

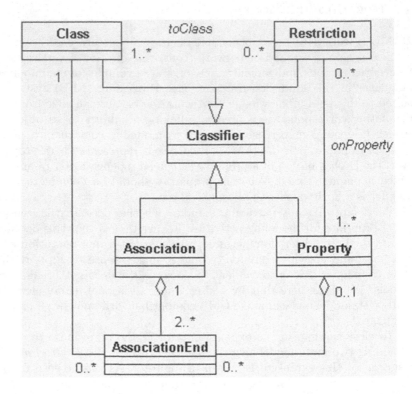

Fig. 9. The MOF Specification of the UML Extension

introduce `allPropConnections` to be the set of all Property classifier of an Association. If T is the intersection of the allConnections and allPropConnections sets, then T has cardinality at most 1. More formally:

```
allConnections: Set(AssociationEnd);
allPropConnections: Set(Property);
self.allConnections->intersection(self.allPropConnections:Set(T)):Set(T);
size(#T)<=1
```

In addition, one must specify that Property classifier can only be specializations or generalizations of other Property classifier.

7.2   Restriction Semantics

A restriction is a classifier for objects. The instances of the restriction are the objects that satisfy a condition on one or more properties associated with the restriction. A restriction is imposed on a class by specifying that the class is a specialization of the Restriction classifier.

If a Restriction classifier is linked with a Property classifier, and if the Restriction classifier is linked with Classes (via the `toClass` meta-Association), then the instances of the Restriction classifier can only link with objects that are in one of the specified classes.

As with the Property classifiers, the Restriction classifiers can only be generalizations and specializations of other Restriction classifiers.

8   Conclusion

In this paper we have reported on our work in progress on a UML as an ontology development environment. We have identified similarities and differences between UML and DAML, and we have discussed how they can be mapped to each other. In the "similarities" discussion we showed how UML concepts can be mapped to DAML. In the "incompatibilities" discussion we identified differences between the two representations. In the "mapping" discussion, we made an attempt to give rules for translating UML concepts to DAML concepts. As a result of our analysis, we came to the conclusion that some of the concepts are significantly incompatible. In particular, the concept of DAML `Property`, although somewhat similar to the UML `Association` concept, cannot be mapped easily. We believe that this is the main obstacle to using UML (and UML tools) for DAML-based ontology development. We believe this obstacle could be reconciled by a modest extension to the UML. We proposed the main idea of such an extension in this paper. We also explained the advantages and disadvantages of having the concept of Association and Property. If the extension as proposed in this paper is accepted, then the two concepts can be mapped consistently. This might lead to the acceptance of UML by the knowledge representation community as the preferred graphical notation for KR languages, such as DAML, that are based on graphs.

Acknowledgements. This material is based upon work supported by the Air Force Research Laboratory, Contract Number F30602-00-C-0188.

Any opinions, findings and conclusions or recommendations expressed in this material are those of the author(s) and do not necessarily reflect the views of the Unites States Air Force.

References

1. R. Abbott. Program design by informal english descriptions. *Comm. ACM*, 26(11), 1983.
2. T. Berners-Lee, J. Hendler, and O. Lassila. The semantic web. *Scientific American*, May 2001.
3. G. Booch, I. Jacobsen, and J. Rumbaugh. *OMG Unified Modeling Language Specification*, March 2000. Available at `www.omg.org/technology/documents/formal/-unified_modeling_language.htm`.
4. S. Cranefield. Networked knowledge representation and exchange using uml and rdf. *J. of Digital information*, 1(8), February 2001.

5. S. Decker, D. Brickley, J. Saarela, and J. Angele. A query and inference service for RDF. In *QL'98 - The Query Language Workshop*. W3C, 1998.
6. M. Genesereth. Knowledge interchange format draft proposed american national standard (dpans) ncits.t2/98-004, 1998. Available at `logic.stanford.edu/kif/dpans.html`.
7. Object Management Group. *Meta Object Facility (MOF) Specification, Version 1.3*, April 2000. Available at `www.omg.org/technology/documents/formal/-meta.htm`.
8. J. Heflin, J. Hendler, and S. Luke. Coping with changing ontologies in a distributed environment. In *AAAI-99 Workshop on Ontology Management*. MIT Press, 1999.
9. J. Heflin, J. Hendler, and S. Luke. SHOE: A knowledge representation language for Internet applications. Technical Report `www.cs.umd.edu/projects/plus/SHOE`, Institute for Advanced Studies, University of Maryland, 2000.
10. J. Hendler and D. McGuinness. The DARPA Agent Markup Language. *IEEE Intelligent Systems*, 15, No. 6:67–73, 2000.
11. D. McGuinness. Ontologies and online commerce. *IEEE Intelligent Systems*, Vol. 16, No. 1:8–14, 2001.
12. D. L. McGuinness, R. Fikes, J. Rice, and S. Wilde. An environment for merging and testing large ontologies. In *Proceedings of the Seventh International Conference on Principles of Knowledge Representation and Reasoning (KR2000)*, 2000.
13. E. Miller, R. Swick, D. Brickley, and B. McBride. Semantic web activity page, April 2001. Available at `www.w3.org/2001/sw/`.
14. Resource Description Framework (RDF) Model and Syntax Specification. `www.w3.org/tr/rec-rdf-syntax`, Feburary 1999.
15. DAML+OIL Design Rationale. `www.cs.man.ac.uk/horrocks/Slides/index.html`, 2001.
16. DARPA Agent Markup Language Web Site. `www.daml.org`, 2001.
17. J. Smith. *UML Formalization and Transformation*. PhD thesis, Northeastern University, Boston, MA, December 1999.
18. J. Smith, M. Kokar, and K. Baclawski. Formal verification of UML diagrams: A first step towards code generation. In *Eighth OOPSLA Workshop on Behavioral Semantics*, pages 206–220, November 1999.
19. J. Smith, M. Kokar, K. Baclawski, and S. DeLoach. UML formalization and transformation. In *ECOOP*, 2000.
20. J. Sowa, editor. *Knowledge Representation: Logical, Philosophical, and Computational Foundations*. PWS Publishing, 2000.
21. DAML+OIL Specification. `www.daml.org/2001/03/daml+oil-index.html`, 2001.

On Associations in the Unified Modelling Language

Perdita Stevens*

Division of Informatics
University of Edinburgh
Perdita.Stevens@dcs.ed.ac.uk.
Fax: +44 131 667 7209

Abstract. Associations between classifiers are among the most fundamental of UML concepts. However, there is considerable room for disagreement concerning what an association is, semantically. These have
implications for the modeller because they can result in serious misunderstandings of static structure diagrams; similarly, they have implications
for tool developers. In this paper we describe and classify the variants
which have implicitly or explicitly been described. We discuss the scope
for, and difficulties in, understanding these as specialisations of a more
general notion and we address the implications for future versions of
UML.

1 Introduction

The Unified Modelling Language has been widely adopted as a standard language
for modelling the design of (software) systems. Nevertheless, certain aspects of
UML are not yet defined precisely. This paper is concerned with one such aspect:
associations.

The paper is structured as follows. The remainder of this section gives background information and introduces the main problems we address. In Section 2,
we carefully discuss the definition of Association in the latest version of UML and
explore the implications of the ambiguities and contradictions it includes and of
the different possible resolutions. Section 3 discusses interactions between associations and generalisation; Section 4 discusses association classes. Section 5
mentions some related work, and finally Section 6 concludes and discusses the
implications for the UML standard.

This paper is based on the UML Revision Task Force's recommendation for
UML1.4 [5], the latest version at the time of writing. It is hoped that this work
may feed into the ongoing construction of UML2.0, which is intended to increase
the precision of UML. A major aim of the paper is to be readable by anyone who
can read the UML standard. At the end of the paper we will briefly discuss work
that gives formal semantics for UML associations, but this paper will not add to
their number: rather, we are concerned with making UML *formalisable*. A main
purpose of formal semantics work with UML is often to find the ambiguities and

---

* Supported by an EPSRC Advanced Research Fellowship.

M. Gogolla and C. Kobryn (Eds.): UML 2001, LNCS 2185, pp. 361–375, 2001.
© Springer-Verlag Berlin Heidelberg 2001

contradictions in the informal specification, and such approaches can be very effective at fulfilling that aim. However, there is a serious drawback in that the formalisations are then not readable except by those familiar with the formalism used; so the vital process of gaining consensus for a modification is hindered. Perhaps more damagingly, the process of formalising UML in one's favourite formalism often suggests assumptions natural in that formalism, the following of which may obscure the very ambiguities we seek. In this paper, we take the view that once the meanings of UML's concepts are informally clear, the way to (perhaps various) formalisations will be clearer. This is our reason – some will say excuse – for not giving here such fundamentals as a programming language independent semantics for attributes of classes, which would be required to cover this material in a fully formal way.

The reader is naturally assumed to be familiar with UML. We cite material from [5] by page; thus, [5] (3-90) indicates page 90 of section 3 of the UML standard, that is, of the Notation Guide.

We will use the usual convention of writing "an A" for "an instance of classifier A" etc., where no confusion results. We write $a : A$ etc. for "a is an instance of classifier A" etc..

One reason why the topic of making associations precise has not attracted more attention in the past is that for purposes of informal design, an ambiguity about exactly which systems correctly implement which UML models – which is at the heart of this issue – is not fatal. Association information provided by a designer in a model can be treated by a programmer (who may or may not be the same person) as guidance, and may be interpreted in different ways for different associations even within the same model.

For other communities this may not suffice. In the reverse engineering community, for example, tools are required to produce UML models from existing code, as an aid to understanding legacy systems. If the tools are to be maximally useful it must be clear to the user what the presence or absence of an association means. Recently there have been several serious efforts to enable interoperability of reengineering tools; representatives of the major ones came together at a Dagstuhl workshop earlier this year, and detailed discussions of these issues took place. Careful consideration was paid to using UML as an interoperability metamodel (or as part of it, for recording the recovered design information; information about the code structure is also vital in such applications but is outside the scope of UML). However, to the disappointment, but with the eventual agreement, of the author it was concluded that this was impossible. The problems addressed in this paper were part of the reason, so those discussions motivate the paper.

More concretely, to introduce the problem, we present some questions which illustrate the legitimate disagreements that can arise as a result of readers of the current UML standard interpreting it differently. Readers are quite likely to have their own strongly preferred answers to these questions, and indeed, some of them are unequivocally answered by the UML specification. Others do lead, as we shall show, to exposing flat contradictions in the current UML specification. However, the main purpose of giving the examples is to demonstrate how easily modeller's expectations may be frustrated. Such arguments are dangerous of course in their informality, but vital where humans are using a large language like UML whose definition they inevitably do not carry in full detail in their heads. Therefore we will not be ashamed to talk about developers expecting something which a perfect reasoner from the UML specification would not expect.

For clarity we present trivial versions of the problems, but it is clear that non-trivial versions do arise in practice, and in particular, that a developer of certain tools would have to make decisions about the answers.

```
class A {
  public void doA(B b) {b.doB();}
}

class B {
  public void doB() {;}
}

class C {
  private A myA;
  private B myB;
  public void doC() {myA.doA(myB);}
}
```

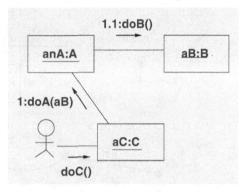

Fig. 1. Java code

Fig. 2. A collaboration including an implicit ≪parameter≫ link

Consider first fragment of Java shown in Fig. 1. Of which class models is this a correct implementation? Specifically, what associations may or must appear between classes A, B and C? Everyone will agree that there must be an association between A and C, because C is declared to hold a reference to an A and there is a method of C which uses this reference to send a message to an A. Most people will argue that there must be an association between B and C because C is declared to hold a reference to a B. Some, however, will argue that there must not be, because no message ever passes between a B and a C. The opposite situation holds between A and B: most will say that there is no association, because the static structure of neither declares a reference to an instance of the other; however, as instances of A may send messages to instances of B, it may also be argued that this should be recorded in an association.

Now let us go on to consider collaborations. Most people would expect C's reaction to message doC() to be shown in an (instance level) collaboration diagram like Fig. 2. That is, even those who do not expect an association between A and B certainly will expect a link between instances of those classifiers: the alternative is to show a stimulus with no link.

This pair of expectations contradicts another universal expectation, that any link is an instance of an association.

Lastly consider Fig. 3. In my experience most people will happily accept the class diagram as representing graphs, including the graph illustrated. They will draw the object diagram shown – or possibly, a variant with two links of is incident on both linking e2 to n2 – to represent the graph. In UML1.4, however, neither variant legally conforms to the class diagram. We will consider this example in Section 2.3.

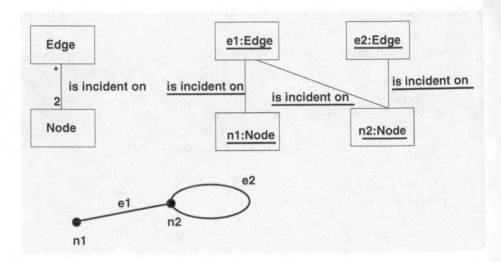

Fig. 3. An incorrect way to use UML1.4 multiplicities

2   Associations in the UML1.4 Standard

In this section we address several issues that arise when we consider UML1.4's treatment of associations in detail.

2.1   Dynamic or Static?

Suppose objects $p : P$ and $q : Q$ are linked within association A which associates classifier P with Q. There are two main ways of interpreting this. We refer to the first notion (labelled S) as *static association* and to the second (labelled D) as *dynamic association*. Because it is important to consider the consequences for both the association and the link, we give the alternatives from both points of view. First, the fact that there is an association A between classifiers P and Q may be informally defined in either of the following ways:

S There is a structural relationship between the classifiers: for example, they should eventually be implemented by class definitions in which one of P, Q will include an attribute which is expected to contain a value which is an object of the other class. (We say "expected" because it is legitimate to use UML to model systems which are implemented in untyped languages, in which the expectation could not be verified from the code.)

D There is a behavioural relationship between the classifiers: that is, the system should be implemented such that it may happen (or perhaps, it is expected to happen: see below) that instances of classifiers P, Q exchange a message.

From the point of view of instances, these views become:

S One of these objects contains data which references the other: for example, p has an attribute whose value *at the moment* is (a reference to) the object q;

D These objects may at some stage exchange a message.

To explain the choice of terminology, notice that under the "static" interpretation, given the code of a system that is claimed to implement a model, we can trivially check whether the associations in the model are reflected in the code and vice versa by inspecting the code; there is no need to run the code. The "dynamic" notion, by contrast, permits associations that may be observable only in the behaviour of the system, not from static analysis of the code alone.

Notice the cautious wording of the dynamic notion of association; the fact that we need to be so cautious is in fact the strongest argument against this notion. Granted that our aims are pragmatic – we want to be able to manipulate UML models reliably and check code against them – we could not usefully define instances $p : P$ and $q : Q$ to be linked exactly if they *do* exchange a message, or define P and Q to be associated if and only if some instances of those classifiers do exchange a message. Quite apart from the fact that for real systems such things will be affected by the environment of the system, including the behaviour of its actors, the notions will be undecidable (that is, it is impossible even in principle to write a program for this family of questions that could always terminate and answer the given question correctly). This is because to decide, given the code of a system, whether any instances of two given classes exchange a message, is at least as hard as the Halting Problem[1]. For this reason we have to settle for an approximation; under suitable assumptions it is possible to provide syntactic conditions sufficient to guarantee that instances of the classes *cannot* exchange a message, although the failure of these conditions will not guarantee that they *do*.

Oddly, therefore, from the point of view of the *links* (as opposed to the associations) the "static" view is in some sense more dynamic: the existence of

---

[1] To be explicit: consider the family of systems in which the nth system simply invokes method f of P with argument n, where f's behaviour given n is that it simulates the behaviour of the nth Turing machine, sending a message to an instance of Q after the Turing machine terminates, if it ever does. Then if we could decide for each system whether an instance of P ever sent a message to an instance of Q, we could also decide whether the corresponding Turing machine halted; which is impossible.

a link between a given pair of objects is a property of one certain point in an execution. (As in the dynamic case, so in the static case we will not be able to decide in general whether two given instances will ever be linked. But this may not concern us, given that we can decide whether their classifiers are associated.)

Notice that in the dynamic view the *non*-existence of an association between P and Q implies by definition that instances of P and Q will never exchange a message; this can be useful in modelling as it provides a way to understand how far the effect of changing an object's interface can spread. In the static view, there is no such guarantee: objects may exchange messages without their classifiers being associated, as with A and B in Fig. 2. It is interesting to observe in passing that the effect of following the Law of Demeter[4] is to limit the extent to which this fact leads to uncontrolled message passing between instances of remote classifiers; in fact, in a system whose design obeys that law the difference between static and dynamic association, while still real, is far more manageable. In other words, by limiting the design space we can get something approaching the best of both worlds.

This discussion shows that the two notions of association, static and dynamic, each have their own advantages to the designer. At this stage the case is strong for allowing both versions in UML, though of course any modeller must be aware of which they are using. In order to explore the implications of the choice further, we need to settle another question about what an association is.

2.2 Tuple or Model Element?

We come now to the issue which, though important and exposing contradictions in the UML standard, is more easily resolved: is a link simply a tuple, or is it more than that?

Consulting the definition of Association first, [5] 2-20 says:

> The instances of an association are a set of tuples relating instances of the classifiers. Each tuple value may appear at most once. [...] An instance of an Association is a Link, which is a tuple of Instances drawn from the corresponding Classifiers.

That is, a link is completely determined by the instances it links. Moreover, and more controversially, 3-87 says: Links do not have instance names, they take their identity from the instances that they relate.

If we take literally the statement that a link "is" a tuple of instances, then a link has no identity of its own: [2] and cannot have any kind of data beyond

---

[2] We do not wish to get into a philosophical discussion of what identity means. For the purposes of this paper, a class of things informally *has (the property) identity* if two elements of that class may own the same data (where "data" of course does not include "the identity of the element") and may nevertheless be distinguishable. It will suffice to say that if it is *meaningful* to ask "Is this a perfect copy of that, or is it actually the same thing?" – whether or not the question can be answered in a given computation framework – then the things concerned have identity.

the literal tuple. In particular, it cannot be possible to navigate from a Link to anything else. (This is for the same reason that an Interface in a model cannot have associations that it can navigate.) Thus in this interpretation we do not need to impose, as a constraint, the fact that the set of links which are instances of a given association cannot include two different links of an association between the same two instances; it is automatic from the fact that a link is a tuple (and the definition of "set").

However, Link does in fact have navigable associations, as described in [5]. Nor would altering the specification of Link specifically help to resolve this, since a Link is also a ModelElement. A ModelElement is *not* just a tuple: for example, any model element has a name and an identity of its own. These are automatically inherited by Link[3], so we have an inescapable contradiction: from the fact that a Link is a tuple we deduce that it cannot have data beyond the tuple, from the fact that it is a ModelElement we deduce that it must.

The easiest way to resolve this – in the sense that it involves a minimal change to the UML1.4 specification – is to decide that the wording of 2-20 and 3-87 is misleading; rather than literally *being* a tuple, a Link simply *determines and is determined by* a tuple: it determines a tuple via its association (connection) with LinkEnd, and to ensure that it is determined by a tuple we do need to add a constraint which forbids that two Links of a given association determine the same tuple. Indeed, [5] has such a constraint on page 2-115, further supporting the view that this is what is intended.

Henceforth we will reject the view that a link is (simply) a tuple: instead, we view a Link as a ModelElement in its own right. However, as a link *determines* a tuple, an Association *determines* a set of tuples. When it is convenient to talk about the set of tuples – that is, the relation – determined by an association A we will denote this A_R.

2.3   Multiplicity and Multiple Links

Next we address the implications of our choices for the definition of multiplicity of associations, which leads us into a consideration of whether multiple links between the same pair of instances should be permitted. [5] 2-71 specifies clearly enough:

> The multiplicity property of an association end specifies how many instances of the classifier at a given end (the one bearing the multiplicity value) may be associated with a single instance of the classifier at the other end. A multiplicity is a range of nonnegative integers.

---

[3] UML frequently specifies that certain things are *not* inherited; this is type-theoretically problematic. Pragmatically, it seems like nonsense that two instances could be indistinguishable when viewed as elements of a subclassifier – which by UML's intention carries more information than (is more specialised than, is a subtype of) its parent – but distinct viewed as elements of the parent.

This is a natural definition *which is based solely on the relation A_R determined by an association A*, and therefore makes sense for both static and dynamic associations. It is often what the modeller wants; but as usual, there are tradeoffs. To see one pragmatic disadvantage of this definition, consider the example given above in Fig. 3. Because the edge $e2$ is linked by "is incident on" to just one Node, $n2$, the multiplicity constraint is violated; although the modeller probably intended it simply to represent the domain-level constraint that any edge has two ends. Replacing the multiplicity with 1,2 makes this object diagram legal, but also allows some unintended configurations.[4]

This is a possibly unintended feature rather than a bug: there is nothing wrong with leaving the multiplicity definition as it is, whichever interpretation of association we are using; the worst that will happen is that a modeller will be inconvenienced.

Notice that because of the constraint on page 2-115 which says that there may be at most one link of an association which links a given pair of objects – which we refer to for short as C – it would be illegal to show two links between $e2$ and $n2$. Pragmatically, however, it is tempting for the modeller to do so and to consider that the resulting instance diagram should conform to the class diagram, and it is not obvious why this should be forbidden. Indeed, it has been argued, for example by Genilloud [2], that it is useful to allow multiple links between the same instances in a given association. Of course, a *set* of tuples of instances by definition does not include the same tuple more than once, so someone who takes the view that an association *is* a set of tuples does not have this option. Given, however, that we have here rejected the "pure tuple" view, it would be a simple matter to remove the constraint C from the UML standard, thus permitting multiple links of an association A between the same instances. (A_R, being a set of tuples, would of course still include the tuple of instances just once. One could consider *defining* an association as a *bag* of tuples, but this gives something close to the worst of all worlds.)

Would dropping constraint C so as to permit multiple links between the same instances be an improvement, perhaps with some appropriate adjustment to the definition of multiplicity? The answer depends crucially on whether we take the dynamic or static view of associations.

S In the static view, removing C can be seen as an attempt to help the modeller trying to model a graph with classes Edge and Node and a single association "is incident on", discussed above. We could replace the definition of multiplicity in the current standard by one that specified that an association end of association A having multiplicity m is not a statement about the tuples in A_R, but instead a structural statement about the classifiers associated by A; for example, if the implementation of class P will have a member which is an array of 3 Qs, then the corresponding association of P and Q will have

---

[4] In fact, the most practical solution might be to interpose a "fictional" (in the sense that it does not model an obvious real-world entity) EdgeEnd, so that an edge connecting a node to itself would have two distinct EdgeEnds, which just happened to refer to the same Node. C.f. AssociationEnd etc. in the UML standard!

multiplicity 3, and the correctness of the implementation will not be affected by the possibility that two or more of the array's elements are the same Q. Whether this would be an improvement is a matter of modellers' taste. In its favour, it can be argued that, given this suggested definition, it is easy to impose an additional constraint on the number of *distinct* instances, at any level (for one association, for one model, in a profile). That is, the current definition is easily recoverable by modellers who want it. The graph example demonstrated that the reverse adaptation is less easy, so we could argue that this suggested definition provides modellers with more flexibility than UML's current definition. Whereas UML's current definition of multiplicity is independent of the choice of a static or dynamic notion of associations, however, this proposed replacement only seems sensible with a static notion. UML could permit both variants of association and both variants of multiplicity, but would have to ensure that nonsensical combinations were excluded: this is likely to be a recurring problem when resolving disagreements about intended interpretations of parts of UML by allowing a choice between the interpretations.

D In the dynamic view, removing C could be seen as an attempt to model the fact that a single association may be used by the same tuple of instances to exchange more than one message; for example, if Edge's code at some point requires that both Nodes linked to the Edge be notified of some change, we might allow two links determining the tuple $(e2, n2)$ to represent the fact that $n2$ will receive the message twice. But this is an unfruitful view: not only is there a difficulty about defining which messages "count" for a given association, but also, for any reasonable definition the question of whether given code correctly implemented a given UML class diagram would be undecidable.[5]

2.4   Links, Associations, and Collaborations

Up to this point, it has been defensible to view the static version of association as correct and the dynamic version as a mistake. This view becomes harder to defend when we consider the behaviour (the dynamics!) of the system.

LinkEnds are provided with stereotypes ≪association≫, ≪global≫, ≪local≫, ≪parameter≫, ≪self≫ corresponding to the different reasons why the instance is visible [5](2-108). However, any LinkEnd occurs in exactly one Association (because of the two relevant multiplicities of 1 in Fig. 2.17 on 2-103). If the corresponding instance is visible for any reason other than because of the existence of an association, there will in general *be* no Association with which the LinkEnd can be linked; contradicting the multiplicity constraint.

This appears to be a serious problem, not resolvable by interpretation – at least, not in the presence of the popular static interpretation of associations –

---

[5] We emphasise: class diagram. Of course, as soon as a UML model includes behavioural information, it is to be expected that such questions will be undecidable, but we may hope to avoid this at the level where we consider only the information contained in a static structure diagram.

but definitely requiring a modification of the standard. There are two obvious approaches to fixing it. We could change the specification so that some Links are allowed not to be instances of any Association. Alternatively, we could allow some Associations not to be static. For example, we could add submetaclasses StaticAssociation and DynamicAssociation, and permit Links to be instances of either. Those favouring the static view of Association would then choose to record only the StaticAssociations in their class models, but could still use Links that were instances of DynamicAssociations in their collaborations.

(We might also attempt to resolve this by supposing that the stereotyped versions of LinkEnd, corresponding to sub-metaclasses of LinkEnd, might relax the multiplicity constraints in Fig. 2.17. But this would be odd, given that subclassifiers in a model are supposed to inherit participation in associations "subject to all the same properties": why would we have one rule for models and another for metamodels?)

We now leave the basic definition of associations and move on to slightly more esoteric matters.

3   Associations and Generalisation

Generalisation and associations interact in two related ways: first, we need to understand the implications of a classifier being involved both in an association and in a generalisation, and second, we need to understand the implications of the fact that Association is itself a GeneralizableElement.

3.1   Associations between Generalised/Specialised Classifiers

If classifier P' is a specialisation of P, and P and Q are associated by A, then because of substitutability considerations we expect P' and Q to be associated. Specifically, the restricted relation $\{(p,q) : p \in P', q \in Q, (p,q) \in A_R\}$ (in which an instance p of P' is linked to an instance q of Q iff p is linked to q when p is regarded as an instance of P) will often be an interesting design object. How is it reflected in the UML metamodel? On page 2-33 we read that any Classifier, being a GeneralizableElement, inherits associationEnd from its parent, meaning that The child class inherits participation in all associations of its parent, subject to

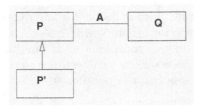

Fig. 4. A situation in which we expect an "induced" association between P' and Q

all the same properties. That is, P' and Q are intended to be associated *by the same association A as P and Q*. By applying this notion twice, we get also that if A relates P and Q, and if P', Q' are specialisations of P, Q respectively, then A is to be regarded as also associating P' and Q'.

This cannot quite be taken literally; the Association "knows" what classifiers it relates, and in our example, that will include P, not P'. However, it probably falls within the "by abuse of notation" family of pseudo-errors dear to mathematicians: that is, although to be completely formal we *could* invent the notion of a Generalization inducing, for every association A participated in by the parent GeneralizableElement, a new association participated in by the child GeneralizableElement, whose determined relation would be the restriction of A_R to instances of the child, it is not immediately clear that there is any advantage to modellers to be gained by so doing. We might feel that it was an advantage to have a distinct Association in the model for every pair of associated classifiers. Note that this need not have any impact on the diagrams. When an association is "simply" inherited in this way, modellers would not normally redraw the association at the P', Q' level, but we could if we chose regard this as mere notational convention: it does not have to determine whether there is or is not a new Association in the model. An alternative means to the same end is to regard this as a first example of generalisation of associations, which we consider next.

3.2   Association as GeneralizableElement

In the UML1.4 metamodel Association inherits from GeneralizableElement; that is, it is permitted for a model to contain an association which is said to be a generalisation of another. What should this most usefully mean? Note first that the "segment descriptor" style of definition, see e.g. [5] 2-75, is quite unhelpful in this context. [5] 2-21 makes a start[6]:

> The child must have the same number of ends as the parent. Each participant class must be a descendant of the participant class in the same position in the parent. If the Association is an AssociationClass, its class properties (attributes, operations, etc.) are inherited. Various other properties are subject to change in the child. This specification is likely to be further clarified in UML 2.0.

When we regard one association as a more exacting, or more specialised, version of another, it is natural to expect that a link of the more specialised association may be regarded as a link of the more general association, but not the other way round. Going further than this is problematic: notice that it is not completely clear what else subtyping for associations should really mean, or in what contexts substitutability should apply. We do not attempt to solve the problem here, partly because it seems futile given that the issue is already

---

[6] There is also the non-sentence on 2-71: "Moreover, the classifier, or (a child of) the classifier itself." which may be connected

highly complex and controversial for classes (although the controversy there is so old that it is often possible to overlook it). On a more technical UML note, notice that an AssociationEnd is *not* a GeneralizableElement, so the option of interpreting a subassociation between subclassifiers by subclassing all of the model classes involved is not available to us.

This will tend to lead us to a notion of generalisation of association which is merely a dressed-up version of subset inclusion of the links. In the absence of a clearly useful notion of subtyping for Associations, one could argue that it would be better to use a new name for these subset relationships, rather than allowing Association to participate in Generalizations. (The counter argument is that this would interfere with AssociationClass, which we consider in the next section.) This simple notion may well be sufficient for modelling purposes, however. A particularly simple case is when there are two different associations, say A and B, between the *same* classifiers, with the property that instances i and j are associated by A if they are associated by B, but may also be associated by A without being associated by B: that is, $B_R \subseteq A_R$. This situation rather frequently arises in modelling; consider, for example, relationships "is a member of" and "is captain of" between TeamMember and Team.

The other context in which generalisation of associations is often mentioned is the "animals eat food, cows eat grass" problem. For the benefit of any reader who has not met this classic before: suppose that classifier Cow is a specialisation of Animal whilst Grass is a specialisation of FoodStuff. The two specialisations of classifiers are quite independent: the inheritance of association "eats" does not ensure that Cows eat Grass, that is, that a Cow is linked by "eats" *only* to Grasses. (Nor should it, of course: the designer might have intended the specialisations to be independent.) However, we have already pointed out that the fact that subclassifiers inherit AssociationEnds means that there is an induced association between Cow and Grass whose links are exactly those that link instances of Cow to instances of Grass, and we have mentioned the possibility of modelling this, and the other associations induced by generalisations of classifiers, as a specialisation of the original "eat" association. Indeed, the confusion which may result from regarding all the various associations between FoodStuff, Grass, Cow and Animal as the same association "eats" in different guises argues for that approach.

4   Relationship with AssociationClass

In UML, an AssociationClass is both an Association and a Class. The idea is that this allows something which, conceptually, is a link between two objects also to own data and even provide behaviour in its own right. The classic example is the Account AssociationClass between two classes Bank and Customer.[7]

---

[7] Notice, however, that it is *not* permitted in UML1.4 for the same customer to have two or more accounts with the same bank, because the constraint we called C still applies! This is another argument for removing it.

In the metamodel, AssociationClass and Association are significantly different; it is not the case, formally, that an AssociationClass which does not happen to have any Features is the same as an Association. This is contradicted in the Notation Guide (3-89, my italics):

> Generalization may be applied to associations as well as to classes. To notate generalization between associations, a generalization arrow may be drawn from a child association path to a parent association path. This notation may be confusing because lines connect other lines. An alternative notation is to represent each association as an association class and to draw the generalization arrow between the rectangles for the association classes, as with other classifiers. This approach can be used even if an association does not have any additional attributes, because *a degenerate association class is a legal association*.

It would arguably be sensible to make the quotation from the Notation Guide above true: make Association a Classifier (so that it is automatically a GeneralizableElement, automatically has Instances, etc., rather than having these properties specifically added). We could then use the terms "association class" and "plain association" where it was necessary to distinguish between associations that do and do not have added features. It is not quite clear why this has not been the approach taken by the UML standard-writers. Perhaps the most likely explanation was that there was a desire to keep associations simple, reflected in the statement that an association is (simply) a set of tuples. However, we have argued against the idea that this view is tenable, and it is not clear what the remaining objections might be. The change would simplify the UML definition, in which there are currently many concepts which are defined twice, once for Classifiers and once for Associations (the family of XRoles, for example).

5   Related Work

Rumbaugh's paper [8] contains an interesting discussion of relationships in UML; his "contextual associations" are ancestors of my "dynamic associations".

Övergaard has considered the formalisation of associations as part of his remarkably complete operational semantics for UML [7]; see also [6]. His approach, however, is very complex, and it is not clear how to relate it to other approaches; at the least, neither of the cited references address the issues considered here explicitly.

Many people have formalised parts of UML's class diagrams, including associations. Almost all model associations as relations between sets of instances, discarding the conflicts principally considered here at an early stage: we may mention particularly [9], [3] (using Z and B respectively). Tenzer [10] takes a slightly different approach based on algebraic specification, but still with concerns different from those of the present paper. Most interesting for our purposes is [1], which (whilst also settling for modelling associations as relations) addresses some issues which have (deliberately) not been considered here, such as the changeability property of AssociationEnd.

6   Conclusions and Implications

In this paper we have attempted to shed light on the root causes of some persistent disagreements about the use of associations in modelling and their definition in UML.

The inclusive spirit of UML leads us initially to hope that it is possible to allow all of the variants described here, leaving the choice of which is appropriate to the designer. To a certain extent this is possible. The problem described in Section 2.4 needs to be fixed. However, we may certainly allow the designer to choose whether a dynamic or a static association is what they wish to represent, and it is straightforward, if we wish, to define stereotypes ≪static≫ and ≪dynamic≫ for the variants. Even for multiplicities, there seems to be no good reason why both of the definitions considered here should not be available. Thus particular profiles for UML could choose the appropriate variant.

We must leave open the question of whether Associations should be Classifiers: the idea is attractive, but this paper has not proposed the details of the considerable modification that this would require to the UML standard. We do recommend, however, that it should be seriously considered.

However, the question about whether a link is just a tuple or is a model element in its own right is more fundamental. There is no sensible way to make a notion of association that is just a set of tuples have a common ancestor with a notion in which instances of associations have identity. The former would have to avoid allowing a tuple to be a model element at all, because model elements, being instances, automatically have identity. In principle, we could make the core of UML define Association (and AssociationEnd etc.) but not Link; then another member of the UML family of languages (which for technical reasons would have to be a Preface, not a Profile as currently considered) could specify that its Associations were composed of Links. However, this would mean that core UML would not be able to make any use of Links, which would be an intolerably large change.

Fortunately, we hope to have convinced the reader that there is no need to insist on links being simply tuples: all the same benefits can accrue from having links which determine tuples, possibly with the constraint that no distinct links in the same association determine the same tuple.

Finally, it is important to point out one non-consequence of this decision. A major, perhaps the major, reason for wanting associations to be just relations is that relations are familiar mathematical objects which are easy to manipulate, and giving a UML diagram a semantics in such terms permits the use of such mathematical manipulations. The reader should not imagine that a refusal to define associations as being relations in the UML metamodel implies that this avenue is closed. The UML metamodel is not the semantics of UML, or at the very least, is not the only semantics of UML; semantic functions can and do define mappings from the metamodel to convenient mathematical domains. There is no reason why such a mapping should not map an Association to a relation, if the other information carried by the Association is not relevant for the purposes of the semantics. Indeed, the power of semantics is precisely this power to discard what is irrelevant *for some particular purpose*.

Acknowledgements. I would like to thank all the members of the pUML mailing list who participated in the discussion that provoked this work and in some private email. Especially, I thank Guy Genilloud for pointing out several problems with my early thoughts on the subject. Remaining mistakes are of course my own. I would also like to thank the participants in Dagstuhl Seminar 01041, especially the DMM group, for illuminating discussions. Gonzalo Génova and the anonymous referees also made helpful suggestions, though for space reasons not all were implemented.

References

1. Robert France. A problem-oriented analysis of basic UML static modeling concepts. In Loren Meissner, editor, *Proceedings of the 1999 ACM SIGPLAN Conference on Object-Oriented Programming, Systems, Languages & Applications (OOPSLA'99)*, volume 34.10 of *ACM Sigplan Notices*, pages 57–69, N. Y., November 1–5 1999. ACM Press.
2. Guy Genilloud. Informal UML 1.3 - remarks, questions and some answers. Contributed to the ECOOP Workshop on UML Semantics, Lisbon, Portugal, June 1999. Available from `http://icawww.epfl.ch/genilloud/`.
3. Régine Laleau and Fiona Polack. Metamodels for static conceptual modelling of information systems. Workshop on Defining Precise Semantics of UML, ECOOP, 2000.
4. Karl J. Lieberherr and Ian Holland. Formulations and benefits of the Law of Demeter. *ACM SIGPLAN Notices*, 24(3):67–78, March 1989.
5. OMG. *Unified Modeling Language Specification version 1.4 draft*, February 2001. OMG document 01-02-14 available from www.omg.org.
6. Gunnar Övergaard. A formal approach to relationships in the Unified Modeling Language. In Manfred Broy, Derek Coleman, Tom S. E. Maibaum, and Bernhard Rumpe, editors, *Proceedings PSMT'98 Workshop on Precise Semantics for Modeling Techniques*. Technische Universität München, TUM-I9803, 1998.
7. Gunnar Övergaard. *Formal Specification of Object-Oriented Modelling Concepts*. PhD thesis, Department of Teleinformatics, Royal Institute of Technology, Stockholm, Sweden, November 2000.
8. James Rumbaugh. Modeling and design. *Journal of Object Oriented Programming*, 11(4), 1998.
9. M. Shroff and R. B. France. Towards a formalization of UML class structures in Z. In *Proceedings of COMPSAC'97*, 1997.
10. Jennifer Tenzer. Translation of UML class diagrams into diagrams of transformation specifications.

iState: A Statechart Translator

Emil Sekerinski and Rafik Zurob

McMaster University, Department of Computing and Software
Hamilton, Ontario, Canada, L8S 4K1
emil|zurobrs@cas.mcmaster.ca

Abstract. We describe formal steps in the design of *iState*, a tool for translating statecharts into programming languages. Currently *iState* generates code in either Pascal, Java, or the Abstract Machine Notation of the B method. The translation proceeds in several phases. The focus of this paper is the formal description of the intermediate representations, for which we use class diagrams together with their textual counterparts. We describe how the class diagrams are further refined. The notions of representable, normalized, and legal statecharts are introduced, where normalized statecharts appear as an intermediate representation and code is generated only for legal statecharts.

1   Introduction

Statecharts, conceived as a visual formalism for the design of reactive systems [3], extend finite state diagrams by *hierarchy*, *concurrency*, and *communication*. These three extensions allow the specification of complex reactive systems that would be impractical without them. Because of the appeal of the graphical notation, statecharts have gained popularity and are now part of object-oriented modeling techniques [4,8,9].

The concepts of hierarchy, concurrency and communication, while intuitive on their own, interact in intricate ways. As a result, various formal semantics of statecharts and statechart tools interpret their interaction in different ways or impose different constraints, e.g. [2,5]. Our approach is to use a semantics of statecharts defined by a direct translation into a (nondeterministic) programming language, with the goal of the generated code being *comprehensible*: Having readable code allows us to get confidence in the translator and in the original statechart. Furthermore, we can use the translation scheme for explaining statecharts and illustrate this by the translator, rather than having to use a "third domain" for the definition. Finally, in order to allow the generated code to be further analyzed, it must be understood in the first place.

Such a translation scheme from statecharts into the Abstract Machine Notation of the B method [1], an extension of Dijkstra's guarded commands, was presented in [10]. The use of AMN is motivated by three aspects: first, AMN supports nondeterminism, allowing nondeterministic statecharts to be translated to nondeterministic AMN machines (that can be further refined into executable machines). This way, the nondeterminism is being preserved rather than eliminated by the translation, as other tools typically do. Secondly, AMN supports the *parallel* or *independent* composition of statements, which allows a simple translation of concurrent states. Thirdly, the B method allows invariants to be

M. Gogolla and C. Kobryn (Eds.): UML 2001, LNCS 2185, pp. 376–390, 2001.

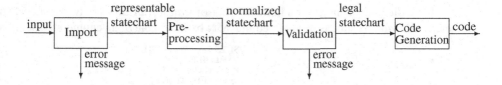

Fig. 1. Phases and intermediate representations of *iState*.

stated and checked. Invariants can express safety conditions and checking the invariant will then ensure that every event is going to preserve all safety conditions.

Compared to translation schemes used by other tools, ours can be characterized as *event-centric* rather than *state-centric*, as the main structure of the code is that of events. The scheme is suitable for those kind of reactive systems where events are processed quickly enough so that no queuing of events is necessary and where blocking of events is undesirable. To our experience so far, the resulting code is not only comprehensible, but compact and efficient as well.

The tool we built for implementing this translation scheme, *iState*, operates in four phases as shown in Figure 1. In this paper we focus on formally describing the intermediate representations, namely the *representable*, *normalized*, and *legal* statecharts. We refer to [10] for an illustration of the translation scheme and to [11] for details on the translation algorithms and for larger examples.

The input to *iState* is a textual representation of statecharts that is defined by a grammar. This representation can also be visualized through a LaTeX package. However, the *Strategy* pattern has been used for allowing other importers to be added, for example a graphical front end. Currently *iState* generates code in AMN, Pascal, and Java. The code generator uses an intermediate representation (which is similar to AMN) so that other languages can be added as needed. All complete statecharts in this paper have been processed and drawn by *iState* and its accompanying LaTeX package.

Section 2 presents briefly all statechart elements and the event-centric translation scheme. This prepares for the formalization of statecharts by class diagrams, together with their textual counterpart, in Section 3. This section illustrates a general way of translating class diagrams into a textual form. Normalized and flawed statecharts are characterized in Section 4 and legal statecharts are characterized in Section 5. The statechart model is refined by eliminating associations and basic algorithms on statecharts are discussed in Section 6. We give an example in Section 7 and conclude with a discussion in Section 8.

2 An Event-Centric Translation Scheme

We give the translation scheme of statecharts to AMN first for plain state diagrams, then for hierarchy, concurrency, and communication. Programs in AMN, called *machines*, consists of a section declaring sets (types), a section declaring variables, an invariant section, an initialization section, and a section with operations. The initialization has to establish the invariant and all operations have to preserve it.

State diagrams consists of a finite number of *states*, *transitions* between states, and an *initial state*. Its state is represented in AMN by a variable of an enumerated set type.

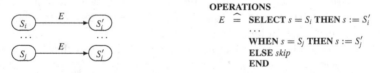

SETS $S = \{S_1, \ldots, S_n\}$
VARIABLES s
INVARIANT $s \in S$
INITIALISATION $s := S_1$

Upon an *event*, a state machine can make a transition from one state to another. Events may be *generated* by the environment. Transition arrows are labeled with an event and optionally labeled with a *parameter*, a *guard*, or an *action*. Events are translated to operations that may be called from the environment. The guard is an expression over the global variables and the action is a statement over the global variables.

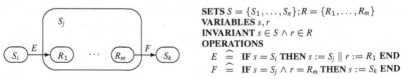

OPERATIONS
$E(p) \;\hat{=}\; \mathbf{IF}\ s = S_1 \wedge g\ \mathbf{THEN}\ s := S_2 \parallel a\ \mathbf{END}$

The operator $P \parallel Q$ stand for the parallel composition of statements P and Q: only the variables assigned by P and Q must be distinct. For brevity, we omit parameters, guards, and actions from now on. In general, several transitions can be labeled with the same event. Let $S_i, \ldots, S_j$ and $S'_i, \ldots, S'_j$ be all (not necessarily distinct) elements of S. If some of the *source states* of the transitions below coincide, several of the conditions in the select statement may be true, leading to a nondeterministic choice.

OPERATIONS
$E \;\hat{=}\; \mathbf{SELECT}\ s = S_i\ \mathbf{THEN}\ s := S'_i$
$\quad \ldots$
$\quad \mathbf{WHEN}\ s = S_j\ \mathbf{THEN}\ s := S'_j$
$\quad \mathbf{ELSE}\ skip$
$\quad \mathbf{END}$

Hierarchy. States can have two kinds of *substates* or *children*, *XOR states* and *AND states*. If a state has XOR children, then whenever the statechart is in that state, it is also in exactly one of its child states. We represent child states by an extra variable for each parent state. This generalizes to children having further offsprings. Transitions can break this hierarchy.

SETS $S = \{S_1, \ldots, S_n\}; R = \{R_1, \ldots, R_m\}$
VARIABLES s, r
INVARIANT $s \in S \wedge r \in R$
OPERATIONS
$E \;\hat{=}\; \mathbf{IF}\ s = S_i\ \mathbf{THEN}\ s := S_j \parallel r := R_1\ \mathbf{END}$
$F \;\hat{=}\; \mathbf{IF}\ s = S_j \wedge r = R_m\ \mathbf{THEN}\ s := S_k\ \mathbf{END}$

Transitions between child states are only taken if the statechart is in all their parent states. Transitions leaving a parent state also leave all the child states.

OPERATIONS
$E \;\hat{=}\; \mathbf{IF}\ s = S_i \wedge r = R_k\ \mathbf{THEN}\ r := R_l\ \mathbf{END}$
$F \;\hat{=}\; \mathbf{IF}\ s = S_i\ \mathbf{THEN}\ s := S_j\ \mathbf{END}$

Concurrency. If a state has AND children, then if the statechart is in that state, it is also in all its child states. AND states always have XOR children. AND states or *concurrent states* are separated by a dashed line in statecharts.

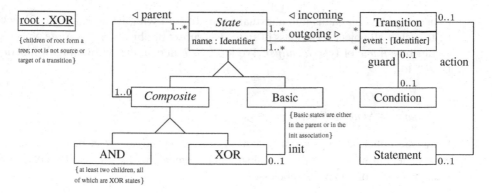

Fig. 2. Representable statecharts defined by a class diagram.

SETS $S = \{S_1, \ldots, S_n\}; Q = \{Q_1, \ldots, Q_l\}; R = \{R_1, \ldots, R_m\}$
VARIABLES s, q, r
INVARIANT $s \in S \wedge q \in Q \wedge r \in R$

Transitions can *fork* to several AND states and can *join* from several AND states.

OPERATIONS
$E \mathrel{\widehat{=}} \textbf{IF } s = S_i \textbf{ THEN } s := S_j \parallel q := Q_1 \parallel r := R_1 \textbf{ END}$
$F \mathrel{\widehat{=}} \textbf{IF } s = S_j \wedge q = Q_l \wedge r = R_m \textbf{ THEN } s := S_k \textbf{ END}$

Transitions in concurrent states labeled with the same event can be taken simultaneously. This is expressed by using parallel composition.

OPERATIONS
$E \mathrel{\widehat{=}} \textbf{BEGIN}$
$\quad \textbf{IF } s = S_i \wedge q = Q_j \textbf{ THEN } q := Q_j' \textbf{ ELSE } \textit{skip} \textbf{ END} \parallel$
$\quad \textbf{IF } s = S_i \wedge r = R_k \textbf{ THEN } r := R_k' \textbf{ ELSE } \textit{skip} \textbf{ END}$
$\textbf{END}$

Communication. Guards may contain *state tests* of the form **in** Q_i. These are translated to conditions of the form $q = Q_i$. Actions may contain statements that *broadcast* an event. These are translated by calling the the operation corresponding to that event. Section 7 presents an example.

3   The Statechart Model

We define *representable* statecharts in two ways, first graphically by the class diagram in Figure 2 and then in an equivalent textual form; this also illustrates a general way of translating class diagrams into a textual form. To start with, let us introduce *Object* to be the set of all objects. The class of states is a subset of objects. Every *State* object has an attribute *name* of type *Identifier*. We let $S \rightarrow T$ denote the set of all total functions from S to T.

> *State* $\subseteq$ *Object*
>
> *name* $\in$ *State* $\rightarrow$ *Identifier*

States are either composite states or basic states, but no state can be both basic and composite. Furthermore, *State* is an abstract class, meaning that all objects of class *State* must belong to of one of its subclasses.

> *Composite* $\subseteq$ *State* $\wedge$ *Basic* $\subseteq$ *State*
>
> *Composite* $\cap$ *Basic* $= \emptyset \wedge$ *Composite* $\cup$ *Basic* $=$ *State*

Likewise, composite states are either AND states or XOR states, but no state can be both an AND state and an XOR state. The class *Composite* is also abstract.

> *AND* $\subseteq$ *Composite* $\wedge$ *XOR* $\subseteq$ *Composite*
>
> *AND* $\cap$ *XOR* $= \emptyset \wedge$ *AND* $\cup$ *XOR* $=$ *Composite*

Transitions are also objects. Each transition has an optional attribute *event* of type *Identifier*. Spontaneous transitions have no event name attached to them. We let $S \nrightarrow T$ denote the set of all partial functions from S to T.

> *Transition* $\subseteq$ *Object*
>
> *event* $\in$ *Transition* $\nrightarrow$ *Identifier*

Conditions and statements are objects as well.

> *Condition* $\subseteq$ *Object* $\wedge$ *Statement* $\subseteq$ *Object*

The *guard* association relates every transition to at most one condition. Likewise, the *action* association relates every transition to at most one statement. We do not require that every condition and every statement relate to exactly one transition, as conditions and statements may appear as part of other conditions and statements, respectively. We let $S \nrightarrowtail T$ denote the set of partial, injective functions from S to T.

> *guard* $\in$ *Transition* $\nrightarrowtail$ *Condition*
>
> *action* $\in$ *Transition* $\nrightarrowtail$ *Statement*

The *outgoing* association relates every state to all the transitions leaving it. Any state may have zero or more transitions leaving it but every transition must have at least one state as origin. We let $S \leftrightarrow T$ denote the set of relations from S to T and $ran(R)$ the range of relation R.

> *outgoing* $\in$ *State* $\leftrightarrow$ *Transition*
>
> *ran*(*outgoing*) $=$ *Transition*

The *incoming* association relates every transition to all the states to which it leads. Any state may have zero or more transitions leading to it but every transition must have at least one state as destination. We let $dom(R)$ denote the domain of relation R.

$incoming \in Transition \leftrightarrow Transition$

$dom(outgoing) = Transition$

The *init* association relates every XOR state to exactly one basic state, which we call the *init* state. This is the state from which all the initializing transitions are leaving, the destinations of which are the initial states. *Init* states do not appear graphically in the statecharts, or perhaps just as fat dots. They are added here for allowing initializing and proper transitions to be treated uniformly. We let $S \rightarrowtail T$ denote the set of all total, injective functions from S to T.

$init \in XOR \rightarrowtail Basic$

The *parent* association relates states to their parent states, which must be composite states. Every state has at most one parent and every composite state must have at least one child.

$parent \in State \twoheadrightarrow Composite$

$ran(parent) = Composite$

We define the relation *children* to be the inverse of the function *parent*. We let R^{-1} denote the inverse of relation R.

$children \mathrel{\widehat{=}} parent^{-1}$

Every AND state has at least two children and all children of AND states are XOR states. We let $R[S]$ denote the image of set S under relation R and $card(S)$ the cardinality of the set S.

$\forall as \in AND . card(children[\{as\}]) \geq 2)$

$children[AND] \subseteq XOR$

All basic states are either in the *init* or *parent* association.

$ran(init) \cup dom(parent) = Basic$

The root state is an XOR state. Every composite state is a descendant of root. We let R^* denote the transitive and reflexive closure of relation R.

$root \in XOR$

$Composite \subseteq children^*[\{root\}]$

The root state must not be the source or target of a transition.

$root \notin dom(outgoing)$

$root \notin ran(incoming)$

This completes the textual definition of statecharts. For brevity, we define the conditions of guards and the statements of actions only graphically by the class diagrams in Figures 3 and 4. Their textual counterpart is derived analogously.

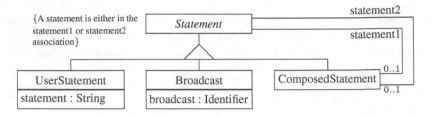

Fig. 3. Statements defined by a class diagram.

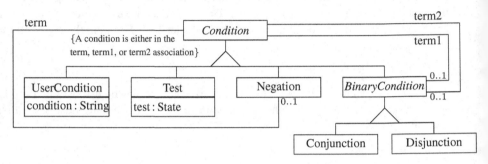

Fig. 4. Conditions defined by a class diagram.

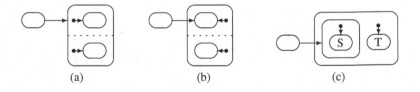

(a)   (b)   (c)

Fig. 5. (a) A statechart violating *targetsProper*. (b) A statechart violating *transitionsComplete*. (c) A statechart with two initial states S and T, both of which have reachable parents, but S is reachable and T is unreachable.

4   Normalized and Flawed Statecharts

The purpose of defining normalized statecharts is that recognizing whether a statechart is flawed or illegal is simplified. Normalization is also a first step in translating to code. Normalization adds those transition arrows to a representable statechart that are allowed to be left out. A statechart is normalized if two conditions hold, *targetsProper* and *transitionsComplete*, see Fig. 5 (a) and (b).

Targets of transitions must be either Basic or XOR states—if a target were an AND state, then that transition can be replaced by one that forks to all the XOR children of that AND state:

$$targetsProper \; \hat{=} \; ran(incoming) \subseteq Basic \cup XOR$$

As all XOR states have an *init* state, this condition allows the set of all basic target states to be determined by transitively following the *init* association.

If an AND state is entered by a transition, then all XOR children must be entered by that transition as well. We define the *closest common ancestor* of a set *ss* of states to be that state that is an ancestor of each state in *ss* and all other common ancestors are also its ancestor, where each state is also its own ancestor. We let $x\ R\ y$ denote that the pair of x and y is in relation R. For any $ss \subseteq State$ we define $cca(ss)$ by:

$$c = cca(ss) \Leftrightarrow \forall s \in ss \ . \ (c \ parent^* \ s \wedge \forall a \in State \ . \ (a \ parent^* \ s \Rightarrow a \ parent^* \ c))$$

The closest common ancestor exists for any set of states that consists of non-*init* states. The *path* from state s to a set ss of children of s is the set of all states that are on the paths from s to a state of ss. Formally, $path(s, ss)$ is defined as those states that are descendants of s and ancestors of states in s, excluding s but including the states of ss.

$$paths(s, ss) \ \hat{=} \ children^+[\{s\}] \cap parent^*[ss]$$

Following [5], the *scope* of a transition is the state closest to the root through which the transition passes.

$$scope(tr) \ \hat{=} \ cca(from(tr) \cup to(tr))$$

The states *entered* by a transition are all the states on the path from the scope of the transition to the targets of the transition. For symmetry, we define the states *exited* by a transition as all the states on the path from the scope of the transition to the sources of the transition.

$$entered(tr) \ \hat{=} \ path(scope(tr), to(tr))$$
$$exited(tr) \ \hat{=} \ path(scope(tr), from(tr))$$

This finally allows us to state the requirement that for all states entered by a transition, if the state is an AND state, then all children of that state must be entered by the transition as well. We let $R \rhd S$ denote the restriction of the range of relation R to set S, formally defined as $R; id(S)$.

$$transitionsComplete \ \hat{=} \ (entered \rhd AND); children \subseteq entered$$

Flawed statecharts are those that are legal but are likely incorrect. Flawed statecharts can appear while they are still being worked on, so by allowing them to be translated they can also be tested. However, *iState* issues a warning. More precisely, a statechart is *flawed* if a non-*init* state is unreachable, formally $\neg statesReachable$. Reachability is defined here solely based on the existence of transitions. A more involved definition taking the enabledness of transitions into account is possible, but quickly leads to conditions that are outside the scope of the tool.

A state is reachable if it is a target of a transition leaving a reachable state, or if it has a reachable descendant. The root state is assumed to be reachable. We define the relation *connected* to relate two states if there is a transition between them, including an *init* transition. We let $R; S$ denote the relational composition of relations R and S:

$$connected \ \hat{=} \ (outgoing; incoming) \cup init$$

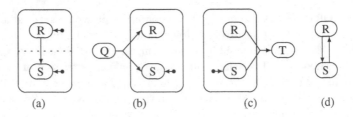

Fig. 6. Statecharts violating (a) *transitionsBetweenXORstates*, (b) *forksToANDstates*, (c) *joins-FromANDstates*, and (d) *spontaneousAcyclic*.

Then $connected^*[\{root\}]$ is the set of all states explicitly reachable from root. States may be reachable even if there is no transition leading to them, but they have a reachable child, see Fig. 5 (c). We therefore consider the ancestors of reachable states as reachable as well. The set of reachable states must be equal to the set of non-*init* states.

$$statesReachable \ \widehat{=} \ (connected^*; parent^*)[\{root\}] = ran(parent)$$

5   Legal Statecharts

Legal statecharts have to satisfy a number of conditions: *transitionsBetweenXORstates*, *forksToANDstates*, *joinsFromANDstates*, *spontaneousAcyclic*, *initTransitionsComplete*, *initToChildren*, *initNotTarget*, *initUnlabeled*, *noSpontaneousLeavingInitial*, *broadcasts-Acyclic*, see Fig. 6 and 7. All legal statecharts can be translated to code, even if they are flawed.

No transition must cross a concurrency line. This would be the case if the scope of a transition is an AND state.

$$transitionsBetweenXORstates \ \widehat{=} \ ran(scope) \subseteq XOR$$

Transitions must not fork to different children of an XOR state. More precisely, the closest common ancestor of any pair of targets of a transition must be an AND state.

$$forksToANDstates \ \widehat{=}$$
$$\forall tr \in Transition \ . \ (\forall s \in to(tr), t \in to(tr) \ . \ (s \neq t \Rightarrow cca(\{s,t\}) \in AND))$$

Dually, transitions must not join from different children of an XOR state. More precisely, the closest common ancestor of any pair of sources of a transition must be an AND state.

$$joinsFromANDstates \ \widehat{=}$$
$$\forall tr \in Transition \ . \ (\forall s \in from(tr), t \in from(tr) \ . \ (s \neq t \Rightarrow cca(\{s,t\}) \in AND))$$

A chain of spontaneous transitions must not contain a cycle. We define *spontaneous-Connected* to be the relation between states with a spontaneous transition between them, including *init* transitions. We let $R \rhd S$ denote the restriction of the range of relation R to those elements not in S; formally defined as $R; id(ran(R) - S)$.

$$spontaneousConnected \ \widehat{=} \ ((outgoing \rhd dom(event); incoming) \cup init$$

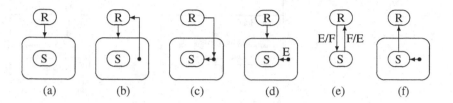

Fig. 7. Statecharts violating (a) *initTransitionsComplete*, (b) *initToChildren*, (c) *initNotTarget*, (d) *initUnlabeled*, (e) *broadcastsAcyclic*, and (f) *noSpontaneousLeavingInitial*

We let $id(S)$ denote the identity relation on set S.

$$spontaneousAcyclic \; \widehat{=} \; id(Transition) \cap spontaneousConnected^* = \emptyset$$

Every XOR state has a basic *init* state and there must be a transition leaving it.

$$initTransitionsComplete \; \widehat{=} \; ran(init) \subseteq dom(outgoing)$$

The transitions leaving the *init* state, the *init* transitions, must go to a child of the state to which the *init* state belongs.

$$initToChildren \; \widehat{=} \; init; connected \subseteq children$$

No *init* state must be a target of a transition.

$$initNotTarget \; \widehat{=} \; ran(init) \cup ran(incoming) = \emptyset$$

We define *initTransitions* to be the set of all transitions leaving some *init* state.

$$initTransitions \; \widehat{=} \; outgoing[ran(init)]$$

These transitions must not be labeled with an event or be associated with a guard or an action.

$$initUnlabeled \; \widehat{=}$$
$$initTransitions \cap (dom(event) \cup dom(guard) \cup dom(action)) = \emptyset$$

Transitions leaving an initial state must not be spontaneous.

$$noSpontaneousLeavingInitial \; \widehat{=} \; connected[initTransitions] \cap dom(event) = \emptyset$$

Finally, broadcasting must not be cyclic. For example, if on event E a transition broadcasts event F then no other transition must on event F broadcast event E. This generalizes to a cycle involving more than two transitions and it generalizes to the case when, say, on event E a transition does not itself broadcast event F but is followed by a chain of spontaneous transitions of which one broadcasts event F. We define *spontaneousSuccessor* to be the relation between transitions that relates a transition to all spontaneous transitions immediately following it.

$$spontaneousSuccessor \; \widehat{=} \; incoming; (outgoing \rhd dom(event))$$

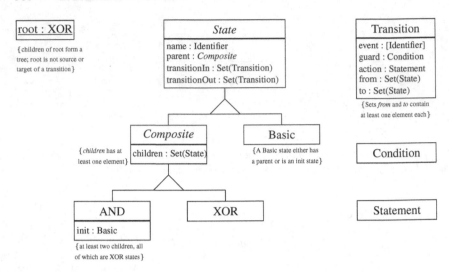

Fig. 8. Refined class diagram of representable statecharts. Associations with a zero-or-one multiplicity are refined by attributes that can be *null*. Associations with higher multiplicity are replaced by *set*-valued attributes that must not contain *null*.

The relation *transitionBroadcast* between *Transition* and *Identifier* relates each transition to all events that the action of the transition can broadcast, taking into account the way broadcast statement may be composed.

$$transitionBroadcast \ \widehat{=} \ action; (statement1 \cup statement2)^*; broadcast$$

The relation *triggers* between identifiers representing events relates each event to all events possibly triggered by that event, taking into account that transitions may be followed by a spontaneous transition also broadcasting events.

$$triggers \ \widehat{=} \ event^{-1}; spontaneousSuccessor^*; transitionBroadcast$$

The condition that broadcasting must not be cyclic is expressed by stating that *triggers* is not cyclic.

$$broadcastsAcyclic \ \widehat{=} \ id(Identifier) \cap triggers^* = \emptyset$$

6   Refinement of the Statechart Model

We refine the model of representable statecharts by replacing associations with attributes. For brevity we give only the class diagram, see Fig. 8. On the refined model, we formulate algorithms for validating statecharts. In formulating the algorithms we use some object-oriented notation. Let x be an object reference, a an attribute, C a class.

$$x.a \ \ \widehat{=} \ a(x)$$
$$x \ \textbf{is} \ C \ \widehat{=} \ x \in C$$

The procedure $cca(s,t)$ computes the closest common ancestor of non-*init* states s and t by first constructing paths from *root* to s and t, respectively, and then returning the last common state in those paths. The running time is bounded by the height of the tree, which is usually a small number.

```
procedure cca(s,t : State) : State
    var l,m : seq(State) ; r : State ;
    begin l := ⟨s⟩ ; m := ⟨t⟩ ;
        while s ≠ root do begin s := s.parent ; l := l ∘ ⟨s⟩ end ;
        while t ≠ root do begin t := t.parent ; m := m ∘ ⟨t⟩ ∘ m end ;
        repeat r := head(l) ; l := tail(l) ; m := tail(m)
        until l = ⟨⟩ ∨ m = ⟨⟩ ∨ head(l) ≠ head(m) ;
        return r
    end
```

The procedure $scope(tr)$ determines the scope of transition tr by repeatedly taking the closest common ancestor of the scope computed so far and an arbitrarily chosen element of the *to* and *from* set of that transition. It running time is proportional to the size of the *to* and *from* sets. We let $x :\in e$ denote the nondeterministic assignment of an element of the set e to x.

```
procedure scope(tr : Transition) : State
    var r : State ;
    begin {tr.from ≠ ∅ ∧ tr.to ≠ ∅}
        r :∈ tr.from ∪ tr.to ;
        for s ∈ tr.from ∪ tr.to − {r} do r := cca(r,s) ;
        return r
    end
```

The procedure *transitionsBetweenXORstates* checks for transitions crossing concurrency lines by checking whether the scope of each transition is and AND state. Its running time is proportional to the sum of the sizes of the *to* and *from* sets of each transition.

```
procedure transitionsBetweenXORstates : boolean
    begin
        for tr ∈ Transition do
            if scope(tr) is AND then return false ;
        return true
    end
```

The procedure *forksToANDstates* checks whether the targets of transitions go to different AND states. Its running time is proportional to the sum of the squares of the sizes of the *to* sets of all transitions.

```
procedure forksToANDstates : boolean
    var ss : set(State) ; s : State ;
    begin
        for tr ∈ Transition do
            begin ss := tr.to ;
```

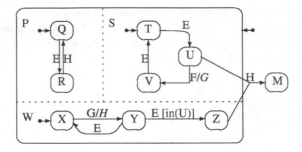

Fig. 9. An example with concurrent states, broadcasting, state tests, and nondeterminism.

```
        while ss ≠ ∅ do
            begin s :∈ ss ; ss := ss − {s} ;
                for t ∈ ss do if cca(s,t) is XOR then return false
            end
        end ;
    return true
end
```

An extended report contains the remaining algorithms [11]. In *iState* these are directly implemented in Java using the collection classes, some as part of the code generation.

7   Example

Below is the AMN code generated for the statechart of Figure 9. If the system is in substate Y of W and in substate U of S, then on event E the next substate of W could be either X of Z. This is reflected by the nondeterministic select statement in the B code. For Pascal and Java, a deterministic if-then-else statement is generated instead. A case statement is generated instead of a select statement if the selection is among different states, hence is deterministic. Pascal and B require that operations are defined before they are called. The code generator achieves this by a topological sort of the operations. For B, additionally auxiliary definitions have to be generated to avoid calls between operations. In any case, the resulting code will never contain circular calls.

```
MACHINE example
SETS
    ROOT = {noname0, M};
    S = {V, T, U};
    W = {Y, Z, X};
    P = {Q, R}
VARIABLES
    root, s, w, p
INVARIANT
    root ∈ ROOT ∧ s ∈ S ∧ w ∈ W ∧ p ∈ P
INITIALISATION
    root := noname0 || s := T || w := X || p := Q
DEFINITIONS
DEF_H ==
    IF root = noname0 THEN
```

```
            IF (w = Z) ∧ (s = U) THEN
                 root := M
            ELSE
                 IF p = R THEN
                      p := Q
                 END
            END
      END
   ;
   DEF_G ==
      IF (w = X) ∧ (root = noname0) THEN
            DEF_H ||
            w := Y
      END

OPERATIONS
H = DEF_H
;
E =
      IF root = noname0 THEN
            CASE s OF
                 EITHER V THEN s := T
                 OR T THEN s := U
                 OR U THEN skip
                 END
            END ||
            SELECT w = Y THEN
                 w := X
            WHEN (w = Y) ∧ (s = U) THEN
                 w := Z
            ELSE skip
            END ||
            SELECT p = Q THEN
                 p := R
            END
      END
;
G = DEF_G
;
F =
      IF (s = U) ∧ (root = noname0) THEN
            DEF_G ||
            s := V
      END
END
```

8   Discussion

We differ from UML statecharts in that we allow an *init*-state to have several outgoing
transitions, like any other state, possibly leading to nondeterminism. On the other hand,
we do require that the children of an AND state must be XOR states and not other AND
states. Currently *iState* does not support enter and exit actions, internal actions which
leave the system in the substate it was, history states for returning to the same substates
from which a superstate was left, timeout events $timeout(E, d)$, which are generated d
time units after event E is generated histories, overlapping states, sync states, and boolean
expressions for events, e.g. $E \wedge F$. These remain the subject of ongoing research. We
believe that most can be treated as straightforward extensions, possibly with the exception
of the last one.

There has been some controversy whether the changes of a transition are visible
in the current step or in the next step, see [5] for a recent discussion. Using parallel

(independent) composition for updating the states of concurrent states we follow [5] by adopting the next step approach: updating concurrent states results in compositions of the from **SELECT** g **THEN** $x := e \ldots \parallel$ **SELECT** h **THEN** $y := f \ldots$, in which the initial values of x and y is taken for evaluating expressions e, f, g, h—a generalization of the multiple assignment $x, y := e, f$.

A number of tools support code generation from statecharts, including xjCharts, withClass, and Rhapsody. The code generated by Rhapsody differs from ours in being state-centric rather than event-centric: Methods corresponding to each state are generated. Events, represented by event objects, are passed to these methods. If a state has a transition using the passed event, it *consumes* the event by initiating the transition and stopping other states from seeing the event.

Another class of tools is based on a semantics of statecharts by (extended) state machines, for example [5,6,7]. The essence of these approaches is that statecharts are first compiled into a state transition table which is then interpreted by a universal algorithm. The states correspond to *configurations* of the statechart, i.e. they correspond to sets of states in which the statechart can be at any time. Our translation scheme avoids the introduction of configurations by having a separate variable for each state and it avoids the generation of state transition tables.

Acknowledgement. We are grateful to the reviewers for their careful comments.

References

1. J.-R. Abrial. *The B Book: Assigning Programs to Meaning.* Cambridge University Press, 1996.
2. M. von der Beck. A comparison of statechart variants. In H. Langmaack, W.-P. deRoever, and J. Vytopil, editors, *Formal Techniques in Real-Time and Fault-Tolerant Systems*, Lecture Notes in Computer Science Vol. 863, pages 128–148. Springer Verlag, 1994.
3. D. Harel. Statecharts: A visual formalism for complex systems. *Science of Computer Programming*, 8:231–274, 1987.
4. D. Harel and E. Gery. Executable object modeling with statecharts. *IEEE Computer*, 30(7):31–42, 1996.
5. D. Harel and A. Naamad. The statemate semantics of statecharts. *ACM Transactions on Software Engineering and Methodology*, 5(5):293–333, 1996.
6. J. Lilius and I. P. Paltor. Formalising UML state machines for model checking. In R. France and B. Rumpe, editors, *UML'99 – The Unified Modeling Language Beyond the Standard*, Lecture Notes in Computer Science Vol. 1723, Fort Collins, Colorado, 1999.
7. E. Mikk, Y. Lakhnech, M. Siegel, and G. J. Holzmann. Implementing statecharts in Promela / Spin. In *Workshop on Industrial-Strength Formal Specification Techniques*, Boca Raton, 1998. IEEE Computer Society Press.
8. J. Rumbaugh, M. Blaha, W. Premerlani, F. Eddi, and W. Lorensen. *Object-Oriented Modeling and Design.* Prentice-Hall, 1991.
9. J. Rumbaugh, I. Jacobson, and G. Booch. *The Unified Modeling Language Reference Manual.* Addison-Wesley, 1999.
10. E. Sekerinski. Graphical design of reactive systems. In D. Bert, editor, *2nd International B Conference*, Lecture Notes in Computer Science Vol. 1393, Montpellier, France, 1998. Springer-Verlag.
11. E. Sekerinski and R. Zurob. From statecharts to code: A tool for the graphical design of reactive systems. Technical report, McMaster University, 2001.

Specifying Concurrent System Behavior and Timing Constraints Using OCL and UML

Shane Sendall and Alfred Strohmeier

Swiss Federal Institute of Technology Lausanne (EPFL)
Software Engineering Laboratory
1015 Lausanne EPFL, Switzerland
{Shane.Sendall,Alfred.Strohmeier}@epfl.ch

Abstract. Despite advances in implementation technologies for distributed systems during the last few years, little attention has been given to distributed systems within software development methodologies. The contribution of this paper is a UML-based approach for specifying concurrent behavior and timing constraints—often inherent characteristics of distributed systems. We propose a novel approach for specifying concurrent behavior of reactive systems in OCL and several constructs for precisely describing timing constraints on UML statemachines.

More precisely, we show how we enriched operation schemas—pre- and postcondition assertions of system operations written in OCL—by extending the current calculus with constructs for asserting synchronization on shared resources. Also, we describe how we use new and existing constructs for UML statemachines to specify timing constraints on the system interface protocol (SIP)—a restricted form of UML protocol statemachine. Finally, we discuss how both the extended system operation and SIP models are complementary.

Keywords: Unified Modeling Language (UML), Object Constraint Language (OCL), Pre- and Postcondition, Software System Specification, Concurrent Programming, Timing Constraints.

1 Introduction

Software-intensive systems are becoming an increasingly important and integral part of everyday life, many of which are distributed and constrained by long lists of non-functional requirements. Expectation and reliance on such software is making the software industry reevaluate the importance of software quality. Assuring that the software has a certain level of quality is a direct concern of the developer. Consequent to this, we believe that there is an increasing need for approaches that target the development of distributed systems and that can provide a reasonable level of quality assurance and rigor in development but still remain cost-effective in terms of time and effort.

In this paper, we propose an approach for specifying two common characteristics of distributed systems: concurrency and timing constraints. Even though such characteristics are inherent in more and more systems, largely due to the increasing amount of internet-based software, UML-based development approaches have paid surprisingly little attention to integrating timing constraints into specifications of functional requirements and to providing guidelines for dealing with synchronization dependencies between operations and resources. This is further compounded by UML's limited support, in general, for the specification of timing constraints and for mechanisms to describe synchronization of concurrent activities.

Our proposal extends our previous work: an approach that uses UML [10] and OCL [16] to specify the behavior of reactive systems [12][13]. Our approach has three principal views [11]:

M. Gogolla and C. Kobryn (Eds.): UML 2001, LNCS 2185, pp. 391–405, 2001.

- a model composed of descriptions of the effects caused by operations, which uses pre- and postcondition assertions written in OCL, called operation schemas;
- a model of the allowable temporal ordering of operations, called the system interface protocol (SIP); and
- a model that describes the system state used in the operation schemas, called the analysis class model (ACM).

In this paper, we show how we enriched operation schemas by extending the current calculus with constructs for asserting synchronization on shared resources. Also, we describe how we use new and existing constructs for UML statemachines to specify timing constraints on the system interface protocol (SIP)—a restricted form of UML protocol statemachine. Furthermore, we discuss how both the extended system operation and SIP models are complementary.

Our aim with this approach is to support the specification of distributed systems in software development practice. And therefore provide the designer with guidelines on synchronization dependencies between operations and timing constraints on their execution. We have a number of criteria that we use to evaluate and guide the development of our approach; for a full list and discussion see [13]. In this paper, we concentrate on two of them:

The descriptions of our approach should support the specification of:

- "quantifiable" non-functional requirements, such as performance constraints, in an integrated way with respect to the functional requirements;
- inherent concurrent properties of the system and quality of service properties.

The paper is composed of six sections. Section 2 briefly presents a case study of an auction system, which is used to highlight our approach and proposals for extending it for specifying concurrency and timing constraints. Section 3 describes our proposals for modeling timing constraints in UML protocol statemachines. Section 4 describes our proposals for specifying concurrent system operations with operation schemas. Section 5 presents related work and section 6 concludes the paper.

2 Auctioning System Case Study

For illustrating our proposals and for use as a common example throughout this paper, we describe an auctioning system, adapted from [6] and [7]. It has many similarities to internet auctioning sites, such as, eBay (www.ebay.com), and uBid (www.ubid.com), although it takes a more conservative view on bid validation. The auctioning system allows people to negotiate over the buying and selling of goods in the form of English-style auctions over the world-wide web. All potential users of the system must first enroll with the system; once enrolled they have to log on to the system for each session, where they are able to sell, buy, or browse the auctions currently running. Customers have credit with the system that is used as security on each and every bid. Customers can increase their credit by asking the system to debit a certain amount from their credit card.

A customer that wishes to sell initiates an auction by informing the system of the goods to auction with the minimum bid price and reserve price for the goods, the start date of the auction, and the duration of the auction, e.g., 30 days. The seller has the right to cancel the auction as long as the auction's start date has not been passed, i.e., the auction has not already started.

Customers that wish to follow an auction must first join the auction. Note that it is only possible to join an active auction. Once a customer has joined the auction, he/she may make a bid. A bid is valid if it is higher than the previous high bid augmented by the minimum bid increment (calculated purely on the amount of the previous high bid, e.g., 50 cent increments when bid is between $1-10, $1 increment between $10-50, etc.), and if the bidder has sufficient funds: the customer's credit with the system is at least as high as the sum of all his/her pending bids. Bidders are allowed to place their bids until the auction closes, and place bids across as many auctions as they please. Once an auction closes, the system calculates whether the highest bid meets the reserve price given by the seller (English auction style reserve price), and if so, the system deposits the highest bid price minus the commission taken for the auction service into the credit of the seller (credit internal to system). The auction system is highly concurrent—clients bidding against each other in parallel, and a client placing bids at different auctions and increasing his/her credit in parallel.

The system operations for the auctioning system are derived from the use case descriptions of the system, not supplied in this paper. A partial view of the input and output events exchanged between the system and its actor is shown, in figure 1, by a UML (specification-level) collaboration diagram. It shows only those events that interest us for the purposes of this paper, i.e., eleven different input events: proposeAuction, joinAuction, cancelAuction, increaseCredit, autoWithdraw, cancelAutoWithdraw, placeBid, logOff, logOn, enrolCustomer, and tick. The tick event from the clock triggers the system operations, closeAuction, increaseCredit and logOff. We use a special icon for the clock actor because we want to highlight that the actor and related events are special.

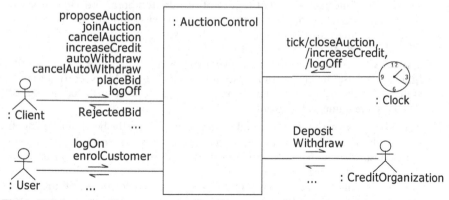

Fig. 1. Collaboration diagram summarizing the interaction between the system and its actors

The analysis class model for the auction control system is shown in figure 2. It shows all the domain concepts and relationships between them, the combination of which provides an abstract model of the state space of the system and defines the system boundary. This model is used as the basis for writing operation schemas, i.e., pre- and postcondition assertions for each system operation. Inside the system there are five classes, Auction, Bid, Goods, Customer, and Credit, and outside four actor classes, Clock, User, Client, and CreditOrganization. The system has six associations: HasHighBid links an auction with the current high bid if it has one, SellsIn links an auction with its respective seller (customer), Makes links a customer to his/her bids, JoinedTo links an auction to all its participants (customers), Has links a customer with his/her credit, and Guarantees links a bid with the credit that ensures its solvency. Finally, an <<id>> stereotyped association means that the system can identify an actor starting from an object belonging to the system. For example, given a Customer, cust, we can find its corresponding client actor with the navigation expression, cust.represents.

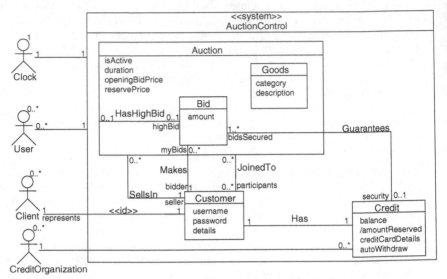

Fig. 2. Analysis class model for the **AuctionControl** system

The System Interface Protocol (SIP) defines the temporal ordering of system operations—one aspect of the behavior model of the system. An SIP is described with a UML state diagram. A transition in the SIP is triggered by an input event only if the SIP is in a state to receive it, i.e., there exists an arc with the input event and the guard evaluates to true. If not, the input event that would otherwise trigger an operation is ignored. We use the convention, also mentioned in the UML specification for protocol statemachines [10], that the action (in our case the operation) need not be explicit if it has the same name as the event.

The SIP for sequential and trivial systems can normally be described with a single statemachine. We have made the observation, however, that concurrent systems are better described with multiple views, one view per perspective on the concurrency. Apart from providing a clearer description of the protocol, a multi-view approach also has the advantage that it allows one to focus on and formulate intuitive timing constraints, i.e., one can define views that facilitate the description of certain timing constraints. However, a multi-view SIP requires rules for composing the different views to form the ensemble. Rules for composition, completeness, consistency, etc. are out of the scope of this paper.

We realize the concept of a "view of the SIP" in UML by introducing the stereotype <<SIPView>> to label the corresponding statemachines that describe a view. The SIP is defined by the composition of all the statemachines that are members of the same UML package and that are stereotyped <<SIPView>>.

Two SIP views for the AuctionControl system are shown in figure 3 and figure 4.

Figure 3 shows an <<SIPView>> statemachine that focuses on the concurrency related to clients interacting with the system. The ClientActivity state is an auto-concurrent statemachine, indicated by a multiplicity of many ('*') in the upper right-hand corner.

There is a statemachine for each client activity but their number is not predefined, hence the multiplicity many. The main substate of ClientActivity consists of three parallel states. The top-most state, SellingByAuction, is also auto-concurrent with the meaning that the respective client can be selling in many auctions in parallel. The time-triggered termination of the auction is specified by the time event, **after** (auctionPeriod). Similarly, the state in the middle, BiddingInAnAuction, is auto-concurrent with the meaning that the client can be participating (bidding) in many auctions in parallel. Finally, the unnamed, bottom-most state shows that the client may increase his/her credit at any moment. The client has also the option to allow the system to automatically debit his/her credit card once the customer's credit in the system drops below a certain amount. This is realized by the time event, **when** (creditIsBelowThreshold), which triggers the increaseCredit operation. Finally, the customer may log out explicitly or be logged out automatically if he/she has been inactive for a certain period of time, **when** (maxIdlePeriodExpired).

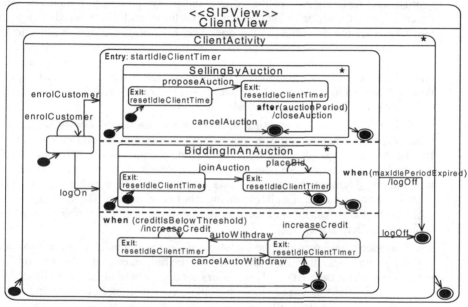

Fig. 3. Client view of the SIP for the AuctionControl system

The client SIP view is complete with respect to the criterion that all (input) events are accounted for, i.e., with respect to figure 1. However, it does not take into account the fact that an auction continues regardless of who logs on and off, and for example an auction may terminate, triggered by **after** (auctionPeriod), without the seller or any other participants being logged in. As a consequence, the event would be ignored because the statemachine is not in a state to trigger a transition. Hence, we need an additional view to model the case that is unaccounted for.

Figure 4 shows an <<SIPView>> statemachine that focuses on the concurrency related to auctions in the system. The AuctionActivity state is auto-concurrent with the meaning that many auctions can take place in parallel, one auction per state. This SIP view covers the full lifecycle of the auction and is thus independent of whether the seller and/or participants are logged on or not.

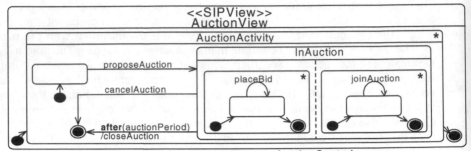

Fig. 4. Auction view of the SIP for the AuctionControl system

We now give a brief overview of the syntax, usage, and semantics of operation schemas. An operation schema declaratively describes the effect of the operation on a conceptual state representation of the system and by events sent to the outside world. It describes the *assumed* initial state by a precondition, and the required change in system state after the execution of the operation by a postcondition, written in UML's OCL formalism [16]. Moreover, we use the same interpretation of assertions as Larch [2]: when the precondition is satisfied, the operation must terminate in a state that satisfies the postcondition. Operation schemas as we define them here specify operations that are assumed to be executed atomically and instantaneously, hence no interference is possible (this assumption is revised in section 4).

Each system operation, proposeAuction, joinAuction, cancelAuction, increaseCredit, autoWithdraw, cancelAutoWithdraw, placeBid, logOff, logOn, enrolCustomer, and closeAuction (highlighted in figure 1) is described by an operation schema. However for reasons of size, we highlight just the placeBid operation schema, shown in figure 5. The placeBid operation schema describes the placeBid system operation. The placeBid system operation occurs as a consequence of a client placing a bid in an auction. The system must decide whether the bid is realistic and solvent; if so, the bid is recorded and the credit of the customer is decremented.

The **Operation** clause provides the signature of the placeBid indicating that the operation has three parameters: the target auction, auct, the bidder, cust, and the amount bid, proposedAmount. The **Description** clause offers a concise natural language description of the operation. The **Use Cases** clause provides cross-references to referring use cases. The **Scope** clause defines all the classes, and associations from the analysis class model defining the name space of placeBid. The last element of the **Scope** clause is an unnamed association that represents the composition association between Bid and Auction: the only unnamed association between the two classes. The **Declares** clause provides two kinds of declarations: naming, and aliases. The first in the list is a variable name, and the last three in the list are aliases, which are used as name substitutes. The **Sends** clause shows that only one type of event may be output by the operation, i.e., the event RejectedBid may be sent to Client actors. The **Pre** clause states that our assumption is that the operation is called while the auction is still active and the customer placing the bid is a participant in the auction.

The **Post** clause states that if the bid is realistic (first **if** block) and solvent (second **if** block) then the system decrements the amount bid from the credit of the bidding customer and records the bid in the system as the current high bid, and if there was a previous bid stored then the customer that held the previous high bid is reimbursed with the amount which he/she bid. Reimbursing a customer once his/her bid is no longer the current high bid allows him/her to immediately reuse the money, e.g., for bidding again or for bidding on other goods. If either the bid was not realistic or solvent then the client was sent an exception indicating that the bid was rejected. An event or exception is specified as sent by placing it in the event queue of the actor instance—**sent** is used as a shorthand for this purpose. For example, the second-to-last line of the **Post** clause states that an event occurrence of type RejectedBid, whose formal parameter reason matches the value #impossibleBid, was placed in the event queue of the client actor, denoted by the navigation expression cust.represents. Further details on the syntax, informal semantics, and usage of operation schemas can be found in [13][15].

Operation: AuctionControl::placeBid (auct: Auction, cust: Customer, proposedAmount : Money);
Description: A bid is placed with the system. The bid is accepted if it is >= to the highest bid so far plus the minimum increment or >= to the min. initial price if it is the first bid in the auction;
Use Cases: buy item under auction;
Scope: Auction; Bid; Customer; Credit; HasHighBid; Makes; Guarantees; JoinedTo; Has;
(Auction, Bid); -- the syntax we use for denoting an unnamed association
Declares:
    bid: Bid;
    prevHighBid: Bid **is** auct.highBid;
    creditOfPrevHighBid: Credit **is** prevHighBid.customer.credit;
    isFirstBid: Boolean **is** auct.bid->isEmpty ();
Sends:
    Type: Client::{RejectedBid};
Pre: auct.isActive **and** auct.participants->includes (cust); -- auction has not finished and cust is a participant
Post:
if (isFirstBid **and** proposedAmount >= auct.openingBidPrice) **or**
  (proposedAmount >= prevHighBid.amount + minBidIncrement (prevHighBid.amount)) **then**
    if cust.credit.balance@pre >= amount **then** -- if cust has sufficient funds
        cust.credit.balance -= proposedAmount & -- x -= 1 <==> x = x@pre + 1
        bid.oclIsNew (amount => proposedAmount) & -- attr of new bid, amount, has value proposedAmount
        cust.myBids->includes (bid) & -- <==> cust.bid = cust.bid@pre->including (bid)
        auct.bid->includes (bid) &
        bid.security = cust.credIt &
        auct.highBid = bid &
        if prevHighBid->notEmpty () **then** -- if there was a previous bid
            creditOfPrevHighBid.balance += prevHighBid.amount &
            prevHighBid.security->isEmpty ()
        endif
    else
        (cust.represents).**sent** (RejectedBid ((reason => #insufficientFunds)))
    endif
else
    (cust.represents).**sent** (RejectedBid ((reason => #impossibleBid)))
endif;

Fig. 5. Operation schema for the placeBid system operation

3 Modeling Timing Constraints

Many real-time and reactive systems exhibit behavior that is constrained by time-related factors, such as response time, waiting time, arrival rate, the number of events processed in some interval of time, etc. Specifying timing constraints is therefore an important activity in the development of such systems. Approaches that support the specification of real-time and reactive systems should support the notion of time-based constraints.

In our approach, the best candidate model for specifying timing constraints is the SIP. This is because statemachines already define part of the necessary vocabulary, such as, event dispatching, event triggered actions, time events, and ordering of events. We choose to keep timing constraints exclusive to the SIP, i.e., we disallow timing constraints in operation schemas, because we want to keep a clean separation of concerns between the functional description of operations, i.e., operation schemas, and their temporal ordering, i.e., the SIP.

We now describe the extensions that we have made to UML protocol statemachines for modeling timing constraints. We propose five time-based properties of transitions, summarized in figure 6. The first two denote absolute time, befT and aftT; the second two denote time periods, durT, distT; and the last one denotes a time frequency, freqT. Such variables provide direct access to timing information related to transitions, facilitating the expression of timing constraints.

Property	Description
befT	The (absolute) dispatching time for the last event that could trigger the transition (note the transition may or may not be taken; firing depends on whether the guard was true or not).
aftT	The (absolute) time at which the last transition completed (i.e., entered the destination state).
durT	The duration in time of the last transition from the source to the destination state (aka. execution time of the operation). It is equivalent to: aftT - befT, if and only if the guard holds.
distT	The amount of time since the last event was fired in the same activity at the *same* level in the state hierarchy, i.e., its destination was the source state of this transition.
freqT	The frequency with which the transition is taken, i.e., the number of times the transition was taken over a certain sampling period: #transitions/period.

Fig. 6. A summary of the five proposed time-based transition properties in UML statemachines

Some timing constraints are invariant. Consider the example where the system must enforce that an operation opX never takes longer than 5 seconds to execute. This is a constraint on the performance of the system. In OCL, we could formulate this with the following invariant that is attached to the respective transition (the transition that triggers the operation opX):

```
<<invariant>>
self.durT <= 5*Sec
```

The interpretation of this invariant is that every time the transition is fired (i.e., the guard evaluates to true) its duration, the time from source to destination states, is always less than or equal to five seconds. In the case that an event is dispatched but rejected, the durT variable is not affected and thus there is no obligation from the invariant.

Note that the context is the transition, which is referred to as self. According to OCL, the self keyword is optional, i.e., it may be dropped when the context is clear.

Apart from stating timing invariants, it is often necessary to state the circumstances in which events can not or should not be served by the system. Guards on transitions can be used for that purpose. Using the transition properties summarized in figure 6, we can define time expressions in guards. For example, we could define a transition with a guard that rejects all eventXs that are dispatched less than 3 seconds after the previous event that entered the source state:

```
[distT >= 3*Sec] eventX / action
```

In this case, we used the distT variable, which can be thought of as defining the amount of time spent in the source state of the transition. We could have equally, and perhaps more intuitively, defined distT as a property of states rather than transitions.

It is also useful to be able to relate an action to a timing constraint failure (defined by a guard), e.g., output an exception if a time expression in the guard fails. However, according to the UML specification (pp. 2-170 of [10]), guards on transitions should not use expressions that cause side-effects. In figure 7 (top), we show how we might model such "guard failure" actions in standard UML (plus our proposed time-based properties of transitions), where **now** is a variable denoting the current time. In the same figure (bottom) we show our proposed equivalent shorthand notation. Note that {transA} is a transition label used to identify the transition.

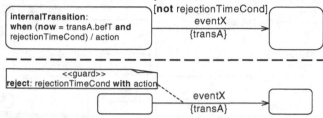

Fig. 7. Proposed "guard failure" actions in UML statemachines; *Top*: Using standard UML notation; *Bottom*: Using our proposed shorthand notation;

The BNF-like grammar of our proposed shorthand notation is as follows:

guard == ["**cond**:" boolean_expression ';'] ("**reject**:" boolean_expression ["**with**" action ';'])*

The "transition guard" shorthand contains two types of clauses: **cond** and **reject**. **cond** indicates the condition that must hold for the transition to be fired; it is equivalent to the original guard definition. We do not, however, allow time expressions to be written in this clause. **reject** defines a time-based boolean expression and an optional action. If the boolean expression evaluates to true then the dispatched event is rejected and the action is executed, if there is one. There may be many **reject** clauses, where the meaning is the disjunction of the boolean expressions of each **reject** clause. The meaning of the proposed guard as a whole is thus defined by the combination of its two parts: the condition of the **cond** clause must be true and the boolean expressions of all the **reject** clauses must be false for the transition to have permission to fire. For example, we attach a guard, which makes use of the "transition guard" shorthand, to the increaseCredit event transition of figure 3. It ensures that all increaseCredit events that are made at a frequency greater than 1 per second are rejected and a SystemOverload exception is output:

<<guard>>
reject: freqT > 1*Hz **with** ^SystemOverload;

We emphasize that all time-related guard expressions are to be placed in the **reject** clause and not in the **cond** clause nor in the operation schemas.

Applying the proposals for time-based constraints made up until now, we present a number of timing constraints on two SIP views of the AuctionControl system: AuctionView and BiddingView, shown in figure 8. Note that to be able to identify transitions easily, we label the ones we reference, e.g., {a}. Also, we attach guards to transitions by UML notes, which use <<guard>> stereotypes. In this way, we can avoid transition clutter, i.e., we avoid to put all the information directly on the transition.

The invariant in the UML note 1 states that the system must guarantee that an auction starts within 5 seconds provided that there are less than or equal to 500 active auctions, and within 10 seconds if the number of active actions is between 500 and 1000. The invariant in the UML note 2 makes references to the two labels, {a} and {b}, which are used to identify the respective transitions. The constraint states that every time an auction activity fires transition a, then b does not occur within 15 minutes of it nor more than 1 year afterwards. Note that in this example we changed the AuctionView SIP view from a definitive auction deadline (i.e., **after** (AuctionPeriod) / closeAuction) to one that depends on the idle period between bids (i.e., **when** (MaxIdleBidPeriodExpired) / closeAuction). These two invariants are performance constraints.

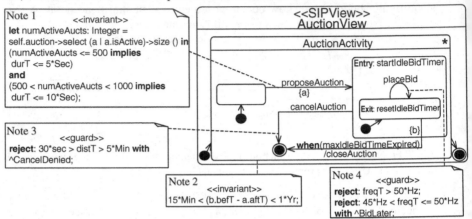

Fig. 8. Timing constraints attached to two SIP views

The constraint in the UML note 3 specifies a guard on the cancelAuction event transition with the meaning: any cancelAuction event that is dispatched within 30 seconds of the proposeAuction transition or more than 5 minutes after it is rejected and an exception CancelDenied is output. The guard in the UML note 4 states, for a particular auction, that all bids received when the frequency of the transition exceeds 50 Hertz are simply rejected; and that all bids that are received between 45 and 50 Hertz will receive a BidLater exception.

When timing invariants and guards are united with time activated transitions as shown in figure 3 and figure 4 (**when** and **after** time events), we have quite some possibilities for defining behavior that is constrained by time-related factors.

4 Modeling Concurrent Operations by Schemas

The online auction system is inherently concurrent at the auction level—clients placing bids in parallel—and at the level of the client's credit—a client placing bids at different auctions and increasing his/her credit in parallel. The different views of the SIP highlight the concurrency between operations. Nevertheless the instantaneous and atomic execution assumption on operations means that operation schemas describe operations that execute in isolation, i.e., there is no interference between operations. Furthermore, if the developer was to design from the placeBid operation schema in figure 5, s/he would be given no help whatsoever as to which resources are possibly shared and what synchronization dependencies on resources there are between these operations.

In this section, we propose extensions to the calculus of operation schemas for the purpose of providing such information to designers, according to the concurrency defined by the SIP. We therefore release the atomicity and instantaneity hypothesis on operations (that was defined in section 2) and allow the specification of fully concurrent operations—operations that are possibly changing the state of the system in parallel.

Absence of interference when updating a shared resource is a safety property of the system. Interference can result in corruption of the resource and erroneous behavior. Exclusive access to a shared resource when updating it is a property that we want all possible solutions to exhibit. We propose to impose it in the model as part of the contract on the software. To highlight this constraint on shared resources in operation schemas, we add a clause to the operation schema format called **Shared**. Resources listed in this clause are constrained to be updated in mutual exclusion by the operation.

When writing operation schemas for concurrent operations, the easiest way to formulate the pre- and postconditions is to write them like we would do if there were no interference by other concurrent operations. Unfortunately, this is not possible when describing changes to a shared variable that can be changed by competing concurrent operations. In particular, the OCL @pre and the implicit "@post" suffixes are almost meaningless for shared variables when describing system state changes in postconditions. Instead, the values of shared variables immediately before and after an update under mutual exclusion are of prime importance. For example, if an operation adds 7 to a shared integer variable val, the effect that one wishes to state is that 7 was added to the value of the variable that was observed immediately before the mutually exclusive update. We, therefore, introduce the suffixes @preAU and @postAU for shared variables, which signify the state of the prefix variable immediately before and after an Atomic Update by the operation, respectively. Thus, we would state the following to signify that 7 was added to the shared variable val:

   val@postAU = val@preAU + 7

Furthermore, when we need to read the value of a shared variable, we need to ensure that we are referring to a consistent value of the variable, i.e., the variable was read outside of any period where the variable was updated. Any consistent value of a shared variable that is taken within the period of the operation's execution is denoted by suffixing the variable name by @rd. The possible suffixes for shared and unshared variables and their meanings are summarized in figure 9.

Schemas can still be structured with *if-then-else* blocks. The branch conditions are evaluated atomically with respect to the blocks, i.e., there is no possibility for racing between the evaluation of the branch conditions and the evaluation of the effects. Also, *if-then-else* blocks are evaluated immediately, i.e., a condition is either true or false, and there is no waiting for the condition to become true.

Also, a situation that can arise in a concurrent environment is when a group of effects relies on a certain condition to stay true during its whole "execution". We model such situations with *rely* blocks (based on the concept of rely conditions, first introduced by Jones [3], see section 5). The *rely* block states a condition that must be true immediately before, immediately after, and during the execution of the body of the block for the body to take effect. If the rely condition does not stay true throughout execution, then the effect of the *fail* part of the rely block is observed to execute instead. The *rely* block imposes neither immediate nor wait semantics on the condition, i.e., an implementation that does a wait until the condition becomes true and then tries to execute the body, or one that fails if the condition is not initially true are both valid refinements. Also, the *rely* block does not stop the implementation from making several attempts (and associated rollbacks) at executing the body of the block. It does however require that if the condition remains true, then the effect described by the body of the block will hold. Also, *rely* blocks should not be nested in *if* blocks due to the immediate evaluation semantics of the *if*. But, *rely* blocks nested in *rely* blocks, and *if* blocks nested in *rely* blocks are possible.

	Shared variables	Unshared variables
x@pre	The last possible *consistent* value of x immediately before the start of the operation's execution.	The value of x immediately before the execution of the operation.
x@post	The first possible *consistent* value of x immediately after the termination of the operation's execution.	"@post" is normally implicit (see x).
x@preAU	The value of the variable immediately before the operation's (atomic) update of x.	– (unused)
x@postAU	The value of the variable immediately after the operation's (atomic) update of x.	– (unused)
x@rd	Any *consistent* value of x inside the bounds of the operation execution (but outside of any updates to x).	– (unused)
x	only allowed in eventually functions.	The value of x immediately after the execution of the operation.

Fig. 9. A summary of the possible variable suffixes in postconditions

Figure 10 shows the operation schema (minus a few clauses that stay unchanged) for the placeBid system operation. It applies our proposed extended calculus to the placeBid operation schema of figure 5. The **Operation** and **Pre** clauses have not changed from figure 5. The **Declares** clause is also similar except it uses time expressions in the name substitute. The **Shared** clause defines all associations and variables that are shared. The **Post** clause shows a number of differences from the schema of figure 5. The *rely* block requires that the balance of the bidder's credit stays above or equal to zero and the auction stays active for the body to have effect. If this condition cannot be guaranteed then one or more of the *fail* parts are observed to execute, e.g., one or two RejectedBid exceptions are output to the bidding client. The body of the *rely* block changes the state of the system in the same way as described by the schema in figure 5, except there are shared variables, which are updated in mutual exclusion. It states that if the proposed bid is realistic (because we rely on the fact that it is solvent), then it is recorded and set as the high bid; also the bidder gets the proposed amount debited from his/her credit, and if there was a previous bid, then the corresponding bidder is reimbursed the credit that was previously taken for the bid.

Both the schemas of figure 5 and figure 10 place an obligation on the system to reimburse the previous high bid. This "undoing" obligation gives bidders the freedom to use the credit on other auctions and not to have it pointlessly locked up on a bid that will not win. One could nevertheless argue that this is overly restrictive and that abstracting at a higher level would make the feature useless and the specification more concise. We can realize such an abstraction by using the temporal logic operator, *eventually* [1]. The *eventually* operator evaluates to true if its corresponding condition becomes true in some future state. We propose to denote this operator in our calculus by the function eventually (...), which takes a boolean expression as parameter.

Using *eventually* we can oblige the system to only debit the bidder's credit, if and only if the bid wins the auction (i.e., in the future). Highlighting this in the placeBid operation schema, we could integrate the following *if* block into the body of the *rely* block, and remove the effects that debit and credit the current and previous bidders' balance. We refer to the schema that includes this constraint as version 2, and the original, shown in figure 10, as version 1.

```
    if eventually (not auct.active and auct.highBid = bid) then  -- if, in the future, the bid wins then
        cust.credit.balance@postAU = cust.credit.balance@preAU - proposedAmount &
        bid.security@postAU = cust.credit
    endif
```

The constraint states that if some time in the future the auction is closed and the current bid is in fact the winner, then the bidder's credit is debited by the bid amount and set as security on the bid. Note that in most cases it should be insured that the *eventually* function can be evaluated after some finite time or when some combination of events occur. In the previous example, for instance, when the auction closes, the *eventually* function can be evaluated.

```
Operation: AuctionControl::placeBid (auct: Auction, cust: Customer, proposedAmount : Money);
Declares: bid: Bid;
        prevHighBid: Bid is auct.highBid@preAU; -- name substitution
        creditOfPrevHighBid: Credit is prevHighBid.customer.credit;
        isFirstBid: Boolean is auct.bid@preAU->isEmpty ();
Shared:  Collection(Bid): Makes; Bid: HasHighBid; Collection(Bid): Guarantees;
        Collection(Bid): (Auction, Bid); isActive::Auction; balance::Credit;
Pre: auct.isActive and auct.participants->includes (cust);
Post:
rely cust.credit.balance@rd >= 0 and auct.isActive@rd then
    if (isFirstBid and proposedAmount >= auct.openingBidPrice) or
    (proposedAmount >= prevHighBid.amount + minBidIncrement (prevHighBid.amount)) then
        cust.credit.balance@postAU = cust.credit.balance@preAU - proposedAmount &
        bid.ocllsNew ((amount => proposedAmount)) &
        cust.myBids@postAU->includes (bid) &
        auct.bid@postAU->includes (bid) &
        bid.security@postAU = cust.credit &
        auct.highBid@postAU = bid &
        if prevHighBid->notEmpty () then -- there was a previous bid
            creditOfPrevHighBid.balance@postAU =
                creditOfPrevHighBid.balance@preAU - prevHighBid.amount &
            prevHighBid.security@postAU->isEmpty ()
        endif
    else
        (cust.represents).events-> includes (RejectedBid ((reason => #impossibleBid)))
    endif
fail (cust.credit.balance@rd >= 0) then
    (cust.represents).events-> includes (RejectedBid ((reason => #insufficientFunds)))
fail (auct.isActive@rd) then
    (cust.represents).events-> includes (RejectedBid ((reason => #auctionClosed)))
endre;
```

Fig. 10. Operation schema for placeBid system operation; non-atomic & non-instantaneous version

How an implementation meets the schema be it version 1 or version 2 is another issue that we now discuss. An implementation could, for example, encapsulate the placeBid operation by a transaction and simply abort and rollback once it finds out that it was outbid [7]. This solution would be the most obvious given the schema version 1. However, schema version 2 is less restrictive. For example, a naive implementation could grab the lock on the bidder's credit and hold onto it until the end of the auction. This would mean that all bids on other auctions by the same bidder that come afterwards would be blocked waiting on the end of the auction of the first bid. This could lead to starvation, for instance, the auctions for later bids could finish before the auction of the first bid, etc.

Research is ongoing on integrating a design of a concurrent system into an architecture [5].

5 Related Work

Formal methods have much to say about the specification of concurrency and timing constraints in systems. The approach described by Lano in [8] provided some motivation for this work. It described extensions to Z and VDM for describing concurrency and timing constraints. Z [14] and VDM [4] are both rich formal notations but they suffer from the problem that they are very costly to introduce into software development environments, as is the case with most formal methods, because of their high requirements in mathematical mastery.

A number of temporal logic operators have been proposed over the years to describe concurrent and reactive systems [1]. The advantage of temporal logic operators is that one can obtain an abstract and concise description of a concurrent system. The disadvantage, however, is that the designer is not given much information on how s/he might go about tackling the problem.

Meyer proposes a programming model for concurrent programming called Simple Concurrent Object-Oriented Programming (SCOOP) [9]. SCOOP reinterprets the preconditions of design-by-contract as guards and enforces that all methods are atomically accessed. Therefore, SCOOP assumes a particular object-oriented concurrency framework. In the context of system-level operations, we prefer to take a more fine-grained approach to concurrency control—giving the developer more freedom in designing a solution.

Our motivation for the rely conditions of section 4 comes from the work by Jones [3]. He proposed supplementary clauses to pre- and postconditions called rely and guarantee conditions; they allow one to state under what circumstances the postcondition makes sense in the presence of concurrency. If an operation is invoked in a situation when the precondition is false, or if during the execution of the operation the rely condition becomes false, then the specification does not state what the outcome should be. Otherwise the postcondition will be true at the end of the execution and the guarantee condition will have been maintained throughout. However, it often the case that the enforcement of the rely condition during the whole execution of the operation is a constraint too strong. This is a consequence of stating concurrency constraints at a coarse grain, in a top-down approach. For this reason, we propose a rely condition that can be used at a finer-grain level.

6 Conclusion

The contribution of this paper is a UML-based approach for specifying concurrent behavior and timing constraints. We proposed a novel approach for specifying concurrent behavior of reactive systems based on joint use of operation schemas and UML protocol statemachines (SIP). We also proposed constructs for precisely describing timing constraints in the SIP. The operation schemas and the SIP are complementary: the operation schemas describe the functional responsibilities of the system and the SIP defines the temporal ordering between operations. The extensions to the SIP for specifying timing constraints allow one to formalize behavior that is constrained by time-related factors. The extensions to operation schemas provide guidelines to developers for dealing with synchronization dependencies between operations and resources. Consequently, we believe our approach offers developers better support for designing distributed systems that exhibit concurrent and time-constrained behavior.

References

[1]   E. Emerson; *Temporal and Modal Logic*. In J. van Leeuwen (Ed.), Handbook of Theoretical Computer Science, Amsterdam, 1989, pp. 995-1072.

[2]   J. Guttag et al. *The Larch Family of Specification Languages*. IEEE Trans Soft Eng 2(5), Sept. 1985.

[3]   C. Jones; *Tentative steps toward a development method for interfering programs*. ACM Transactions on Programming Languages and Systems, 5(4):596-619, 1983.

[4]   C. Jones; *Systematic Software Development Using VDM*. Prentice Hall, 1986.

[5]   M. Kandé and A. Strohmeier; *Towards a UML Profile for Software Architecture*. UML 2000 — The Unified Modeling Language: Advancing the Standard, Third International Conference, York, UK, October 2-6, 2000, S. Kent and A. Evans (Ed.), LNCS (Lecture Notes in Computer Science), no. 1939, pp. 513-527; Also available as Technical Report (EPFL-DI No 00/332).

[6]   J. Kienzle, A. Romanovsky and A. Strohmeier; *Open Multithreaded Transactions: Keeping Threads and Exceptions under Control*. 6th International Workshop on Object-Oriented Real-Time Dependable Systems, Italy, January 2001.

[7]   J. Kienzle; *Open Multithreaded Transactions: A Transaction Model for Concurrent Object-Oriented Programming*. Ph.D. Thesis EPFL-DI, no 2393, Swiss Federal Institute of Technology in Lausanne, Software Engineering Lab., 2001.

[8]   K. Lano; *Formal Object-Oriented Development*. Springer-Verlag, 1995.

[9]   B. Meyer; *Object-Oriented Software Construction*. Second Edition, Prentice Hall, 1997.

[10] OMG Unified Modeling Language Revision Task Force; *OMG Unified Modeling Language Specification*. Version 1.4 draft, February 2001. http://www.celigent.com/omg/uml-rtf/

[11] S. Sendall and A. Strohmeier; *UML-based Fusion Analysis*. UML '99 - The Unified Modeling Language: Beyond the Standard, Second International Conference, Fort Collins, CO, USA, October 28-30, 1999, R. France and B. Rumpe (Ed.), LNCS (Lecture Notes in Computer Science), no. 1723, 1999, pp. 278-291, extended version also available as Technical Report (EPFL-DI No 99/319).

[12] S. Sendall and A. Strohmeier; *From Use Cases to System Operation Specifications*. UML 2000 — The Unified Modeling Language: Advancing the Standard, Third International Conference, S. Kent and A. Evans (Ed.), LNCS (Lecture Notes in Computer Science), no. 1939, pp. 1-15; Also available as Technical Report (EPFL-DI No 00/333).

[13] S. Sendall and A. Strohmeier; *Using OCL and UML to Specify System Behavior*. Technical Report (EPFL-DI No 01/359), Swiss Federal Institute of Technology in Lausanne, Software Engineering Lab. 2001; to be published in Lecture Notes in Computer Science, Springer-Verlag.

[14] J. Spivey; *The Z Notation: A Reference Manual*. Prentice Hall, 1989.

[15] A. Strohmeier and S. Sendall; *Operation Schemas and OCL*. Technical Report (EPFL-DI No 01/358), Swiss Federal Institute of Technology in Lausanne, Software Engineering Lab., 2001.

[16] J. Warmer and A. Kleppe; *The Object Constraint Language: Precise Modeling With UML*. Addison-Wesley 1998.

Formalization of UML-Statecharts

Michael von der Beeck

BMW Group
Michael.Beeck@bmw.de

Abstract. The Unified Modeling Language (UML) has gained wide acceptance in very short time because of its variety of well-known and intuitive graphical notations. However, this comes at the prize of an unprecise and incomplete semantics definition. This insufficiency concerns single UML diagram notations on their own as well as their integration. In this paper, we focus on the notation of UML-Statecharts. Starting with a precise textual syntax definition, we develop quite a concise structured operational semantics (SOS) for UML-Statecharts based on labeled transition systems. Besides the support of interlevel transitions and in contrast to related work, our semantics definition supports characteristic UML-Statechart features like the history mechanism as well as entry and exit actions.

1 Introduction

The Unified Modeling Language (UML) [20] has become quite a successful specification language in very short time. It already constitutes a de-facto-standard in industrial applications. Its very advantages are given by a great variety of intuitive and mostly well-known notations for different kind of information to be specified: requirements, static structure, interactive and dynamic behaviour as well as physical implementation structures. However, this intuitive appeal comes at the prize of an insufficient definition. Whereas the UML syntax is defined in quite a precise and complete manner, its semantics is not. The official UML documentation [13] contains a chapter titled "semantics", but on the one hand quite a big part of it only considers what is usually called "static semantics" in compiler theory, i.e. the parts of the syntax which are not context-free, on the other hand the parts which in fact consider semantics contain English prose and therefore lack preciseness and completeness.

This serious insufficiency concerns single diagram notations like Statecharts, sequence diagrams, and class diagrams as well as their integration. In this paper we focus on the Statecharts version contained in UML – in the following denoted as UML-Statecharts.

The "classical" Statecharts language, developed by Harel [5], constitutes a very successful intuitive state-based graphical specification language which enhances finite automata by hierarchy, concurrency, and a sort of broadcast communication. However, its semantics definition required tremendous efforts. A lot of work deals with precisely defining the Statecharts semantics in such a way that certain semantic properties – Statecharts specific like causality as well as general ones like compositionality – are fulfilled [17,21,11,6,12,9,10,22]. Some of the semantic difficulties therein also exist for UML-Statecharts e.g. with respect to interlevel transitions, whereas some intricacies – like those caused by set-valued events or negated events – do not exist. However, only a small amount of work has been published on UML-Statecharts in the past.

M. Gogolla and C. Kobryn (Eds.): UML 2001, LNCS 2185, pp. 406–421, 2001.

The main contribution of this paper consists of a formal, SOS-style semantics definition for UML-Statecharts. The SOS-approach of Plotkin [16] combines an intuitive operational understanding with precisenenss and supports the definition of a compositional semantics. Our work is partly based on earlier work of Latella, Majzik, and Massink [8] for UML-Statecharts, but to some extent also on previous work for classical Statecharts, namely on the work of Mikk, Lakhnech, and Siegel [12], on the work of Lüttgen, von der Beeck, and Cleaveland [9,10], as well as on our work [22].

In contrast to the work of Latella et al. [8][1] our approach

- incorporates the history mechanism (**shallow** and **deep** cases)[2]
- supports entry and exit actions
- uses Statecharts terms as "intermediate language" which are "more similar" to the original UML-Statecharts syntax than Enhanced Hierarchical Automata which are used in [8] (and [12]), and
- enables a more liberal modeling of interlevel transitions, because we use complete as well as incomplete configurations for specifiying the source states and the target states of interlevel transitions.

The rest of the paper is organized as follows: We briefly discuss differences between classical Statecharts and UML-Statecharts in section 2. In section 3, we define our textual syntax of UML-Statecharts. Prerequisites for our semantics definition are dealt with in section 4, whereas section 5 presents our formal operational semantics for UML-Statecharts. Related work is discussed in section 6. We conclude and briefly discuss future work in section 7.

2   UML-Statecharts versus Classical Statecharts

Some of the problems inherent in classical Statecharts also exist in UML-Statecharts. However, there are some important differences which simplify or complicate the semantics definition, respectively. In contrast to classical Statecharts, for UML-Statecharts the following can be stated:

- Only one triggering event is processed at each point of time. Especially, a generated event is not sensed within the same "step", i.e. it can not trigger a transition within the same step. Therefore the UML-Statecharts semantics need not be defined in a two-level micro/macro step approach.
- The trigger part of a transition label neither contains conjunctions of events nor negated events. Therefore the problem of achieving global consistency does not exist.
- If an event occurs, but no transition is enabled, then this event is simply ignored.

---

[1] The work of Latella et al. [8] for UML-Statecharts is based on the work of Mikk et al. [12] for classical Statecharts.

[2] Note that the history mechanism has been neglected in most of the semantics definitions of classical Statecharts.

- If several conflicting transitions, i.e. transitions which must not be taken simultaneously, are simultaneously enabled, then a transition on a lower level has priority over transitions on a higher level (for short: lower-first priority). In the case of classical Statecharts either no priority or upper-first priority (STATEMATE) is given.
- Entry/exit actions associated to states exist, which are executed whenever the corresponding state is entered or exited, respectively.

3   Syntax

UML-Statechart Terms. UML-Statecharts is a visual language. However, for our aim to define a formal semantics, it is convenient to represent UML-Statecharts not visually but by textual terms. This is also done in related work for "classical" Statecharts [11, 21] as well as for UML-Statecharts [8]. Essentially, our term syntax enhances the syntax presented in [11] by entry and exit actions and by a possibility to model interlevel transitions.

Let $\mathcal{N}, \mathcal{T}, \Pi, \mathcal{A}$ be countable sets of state names, transition names, events, and actions, respectively, with $\Pi \subseteq \mathcal{A}$. We denote events and actions by $a, b, c, \ldots$ and sequences of events and sequences of actions by $\alpha, \beta, \gamma, \ldots$. For a set M let M^* denote the set of finite sequences over M. Then, the set **UML-SC** of *UML-Statechart terms* is inductively defined to be the least set satisfying the following conditions, where $n \in \mathcal{N}$ and $en, ex \in \mathcal{A}^*$. (The interpretation of n, en and ex will be given later.)

1. **Basic term:** $s = [n, (en, ex)]$ is a UML-Statechart term with $\mathsf{type}(s) = \mathsf{basic}$. Therefore s is also called a *basic term*.
2. **Or-term:** If $s_1, \ldots, s_k$ are UML-Statechart terms for $k > 0$, $\rho = \{1, \ldots, k\}$, $l \in \rho$, $\mathsf{HT} = \{\mathsf{none}, \mathsf{deep}, \mathsf{shallow}\}$, and $T \subseteq \mathsf{TR} =_{\mathrm{df}} \mathcal{T} \times \rho \times 2^{\mathcal{N}} \times \Pi \times \mathcal{A}^* \times 2^{\mathcal{N}} \times \rho \times \mathsf{HT}$, then $s = [n, (s_1, \ldots, s_k), l, T, (en, ex)]$ is a UML-Statechart term with $\mathsf{type}(s) = \mathsf{or}$. Therefore, s is also called an *Or-term*. Here, $s_1, \ldots, s_k$ are the *subterms* of s, T is the set of *transitions* between these terms, s_1 is the *default subterm* of s, l is called the *index*, and s_l is the *currently active* subterm of s (or for short: s_l is *active*).[3]
   For each transition $t = (\hat{t}, i, sr, e, \alpha, td, j, ht) \in T$ we require that $sr \in \mathsf{confAll}(s_i)$ and $td \in \mathsf{confAll}(s_j)^4$. Furthermore, we define $\mathsf{name}(t) =_{\mathrm{df}} \hat{t}$, $\mathsf{sou}(t) =_{\mathrm{df}} s_i$, $\mathsf{souRes}(t) =_{\mathrm{df}} sr$, $\mathsf{ev}(t) =_{\mathrm{df}} e$, $\mathsf{act}(t) =_{\mathrm{df}} \alpha$, $\mathsf{tarDet}(t) =_{\mathrm{df}} td$, $\mathsf{tar}(t) =_{\mathrm{df}} s_j$, and $\mathsf{historyType}(t) =_{\mathrm{df}} ht$. $\mathsf{name}(t)$ is called the *transition name* of t, the sets $\mathsf{ev}(t)$ and $\mathsf{act}(t)$ are called the *trigger part* and *action part* of t, respectively,[5] $\mathsf{sou}(t)$ and $\mathsf{tar}(t)$ are called the *source* and *target* of t, respectively, whereas $\mathsf{souRes}(t)$ and $\mathsf{tarDet}(t)$ are called the *source restriction* and *target determinator*. Source restriction and target determinator provide a means for modelling an interlevel transition by

---

[3] Note that according to our definition of Or-terms a UML-Statechart term does not only contain the static term structure (e.g. the information which subterms exist), but also dynamic information, i.e. the information which of the subterms of an Or-term is the currently active one.

[4] The definition of $\mathsf{confAll}(s_j)$ is postponed to the end of this section.

[5] Note that the trigger part e is a single element of Π, whereas the action part a is a sequence of elements of $\mathcal{A}$ (with $\Pi \subseteq \mathcal{A}$).

a simple transition on the level of the uppermost states the interlevel transition exits and enters. The source and target of the interlevel transition are represented as additional label information by the source restriction and the target determinator.[6]

3. **And-term:** If $s_1, \ldots, s_k$ are UML-Statechart terms for $k > 0$, then term $s = [n, (s_1, \ldots, s_k), (en, ex)]$ is a UML-Statechart term with $\mathsf{type}(s) = \mathsf{and}$. Thus, s is also called an *And-term*. Here, $s_1, \ldots, s_k$ are the (parallel) *subterms* of s.

In all three cases we refer to n as the *root name* of s and write $\mathsf{root}(s) =_{\mathrm{df}} n$. Furthermore, en and ex are the *sequence of entry* and the *sequence of exit actions* of s, respectively. If $a_1, \ldots, a_k$ are actions, then the sequence of actions $a_1, \ldots, a_k$ is denoted by $\langle a_1, \ldots, a_k \rangle$. Especially, the empty sequence is denoted by $\langle \rangle$. We assume that all root names and transition names are mutually disjoint so that terms and transitions within UML-Statechart terms are uniquely referred to by their names. For convenience, we sometimes write "state" instead of "term". and abbreviate $(s_1, \ldots, s_k)$ by $(s_{1..k})$.

We explain our term syntax with Fig. 1:

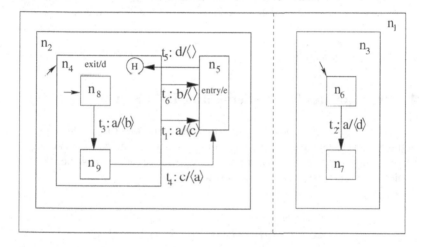

Fig. 1. UML-Statechart Example

The term syntax of the UML-Statechart of Fig. 1 is as follows:

$$s_1 = [n_1, (s_2, s_3), (\langle \rangle, \langle \rangle)] \qquad s_2 = [n_2, (s_4, s_5), 1, \{t_1, t_4, t_5, t_6\}, (\langle \rangle, \langle \rangle)]$$
$$s_3 = [n_3, (s_6, s_7), 1, \{t_2\}, (\langle \rangle, \langle \rangle)] \qquad s_4 = [n_4, (s_8, s_9), 1, \{t_3\}, (\langle \rangle, \langle d \rangle)]$$
$$s_5 = [n_5, (\langle e \rangle, \langle \rangle)] \qquad\qquad\qquad s_i = [n_i, (\langle \rangle, \langle \rangle)] \; (6 \le i \le 9)$$

where s_1 is an And-state, s_2, s_3, and s_4 are Or-states, and $s_5, \ldots, s_9$ are basic states. Only s_4 has an exit action and only s_5 has an entry action. For the Or-states, we have selected the default substate as the currently active substate. Therefore, the index equals 1 for all these Or-states.

---

[6] This idea stems from Mikk et al. [12].

A UML-Statechart a transition $(\hat{t}, i, sr, e, \alpha, td, j, ht)$ with $sr = \emptyset = td$ and $ht =$ none is represented by an arrow from state s_i to s_j with label $t : e/\alpha$. Therefore, the transitions $t_1, t_2, \ldots, t_6$ are given as follows:

$$t_1 = (\hat{t}_1, 4, \emptyset, a, \langle c \rangle, \emptyset, 5, \text{none}) \qquad t_2 = (\hat{t}_2, 6, \emptyset, a, \langle d \rangle, \emptyset, 7, \text{none})$$
$$t_3 = (\hat{t}_3, 8, \emptyset, a, \langle b \rangle, \emptyset, 9, \text{none}) \qquad t_4 = (\hat{t}_4, 4, \{n_9\}, c, \langle a \rangle, \emptyset, 5, \text{none})$$
$$t_5 = (\hat{t}_5, 5, \emptyset, d, \langle \rangle, \emptyset, 4, \text{shallow}) \qquad t_6 = (\hat{t}_6, 4, \emptyset, b, \langle \rangle, \emptyset, 5, \text{none})$$

Transition t_4 is the only interlevel transition and only transition t_5 uses the history mechanism. Lateron these issues will be dealt with in more detail.

As can be seen from our UML-Statecharts term syntax and as in the work of [8] we do not consider the following features of UML-Statecharts:

- initial, final, and junction pseudostates,
- time, change and deferred events,
- branch segments and completion transitions,
- guards, variables, and data dependencies in transition labels,
- termination, creation, destruction of objects and send clauses within actions as well as do actions, and
- dynamic choicepoints.

4   Prerequisites for the Semantics Definition

We consider different kinds of configurations. Function conf : UML-SC $\longrightarrow 2^{\mathcal{N}}$ which is inductively defined along the structure of UML-Statechart terms computes the *complete current configuration* of a given UML-Statechart term s, i.e. the set of the root names of all currently active substates within s.[7]

$$
\begin{array}{ll}
\text{conf}([n, \_]) & =_{\text{df}} \{n\} \\
\text{conf}([n, (s_{1..k}), l, T, \_]) & =_{\text{df}} \{n\} \cup \text{conf}(s_l) \\
\text{conf}([n, (s_{1..k}), \_]) & =_{\text{df}} \{n\} \cup \bigcup_{i=1}^{k} \text{conf}(s_i)
\end{array}
$$

For example in the UML-Statechart of Fig. 1 we have:

$$\text{conf}(s_1) = \{n_1, n_2, n_4, n_8, n_3, n_6\} \qquad \text{conf}(s_2) = \{n_2, n_4, n_8\}$$

In contrast, function confAll : UML-SC $\longrightarrow 2^{2^{\mathcal{N}}}$ applied to UML-Statechart s computes the set of all *potential* configurations of s, which can be complete or *incomplete*.[8]

- The term "potential" denotes that not only the currently active substate of each Or-state s' within s is considered, but all possibilities for choosing a substate of s'. This difference between conf and confAll implies that $\text{conf}([n, (s_{1..k}), l, T, \_])$ depends on index l, whereas $\text{confAll}([n, (s_{1..k}), l, T, \_])$ does not.

---

[7] The underscore "$\_$" is used as a placeholder for arguments which are neglected for the present consideration.

[8] Remember that we have used function confAll to define constraints on the transition syntax.

- The term "incomplete" denotes a configuration which results from an application of confAll to state s, where the recursion within confAll terminates before the basic states of s are reached. Therefore, an incomplete configuration is upward-closed with respect to the state hierarchy, but not downward-closed, whereas a complete configuration is both.

$$\text{confAll}([n, \_]) \qquad\qquad\qquad =_{\text{df}} \{\{n\}\}$$
$$\text{confAll}([n, (s_{1..k}), l, T, \_]) =_{\text{df}} \{\{n\} \cup c \mid c \in \text{confAll}(s_j), 1 \le j \le k\} \cup \{\{n\}\}$$
$$\text{confAll}([n, (s_{1..k}), \_]) \qquad =_{\text{df}} \{\{n\} \cup \bigcup_{i=1}^{k} c_i \mid c_i \in \text{confAll}(s_i)\} \cup \{\{n\}\}$$

Incomplete configurations are realized in the second and third case of the definition of confAll by the union with term $\{\{n\}\}$. Note that $\text{conf}(s)$ is an element of $\text{confAll}(s)$ for each UML-Statechart term s, formally $\forall s \in \text{UML-SC} : \text{conf}(s) \in \text{confAll}(s)$.

We explain the notion of confAll by the UML-Statechart of Fig. 1:

$$\text{confAll}(s_1) \supseteq \{\{n_1, n_2, n_4, n_8, n_3, n_6\}, \{n_1, n_2, n_4, n_9, n_3, n_6\},$$
$$\{n_1, n_2, n_5, n_3, n_6\}, \{n_1, n_2, n_4, n_8, n_3, n_7\},$$
$$\{n_1, n_2, n_4, n_9, n_3, n_7\}, \{n_1, n_2, n_5, n_3, n_7\}\}$$
$$\text{confAll}(s_2) \supseteq \{\{n_2, n_4, n_8\}, \{n_2, n_4, n_9\}, \{n_2, n_5\}\}$$

In this example, we have only listed the set of all complete potential configurations, but not the incomplete potential ones.

Having defined confAll and assuming that transition $t = (\_, i, sr, \_, \_, td, j, \_)$ with source s_i, target s_j, source restriction $sr \ne \emptyset$, and target determinator $td \ne \emptyset$ is given, now the reason for the above-mentioned constraints $sr \in \text{confAll}(s_i)$ and $td \in \text{confAll}(s_j)$ becomes clear. The source restriction and the target determinator are (possibly incomplete) configurations of s_i and s_j and specify that transition t models an interlevel transition as follows:

- Source restriction sr of t specifies the source state of the interlevel transition.
- Target determinator td of t specifies the target state of the interlevel transition.

Let us consider an example: The only interlevel transition of UML-Statechart term s_1 of Fig. 1 is $t_4 = (\hat{t}_4, 4, \{n_9\}, c, \langle a \rangle, \emptyset, 5, \text{none})$, because in all other transitions both the source restriction as well as the target determinator equal the empty set. Due to the source restriction $\{n_9\}$ of t_4 this transition is represented in Fig. 1 by an arrow from state s_9 (instead of s_4) to s_5 with label $t_4 : c/\langle a \rangle$.

Note that our definition of confAll which allows *incomplete* configurations enables – together with the conditions $sr, td \in \text{confAll}(s_i)$ – a more liberal modeling of interlevel transitions than the definition of transitions in the work of Mikk et al. [12], where source restriction and target determinator must be *complete* configurations.

5 Semantics

In the following subsections, we proceed as follows: At first we recall the intuitive semantics definition of UML-Statecharts. Then we present the general approach of our semantics definition. Afterwards we formalize the treatment of entry and exit actions. Then we define how the state resulting from transition execution is computed. Finally, we use the achieved results to formally define the semantics of UML-Statecharts.

5.1 Intuition

We recall the intuitive semantics definition of UML-Statecharts by considering again our example of Fig. 1.[9] Initially, UML-Statechart term s_1 is in subconfiguration $\{n_8, n_6\}$. If the environment offers event

- b, then transition t_6 can be taken, so that the next subconfiguration of s_1 will be $\{n_5, n_6\}$ and the sequence $\langle d, e \rangle$ of actions is executed, because $\langle d \rangle$ is the sequence of exit actions of state s_4, t_6 has the empty sequence $\langle \rangle$ as action part, and $\langle e \rangle$ is the sequence of entry actions of state s_5,
- a, then transitions t_3 and t_2 can simultaneously be taken[10], so that $\{n_9, n_7\}$ will be the next subconfiguration and the sequence $\langle b, d \rangle$ of actions will be executed. Note that due to the lower-first priority in UML-Statecharts the transition t_1 can not be taken if state s_8 is active, because the source s_8 of transition t_3 is on a lower level than the source s_4 of transition t_1,[11]
- $e \in \Pi \setminus \{a, b\}$, then the configuration does not change, because no transition can be taken.

Now we focus on the history mechanism. Harel already presented it in his classical Statecharts paper [5]. However, most proposals for a precise semantics definition of classical Statecharts neglected it. The history mechanism allows to reenter an Or-state s, such that the same substate of s becomes the currently active substate as it has been the case, when s has been active the last time. If the Or-state has never been active before, the default substate of the Or-state becomes the currently active substate.

The history mechanism allows two kinds of scoping: the "memory" effect can be restricted to the direct substates of the considered Or-state ("shallow", graphical symbol: "H") or can be unrestricted ("deep", graphical symbol: "H*"), such that it recursively remembers the active substates along the state hierarchy down to the basic states. We will consider both cases in our semantics. In our syntax the history mechanism is used by every transition t which has an Or-state as target and for which historyType$(t) \in$ {deep, shallow}. In the UML-Statechart of Fig. 1 only transition t_5 uses the history mechanism – with historyType$(t_5) =$ shallow. If t_5 is performed, then state s_4 becomes active. Furthermore, substate s_8 (s_9) becomes active, if s_8 (s_9) has been active, when s_4 has been active last time before. In the case that s_4 has never been active before, then the default state s_8 of s_4 becomes active.

5.2 General Approach for the Semantics Definition

To achieve a precise, but nevertheless intuitive semantics definition, we take labeled transition systems as semantic domain and use SOS-rules to define the semantics of UML-Statecharts.

The main difficulty in our enhancements with respect to the work of Latella et al. [8] (and Mikk et al. [12]) arises from the fact that we additionally support the history

---

[9] For the sake of brevity, in the following we sometimes abbreviate a configuration c by its *subconfiguration*: This is the set of those state names of c which denote basic states.

[10] In this case it is not allowed that only one of both transitions is taken.

[11] The level of a transition t is defined by the level of the source of t, not by the level of its source restriction.

mechanism which exhibits quite intricate dependencies with interlevel transitions.[12] To clarify this point let us assume that transition t_5 in Fig. 1 which uses the history mechanism (cf. historyType(t_5) = shallow) is modified to an interlevel transition t_5' by changing its target determinator from empty set $\emptyset$ to n_8. If t_5' is taken one could argue that due to the history mechanism the next currently active subterm of s_4 should be s_9 if s_9 had been the last active subterm of s_4. Alternatively, one could argue that due to the target determinator n_8 of t_5' the next currently active subterm of s_4 should be s_8. However, we will define the semantics such that the target determinator information of a transition has priority over the history mechanism. For our example this means that the second possibility is chosen.

As opposed to the work of Latella et al. [8] we do not parameterize our semantics definition with a priority mechanism for transition execution, since lower-first priority is stipulated for UML-Statecharts.

5.3 Entry and Exit Actions

When a UML-Statechart transition t is taken, a (possibly empty) set of actions is executed: at first the sequence of exit actions of the source of t is executed (in an inner-first approach), then the action part act(t) of t, and finally the sequence of entry actions of t (in an outer-first approach).

We explain the execution of entry and exit actions with the UML-Statechart example of Fig. 1. If transition t_1 is taken then the action sequence $\langle d, c, e \rangle$ is generated, because at first the sequence $\langle d \rangle$ of exit actions of source s_4 of transition t_1 is executed, then the action part $\langle c \rangle$ of t_1, and finally the sequence $\langle e \rangle$ of entry actions of target s_5 of t_1.

In general, if a transition $(\_, l, \_, \_, \alpha, \_, i, \_)$ from state s_l to state s_i with action part α is taken, then the sequence exit(s_l) :: α :: entry(s_i) of actions is executed, where exit(s_l) is the sequence of exit actions of s_l and entry(s_i) is the sequence of entry actions of s_i. Here, we assume that :: is an operator (in infix-notation) which concatenates action sequences. The above-mentioned term exit(s_l) :: α :: entry(s_i) will be used (in a slightly modified form) in SOS rule OR-1 of the (auxiliary) semantics of UML-Statecharts to be presented in section 5.5. The functions entry : UML-SC $\longrightarrow \mathcal{A}^*$ and exit : UML-SC $\longrightarrow \mathcal{A}^*$ are inductively defined along the structure of UML-SC terms as follows:[13]

entry($[n, (en, ex)]$)	$=_{\mathrm{df}} en$
entry($[n, (s_{1..k}), l, T, (en, ex)]$)	$=_{\mathrm{df}} en$ :: entry(s_l)
entry($[n, (s_{1..k}), (en, ex)]$)	$=_{\mathrm{df}} en$ :: entry(s_1) :: ... :: entry(s_k)

---

[12] Remember that our UML-Statecharts term syntax represents interlevel transitions using additional information in the transition labels (i.e. source restriction and target determinator) based on the approach of [12].

[13] The UML definition in [13] does not define in which order the entry actions of the substates of an And-state $[n, (s_{1..k}), (en, ex)]$ have to be executed with respect to each other. The same is valid for the exit actions of the substates of an And-state. However, we define that the sequence of entry/exit actions of a state s_i is executed before the sequence of entry/exit actions of a state s_{i+1} (for $1 \le i < k$).

$$\begin{aligned}
\mathsf{exit}([n, (en, ex)]) &=_{\mathrm{df}} ex \\
\mathsf{exit}([n, (s_{1..k}), l, T, (en, ex)]) &=_{\mathrm{df}} \mathsf{exit}(s_l) :: ex \\
\mathsf{exit}([n, (s_{1..k}), (en, ex)]) &=_{\mathrm{df}} \mathsf{exit}(s_1) :: \ldots :: \mathsf{exit}(s_k) :: ex
\end{aligned}$$

5.4   Computing the Next State

If a UML-Statecharts transition t is executed, especially the history mechanism and – if t is an interlevel transition – t's target determinator have to be considered. Therefore we define a function next which computes the state which results from a transition execution. Later on this function is used in the SOS rule which handles transition execution (in an OR-state). Function $\mathsf{next} : \mathsf{HT} \times \mathcal{N} \times \mathsf{UML\text{-}SC} \longrightarrow \mathsf{UML\text{-}SC}$ computes for the history type ht and for the target determinator $N = \mathsf{tarDet}(t)$ of a UML-Statechart transition t with target s the UML-Statechart term $s' = \mathsf{next}(ht, \mathsf{tarDet}(t), s)$ which results after execution of transition t. Note that the terms s and s' have an identical static structure, only their dynamic information – specifying the currently active substates – may differ. In order to simplify the presentation of next as well as of several subsequent definitions (functions next_stop, default, and the SOS rules), we abstract from entry and exit actions within UML-Statecharts terms: for example, we write $[n]$ instead of $[n, (en, ex)]$, we write $[n, (s_{1..k}), l, T]$ instead of $[n, (s_{1..k}), l, T, (en, ex)]$, and we write $[n, (s_{1..k})]$ instead of $[n, (s_{1..k}), (en, ex)]$.

$$\begin{aligned}
\mathsf{next}(ht, N, [n]) &=_{\mathrm{df}} [n] \\[1ex]
\mathsf{next}(ht, N, [n, (s_{1..k}), l, T]) &=_{\mathrm{df}}
\begin{cases}
[n, (s_{1..k})_{[s_j/\mathsf{next}(ht,N,s_j)]}, j, T] & \text{if } \exists n' \in N, \\
& \quad j \in \{1, \ldots, k\}. \\
& \quad n' = \mathsf{name}(s_j) \\
\mathsf{next\_stop}(ht, [n, (s_{1..k}), l, T]) & \text{otherwise}
\end{cases} \\[1ex]
\mathsf{next}(ht, N, [n, (s_{1..k})]) &=_{\mathrm{df}} [n, (\mathsf{next}(ht, N, s_1), \ldots, \mathsf{next}(ht, N, s_k))]
\end{aligned}$$

Here the second case of the definition requires some explanation:

- If N contains a name n' of one of the state names of the substates $s_1, \ldots, s_k$, i.e. $\exists n' \in N, j \in \{1, \ldots, k\}$, such that $n' = \mathsf{name}(s_j)$ (condition $*$), then index l will be replaced by index j and function next is recursively applied to s_j. Therefore, if $N = \mathsf{tarDet}(t)$, then the target determinator information of t is exploited in function next when zooming into the state hierarchy as long as condition $*$ is fulfilled, i.e., as long as adequate target determinator information exists.
- Otherwise, function $\mathsf{next\_stop} : \mathsf{HT} \times \mathsf{UML\text{-}SC\text{-}OR} \longrightarrow \mathsf{UML\text{-}SC\text{-}OR}$ is called which uses the history type information to determine currently active substates of a state.[14] In the definition of function next_stop the following case distinction occurs:
  - If $\mathsf{historyType}(t) = \mathsf{deep}$, then the state does not change at all.
  - If $\mathsf{historyType}(t) = \mathsf{none}$, then index l is replaced by index 1 and function default is used to initialize substate s_1.
  - If $\mathsf{historyType}(t) = \mathsf{shallow}$, then index l does not change, but function default initializes all lower levels of s_l.

---

[14] $\mathsf{UML\text{-}SC\text{-}OR} =_{\mathrm{df}} \{s \mid s \in \mathsf{UML\text{-}SC}, \mathsf{type}(s) = \mathsf{or}\}$

$$\text{next\_stop}(ht, [n, (s_{1..k}), l, T]) =_{df} \begin{cases} [n, (s_{1..k}), l, T] & \text{if } ht = \text{deep} \\ [n, (s_{1..k})_{[s_1/\text{default}(s_1)]}, 1, T] & \text{if } ht = \text{none} \\ [n, (s_{1..k})_{[s_l/\text{default}(s_l)]}, l, T] & \text{if } ht = \text{shallow} \end{cases}$$

Note the difference between the second and third case of the definition of next_stop: the second case (historyType$(t) = $ none) is independent from l, i.e. from the index of the currently active substate of the Or-state – default(s_1) becomes the new currently active substate of s_1. In contrast the third case (historyType$(t) = $ shallow) depends on l, because default(s_l) becomes the new currently active substate of the Or-state.

The definition of next_stop uses function default : UML-SC $\longrightarrow$ UML-SC which defines for an Or-state that its currently active substate is given by its default substate.

$$\begin{aligned} \text{default}([n]) & =_{df} [n] \\ \text{default}([n, (s_{1..k}), l, T]) & =_{df} [n, (s_{1..k})_{[s_1/\text{default}(s_1)]}, 1, T] \\ \text{default}([n, (s_{1..k})]) & =_{df} [n, (\text{default}(s_1), \dots, \text{default}(s_k))] \end{aligned}$$

5.5 Semantics Definition

Let LTS be the set of *labeled transition systems*. In a first step, we define an auxiliary semantics $[\![.]\!]_{aux}$: UML-SC $\longrightarrow$ LTS where the (semantic) transitions work on single input events. In a second step, we use $[\![.]\!]_{aux}$ to define our (final) semantics $[\![.]\!]$: UML-SC $\longrightarrow$ LTS for UML-Statechart terms where the (semantic) transitions work on sequences of input events. This two-step approach simplifies the SOS rules to be defined.

Auxiliary Semantics. The auxiliary semantics $[\![s]\!]_{aux}$ of a UML-Statecharts term $s \in$ UML-SC is given by the labeled transition system $(\text{UML-SC}, L, \longrightarrow, s) \in$ LTS, where

- UML-SC is the set of states,[15]
- $L = \Pi \times \mathcal{A}^* \times \{0, 1\}$ is the set of labels,
- $\longrightarrow \subseteq \text{UML-SC} \times L \times \text{UML-SC}$ is the transition relation, and
- s is the start state.

For the sake of simplicity, we write $s \xrightarrow[\alpha]{e}_f s'$ instead of $(s, (e, \alpha, f), s') \in \longrightarrow$ and $s \xrightarrow{e}{}_f$ instead of $\not\exists s', \alpha . s \xrightarrow[\alpha]{e}_f s'$, where s and s' are called the *source* and the *target* of these (semantic) transitions[16], respectively, e and α are called the *input* and *output*, respectively, and f is called the *flag*. We say that term s may perform a (semantic) transition with input e, output α, and flag f to term s'. If appropriate, we do no mention the input, output, and/or target of the transition. Intuitively, flag f states whether a semantic transition is performed according to taking at least one Statechart transition (in this case $f = 1$, denoted as *positive flag*) or without taking any Statechart transition (in this case $f = 0$, denoted as *negative flag*). In the later case only the input event is "consumed",

---

[15] This implies that each state of the transition system is given by a UML-Statechart term.

[16] We use the term "semantic transition" in order to distinguish transitions of the semantics of UML-Statecharts from "UML-Statechart transitions", which occur in the syntax of UML-Statecharts (within an Or-state).

whereas the source and the target are identical. In contrast to the work of Latella et al. [8] we do not need to annotate a semantic transition with the explicit set of UML-Statechart transitions which are taken when the semantic transition is performed. Instead, in our case it suffices to annotate the boolean information whether at least one UML-Statechart transition is taken. For $l \in \{1, \ldots, k\}$ we abbreviate $(s_1, \ldots, s_{l-1}, s_l', s_{l+1}, \ldots, s_k)$ by $(s_{1..k})_{[s_l / s_l']}$. Then transition relation $\longrightarrow$ is defined as presented in Table 1 by five SOS rules.

Table 1. SOS rules of the auxiliary semantics

BAS
$$\frac{\text{true}}{[n] \xrightarrow[\langle\rangle]{e}_0 [n]}$$

OR-1
$$\frac{(\_, l, sr, e, \alpha, td, i, ht) \in T, \ sr \subseteq \mathsf{conf}(s_l), \ s_l \xrightarrow{e}\!\!\!\!\!/\,_1}{[n, (s_{1..k}), l, T] \xrightarrow[\mathsf{exit}(s_l)::\alpha::\mathsf{entry}(\mathsf{next}(ht,td,s_i))]{e}_1 [n, (s_{1..k})_{[s_i / \mathsf{next}(ht,td,s_i)]}, i, T]}$$

OR-2
$$\frac{s_l \xrightarrow[\alpha]{e}_1 s_l',}{[n, (s_{1..k}), l, T] \xrightarrow[\alpha]{e}_1 [n, (s_{1..k})_{[s_l / s_l']}, l, T]}$$

OR-3
$$\frac{s_l \xrightarrow[\langle\rangle]{e}_0 s_l, \ [n, (s_{1..k}), l, T] \xrightarrow{e}\!\!\!\!\!/\,_1}{[n, (s_{1..k}), l, T] \xrightarrow[\langle\rangle]{e}_0 [n, (s_{1..k}), l, T]}$$

AND
$$\frac{\forall j \in \{1, \ldots, k\} \cdot s_j \xrightarrow[\alpha_j]{e}_{f_j} s_j'}{[n, (s_{1..k})] \xrightarrow[\alpha_1::\ldots::\alpha_k]{e}_{\vee_{j=1}^{k} f_j} [n, (s_{1..k}')]}$$

Explanation of the SOS rules:

– BAS (stuttering)
A basic state may perform a semantic transition with arbitrary input event e, empty output, and negative flag such that the state does not change, i.e., that the input event is just consumed.

– OR-1 (progress)
If t is a UML-Statechart transition of an Or-state s with trigger part e, then s can perform a semantic transition with input e and positive flag
  • if the source restriction sr of t is a subset of the complete current configuration of the currently active substate s_l of s ($sr \subseteq \mathsf{conf}(s_l)$) and
  • if s_l cannot perform a semantic transition with input e and positive flag ($s_l \xrightarrow{e}\!\!\!\!\!/\,_1$).

The former condition assures the enabledness of transition t, whereas the last condition assures the lower-first priority of UML-Statecharts. Rule OR-1 treats the execution of entry and exit actions: it is the only rule in which additional entry and exit actions, i.e. entry and exit actions not already occuring in the output part of the transition in the rule's premise, can occur in the output part of the transition in the conclusion. Note that the source restriction sr and the target determinator td of a UML-Statechart transition only appear in this rule: $sr \subseteq \mathsf{conf}(s_l)$ assures the enabledness of the considered transition, whereas td – used within $\mathsf{next}(ht, td, s_i)$ – precisely defines the target state and therefore also the sequence of entry actions to be executed. The target of the semantic transition differs from its source by changing the currently active substate from s_l to s_i because s_l and s_i are the source and target of the (syntactic) transition t, respectively. Furthermore, the dynamic information of s_i is updated according to the history type ht and the target determinator td of t using function next. This update is performed by the substitution $(s_{1..k})_{[s_i/\mathsf{next}(ht,td,s_i)]}$. Finally, the output of the semantic transition is given by concatenating the sequence $\mathsf{exit}(s_l)$ of exit actions of the old currently active substate s_l with the output part α of the (syntactic) transition t and with the sequence $\mathsf{entry}(s_i')$ of the entry actions of the new currently active substate s_i', where s_i' is the result of updating s_i using function next as explained before.

- OR-2 (propagation of progress)
  If a substate of an Or-state may perform a semantic transition with a positive flag, then the Or-state may perform a semantic transition with the same label.

- OR-3 (propagation of stuttering)
  If a substate of an Or-state may perform a semantic transition with a negative flag, i.e. intuitively that no Statechart transition can be taken within the Or-state, and if furthermore the Or-state cannot perform a semantic transition with positive flag, then the Or-state may also perform a semantic transition with the same label (especially with negative flag).

- AND (composition)
  If every substate s_j of an And-state s can perform a semantic transition with input e, output α_j, and flag b_j, then And-state s can also perform a semantic transition with the same input e, but with output $\alpha_1 :: \ldots :: \alpha_k$ resulting from concatenating all substate outputs α_j, and with flag $\bigvee_{j=1}^{k} f_j$ given by the logical disjunction of all flags f_j. Here, we identify "0" and "1" with the boolean values "false" and "true", respectively, to evaluate term $\bigvee_{j=1}^{k} f_j$.

Summing up, the SOS rules define that for every input event $e \in \Pi$ and for every state $s \in$ UML-SC either a semantic transition $s \xrightarrow{e}_\alpha {}_1 s'$ with output $\alpha \in \mathcal{A}^*$ and state $s' \in$ UML-SC exists or a semantic transition $s \xrightarrow{e}_{\langle\rangle} {}_0 s$ exists.

Fig. 2 presents the auxiliary semantics, i.e., a labeled transition system for the UML-Statechart of Fig. 1 graphically as state transition diagram. For the sake of simplicity, Fig. 2 only presents those semantic transitions which have positive flags. Semantic transitions with negative flags would have to be presented by cyclic transitions at every state.[17] Furthermore, Fig. 2 only shows those states which are reachable from the start state (n_8, n_6).

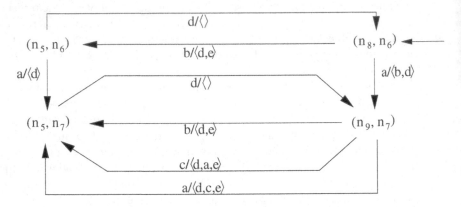

Fig. 2. Auxiliary semantics of UML-Statechart from Fig. 1

Final Semantics. After having defined the auxiliary semantics $[\![.]\!]_{aux}$ we are now able to define the (final) semantics $[\![.]\!]$: UML-SC $\longrightarrow$ LTS. Very similar to the auxiliary semantics $[\![s]\!]_{aux}$, the (final) semantics $[\![s]\!]$ of a UML-Statechart term $s \in$ UML-SC is given by a labeled transition system (UML-SC, L', $\longrightarrow$, s) $\in$ LTS, where

- UML-SC is the set of states,
- $L' = \Pi^* \times \mathcal{A}^*$ is the set of labels,
- $\longrightarrow \subseteq$ UML-SC $\times L' \times$ UML-SC is the transition relation, and
- s is the start state.

Note the differences between label set L' of the final semantics and label set L of the auxiliary semantics: transition labels of the final semantics work on sequences of trigger events, not on single events and they do not contain flags.

For the sake of simplicity, we write $s \xrightarrow{\epsilon}_{\alpha} s'$ instead of $(s, (\epsilon, \alpha), s') \in \longrightarrow$. Only one SOS rule is needed to define the final semantics based on the auxiliary semantics.

$$\frac{s \xrightarrow{e}_{\alpha}{}_f s'}{s \xrightarrow{\epsilon}_{\mathrm{join}(\alpha, \epsilon')} s'} \quad \mathsf{sel}(\epsilon) = (e, \epsilon')$$

Explanation of the SOS rule:

If a sequence ϵ of events is given, such that function sel separates it in a single event e and the rest sequence ϵ' and if a state s may perform a transition according to transition

---

[17] More precisely for every state s of the transition diagram of Fig. 2 for which there does not exist an outgoing transition with input $e \in \Pi$ a cyclic transition with label $e/\langle\rangle$ at state s would have to be drawn.

relation $\longrightarrow$ with input e (being a single event), output α, and flag f to state s', then state s may also perform a transition according to transition relation $\longrightarrow\!\!\!\blacktriangleright$ to state s', but with input ϵ (being a sequence of events) and output $\mathsf{join}(\alpha, \epsilon')$.

According to the UML definition which neither defines the scheduling of the input queue nor the output queue of a Statechart (and thereby following [8]) we use two functions $\mathsf{sel} : \Pi^* \longrightarrow \Pi \times \Pi^*$ and $\mathsf{join} : \Pi^* \times \Pi^* \longrightarrow \Pi^*$ which still have to be defined accordingly for a concrete scheduling strategy.

We finish this section with a few remarks concerning the use of interlevel transitions.

– On the one hand interlevel transitions are allowed in Harel's classical Statecharts and in UML-Statecharts.
– On the other hand interlevel transitions imply that (UML-)Statecharts are not defined in a modular way, so that e.g. the definition of a compositional Statecharts semantics is impeded. Therefore interlevel transition are not allowed in most work related to the formalization of Statecharts semantics [17,21,11] (especially in our previous work [9,10,22]).
– However, in the present work we have incorporated interlevel transitions within our UML-Statechart term syntax, although their prohibition would have significantly simplified our syntax and semantics definition of UML-Statecharts:
  • Syntax: Transitions of Or states would neither contain source restriction nor target determinator information. Therefore also function confAll would not be necessary any more.
  • Semantics: We could skip function conf which is used in SOS-rule OR-1. Furthermore, the definition of function next would be significantly less complex.

6   Related Work

Most work on the formalization of the UML semantics focuses on one single diagram type – as we do. As far as we know the overall integration aspect is only treated by Reggio et al. in [19] and by the precise UML group [3]. In the following we focus on related work for UML-Statecharts.

– The work of Latella et al. [8] has been one starting point of our work. The enhancements of our work w.r.t. their work have already been described before.
– Paltor and Lilius [15] as well as Kwon [7] define an operational semantics for UML-Statecharts in terms of rewrite rules. Since Paltor et al. do not use a structured approach like SOS their semantics does not offer the same level of clarity as ours.
– Compton et al. [1] outline a UML-Statecharts semantics based on Abstract State Machines. They consider entry and exit actions, but not the history mechanism.
– Gogolla et al. [4] present a formal semantics of UML-Statecharts by mapping UML-Statecharts into a more simplified machine using graph rewriting techniques.
– Reggio et al. [18] define the semantics of a UML-Statechart associated with an active UML-class by a labeled transition system which is formally specified by the algebraic specification language CASL. In contrast to our approach neither entry and exit actions nor the history mechanism are considered.

- Padawitz [14] formalizes parts of UML-Statecharts (as well as of class diagrams) by use of swinging types which are based on terms of many-sorted logic and which comprise functions, relations, and transition systems.
- Engels, Hausmann, Heckel, and Sauer [2] propose a meta modeling approach to define the operational semantics of behavioural UML diagrams – especially a fragment of UML-Statecharts – based on collaboration diagrams. The way how collaboration diagrams are used resembles Plotkin's Structured Operational Semantics.

7 Conclusions and Further Work

We presented a formal semantics of UML-Statecharts. In contrast to related work (like the approach of Latella et al. [8] which is quite similar to our approach) we additionally include UML-Statechart features like the history mechanism (in both kinds) as well as entry and exit actions. Furthermore the use of our syntax, namely UML-Statechart terms, as well as our approach of defining an SOS-style semantics results in quite a succinct and well adaptable semantics which could be used as the basis for formal analysis techniques like model checking or for defining transformations between tools which support different UML-Statechart dialects.

In future, we will consider additional features of UML-Statecharts. However, a formalization of the complete UML constitutes the global aim.

References

1. K. Compton, J. Huggins, and W. Shen. A Semantic Model for the State Machine in the Unified Modeling Language. In *Proc. Dynamic Behaviour in UML Models: Semantic Questions*, pages 25–31. LMU München, Institut für Informatik, Bericht 0006, 2000.
2. G. Engels, J. H. Hausmann, R. Heckel, and S. Sauer. Dynamic meta modeling: A graphical approach to the operational semantics of behavioral diagrams in UML. In A. Evans, S. Kent, and B. Selic, editors, *UML 2000 - The Unified Modeling Language. Advancing the Standard. Third International Conference, York, UK, October 2000, Proceedings*, volume 1939 of *LNCS*, pages 323–337. Springer, 2000.
3. A. Evans and S. Kent. Core meta-modelling semantics of UML: The pUML approach. In R. France and B. Rumpe, editors, *UML'99 - The Unified Modeling Language. Beyond the Standard. Second International Conference, Fort Collins, CO, USA, October 28-30. 1999, Proceedings*, volume 1723 of *LNCS*. Springer, 1999.
4. M. Gogolla and F. Parisi-Presicce. State diagrams in UML: A formal semantics using graph transformations. In M. Broy, D. Coleman, T. S. E. Maibaum, and B. Rumpe, editors, *Proceedings PSMT'98 Workshop on Precise Semantics for Modeling Techniques*. Technische Universität München, TUM-I9803, 1998.
5. D. Harel. Statecharts: A visual formalism for complex systems. *Science of Computer Programming*, 8:231–274, 1987.
6. D. Harel and A. Naamad. The STATEMATE semantics of Statecharts. *ACM Transactions on Software Engineering*, 5(4):293–333, October 1996.
7. G. Kwon. Rewrite rules and operational semantics for model checking UML statecharts. In A. Evans, S. Kent, and B. Selic, editors, *UML 2000 - The Unified Modeling Language. Advancing the Standard. Third International Conference, York, UK, October 2000, Proceedings*, volume 1939 of *LNCS*, pages 528–540. Springer, 2000.

8. D. Latella, I. Majzik, and M. Massink. Towards a formal operational semantics of UML Statechart diagrams. In *Formal Methods for Open Object-based Distributed Systems*. Chapman & Hall, 1999.

9. G. Lüttgen, M. von der Beeck, and R. Cleaveland. Statecharts via process algebra. In *Concurrency Theory (CONCUR '99)*, volume 1664 of *Lecture Notes in Computer Science*, pages 399–414. Springer-Verlag, 1999.

10. G. Lüttgen, M. von der Beeck, and R. Cleaveland. A Compositional Approach to Statecharts Semantics. In *Proc. of ACM SIGSOFT Eighth Int. Symp. on the Foundations of Software Engineering (FSE-8)*, pages 120–129. ACM, 2000.

11. A. Maggiolo-Schettini, A. Peron, and S. Tini. Equivalences of Statecharts. In U. Montanari and V. Sassone, editors, *CONCUR '96 (Concurrency Theory)*, volume 1119 of *Lecture Notes in Computer Science*, pages 687–702, Pisa, Italy, August 1996. Springer-Verlag.

12. E. Mikk, Y. Lakhnech, and M. Siegel. Hierarchical automata as model for Statecharts. In *Proceedings of Asian Computing Science Conference (ASIAN '97)*, volume 1345 of *Lecture Notes in Computer Science*. Springer-Verlag, December 1997.

13. OMG. OMG Unified Modeling Language Specification. Version 1.3 alpha R5, 1999.

14. P. Padawitz. Swinging UML: How to make class diagrams and state machines amenable to constraint solving and proving. In A. Evans, S. Kent, and B. Selic, editors, *UML 2000 - The Unified Modeling Language. Advancing the Standard. Third International Conference, York, UK, October 2000, Proceedings*, volume 1939 of *LNCS*, pages 162–177. Springer, 2000.

15. I. Paltor and J. Lilius. Formalising UML state machines for model checking. In R. France and B. Rumpe, editors, *UML'99 - The Unified Modeling Language. Beyond the Standard.*, volume 1723 of *LNCS*. Springer, 1999.

16. G. Plotkin. A structural approach to operational semantics. Technical Report DAIMI-FN-19, Computer Science Department, Aarhus University, Denmark, 1981.

17. A. Pnueli and M. Shalev. What is in a step: On the semantics of Statecharts. In *Theoretical Aspects of Computer Software (TACS '91)*, volume 526 of *Lecture Notes in Computer Science*, pages 244–264. Springer-Verlag, 1991.

18. G. Reggio, E. Astesiano, C. Choppy, and H. Hussmann. Analysing UML Active Classes and Associated State Machines – A Lightwight Formal Approach. In *Fundamental Approaches to Software Engineering*, number 1783 in LNCS, pages 127–146. Springer, 2000.

19. G. Reggio, M. Cerioli, and E. Astesiano. Towards a Rigorous Semantics of UML Supportin its Multiview Approach. In *Proceedings Dynamic Behaviour in UML Models: Semantic Questions*, pages 86–91. Ludwig-Maximilians-Universität München, Institut für Informatik, Bericht 0006, 2000.

20. J. Rumbaugh, I. Jacobson, and G. Booch. *The Unified Modeling Language Reference Manual*. Addison-Wesley, 1998.

21. A. Uselton and S. Smolka. A compositional semantics for Statecharts using labeled transition systems. In B. Jonsson and J. Parrow, editors, *CONCUR '94 (Concurrency Theory)*, volume 836 of *Lecture Notes in Computer Science*, pages 2–17. Springer-Verlag, 1994.

22. M. von der Beeck. A Concise Compositional Statecharts Semantics Definition. In *Proc. of FORTE/PSTV 2000*, pages 335–350. Kluwer, 2000.

UML for Agent-Oriented Software Development: The Tropos Proposal*

John Mylopoulos[1], Manuel Kolp[1], and Jaelson Castro[2]

[1]Department of Computer Science, University of Toronto, 10 King's College Road, Toronto
M5S 3G4, Canada
{jm, mkolp}@cs.toronto.edu
[2] Centro de Informática, Universidade Federal de Pernambuco, Av. Prof. Luiz Freire S/N,
Recife PE, Brazil 50732-970
jbc@cin.ufpe.br

Abstract. We describe a software development methodology called *Tropos* for agent-oriented software systems. The methodology adopts the *i** modeling framework [29], which offers the notions of *actor*, *goal* and (actor) *dependency*, and uses these as a foundation to model early and late requirements, architectural and detailed design. The paper outlines the methodology, and shows how the concepts of *Tropos* can be accommodated within UML. In addition, we also adopt recent proposals for extensions of UML to support design specifications for agent software. Finally the paper compares *Tropos* to other research on agent-oriented software development.

1 Introduction

The explosive growth of application areas such as electronic commerce, enterprise resource planning and mobile computing has profoundly and irreversibly changed our views on software and Software Engineering. Software must now be based on open architectures that continuously change and evolve to accommodate new components and meet new requirements. Software must also operate on different platforms, without recompilation, and with minimal assumptions about its operating environment and its users. As well, software must be robust and autonomous, capable of serving a naïve user with a minimum of overhead and interference. These new requirements, in turn, call for new concepts, tools and techniques for engineering and managing software.

For these reasons -- and more -- agent-oriented software development is gaining popularity over traditional software development techniques. After all, agent-based architectures (known as multi-agent systems in the Agent research community) *do* provide for an open, evolving architecture which can change at run-time to exploit the services of new agents, or replace under-performing ones. In addition, software agents can, in principle, cope with unforeseen circumstances because they include in their architecture goals, along with a planning capability for meeting them. Finally, agent technologies have matured to the point where protocols for communication and negotiation have been standardized [12].

What would it take to adopt a popular software modeling language such as UML [2] and turn it into one that supports *agent*-oriented software development? This paper

---

* For further detail about the *Tropos* project, see http://www.cs.toronto.edu/km/tropos.

M. Gogolla and C. Kobryn (Eds.): UML 2001, LNCS 2185, pp. 422-441, 2001.

sketches an agent-oriented software development methodology and proposes extension to UML to accommodate its concepts and features. Our proposal is based on on-going research within the *Tropos* project [3, 23].

Tropos is founded on the premise that in order to build software that operates within a dynamic environment, one needs to analyze and model explicitly that environment in terms of "actors", their goals and dependencies on other actors. Accordingly, Tropos supports four phases of software development:

- Early requirements, concerned with understanding the problem by studying an organizational setting; the output of this phase is an organizational model which includes relevant external actors, their respective goals and their inter-dependencies.
- Late requirements, where the system-to-be is described within its operational environment, along with relevant functions and qualities.
- Architectural design, where the system's global architecture is defined in terms of subsystems, interconnected through data, control and other dependencies.
- Detailed design, where behaviour of each architectural component is defined in further detail.

To support modeling and analysis during each of these phases, we adopt the concepts offered by *i** [29], a modeling framework offering concepts such as *actor* (actors can be *agents, positions* or *roles*), as well as social dependencies among actors, including *goal, softgoal, task* and *resource* dependencies. These concepts are used to support modeling during the four phases listed above. This means that both the system's environment and the system itself are seen as organizations of actors, each having goals to be fulfilled and each relying on other actors to help them with goal fulfillment.

In order to illustrate the *Tropos* software development methodology, we use a small case study for a B2C (business to consumer) e-commerce application. *Media Shop* is a store selling and shipping different kinds of media items such as books, newspapers, magazines, audio CDs, videotapes, and the like. *Media Shop* customers (on-site or remote) can use a periodically updated catalogue describing available media items to specify their order. *Media Shop* is supplied with the latest releases from *Media Producer* and in-catalogue items by *Media Supplier*. To increase market share, *Media Shop* has decided to open up a B2C retail sales front on the internet. With the new setup, a customer can order *Media Shop* items in person, by phone, or through the internet. The system has been named *Medi@* and is available on the world-wide-web using communication facilities provided by *Telecom Co*. It also uses financial services supplied by *Bank Co.*, which specializes on on-line transactions.

The basic objective for the new system is to allow an on-line customer to examine the *Medi@* internet catalogue, and place orders. There are no registration restrictions, or identification procedures for *Medi@* users. Potential customers can search the on-line store by either browsing the catalogue or querying the item database. The catalogue groups media items of the same type into (sub)hierarchies and genres (e.g., audio CDs are classified into pop, rock, jazz, opera, world, classical music, soundtrack, ...) so that customers can browse only (sub)categories of interest. An on-line search engine allows customers with particular items in mind to search title, author/artist and description fields through keywords or full-text search. If the item is not available in the catalogue, the customer has the option of asking *Media Shop* to order it, provided the customer has editor/publisher references (e.g., ISBN, ISSN), and identifies herself (in terms of name and credit card number). For detailed descriptions of the medi@ case study, see [3] and [20].

Section 2 introduces the primitive concepts offered by *i** and illustrates their use for early requirements analysis. Section 3 sketches how the *Tropos* methodology works for later phases of the development process. Section 4 presents fragments of *Tropos* models in UML using existing and extended UML diagrammatic techniques. Section 5 compares our proposal with others in the literature, offers an initial assessment of UML's suitability for modeling agent-oriented software, and outlines directions for further research.

2 Early Requirements with *i**

Early requirements analysis focuses on the intentions of stakeholders. These intentions are modeled as goals which, through some form of a goal-oriented analysis, eventually lead to the functional and non-functional requirements of the system-to-be [8]. In *i** (which stands for "distributed intentionality"), stakeholders are represented as (social) actors who depend on each other for goals to be achieved, tasks to be performed, and resources to be furnished. The *i** framework includes the *strategic dependency model* for describing the network of relationships among actors, as well as the *strategic rationale model* for describing and supporting the reasoning that each actor goes through concerning its relationships with other actors. These models have been formalized using intentional concepts from Artificial Intelligence, such as goal, belief, ability, and commitment (e.g., [6]). The framework has been presented in detail in [29] and has been related to different application areas, including requirements engineering [27], business process reengineering [30], and software processes [28].

A strategic dependency model is a graph involving *actors* who have *strategic dependencies* among each other. A dependency describes an "agreement" (called *dependum*) between two actors: the *depender* and the *dependee*. The *depender* is the depending actor, and the *dependee,* the actor who is depended upon. The type of the dependency describes the nature of the agreement. *Goal* dependencies are used to represent delegation of responsibility for fulfilling a goal; *softgoal* dependencies are similar to goal dependencies, but their fulfillment cannot be defined precisely (for instance, the appreciation is subjective, or the fulfillment can occur only to a given extent); *task* dependencies are used in situations where the dependee is required to perform a given activity; and *resource* dependencies require the dependee to provide a resource to the depender. As shown in Figure 1, actors are represented as circles; dependums -- goals, softgoals, tasks and resources -- are respectively represented as ovals, clouds, hexagons and rectangles; and dependencies have the form *depender* → *dependum* → *dependee*.

These elements are sufficient for producing a first model of an organizational environment. For instance, Figure 1 depicts an *i** model of our *Medi@* example. The main actors are *Customer, MediaShop, MediaSupplier* and *MediaProducer. Customer* depends on *MediaShop* to fulfill her goal: *Buy Media Items.* Conversely, *MediaShop* depends on *Customer* to *increase market* share and make *"customers happy".* Since the dependum *HappyCustomers* cannot be defined precisely, it is represented as a softgoal.

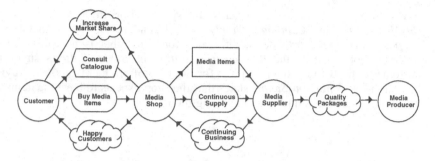

Fig. 1. *i** Model for a Media Shop

The *Customer* also depends on *MediaShop* to *consult the catalogue* (task dependency). Furthermore, *MediaShop* depends on *MediaSupplier* to supply media items in a continuous way and get a *Media Item* (resource dependency) . The items are expected to be of good quality because, otherwise, the *Continuing Business* dependency would not be fulfilled. Finally, *MediaProducer* is expected to provide *MediaSupplier* with *Quality Packages.*

We have defined a formal language, called *Formal Tropos* [13], that complements *i** in several directions. First of all, it provides a textual notation for *i** models and allows us to describe dynamic constraints among the different elements of the specification in a first order, linear-time temporal logic. Second, it has a precisely defined semantics that is amenable to formal analysis. Finally, *Formal Tropos* comes with a methodology for the automated analysis and animation of specifications [13], based on model checking techniques [5].

Entity MediaItem
  Attribute constant itemType : ItemType, price : Amount,
                    InStock : Boolean

Dependency BuyMediaItems
 Type goal
 Mode achieve
 Depender Customer
 Dependee MediaShop
 Attribute constant item : MediaItem
 Fulfillment
    condition for depender
        $\forall media : MediaItem(self.item.type =$
      $media.type \rightarrow item.price <= media.price)$
      [the customer expects to get the best price for the type of item]

Dependency ContinuousSupply
 Type goal
 Mode maintain
 Depender MediaShop
 Dependee MediaSupplier
 Attribute constant item : MediaItem
 Fulfillment
    condition for depender
        $\exists buy : BuyItem(JustCreated(buy) \rightarrow buy.item.inStock)$
    [the media retailer expects to get items in stock as soon as someone is interested in buying them]

Fig. 2. *Formal Tropos* Specifications

As an example, Figure 2 presents the specification in *Formal Tropos* for the *BuyMediaItems* and *ContinuousSupply* goal dependencies. Notice that the *Formal Tropos* specification provides additional information that is not present in the *i** diagram. For instance, the *fulfillment condition* of *BuyMediaItems* states that the customer expects to get the best price for the type of product that she is buying. The condition for *ContinuousSupply* states that the shop expects to have the items in stock as soon as someone is interested in buying them.

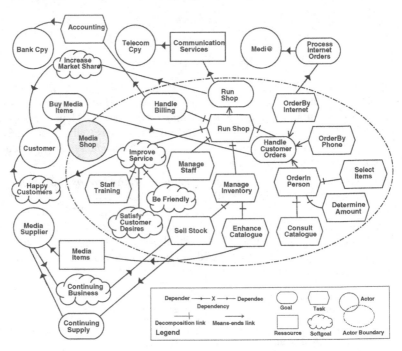

Fig. 3. Means-Ends Analysis for the Softgoal *Increase Market Share*

Once the relevant stakeholders and their goals have been identified, a strategic rationale model determines through a means-ends analysis how these goals (including softgoals) can actually be fulfilled through the contributions of other actors. A strategic rationale model is a graph with four types of nodes -- *goal, task, resource,* and *softgoal* -- and two types of links -- means-ends links and task decomposition links.   A strategic rationale graph captures the relationship between the goals of each actor and the dependencies through which the actor expects these dependencies to be fulfilled.

Figure 3 focuses on one of the (soft)goal dependency identified for *Media Shop*, namely *Increase Market Share*. To achieve that softgoal, the analysis postulates a goal *Run Shop* that can be fulfilled by means of a task *Run Shop*. Tasks are partially ordered sequences of steps intended to accomplish some (soft)goal. Tasks can be decomposed into goals and/or subtasks, whose collective fulfillment completes the task. In the figure, *Run Shop* is decomposed into goals *Handle Billing* and *Handle Customer Orders*, tasks *Manage Staff* and *Manage Inventor,* and softgoal *Improve Service* which together accomplish the top-level task. Sub-goals and subtasks can be specified more precisely through refinement. For instance, the goal *Handle Customer*

Orders is fulfilled either through tasks *OrderByPhone*, *OrderInPerson* or *OrderByInternet* while the task *Manage Staff* would be collectively accomplished by tasks *Sell Stock* and *Enhance Catalogue*.

3 Other Phases

3.1 Late Requirements Analysis

Late requirements analysis results in a requirements specification which describes all functional and non-functional requirements for the system-to-be. In *Tropos*, the information system is represented as one or more actors which participate in a strategic dependency model, along with other actors from the system's operational environment. In other words, the system comes into the picture as one or more actors who contribute to the fulfillment of stakeholder goals.

For our example, the *Medi@* system is introduced as an actor in the strategic dependency model depicted in Figure 4. With respect to the actors previously identified, *Customer* depends on *Media Shop* to buy media items while *Media Shop* depends on *Customer* to increase market share and remain happy (with *Media Shop* service). *Media Shop* depends on *Medi@* for processing internet orders and on *Bank Cpy* to process business transactions. *Customer*, in turn, depends on *Medi@* to place orders through the internet, to search the database for keywords, or simply to browse the on-line catalogue. With respect to relevant qualities, *Customer* requires that transaction services be secure and usable, while *Media Shop* expects *Medi@* to be easily adaptable. Further dependencies are shown on Figure 4 and explained in [3].

Although a strategic dependency model provides hints about why processes are structured in a certain way, it does not sufficiently support the process of suggesting, exploring, and evaluating alternative solutions.

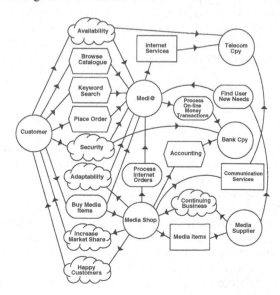

Fig. 4. Strategic Dependency Model for a Media Shop

As late requirements analysis proceeds, *Medi@* is given additional responsibilities, and ends up as the depender of several dependencies. Moreover, the system is decomposed into several sub-actors which take on some of these responsibilities. This decomposition and responsibility assignment is realized using the same kind of means-ends analysis along with the strategic rationale analysis illustrated in Figure 3. Hence, the analysis in Figure 5 focuses on the system itself, instead of an external stakeholder.

The figure postulates a root task *Internet Shop Managed* providing sufficient support (++) [4] to the softgoal *Increase Market Share*. That task is firstly refined into goals *Internet Order Handled* and *Item Searching Handled*, softgoals *Attract New Customer*, *Secure* and *Usable* and tasks *Produce Statistics* and *Adaptation*. To manage internet orders, *Internet Order Handled* is achieved through the task *Shopping Cart* which is decomposed into subtasks *Select Item*, *Add Item*, Check *Out*, and *Get Identification Detail*. These are the main process activities required to design an operational on-line shopping cart [7]. The latter (goal) is achieved either through sub-goal *Classic Communication Handled* dealing with phone and fax orders or *Internet Handled* managing secure or standard form orderings. To allow for the ordering of new items not listed in the catalogue, *Select Item* is also further refined into two alternative subtasks, one dedicated to select catalogued items, the other to preorder unavailable products.

To provide sufficient support (++) to the *Adaptable* softgoal, *Adaptability* is refined into four subtasks dealing with catalogue updates, system evolution, interface updates and system monitoring.

The goal *Item Searching Handled* might alternatively be fulfilled through tasks *Database Querying* or *Catalogue Consulting* with respect to customers' navigating desiderata, i.e., searching with particular items in mind by using search functions or simply browsing the catalogued products.

In addition, as already pointed, Figure 5 introduces softgoal contributions to model sufficient/partial positive (respectively ++ and +) or negative (respectively - - and -) support to softgoals *Secure*, *Available*, *Adaptable*, *Attract New Customers* and *Increase Market Share*. The result of this means-ends analysis is a set of (system and human) actors who are dependees for some of the dependencies that have been postulated.

Resource, task and softgoal dependencies correspond naturally to functional and non-functional requirements. Leaving (some) goal dependencies between system actors and other actors is a novelty. Traditionally, functional goals are "operationalized" during late requirements [8], while quality softgoals are either operationalized or "metricized" [9]. For example, a security softgoal might be operationalized by defining interfaces which minimize input/output between the system and its environment, or by limiting access to sensitive information. Alternatively, the security requirement may be metricized into something like "No more than X unauthorized operations in the system-to-be per year".

Leaving goal dependencies with system actors as dependees makes sense whenever there is a foreseeable need for flexibility in the performance of a task on the part of the system. For example, consider a communication goal "communicate X to Y". According to conventional development techniques, such a goal needs to be operationalized before the end of late requirements analysis, perhaps into some sort of a user interface through which user Y will receive message X from the system. The problem with this approach is that the steps through which this goal is to be fulfilled (along with a host of background assumptions) are frozen into the requirements of the system-to-be. This early translation of goals into concrete plans for their fulfillment makes systems fragile and less reusable.

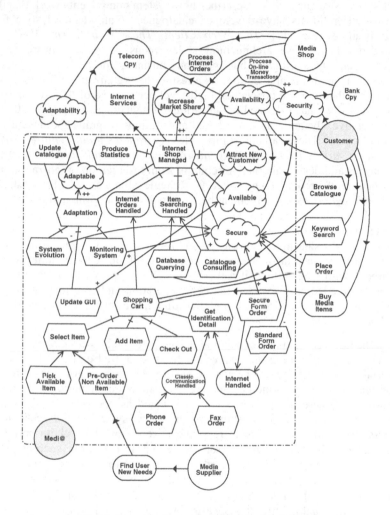

Fig. 5. Strategic Rationale Model for *Medi@*

In our example, we have left three (soft)goals (*Availability, Security, Adaptability*) in the late requirements model. For instance, we have left *Availability* because we propose to allow system agents to automatically decide at run-time which catalogue browser, shopping cart and order processor architecture fit best customer needs or navigator/platform specifications. Moreover, we would like to include different search engines, reflecting different search techniques, and let the system dynamically choose the most appropriate.

3.2 Architectural Design

A system architecture constitutes a relatively small, intellectually manageable model of system structure, which describes how system components work together. By now, software architects have developed catalogues of architectural style for e-business applications (e.g., [7]: *Thin Web Client, Thick Web Client, Web Delivery, ...*) Unfortunately, these architectural styles focus on web concepts, protocols and underlying technologies but not on business processes nor non functional requirements of the application. As a result, the organizational architecture styles are not described nor the conceptual high-level perspective of the e-business application. In *Tropos*, we have defined organizational architectural styles [19, 20, 14] for agent, cooperative, dynamic and distributed applications to guide the design of the system architecture. These architectural styles (*pyramid, joint venture, structure in 5, takeover, arm's length, vertical integration, co-optation, bidding, ...*) are based on concepts and design alternatives coming from research on organization management : organization theory, agency theory, strategic alliances, ... For instance, the *joint venture* style involves agreement between two or more principal partners to obtain the benefits of larger scale, partial investment and lower maintenance costs. Through the delegation of authority to a specific *Joint Management* actor that coordinates tasks and manages sharing of knowledge and resources, they pursue joint objectives. Each principal partner can manage and control itself on a local dimension and interact directly with other principal partners to exchange, provide and receive services, data and knowledge. However, the strategic operation and coordination of such a system and its partner actors on a global dimension are only ensured by the *Joint Management* actor.

The first task during architectural design is to select among alternative architectural styles using as criteria the desired qualities identified earlier. The analysis involves refining these qualities, represented as softgoals, to sub-goals that are more specific and more precise and then evaluating alternative architectural styles against them, as shown in Figure 6. The styles are represented as operationalized softgoals (saying, roughly, "make the architecture of the new system *pyramid-/joint venture-/co-optation*-based, ... "). Design rationale is represented by claim softgoals drawn as dashed clouds. These can represent contextual information (such as priorities) to be considered and properly reflected into the decision making process. Exclamation marks (! and !!) are used to mark priority softgoals. A check-mark "✓" indicates a fulfilled softgoal, while a cross "✗" labels an unfulfillable one.

Software quality attributes *Security*, *Availability* and *Adaptability* have been left in the late requirements model (See Section 3.1). They will guide the selection process of th appropriate architectural style.

In Figure 6, *Adaptability* has been AND-decomposed into *Dynamicity* and *Updatability*. For our e-commerce example, *dynamicity* should deal with the way the system can be designed using generic mechanisms to allow web pages and user interfaces to be dynamically and easily changed. Indeed, information content and layout need to be frequently refreshed to give correct information to customers or simply be fashionable for marketing reasons. Frameworks like Active Server Pages (ASP), Server Side Includes (SSI) to create dynamic pages make this attribute easier to achieve. *Updatability* should be strategically important for the viability of the application, the stock management and the business itself since *Media Shop* employees have to very regularly bring up to date the catalogue by for inventory consistency. Comparable analyses are carried out in turn for newly identified quality sub-attributes and for the other top-level quality softgoals *Security* and *Availability*.

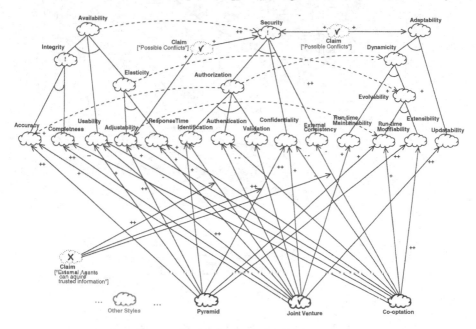

Fig. 6. Selecting the Architecture

Eventually, the analysis shown in Figure 6 allows us to choose the joint venture architectural style for our e-commerce example (the operationalized attribute is marked with a "✓"). More details about the selection and non-functional requirements decomposition process can be found in [19, 20]. In addition, more specific attributes have been identified during the decomposition process, such as *Integrity* (*Accuracy, Completeness*), *Usability*, *Response Time*, *Maintainability*, *Updatability*, *Confidentiality*, *Authorization* (*Identification*, *Authentication*, *Validation*) and need to be considered in the system architecture.

Figure 7 suggests a possible assignment of system responsibilities, based on the joint venture architectural style for our e-business application. The system is decomposed into three principal partners (*Store Front*, *Billing Processor* and *Back Store*) controlling themselves on a local dimension and exchanging, providing and receiving services, data and resources with each other.

Each of them delegates authority to and is controlled and coordinated by the joint management actor (*Joint Manager*) managing the system on a global dimension. *Store Front* interacts primarily with *Customer* and provides her with a usable front-end web application. *Back Store* keeps track of all web information about customers, products, sales, bills and other data of strategic importance to *Media Shop*. *Billing Processor* is in charge of the secure management of orders and bills, and other financial data; also of interactions to *Bank Cpy*. *Joint Manager* manages all of them controlling *security* gaps, *availability* bottlenecks and *adaptability* issues.

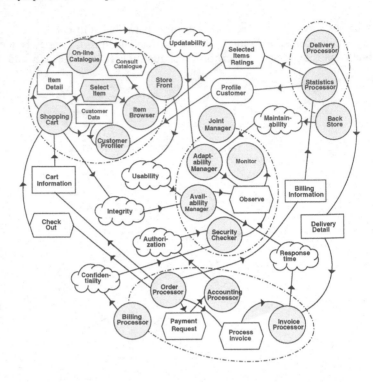

Fig. 7. The E-commerce System in Joint Venture Architecture

To accommodate the responsibilities of *Store Front*, we introduce *Item Browser* to manage catalogue navigation, *Shopping Cart* to select and custom items, *Customer Profiler* to track customer data and produce client profiles, and *On-line Catalogue* to deal with digital library obligations. To cope with the identified software quality attributes (*Security*, *Availability* and *Adaptability*), *Joint Manager* is further refined into four new system sub-actors *Availability Manager*, *Security Checker* and *Adaptability Manager* each of them assuming one of the main softgoals (and their more specific subgoals) and observed by a *Monitor*. Further refinements are shown on Figure 7 and explained in [19, 20].

3.3 Detailed Design

The detailed design phase is intended to introduce additional detail for each architectural component of a system. In our case, this includes actor communication and actor behavior. To support this phase, we propose to adopt agent specifications proposed by FIPA (Foundation for Intelligent Agents) [12] notably agent role and patterns (see [14, 20]) that can be found in agent communication languages like FIPA-ACL [12] or KQML [12].

For instance, the *matchmaker* agent pattern locates a provider corresponding to a consumer request for service, and then hands the consumer a handle to the chosen provider. Contrary to the broker pattern who directly handles all interactions between the consumer and the provider, the negotiation for service and actual service provision are separated into two distinct phases.

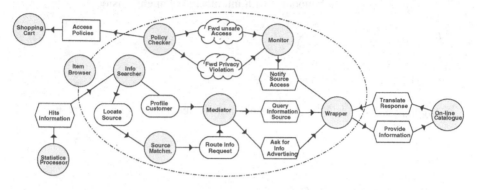

Fig. 8. Detailing Item Browser with Agent Patterns

Figure 8 shows a possible use of the patterns in the e-business system depicted in Figure 7. In particular, it describes how to solve the goal of managing catalogue navigation that the *Store Front* has delegated to the *Item Browser*. The goal is decomposed into different subgoals and solved with a combination of patterns. The broker pattern is applied to the *Info Searcher*, which satisfies requests of searching information by accessing *On-line Catalogue*. The Source *Matchmaker* applies the matchmaker pattern locating the appropriate source for the *Info Searcher*, and the monitor pattern is used to check any possible change in the *On-line Catalogue*. Finally, the mediator pattern is applied to mediate the interaction among the *Info Searcher*, the *Source Matchmaker*, and the *Wrapper*, while the wrapper pattern makes the interaction between the *Item Browser* and the *On-line Catalogue* possible. Of course, other patterns can be applied [20]. For instance, we could use the contract-net pattern to select a wrapper to which delegate the interaction with the *On-line Catalogue*, or the embassy to route the request of a wrapper to the *On-line Catalogue*.

4 *Tropos* Models in UML

We have defined a set of stereotypes, tagged values, and constraints to accommodate *Tropos* concepts within UML. This section briefly describes some of them according to GRL (Goal-oriented Requirement Language) [15]. For an exhaustive and formal definition of the *Tropos* ontology see [15].

Stereotypes

i* actor

Metamodel class   Actor

Description	An actor is an active entity that carries out actions to achieve goals by exercising its know-how. An actor may optionally have a boundary, with intentional elements inside.

Icon

Constraints	None
Tagged values	Actor_id, external_name, description, goal_model_id

Task

Metamodel class	Use Case
Description	A task specifies a particular way of doing something. Tasks can also be seen as the solutions in the target system, which will satisfice the softgoals (operationalizations). These solutions provide operations, processes, data representations, structuring, constraints and agents in the target system to meet the needs stated in the goals and softgoals.

Icon

Constraints	None
Tagged values	Task_id, external_name, owner_id, description

Goal

Metamodel class	Class
Description	A goal is a condition or state of affairs in the world that the stakeholders would like to achieve. How the goal is to be achieved is not specified, allowing alternatives to be considered. A goal can be either a business goal or a system goal.

Icon

Constraints	None
Tagged values	Goal_id, external_name, owner_id, description

i dependency*

Metamodel class	Association
Description	The Dependency statement describes an intentional relationship between two actors, i.e., one actor (<Depender>) depends on another actor (<Dependee>) on something (<Dependum>).
Constraints	Dependencies must have at least one depender and one dependee.
Tagged values	Dependency_id, dependency_name, dependum_type, depender_id, dependee_id

Means-ends

Metamodel class	Association
Description	The Means-ends statement describes how goals are in fact achieved. Each task provided is an alternative means for achieving the goal. Normally, each task would have different types of impacts on softgoals, which would serve as criteria for evaluating and choosing among each task alternative.
Constraints	Only goals are applicable to means-ends links.
Tagged values	Means-ends_id, means_element_id, ends_element_id

Task Decomp.

Metamodel class	Aggregation
Description	The decomposition relationship provides the ability to define what other elements need to be achieved or available in order for a task to perform.
Constraints	Only tasks are decomposable. Sub-components of tasks are goals, tasks, resources, and softgoals.
Tagged values	Decomposition_id, sub-element_id, decomposed_element_id

For instance, Figure 9 depicts the i* model from Figure 1 in UML using the stereotypes we have defined, notably <<*i* actor*>> and <<*i* dependency*>>. Such mapping in UML could also be done in a similar way for strategic rationale (e.g., Figure 3) or goal analysis (e.g., Figure 6) models.

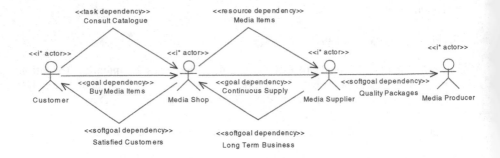

Fig. 9. Representing the *i** Model from Figure 1 in UML with stereotypes

In addition to the introduction of *Tropos* concepts in UML through stereotypes, we also adopt UML extensions proposed by FIPA and the OMG Agent Work group [1, 21, 22]. The rest of the section concentrates on the *Shopping cart* actor and the *check out* dependency. Figure 10 depicts a partial UML class diagram focusing on that actor that will be implemented as an aggregation of several *CartForm*s and *ItemLine*s. Associations *ItemDetail* to *On-line Catalogue*, aggregation of *MediaItem*s, and *CustomerDetail* to *CustomerProfiler*, aggregation of *CustomerProfileCard*s are directly derived from resource dependencies with the same name in Figure 7.

i* tasks will be implemented as agent plans represented as methods following the label "*Plans*".

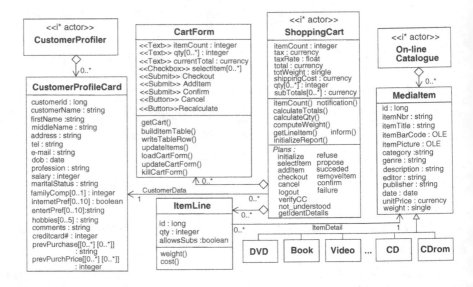

Fig. 10. Partial Class Diagram for *Store Front* Focusing on *Shopping Cart*

To specify the *checkout* task, for instance, we use AUML - the Agent Unified Modeling Language [1], which supports templates and packages to represent *checkout* as an object, but also in terms of sequence and collaborations diagrams.

Figure 11(a) introduces the *checkout* interaction context which is triggered by the *checkout* communication act (CA) and ends with a returned information status. This diagram only provides basic specification for an intra-agent order processing protocol. In particular, the diagram stipulates neither the procedure used by the *Customer* to produce the *checkout* CA, nor the procedure employed by the *Shopping Cart* to respond to the CA.

As shown in Figure 11(b), such details can be provided by using *levelling* [22], i.e., by introducing additional interaction and other diagrams. Each additional level can express *inter-actor* or *intra-actor* dialogues. At the lowest level, specification of an actor requires spelling out the detailed processing that takes place within the actor.

Figure 11(b) focuses on the protocol between *Customer* and *Shopping Cart* which consists of a customization of the Contract Net FIPA agent pattern [21]. Such a protocol describes a communication pattern among actors, as well as constraints on the contents of the messages they exchange.

We use plan diagrams [18], based on state charts and activity diagrams, to specify the internal processing (tasks) of atomic actors. The initial transition of the plan diagram is labeled with an activation event (*Press checkout button*) and activation condition (*[checkout button activated]*) which determine when and in what context the plan should be activated. Transitions from a state automatically occur when exiting the state and no event is associated (e.g., when exiting *Fields Checking*) or when the associated event occurs (e.g., *Press cancel button*), provided in all cases that the associated condition is true (e.g., *[Mandatory fields filled]*). When the transition occurs, any associated action is performed (e.g., *verifyCC()*).

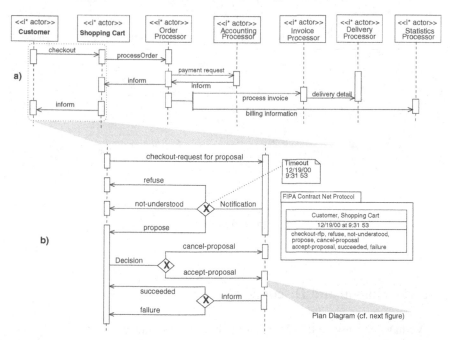

Fig. 11. Sequence Diagram to Order Media Items (a), and Agent Interaction Protocol Focusing on a *Checkout* Dialogue (b)

An important feature of plan diagrams is their notion of failure. Failure can occur when an action upon a transition fails, when an explicit transition to a fail state (denoted by a small no entry sign) occurs, or when the activity of an active state terminates in failure and no outgoing transition is enabled.

Figure 12 depicts the plan diagram for *checkout*, triggered by pushing the checkout button. Mandatory fields are first checked. If any mandatory fields are not filled, an iteration allows the customer to update them. For security reasons, the loop exits after 5 tries ([i<5]) and causes the plan to fail. Credit Card validity is then checked. Again for security reasons, when not valid, the CC# can only be corrected 3 times. Otherwise, the plan terminates in failure. The customer is then asked to confirm the CC# to allow item registration. If the CC# is not confirmed, the plan fails. Otherwise, the plan continues: each item is iteratively registered, final amounts are calculated, stock records and customer profiles are updated and a report is displayed. When finally the whole plan succeeds, the *ShoppingCart* automatically logs out and asks the *Order Processor* to initialize the order. When, for any reason, the plan fails, the *ShoppingCart* automatically logs out. At anytime, if the cancel button is pressed, or the timeout is more than 90 seconds (e.g., due to a network bottleneck), the plan fails and the *Shopping Cart* is reinitialized.

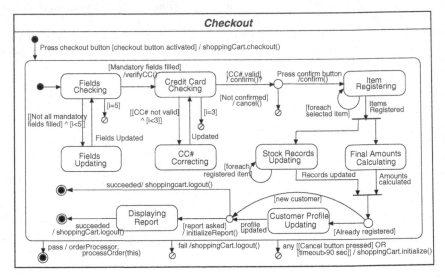

Fig. 12. A Plan Diagram for *Checkout*

5 Conclusion and Discussion

We have proposed a development methodology founded on intentional concepts, and inspired by early requirements modeling. We have also sketched how these concepts can be accommodated within UML, and how they can incorporate recent proposals for UML extensions. We believe that the methodology is particularly appropriate for generic, componentized software systems, such as e-business applications that can be downloaded and used in a variety of operating environments and computing platforms around the world. Preliminary results (e.g., [20, 23]) suggest that the methodology complements well proposals for agent-oriented programming environments.

As a matter of fact, unlike UML and existing UML extensions for agent software development such as AUML [22], the *Tropos* approach is requirement- and goal-oriented, i.e., based and driven by intentional and social primitives. Besides, in *Tropos*, we do not necessarily operationalize or metricize these intentional an social structures early on during the development process, avoiding to freeze solutions to a given requirement in the produced software designs. This kind of approach is especially relevant for developing agent applications since, in addition to be systems requiring flexibility and dynamicity, they are built on mental states like beliefs, intentions, desires or commitments and considered "societies" of software entities.

On the other hand, there already exist some proposals for agent-oriented software development like [10, 16, 17, 18, 25]. Such proposals are mostly extensions to known object-oriented and/or knowledge engineering methodologies. Moreover, all these proposals focus on design -- as opposed to requirements analysis -- and are therefore considerably narrower in scope than *Tropos*. Indeed, *Tropos* proposes to adopt the same concepts, inspired by requirements modeling research, for describing requirements *and* system design models in order to narrow the semantic gap between them. The architecture and software design models produced within our framework are intentional in the sense that system components have associated goals that are supposed to be fulfilled. They are also social in the sense that each component has obligations/expectations towards/from other components. Obviously, such models are best suited to cooperative, dynamic and distributed applications like multi-agent systems.

The research reported here is still in progress. Much remains to be done to further refine the proposed methodology and validate its usefulness with real case studies. We are currently working on the development of additional formal analysis techniques for *Tropos* including temporal analysis (using model-checking), goal analysis and social structures analysis, also the development of tools which support different phases of the methodology and the definition of the *Formal Tropos* language.

References

[1] Bauer, B., *Extending UML for the Specification of Agent Interaction Protocols,* OMG document ad/99-12-03, FIPA submission to the OMG's Analysis and Design Task Force (ADTF) in response to the Request of Information (RFI) entitled "UML2.0 RFI", December 1999.

[2] Booch, G., Rumbaugh, J. and Jacobson, I., *The Unified Modeling Language User Guide,* The Addison-Wesley Object Technology Series, Addison-Wesley, 1999.

[3] Castro, J., Kolp, M. and Mylopoulos, J., "A Requirements-Driven Development Methodology", *Proceedings of the 13th International Conference on Advanced Information Systems Engineering* (CAiSE'01), Interlaken, Switzerland, June 2001.

[4] Chung, L. K., Nixon, B. A., Yu, E. and Mylopoulos, J., *Non-Functional Requirements in Software Engineering,* Kluwer Publishing, 2000.

[5]   Clarke, E., Grumberg, O. and Peled, D., *Model Checking*, MIT Press, 1999.
[6]   Cohen, P. and Levesque, H., "Intention is Choice with Commitment", *Artificial Intelligence, 32(3)*, 1990, pp. 213-261.
[7]   Conallen, J., *Building Web Applications with UML*, The Addison-Wesley Object Technology Series, Addison-Wesley, 2000.
[8]   Dardenne, A., van Lamsweerde, A. and Fickas, S., "Goal–directed Requirements Acquisition", *Science of Computer Programming, 20*, 1993, pp. 3-50.
[9]   Davis, A., *Software Requirements: Objects, Functions and States*, Prentice Hall, 1993.
[10] DeLoach, S. A. and Wood, M., "Developing Multiagent Systems with agentTool", *Proceedings of the 7th The Seventh International Workshop on Agent Theories, Architectures, and Languages* (ATAL'00), Boston, USA, July, 2000.
[11] DeMarco, T., *Structured Analysis and System Specification*, Yourdon Press, 1978.
[12] *The Foundation for Intelligent Physical Agents*, http://www.fipa.org, 2001.
[13] Fuxman, A., Pistore, M., Mylopoulos, J. and Traverso, P., "Model Checking Early Requirements Specification in Tropos", *Proceedings of the Fifth IEEE International Symposium on Requirements Engineering* (RE'01), Toronto, Canada, August 2001.
[14] Fuxman, A., Giorgini, P., Kolp, M. and Mylopoulos, J., "Information Systems as Social Structures", *Proceedings of the Second International Conference on Formal Ontologies for Information Systems* (FOIS'01), Ogunquit, USA, October 2001.
[15] *Goal Oriented Requirement Language*, http://www.cs.toronto.edu/km/GRL
[16] Iglesias, C., Garrijo, M. and Gonzalez, J., "A Survey of Agent-Oriented Methodologies", *Proceedings of the 5th International Workshop on Intelligent Agents: Agent Theories, Architectures, and Languages* (ATAL'98), pp. 317-330, Paris, France, July 1998.
[17] Jennings, N. R., "On agent-based software engineering", *Artificial Intelligence, 117*, 2000, pp. 277-296.
[18] Kinny, D. and Georgeff, M., "Modelling and Design of Multi-Agent System", *Proceedings of the Third International Workshop on Agent Theories, Architectures, and Languages* (ATAL'96), pp. 1-20, Budapest, Hungary, August 1996.
[19] Kolp, M., Castro, J. and Mylopoulos, J., "A Social Organization Perspective on Software Architectures", *Proceedings of the First International Workshop From Software Requirements to Architectures* (STRAW'01), pp. 5-12, Toronto, Canada, May 2001.
[20] Kolp, M., Giorgini, P. and Mylopoulos, J., "A Goal-Based Organizational Perspective on Multi-Agents Architectures", *Proceedings of the 9th International Workshop on Intelligent Agents: Agent Theories, Architectures, and Languages* (ATAL'01), Seattle, USA, August 2001.
[21] Odell, J. and Bock, C., *Suggested UML Extensions for Agents*, OMG document ad/99-12-01, Submitted to the OMG's Analysis and Design Task Force (ADTF) in response to the Request of Information (RFI) entitled "UML 2.0 RFI", December 1999.
[22] Odell, J., Van Dyke Parunak, H. and Bauer, B., "Extending UML for Agents", *Proceedings of the Agent-Oriented Information System Workshop at the 17th National Conference on Artificial Intelligence*, pp. 3-17, Austin, USA, July 2000.
[23] Perini, A., Bresciani, P., Giunchiglia, F., Giorgini, P. and Mylopoulos, J., "A Knowledge Level Software Engineering Methodology for Agent Oriented Programming". *Proceedings of the Fifth International Conference on Autonomous Agents* (Agents'01), Montreal, Canada, June 2001.
[24] Wirfs-Brock, R., Wilkerson, B. and Wiener, L., *Designing Object-Oriented Software*, Englewood Cliffs, Prentice-Hall, 1990.
[25] Wooldridge, M., Jennings, N. R. and Kinny D., "The Gaia Methodology for Agent-Oriented Analysis and Design", *Journal of Autonomous Agents and Multi-Agent Systems, 3(3)*, 2000.
[26] Yourdon, E. and Constantine, L., *Structured Design: Fundamentals of a Discipline of Computer Program and Systems Design*, Prentice-Hall, 1979.

[27] Yu, E., "Modeling Organizations for Information Systems Requirements Engineering", *Proceedings of the First IEEE International Symposium on Requirements Engineering* (RE'93), pp. 34-41, San Jose, USA, January 1993.
[28] Yu, E. and Mylopoulos, J., "Understanding 'Why' in Software Process Modeling, Analysis and Design", *Proceedings of the Sixteenth International Conference on Software Engineering* (ICSE'94, , pp. 159-168, Sorrento, Italy, May 1994.
[29] Yu, E., *Modelling Strategic Relationships for Process Reengineering*, Ph.D. thesis, Department of Computer Science, University of Toronto, Canada, 1995.
[30] Yu, E. and Mylopoulos, J., "Using Goals, Rules, and Methods to Support Reasoning in Business Process Reengineering", *International Journal of Intelligent Systems in Accounting, Finance and Management, 5(1),* January 1996, pp. 1-13.

A UML Meta-model for Contract Aware Components*

Torben Weis[1], Christian Becker[1], Kurt Geihs[1], and Noël Plouzeau[2]

[1] J. W. Goethe-University, Dept. of Computer Science, Robert-Mayer-Str. 11-15,
60326 Frankfurt/Main, Germany
[2] IRISA, Campus de Beaulieu, 35042 Rennes Cedex, France

Abstract. We present an extension to the UML meta-model which allows modelling of contract aware components. Contracts are a novel way of describing the functional and non-functional behaviour of components. The usage of contracts in component diagrams allows tools to check whether all requirements for a successful assembly and deployment of the components are fulfilled. Furthermore, we investigate how components can be used in the different development phases and how design phase transitions can be managed.

1 Introduction

Since some software projects became so complex that it took an entire team multiple months to finish them, scientists started to search for technologies and methodologies which allowed to produce high quality software in time and with little human resources. One of the key techniques improving software productivity and cost is reuse of software architectures. Indeed, a reusable architecture can help to produce high quality code, where quality means few bugs, efficiency and easy to understand code. Reuse of well tested software building blocks should lead to less errors or inefficiencies than the development of new code.

Component technology focuses in first place on code reuse. A component can be thought of as a software building block which solves a specific problem. In the absence of a single accepted definition of the word *component* we do assume that a component does by default not include its source code (although that is – especially in the open source community [15] – sometimes the case). And since source code is not available, a component must provide a great deal of information on how it can be used by other software parts.

To achieve this, a component usually specifies interfaces (in the sense of OOP) which it exposes to its users. However, this is not enough for proper reuse of this software building block. Remember that the original goal was to save time in development and to profit from the well tested implementation. But if it is not clear how a component will behave then it is likely that it is used wrongly which would contradict the original goal.

---

* The work presented in this paper is partially funded by the European QCCS project, IST-1999-20122

M. Gogolla and C. Kobryn (Eds.): UML 2001, LNCS 2185, pp. 442–456, 2001.
© Springer-Verlag Berlin Heidelberg 2001

To remove this shortcoming a more precise specification of the component is needed, which covers its functional and non-functional behaviour. As shown in [3] contracts can be used to close the specification gap. However, the current state of the UML standard does not provide tools to model contract aware components. In this paper we present an extension to the UML meta-model which supports improved modelling of components and contracts. After a short introduction to component contracts we will discuss the anatomy of a contract and show how one component can contract another one. We then deal with development phase transitions of component modelling (model refinements) and show how a tool can ensure that contracts made in one phase find their representation in the next phase. Then we will have a look at the support for components in UML 1.4 beta1, present our meta-model extension and discuss its backward compatibility. Finally we illustrate our approach with a comprehensive example, which models the server side of a simple home banking application.

2   Component Contracts

Components are often underspecified which makes their proper reuse a risk in the development process. To remove this shortcoming a more precise specification is needed. Interfaces as we know them from object oriented programming provide a so called *functional* specification of the component. But there are *non-functional* issues which have to be specified, too.

Prominent examples for non-functional aspects of a component are performance and security. For instance, a component customer may be interested in knowing the time complexity of a component's computation (e.g. $O(log(n))$ or $O(n^2)$). Or a component user may want to know whether the component encrypts the data that it sends over the network. Along the same vein, knowledge of bandwidth and latency properties of a component are important issues for component deployment.

Some conceptual tools have been devised to support these various aspects of components properties: instead of just using component interfaces it is possible to extend them with *contracts*. A contract [13] greatly extends the component specification precision. In [3] contracts are divided into four different levels:

1. syntactical contracts,
2. behavioural contracts,
3. synchronisation contracts,
4. quality of service contracts.

Interfaces as offered for example by C++ only cover level one. They describe which methods are available and the structure of incoming and outgoing parameters. In Java the interface is enriched with synchronisation specifications (level 3). But none of the mainstream object oriented programming languages features solutions for level 2 or 4.

Furthermore, we will make the requirements of a component explicit so that the developer can see as early as possible what it takes to get the component up

and running. For example a component for an online shop will offer an interface
for ordering goods. But most likely the component will need some other component which offers a database interface so that the e-shop can store the customer
data.

These requirements are currently not expressed explicitly. Sometimes they
are implicitly given by the interface. The e-shop component may have an interface which features the following method:

```
setDataBase( in db : IDataBase ) : boolean
```

Some written documentation that comes along with the component may explain that the application has to invoke this method first before doing anything
else. That means the requirement was expressed implicitly by one of the component's interfaces. The problem here is that this requirement is hard to detect
at design time.

In the early iterations of the design a developer usually does not spend too
much time on the details of his interfaces nor should he spend too much time
investigating the details of third party components he intends to use. On the
other hand it is important to know that the e-shop requires a database to work
properly.

For this reason requirements have to be explicit. Such requirements are in
general just contracts, with the little difference that the component does not offer
this kind of contracts: it demands them. Hence we have to distinguish between
output contracts which are offered by the component to the outer world and
input contracts on which the component relies.

2.1   Contract Relationships

Components and objects bear different kinds of flexibility. It is generally not
possible to derive from a component and to overload some of its methods. However, a component offers means for interface discovery and configuration management through introspection mechanisms. Therefore a tool can find out at
runtime which properties are available and which type they expect; this facility
helps the user in configuring the component. Most of these properties can be
altered at runtime, but some are static and have to be set during or before deployment. However, this mechanism does not offer more than a tool supported
parametrization of a component which does neither affect the *offered* nor the
required interfaces or non-functional properties.

To illustrate the inherent problem of this approach we come back to our e-
shop component example and we assume that it basically offers two interfaces.
One interface allows to retrieve a list of all products, their detailed description
and availability and a list of "real" shops where people can shop. The other
interface deals with e-payment.

Now the e-payment interface is valid only in some situations, for instance
only if data exchanges can be safely encrypted over the communication link.
Such requirements on a component's environment can be modelled by an input

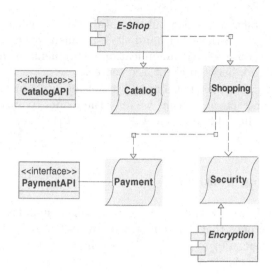

Fig. 1. Modelling of contracts

contract. If this required contract cannot be fulfilled then the component should not offer the e-payment interface. This mechanism prevents the developer from making a fundamental design error. Figure 1 illustrates our example.

In more complex examples the relationships between required contracts and ensured ones can become quite complex, especially when level 4 (QoS) contracts are involved. As we will see later in this paper, an appropriate UML notation is needed to assist designers and design tools in manipulating contracts and contract relationships.

When dealing with QoS contracts we will discover that a set of contracts may have exclusive-or semantics. That means only one contract can be active at a certain time. These contracts often share common subsets. To ease the modelling we introduced the concept of compound contracts. A compound contract is a composition of other contracts. A composed contract can play two different roles. It is either a required or an offered contract.

Another case where compound contracts are useful is the combination of functional and non-functional contracts. For example some component demands a certain throughput for an SQL interface it is using. By grouping the interface and the non-functional contract in a compound contract we can express this relationship.

2.2   Contract Selection and Negotiation

Sometimes the contracts can be selected at design time. But in other cases – especially in QoS-enabled applications – contracts depend on dynamic factors and have to be chosen at runtime. For example a webcast application which transmits a rock concert over the internet may decide to switch to a contract that does not offer any video but acceptable sound when the bandwidth is no longer sufficient. On the other hand the e-payment contract may be selected at design time because some communication component ensures that there will be an encrypted link between client and server.

Since this paper does not aim at presenting mechanisms to select and parametrize the contracts at runtime we refer the reader to our "Management Architecture for Quality of Service (MAQS)" [2] and [11] as an example for dynamic contract negotiation.

2.3   Designing Contracts

Until now we have discussed that a component is manifested by its offered contracts and the ones that it requires. It turns out that contracts often deal with specific dimensions of requirements and offers, such as synchronization paths, delay management, etc.

We claim that such dimensions should be clearly separated by the component designer. More precisely, a component designer should not build contract types that mix specifications of pre- and postconditions, synchronization constraints and QoS issues (such as maximum delays, for instance). The reason for such a separation is simply the well known separation of concerns issue [10]: Developers should minimize unnecessary interactions and constraints between them.

For the component developer it is even more important to practice the separation of concerns. We have already shown in [1] that the implementation of multi-category QoS applications can be quite complicated because the code that implements a certain category cannot be easily separated in methods or classes. Instead cross cuts between the application itself and the QoS mechanisms will show up. Source code written in a language which feature a preprocessor is usually cluttered with #ifdef, #else and #endif instructions. Such code is already hard to understand if the developer knows which parts the preprocessor will throw out and which it will keep. But being aware of all possible combinations is almost impossible in larger projects.

As an example of separation of concerns with contracts let us consider the freely available *zlib* [7] library, which implements compression and is written in ANSI-C. It has many options which can be turned on or off at compile time and it is highly portable. The total line count is 8934, which does already include comments and documentation. The lines which contain preprocessor commands add up to 813. That means almost 10% of the entire code is used to hide or show certain code fragments before the C-compiler sees them. Different compression types and platform support could be modelled as separate contracts. Using an aspect oriented approach [10] it is possible to separate the code for each compression method and the code that is specific for each platform. An aspect weaver can then generate an implementation which supports only the selected contracts. However, this requires the definition and implementation of an appropriate aspect-language which in general is not trivial. Hence the applicability should be high in order to justify the effort.

To sum up we argue that in the common case one should never mix contracts of different levels, because the resulting contract is difficult to understand, not flexible and does not foster tool support. In addition it complicates the component implementors work.

3   Development Phases

A designer might wonder when components show up in the software development process. According to the Unified Process [9] we should distinguish the following phases:

1. Analysis
2. Design
3. Implementation
4. Deployment
5. Runtime

In [4] a component is some physical entity which "ultimately resides on physical nodes". Hence this restricts the component concept to the deployment phase because that is the phase when the physical entities of the system are assigned to concrete nodes. The connection to previous phases is made via interfaces. In the design phase interfaces are defined and used, and later on the components form the code which implements some of these interfaces. In such a scenario components do not support the reuse of code. In [4] it is argued that the advantage of components is the possibility to replace them later easily with a new or better ones. But even that goal is hard to reach, because with these settings components are underspecified. Two components which comply to the same interfaces are not necessarily exchangeable because there may be hidden constraints or non-functional properties which are not part of the components specification.

We are convinced that components should be considered in the design phase already. Component interface definition and implementations belong to this same phase. Therefore it seems to be reasonable to integrate components in earlier design phases and thus provide extensions to the UML.

3.1   Phase Transitions

Since contracts are first class entities in our model framework, we have to take care of their integration into a software development method. Many methods advocate the use of quasi-continuous transformation of models from the specification phase up to deployment and execution. Our contract architecture must then deal with such model transformations.

For instance, in the analysis phase the customer demands high availability for certain actions carried out by the system. In the design phase the developers decide to use an existing component for one of the high availability tasks. The component features a contract which is a specialization of the abstract availability contract which has been used in the analysis phase. The specialized contract offers for example 98% uptime ensured by replica groups. When we finally come into the deployment phase then the component will be split up in several pieces: one which implements the basic functionality, a sequencer and perhaps a monitor. In order of realizing the 98% uptime the replicas have certain constraints. For example there have to be at least 5 of them, each running on a seperate node which has itself an uptime of a certain percentage, a minimum network bandwidth and relies on an independent power supply.

The conclusion that we can draw from the above example is that the component changes drastically from the analysis, through the design and up to the deployment phase. Originally the component offered an availability contract. In the end there exist several subcomponents, and one of them – the replicated one – requires certain contracts from the nodes on which they are to be deployed.

Our component meta-model has been developed with these phase transitions in mind. However, when we just look at a single phase, then we notice that the component can always be described by the contracts it offers and the contracts it requires. So what remains to be done is to describe the transitions using the meta-model, too.

3.2   Modelling Phase Transitions

To support the modelling of phase transitions we introduced the new meta-class *Transition* which is derived from the *Package* meta-class. We do not want to restrict developers in their choice of a model transformation language. So we keep this concept as generic as possible. There are two ways of using the *Transition* meta-class. The first possibility is to describe the model transformation in UML itself. In this case all UML elements which are owned by a *Transition* object describe the transformation. How these UML elements are to be interpreted depends on the transformation language. To cover textual model transformation languages as well, we added the *script* attribute of type *Expression* which consists of a language name and an arbitrary string. This enables support for transformation languages which are themselves not described in UML but in some textual notation. An example of a similar transformation framework is the UMLAUT platform [8], which uses functional programming for UML model transformations.

After creation of the new UML model elements the transformation tool should insert dependency relations between the source and destination elements. The dependencies can be marked with the <<trace>> stereotype [9]. This has two advantages. First the user can see what the tool did and he can find out where a generated UML element originated from. Second, the tool can delete the result of a previous phase transition when the transition has to be repeated. It may happen that the developers have to go back to the design phase, because they discovered some problems with the design. To solve this they might choose other contracts, thereby obsoleting the UML elements which have been created during the first phase transition. With the help of the trace dependency the tool can remove the old transition results and start over again without having to throw everything away.

The developer must be able to find out whether there are still transitions needed for the components he uses in his application. Therefore every component has a boolean attribute called *isDeployable* which determines whether the component has a physical representation that can actually be installed on some node. The opposite is a more abstract representation of a component. When we go back to the availability example we can draw the entire component using a single rectangle in some UML diagram. But underneath it consists of subcomponents: replicas, sequencer, monitor etc. These subcomponents are deployable while the entire component itself is not deployable. That means transitions have to be made until all components are deployable.

Some component or subcomponent is usually not deployable because it can be further decomposed in other subcomponents. Another reason is that the component has at least two contracts which should not appear in the same development phase. For example a component for financial transactions may have special requirements regarding the security policy of the node on which it will be deployed. This required contract does not make much sense in the design phase, simply because it can not be satisfied before deployment. In this example the component can not be decomposed in subcomponents, but it will still not be deployable in the design phase for the above reasons.

It has to be considered whether the *isAbstract* attribute of *GeneralizeableElement* can be used instead of *isDeployable*. In fact these attributes have different semantics. The *isAbstract* means that it is not possible to create instances of the *GeneralizeableElement*, but a derived *Classifier* may be instantiated. This is not the case for our component. It is possible to instanciate a deployable component by deploying and instanciating its subcomponents. However, these subcomponents are not connected with the component by a *Generalization* relationship.

4   Modelling Contracts with the UML

4.1   Component Modelling in UML 1.x

The UML is now the *de facto* standard notation for object oriented systems. But its support for components is still weak. In [4] a component is specified as "a physical and replaceable part of a system that conforms to and provides the realization of a set of interfaces". Furthermore, there exist standard stereotypes named *table*, *file* and *document* which label a component to be a database file, some source file or the like.

That does obviously allow a large range of things to be called a component in UML. That may have historical reasons because calling a table or file a component was unproblematic until this term was overloaded by the rise of component technology. In the latest UML 1.4 beta1 [14] specification there is a suggestion to call everything an *Artifact* which used to be a component but does not comply with the new meaning of this technical term. This change is helpful to give a more precise definition of a component in terms of the UML. However, UML still treats a component as some kind of code that offers certain object oriented interfaces, which is – as discussed above – not sufficient.

4.2   Meta-model Extensions

We propose an extension to the meta-model of the UML 1.4 beta1 specification which allows to model components and contracts as discussed above. Figure 2 shows our new meta-classes and some excerpts from the UML 1.4 beta1 meta-model.

The biggest change is the addition of *Contract* and its subclasses. A *Contract* has the attribute *isOptional* which is set to *true* if the developer can decide not to accept the contract. Some contracts however are mandatory for the use of the component, so they are not optional. The *isStatic* attribute determines whether the contract has to be selected before deployment or whether selection is possible at runtime.

The *Contract* is a superclass of *Interface* and has a *NonFunctionalContract* subclass. The standard *Interface* element is thus redefined in our model. Although we mentioned four levels of contracts we believe there is no need to derive a *QosContract* and a *Synchronisation* meta-class from *NonFunctionalContract* because the nature of the contract can be expressed in some language (for instance QML [6]). This expression can then be stored in the *specification* attribute of the *NonFunctionalContract* instances. And in addition it would not help a generic case tool to see the inner structure of a contract since it has no understanding of it. Once there is a UML standard to describe QoS contracts and the like in UML directly it might make sense to introduce a *QoSContract* subclass.

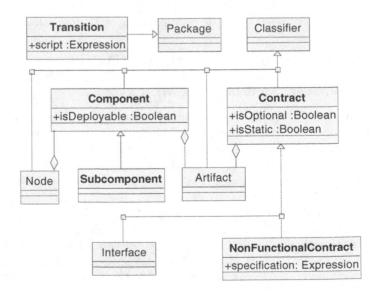

Fig. 2. Extended UML Meta-Model

- *NonFunctionalContract* instances can be associated with *Interfaces*, which represent functional contracts by grouping them in compound contract as shown in figure 2. For example imagine a *NonFunctionalContract* that will deny access to a certain API when the process is running in super-user mode. To model this, one would just draw a *Contract* which has a *Dependency* relationship with the *Interface* and the *NonFunctionalContract*. Connecting the non-functional contract directly with the interface does not work, because that would not allow to model two components which require the same interface but with different non-functional contracts attached to it.
- *Artifact* is a meta-class which was introduced by UML 1.4 beta1; it can be linked to a contract. In this case the artifact which represents some physical data will only be installed if its contract has been selected. If the developer decides not to use an optional contract then there is no need to install the data which is used to implement the functionality offered by this contract.
- *Transition* is a meta-class inherited from *Package*. That allows it to describe the model transformation in UML without polluting the global namespace. Since we do not want to put restrictions on the way such transformations can be described we inserted the *script* attribute. It may contain some textual description of the transformation and the name of its programming language. A transition is connected with its component via a *Dependency* relation.
- *Subcomponent* is derived from *Component*. The reason is that a subcomponent behaves like a component, but it is further restricted: it can not be deployed independently. The word *independently* means here independent of its sibling subcomponents. A subcomponent may be connected to its parent component with a *Dependency* relation which has the <<trace>> stereotype.

We now need a way to describe which contract is offered and which contract is required by a component. If a component offers a contract then they are connected by a *Realization* relationship (dashed line with closed arrow). A normal *Dependency* relationship (dashed line with open arrow) between contract and component indicates that the contract is required by this component. The same applies to compound contracts. They can offer and require subcontracts. An example is shown in figure 1.

4.3   Notation

Our meta-model extension introduces some new meta-classes. Consequently we have to specify their graphical notation. The UML 1.3 already defines the notation for a component but we have altered it slightly. We added the *isDeployable* attribute to components. If this attribute's value is *false* then the components name should appear in italic font. That remains compatible with the current notation since a UML 1.3 component is by definition always deployable.

Subcomponents are displayed like normal components. The only difference is that the top right corner of its rectangle is cut off like shown in figure 8.

The notation for *contracts* is structurally the same as for classes. That means contracts may have compartments, including but not limited to compartments for attributes and operations. The shape of a contract is not a rectangle. Instead it resembles the shape of a convoluted sheet of paper like shown in figure 1.

Interfaces, which are in our meta-model a specialization of the contract meta-class, are an exception to this rule. For the sake of compatibility their notation does not change.

There are two different methods to describe a transition script. If the *Transition* does not own UML elements then it is displayed as an icon. It is the responsibility of the tool to show the content of the *script* attribute on demand of the user. Otherwise the transition is shown like a class: a rectangle which contains the <<transition>> stereotype and the transitions name. The compartment shows the UML elements which describe the transition. A tool may choose to collapse this view and show the icon instead.

4.4   Backward Compatibility

Nowadays component models like JavaBeans/EJB [12], COM+ etc. do not directly support contract aware components. So we took care that the proposed meta-model extension is backward compatible.

First of all we made sure that the current way of modelling components is still valid. Component models may not know the concept of phase transitions. So they will simply not provide *Transition* elements. And since a component is by default deployable it follows automatically that no *Transitions* and *Subcomponents* are needed.

The notation for functional contracts (*Interfaces*) did not change. If component models do not support non-functional contracts then they simply do not use them. The only change is in the inheritance hierarchy of the meta-model: *Interface* does now inherit from *Contract*.

The current way of describing a component that offers an interface is consistent with our way of describing an offered contract. That means existing component diagrams will automatically comply to our extended component diagram definition.

4.5   Example

Let us look at a complete example. We model a simple banking application, which consists mainly of the *Banking* component, *HTTP Server*, *Database* and an implementation of the secure socket layer (*SSL*).

Fig.3 shows the specification of the *Database* component as given by the components vendor. The database realizes two compound contracts (realization is indicated by the closed arrow). One contract combines a *SQL* interface with the non-functional contracts *Availability* and *Thruput*. The other compound contract combines the *Admin* interface with the *Availability* contract. This little example illustrates that different interfaces can be combined with different sets of non-functional contracts.

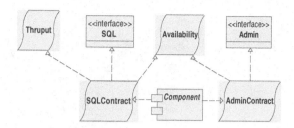

Fig. 3. The database component

Fig.4 shows the banking components specification. It requires two interfaces. For the *SQL* interface it requires two non-functional contracts in addition. Furthermore, it realizes the *Content* compound contract, which in turn offers the *ServeletAPI* interface. However, the compound contract has a dependency on the *Security* contract. That means users of the compound contracts offerings are in turn required to realize the *Security* contract.

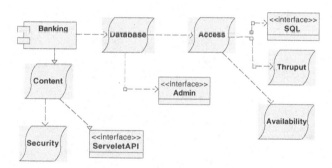

Fig. 4. The banking component

Fig.5 illustrates the *HTTP Server* component, which implements the HTTP protocol on top of a socket-layer. The server offers to handle all data retrieved from the *Servelet* interface in a secure way. To do so it requires that the *Socket Layer* interface uses *Encryption*.

Fig.6 shows that the *SSL* component realizes the *Socket Layer* interface and provides encryption via *RSA* which is a specialization of the *Encryption* contract demanded by the *HTTP Server*.

Fig.7 illustrates how the components fit together. Since the specifications of the single components use different compound contracts we use the *Dependency* relationship with the <<fulfills>> stereotype to match offered contracts with demanded ones.

Fig.8 presents a phase transition. A *Database* component has been split in multiple subcomponents by a tool and traces have been inserted. The developer finally deployed the single subcomponents on different nodes.

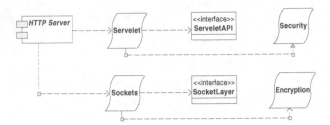

Fig. 5. The http-server component

Fig. 6. The secure socket layer component

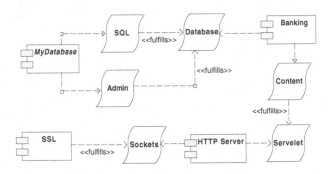

Fig. 7. The application

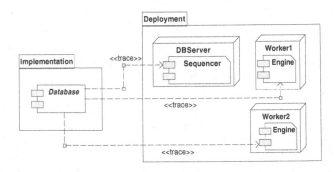

Fig. 8. A phase transition

Fig.9 finally illustrates the details of deployment. The *Engine* subcomponents demand that the hardware of their nodes fulfills certain criteria. The *Sequencer* requires a certain bandwidth for the *Connection* to its engines. The
required *Engines* contract makes sure that at least two engines are deployed on
different nodes. The <<ModelContract>> stereotype shows that this contract
is fulfilled if a certain constraint on the UML model if fulfilled. This constraint
can be expressed via OCL but it is not visible in the diagram.

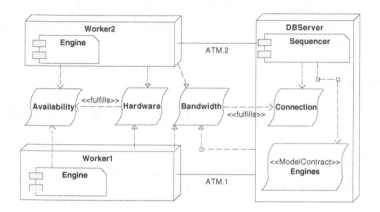

Fig. 9. Deployment of the database component

4.6   Catalysis

Bringing more power to component modelling techniques with the UML is a concern shared by many people. The Catalysis method [5] focuses on issues which
are similar to the ones we address in this paper, especially the use of contracts on
component interfaces. Catalysis adds many extensions to the UML notation and
meta-model to build a complete method, and to support an advanced component
model suited to abstraction and refinement modelling activities. We also consider modelling "model transformations" based on our phase transition notion.
However, our goal is to add as little as needed to the UML standard and reuse
as many concepts as possible. In addition our proposal supports non-functional
contracts between components and allows to automatically decompose a component in subcomponents during phase transitions.

5   Conclusion

We showed that contracts are a modelling technology which fosters the assembly of component-based applications. Non-functional contracts allow to further
describe the properties of a component. By making these properties explicit in
the form of contracts case tools can check whether contracts are fulfilled. For

this purpose we introduced the distinctions between an offered contract and a required contract.

To support modelling of contract aware components in UML we presented an extension to the UML meta-model. Our goal was to keep the changes as little as possible, which means to use existing UML concepts such as dependencies, realization relationships, traces, etc, where they are appropriate. We introduced a total of only four new meta-classes and added some attributes and associations.

Another concern of our meta-model is backward compatibility. We showed that component diagrams which follow the UML 1.4 beta1 meta-model still comply with our extended meta-model. That allows to integrate contracts step by step in the modelling process.

References

1. C. Becker and K. Geihs. Quality of Service - Aspects of Distributed Programs. In *Second Workshop on Aspect-Oriented Programming*, Kyoto, Japan, April 1998.
2. C. Becker and K. Geihs. Generic QoS-Support for CORBA. In *Proceedings of ISCC'00*, Antibes, France, July 2000.
3. A. Beugnard, J.-M. Jézéquel, N. Plouzeau, and D. Watkins. Making components contract aware. *IEEE Computer*, 13(7), July 1999.
4. G. Booch. *The unified modelling language user guide*. Addison Wesley, 2000.
5. Desmond Francis D'Souza and Alan Cameron Wills. *Objects, Components and Framework with UML: the Catalysis Approach*. Addison-Wesley, 1998.
6. S. Frølund and J. Koistinen. Quality of Service Specification in Distributed Object System Design. In *Proceedings of the COOTS 98*, Santa Fee, USA, March 1998.
7. Jean-loup Gailly and Mark Adler. ZLIB Home Site: http://www.gzip.org/zlib, 1996.
8. W.M. Ho, F. Pennaneac'h, and N. Plouzeau. Umlaut: A framework for weaving uml-based aspect-oriented designs. In *Technology of object-oriented languages and systems (TOOLS Europe)*, volume 33, pages 324–334. IEEE Computer Society, June 2000.
9. I. Jacobson. *The unified software development process*. Addison Wesley, 1999.
10. Gregor Kiczales. Aspect oriented programming. *ACM SIGPLAN Notices*, 32(10):162–162, 1997.
11. Stephane Lorcy, Noel Plouzeau, and Jean-Marc Jézéquel. Reifying quality of service contracts for distributed software. In *26th Conference on Technology of Object-Oriented Systems (TOOLS USA '98)*, August 1998.
12. V. Matena. *Applying Enterprise JavaBeans*. Addison Wesley, 2000.
13. B. Meyer. Applying "design by contract". *IEEE Computer (Special Issue on Inheritance & Classification)*, 25(10):40–52, October 1992.
14. UML revision taskforce. UML 1.4 beta1: http://www.celigent.com/omg/umlrtf, 2000.
15. T. Weis and K. Geihs. Components on the desktop. In *Technology of object-oriented languages and systems (TOOLS Europe)*, volume 33, pages 250–261. IEEE Computer Society, June 2000.

A Specification Model for Interface Suites[*]

E.E. Roubtsova[1], L.C.M. van Gool[1], R. Kuiper[1], and H.B.M. Jonkers[2]

[1] Faculty of Mathematics and Computing Science, TU Eindhoven,
Den Dolech 2, P.O. Box 513, 5600MB Eindhoven, The Netherlands.
E.Roubtsova@tue.nl, L.v.Gool@tue.nl, r.kuiper@tue.nl
[2] Philips Research Laboratories Eindhoven, Prof. Holstlaan 4,
5656AA Eindhoven, The Netherlands. hans.jonkers@philips.com

Abstract. The paper describes a model and tool support for a UML-based specification approach, extending UML with templates for structured specifications deriving from the ISpec approach. The approach is component-oriented where the unit of description is an interface suite: a coherent collection of interfaces defining interactions that transcend component boundaries. To handle complexity, descriptions from various points of view are necessary, expressed by UML diagrams, templates, etc. The issue is to ensure that the views are consistent. For this, we provide a model to integrate the views. The model is sequence-based, the elements of the sequences are carefully designed tuples that reflect the interface suite approach. Abstractions from the model reflect the views. The model provides the underlying structure for tooling. We developed extensions to Rational Rose by customizing specifications, automating diagram generation and enabling some consistency checks.

1 Introduction

Modern industry defines new software demands, notably complex functionality, high degree of correctness and short development time. This requires new ways of software development. An important approach in this field is component technology. The Component Object Model (COM, COM+) of Microsoft, Java-Beans technology of Sun and the Common Object Request Broker Architecture (CORBA) of the Object Management Group (OMG) are examples of component based technologies that are used in industry. At Philips, for example, COM technology is used in the development of medical imaging systems and various other new product developments in the professional as well as the consumer domain.

One of the main ideas of component technology is to provide the functionality of a piece of software (component) as a well-defined set of interfaces where an interface is a set of operations. Components can interact in a system only through interfaces. Interfaces abstract from implementation details of a component and allow selecting a part of the functionality of the component. Another advantage of interfaces is that they can be reused on several components. This means

---

[*] Supported by PROGRESS grant EES.5141 and ITEA grant IT990211.

M. Gogolla and C. Kobryn (Eds.): UML 2001, LNCS 2185, pp. 457–471, 2001.

shorter development times but also the use of standardized interfaces, resulting in components that are easier to use.

Interfaces also allow for the specification of interactions of parts in a system at the early stage when the components have not been chosen. A collection of interfaces, called an *interface suite*, together with a corresponding set of interactions thus becomes a new building block. As a suite transcends component boundaries, it is not described in terms of components; it is described in terms of roles and interfaces.

There are several existing approaches that specify behavioural blocks [5,8]. The approaches use different names for a building block: an interface suite, a pattern, a framework. To handle complexity, most of the approaches specify such a building block by different views: different tables, templates and diagrams; they apply different formal notations to represent properties of the block.

Analyzing the approaches we can say that the main problem with specification of behavioural building blocks is the problem of *consistency* of different specification views. The way to solve this problem is to define one model that integrates these views. In this paper we offer such a model and explain our choice.

The connection with UML is two-fold. Firstly, ISpec is a specification approach that uses UML for the descriptions, with the addition of ISpec templates to hierarchically capture behavioural aspects at different levels of formality. Secondly – and this is the main aim in this paper – we provide a semantic specification model to enable dealing with consistency of the various UML views that are used during development. This use of one model comes from the ISpec approach, but it can equally well be applied in other approaches.

The paper is organized as follows. Section 2 describes the ISpec approach. Section 3 shows an example of an interface suite and illustrates the problems with its description using different views. Section 4 describes the model. Section 5 considers the link between various views and the model. In section 6 we discuss the specification tool based upon the interface suite model.

2   The ISpec Approach

In our work we use ideas of the ISpec approach developed by Philips Research [8].

ISpec addresses the problem of specifying the type of interfaces encountered in component technologies such as Microsoft COM, JavaBeans and CORBA. In ISpec an interface specification is perceived as the description of an interaction pattern. It specifies the behaviour of an *interface suite* (i.e. a collection of mutually related interfaces). Interface suites, rather than individual interfaces, are the units of independent specification. An interface specification identifies a number of *roles* that can be seen as abstractions of component object classes [4]. Each interface has a role associated with it and the behavioural aspects of the interfaces including the interactions they are involved in follow from the specification of the roles. ISpec interface specifications are closely related to design patterns [7], role models [16] and contracts [17]. They are referred to as *i-specs*, which can be interpreted as 'interface specifications' as well as 'interaction specifications'.

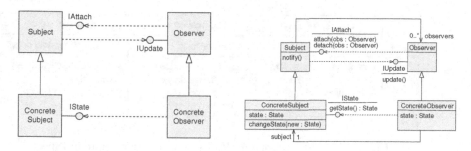

Fig. 1. Interface-Role Diagram and Abstract Model Diagram of the Concrete Observer Interface Suite

ISpec supports the construction of i-specs at different levels of detail and formality, ranging from 'signature only' to 'complete and formal' specifications. ISpec is a model-based approach that uses UML in a number of ways. The modelling concerns are separated into three views: conceptual, specification, and technical.

The *conceptual view* is primarily meant to introduce the necessary terms and concepts and explain the purpose and behaviour of the interfaces in an informal and intuitive way. It uses UML diagrams in an 'impressionistic way', sketching various aspects of interface behaviour using state diagrams, sequence diagrams, etc. These diagrams are typically abstractions, simplifications or snapshots of interface behaviour and need not be complete.

The *specification view* is meant to provide a technology-independent description of the behavioural aspects of the interfaces that is sufficiently precise and detailed. The latter normally implies that the description can be used as a basis for applying, implementing and testing the interfaces. The specification view is based on two types of diagrams: an interface-role diagram and an abstract model diagram [9]. The interface-role diagram is a UML class diagram that can be seen as the 'signature' of an interface suite: it identifies the names of the interfaces and roles, defines the 'provides' and 'requires' relations between roles and interfaces, as well as the specialization relations between roles (The latter relation is not considered in this paper; for more detials see [9]). For example, if we have a set of interfaces supporting the concrete observer pattern [7], the interface role diagram of this interface suite would look something like Fig. 1. The abstract model diagram is a UML class diagram that is a specialization of the interface-role diagram. It associates an abstract representation with each role in terms of attributes and relations, gives the signatures of all interfaces and may introduce additional artifacts such as auxiliary classes and operations, see Fig. 1. The behavioural aspects of the interfaces are directly specified in terms of this model using templates, attached to the diagrams. A template provides slots where information about behaviour can be put in in a structured manner, e.g. pre- and postconditions. Templates also contain action clauses to capture further information, for example about the interactions of roles. The slots in the templates are pieces of text, that may be informal, semi-formal or formal. ISpec

	conceptual view	specification view	technical view
goal	provide *intuition*	provide *precision*	provide *technological details*
model	*implicitly* characterized by - set of UML diagrams - explanatory text	*explicitly* characterized by - interface role diagram - abstract model diagram - (filled) templates	*explicitly* characterized by - specification view - mapping to technology

Fig. 2. The Three Modelling Views of an Interface Suite in ISpec

is neutral with respect to the language used in the placeholders. The formal language that is currently used is the expression language of Z, but OCL could be used as well.

The templates themselves are hierarchically ordered in a tree-structure, allowing behaviour to be specified at different levels of detail. The specification view uses other UML diagrams as well but only in an 'expressionistic' way, i.e. as 'expressions' of the model defined by the interface-role diagram, abstract model diagram and the templates. For example, state diagrams are derived from the abstract state representation of the roles and the pre- and post-conditions of the operations (similar to [10]). Mathematically speaking, the state representation and the pre- and post-conditions are the axioms and the diagrams are the theorems. The advantage of this approach is that it is much easier to ensure consistency of the various diagrams since they have to relate to a single explicit model.

The *technical view* provides the mapping of the interfaces to their concrete representation in a particular component technology or programming language. This concrete representation of the interfaces is important in connection with implementation and testing, but specifying the interfaces directly in terms of this representation will generally mess up specifications (just have a look at some Microsoft COM IDL). By keeping the technical details separated from the essential behavioural details defined by the specification view, the interface specifications can be kept clean and mappings to different component technologies and programming languages can be supported without the need to change the specification view. The key aspects of the three views used in ISpec are summarized in Fig. 2.

The main subject of this paper is the definition of one model for all UML and template views on an interface suite. On the one hand the model will allow to solve the problem of view-consistency, on the other hand, it will help to specify, identify and use existing patterns to reduce the design time and minimize behavioural errors.

3   A Case Study with an Interface Suite

The aim of this section is to illustrate the problems with the specification of interface suites. For this purpose we use different UML diagrams. Our case study

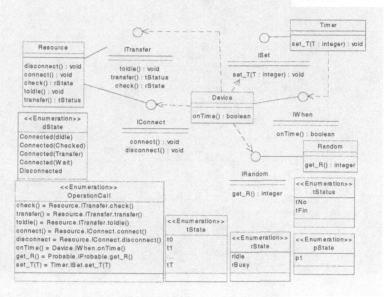

Fig. 3. An abstract class diagram for the role view of the interface suite

is concerned with the interaction in a system for collision detection in local networks (Carrier Sense, Multiple Access, Collision Detection CSMA/CD [1]. Concrete examples are a system for urgent telephone calls as described in [3], or a local network where several computers share a printer or a plotter.

Note that the specification is a conceptual view of ISpec, as introduced in section 2. We briefly remind the reader that we use the term *role* to enable describing an observable behavioural aspect of some class or classes at a stage in the development where the classes have not been specified yet. The decision about the class specification can then be postponed till the behaviour is well understood.

Role view. The first view on the suite is a UML class diagram (classes represent roles in our case, Fig. 3).

There are two main roles in the suite named *Resource* and *Device*. *Resource* provides the interfaces *IConnect* and *ITransfer*. *Device* uses these interfaces of *Resource*. Several devices can be connected to a resource. Connecting and disconnecting is possible at any moment. Using the number of devices, *Resource* defines a maximum time *P* that is allowed for a transfer between a *Resource* and a *Device*.

In a system for collision detection in local networks the channel with multiple access plays the role of resource and a local station plays the role of device.

Details of the role view. The specification of a role can be done at different levels of abstraction. This already introduces the possibility of different, maybe inconsistent views. A role has some interfaces that are detailed by operations. Operations are represented by name, parameters, return value, preconditions,

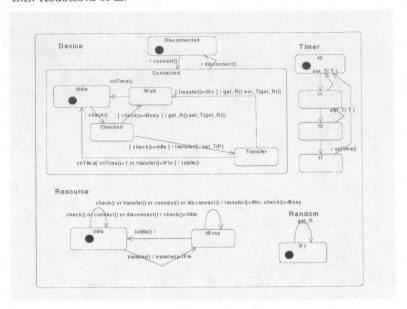

Fig. 4. A statechart diagram of the interface suite

postconditions etc. Such a structure of specifications is given by specification templates.

Statechart view. The behaviour of the suite is shown by a UML statechart, Fig. 4. Each *Device* checks the *Resource*. If there is another device that transfers data, the *Device* waits some time and checks the *Resource* again. If *Resource* is *Idle* the *Device* begins the *transfer* of some data and checks the resource a second time. If no one has begun to transfer at the same time, the device transfers data during some time interval. The time of transfer is controlled by a timer. This time is no more than P time units. The transfer can terminate by itself or be stopped by the timer when time is up.

However, it is possible that two devices begin to transfer simultaneously. In this case both devices stop transferring and try again later. We can compare the behaviour of devices in the suite with a dialog of well-behaved persons: if two of them begin to speak simultaneously, they stop talking for some time interval and then begin their attempt again, hopefully not simultaneously.

Interaction diagram view. Relevant traces are depicted in UML by interaction diagrams. An example of an interaction diagram is presented in Fig. 5.

Consistency checking. Consistency checking even for two diagrams can take a lot of time and effort.

For example, to make the role view (Fig. 3) and the statechart view (Fig. 4) consistent, one would need to check the names of roles and arrow labels that represent operation calls. The list of possible operation calls that is derived from the role view is shown in Fig. 3 as an enumeration type *OperationCall*. An arrow label on the statechart means a call and its return. For the sake of consistency

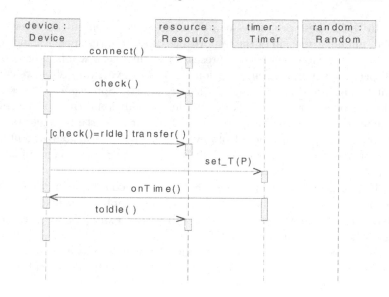

Fig. 5. An interaction diagram of the interface suite

of role and statechart views, arrow labels of the statechart should be taken from *OperationCall.*

We can add state information to the class diagram as attributes. For example attributes of the types defined by the enumeration classes *dState* and *rState* in Fig. 3 that represent the states of *Device* and *Resource* respectively. States in the statechart diagram should be consistent with the class diagram.

During the process of development, a first consistency check might be performed when *Random* and *Timer* were not yet present. When we modeled the behaviour we realized that these two auxiliary roles should be in the model. Role *Random* models a generator of random values in a given value interval $(0..B)$. The current value returned by the generator is of type Real. Role *Random* provides interface *IRandom* with an operation $get\_R()$. Role *Timer* contains a clock. *Timer* provides an interface to reset the clock to zero. After resetting, the value of the clock increases with a constant rate till a certain control value T is reached and operation *onTime()* via interface *IWhen()* of *Device* is called, Fig. 3. So, we changed both class and statechart diagrams and perform the consistency checking again.

Having exemplified the consistency problem, we discuss further examples to clarify where consistency problems occur in practice.

Property view. The next view states the main properties of the suite:

1. Each device that requests a data transfer has access to the resource in a reasonable time interval T.
2. Each moment in time no more then one of the devices transfers data to *Resource*.

In UML these properties can be represented as comments (that we consider as an underestimation of the importance of a property specification) or localized in an aggregation class that represents the suite as a whole. The properties can be specified using different notations [2,6]. However, very often we cannot represent properties without some additional efforts. Sometimes we need additional roles to specify properties. For example, an additional timer is necessary for the specification of property 1. Property 2 of our case study suggests a counter k to count the current amount of devices that use the *Resource*. So the specification of properties of our case study gives rise to new variants of diagrams and complicates the problem of consistency.

Furthermore, at some stage of design we could prefer to adapt the suite to some chosen components or to a concrete application field. New versions of diagrams extend the set of design views. For example, we can split the role *Resource* into *Connector* and *Resource*.

Because the designer has different views on the system, he/she represents his/her knowledge using different languages (graphical, logical etc.). Let's assume that there are four diagrams (Class diagram C, Statechart S, interaction diagrams I_1 and I_2) with precise semantics. Checking pairwise consistency means that we should solve six tasks of consistency: (C, S), (C, I_1), (C, I_2), (S, I_1), (S, I_2), (I_1, I_2). Generally speaking, if we have n diagrams we should perform $\frac{1}{2}n(n-1)$ consistency checks for diagram pairs. And this pairwise consistency does not even guarantee the consistency of the collection of all four diagrams. The way out is to use one specification model. We then have to perform only n consistency checks of type (*View, Model*).

4   The Specification Model for Interface Suites

In this section we introduce the specification model that will enable us to guarantee consistency of views.

Informally, our model consists of a number of *actors* that interact by calling operations of each other. An actor is identified by a *role* name and a *player* identifier. The role names allow us to talk about different kinds of actors and the player identifiers allow us to distinguish between actors that play the same role.

Each actor in our model has a number of *interfaces* that consist of a number of *operations* that can be called on this actor. Operations that have the same name but occur on different interfaces are supposed to be *different* operations. This corresponds to the notion of interface as used in Microsoft COM.

Our model captures the interaction between several actors. More formally, our model is a set of (possibly infinite) sequences of messages where a *message* is either a call of an operation or a return from an operation call.

A *call* is described by

- a *caller role cr*,
- a *caller player cp*,

− a *callee role rr*,
− a *callee player rp*,
− an *interface i*,
− an *operation o* and
− a *parameter x*.

The interpretation of a call $(cr, cp, rr, rp, i, o, x)$ is that player cp of caller role cr calls, with parameter x, operation o of the interface i on player rp of callee role rr.

A *return* is described by

− a *call depth d* and
− a *result y*.

The formal definition of messages is as follows.

Definition 1. *The type of all messages Msg is defined by*

$$Msg ::= call(Role, Player, Role, Player, Interface, Operation, Parameter)$$
$$| \; return(\mathbb{N}, Result)$$

where

− *Role is some set of role names,*
− *Player is some set of player identifiers,*
− *Interface is some set of interface names,*
− *Operation is some set of operation names,*
− *Parameter is some set of parameter values,*
− $\mathbb{N}$ *is the set of the natural numbers and*
− *Result is some set of result values.*

The call depth of a return makes it possible to link each return to its corresponding call. For each sequence of messages we imagine a stack in which each call that occurs is stored. If a return with call depth d occurs, we interpret this as the return with result y of the call that lies d layers deep in the current stack (if the call depth is 0, this is the call on top of the stack). When a return occurs, the corresponding call is removed from the stack.

Notice that it follows from this interpretation that we don't allow every sequence of messages; we have to make sure that the call depth of each return in a trace does not exceed the stack size. A sequence of messages that adheres to this restriction is called a *trace*.

Definition 2. *A trace is a (possibly infinite) sequence with elements of type Msg where the call depth of each return in a trace is smaller than the number of calls preceding this return minus the number of returns preceding this return.*

We now propose the next definition for the specification model for interface suites:

Definition 3. *The specification model for interface suites is a set of traces.*

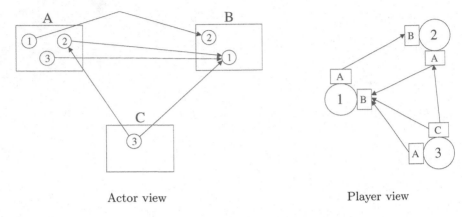

Actor view   Player view

Fig. 6. Two different views on our model

In a trace, each return is associated with exactly one call and each call with at most one return. A crucial concept in connection with our model is the combination of a return and its corresponding call. This will be called a *roundtrip*. The *value* of a roundtrip with call $(cr, cp, rr, rp, i, o, x)$ and return (d, y) is the tuple $(cr, cp, rr, rp, i, o, x, y)$. Notice that it is possible that a call never returns, so not every call needs to be part of a roundtrip.

Roundtrips are the basic communications in our suites. They generalize the communications of standard message passing systems by allowing a reply to a message that is sent. Usually in a message passing system, a reply is just the sending of another message. Roundtrips make the link between the sending of a message and a reply to that message explicit; they bring us closer to the standard functional theory of I/O.

Notice that if for a certain trace, for each return the call-depth is 0 and the caller actor of each call is equal to the callee actor of the call that is on top of the stack then the trace is implementable using a single thread. Our traces are a generalization of single threads and actually abstract completely from the threads in the system. If our traces were single threads then our model could be simplified by omitting the return depths and caller actors.

4.1   Another Look at Our Model

To explain our model, we took *actors* as the main interacting entities. We will call this the *actor view*. In this respect we deviate from common practice (and also from the usual interpretation in ISpec). It is more common to not view the actors, but what we called *players* as the main interacting entities. We will call this the *player view*. In this view, the players are usually called *objects*. Figure 6 illustrates these two views on our model. The boxes represent roles, the circles represent the main interacting entities and the arrows represent messages. The letters 'A', 'B' and 'C' are role names and the numbers '1', '2' and '3' are player identifiers.

The intuition behind the main interacting entities in the actor view is reflected by the phrase "player p of role r" and in the object view it is reflected by the phrase "player (object) p playing role r".

Because of the presence of player names, the two pictures can easily be mapped onto each other. So, the player names allow us to map these different views on our model onto each other. However, if we make explicit that the names of players are not considered to be relevant, the two ideas diverge: if we omit the player names in both pictures, we are not able anymore to map them onto each other! We have made the differences between the two views explicit in terms of refinement, but this is beyond the scope of this paper.

5   The Link between the Views and Our Model

In this section we will show for several views which models correspond to each view. So, if we have a collection of views, we then know whether or not there exists a model that corresponds to each view in this collection.

Each view is an instance of a certain *view type*: a construction in which some aspects of systems can be described. Role diagrams, statecharts and sequence diagrams are examples of view types.

To define for a certain view type which models are associated with a certain view of this type, we need to define a *consistency relation* between models and views of this type that tells which views are consistent with which models. We say that a *collection of views is consistent* if there exists a model that is consistent with each view in this collection.

5.1   Role View

We will now show a way to link a class diagram that represents a role view, to our model. There are several ways to interpret these kind of diagrams. The way that is described here, we think, matches the intuition of UML-users. The key idea is that all interactions that are not explicitly forbidden by the diagram can appear anywhere in a trace. The advantage of this approach is in a simple and natural definition of refinement, but this is beyond the scope of this paper. Interested readers are referred to [12]. However, this approach doesn't correspond to the "closed world" interpretation of these kind of diagrams in ISpec where the only interactions that are allowed are the ones that are explicitly mentioned in the diagram. As explained in [9], these are important choices as they influence the feasibility of, for example, a compositional approach of interface suites. Our model enables to accommodate such choices through different interpretations of the diagrams or different notions of refinement. This is the subject of current research.

A role view expresses *static* aspects of a system. We introduce the notion of a *signature* as a formal description of these static aspects. For our kind of systems, these static aspects are expressed by a set of allowed roundtrip values. Formally a signature is a set

$$S \subseteq Role \times Player \times Role \times Player \times Interface \times Operation \times Parameter \times Result$$

Definition 4. *A model is consistent with a signature S exactly when the value of each roundtrip in the model is an element of S.*

By means of an example, using the role view of Fig. 3, we explain how a role view defines (in the intuitive UML sense) a signature S. This signature consists exactly of all tuples $(cr, cp, rr, rp, i, o, x, y)$ that satisfy the next constraint (the type *void* consists of the single element ()).

$$
\begin{aligned}
(cr, rr, i, o, x) &= (Device, Resource, ITransfer, check, ()) &\Rightarrow y \in rState \\
(cr, rr, i, o, x) &= (Device, Resource, ITransfer, transfer, ()) &\Rightarrow y \in tStatus \\
(cr, rr, i, o, x) &= (Device, Resource, ITransfer, toIdle, ()) &\Rightarrow y \in void \\
(cr, rr, i, o, x) &= (Device, Resource, IConnect, connect, ()) &\Rightarrow y \in void \\
(cr, rr, i, o, x) &= (Device, Resource, IConnect, disconnect, ()) &\Rightarrow y \in void \\
(cr, rr, i, o) &= (Device, Timer, ISet, set\_ T) \wedge x \in (T{:}integer) &\Rightarrow y \in boolean \\
(cr, rr, i, o, x) &= (Timer, Device, IWhen, onTime, ()) &\Rightarrow y \in boolean \\
(cr, rr, i, o, x) &= (Device, Probable, IProbable, get\_R, ()) &\Rightarrow y \in integer
\end{aligned}
$$

5.2   Statecharts and other Interaction Diagrams

UML statecharts can be given a semantics in terms of our model. The idea is to represent calls and returns as separate actions and have a stack of calls that have not returned yet. This is similar to the semantics presented in [13].

Assume that we have two devices that can be connected to one resource (Fig. 3, 4). Both of them call the operation *connect*() of role *Resource* via interface *IConnect*. The returns of both connects can come in any order. One of the legal traces, derived from the statechart diagram in our case study (Fig. 4) is the following:

$call(Device, 1, Resource, 1, IConnect, connect, ())$
$call(Device, 2, Resource, 1, IConnect, connect, ())$
$return(1, ())$
$return(0, ())$
$call(Device, 1, Resource, 1, IConnect, disconnect, ())$
$return(0, ())$
$call(Device, 2, Resource, 1, IConnect, disconnect, ())$
$return(0, ())$.

According to the statechart diagram (Fig. 4) a device can not be connected twice without disconnecting. Thus, an illegal trace is

$call(Device, 1, Resource, 1, IConnect, connect, ())$
$return(0, ())$
$call(Device, 1, Resource, 1, IConnect, connect, ())$
$return(0, ())$.

Note, that this trace *is* consistent with the signature of the operations. So we use the expressive power of sets of traces to define consistency of statecharts with respect to our model.

Assume that a straightforward trace semantics as indicated at the beginning of this section, is available.

Definition 5. *A statechart is consistent with exactly one model, being its trace set.*

Here we assume that we have exactly one statechart for the entire system behaviour. However, a statechart could describe only part of the system behaviour. We then also need to give a signature (in the closed world interpretation, see section 5.1) that describes which messages the statechart talks about. A statechart is then consistent with exactly all models that, after projection to this signature, are equal to the statechart's trace set.

Dynamic diagrams like statecharts, interaction diagrams, activity charts, collaboration diagrams, can be handled in a similar way.

6   Specification Tool

The use of our model for the specification of interface suites is viable only with tool support.

First of all, the complex structure of a message in the form of a tuple allows to restrict the set of possible messages using a hierarchy of specifications: for a role, interfaces provided by the role, interfaces required by the role and operations belonging to interfaces. To make practical use of such restrictions we need a tool.

Second, the conceptual description of the traces that comprise the specification model is realized in practice by statechart diagrams and sets of interaction diagrams. A natural way to obtain a suite specification model is to automatically derive the corresponding set of traces from such views. The model can be made more precise in the specification view as proposed in ISpec [8].

Third, the consistency check of models derived from different views supposes to compare sequences of strings (names), which can be hardly realized without tooling.

We have chosen the UML to describe interfaces suites, because the UML is a standard in the specification of object-oriented and component-based systems at different levels of abstraction. Some approaches that are based on the UML also use the notion of 'role' to represent abstract system structure and behaviour [5, 18]. A difference with our approach is that we use the role notion in the context of the specification of interaction through interfaces. We combine the interface signature specification that is used in approaches based on Interface Definition Languages (IDL) [11] and the description of the interactions they are involved in.

We use our formal model of interface suites to customize the specification in the UML-based tool Rational Rose [14] using the Rose Extensibility Interface [15]. We have developed a Rational Rose add-in as a Visual Basic(VB)

ActiveX DLL because VB is easily integrated with Rational Rose [15]. The add-in reacts on the Rose event that allows to replace the standard Rational Rose specification of an empty class by our own specification. The hierarchy of specification windows for roles, constraints, interfaces, operations, attributes allows to ensure the consistency between name spaces. The hierarchy is based on the model defined in section 4.

The tool is used as follows. First of all we define empty roles by Rose. Then we fill in our specification templates. The role diagram is automatically generated consistent with these templates.

The specifications of suites in the specification model are saved in model files of Rational Rose and in HTML format as documentation for verification and for reuse in design. Collecting and identifying interface suites during the design ensures the correctness of the design decisions and reduces the development time. The model also makes it possible to connect to simulation and verification tools for the verification of interface suites.

Acknowledgements. We thank the anonymous referees for helpful comments and the TU/e SOOP group, Loe Feijs and Natalia Belousova for helpful comments.

References

1. Carrier Sense Multiple Access\Collision Detection (CSMA\CD), *http : //webopedia.internet.com/TERM/C/CSMA_CD.html*. 1998.
2. A. Evans and R. France and K. Lano and B.Rumpe. The UML as a Formal Modeling Notation. *The Unified Modeling Language. UML'98: Beyond the Notation*, LNCS 1618:336–348, 1998.
3. G. Booch, J. Rubaugh, and I. Jacobson. *The Unified Modeling Language User Guide.* Addison-Wesley, Amsterdam, 1999.
4. C. Szyperski. *Component Software Beyond Object-Oriented Programming.* Addison-Wesley, New-York, 1998.
5. D. D'Souza and A. Wills. *Objects, Components and Frameworks with UML. The Catalysis Approach.* Addison-Wesley , 1999.
6. E.E. Roubtsova and J.van Katwijk and W.J. Toetenel and C. Pronk and R.C.M.de Rooij. The Specification of Real-Time Systems in UML. *MCTS2000*, http://www.elsevier.nl/locate/entcs/volume39.html , 2000.
7. E. Gamma, R. Helm, R. Johnson, and J. Vlissides. *Design Patterns. Elements of Reusable Object-Oriented Software.* Addison-Wesley, New-York, 1994.
8. H.B.M. Jonkers. ISpec: Towards Practical and Sound Interface Specifications. *Integrated Formal Methods*, LNCS1945:116–135, 2000.
9. H.B.M. Jonkers. Interface-Centric Architecture Descriptions. *WICSA 2001, The Working IEEE/IFIP Conference on Software Architecture* , August 2001.
10. J. Cheesman, and J. Daniels. UML Components: A Simple Process for Specifying Component-Based Software. *Addison Wesley*, 2000.
11. R. Kling. *Application Development with IDL.* Ronn Kling Consulting, http://www.rlkling.com , 1999.
12. L.C.M. van Gool. Cylindrische Componenten Calculus. (in Dutch). *Eindhoven University of Technology, Department of Computer Science*, 2000.

13. J. Lilius and I.P.Palor. Formalising UML StateMachines for Model Checking. *UML'99. Beyond the Standard, LNCS 1723*, pages 430–445, 1999.
14. Rational Software Corporation. *Rational Rose.*
    http : //www.rational.com/ products/rose, 2000.
15. Rational Software Corporation. *Rose Extensibility Reference 2000e*, 2000.
16. T. Reenskaug. *Working with objects*. Manning Publications, 1995.
17. R.Helm and I.M.Holland and D. Gangopadhyay. Contracts: Specifying Behavioral Compositions in Object-Oriented Systems. *Proc. ECOOP/OOPSLA '90, ACM*, pages 169–180, 1990.
18. D. Riehle. *Framework Design: A Role Modeling Approach. Ph.D. Thesis, No. 13509.* Zurich, Switzerland, ETH Zurich , 2000.

Against Use Case Interleaving

Pierre Metz[1], John O'Brien[1], and Wolfgang Weber[2]

[1] Dept. of Mathematics & Computing, Cork Institute of Technology,
Ireland,
{pmetz, jobrien}@cit.ie

[2] Dept. of Computer Science, Darmstadt University of Applied
Sciences, Germany,
w.weber@fbi.fh-darmstadt.de

Abstract. Use cases are a powerful and widely recognised tool for functional requirements elicitation and specification of prospective software applications. However, there still are major problems and misunderstandings about the use case approach. One of these is the troublesome notion of use case interleaving which is discussed in this work. Interleaving is still present in the current UML specification. A. Simons correctly realised that interleaving compares with goto/comefrom semantics that were already judged harmful by Dijkstra at the emergence of the Structured Programming era. Simons, thus, has requested the explicit dropping of interleaving semantics. The authors give further support for Simons´ request by showing that interleaving causes severe inconsistencies within UML and contradicts other proven and practically relevant use case concepts such as Goal-Based Use Cases of A. Cockburn, and contractual specifications of use cases expressed by pre- and postcondition approaches. Significant fixes to UML are proposed, in addition to those suggested by Simons. These will dramatically clarify prevailing problems and confusion with use cases and use case relationships among both practitioners and researchers.

1 Use Case Interleaving Semantics from Jacobson to UML v1.2

In [14], Jacobson et al. introduced the notion of use case *interleaving*. On the one hand, abstract use cases[1] that are attached by a use case relationship may represent continuous interaction courses which are plugged into another use case as a whole [7], [8], [14], [21]. On the other hand, instead of embedding an abstract use case as a unit, it is also proposed to interleave the interaction elements of an abstract use case into the base use case [7], [8], [14]. Interleaving can be understood as cutting a given use case interaction into pieces and weaving them into the interaction description of another use case (see Fig. 1). Any interleaving is possible as long as the relative order of all use case elements is preserved [14], [20]. Originally, interleaving was intro-

---

[1] An *abstract use case* does not represent a complete external system functionality. Abstract use cases are a mechanism for structuring and refactoring descriptions of complete system behaviour [14]. They represent extracted parts of other use cases and are meaningful only in the context of the surrounding base use case definition. Hence, abstract use cases cannot be processed in isolation; thus, in the use case model, they do not have an actor attached directly.

M. Gogolla and C. Kobryn (Eds.): UML 2001, LNCS 2185, pp. 472–486, 2001.
© Springer-Verlag Berlin Heidelberg 2001

duced for the Uses relationship only [14] (predecessor of UML v1.3´s «include» relationship), but not for Jacobson et al.´s Extends relationship (predecessor of UML v1.3´s «extend» relationship).

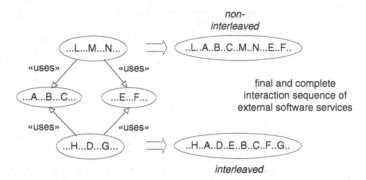

Fig. 1. Examples of uses-relationships with interleaving, adapted from [14], UML v1.1 notation

The idea of use case interleaving for the Uses relationship is explicitly upheld in UML up to version 1.1 [7], [8]. In contrast to Jacobson et al. [14], UML v1.1 seems to have expanded interleaving semantics to the «extends» relationship as well. We may conclude this from statements such as "*Different parts of the extending use case sequence may be inserted at different extension points in the original sequence*" [7] (p. 2-95), [8] (p. 2-104). How interleaving works exactly can be best understood by investigating UML´s *Classifier* foundation of use cases. In the following, we will take a closer look at the Classifier concept and how it relates to use cases.

1.1   Understanding Use Cases as UML Classifiers

Since version v1.1, UML has been aiming to formalise use cases through object-oriented semantics, rather than procedural semantics. This has been achieved by declaring the metamodel element *UseCase* as a subtype of Classifier [7], [8], [9], [10]. The introduction of use cases as Classifiers gives use cases an explicit type level representation which adopts Jacobson´s meta-perception of a use case as a class [14], [21], [22]. Fig. 2 depicts sections of the UML metamodel Core Package and UML Behavioral Elements Package Use Cases which are identical in UML v1.1. and v1.4[2]. A Classifier may contain structural and behavioural features which can be *Attributes*, *Operations* and *Methods*. The meta-element *Operation* defines a service of an object having a signature to effect behaviour. A *Method* is the realisation of an operation obeying its signature. A Classifier is a subtype of *GeneralizableElement* which denotes entities that can participate in generalisation relationships.

---

[2] Not all entities and elements are shown, attributes of the entities are omitted.

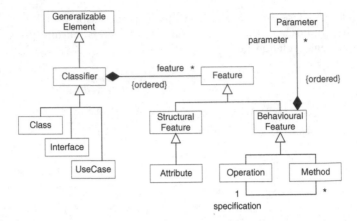

Fig. 2. Extraction from UML v1.4 metamodel Core Package and Behavioral Elements Package Use Cases

A use case run is commonly considered a *use case instance*[3] [9], [10], [11], [12], [14], [18], [20], [21], [22]. At the meta-level, a use case operation can be perceived as the formalisation of possible asynchronous actor input to the system, i.e. a message. In turn, a method defines the immediate and full reaction of the system to such an input (see Fig. 3). A use case operation can specify parameters when the system requires information which must be delivered by an actor. One of the key properties of use cases is *sequence*: a use case has sequence in terms of determining the partial order of interaction steps that must be taken [14], [21], i.e. the order of operation invocations. For UML Classifiers, this can be specified by a state machine.

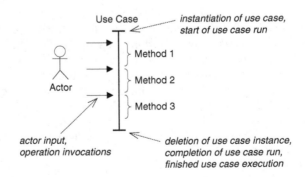

Fig. 3. Graphical explanation of terms *use case instance*, *use case operation* and *use case method*

---

[3] Only concrete use cases can be instantiated [14], [20]. Abstract use cases cannot because they do not represent complete external system services. They form extracted parts of system services for refactoring purposes.

At the meta-level, we can understand attributes of a use case as data which is available during a use case run and are lost when the use case is completed, i.e. when the use case instance is destroyed. Such data refers to information provided by the actor from outside to feed the system with, i.e. parameters handed in to a use case operation; it may, also, refer to information which is retrieved from inside the system for displaying and modification at the use case interface by an actor, i.e. business objects, persistent storages etc. The use case instance holds this data, modified or not, until it is sent into the system or to the actor instance.

1.2   Named and Unnamed Use Case Methods

In [20], the notion of use case interleaving is confirmed and further refined, based on the Classifier foundation of UML v1.1. In this context, the notions of *Named Methods* and *Unnamed Methods* of use cases are introduced, by which interleaving capabilities are explained.

A Named Method is a complete behavioural body of a use case operation, i.e. a complete system response to an actor input. It is processed when an actor input, described by the corresponding operation, is received. A Named Method "is named by its operation".
Conversely, an Unnamed Method is explained as a fragment of system behaviour which does not completely realise an operation. It is not supposed to be a full reaction to an operation invocation on its own; it is only a *part* of a full system reaction to a particular actor input. An Unnamed Method is subject to insertion into a Named or Unnamed Method of another use case. Ultimately, it will form a part of a Named Method. Unnamed methods are defined within abstract use cases only. Insertion of Unnamed Methods is not meant to follow function call semantics or reference semantics; it can be considered acting like a macro. Unnamed methods are directly embedded in methods of other use cases (see Fig. 3 and Fig. 4).
With respect to Named and Unnamed Methods, interleaving is twofold: first, interleaving of Named Methods means mixing them with the interaction sequence of Named Methods of the base use case while preserving the relative order. Second, interleaving of Unnamed Methods means embedding these in use case operation realisations (i.e., system reactions) of a base use case. Thus, interleaving of Unnamed Methods does not affect the order of interaction but the definition of system responses.

With these explanations it becomes clear why interleaving does not mean a communication between a base use case A and an abstract use case B, but means composing A´s behaviour from local parts defined in A and parts of B: abstract use cases are considered non-instantiable   [4], [14], [16], [20] because they do not form complete system services, i.e. they are not runnable individually. Though modelled as distinct use cases, abstract use cases represent extracted behavioural compositional parts of a base use case [4]. Thus, there is no message interchange between a concrete use case and an abstract use case because message interchange requires unique instances to address (client-server collaboration semantics). Hence, connecting abstract use cases by use case relationships means pure static composition. Only a concrete use case, as the complete composite of all its behavioural descriptions, is instantiable. Clearly, interleaving means embedding behaviour within a base use case to form a complete interaction description of a single system functionality as shown in Fig. 1.

2   Interleaving Semantics Considered Harmful

Simons [21] shows that use case interleaving is a harmful and unreasonable concept by demonstrating that interleaving corresponds to repeated *goto* and *comefrom* statements in the sense of a "breaking into blocks and jumping out of blocks" programming style which was already strongly discouraged by Dijkstra at the dawn of the Structured Programming era [21]. Interleaving produces highly interdependent use cases resulting in a huge, arbitrary and complex flow of control [21]. As a consequence, the use case model is hard to read and maintain, thus impacting the verification by subject matter experts within requirements engineering. Moreover, developers must resolve and deconstruct these interdependencies before they can advance to constructive analysis modelling [21].

As a result, use case interleaving is in direct conflict with two major and essential software engineering principles, *Separation of Concerns* and *Encapsulation*, which have been emphasised over the last decades in order to improve and advance software construction and software development methodologies.

The following Section 3 reflects the changes to the use case relationships made in UML v1.3. It is shown that these changes are not sufficiently discouraging use case interleaving. Subsequently, Section 4 explains in detail why use case interleaving violates the Encapsulation principle; furthermore, Section 6 shows why use case interleaving is in conflict with the Separations of Concerns principle.

3   Changes Made in UML v1.3 and Remaining Inconsistencies

Use case interleaving semantics are no longer explicitly mentioned in UML v1.3 and v1.4 [9], [10]. UML v1.3 has divided the former Uses relationship into the «include» relationship and an explicit use case generalisation relationship; the former «extends» relationship has been renamed to «extend» relationship[4]. However, different opinions exist about whether interleaving is still possible or not.

From the way the «include» relationship is defined in the current UML it may be concluded that this relationship is now meant to follow straightforward compositional subroutine semantics [9], [10], [21], [22] a view which is proposed by Simons [21], Graham/Simons [22] and which has been adopted by practitioners like Armour/Miller [1], Cockburn [11] and Kulak/Guiney [18] as well as by the IBM Global Services Method [13]. Accordingly, Jacobson as one of the UML authors states in one of his recent publications that "... *the behavior sequence and the attributes of an included*

---

[4] Presumably, this renaming aims to prevent the confusing of this use case relationship with Java's implementation inheritance syntax. See also [21].

use case are encapsulated and cannot be changed or accessed – only the result (or function) of the included use case can be exploited" [16] (p. 191) which supports our interpretation from the official UML v1.3 and v1.4 Semantics [9], [10], [21], [22]. Unfortunately, this is not made explicit in official UML semantics [9], [10], [21], [22]. Moreover, Simons has observed that explanations and examples for «include» given in the UML User Guide publication [5] by the authors of UML are ambiguous, thus there is no clear and reliable assertion of «include» to represent subroutines [21], [22].

However, for «extend» interleaving semantics are still evident in statements such as *"The relationship consists of a condition, which must be fulfilled if the extension is to take place, and a sequence of references to extension points in the base use case where the additional behaviour fragments are to be inserted"* [9] (p. 2-119), [10] (p. 2-143) and *"The different parts of the extending use case are inserted at the locations defined in the sequence of extension points in the relationship - one part at each referenced extension point"* [9] (p. 2-127), [10] (p. 2-151). This view is also supported by the UML Reference Manual publication [4]. These statements indicate that interleaving is inherent to «extend» relationships. Most likely, an extending use case being fragmented and distributed across multiple extension points in the base use case relates to pieces of behaviour that are extracted because they are subject to the same business condition. However, the disadvantages described in Section 2 still remain, and Sections 4 and 6 identify further inconsistencies.

Finally, we must realise that we cannot prove interleaving semantics to be absent from «extend» and «include». Therefore, the exact distinction between use case generalisation and use case relationships as well as the distinction between «include» and «extend» remain unclear. Precise definitions of terms are missing. Practitioners are left to their own devices when interpreting UML semantics.

In the following, the authors give further counter arguments against use case interleaving in addition to those presented so far. These arguments demonstrate that interleaving semantics cannot be upheld for both «extend» and «include» because this would contradict the UML Classifier core foundation.

4   Interleaving Violates UML Classifier Encapsulation

Since encapsulation is one of the four basic software engineering principles upon which the object-oriented paradigm is built [1], UML preserves this principle for Classifiers. This is evident in the definition of Classifiers as shown in Fig. 2. As we see, all *Features* of a Classifier, either *StructuralFeatures* or *BehavioralFeatures*, are associated by compositional aggregation which enforces encapsulation: UML Semantics from v1.1 to v1.4 state that in a composition relationship *"The part is strongly owned by the composite and may not be part of any other Composite."* [7] (p. 2-16), [8] (p. 2-16), [9] (p. 2-21), [10] (p. 2-23). UML v1.3 Notation Guide additionally states that *"Composition is a strong form of ownership and coincident lifetime of part with the whole"* [9] (p. 3-74), which is further refined by the UML v1.4 Notation Guide by defining that *"Composite aggregation is a strong form of aggregation which requires that a part instance be included in at most one composite at a time and that the composite object has sole responsibility for the disposition of its parts."* [10] (p. 3-82).

As a consequence, the encapsulation principle is adopted for use cases since use cases are special Classifiers. This seems to be further supported by the UML v1.4 definition of the «include» relationship: *"The included use case may not be dependent on the base use case. In that sense the included use case represents encapsulated behavior which may easily be reused in several use cases. Moreover, the base use case may only depend on the results of performing the included behavior and not on structure, ..., of the included use case."* [10] (p. 2-150). In one of his recent publications, Jacobson even strengthens the UML statement on the «include» relationship by saying that *"... the behavior sequence and the attributes of an included use case are encapsulated and cannot be changed or accessed – only the result (or function) of the included use case can be exploited"* [16] (p. 191). To date, this is the strongest and most noticeable informal confirmation of «include» preserving encapsulation. It comes very close to Graham and Simons´ demand of subroutine call semantics.

Based on the above, the following two cases provide explanations for why interleaving violates encapsulation of use cases as Classifier*s*. This is done by examining use case property access scopes. With respect to interleaving, we show that this violation results from both Named and Unnamed Use Case Methods.

(i)   Accessing Properties of a Base Use Case by an Abstract Use Case

Consider the example in Fig. 4. It shows a simplified example of registering native students and foreign exchange students having been granted a scholarship. Further consider A being an abstract use case and B being a concrete use case. Use case B has an operation op_2 and a corresponding method m_2. Use case A has an Unnamed Method m_U, and an operation op_1 with a corresponding method m_3. A connects B with an «extend» relationship; A represents optionally included behaviour. The condition distinguishes whether the student to be registered is native or foreign.

Interleaving means assembling B´s and A´s behaviour within B. Consider the underlying condition to be met; further consider m_U being integrated in m_2 of B (see Fig. 4). Clearly, m_2 can access the attributes of B as well as the parameters of op_2. Since the behaviour of op_2 is assembled from both m_2 and m_U, m_U becomes an integral part of op_2´s realisation. This means that m_2 and m_U share the same scope. This further implies that B´s attributes and op_2´s parameters are accessible to m_U as well. Now consider op_1 being interleaved into B. In this case, m_1 may also access B´s attributes because it is part of B´s behavioural specification. This implies that if m_1 and m_U actually access B´s attributes and op_2 arguments, this would have to be "encoded" within A since this is the location where m_U and m_1 are realised. This would mean that from within A there is access to properties which cannot be found. Since A is modelled as a distinct use case, this violates the encapsulation principle of use case properties and is thus contradictory to UML. This contradiction becomes worse if we consider a third use case C coming into play that connects A as well (see Fig. 4). In this situation, access to B´s attributes is incorporated in C through A and vice versa.

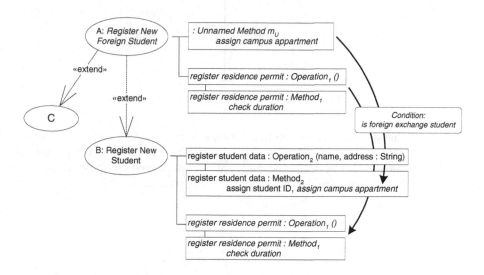

Fig. 4. Example of an interleaved Unnamed Method

However, this reasoning seems to be artificial. If m_1 or m_U should access B´s or C´s properties, this actually proves m_U and m_1 not being common to B and C; there is no redundancy. In this case, there does not exist such an abstract use case A. Modelling use case A then is needless and even wrong.

An apparently obvious solution is to demand that use case A works with A´s locally defined properties only. These are properties B and C have in common which are thus moved to A. In this case, encapsulation of use case B is guaranteed and the above mentioned problems do not arise. However, the following reasoning, (ii) below, shows that this does not suffice for interleaving semantics to be upheld, either for «extend» or for «include».

(ii)   Accessing Properties of an Abstract Use Case by a Base Use Case

Consider that in Fig. 4 the local methods of A and B access only their own local use case attributes. Now consider interleaving of Named and Unnamed Use Case Methods. Remember that interleaving does not mean a collaboration of two distinct use cases but static interweaving of use case behaviour (see Section 1.2). Fig. 4 shows the assembly of B´s and A´s behaviour within B to form B´s final definition as a result of interleaving. In this situation, op_1 together with m_1 is directly incorporated into B. Method m_U remains embedded into m_2. Still, m_1 and m_U access A´s attributes. This directly implies that attributes of A are accessible within B. Actually, at the level of B, attributes of both A and B have the same scope (see Fig. 5).

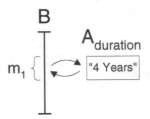

Fig. 5. Interleaving means embedding of behaviour

This situation is different to subroutine semantics: in a subroutine situation, the attribute is accessed where it is located (encapsulation) which is inside use case A (see Fig. 6). If use cases are not interleaved but plugged in as a whole, then we can consider this following subroutine semantics.

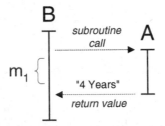

Fig. 6. Subroutine semantics

In this sense, if, potentially, base use case B actually needs the information stored within the attribute of A, its *value* is to be returned which is not the same as accessing the attribute directly (see Fig. 6). This compares with client-server collaboration semantics. In contrast to this, the direct access to A's attribute within B (as shown in Fig. 5 and Section 1.2) represents embedded behaviour.

The understanding of properties of different use cases having the same scope within the base use case corresponds with OO structural inheritance semantics of classes. Indeed, UML v1.3 and v1.4 explain use case generalisation as "A *generalization relationship between use cases implies that the child use case contains all the attributes, sequences of behavior, and extension points defined in the parent use case, and participate in all relationships of the parent use case.*" [9] (p. 2-126), [10] (p. 2-150). We realise that interleaving implies the existence of inheritance semantics. Inheritance semantics allow an entity to share the property access scope of its parent entities. However, UML [9], [10] keeps «extend» and «include» explicitly separate from use case generalisation. This implies that «extend» and «include» are not meant to have inheritance semantics since otherwise UML's distinction would be meaningless and even create superfluous redundancy within the metamodel. As a consequence, this finally means that applying interleaving to «extend» or «include» directly violates encapsulation of UML Classifiers, and would further be contrary to Jacobson´s statement in [16] (see above).

Note that the authors do not state that use case generalisation semantics necessarily include interleaving semantics. The proof that interleaving implies the existence of structural inheritance semantics comes solely from reasoning on property access scopes. This does not imply that use case inheritance implies interleaving.

Apart from the fact that use case interleaving violates encapsulation of UML Classifiers, the authors further present an additional set of counter arguments below. These arguments show that use case interleaving reveals further inconsistencies within UML, and fails under the Use Case Goal theory of Cockburn [11]. Cockburn´s approach is, initially, briefly explained; arguments are presented subsequently.

5   Goal-Based Use Cases

5.1   Goals and Interaction

Cockburn´s approach is a more refined and detailed view of Jacobson et al.´s [14] explanation of how use cases are found through actor identification. Cockburn further refines the notion of actor.

Each actor has certain responsibilities imposed by the business processes of the business domain. In order to fulfil its responsibilities, the actor has to perform some operations. An actor wants some of these operations to be facilitated by a software application. Thus, it sets goals for the system to deliver. These goals lead to desired system functionalities expressed by use cases. Each use case takes a single business goal.

A goal needs to be accomplished; therefore, some action has to be taken to achieve it. Hence, a use case goal leads to an interaction with the system in order to deliver this goal. An interaction always relates to a single goal; the goal holds together all action and interaction to be taken. The goal makes the related behaviour coherent.

An important property of goals is that they can be *nested*, i.e. they can have hierarchical dependencies. Any goal has sub-goals which make up the super goal. Since goals lead to interaction, goal unfolding results in interaction refinement. In fact, any sentence in a use case interaction description can be considered a sub-goal, which is also considered a "sub use case" in [11], and, thus, can be further unfolded. Unfolding can only be done downwards, i.e. adding more detail. Conversely, each goal and its corresponding interaction can also be rolled up, i.e. abstraction.

5.2   Use Cases as Contracts of System Behaviour

The system aims to reach the use case goals derived from the actors. In many cases, a use case requires some condition before it can be initiated and executed by an actor.

These are called *Preconditions* following the idea of *Design-by-Contract* [19]. Use Case Preconditions are derived from the surrounding business processes, business rules, and from the actor´s operational responsibilities; however, since a use case is the specification of a software-supported business task, use case preconditions are checked and ensured by the software application.

Use case postconditions relate to goal achievement. The fact that use case goals may be fully delivered, partially delivered or abandoned depending on failure recovery, i.e. alternative interaction courses, backup actions, backup goals, leads to the specification of *Minimal Guarantees* and a *Success Guarantee* [11]. Minimal Guarantees specify the least promise when the main use case goal is abandoned. The Success Guarantee represents additions to the Minimal Guarantees if the use case main goal is achieved. By introducing these two kinds of guarantees, Cockburn refines the notion of use case postconditions.

Altogether, the view of use case pre- and postconditions fits with the goal-based approach of use cases. Use case goals are "*System Service Promises*" described by a contractual specification [11]. Therefore, a use case is called a "*Contract of System Behaviour*" [11]. Such a contractual view is also proposed in [18]. Generally, pre- and postconditions for use cases is a widely shared approach for use case specification [1], [7], [8], [9], [10] [13], [16], [18]. Since goals and interaction are nested, the notion of contracts of system behaviour refers to concrete as well as abstract use cases following Jacobson et al.´s terminology [14].

6   Interleaving Violates Continuity of Interaction Sequence and Behavioural Coherence of Functional System Service Descriptions

Jacobson et al. defined a use case as "*... a complete course of events initiated by an actor ...*" [14] (p. 159). This is confirmed in [20] where it is stated that "*... a use case specifies a set of complete sequences of actions which the system can perform*", "*...each sequence of a Use Case is complete in itself*". The term "complete" thereby means that external system services are performed entirely, which is exactly the view of Jacobson et al. when saying that a use case is a "*... specific way of using the system by performing some part of the functionality*" [14] (p. 159). In addition to emphasising completeness, these statements implicitly define a use case as a continuous and coherent flow of interaction; otherwise, it cannot be complete.

Continuity of interaction sequence and completeness of use cases is adopted by UML v1.3 and v1.4. This is evident in statements such as "*A pragmatic rule of use when defining use cases is that each use case should yield some kind of observable result to (at least) one of its actors. This ensures that the use cases are complete specifications and not just fragments.*" [9] (p. 2-127), [10] (p. 2-151) as well as "*Each use case specifies a sequence of actions including variants, that the entity can perform, ...*" [9] (p. 2-120), [10] (p. 2-144). It can be assumed that completeness here does not mean an entire and externally available system service. Rather, it generally means coherence of the behavioural specification of a piece of system behaviour, which may either be a concrete or an abstract use case[5]. In particular, the suggestion of an *observable result* and the emphasis on a use case not containing fragments confirms continuity of interaction sequence and behavioural coherence clearly.

UML´s view of an observable result is supported in Jacobson´s recent publication where he confirms a good use case as one that yields "*a measurable result of values*"[6] [16] (p. 173). Such Quantifiable results, each of them being meaningful to and of value to the business process that the use case under discussion is associated with, and delivered to a particular actor, are also recommended by Cockburn [11], Jacobson et al. [15] and Kulak/Guiney [18]. Altogether, the emphasis on measurable business results requires a use case being a coherent piece of external system behaviour having continuous sequences of interaction.

Cockburn´s goal theory of use cases refines the notion of a measurable business result thus giving further support for interaction continuity and behavioural coherence. A use case goal corresponds with a demand for a measurable use case result being of value to the business. A goal leads to interaction. An interaction directly relates to its goal. Hence, interaction derived from a goal must be continuous in order to fulfil this goal. This is true for goals and interaction at any level; i.e. for concrete use cases as well as for abstract use cases. Further, any use case is specified as a contract of behaviour stating what system state is assumed at the beginning and what can be guaranteed after completion [11]. As a consequence, contractual system behaviour specification and use case goals also demand coherence of behaviour and continuous interaction sequences.

However, interleaving disregards the fact that goals and interaction are nested and hierarchical. Interleaving explicitly allows use cases to form a pool of incoherent but coupled behavioural interaction fragments. This breaks continuity of interaction courses, thereby clearly violating behavioural coherence. This proves the absence of a meaningful goal which must exist for any use case at any level because goals are nested: a use case which is subject to interleaving and thus does not show a continuous interaction flow cannot have a goal provable in the problem domain of the underlying business semantics. What business goal does a pool of disassembled interaction fragments have? This in turn means that an interleaved use case cannot reveal any measurable result. Furthermore, a pool of behavioural fragments to be interleaved cannot form a contractual specification expressed by pre- and postconditions since a contract demands encapsulation of service (see also Section 4).

We now understand why use case interleaving violates the software engineering principle Separations of Concerns (see Section 2): a use case goal is a business

---

[5] Unfortunately, the UML metamodel does not explicitly distinguish between abstract use cases and concrete use cases. However, such a distinction is needed. The reason for this is that the exact meaning of the application of use case relationships to concrete use cases, in contrast with abstract use cases, must be defined. Details and related issues are addressed in a later paper.

[6] Though vague and imprecise, the idea of requiring measurable results aims to find a correct and suitable level of specification detail [21] which is one of the greatest problems in practice.

concern provable in the business domain. Since a use case has a single goal independent of its level of abstraction and level of detail, a use case is a single business concern. Further, a use case goal leads to a set of possible interactions, i.e. solutions, for achieving this goal. This means that a use case being a business concern subsumes the use case goal, all related interaction, and the measurable results of business value. This implies that if two interactions represent solutions for different goals, then they belong to different concerns, i.e. different use cases; otherwise, their goals would be identical and, thus, they would belong to the same use case.

If two interactions being part of different use cases are interleaved, then either the supporting use case does prove not having a goal (as shown above) or the Separations of Concern principle is violated.

7   Solution Proposals and Remaining Problems

The authors support Graham's and Simons' request for the explicit dropping of interleaving semantics for «include» [21], [22]. Furthermore, the authors encourage the extending of this request to the «extend» relationship. The following provides explanations for these requests; it also proposes corresponding UML changes to meet these. These change proposals address the issue of removing the aforementioned problems and inconsistencies.

7.1   UML Metamodel Element *UseCase*

The definition of the UML metamodel element *UseCase* should assert and refine:

1. Partial order of interaction sequence;
2. Continuity of interaction;
3. A single business-motivated goal;
4. At least one measurable result being of value to the business process the use case is associated with.

This set of assertions excludes any kind of use case interleaving; also, it excludes the disadvantageous notion of Unnamed Use Case Methods. Hence, coherence of a use cases's behavioural properties is guaranteed. As a consequence, the UML metamodel should be adapted in a way that it becomes clear that for the «extend» relationship an extension use case is placed into the base use case as a whole. The extension use case may still be added to the base use case at more than one location, i.e. if the extension is redundant to the base use case and is thus extracted. However, a fragmentation of the extension use case is disallowed. An Extension Point remains associated with the «extend» relationship and represents the label of a single insertion point within the base use case.

As mentioned in Section 3, different extension use cases may be subject to the same business condition. In order to guarantee this while maintaining non-fragmented extension use cases, the condition of an extend-relationship is no longer maintained as an attribute of the UML metamodel element *Extend*. Rather, the condition becomes an explicit metamodel element *Condition* instead. Altogether, the corresponding part of the UML Abstract Syntax may appear as shown in Fig. 7.

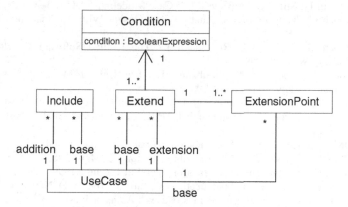

Fig. 7. Change proposals for the UML Abstract Syntax

7.2   Semantics of the Use Case Relationships «Include» and «Extend»

Following the suggestions of Graham and Simons [21], [22] UML should explicitly confirm «include» as following subroutine semantics. Additionally, the authors propose to define «extend» as, also, following subroutine semantics. Subroutine semantics for use cases should encompass at least:

* Parameters;
* Return values;
* Single flow of control: the base use case interaction course is discontinued at the specified location, i.e. an Extension Point or the inclusion point named by the base use case, and follows the behaviour specified in the extension use case; the base use case resumes execution after the extension use case has terminated (synchronous flow of control).

We need to demand subroutine semantics including parameters and return values. The reason is that because of encapsulation, properties of a Classifier are distinct: if an extension use case B needs information kept within the base use case A, it must be passed as arguments. Use case B cannot access A´s properties directly. The same reasoning applies to information present within B but needed within A after B has finished execution, i.e. return values.

Single flow of control is needed in order to ensure the sequence property, i.e. continuity of interaction, of a concrete use case as a system functionality exposed to an actor (see Section 7.1). If multiple flows of control is assumed, a use case interaction cannot follow a strict order while being continuous with regard to fulfilling its goal.

References

1. Armour F., Miller G. "Advanced Use Case Modeling", Addison-Wesley, 2001
2. Booch G. "Object-Oriented Analysis and Design With Applications", Addison-Wesley, 1994
3. Booch G., Jacobson I., Rumbaugh J. "The Unified Software Development Process", Addison-Wesley, 1999
4. Booch G., Jacobson I., Rumbaugh J. "The Unified Modeling Language Reference Manual", Addison-Wesley, 1999
5. Booch G., Jacobson I., Rumbaugh J. "UML User Guide", Addison-Wesley, 1998
6. Booch G., Jacobson I., Rumbaugh J. UML v1.0 Semantics and Notation Guide, Rational Software Corporation, 1997
7. OMG Unified Modeling Specification, Version 1.1, March 1998
8. OMG Unified Modeling Specification, Version 1.2, May 1998
9. OMG Unified Modeling Specification, Version 1.3, June 1999
10. OMG Unified Modeling Specification, Version 1.4 (beta R1), November 2000
11. Cockburn A. "Writing Effective Use Cases", Addison-Wesley, 2001
12. Henderson-Sellers B., Simons A., Younessi H. "The OPEN Toolbox of Techniques", Addison-Wesley, 1998
13. IBM Global Services, IBM Global Services Method Release 3.0, IBM Corporation, 1998, 2000
14. Jacobson I. Christerson M., Jonsson P., Övergaard, G. "Object Oriented Software Engineering – A Use Case Driven Approach", Addison-Wesley, 1992
15. Jacobson I., Griss M., Jonsson P. " Software Reuse - Architecture Process and Organization for Business Success", Addison-Wesley, 1997
16. Jacobson I. "The Road to the Unified Software Development Process", Cambridge University Press, SIGS Reference Series, 2000, (Compilation of formerly published articles of I. Jacobson, revised and updated by S. Bylund)
17. Korson T. "The Misuse of Use Cases", Object Magazine, May 1998, available on http://www.software-architects.com/publications/korson/
18. Kulak D., Guiney E. "Use Cases – Requirements In Context", Addison-Wesley, ACM Press, 2000
19. Meyer B. "Object-Oriented Software Construction", 2nd Edition, Prentice Hall, 1997
20. Övergaard G, Palmkvist K. "A Formal Approach to Use Cases and Their Relationships", Proceedings of "UML'98: Beyond the Notation", Lecture Notes in Computer Science 1618, available on http://www.it.kth.se/~gunnaro/www/index.html
21. Simons A. "Use Cases Considered Harmful", Proceedings of TOOLS-29 Europe, eds. R Mitchell, A C Wills, J Bosch and B Meyer (Los Alamitos, CA: IEEE Computer Society, 1999), p. 194-203, available on http://www.dcs.shef.ac.uk/~ajhs/abstracts.html#harmful
22. Simons A., Graham I. "30 Things That Go Wrong in Object-Oriented Modeling With UML 1.3", in "Behavioral specifications of businesses and systems", Kilov, Rumpe, Simmonds (eds.), Kluwer Academic Publishers, 1999, available on http://www.dcs.shef.ac.uk/~ajhs/publish.html#uml30thg

Estimating Software Development Effort Based on Use Cases – Experiences from Industry

Bente Anda[1], Hege Dreiem[2], Dag I.K. Sjøberg[1,3], and Magne Jørgensen[1,3]

[1]Department of Informatics
University of Oslo
P.O. Box 1080 Blindern
N-0316 Oslo
NORWAY
{bentea,dagsj,magnej}@ifi.uio.no

[2]Mogul Norway AS
Drammensveien 134
N-0277 Oslo
NORWAY
{hege.dreiem@mogul.com}

[3]Simula Research Laboratory
P O Box 1080 Blindern
N-0316 Oslo
NORWAY

Abstract. Use case models are used in object-oriented analysis for capturing and describing the functional requirements of a system. Several methods for estimating software development effort are based on attributes of a use case model. This paper reports the results of three industrial case studies on the application of a method for effort estimation based on *use case points*. The aim of this paper is to provide guidance for other organizations that want to improve their estimation process applying use cases. Our results support existing claims that use cases can be used successfully in estimating software development effort. The results indicate that the guidance provided by the use case points method can support expert knowledge in the estimation process. Our experience is also that the design of the use case models has a strong impact on the estimates.

Keywords: Use cases, estimation, industrial experience

1. Introduction

Use case modelling is a popular and widely used technique for capturing and describing the functional requirements of a software system. The designers of UML recommend that developers follow a use case driven development process where the use case model is used as input to design, and as a basis for verification, validation and other forms of testing [11].

M. Gogolla and C. Kobryn (Eds.): UML 2001, LNCS 2185, pp. 487–502, 2001.
© Springer-Verlag Berlin Heidelberg 2001

A use case model defines the functional scope of the system to be developed. The functional scope subsequently serves as a basis for top-down estimates[1]. A method for using use case models as a basis for estimating software development effort was introduced by Karner [13]. This method is influenced by the function points method and is based on analogous use case points. The use of an adapted version of the use case points method is reported in [3] where it was found that attributes of a use case model are reliable indicators of the size of the resulting functionality. Use case models have also been found well suited as a basis for the estimation and planning of projects in a software improvement project [16]. However, we have been unable to find studies that describe the use case points estimation process in details. This paper describes a pilot study on three system development projects. The aim of this paper is to provide a detailed description of the method used and experiences from applying it.

Our study was conducted in a software development company located in Norway, Sweden and Finland. The company has a total of 350 employees; 180 are located in Norway. Its primary areas of business are solutions for e-commerce and call-centers, in particular within banking and finance. The company uses UML and RUP in most of their software development projects, but currently there is neither tool nor methodological support in place to help the estimation process. The company wishes to improve the process of estimating software development effort. This is the origin of the process improvement initiative reported in this paper.

We compared estimates based on use case points for three development projects with estimates obtained by experts, in this case senior members of the development projects, and actual effort. Our results support findings reported elsewhere [3,13,16] in that use case models may be suitable as a basis for effort estimation models. In addition to supporting other studies, we have experienced that the guidance provided by the use case points method appears to reduce the need for expert knowledge in the estimation process.

UML does not go into details about how the use case model should be structured nor how each use case should be documented [17]. Therefore, use case models can be structured and documented in several alternative ways [19]. An experiment described in [2] indicated that the understandability of a use case model is influenced by its structure, and our results show that the structure of the use case model has a strong impact on the precision of the estimates. In particular, we experienced that the following aspects of the structure had an impact:

- the use of generalization between actors[2]
- the use of included and extending use cases[3]
- the level of detail in the use case descriptions

---

[1] In general, a top-down estimate is produced applying an estimation method to factors believed to influence the effort necessary to implement a system. The estimation method gives the total software development effort, which may then be divided on the different activities in the project according to a given formula. Adding up expected effort for all the activities planned in a project, on the contrary, produces a bottom-up estimate.

[2] Two actors can be generalized into a *superactor* if there is a large description that is common between those two actors.

[3] Common behaviour is factored out in included use cases. Optional sequences of events are separated out in extending use cases [17].

An important prerequisite for applying a use case based estimation method is that the use cases of the system under construction have been identified at a suitable level of detail. The use case model may be structured with a varying number of actors and use cases. These numbers will affect the estimates. The division of the functional requirements into use cases is, however, outside the scope of this paper.

The remainder of this paper is organized as follows. Section 2 gives an overview of the use case points method. Section 3 describes related work and presents alternative methods and tools for estimation based on use cases. Section 4 describes the three development projects that were used as case studies and how data was collected from them. Our results are reported in Section 5. Lessons learned are reported in Section 6. Section 7 discusses threats to the validity of our results. Section 8 concludes and suggests directions for future work.

2. The Use Case Points Method

This section gives a brief overview of the steps in the use case points method as described in [18]. This estimation method requires that it should be possible to count the number of transactions in each use case. A transaction is an event occurring between an actor and the system, the event being performed entirely or not at all.[4] The four steps of the use case points method are as follows:

1. The actors in the use case model are categorized as *simple*, *average* or *complex*. A simple actor represents another system with a defined API; an average actor is another system interacting through a protocol such as TCP/IP; and a complex actor may be a person interacting through a graphical user interface or a web-page. A weighting factor is assigned to each actor category:
   - Simple: Weighting factor 1
   - Average: Weighting factor 2
   - Complex: Weighting factor 3

   The total *unadjusted actor weight* (UAW) is calculated counting the number of actors in each category, multiplying each total by its specified weighting factor, and then adding the products.

2. The use cases are also categorized as *simple*, *average* or *complex*, depending on the number of transactions, including the transactions in alternative flows. Included or extending use cases are not considered. A simple use case has 3 or fewer transactions; an average use case has 4 to 7 transactions; and a complex use case has more than 7 transactions. A weighting factor is assigned to each use case category:

---

[4] Appendix A shows a use case from one of the development projects used in this study. The basic flow of events in the use case consists of 7 transactions. The use case is documented according to a template used throughout the company. The template ressembles those recommended in [6].

- Simple: Weighting factor 5
- Average: Weighting factor 10
- Complex: Weighting factor 15

The *unadjusted use case weights (UUCW)* is calculated counting the number of use cases in each category, multiplying each category of use case with its weight and adding the products. The UAW is added to the UUCW to get the *unadjusted use case points (UUPC)*.

3. The use case points are adjusted based on the values assigned to a number of technical factors (Table 1) and environmental factors (Table 2).

Table 1. Technical complexity factors

Factor	Description	Wght
T1	Distributed system	2
T2	Response or throughput performance objectives	2
T3	End-user efficiency	1
T4	Complex internal processing	1
T5	Reusable code	1
T6	Easy to install	0.5
T7	Easy to use	0.5
T8	Portable	2
T9	Easy to change	1
T10	Concurrent	1
T11	Includes security features	1
T12	Provides access for third parties	1
T13	Special user training facilities are required	1

Table 2. Environmental factors

Factor	Description	Wght
F1	Familiar with Rational Unified Process	1.5
F2	Application experience	0.5
F3	Object-oriented experience	1
F4	Lead analyst capability	0.5
F5	Motivation	1
F6	Stable requirements	2
F7	Part-time workers	-1
F8	Difficult programming language	-1

Each factor is assigned a value between 0 and 5 depending on its assumed influence on the project. A rating of 0 means the factor is irrelevant for this project; 5 means it is essential.

The *Technical Factor (TCF)* is calculated multiplying the value of each factor (T1 –T13) in Table 1 by its weight and then adding all these numbers to get the sum called the *TFactor*. Finally, the following formula is applied:

$$TCF = 0.6 + (.01*TFactor)$$

The Environmental Factor (EF) is calculated accordingly by multiplying the value of each factor (F1 – F8) in Table 2 by its weight and adding all the products to get the sum called the *Efactor*. The formula below is applied:

$$EF = 1.4+(-0.03*EFactor)$$

The *adjusted use case points (UCP)* are calculated as follows:

$$UCP = UUCP*TCF*EF$$

4. Karner [13] proposed a factor of 20 staff hours per use case point for a project estimate, while Sparks states that field experience has shown that effort can range from 15 to 30 hours per use case point [21]. Schneider and Winters recommend that the environmental factors should determine the number of staff hours per use case point [18]. The number of factors in F1 through F6 that are below 3 are counted and added to the number of factors in F7 through F8 that are above 3. If the total is 2 or less, use 20 staff hours per UCP; if the total is 3 or 4, use 28 staff hours per UCP. If the number exceeds 4, they recommend that changes should be made to the project so the number can be adjusted. Another possibility is to increase the number of staff hours to 36 per use case point.

3. Related Work

This section reports two experiences with estimation based on use case points. Two alternative methods and one tool for estimation based on use cases are described. Finally, use case points are compared to function points.

3.1 Reported Experiences with Estimation Based on Use Cases

Arnold and Pedross reported experiences from using use case points to measure the size of 23 large-scale software systems [3]. Their method for counting use case points was inspired by, but not identical to, Karner's method. Their experience was that the use case points method is a reliable indicator of the size of the delivered functionality. However, they observed that the analyzed use case models differed much in the degree of details and believed that the measured size may have differed according to this degree. They also found that free textual use case descriptions were insufficient to measure the software size.

Martinsen and Groven reported a software process improvement experiment aimed at improving the estimation process using a use case model in estimating a pilot project [16]. Before the improvement project, the requirements specification was only loosely coupled with the effort and cost estimates. The requirement specification was written in natural language, which was found too informal to be a good basis for the necessary revision of the cost estimate or for restricting the implementation within the cost estimate. Adopting use case modelling, the customer and developers had a common, documented understanding of the requirements. The pilot project experienced an overrun on the estimates, but the overrun was smaller than the average for previous, similar projects. Hence, they found use cases useful as a basis for estimation and planning.

3.2 Methods and Tools for Use Case Estimation

Alternative methods for estimation based on use cases are described in [7] and [20]. In [7] the use case model is a basis for counting function points, which in turn may be used to obtain an estimate of effort. In [20] the use case model is used to estimate the number of lines of code (LOC) in the finished system. This number of LOC is subsequently used as the basis for an estimate.

These two methods appear more complex than the one we have used as they respectively make assumptions on the relationship between use cases and function points, and between use cases and the number of LOC in the finished system. These assumptions have not been tested. The advantage of these methods, however, is that they may exploit the extensive experience with estimation using function points or lines of code.

Optimize [22] is a tool that provides estimates based on use case models. Optimize measures the size of the problem counting and classifying scope elements in a project. The set of use cases in the project's use case model is one kind of scope element. Other possibilities are, for example, the project's classes, components and web-pages. Qualifiers are applied to each scope element. The complexity qualifier defines each scope element as simple or complex. The tool provides a set of default metrics, extrapolated from experience on more than 100 projects. The user can also customize metric data to produce estimates calibrated for an organization. Optimize organizes the scope elements and metric data to compute an estimate of effort and cost. We intend to evaluate this tool more thoroughly. So, far we have only tried it briefly on data from one of the development projects. Our impression is that the tool requires calibration to the particular organization to provide a reasonable estimate. Moreover, the cost of purchase and training makes it less accessible than the method with associated spreadsheet that we have used.

3.3 Use Case Points and Function Points

The number of function points measures the size of a software application in terms of its user required functionality [1]. Although the calculation of use case points has been strongly influenced by function points, there are several important differences leading to different strengths and weaknesses:

- The function point standards do not require that the input documents follow a particular notation. Use case points are based on the use case model. This means that it is easier to develop estimation tools that automatically count use case points; the counting is based on available documents (use case models). This is an important difference, since counting function points frequently requires much effort and skill.
- There are international standards on how to count function points. The concept of use case points, on the other hand, has not yet reached the level of standardization. Without a standard describing the appropriate level of detail in the requirement description, i.e., the use case model, there may be very large differences in how different individuals and organizations count use case points. Hence, it may currently be difficult to compare use case point values between companies. As reported in [12;14], even with a counting standard there may be significant differences in how people count function points.

4. Data Collection

Table 3 shows some characteristics of the three software development projects used in our case studies.

Table 3. Characteristics of three software development projects

Characteristic	Project A	Project B	Project C
Size	7 months elapsed time, 4000 staff hours	3 months elapsed time, 3000 staff hours	4 months elapsed time, 3000 staff hours
Software architecture	Three-tier, established before the project	Three-tier, known, but not established in advance	As project B
Programming environment	Java (Visual Café and JBuilder), Web Logic	MS Visual Studio	Java (Jbuilder), Web Logic
Project members	6 developers with 0 to 17 years experience	6 developers with 0 to 12 years experience	5 developers with 2 to 10 years experience, 4 consultants were involved part time.
Application domain	Finance	CRM (Customer relationship manage-ment within banking), part of a larger solution	Banking (support for sale of credit cards)

Our research project was conducted in parallel with project A during a period of seven months. Projects B and C, on the other hand, were finished before the start of our research. We collected information about the requirements engineering process and about how the expert estimates were produced. We also collected information about the use case models and actual development effort.

Data from project A was collected from the project documents, i.e., the use case model, iteration plan and spreadsheets with estimates and effort, and from several interviews with project members. Data from project B was collected from project documents, and from e-mail communication with people who had participated in the project. In this project the available documentation consisted of a detailed requirements specification with several use case diagrams and textual descriptions of use cases, project plan and time sheets recording the hours worked on the project. Data from project C was collected from project documents, including a requirements specification with brief textual descriptions of each use case, a use case model in Rational Rose with sequence diagrams for each use case, project plan and initial estimates, and from an interview with two of the project members. The collected data is shown in Table 4.

Table 4. Data collection in the three development projects

Data element	Project A	Project B	Project C
Requirements engineering	600 hours spent on requirements specification. Relatively stable throughout the project.	Effort not available. Some serious changes in the requirements during the project.	Effort not available. Stable requirements throughout the project.
Expert estimate	Produced by a senior developer with 17 years experience. The esti-mation process was influenced by the function points method; effort was estimated per screen.	Produced by a senior developer with 7 years experience.	Produced by three developers with between 6 months and 9 years experience.
The use case model	No included or extending use cases. Example of a use case in Appendix A. The customer reviewed the use case model and read through the use cases.	Included many small use cases (containing only 1 or 2 transactions). Contained many included and extending use cases as and a large number of actors.	Contained many included and extending use cases. Each use case was described by a brief textual description and a sequence diagram.
The use case estimation process	A senior member of the project team counted and assessed actors and use cases and assigned values to the technical and environmental factors. Values were inserted into a spread-sheet to produce an estimate. The estimation process took approxi-mately one hour when the use case model was completed and well understood by the person performing the estimation.	The senior developer who had produced the initial expert estimate counted and assessed actors and use cases and assigned values to the technical and environ-mental factors. An alternative estimate was produced by the first author counting and assessing actors and use cases based on the textual requirements documents. A spread-sheet was used in the estimation.[1]	The project manager assigned values to the technical and environ-mental factors and also assessed the complexity of each actor. The first author counted use cases from the requirements document and a Rational Rose Model and assessed their complexity. A spread-sheet was used to produce an estimate.
Time sheets	Actual effort was computed from time sheets. The time sheets were structured to enable registering effort on each use case.	Hours were recorded according to some predefined activities. Actual effort was calcu-lated adding up all the activities in the project.	As project B

[1]Two different estimates were produced due to different interpretation on how to count actors and usecases.

5. Results

The results are shown in Table 5. Despite of no customisation of the method to this particular company, the use case estimates are fairly close to the estimates produced by the experts.

Table 5. Expert estimate, use case estimate and effort (in hours)

Project	Expert estimate	Use case estimate		Actual effort
A	2730	2550		3670
B	2340	3320	2730	2860
C	2100	2080		2740

In projects A and C, the use case estimate ended up only slightly below the expert estimate but a bit below the actual effort. The use case estimate for project B is close to actual effort and somewhat higher than the expert estimate.

The first use case based estimate for project B (3320) was produced by the authors with information about actors and use cases given by the senior developer in the project. This estimate was very much higher than the original expert estimate, and it was also higher than the actual effort. We believe that this is because trivial actors were counted, such as printer and fax, and also included and extending use cases. We therefore decided to calculate a second estimate where actors and use cases were counted from the use case model. The actors that provided input to the system or received output from it were generalized into two superactors. Only those two were counted, not the individual actors. This reduced the number of actors from 13 to 6. The included and extending use cases were omitted. We used the same technical and environmental factors in the second estimate as in the first estimate. This resulted in an estimate of 2730 hours, which is very close to the actual effort on the project (2860 hours).

One reason why the use case estimate for project C ended up a bit below the actual effort may be that the project manager assigned too high values to the environmental factors regarding experience and capabilities of the team. For example, he assigned higher values than did the project manager of project B even though the two projects were conducted with similar teams regarding size and experience with software development. Using the same environmental factors as for project B, project C would get a use case estimate of 2597 hours which is very much closer to the actual effort.

The use case estimates for projects B and C were made after the completion of the projects. It was therefore easier to assess values for the technical and environmental factors than in a normal situation because the choice of values could be based on experience with the actual project. This indicates that the technical and environmental factors in the method are appropriate for this company, although there may be a need for some, but not extensive adjustments.

We consider these results promising for the use case points method. The expert estimates were produced by very competent senior developers with good knowledge of both the technology and the application domain. The results were obtained without any particular calibraton of the method, so it is likely that the use case estimates can be improved. Independent of the method used for estimation, we must expect inaccuracies. Boehm states that these inaccuracies range up to 60 percent or more during the requirements phase [4]. The use case estimate for project A, the project with the largest difference, is 30 percent below actual effort.

Table 5 indicates a relationship between the use case estimate for a project and the effort needed to implement it. Based on this, we would expect a relationship between the size of each use case, measured in number of transactions and the actual effort on implementing the use case. The result of investigating this relationship is shown in Table 6.

Table 6. Size and effort for each use case in project A

Use case	Number of transactions	Use case points	Deve-loper	Iteration	Expert estimate	Actual effort
1. Fetch application	16	15	A	0 and 1	42 h	224 h
2. Simulate application	22	15	B	1 and 2	64 h	301 h
3. Automatic scoring	11	15	C	1 and 2	86 h	267 h
4. Change application	13	15	C	2	124 h	144 h
5. Assess credit-worthiness	31	15		2	170 h	
6. Produce documents	7	10	B + D	1 and 3	152 h	122 h
7. Register new application	14	15	All	2 and 3	936 h	647 h
8. Notification of application	5	10		3	132 h	
9. Transfer application to new responsible	9	15		3	82 h	

For each use case, Table 6 shows the number of transcations, the number of use case points, the developer (anonymized), in which iteration the use case was developed, the expert estimate and the actual effort. The system was developed in four iterations, in the first iteration (iteration 0) the architecture was established and in the subsequent iterations the system was constructed. The realization of the use cases was divided on these iterations.

The functionality described in use cases 5, 7, 8 and 9 was realized as one unit. The total corresponding effort was registered on use case 7. Hence, six cells in the table are empty.

The use cases contain between 5 and 31 transactions. The number of use case points for each use case is calculated according to the description in Section 2. Use cases 1 through 4 were implemented by a single developer; use case 6 was implemented by two developers; and all the developers participated on use case 7. For most of the use cases, the basic flow was implemented in one iteration. Those use cases were then completed by the implementation of alternative flows in a later iteration. Originally, the expert had estimated effort per screen, but the screens were associated with use cases, so he managed to re-organize the estimates in order to show expected effort per use case. Actual effort shows effort on analysis, design and implementation for each use case and was calculated from the time sheets.

The sum of effort registered on the use cases is smaller than the total effort registered on the project because much of the effort was registered on activities that were not related to a particular use case.

Table 6 shows no relationship between the size of each use case measured as the number of transcations and the effort necessary to implement it. Possible reasons are:

- Estimates based only on the number of use cases, or on a division into simple and complex use cases, are equally precise to counting all the transactions. One way of investigating this further is to compare the size of each use case with the number of classes or lines of code necessary to implement it.
- Many factors influenced the registered effort for each use case, for example:
  - There were different levels of experience among the members of the project.
  - The use cases implemented in the last iterations could reuse design and code.
  - The structure of the time sheets was new to the project members, and they did experience some difficulties in registering effort exactly as intended.

With relatively few data, we are unable to correct for these confounding factors. Therefore, we need more data to further investigate the relationship between the size of a use case and the required effort to implement it.

6. Lessons Learned

This section presents a number of lessons learned from applying the use case points method.

6.1 The Impact of the Structure of a Use Case Model

When we applied the use case points method to the three projects, we experienced that the following aspects of the structure of a use case model had an impact on the estimates:

- The use of generalization between actors. The number of actors in a use case model affects the estimate. Our experience is that if the descriptions of two or more actors have a lot in common, the precision of the estimate is increased by generalizing the actors into a superactor and hence counting the actors only once.
- The use of included and extending use cases. Karner recommends that included and extending use cases should not be counted. Omitting such use cases for project B resulted in an estimate that was closer to the expert estimate and to the actual effort than if they were included. However, in project C we found it necessary to count the included and extended use cases as very much of the essential functionality was described using these constructs. In our opinion there is definitely a need to investigate this further. Separating out functionality in included and extending use cases reduces the number of transactions in the use cases from which the functionality is separated out, hence the estimate is reduced, but the functionality will still have to be implemented. Optional functionality can be described either in an extending use case or in an alternative flow of events.

This complicates the estimation process, because choosing an extending use case will result in a lower estimate than if an alternative flow is chosen.

- The level of details in the use case descriptions. The size of each use case is measured as the number of transactions. We experienced the following difficulties when counting transactions for each use case.
    - Almost all the use cases in project A were classified as complex. We believe that this indicates that the classification of complexity of the use cases should also include an alternative for very complex use cases, for example use cases with 15 or more transactions.
    - It is a challenge to decide the appropriate level of detail in each transaction when structuring a use case, as there are no metrics established to determine correct level of detail for all projects [15]. The level of detail in each transaction will affect the number of transactions, which subsequently has an impact on the estimate obtained with the use case points method.

6.2 Assigning Values to Technical and Environmental Factors

We experienced difficulties when trying to assign values to the technical and environmental factors because we lacked a basis for comparison. In some cases we had to guess what was meant by each factor and we had to try to recapture other projects with which this project could be compared. A particular problem here is that the environmental factors require an evaluation of the competency of the project team. People often have difficulties being neutral when they are asked to evaluate their own work. This may lead to problems if the project members themselves perform the use case estimation and have to assign values to the environmental factors. With more experience from using the method, it will be possible to reuse experiences from earlier projects and calibrate the method to fit the organization. However, this will require that use case models for different projects are structured with a consistent level of detail.

The choice of productivity rate for each use case point may also need calibration. We used a productivity rate of 20 staff hours pr. use case point, but we believe that this choice will depend on whether some activities are estimated outside the use case point method or not.

6.3 Time Sheets

We believe that the entities used in the estimation should correspond to the structure of the time sheets to enable feedback on the precision of the estimates to gradually improve the estimation process. In project A, the time sheets were organized as a table with five columns:

Activity, Use case, Functionality, Name of developer, Hours

Examples of activities are analysis and design, implementation and administration. There was, however, effort in the project that the developers found difficult to register on one particular use case, for example effort related to establishing the database and the client framework. It was some disagreement as to whether this effort should be registered on the first use case that was implemented or as a separate activity not related to a use case. The developers decided to do the latter.

We included all the activities performed after the use case model was completed in the actual effort. Some of the activities were untypical; that is, they would usually not be included in the organization's software development projects. Examples are effort on upgrading to a new version of a development tool and training in the development method and tools for new project members. We decided to include untypical activities also, because we believe that every project is special somehow. In our opinion, if the application of the use case model shall result in a complete top-down estimate, it must produce an estimate with some surplus time for unexpected activities.

6.4 Using Use Case Estimates

In our opinion, use case estimates should not substitute expert estimates. It seems sensible to combine models and human judgement [5]. We therefore believe that use case estimates can be used successfully in conjunction with expert estimates.

For estimators with little experience, the use case points method gives good support for estimation. Estimators may also find it useful to compare the unadjusted use case points for a system with unadjusted use case points from previous projects. Expert estimators may be strongly influenced by, for example, previous estimates or what the estimators believe will be the price to win [9;10], which in turn may result in large deviations from actual effort. The use of function points together with expert estimates has reduced such large deviations [8]. Use case points may be used to obtain the same effect. We also believe that the customers may more easily accept estimates if they know that an established method have been used to produce them.

7. Threats to Validity

In project A, the use case estimate and the expert estimate were produced in parallel. Hence, some of the information used in the expert estimate may have been reused in the use case estimate because of communication between the project members involved in producing the two estimates. We do not know whether this influence had any impact on the estimates.

Project B and C were finished before the start of the research project, so the actual effort was known when the use case estimates were produced. However, the project members who provided information to the estimation method were unable to make use of the information about the actual effort because they did not know the formula behind the use case estimate. Therefore, we believe that the actual effort had no impact on the use case based estimate.

In Project C there were no detailed textual descriptions of the use cases so the number of transactions in each use case was counted from sequence diagrams. Sequence diagrams typically describe the functionality at a lower level of detail than the textual use cases so there will usually not be equally many functions in a sequence diagram as there are transactions in the corresponding use case description. This means that the use case estimate for project C might have been slightly different if it had been produced from use case descriptions instead. After considering the actual sequence diagrams, we do not believe that this had a serious effect on the estimate in this case.

8. Conclusions and Future Work

We conducted three case studies on applying a method for estimating software development effort based on use cases, the use case points method. The results indicate that this method can be used successfully since the use case estimates were close to the expert estimates in our three case studies. In one case it was also very close to the actual effort. It is therefore our impression that the method may support expert knowledge. We intend to further study the precision of the use case point method compared with expert estimates. In our three projects the experts had much experience from similar projects. We will therefore conduct a study where the estimators have different levels of experience.

Moreover, our experience is that applying the use case point method in practice is not straightforward. For example, the choice of structure for the use case model has an impact on the estimates. There is consequently a need for further studies on the precision of the estimates when using the use case points method in different types of projects.

We also believe that it would be useful to investigate how the use case points method, which provides top-down estimates based on a measure of size, can be combined with other methods that provide bottom-up estimates. The purpose of using the estimation method investigated in this paper is to provide a complete estimate for all the activities in the project. Nevertheless, we believe that some of the activities in a development project do not depend on size or use case points, for example, training and establishing a new programming environment. Therefore, such activities should be estimated in alternative ways and then be added to the use case estimate to provide a final estimate.

Another direction we intend to pursue is comparing the different methods for use case estimation described in Section 3 with regards to precision of the estimates and the effort needed to produce them. The use case points method requires use cases to be described at a level of detail where each transaction is specified. This is not always the case in practice. We therefore believe it is useful to investigate whether other methods for use case estimation are suitable for use case models with less detail. The way use case models are described in a company should guide the choice of method for use case based estimation, or vice versa, a specific method for use case based estimation should guide the way the use case models are described in the company.

Acknowledgements. We gratefully acknowledge the support from our industrial partner, Mogul, in particular Jon Ola Hove, Trond Andersen, Anne Hurlen, Skule Johansen, Helge Aarstein and Sigurd Stendal. The reported work was funded by The Research Council of Norway through the industry-project PROFIT (PROcess improvement For the IT industry).

References

1. Albrecht, A.J. Measuring Application Development Productivity. Proceedings of Joint SHARE, GUIDE, and IBM Application Development Symposium. 1979.
2. Anda, B., Sjøberg, D., and Jørgensen, M. Quality and Understandability in Use Case Models. In Proc. 13th European Conference on Object-Oriented Programming (ECOOP'2001), Jørgen Lindskov Knudsen (editor), June 18-22 2001, Budapest, Hungary, LNCS 2072, Springer Verlag, pp. 402-428.
3. Arnold, P. and Pedross, P. Software Size Measurement and Productivity Rating in a Large-Scale Software Development Department. Forging New Links. IEEE Comput. Soc, Los Alamitos, CA, USA, pp. 490-493. 1998.
4. Boehm, B.W. *Software Engineering Economics*. Prentice-Hall. 1981.
5. Blattberg, R.C. and Hoch, S.J. Database models and managerial intuition: 50% model + 50% manager, *Management Science,* Vol. 36, No. 8, pp. 887-899. 1990.
6. Cockburn, A. Writing Effective Use Cases. Addison-Wesley. 2000.
7. Fetcke. T., Abran, A. and Nguyen, T.-H. Mapping the OO-Jacobson Approach into Function Point Analysis. International Conference on Technology of Object-Oriented Languages and Systems (TOOLS-23). IEEE Comput. Soc, Los Alamitos, CA, USA, pp. 192-202. 1998.
8. Jørgensen, M. An empirical evaluation of the MkII FPA estimation model, Norwegian Informatics Conference, Voss, Norway. 1997.
9. Jørgensen, M., Kirkebøen, G., Sjøberg, D., Anda and B., Bratthall, L. Human judgement in effort estimation of software projects, Beg, Borrow, or Steal Workshop, International Conference on Software Engineering, Limerick, Ireland. 2000.
10. Jørgensen, M. and Sjøberg, D.I.K. Software Process Improvement and Human Judgement Heuristics, *Accepted for publication in: Scandinavian Journal of Information Systems.* 2001.
11. Jacobson, I., Christersson, M., Jonsson, P. and Övergaard, G. *Object-Oriented Software Engineering. A Use Case Driven Approach.* Addison-Wesley. 1992.
12. Jeffery, D.R., Low, G.C. and Barnes, M. A comparison of function point counting techniques. *IEEE Transactions on Software Engineering.* Vol. 19, No. 5, pp. 529-532. 1993.
13. Karner, G. Metrics for Objectory. Diploma thesis, University of Linköping, Sweden. No. LiTH-IDA-Ex-9344:21. December 1993.
14. Kemerer, F.K. Reliability of Function Points Measurement. *Communications of the ACM.* Vol. 36, No. 2, pp. 85-97. February 1993.
15. Kulak, D. and Guiney, E. *Use Cases: Requirements in Context.* Addison-Wesley. 2000.
16. Martinsen, S.A. and Groven, A-K. Improving Estimation and Requirements Management Experiences from a very small Norwegian Enterprise. Improvement in Practice: Reviewing Experience, Previewing Future Trends. The European Conference on Software Process Improvement (SPI 98). Meeting Management, Farnham, UK. 1998.
17. OMG Unified Modeling Language Specification, Version 1.3. June 1999. (http://www.rational.com/media/uml/post.pdf).
18. Schneider, G. and Winters, J. *Applying Use Cases – A Practical Guide.* Addison-Wesley. 1998.
19. Sendall, S. and Stroheimer, A. From Use Cases to System Operation Specification. Third International Conference on the Unified Modeling Language (UML'2000), York, UK. LNCS 1939; Springer Verlag, pp. 1-15. 2000.
20. Smith, J. The Estimation of Effort Based on Use Cases. Rational Software, White paper. 1999.
21. Sparks, S. and Kaspcynski, K. The Art of Sizing Projects, Sun World. 1999. (http://www.sunworld.com/sunworldonline/swol-12-1999/swol-12-itarchitect.html).
22. The Object Factory. Estimating Software Projects using ObjectMetrix, White paper. April 2000.

Appendix A

Use Case Specification : Transfer loan application to new responsible

1.   Use Case Name: Transfer loan application to new responsible

1.1   Brief description

The use case describes how a person responsible for a loan application can transfer it to another responsible.

2.   Flow of Events

2.1   Basic Flow

1.   The responsible notifies the system that he wants to transfer a specific loan application to another responsible.
2.   The system displays the name of the applicant and the reference number of the application.
3.   The responsible verifies that the application is correct based on the name of the applicant and the reference number.
4.   The system presents a list of groups of responsibles and users within each group.
5.   The responsible may choose one group of responsibles and possibly one particular responsible.
6.   The responsible requests the loan application to be transferred to the chosen (group of) responsible(s).
7.   The system transfers the application to the chosen (group of) responsible(s).

The use case ends successfully.

2.2   Alternative Flows

2.2.1   The responsible cancels the transfer

The responsible can cancel the transfer at any time and the use case ends.

2.2.2   Additional notification by mail

After the 5th step:

5.1 The responsible indicates that the new responsible should receive an e-mail telling him that he has received a new application for consideration.

5.2 The system automatically produces an e-mail message to the new responsible.

The use case resumes at step 6.

3.   Special Requirements

4.   Pre-Conditions

4.1   The responsible must be logged on to the system

The system must be started and the responsible must be logged on correctly.

5.   Post-Conditions

5.1   The application has a valid status after saving

The application should be saved in he database with a valid status and in a consistent state.

5.2   The application is assigned to one responsible or to a group of responsibles

The application should be assigned to one responsible or to a group of responsibles after the transfer is completed.

6.   Extension Points

Workshops and Tutorials at the UML 2001 Conference

Heinrich Hussmann

Dresden University of Technology, Department of Computer Science

Abstract. As part of the UML 2001 conference, nine tutorials and five workshops were held. In the following a brief summary of these events is given, including references for further information.

1 Workshops

A workshop at the UML conference provides a forum for groups of (typically 20 to 25) researchers and practitioners to meet for one day and to exchange opinions, advance ideas, and share preliminary results on focused issues in an atmosphere that fosters interaction and problem solving. Typically, most of the results of a workshop are generated on-site during the workshop and not in advance of the workshop. Therefore, there are no specific proceedings of the workshops. Workshop organizers, however, were encouraged to set up a web page where the contributions and results of the workshop are publicly available. Where known at publication time, the respective URLs are given below.

Workshop 1: Agile Modeling (AM) - A Discussion of Principles and Practices and Their Application

Organizer: Scott Ambler (Ambysoft/Ronin Intl., Canada)
Further information:
http://www.agilemodeling.com/workshopUML2001.htm

Abstract: Contrary to (un)popular belief, modeling can be an integral part of agile methodologies such as eXtreme Programming (XP) perhaps because of XP's name this fact is often overlooked. Furthermore, modeling in heavy-weight processes such as the Rational Unified Process (RUP) or Enterprise Unified Process (EUP) can certainly be made more agile. In this workshop participants will explore the underlying values, principles, and practices of Agile Modeling (AM), to determine how and if it can be used to enhance XP.

Workshop 2: Teaching UML to Non-technical Staff

Organizers: Ron Suarez (Object Insight, USA), Christoph Crasemann (IC&C, Germany)
Further information: http://www.object-insight.com/pdf/call_for_papers.pdf

M. Gogolla and C. Kobryn (Eds.): UML 2001, LNCS 2185, pp. 503–507, 2001.

Abstract: While UML notation offers great potential, many efforts to introduce UML into corporate environments have failed. This workshop will explore how methodologies and practices need to be adapted to insure greater participation from the non-technical members of development teams. Currently only a small percentage of the developer population actively uses UML and few people even consider how UML could be utilized by business people to do domain modeling of business objects with simple class diagrams or Use Case modeling of business processes. In addition, UML Use Case diagrams, in particular, offer opportunities for business people to model processes in their organization even when those processes may not currently or ever be a target for automation through software development. Thus, the focus of this workshop will be on selecting a minimal set of constructs from UML and developing recommendations for a simpler process that can be adopted by even the non-technical business members of a project team. In addition, the workshop will seek to define the web based collaborative tools that will make the practice of employing this simplified process more practical for geographically distributed teams.

Workshop 3: Concurrency Issues in UML

Organizers: Colin Atkinson (Fraunhofer IESE, Germany), Bruce Douglass (I-Logix, USA), Sébastien Gérard (CEA-LIST, France), Alan Moore (ARTiSAN, UK), Ileana Ober (Telelogic, France), Bran Selic (Rational, Canada), François Terrier (CEA-LIST, France)
Further Information: http://wooddes.intranet.gr/uml2001/Home.htm

Abstract: This workshop aims to gather academics people to discuss concurrency issues within UML, possibly connected with the development of embedded real-time systems. In particular, we are interested in focused discussions and survey contributions on (but not restricted to) the following subject categories:

- Relationship between active objects and behavior specification;
- Concurrency and communication inter objects;
- Active object and inter or/and intra concurrency;
- Adapted frameworks to support concurrency with UML;
- Interaction between various mechanisms for specifying concurrency;
- Object models compliant with the UML definition.

Workshop 4: Practical UML-Based Rigorous Development Methods - Countering or Integrating the eXtremists?

Organizers: Andy Evans (University of York, UK), Robert France (Colorado State University, USA), Ana Moreira (Universidade Nova de Lisboa, Portugal), Bernhard Rumpe (Technische Universitat Munchen, Germany)
Further information: http://ctp.di.fct.unl.pt/ amm/wrkUML2001.html

Abstract: This workshop will focus on techniques and concepts related to rigorous software development methods based on the Unified Modeling Language (UML). During the workshop the following methodical issues will be explored:

- Challenges to defining methodical software development processes based on the UML.
- Proposed methods and techniques that have proven industrial applicability or have the potential to scale up to industrial applications.
- Formal underpinnings for modeling and analyses techniques.

The workshop will provide attendees with a forum for discussing issues that can lead to a better understanding of how the UML can be used to support systematic and rigorous development of software. Relevant topics include all techniques and concepts useful for rigorous development methods, and in particular:

- Model refactoring, refinement, abstraction, and composition;
- Model realization, code generation, and round-trip-engineering;
- Generating test artifacts (e.g., test criteria, test cases) from UML models;
- Rigorous analysis of UML models: formal verification and validation;
- Usage of meta-modeling concepts in the development process.

Workshop 5: The Constraint Language for UML 2.0

Organizers: Tony Clark (King's College, UK), Jos Warmer (Klasse Objekten, Netherlands), Jonas Hogstrom (Boldsoft, Sweden)
Further information: http://www.klasse.nl/ocl/workshop-uml-2001.html

Abstract: The organizers of the workshop belong to a team of persons which is working on a submission to the OMG proposing an OCL specification for UML 2.0. The goal of the workshop is to perform an in-depth review of the initial submission and to help in achieving a high quality specification of OCL. The review will focus on:

- Solving issues within the initial submission.
- Integrating additional functionality in the initial submisison.
- Any other useful input for the submission.

2   Tutorials

During the UML 2001 conference, tutorials on advanced topics related to the UML are presented. In all tutorials, a target audience is assumed which comprises practitioners, industrial researchers and developers familiar with and already working with UML. There are no no introductory tutorials on UML, and too vague and general discussions are avoided as well.

Below follows a list of the tutorials together with references for further information.

Tutorial 1: Describing Software Architecture with the UML

Presenters: Bran Selic (Rational, Canada) , Wojtek Kozaczynski (Rational, Canada)
Further information:
See http://www.cs.toronto.edu/uml2001/workshop.html

Tutorial 2: Designing Concurrent, Distributed, and Real-Time Applications with UML

Presenter: Hassan Gomaa (George Mason University, USA)
Further information:
See http://www.cs.toronto.edu/uml2001/workshop.html

Tutorial 3: A Revolution in UML Tool Use? Tool Adaptation, Extension and Integration Using XMI

Presenter: Perdita Stevens (University of Edinburgh, UK)
Further information: http://www.dcs.ed.ac.uk/home/pxs/UML2001/

Tutorial 4: From Requirements to UML Models with Use Case Maps (UCMs)

Presenters: Daniel Amyot (Mitel Networks, Canada), Gunter Mussbacher (Mitel Networks, Canada)
Further information: http://micmac.mitel.com/UML2001/UCMTutorial.htm

Tutorial 5: Creating Evolvable, Embedded, Time-Critical Systems with UML and MetaH

Presenters: Bruce Lewis (US Army SED Redstone, USA), Edward Colbert (Absolute Software, USA)
Further information:
See http://www.cs.toronto.edu/uml2001/workshop.html

Tutorial 6: Realising MDA: A Precise Meta-modelling Approach

Presenters: Tony Clark (King's College, UK), Andy Evans (University of York, UK), Stuart Kent (University of Canterbury, UK)
Further information: http://www.puml.org/mmf

Tutorial 7: Quality Assurance for UML-Based Projects: Process and Techniques

Presenter: Bhuvan Unhelkar (MethodScience, Australia)
Further information: http://www.methodscience.com

Tutorial 8: Designing Effective Diagrammatic Languages for Software Engineering

Presenter: Corin Gurr (University of Edinburgh, UK)
Further information:
See http://www.cs.toronto.edu/uml2001/workshop.html

Tutorial 9: Executable UML (xUML): An Interactive Tutorial

Presenters: Chris Raistrick (Kennedy-Carter, UK), Ian Wilkie (Kennedy-Carter, UK)
Further information: http://www.actionsemantics.org

Author Index

Lecture Notes in Computer Science

For information about Vols. 1–2112
please contact your bookseller or Springer-Verlag